EARLY AMERICAN FURNITURE

a guide to

WHO, WHEN, *and* WHERE

John W. Obbard

Illustrated by

Brenda Bechtel

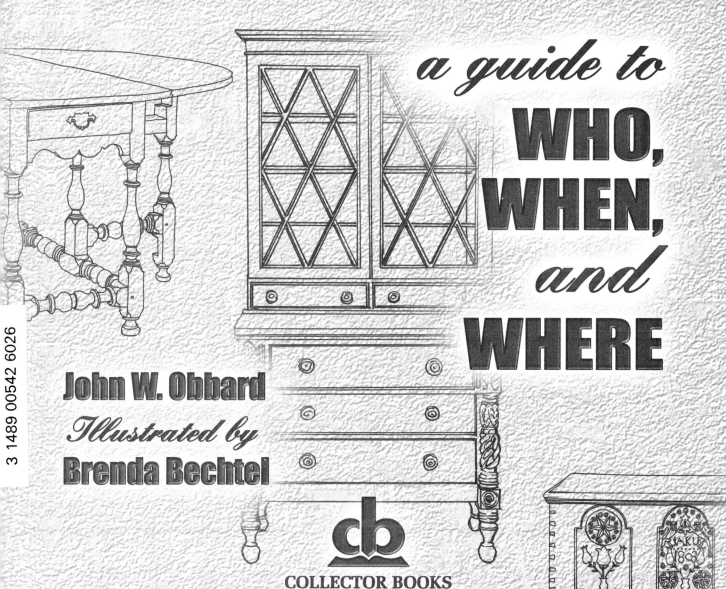

COLLECTOR BOOKS

A Division of Schroeder Publishing Co., Inc.

Cover design by Beth Summers
Book design by Allan Ramsey

COLLECTOR BOOKS
P.O. Box 3009
Paducah, Kentucky 42002-3009

www.collectorbooks.com

Copyright © 2006 John W. Obbard

Searching for a Publisher?

We are always looking for people knowledgeable within their fields. If you
feel that there is a real need for a book on your collectible subject and have a
large comprehensive collection, contact Collector Books.

Proudly printed and bound in the
United States of America

CONTENTS

✳ — ✳ — ✳ — ✳ — ✳ — ✳ — ✳ — ✳ — ✳

Acknowledgments

The many subtle little regional differences that characterize early American furniture, that tell us where and when it was produced, are so diverse a subject that I would be less than honest if I did not acknowledge the help that went into developing this survey of American period furniture.

First off, I would like to thank illustrator Brenda Bechtel for preparing the lion's share of the almost seven hundred illustrations that are scattered throughout the text. Brenda worked tirelessly for more than half a year, frequently with the aid of a magnifying glass, to translate the often less-than-clear auction catalog photographs into detailed line drawings. Many of these are little works of art in themselves, and it is a pity that they have had to be reduced in size for publication.

Permission to make drawings from their catalogs was generously provided by Northeast Auctions, Skinner, Sotheby's, and Christie, Manson and Woods. It was from these that I culled the many thousands of illustrations that formed the core of this study, that helped determine both the most salient characteristics and the relative frequency of different forms of regional furniture.

The many scholarly books on American period furniture, especially those on major exhibitions and museum and historical society collections, were invaluable sources of information. They provided both additional data and verified much of the informative detail found throughout this book.

Much credit should also go to Gail Ashburn, editor of Collector Books, and to Billy Schroeder, President of Schroeder Publishing, for backing a very much one-of-a-kind effort, and to Allan Ramsey for the design and layout that does so much toward making this sort of book easy to read and use.

Finally, I would like to thank both Brenda and my very dear wife for reviewing almost seven hundred pages of manuscript for errors in punctuation and wording, particularly my unfortunate habit of randomly omitting small words, as though in some way they were less important. Without Brenda's work and Evie's support, this book would never have come into existence.

Introduction

This book is a guide to regional differences in early American furniture. It will help the reader determine when and where a piece of furniture was made, and if it does not identify a specific location, it will suggest a region and then recommend other books and articles in which the answer might be found.

There are so many regional variations in the design and construction of furniture made in 13 colonies spread up and down a thousand miles of coastline that no single book can cover everything. There is no way to describe in one volume the hundreds of subtle little regional idioms and local practices found among the thousands of turners, joiners, and cabinetmakers that worked in Colonial and Federal America. A thorough survey would require a whole shelf of books. Instead, we will focus on the more common regional characteristics — those that the reader is most likely to encounter in furniture made between the late seventeenth and early nineteenth centuries. We will also favor features that are easy to observe rather than the subtle little differences so beloved of the scholar. Whenever possible, the figures illustrate the average grade of furniture on the premise that the reader is unlikely to be dealing with the very best workmanship, if for no other reason than that much is in museums and major private collections, and in any event, has already been carefully examined and thoroughly documented. The very best is also fairly rare, and is unlikely to be encountered in the home or marketplace. However, for completeness, I have included some things that you are unlikely to see outside of a museum. But then, you never know. One of the Newport block-and-shell dressing tables was found set out on a porch. It had been painted white.

To be most representative, the illustrations in the following chapters were selected from among many thousands of auction catalog illustrations on the assumption that the market is a fair representation of the whole. Things seen with some frequency in the marketplace are the same things that the reader is most likely to encounter among dealers, at auctions, and in the home. When given a choice of illustrations, I have favored the simpler, what in the past would have been the less expensive, on the premise that these would have been the more common and two hundred years later will be those you are most likely to encounter.

Identifying a region — and even a specific city or town — is not as difficult as it might seem, for Colonial America was not the homogeneous America we see today, where furniture manufactured in North Carolina is shipped over interstate highways to customers in every state in the union. America then was a group of separate colonies, each settled at different times by different peoples with very different cultural backgrounds: New England by immigrants from the south of England, New York and the Hudson River Valley by the Dutch, and the counties north and west of Philadelphia by the Welsh and the German. Except where brought together by coastal trade, or in response to a common enemy, the colonies relationships were as much with England and the Continent as they were with each other.

Our search is also much helped in that craftsmen, particularly in urban centers but also in clusters of towns, shared, or perhaps copied, popular and successful designs. In the following chapters, you will see again and again that cabinetmakers in these areas favored certain woods, designs, and construction methods. Because skilled trades tend to stay within families, cabinetmaking was often followed by members of the same family for two or three generations, and here also we will see the transmission of design and construction methods through family descent and intermarriage. America in the eighteenth century was so rural and thinly populated that relatively small family groups — the Dunlaps in southcentral New Hampshire, the Townsends and Goddards in Newport, and the Chapins in Connecticut — had a major influence on a region's furniture.

It is useful to remember what America was like in the past. Today our country is a mix of rural, suburban, and urban communities, all linked by modern high-speed highways. Raw materials and finished goods are easily shipped long distances. The same products are available everywhere. Without the manufacturer's label, we would have no idea where a piece of furniture was made. However, America in the eighteenth century was very isolated and very rural. Most people either worked on farms or in the small towns that supported the agricultural community. In 1775, just prior to the Revolution, America had a population of about four million, of which perhaps nine in ten people worked directly on the land. There were only five cities of any significance, and Philadelphia, by far the largest, was home to no more than about 40,000 people. Most transportation was by water, for the highways, even by eighteenth century standards, were terrible. Water transport was faster and much less expensive. Excepting Lancaster, Pennsylvania, every major population center was either on a harbor or on a river at the head of navigation.

Timber was heavy, inexpensive, and available almost everywhere. It was seldom shipped overland any great distance. For the most part, rural craftsmen used locally available woods. Furniture of imported mahogany was seldom made any great distance from the sea or from a navigable river. Difficulties in transportation, communication, and finance also seem to have limited the hardware and inlay available to the cabinetmaker, for in rural workmanship we often see hinges and latches that are obviously of local manufacture, and simple, unsophisticated inlays made up of local woods.

Because the majority of furniture was produced in urban centers, it is helpful to keep in mind the relative sizes of cities prior to the Revolution. For instance, Philadelphia was far larger than New York, and Baltimore was little more than a good-sized village. All else being equal, we would expect that from this period there would be more surviving Philadelphia than New York furniture, and that Baltimore furniture would be quite rare. Later, when discussing the specific regions, we will go into this subject further, for size — as well as history — is important in determining where furniture is likely to have been made.

You will notice that the great majority of the furniture illustrated in the following chapters is both urban and relatively early, that is, produced in or around an urban center prior the second decade of the nineteenth century. There is good reason for this. First off, rural cabinetmakers were often part-time artisans, mixing cabinetry with other endeavors, often not producing more than half a dozen pieces per year. Except for Windsor and the later fancy chairs, not a great deal of furniture was produced in rural areas. Also, rural work tends to be unique, or part of a very small group, and there is often very little to link the workmanship to a particular region or style center.

The other problem is that after the Revolution, American furniture began to lose its regional individuality. Due to a variety of reasons — the rapid growth of interstate commerce, the continual movement of journeymen, and perhaps a greater feeling of national identity — Federal furniture became increasingly homogeneous, so much so that by the late Federal or classical period, there was much less regional difference among furniture. In books and catalogs you will notice that the later the piece, the more nebulous is the identification, with increasing use of such words as *perhaps* or *probably*. Even side chairs, normally easy to place, may be identified as "Boston or New York." This survey ends with the late Federal, not so much because the average grade of American furniture ceases to have any great value, but because it has lost so much of its regional identity.

In determining source, it is helpful to differentiate between urban and rural workmanship, for this will tell us if our piece was made in an urban center or in an adjacent rural area; for instance, whether a piece was a product of Philadelphia or a product of nearby Chester or Lancaster counties. The best way to understand the difference is to remember that the urban cabinetmaker was a full-time professional with a complete set of tools and access to imported cabinet woods, hardware, inlay, the services of turners, carvers, and upholsterers, and perhaps most importantly, the work of peers within the furniture making community. For the most part, urban production is consistent in form, in scale, and in the use of primary and secondary woods. The average grade of furniture was produced in quantity to standard designs, so much so that today it is not all that difficult to assemble a group of side chairs so nearly identical that only close inspection will show they are not a set.

In contrast, the rural cabinetmaker worked very much on his own, and often turned to other trades to supplement his income. While not lacking in talent, he seldom had access to the services, supplies, and tools available to the urban craftsman. He often employed wooden latches, made up his own inlay, and turned to the local blacksmith for hardware. When we see professionally made inlay, it will sometimes be inappropriate for its location, suggesting that this was all that was available. When there is carving, it will usually be no more than a simple fan that could be laid out with a compass and shaped up with a couple of chisels. The rural cabinetmaker seldom had a large tool set, and furniture was often made with an absolute minimum of molding planes. Very neatly cut dovetails required the use of a fine dovetail saw and are usually a sign of urban workmanship. The rural cabinetmaker also did not have access to a large stock of lumber, and secondary woods were apt to be a mixture of whatever was available. Also, rural furniture was often overbuilt, perhaps due to lack of experience or because a piece was expected to endure hard use, but probably also because it was difficult to obtain thin stock.

The rural artisan also lacked the examples of others on which to base his work. Rural furniture will emulate the features of urban furniture, but often without the same balance and restraint. When an area was only semirural — what we might see now as a suburb — design would differ only slightly from the urban norm; but the farther away, the greater would be the difference, a phenomenon known as cultural drift. In country work, we may also see a naive enthusiasm expressed in unusual proportions or exaggerated design features — oversized case work, deeply bowed cabriole legs, or an excessive amount of decoration.

In a general way, quality furniture will be from areas where there was the money to pay for quality. This is helpful when trying to place rural workmanship. Well-made rural furniture will most likely be from very prosperous areas such as the Connecti-cut River Valley and the counties north and west of Philadel-phia. Nowhere is the poverty of much of the Southern backcountry so evident as in this region's furniture.

One of the most engaging features of early American furni-ture is the way in which regional design and construction features seeped into adjacent areas. There was never a clear boundary between style centers. Influences moved in all directions, overlap-ping and intertwining between adjacent areas. Boston style did not end at the Massachusetts border, nor Philadelphia at the Delaware River. The Boston owl's-eye splat is found all up and down coastal New England, Philadelphia through tenoning in New York and Connecticut. Work from colonies that lacked a major urban center to guide fashionable styles typically exhibits a mix of different regional characteristics. Connecticut furniture is a wonderful mix of Boston, Newport, New York, and Philadelphia influences — which contributes much to its charm.

Design features or motifs popular to a region are often found in more than one form of furniture. Quarter columns are seen on all sorts of Delaware Valley case furniture, and stop-fluted legs are found on many Rhode Island tables and chairs. Later we will see marked regional similarities in the shape of the tops of breakfast and card tables. Local preferences sometimes even survived major changes in style. The Philadelphia affection for round tabletops that would both turn and tilt continues to be seen in Federal can-dlestands with rectangular tops, where this feature would not seem to be very useful. The popularity of these features helps in identification, for as a rule the features are both easy to spot and are reliable indicators of region.

Local construction practices not only appeared in adjacent regions, but also in different forms of furniture in areas where they were popular. The New Hampshire practice of joining the legs of candlestands by tenoning, rather than blind dovetailing, is also seen in tea tables; and the Philadelphia practice of through tenoning the seat rails on cabriole leg chairs is also found in Marlborough leg side chairs, in easy chairs in which the extra cost of this feature would have been hidden by the fab-ric, and even in sofas in which the additional strength would hardly seem to have been necessary.

From regional preferences in design, style, and construction, as well as the craftsman's choice of primary and secondary woods, it is often possible to determine the source of a piece of furniture, even though no similar example is found in any reference book. Although cabinetmakers generally produced to popular and suc-cessful designs, handmade furniture can follow any form, and there is a considerable body of period workmanship for which there are no published examples. Even longtime collectors and dealers encounter pieces the likes of which they have never seen before. The real world among the average grade of period furniture is at times a lot messier than the carefully organized sections of this book would suggest. However, it is usually possible to assign region on the basis of design and construction features, as well as the choice of primary and secondary woods.

Leaf through any good auction catalog and you cannot help but be impressed with the regional expertise of the major auc-tion houses. Although auction house furniture specialists are good, and frequently very good, the information describing each lot is often derived from knowing the source or family his-tory of the consignment. This suggests that your first step in identifying region is simply to inquire if the item in question has any provenance, or history. Even if the maker is unknown, that the piece spent many years in a certain area is suggestive of region, for until fairly recently, it was expensive and difficult to move furniture any great distance. It still is expensive.

The next step is a really thorough inspection. After perhaps an initial check for features suggestive of region, take out all the drawers, or if a chair, the drop seat, and inspect every sur-face. Note the secondary woods and any unusual construction features. Look for labels, signatures, or inscriptions. You may come across shop marks such as "L," "R," and "Bottom"; and in chairs, assembly numbers such as "2" and seat numbers such as "IV," but these tell almost nothing of region. While it is true that only a small percentage of early furniture was labeled, sur-viving labels and signatures are more common than you might think, particularly among Federal furniture, which was often produced for sale in warerooms. Labels may be found on any inside surface where they would be protected and not too diffi-cult to locate — on the insides and bottoms of drawers, inside cupboard doors, and on the bottoms of small tables and stands. On desks and secretaries they are usually found inside one of the little drawers. Some carry the date the piece was made, and some also have the initials of the journeyman that made the piece. Look carefully, because only a fragment of the label may remain, or the label may be so dark with grime and oxidation as to blend into the background.

Windsor chairs, which were made in quantity and shipped everywhere, at times with Windsors from other manufacturers, frequently carry the maker's name on the underside of the seat. Sometimes there will be a paper label, but more frequently you will find a stamp or brand, maybe because a label could have been lost if the chair got wet in shipment. There is also a consid-erable body of furniture that carries the owner's brand. While found to some extent on New York, Boston, and Salem furniture, branding was particularly common in Portsmouth, New Hamp-shire, perhaps because so many Portsmouth merchants were engaged in shipping and employed branding irons to identify their goods. In appendix B of Brock Jobe's *Portsmouth Furni-ture: Masterworks from the New Hampshire Seacoast*, almost fifty of these brands are listed and illustrated. Normally they are about one half an inch high and consist of the first initial and the surname, usually separated with a period or dot.

Cabinetmakers, journeymen, and apprentices sometimes signed their work in chalk, ink, or pencil on the bottoms of drawers and the backs of cases. Sometimes this had little rele-vance to the furniture itself and was just done by an apprentice to identify the boards he had prepared. Federal card tables are apt to be signed on the bottom in pencil or chalk, this probably not so much for advertisement as to identify the maker to the retailer, for many card tables were produced for sale in ware-rooms. In your enthusiasm to find a signature, do not read more into a faint inscription than is actually there. Shop marks are not uncommon, and you do not want to mistake "Bottom" for "Boston" as was once done many years ago.

Most labels also identify location, but should you locate a label without this information, or perhaps just a signature, you may be able to identify who, when, and where in *American Cabinetmakers: Marked American Furniture, 1640 – 1940* by William C. Ketchum. Finally, it should be noted that a label is not a sure indicator of region, for imported furniture was sometimes labeled by the retailer. The well-known Elliot family of Philadelphia labeled both the mirrors they made and the mirrors they imported from Europe, and Duncan Phyfe is known to have added his label to some imported Boston furniture.

When examining old furniture, always be on the lookout for family data. When a piece of furniture becomes notable for its age and family associations, it may be inscribed in pencil or pen with some family history. Check unfinished surfaces that can be brought to an easy writing level, usually the sides and bottoms of drawers, particularly the small drawers in desks and secretaries. Sometimes there will just be a name, but more often you will find a complete little history of the piece, with the name of the original owner and the descent to the family of the writer.

Lacking the good fortune of finding a label, a signature, or some family history, we are on our own. Then the piece must speak to us. It must tell us where it was made. This is often not too difficult, for its voice tends to be clear, and usually it is possible to identify not only the region but also the specific area or location where a piece was made. The chapters that follow will assist the reader by first discussing the range and characteristics of the major cabinet woods, then by telling something about each region, and then by covering the different types of furniture made in these regions. However, a word of caution: in determining source, you need to be careful to avoid snap judgments based on the use of a certain secondary wood or the presence of a common regional feature. Always take the time to consider the sum of the evidence, for among period furniture, there is almost no rule for which there is not an exception. When we consider that the birdcage mechanism so popular to Philadelphia is occasionally found in Boston tea tables, and that Colonial Williamsburg has in its collection a "New England" blockfront desk that appears to have been made in Norfolk, Virginia, we realize that determining source is far more complicated than using such simple generalizations as saying that cherry furniture is from Connecticut and walnut furniture is from Philadelphia. Even the construction practices associated with different regions are not a sure guide, for methods that were both simple and logical can turn up almost anywhere. In the research that led to this book, I found that there was hardly a rule for which there was not the occasional exception. To this may be added the insidious influence of a sloppy restoration, such as replacing a splat on a Philadelphia chair with one with a Boston pattern, or replacing the feet on a New York work table with New England double-tapered feet. At times you will have to deal with conflicting evidence to arrive at the truth of the matter of origin. Like a judge or jury, you must consider the sum of the evidence.

Also, you should be careful not to read more into a description than is warranted by the actual wording. In the following chapters, adverbs such as *often*, *generally*, *usually*, and *typically* have been selected after careful thought, and they mean just what they say — and nothing more. That Philadelphia side chairs typically have the seat rails mortised through the stiles does not mean that all Philadelphia chairs are through tenoned, nor does it mean that chairs made elsewhere may not also be through tenoned.

Cabinetmakers were always under pressure to produce the most work in the least amount of time, and to produce furniture that would be accepted by local customers. In slack times furniture was made up on speculation, and it had to appeal to as many shoppers as possible. These economic pressures led to much local standardization that today, two hundred years later, can help us in identification. Also, cabinetmakers saved time by employing carvers to produce ball and claw feet, which is probably why they are so regionally distinct. They also went to turners for their lathe work, and turners tended to produce standard shapes that were acceptable to cabinetmakers and their patrons. Perhaps the best known turning is the Philadelphia compressed ball, but dozens of others have been identified by scholars, particularly in the columns of tea tables and the legs and feet of Federal Sheraton furniture. We will see many of these when we get to the chapters on chairs and tables.

To save time, cabinetmakers employed patterns whenever possible. They would never lay out cuts if they had patterns that could be used. Sometimes this lets us identify the work of a particular individual, when an identified piece exists as a reference. Also, a craftsman might employ the same pattern on different types of furniture if the shape was appropriate — a bracket foot would do equally well on both a desk and a chest of drawers. In addition, there were the dictates of local fashion. Popular and accepted patterns in the turnings of legs and stretchers, in the shapes of aprons and feet, and in the size and position of drawers, were apt to be used by many area craftsmen.

When puzzling over a piece, keep in mind that the subject may not be native to its present region. Even though family history may place it in a particular locale from its apparent time of manufacture, it may have come from elsewhere. Almost from the beginning of our country, furniture was manufactured for export to the other colonies. It was a major business. Probate inventories indicate that New England chairs were being sold in Maryland by the 1670s, and so many Boston Queen Anne chairs were sold in Philadelphia that they were known as "Boston" chairs. In our time of interstate motor transport, it is easy to overlook the enormous amount of coastal trade between the colonies, often by small ships with a crew of no more than the master, a mate, and one strong boy. Old marine paintings and prints almost invariably depict a number of ships on the horizon. While much of the traffic was in chairs, desks and dining tables were shipped from Newport, and card tables from New York and Philadelphia. Most all of this traffic was from north to south, which suggests that if a piece does not appear local to a region, one should look north for the source.

Much English furniture has been brought to America, but aside from innumerable Chippendale mirrors and Restoration chairs, it is rare to find English furniture that was imported in the period in which it was made. However, much English furniture has been brought over in the past century, and should you have difficulty in determining region, it may be that while your subject is the product of a region, it is not the product of an American region.

A more subtle problem is American furniture that is incorrectly identified as English, either because it left America two centuries ago, when many loyalists left America, or because it apparently did not occur to the owners that their fine old family furniture had actually been produced in this country. This sort of error is rare now that so much is known about American furniture, but it must have been fairly common at one time, for among museum collections there are a number of pieces with family inscriptions that identify them as being English rather than American.

Do not be discouraged if you have difficulty in assigning region, for even the experts are puzzled at times. Leaf through any of the books on museum collections and you will see pieces with "probably" or "possibly" before the city or town, some that are identified only by region, and even an occasional entry that is simply identified as being "American." In spite of significant regional differences, there is much furniture, particularly of rural workmanship, that can be identified no more accurately than as being from New England or from the Middle Atlantic or from the South. Simple furniture within the capability of a talented carpenter often exhibits no more regionalism than the selection of secondary woods.

This book has been organized for ease of use. After a chapter about cabinet woods and discussions of the major regions, furniture has been arranged by type in order to facilitate comparison between different regions. Thus, we will first cover the framed chairs made by cabinetmakers, then turned chairs, Windsors, and upholstered seating furniture; then we will go on to different types of case furniture and tables. You will see that some types of furniture were very popular in one region, less so in another, and almost never produced in a third. In some measure, one can determine source by the simple expedient of eliminating the unlikely, by noting what forms were seldom produced in certain areas.

In these chapters I will direct your attention to illustrations by use of figure numbers, and I will also reference figures in other chapters by figure numbers placed within parentheses, for example, "(5-21B)." These figure numbers have three parts; first is the chapter number, then the section number within the chapter, and last, the position within the section. For example, "5-21B" would direct us to the second illustration of section 21 in chapter 5.

Because you may need to do additional research, I have included a bibliography that focuses on books and articles that are useful in identifying region and are available. Should you be interested in a particular region, you may wish to add some of these books to your own library.

Lastly, something might be said about the captions that accompany the many furniture illustrations. When applicable, in addition to the area or place of manufacture, furniture has been identified as to style, this to assist the reader in understanding the progression, and at times, the lack of progression, of design and style in American furniture, which can be puzzling as it frequently has little relation to the time of manufacture. The dates that accompany the illustrations have been derived from the most current studies of American furniture. To this there is a bias to later rather than earlier, for styles, particularly among the average grade of furniture, are far more long lasting than is suggested by the best work of a period. In addition, there is some question as to the amount of manufacture during the decade and a half between 1776 and 1790 when America was engaged in, and then recovering from, the prolonged struggle to secure independence from Great Britain. Following the Revolution, cabinetmakers picked up where they stopped, and in rural areas furniture in Queen Anne and Chippendale styles continued to be produced well into the nineteenth century. The new neoclassical styles so associated with the Federal period do not appear until the early 1790s, and then first in the urban centers, particularly in New York City.

Cummaquid, Massachusetts, 2005

Today you can go to any lumber yard and buy board taken from a tree thousands of miles away. Should you make a bookcase from the board, the species of wood would offer no clue as to where the bookcase had been made. But in the past, this was not so. Except for timber growing close to a sea or a navigable river, which could be transported by water, most wood was used within a few miles of where it had been cut. Prior to the advent of railroads, overland transportation was so slow and difficult that both primary and secondary woods can tell us much about where a piece of furniture was made, so long as we also keep in mind the patterns of coastal trade.

In considering region we should, moreover, remember the woods that were in fashion during different periods, for this also influenced their use. Perhaps the best example is walnut, which was fashionable in England and America in the first half of the eighteenth century. Walnut is usually associated with Philadelphia and the South, but during this period it was employed in better quality Boston and Newport furniture. Not until after about 1760 did mahogany replace walnut as the fashionable wood in Massachusetts. Thus, a walnut Queen Anne chair could very well have been made in Boston, while a walnut Chippendale chair would probably be from somewhere else.

Before discussing individual species, it might be helpful to say something about cabinet woods. Of the many species of woods found in the New World, only a few are suitable for cabinet work. Most are either too small in diameter or too difficult to work or too prone to shrinking and warping to be used for any but the simplest pieces of furniture. Black locust is perfect for fence posts, but it is difficult to work and lacks the size, stability, color, and figure needed for furniture. That most woods are unsuitable for cabinetry is something of a blessing, for it leaves us only a relative handful that we need to identify.

All species of trees are divided into either broad-leaf deciduous hardwoods or conifers, cone-bearing softwoods, although the distinction, based on the method of reproduction, has only a general correlation to relative hardness and softness. The balsa tree, whose wonderfully soft and light wood has been used by generations of hobbyists for model airplanes, is a deciduous tree — a hardwood.

In old furniture, hardwoods were normally employed for the visible primary woods, softwoods for the invisible secondary woods, structural members, drawer framing, and backboards — the parts that did not show. However, there are so many exceptions that is a mistake to arbitrarily associate hardwood with primary wood and softwood with secondary. Much rural furniture was made entirely of pine or poplar, and in the South, walnut was so common that it was sometimes used for slip-seat framing and drawer sides. Even costly imported woods may be seen in secondary areas. On high-quality furniture, mahogany was employed for small drawers and as a base for veneers.

Boards are cut from logs in two basic ways. The most common method is plane sawing. Here, boards are sawn clear across the log as illustrated in figure 1-1. This is the most economical method, both in terms of cost and waste. It provides the widest possible boards, as the cut is across the whole log, and the most

figure, because the cut is across the annual, or growth, rings. However, these boards are also prone to warping and splitting. In the past, unless maximum width was desired, it was more common to quarter saw logs. Here the log would be first cut lengthwise into four equal sections, then each section would be cut radially into boards as shown in figure 1-2. This limited the width of the lumber, but provided strong boards with harder surfaces that were much less subject to shrinkage and the attendant twisting, warping, and cracking. In quarter-sawn boards the figure is less evident, but the wood rays, particularly in the oaks, are much more pronounced. Unfortunately, the lack of figure in old quartersawn wood makes identification more difficult, and you will find that in the sides of an old drawer, even such dissimilar woods as pine and popular can look very much alike.

Before covering the different species of cabinet woods, we need to discuss the way in which woods are described. We need to consider grain, texture, figure, color, density, and tree size. First off, wood is composed of innumerable tiny cells, and grain is the direction or orientation of these cells, particularly the cells that make up the fibers of the wood. Grain is commonly classified as being either straight, cross, irregular, diagonal, spiral, interlocked, wavy, or curly.

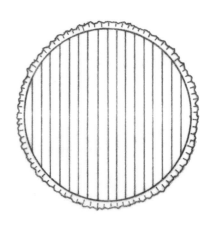

1-1. Plane sawing.

Wood is also described in relation to its texture, which is the relative size and amount of variation in the cells of the wood. For example, oaks are coarsely textured, mahogany medium textured, and fruitwoods very finely textured. Softwoods generally have a rather fine texture. The words grain and texture

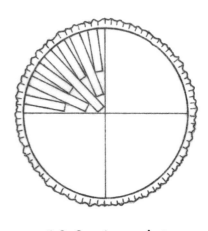

1-2. Quarter sawing.

are often misused, for "coarse grain" and "fine grain" actually describe the surface texture of the wood — not the grain. For instance, red oak is not coarsely grained, it is straight grained and coarsely textured. However, so common is this error that I would not censure you for using grain instead of texture. I tend to do so myself.

Figure is the pattern of color, the natural design on the surface of wood. The variations in color that produce figure are usually found in the growth, or annual, rings, around knots, and in crotches where major limbs branch off from the trunk. Some woods also exhibit decorative figures such as bird's-eye, flame, feather, burl, plum pudding, and the fiddle-back, or striped, pattern that is seen in tiger maple. In addition, many woods have rays that run at right angles to the grain, particularly when the wood has been quartersawn. Most of these are quite small, but some, such as those in oak, may be very pronounced. While some decorative figures are popularly associated with certain species of wood, most are, in fact, not unique to just those woods, and just casually identifying wood by figure alone may lead to an error in identification.

Color is less helpful for identification than it would seem, partly because the softwoods commonly exhibit little color, and partly because some woods exhibit such a wide range of color. The mahogany in old furniture varies from a pale tan to so dark a brown as to appear almost black. Where we get some help, though, particularly in the softwoods, is from the effects of oxidation. With time, all woods react to some extent with the oxygen in the atmosphere. In many woods this results in noticeable changes in color, particularly on the most exposed surfaces. Eastern white pine on the back and bottom of a chest of drawers oxidizes to a rich tobacco brown — very different from tulip poplar, which is apt to have a green or gray cast.

Woods vary widely in density, and this can sometimes help to identify primary woods. While walnut, maple, birch, and many mahoganies are about the same weight, cherry is somewhat lighter than the average hardwood, and some types of mahogany can be very dense, so much so that a chair will seem remarkably heavy, and starting to open the lid on a desk will immediately suggest that the lopers should be pulled out first.

Similarly, the general diameter of the trees and the width of the boards used in period furniture can suggest species. First growth eastern white pine grew up to six feet in diameter, and if you spot an extraordinarily wide softwood board on a table top or on the back of a chest of drawers, you are most probably looking at eastern white pine. Mahogany was also available in wide boards. The tops of mahogany tea tables and the sides of mahogany desks and chests of drawers are typically cut from a single piece of wood. While there are some exceptions, table tops and case sides made up of two or more pieces of wood are probably not mahogany. They will be some other wood, most probably walnut, birch, cherry, or maple.

Two-hundred-year-old cabinet woods can be very difficult to identify, particularly if heavily oxidized and covered with decades of grime. There is so much variation in color and figure that photographs of woods are not much use. Neither are wood samples particularly beneficial except to suggest the general grain and texture to be found in a species. After two centuries or more of drying and oxidizing, old quartersawn wood is quite unlike the plane-sawn boards seen in a lumber yard.

In addition, two hundred years ago trees grew very slowly, for in dense forests there was much competition for sunlight and nutrients. As a result, the growth rings that produce much of the figure in wood are much closer together than those seen

today; sometimes there are more than 70 per inch. Old wood may look very different from modern wood, even if it has been sawn the same way.

Dealers are quite good at identifying cabinet woods, but this is only after years of handling many thousands of pieces of old furniture. Should you be unable to identify a wood, the United States Department of Agriculture's Forest Products Laboratory in Madison, Wisconsin, may be able to help. To identify a wood, the laboratory needs a sample, a chip of solid wood at least ³⁄₁₆" across and ½" long. For determining region, you will usually be interested in the native secondary woods, and it should not be too difficult to obtain a sample from an unobtrusive location. Remove it with a sharp knife or chisel so that there is a clean cross section of the cell structure. Place in a small envelope with a cover letter stating what you know about the piece of furniture, where the sample was taken from, and perhaps what the wood might be, and mail to the Center for Wood Anatomy Research, Forest Products Laboratory, One Gifford Pinchot Drive, Madison, Wisconsin 53726.

If there is more than one sample, use individual envelopes with the identification on each envelope. Make sure that the samples are carefully labeled. Remember that what may be obvious to you may be anything but obvious to the laboratory staff in Wisconsin.

Responses are handwritten on the letter sent with the request, an admirable procedure that links together in one document both the piece of furniture, the source of the sample, and the identity of the wood. Identifications based on wood anatomy are usually accurate to genus rather than to species, although in some cases a subgenera identification may be possible. For example, the laboratory can identify spruce (genus *Picea*), but cannot tell the difference between blue spruce (*Picea pungens*) and white spruce (*Picea glauca*). In most cases, though, identification of genus will be quite enough to suggest region.

Now let's go to individual woods and their properties, always keeping in mind that cabinetmakers, particularly in the countryside, would use any suitable wood that was about the right size. It is not unusual to find two or three different secondary woods on a rural piece, and if some of the woods appear to be a different species, you might want to send the Forest Products Laboratory more than one sample.

Apple (Malus pumilia). A relatively heavy, finely textured (not finely grained) fruitwood with no visible pores and little color and few obvious growth rings. Apple grows to a maximum height of about 50' and grows 2' – 3' in diameter, so the sides of case work are apt to be made of two or more pieces. The wood is light brown, somewhat pinkish in color, and does not darken significantly with age. Apple was employed as both a primary and secondary wood along the eastern seaboard, and although it stains easily, its lack of color and figure usually limited it to budget work. Furniture made of apple is not common, although it was popular on Long Island. Sometimes a light or bleached-out cherry — also a fruitwood — is mistaken for apple.

Ash, White (Fraxinus americana), Black (Fraxinus nigra), and Green (Fraxinus pennsylvanica). These three species of ash are all found east of the Mississippi. Black ash does not grow south of Maryland, but the other varieties are found as far south as northern Florida. Ash is a coarsely textured, heavy, straight-grained wood with large, open pores. Just as apple can be confused with cherry, so also ash can be confused with hickory. Ash turns easily when green, and was often used in turned and Windsor chairs. It was the favorite wood of seventeenth century New England turners. In addition to its coarse texture, ash can be spotted in a table or chair leg by the soft, rounded turnings, as the texture does not allow the sharp, crisp turnings seen in maple.

Of the three species, white ash was most commonly used in furniture. The tree grows to a maximum height of about 80', with a diameter at the base of 4' – 6'. The wood varies in color from grayish white to a light tan. In addition to being used for turnings, ash was employed in urban centers for seat rails, to some extent in Boston and Philadelphia, but mostly in Federal New York where it is not only common in chairs, but is also found as a secondary wood in sofas, card tables, and sideboards. Sadly, ash grows everywhere, so is no particular indicator of region. It was used for turned chairs in both the North and the South, and is found as a secondary wood in both Maryland and Charleston furniture.

Basswood *(Tilia americana)*. Also known as linden and whitewood, basswood grows throughout the eastern half of the United States from Maine to Maryland and at higher elevations as far south as North Carolina. Basswood is a very light wood with a creamy white to creamy brown color. Due to a lack of strength and excessive shrinkage, its use in case work appears to have been limited to northern New England, where it was favored as both a primary and a secondary wood in Vermont and inland Maine, as the primary wood in painted furniture, and as a secondary wood in combination with white pine for drawer bottoms and backboards. Being soft and easy to work, basswood was also employed for feet and cornice moldings in northeastern Massachusetts and inland New Hampshire. For the same reason, it is found in the seats of New England and New York Windsor chairs.

Bay, Red *(Persea borbonia)*. Red bay is a small-to-medium-sized tree that grows along the Atlantic coast beside streams and bogs from Virginia to Florida and as far west as Texas. The reddish colored wood is hard, heavy, and somewhat brittle. It may have pronounced rays. The wood takes an excellent finish and was used to some extent for furniture in the Low Country. Red bay has been described as cherry in color and mahogany in texture. It probably served as an inexpensive substitute for the latter.

Beech, American *(Fagus grandifolia)*. Beech is so often associated with English furniture that it is easy to forget that it was also used to some extent by American cabinetmakers, and for much the same reasons — its toughness and resistance to splitting. Moreover, in America its principal liability, a lack of resistance to furniture beetles, was not a significant problem. If you find badly wormed beech, you are probably looking at a piece of English furniture.

Beech grows from Maine to northern Florida and westward into Wisconsin and Texas. It is a heavy wood with conspicuous rays, a tight straight grain, and tiny pores that result in a fine, even texture. When exposed to air, it ages from a light tan to a deep amber brown. For the most part, beech was used the same way it was used in England, as a secondary wood in chairs for over upholstered rails and slip-seats frames. It is found in Essex County, Massachusetts, chairs, in some New England lolling chairs, in the cross braces in New York City Federal chairs, and in the slip seats of chairs made in the Chesapeake Bay area. Due to its strength and toughness, it was sometimes used in the South for hinge rails on dining room tables. Beech would probably have seen more use in America had there not been so much maple available for turning and chair framing.

Birch, Yellow *(Betula alleghaniensis)*. Birches compose a family of similar woods, of which northern yellow birch was the most commonly used as a cabinet wood, although river birch *(Betula nigra)*, which grows throughout the South, is also found in some Mid-Atlantic and Southern furniture. Because yellow birch is of moderate size, perhaps 60' high and about 3' in diameter, the sides of case work are apt to be pieced. The wood is heavy, very strong, and finely textured; the color is creamy or light brown. When quartersawn, it frequently exhibits a curly pattern not unlike the figuring of curly maple. Yellow and river birch are cousins of the lovely small paper birch *(Betula papyrifera)* that now graces so many suburban lawns.

Yellow birch was used in New England as a primary and a secondary wood. Case furniture of birch usually comes from northern New England, having been produced to some extent in Rhode Island and New London County, but more commonly further north, in Massachusetts, New Hampshire, and in the upper Connecticut River Valley. Portsmouth, New Hampshire, chests of drawers were often made of birch. It was also used for innumerable little rural candlestands, and is occasionally found in side chairs. Birch takes a nice stain and in case work was usually stained up to resemble mahogany. Stands made of birch were often painted, and if you see a black or red painted stand, it is likely to be birch.

The use of birch is somewhat period sensitive; it was seldom employed before the last decades of the eighteenth century and is most commonly seen in furniture produced during the Federal period.

Due to its weight, birch was not employed for drawers. Instead, it was used as a secondary wood where strength was required, for chair frames and the swing rails of card tables. It is the most common wood in Boston and Salem seat rails, and is common in New England lolling chairs. To a lesser extent it was also used in New York furniture in sofa frames, in the medial braces of Federal side chairs, and in the swing rails on card tables.

Finally, it should be noted that figured birch was used everywhere for decorative veneers and inlays, most commonly in Federal New England, where we often find flame birch tablets set into the fronts of chests of drawers and the legs of card tables and sofas.

Butternut *(Juglans cinerea)*. Like a great many species of New World deciduous trees, butternut grows from New England south along the coast through the Middle Atlantic and also inland on higher ground as far south as Georgia. While of the same genus as American black walnut — and sometimes called white walnut — it is a lighter, softer wood with a coarser texture and more open pores. When stained, it resembles an indifferent grade of walnut. Butternut was used as both a primary and a secondary wood, usually as a substitute for walnut in inland rural areas, but also as a secondary wood in New London County furniture. Its use as a primary wood is not particularly region specific, for it is seen in both New England and Middle Atlantic case work. If nothing else, it is evidence of rural workmanship.

Cedar, Atlantic White (Chamaecyparis thyoides). The three types of cedar used in American furniture, Atlantic white, eastern red, and Spanish, are similar in many respects, even though they differ in both species and genus. All are aromatic, and even after two hundred or more years, a faint aroma can be detected in unfinished secondary woods. This is perhaps the easiest way to identify a cedar.

Atlantic white cedar grows everywhere along the seaboard from Maine to northern Florida. It is a medium-sized tree, 60' to 80' high, with a maximum diameter of about 3'. The wood is light in weight with a fine texture. It is quite soft, and can easily be marked with a thumbnail. It was used everywhere as a secondary wood, and by itself is no particular indicator of region, although in Philadelphia and the surrounding area, including southern New Jersey, it was frequently used in drawer bottoms and chair blocking. In addition to a light tan color and the characteristic scent, a cut across the end grain of a drawer bottom will often look coarse and rough due to the softness of the wood.

Cedar, Eastern Red (Juniperus virginiana). Eastern red cedar is a smaller tree, perhaps 40' high and 16" in diameter. It also grows everywhere along the seaboard except in the low country of South Carolina and Georgia. The heartwood oxidizes to a pinkish red. Today it is commonly used in cedar chests, often showing many knots due to the small size of the remaining growth. In the past it was employed both as a primary and a secondary wood, for drawers in Boston and Salem, and in Newport for inexpensive export-quality desks, and also for the small interior drawers of desks and desks and bookcases. Its use is not limited to New England, for red cedar is also found in some Charleston case furniture.

Cedar, Spanish (Cedrela mexicana). Spanish cedar grows in every country south of the United States except Chile. The wood is light red, straight grained, and relatively soft, and resembles mahogany, although a rather coarse, open-textured mahogany. It was brought to Boston and Philadelphia in the early eighteenth century, where it was used as both a primary and a secondary wood. Case furniture made in America of Spanish cedar will be quite early, probably made not much later than 1730. It will also be quite rare.

Cherry, Black (Prunus serotina). Cherry grows throughout the eastern United States, mostly in the higher elevations in New York, Pennsylvania, and West Virginia. While it may grow to a height of 100' and a diameter of 4', most trees are considerably smaller, and case sides and tabletops of cherry are often made up of two or more pieces of wood. The wood is a light-to-medium red that eventually darkens to a deep reddish brown.

When exposed to sunlight, it can bleach to a very pretty orange-red. Rural furniture often exhibits distinctive bands of lighter sapwood that run lengthwise with the direction of the grain. It is seen in rural work because the cabinetmaker has used the full width of a board. In better-quality work, a cabinetmaker would not use sapwood because of the difficulty in matching the color.

In the past, cherry was almost invariably stained to resemble either mahogany or walnut, and occasionally you will see a piece of furniture that retains much of this original stain.

Cherry is a fairly heavy, moderately hard wood with a fine, smooth texture and almost invisible pores. Even if stained up to simulate mahogany or walnut, it will not show the pores seen in these woods. Quartersawn cherry shows a small but distinctive ray pattern and occasionally a curly figuring that resembles maple.

Cherrywood is so often associated with furniture from the Connecticut River Valley that we need to remember that this lovely cabinet wood is by no means unique to Connecticut. It was used almost everywhere from Vermont to Georgia, particularly in rural areas as an inexpensive substitute for mahogany. Furniture was quite frequently made of cherry in Rhode Island, in eastern Massachusetts, throughout the Middle Atlantic, and in the South. It is the most common primary wood in eastern Long Island. In addition, its strength and ease of working made it popular as a secondary wood when strength was required, and it is found in drawers, seat frames, and swing rails of New England and New York furniture.

Where cherry helps us to distinguish Connecticut and the Connecticut River Valley is in the nature of the furniture. Good-quality high-style furniture was customarily made of either walnut or mahogany. However, in Connecticut the preference for cherry was such that the best-quality furniture was generally made of this wood, even though the best was somewhat rural by Boston or Newport standards. Thus, when we see an elegant high chest of drawers, dressing table, or tea table made of cherry, it is very likely to be Connecticut River Valley workmanship. A Queen Anne or Chippendale side chair made of cherry will most probably be from Connecticut. In contrast, a simple late Sheraton breakfast table or corner cupboard made of cherry could have been made almost anywhere.

Chestnut, American (Castanea dentata). In the past, chestnut followed the usual pattern of other eastern deciduous hardwoods by growing all along the coast as far south as Virginia and inland down the Appalachians into Georgia. It was a large tree 60' – 80' high and 5' – 6' in diameter; *was* because the American chestnut was wiped out in the nineteenth century by the chestnut blight.

The wood is light tan in color, with a coarse texture and prominent pores. Old wood will be an even nut brown color. Due to its texture and large open pores, chestnut resembles red oak. However, even when quartersawn, it has no medullary rays, and this the best way to tell it from oak. Sometimes there will be tiny holes caused by pinworms. These should not be confused with the larger holes made by insects that infested the wood after the tree died — the so-called wormy chestnut.

Chestnut is a strong, stable wood that planed easily when green. In the eighteenth century, it was a favorite secondary wood in Rhode Island and in nearby southeastern Massachusetts and eastern Connecticut, where it was used for drawers, backboards, swing rails, and the blocks or plates under the tops of tea tables and candlestands. The drawers in Rhode Island furniture are often made of poplar with chestnut bottoms, or else are all chestnut. However, chestnut is such a useful secondary wood that we should not think that chestnut equals southeastern New England, for it was also used to some extent in furniture produced in westcentral Massachusetts, along the North Shore of Massachusetts, and in Long Island, Philadelphia, and Maryland.

Cypress (Taxodium distichum). Often called bald cypress, this very large tree grows in damp bottomlands and swamps along the coast from Delaware to Florida. It is the largest and longest living tree east of the Mississippi. The wood is medium hard with a fine texture, the color a light yellowish brown that oxidizes to a reddish color. It looks something like a southern pine, but without the strong figuring. As you would expect, it is notably resistant to rot. Unfortunately, it does not plane quite smoothly, leaving a slightly fuzzy surface. I've heard that it has a distinctive damp odor — perhaps a reflection of its source.

Cypress was used along the coast from Maryland down to South Carolina primarily as a secondary wood, most particularly in Charleston, where it was commonly employed for dustboards, drawer sides, and drawer bottoms. High-style furniture containing some cypress will generally be a Charleston product.

Gum, Red (Liquidambar styraciflua). Also known as sweetgum, and in the past, bilsted, red gum grows along the coast from Connecticut down through New Jersey and both inland and along the coast as far south as Florida, with the exception of the southern range of the Appalachians — almost the reverse of the habitat of most deciduous hardwoods. The tree can grow to 120' high and 4' in diameter, although logs are usually not more than 30" in diameter. The wood is light brown, fairly heavy, and moderately strong and stiff. In old furniture, gumwood looks like a very finely textured maple with closed pores and small, random, tight knots. There is seldom much figure. The name comes not from the color of the wood, but rather the color of its autumn leaves. The euphonious Latin name *Liquidambar* refers to its fragrant resin.

Red gum was often used as a primary wood in the Hudson River Valley and in northern New Jersey, particularly for large case work such as kasten and clothespresses. In the eighteenth century it was the favored wood on western Long Island. It is also found as a secondary wood in the medial braces and blocking in New York chairs, and occasionally in Philadelphia and Maryland furniture. The wood takes stain exceptionally well and is now often used by manufacturers — and fakers — as an inexpensive substitute for mahogany.

Hickory (Carya ovata and others). There are no fewer than 16 species of hickory in North America, many of which grow along the East Coast. Of these, shagbark hickory (*Carya ovata*) is the most common. The wood is straight grained and coarsely textured, brown to reddish brown in color. Hickory has a unique combination of strength, toughness, hardness, and stiffness, and today sees much use in tool handles. In the past it was used for rails and stretchers in turned chairs and for the bows and spindles of Windsor chairs. Aside from its strength, hickory is a poor cabinet wood, being prone to shrinking and warping. It grows everywhere, and is no particular indicator of region, although it was especially popular in the South. The wood does not hold paint well, and if you see a chair spindle or stretcher that has lost most of its paint, you are probably looking at hickory.

Magnolia, Southern (Magnolia grandiflora). While now growing in New England, the southern, or laurel, magnolia is a native of the South, growing along the coast in swamps and beside streams, from the southeastern corner of North Carolina to Florida, and along the Gulf Coast as far west as Texas. In the South it is a good-sized tree, growing about 80' high and 3' in diameter. The wood varies in color from a straw to a greenish beige and is of medium weight, is straight grained and finely textured, and has no visible pores. In the Low Country, magnolia was used as both a primary and a secondary wood in rural furniture, and although uncommon, is an almost sure indication of Southern workmanship.

Mahogany, Santo Domingo (Swietenia mahogani) and Honduras (Swietenia macrophylla). Mahogany occupies a unique place in this survey of cabinet woods, for it is the only wood commonly employed in American period furniture that is not native. However, it is the perfect cabinet wood and was well worth the additional cost of importation. It is strong, stable, rich in color and figure, easy to carve, impervious to worms, and was available in widths such that the tops and sides of furniture could be worked out of single boards without having to be pieced together.

Mahogany can be puzzling, for it has the widest ranges of color, figure, and weight found in any cabinet wood. The color varies from a light tan in Honduras mahogany to a deep reddish brown that is little short of black in some Santo Domingo mahogany; figuring includes swirl, plum pudding, blister, stripe, and roe patterns; and densities range from as little as 28 lb. per cubic foot to over 50 lb. per cubic foot in some old-growth wood.

Fortunately, all mahoganies, in addition to having a characteristic reddish color, are medium textured and open pored, and if examined closely, show vessel lines as either dots or short grooves, depending on the angle of the cut in relation to the grain. Under a clear finish, the pores show as masses of short parallel black lines. The only other common cabinet wood with open pores is black walnut, but its pores are smaller and the color is a more true brown. Even so, it is at times difficult to tell them apart.

Although mahogany was being used in furniture from the early years of the eighteenth century, it was not understood until the 1880s that there were actually two species of New World mahoganies, the species growing on the islands of the West Indies, and now named for one of the first settled islands (Santo Domingo mahogany, *Swietenia mahogani*), and the species growing on the mainland of Central and South America and now named for a Central American country (Honduras mahogany, *Swietenia macrophylla*). It is commonly thought that Santo Domingo mahogany is denser and heavier than Honduran mahogany, and while this is generally true, it may be more a result of soil and sunlight than species, for to an unusual extent, mahogany seems to be sensitive to its environment, the wood becoming very hard and dense if it grows but slowly in poor soil or with little sunlight. However, other woods also exhibit this property, and in early furniture we also find very hard first growth cherrywood and pine. It is also believed that mahogany from the islands is darker and has less figure than that from the mainland, and this may be true, if only because Santo Domingo mahogany tends to darken with age while the Honduran species tends to fade to lighter shades.

In the past, mahogany was named for the islands and lands where it had originated, and this has led to a bewildering variety of names. You will read of Cuban, Jamaican, and West Indian mahogany, all of which are actually Santo Domingo mahogany, and baywood, which was shipped from Campechy Bay in the Gulf of Mexico and is Honduras mahogany. To add to the confusion, a wood might be named for the country that occupied the source. Thus we have Spanish mahogany, which came from Spanish possession of Cuba and Puerto Rico, as well as Spanish cedar. The variations in color, figure, and weight found in mahogany may have been just as puzzling to eighteenth century cabinetmakers as it is to us now.

You will sometimes hear that the supply of mahogany from the West Indies was exhausted at an early date. The much quoted 1748 statement that "The true Mahogany; which grows in Jamaica, is at present almost all cut down" gives an impression that most furniture must be made of Honduras mahogany, and that the presence of island mahogany is a sign of very early work. However, the great majority of American mahogany furniture postdates the middle of the eighteenth century, and a substantial amount is made with heavy and dark Santo Domingo wood. It may be just that the easily harvested timber near the coast had been cut down.

Mahogany was used all up and down the eastern seaboard, and by itself is no particular indicator of region except that it suggests work done within a relatively short distance of a seaport or a navigable river. In spite of the local preference for cherry, it is seen in both eastern Connecticut and the Connecticut River Valley, and is sometimes found in western Pennsylvania, southern Ohio, and western Maryland. To a certain extent, mahogany was used less the more distant from the source, with gay abandon in Charleston, South Carolina, and as no more than a veneer in Portsmouth, New Hampshire. While we usually think of mahogany as a primary wood, it was used as a secondary wood in first-class work, particularly in cities, where we may find it in the small drawers of work tables, in the swing rails on card tables, in the square plates in candlestand and tea tables, and as a base for veneer on small drawers.

Maple, Sugar (Acer saccharum), Silver (Acer saccharinum), and Red (Acer rubrum). The more than 20 different species of maple found in North America are divided into hard and soft groups. The best known of the hard group is sugar maple, which follows the usual pattern of eastern deciduous trees by growing from New England to Maryland and inland at higher elevations down into North Carolina. The tree can reach heights of 80' – 100' and diameters of 3' – 4'. Sugar maple is very hard and heavy and, in common with the other maples, has a fine texture and few visible pores. It is the source of the well-known tiger and bird's-eye maples, which are actually abnormal growth patterns found in relatively few trees. In the past tiger maple was called fiddleback because it was commonly used for the backs of violins.

Silver and red maple are both soft maples. They resemble sugar maple in being finely textured, but are much softer and lack the same decorative figuring, although red maple often displays a curl figure. When cut, maples have a light tan to amber color that ages to a very pretty honey yellow. However, maple was usually stained or painted to resemble walnut or mahogany, and if the original finish remains, the surface will be much darker.

Both hard and soft maples were commonly employed as primary woods as far south as eastern Connecticut. Maple was particularly popular in rural New Hampshire, and most highboys, chests on chests, and chests of drawers from this area will be either maple or birch. The striking pattern of tiger maple was everybody's favorite, and not only was it common in New England, but there were even a few Philadelphia-area dressing tables made of the wood. In Rhode Island, tall chests of drawers were often made of tiger maple. Throughout New England, maple was the favored budget wood for chairs, and many Queen Anne chairs were made of maple. It was used everywhere for chair legs, being strong, finely textured, easily turned when green, and — unlike hickory — holding paint well. The legs of Windsor chairs are generally made of maple.

In New England, soft maple also saw much use as a secondary wood in locations where strength was required. It is commonly found in Boston-area seat rails, in drop seats, and in the frames of easy chairs, lolling chairs, and sofas. However, its use should no more than suggest New England, for maple is also found in some New York and Philadelphia seating furniture, and red maple was used in the South for turned chairs.

Mulberry, Black (Morus nigra). Mulberry grows along the entire coast, but seems to have been used only in the South. The wood is a brilliant yellow that ages to a golden brown. It has a fine texture and turns well, and is found to some extent in turned chairs. In common with magnolia, its presence is an almost sure sign of southern workmanship.

Oak, White (Quercus alba) and Red (Quercus rubra, Quercus falcata, and others). The many species of oaks found in North America are separated into two groups, white oaks and red oaks. If you compare the end grains of the two, you will notice that white oak differs from red in that its pores are filled with a substance called tylosis, which makes the white oaks very resistant to moisture and rot. All oaks have in common a coarse texture, and red oaks all have large pores. When quartersawn, oak exhibits prominent medullary rays, which is the simplest way to tell oak from chestnut.

Oak is so common in English furniture that it is easy to overlook its use in America or to conclude that oak is a sure sign of English workmanship. In either event, the European oaks are very different from, and in some ways far superior to, the American products.

Red oak was initially used throughout New England for paneled case furniture, perhaps because of the background and training of the early joiners, and also perhaps because red oak could so easily be split into boards. However, by the second decade of the eighteenth century, paneled furniture was long out of style, and wide boards of other woods were available from dozens of water powered sawmills. Oak furniture then proceeded to go out fashion for almost a century and a half.

However, oak continued to be used as a secondary wood when strength was required, in places its coarse texture would not show. While it was occasionally used everywhere along the eastern seaboard, it is most commonly found in the Philadelphia area, including adjacent New Jersey, and in what might be seen as the near south, in Maryland and eastern Virginia. Here we find both white and red oak used for drawer sides, seat rails, sofa frames, and for the flyleaves and swing rails in tables. Oak is also found to some extent in New York City chairs.

Pine, Eastern White (Pinus strobus). Eastern white pine is the largest and best known of some 35 species of American pine. This grand big tree grows from the Canadian Maritimes south into Maryland and inland down through Virginia and North Carolina. Given enough time, and in favorable conditions, a white pine can grow up to 200' high and 6' or more in diameter. The wood has few knots and is stable and easily worked, and once water-powered mills were available to cut it economically, it was used as both a primary and a secondary wood all over New England. North of Boston there is little other secondary wood.

Eastern white pine is relatively soft, fine textured, and straight grained. A cream to light tan color when first cut, it darkens with age to a light orange-brown, and in unfinished and exposed surfaces, such as the bottoms and backs of chests of drawers, to a rich tobacco brown. When plane sawn, it exhibits the prominent growth-ring veining common to all pines. White pine was used for painted furniture as far south as New Jersey, and is also found in Chester and Lancaster County furniture. It was a common secondary wood, not only in northern New England, but also in the Connecticut River Valley, and it is often found in Rhode Island, eastern Connecticut, and New York furniture.

The wood was so perfect for both room moldings and furniture that vast quantities were shipped down the coast, particularly in the years following the Revolution. Charleston furniture often has drawers and dustboards made of white pine. It is both stable and holds glue well, and is seen everywhere in Federal furniture as glue blocks and as a base for veneer. Unfortunately, this does nothing to help identification, for it no more than suggests region except north of Boston.

Pine, Pitch (Pinus rigida). While on the subject of pines, we should note a smallish pine that grows from Maine to northern Georgia. Although now mostly cut over and reduced to scrub growth, in the past pitch pines grew as tall as 90' with a maximum diameter of perhaps 3'. The wood is quite heavy and resinous, and it is soft and easy to work when green, but becomes very hard as it seasons. It is thought that this is the mysterious wood found in the tops of early New England paneled chests. It also seems to have been used to a limited extent in some early southern furniture.

Pine, Southern Yellow (Pinus teada, Pinus palypins, Pins echinata, and Pinus eliotti) South of the Mason-Dixon Line, identification of pine is not a simple matter, for in addition to pitch pine, at least four different species of pine were commonly used in furniture: loblolly pine (*Pinus taeda*), longleaf pine (*Pinus palustris*), shortleaf pine (*Pinus echinata*), and slash pine (*Pinus elliotti*). However, we may consider them a single *taeda* group, a single southern yellow pine. To a greater or lessor extent these are all hard pines; that is, they are both harder and heavier than eastern white pine, which is classified as a soft pine. As a group they are resinous and resistant to rot. The simplest way to identify a southern pine is by the figure, or veining, which is significantly darker and more pronounced that of than eastern white pine.

The thing to remember about the southern yellow pines is that their use in furniture was not confined to the South, and their presence no more than suggests southern workmanship. To a limited extent yellow pine is found in New England, where it was used in early Connecticut chests and Bible boxes. A bit further south it is found in New York and Long Island furniture, and by the time we reach Philadelphia and adjacent New Jersey, it is a fairly common secondary wood. South of the Mason-Dixon Line, yellow pine was employed everywhere as a primary and secondary wood. There is little Southern furniture that does not have it somewhere, and furniture made entirely of yellow pine is almost certainly a product of the South.

Poplar, Yellow (Liriodendron tulipifera). Yellow poplar is a large tree that in good soil can grow to over 150' high and 6' or more in diameter. Also known as tulip poplar, and in the eighteenth century as tulipwood or whitewood, it grows from New England down the coast as far as Pennsylvania and inland at higher elevations as far west as the Mississippi. The wood is light in weight, finely textured, and without any visible pores. Poplar looks somewhat like pine, but lacks the prominent figure. While reasonably strong, it can be dented with a fingernail. The wood is yellowish or grayish in color, often with distinctive greenish or greenish gray stripes. Available in wide, knot-free boards and easy to work, poplar was a favorite of cabinetmakers. Like white pine, it is excellent at holding paint. Its use as a secondary wood is perhaps second only to eastern white pine. Poplar is found in furniture everywhere from Rhode Island and coastal Connecticut down into the Carolinas, and in this respect provides us with little assistance except to discount northern New England, where white pine was favored, and the coastal South, where it does not grow. Its compatibility with paint made it the choice wood for inexpensive painted furniture in New York, Pennsylvania, and New Jersey, and to some extent in the South, although here it had to compete with the harder and stronger yellow pine.

The combination of light weight and strength made tulip poplar a favorite everywhere for drawers. Drawers were sometimes made entirely of poplar, but were sometimes made with white pine bottoms in southeastern New England and New York or with white cedar bottoms in the area around Philadelphia. Poplar was also used for drawers in Maryland and, to some extent, in the Carolinas.

Sabicu (Lysiloma latsiliqua). A brief mention should be made of sabicu, a tropical hardwood that grows in Cuba and the Bahamas. Although not nearly as large a tree as mahogany, it has many of the same attributes, being hard and strong with a close grain. The wood has a mottled figure and a rich reddish color. It is often highly figured and can easily be mistaken for Santo Domingo mahogany. Also known as horseflesh mahogany, it was frequently employed in England during the latter part of the eighteenth century as a substitute for mahogany, and in America has been found in some Boston and Newport furniture. It may be more common than is generally realized, for at Winterthur there are six New England pieces made all or in part of sabicu. Some of these are a mix of mahogany and sabicu, suggesting that the wood was sometimes employed as a substitute when of adequate width and a of color that would blend in with mahogany. Whatever the reason, its presence is a nice indication of eighteenth century workmanship.

Spruce, White (Picea glauca). On the eastern seaboard, white spruce grows no farther south than Vermont and New Hampshire. It is a conifer with light and finely textured wood. Although available in urban centers, particularly during the Federal period, it was seldom used by American cabinetmakers and is generally associated with English furniture, particularly in the manufacture of mirror frames, for which its combination of strength and light weight was an asset. However, it is sometimes seen as a secondary wood in American furniture, particularly in Portsmouth, New Hampshire, and you should not automatically assume that its presence indicates English workmanship.

Sycamore, American (Platanus occidentalis). Sycamore is found everywhere from southern Maine to northern Florida and west beyond the Mississippi. The wood of this large tree is straight grained and the texture fine and even, and when quartersawn it often produces an attractive curly or wavy figure. Unfortunately, it is difficult to season, exhibiting much shrinkage and being inclined to warp, which limited its use in a land where better cabinet woods were available almost everywhere. Sycamore was sometimes used for Windsor chair seats, and it is found in coastal Connecticut and Long Island furniture; its handsome figure provided the rural cabinetmaker with attractive drawer fronts. Unfortunately, it provides only a suggestion of region, for it is also occasionally seen in the Middle Atlantic.

Walnut, Black (Juglans nigra). Walnut was the premier wood for fine furniture until superseded by mahogany in the eighteenth century. American black walnut is among the best of the genus, and while lacking some of the color and figure found in European species, was available in much greater widths. During the seventeenth and eighteenth centuries it was exported to Europe, first from Virginia and later from North Carolina, Maryland, Pennsylvania, and New York. To this day in the United Kingdom, black walnut is called Virginia walnut.

Walnut grows along the coast from New York into North Carolina, inland through South Carolina and Georgia, and to the west beyond the Mississippi. While it can grow up to 150' high and 6' in diameter, most trees are not more than perhaps 100' high and 3' in diameter, and the tops of walnut tables are often made from several boards. The wood comes in various shades of brown from a light tan to a dark chocolate, differing from mahogany in being a more true brown and not having a reddish tinge. It has a straight, somewhat medium texture that under a clear finish is similar to mahogany, but the pores and vessel lines are much smaller than those in mahogany. Walnut can be found with stripe, crotch, fiddleback, and leaf figuring, and also in a striking burl that was popular as a veneer in Colonial New England.

In the eighteenth century, walnut seldom grew north of New York. It was shipped to Boston and Newport, where it is now commonly found in Queen Anne furniture. Even after being displaced by mahogany, it continued to be used to some small extent in New England, usually in traditional, conservative forms of furniture: easy chairs, chests of drawers, slant lid desks, and candlestands.

Walnut was exceedingly popular in the Delaware Valley, and it continued to be used right up into the nineteenth century. The famous Philadelphia high chests are often made of a figured walnut, even though here cost would not appear to have been a consideration.

South of Pennsylvania, walnut was employed everywhere throughout the eighteenth and nineteenth centuries, particularly in furniture produced outside the urban centers of Baltimore, Annapolis, and Charleston. Here it was the primary wood of choice — the maple, cherry, and birch of New England. So ubiquitous is walnut in Southern furniture that it is not unusual to find it employed to some extent as a secondary wood, in drawer sides, drop seats, sofa frames, and the swing rails of gate-leg tables. Much Southern furniture is a combination of walnut and southern yellow pine.

Before discussing different types of furniture, we should consider the regions in which period furniture was produced, for doing so will not only narrow possible locations of manufacture, but will also, in large measure, help us determine the origins of pieces based on design and construction. The first benefit is obvious. When examining an American Chippendale chair, we have to consider Boston, New York, and Philadelphia, but we do not have to worry about Cleveland, Ohio. Secondly, to a greater or lesser extent, early furniture speaks to us of source. Furniture produced in each of the major regions is distinctive, as is furniture produced in different colonies within the regions, and also frequently that produced in different areas within the colonies. Most early furniture exhibits regional features that suggests where it was made. This is most important when dealing with the average grade of old furniture. Not every Massachusetts chest of drawers has a blocked front, nor is every Philadelphia chest of drawers fitted with quarter columns. Even if faced with something the likes of which we have never seen before, and for which there is no similar illustration in the chapters that follow, we can make an educated guess as to where it was made. We will discuss these regional characteristics in this chapter and in the two that follow.

Something first should be said about Colonial America. In the eighteenth century, there were only three cities of any significant size: Boston, New York, and Philadelphia. Because New York cabinetmakers tended to emulate English fashions, the primary innovative centers of style were Boston and Philadelphia, for many years the largest cities in America. Not only did new types of furniture develop in these two cities, but also, Boston and Philadelphia designs influenced work done in surrounding regions. In the chapters that follow you will often see New Hampshire, Rhode Island, and Connecticut furniture that resembles coastal Massachusetts furniture, and Southern furniture that looks like it might have been made in the Delaware Valley. Another thing to remember is that New England furniture is the least English of American furniture, perhaps because Philadelphia grew to be the major American city in the 1750s, leaving Boston as something of a cultural backwater, and perhaps because immigration into New England slowed to a trickle during much of the eighteenth century, what little good land there was having all been spoken for. Benjamin Franklin, after falling out with his brother in the printing business, left Boston for the bright lights of Philadelphia in 1723.

From its earliest Colonial times, New England was an exporter of furniture, mostly to the coastal areas of the Middle Atlantic and Southern colonies, but also to the West Indies. The majority of this trade was from Portsmouth, Boston, Newport, and coastal Connecticut. The most common product was chairs, either simple turned chairs or the enormously popular William and Mary and Queen Anne leather upholstered chairs that were produced by the thousands in Boston.

The most often exported case furniture seems to have been desks, which is logical when you think about it, for a desk is far more difficult to make than a chest of drawers. The dividers require thin stock, which would have been difficult to obtain outside of an urban center. They must be shaped to exact size with a fine saw and slid into small grooves from the back of the case. Then the desk needs a set of small interior drawers, each drawer carefully made of thin stock and joined with small dovetails.

The furniture export trade was almost invariably from north to south, first from New England to the Middle Atlantic and Southern colonies, and later from New York and Philadelphia to the Southern states. As mentioned earlier, if a piece of furniture does not seem native to its present location, it is most logical to look north.

America in the eighteenth and early nineteenth century was very different from the America we see today, and we should consider New England as it looked then, especially from the viewpoint of furniture production. As we see in figure 2-1, most of the small cities were near the coast, either at natural harbors like Boston and Portsmouth or, like Hartford, at the fall line, the head of navigation on a river. Inland settlements, such as Deerfield, tended to lie in river valleys where there was water transportation and good soil. The industrial mill towns of Lowell, Massachusetts, and Manchester, New Hampshire, did not yet exist, and the present city of Fall River was little more than a fishing village.

New England furniture exhibits remarkable diversity, in part

2-1. The New England colonies.

due to geographical accident, the small size of the northern colonies. The larger Middle Atlantic also comprised just four colonies, the whole vast South just five. To survey this smallest of regions, we will start with Maine and Vermont, which were not among the thirteen colonies, and then proceed south through New Hampshire, Massachusetts, Rhode Island, and Connecticut.

Maine

There is little to say about Maine, as during much of this period, this largest state in New England produced little furniture. Maine began as an extension of the Massachusetts Bay Colony, all the land north of the Piscataqua River having been granted to Sir Ferdinando Gorges in the 1620s. Massachusett's District of Maine did not separate and become the state of

Maine until 1820. Habitation was largely a cluster of small fishing villages along the heavily indented coast. As the fisheries became depleted, the early settlers turned to Maine's other great natural resource, the forests, and began exporting timber. However, the area continued to be thinly populated, and aside from the well documented work of Samuel Sewall of York, little furniture was produced until the late in the eighteenth century.

Then, after the Revolution, between about 1790 and 1830, the economy boomed with increased trade in shipbuilding and timber. The population tripled in these forty years. Neoclassical furniture was produced in coastal communities, primarily in York County, just across the river from Portsmouth, New Hampshire. Here in the larger towns, Portland, Saco, and Kennybunk, there was production of fashionable neoclassical forms, most notably chests of drawers, card tables, and sideboards. As you would expect, this furniture closely followed Portsmouth fashion, particularly in having light wood veneered drawer fronts, although, as befits a more rural environment, it tended to have thicker secondary woods. Very probably some Federal furniture attributed to Portsmouth is actually from southern coastal Maine.

With this late start, the rural character of so much of the state, and the abundance of white pine, it is perhaps to be expected that the major body of Maine furniture is both Empire in style and painted, and indeed, the best-known Maine furniture is the wonderfully exuberant painted furniture that was produced in the 1820 and 1830s, examples of which often appear in books on American painted furniture. Among this furniture, you are most likely to see chests of drawers (11-14), dressing tables, and light stands (19-8B). Painted furniture was popular everywhere at this time, but a wonderfully grain-painted piece made of eastern white pine, perhaps with drawer bottoms or backboards of basswood, will most probably be from somewhere in Maine.

Vermont

We will also just touch on Vermont, for although larger in population than Maine, settlement did not get well underway until the latter part of the eighteenth century, and very little furniture survives prior to the turn of the century. Because of this, Vermont period furniture is mostly Federal and neoclassical. While you may see a bracket-foot chest of drawers, it will most likely be Federal rather than Colonial. In style and in use of woods, Vermont might be seen as an extension of the Connecticut River Valley, with some influence from inland and coastal New Hampshire. Cherry is the favored primary wood for better-quality work, with some use of figured maple. Secondary is almost always eastern white pine, and interestingly, often in combination with some basswood, a pairing also seen in adjacent rural New Hampshire.

While there are some formal and Windsor chairs, cherry candlestands, and cherry birdcage tea tables similar to those made in Connecticut, most identified Vermont period furniture is case work, principally chests of drawers and small sideboards. Quite the best known is a small group of very unusual bombé-front chests of drawers, one of which, signed by George Stedman of Norwich, Vermont, is in Winterthur. Although perhaps inspired by the bombé furniture made earlier in Boston, these chests are quite different, being made of cherry rather than mahogany and swelling only across the fronts rather than on both the fronts and the sides (11-13B). The other distinctive pieces of Vermont case work are small Sheraton half sideboards (14-1), which might be considered rural interpretations of small sideboards being made in Boston and Salem. In any event, their simple construction and small scale made them a natural for this rural area. The inlaid diamond shown in the center of the upper drawer of the sideboard is a feature also seen in Vermont chests of drawers.

Far more common than either of these are a very considerable group of Hepplewhite-style French-foot chests of drawers (11-13A). These seem to have a mix of Connecticut and New Hampshire influences; usually the case is made of cherry and then the drawer fronts are veneered in light contrasting figured maple or birch and bordered with darker mahogany veneer. Even this far inland it would not have been too difficult to obtain a little mahogany for trim. Unlike a great many makers of Federal chests of drawers, Vermont cabinetmakers seem never to have bowed the fronts of furniture, and this, in conjunction with the use of basswood, helps us to distinguish Vermont casework. There may be more of these chests of drawers than we realize, for some have almost certainly been confused with, or passed off as, the work of Connecticut or New Hampshire craftsmen.

New Hampshire

New Hampshire is a more interesting study, for here there were two very different furniture schools, one coastal and urban, the other inland and rural. We will start at the mouth of the Piscataqua River with furniture produced in and around the small city of Portsmouth, then turn inland to consider some equally distinctive furniture produced in a group of small towns near present-day Manchester.

Portsmouth furniture is in many ways an extension of Boston, and here we see Queen Anne chairs and Chippendale block-front chests of drawers that are very similar to those of Boston workmanship but have small differences in proportion and construction. While the early Queen Anne chairs made by John Gaines III are very distinctive (5-12A), they are very uncommon, and the average run of the New Hampshire Queen Anne chair is similar to a great many other New England Queen Anne chairs, differing mostly in having the rush seat set within covering rails, and then one or two semicircular drops in the front rail. Although lacking in the example in figure 5-12B, many have the large, built-up Spanish feet shown in figure 5-12A.

Turned banister-back chairs produced in coastal New Hampshire and adjacent Essex County often have unusual "staghorn" or "fishtail" crest rails (6-3D). The arms are apt to have curved-over, drooping handholds, although this shape is not unique to this area.

With the advent of rococo and Chippendale style there were more differences, due in part to a local preference for English styles and in part to the arrival in the 1760s of a group of English-trained cabinetmakers, most notably Robert Harrold. This influence is seen in a number of very English-looking chairs, basin stands, tea tables, and kettle stands. Of this furniture, you are most likely to encounter a side chair or armchair. These are rather English looking, with wide seats and intricate pierced splats (5-18A). Look under the seat and you may see that the rails are reinforced with the English type of bracing (5-7), a feature also seen in upholstered chairs. In English fashion, upholstered chairs also tend to have overupholstered arms.

However, it is in the Federal period, and in case furniture, that Portsmouth furniture becomes most distinctive. Here we see neoclassical high-style chests of drawers, desks, and sideboards that are notably colorful, even by American standards. The usual treatment was to veneer up the drawer fronts in light-colored figured birch or maple veneers, then provide a contrasting frame by edging the drawers with darker mahogany. They look somewhat naive and flashy — and they are. While there may be but a single panel, the more common treatment was to divide the area into two or three panels by use of vertical bands of mahogany as shown in the chest of drawers in figure 11-15. When a piece has three panels, there will usually be two wide panels on either side of a somewhat narrower center panel, the latter often decorated with a neoclassical oval. Below the bottom drawer, at the center of the apron, there will very often be a similarly veneered rectangular tablet, what is often called a "dropped panel."

While the colorful drawers are what first come to the eye, there are other features that can help identify Portsmouth workmanship, as not all Portsmouth case work has light veneers and dropped panels. Even with better work, the case is frequently constructed of birch that was stained up to resemble mahogany. While a chest of drawers or a desk will appear to be made of mahogany, in fact, the only mahogany will be the bordering veneer on the front of the case. To stiffen the case, there will usually be either a wide cross brace or full-depth dustboard behind the middle drawer divider. The front feet will be high and somewhat narrow, with pronounced flares at the bottoms and small steps or spurs on the insides just below where the legs curve over to join the apron. The back feet will be quite robust, usually having wide, dovetailed diagonal braces across the rear.

Here it should be noted that not all New Hampshire high-style Federal furniture is from Portsmouth. There was some production in nearby coastal towns, in Hampton and Dover, and inland in Concord, which became the capital of New Hampshire in 1808 and was also the home of the famous Concord coaches.

Fifty miles west of Portsmouth, between Concord and the present-day city of Manchester, there is a cluster of small towns in the Merrimack River Valley: Salisbury, Goffstown, Henniker, Antrim, Chester, and Bedford. This is where two brothers, Major John Dunlap and Lieutenant Samuel Dunlap, began making furniture in the 1770s. They would seem to have worked night and day, for almost every maple or birch chest with a little foofaraw in the apron is likely to be attributed to one or the other. Actually, at least eleven children and grandchildren followed in the trade, so a fair amount of rural New Hampshire furniture may indeed be the product of one or another Dunlap, although perhaps not John or Samuel.

Most of this production occurred after the Revolution, and it continued well up into the nineteenth century, when the Queen Anne features so often seen in this rural furniture were long out of fashion in urban areas. As is often the case, the best work was done early on, most of it apparently by John and Samuel before the close of the century. Here we see typical Dunlap features: whimsical carving described as "flowered ogee" on the base moldings of chests of drawers, boldly scrolled knee brackets (11-5A), pierced basketweave cornices (12-3A), and very often, S-scrolls on highboy skirts (12-3A). The Dunlaps are not the only well-known makers of Merrimack Valley furniture. Another is Peter Bartlett (1788 – 1838), who worked in Salisbury. The Queen Anne desk in Figure 13-3 and the tall chest in figure 11-21D are attributed to his shop.

In many respects, Dunlap furniture is just an embellished version of the case furniture being produced all over rural New Hampshire at the turn of the eighteenth century. Here we see a great many simple birch or maple chests of drawers, tall chests, chest-on-chests, and high chests of drawers. In spite of the additional labor, Queen Anne cabriole legs were much in favor and are often seen on furniture from this area. High chests usually have a deep lower case with three rows of drawers that rest on rather short legs, then a tall, five-drawer upper case (12-3B). Often drawers will be doubled up with false fronts that mask large drawers with fake drawer fronts. The high chest of drawers in figure 12-3B would seem to have 12 drawers, but there are actually only eight, for both the three drawers at the top of the upper case and the three at the base of the lower case are but single full-width drawers. This charming little economy is seen all over New England, even in Rhode Island work in which there was an emphasis on quality, but is by far the most prevalent in rural New Hampshire. It should also be noted that in New Hampshire case work, the secondary wood will almost invariably be white pine, sometimes with a little basswood here and there.

Before leaving rural New Hampshire, another characteristic of this area should be noted, this one a construction practice. Normally in period work, the legs of stands and tea tables are fastened to the column or pillar by use of blind dovetail joints. Here a dovetail was cut at the inner ends of the legs, then the legs were joined by sliding them up into matching slots cut into the bottom of the column. However, in rural New Hampshire it was more usual to fasten the legs with mortise and tenon joints. To provide a flat surface for the mortise, the bottom of the column was usually six-sided, and to lock in the leg, the joint was normally pinned at the top and bottom. The column was then extended a few inches below the bottom of the legs to provide adequate stock at the bottom of the mortise. This was usually terminated with a decorative turning as shown in figure 19-1A. While this unusual construction is most often seen in rural New Hampshire candlestands and tea tables, mortised and tenoned cabriole legs should not be taken as certain evidence of New Hampshire workmanship, for it is a logical construction method in any area where the required tools, or the iron strapping, were not available. It is also seen in rural Southern candlestands.

Perhaps the most striking aspect of rural New Hampshire

furniture is the continued use of the Queen Anne style well up into the nineteenth century, many years after it had been superseded first by Chippendale, and then by Hepplewhite and Sheraton in urban New Hampshire and Massachusetts. We will encounter this affection for the Queen Anne style again, but in an urban setting, when we reach Rhode Island.

Massachusetts

Now we come to Massachusetts, the most populous of the northern colonies and the source of the great majority of New England furniture produced both before and after the Revolution. So preeminent was Massachusetts, and Boston in particular, in the production of furniture in the eighteenth and nineteenth centuries, that if a piece of New England furniture has no particular attributes to link it with one of the other New England colonies, it is pretty safe to attribute it to Massachusetts, and to the eastern third of Massachusetts at that. The Massachusetts we will discuss is coastal Massachusetts, the center of population and manufacturing: Boston and the nearby towns of Charlestown, Dorchester, and Roxbury; and the northern coastal communities of Salem, Marblehead, Ipswich, and Newburyport. South of Boston there appears to have been only limited production in some of the larger towns, in Plymouth, Sandwich, Barnstable, and Taunton. Much of the furniture in this area seems to have come down from Boston by packet boat. A considerable body of furniture was also produced in the western part of the state, and while this is indeed part of Massachusetts, it is in the Connecticut River Valley, and will be discussed when we get to Connecticut and the Connecticut River Valley.

From earliest times Boston was a major center of production, and Boston furniture reflects this environment. There is much standardization in popular and successful designs, in the crooked-back chairs that were shipped down to Philadelphia, in the standard cabriole-leg Queen Anne side chair, and in the innumerable block and serpentine front chests of drawers. The retracted ball and claw foot with its backward sloping claws is seen in all types of furniture. By and large, Massachusetts furniture does not have the one-off look seen in items of rural workmanship. With this, there are all sorts of subtle little hints of the casual haste that comes with working in a busy shop. The front legs on turned chairs do not always quite match, drawer slides on a chest of drawers may be simply nailed to the sides of the case, and even on expensive blockfront furniture, drawer dovetails are apt to appear quickly cut and irregular. Carving is uncommon, and where present, is normally quite shallow, as though the carver was working in haste and was loath to do any more work than absolutely necessary. For the most part, New England case work does not have dust boards between the drawers. Such boards are far more common in New York and Philadelphia furniture — and also in English furniture, for which they were such a cachet of quality that they were even fitted on budget chests of drawers.

In addition to standard designs and a standard form of ball and claw foot, Boston-area furniture exhibits a number of construction practices that can help identify Massachusetts workmanship. In common with much other New England case work,

bracket and French feet tend to be high and bold. Perhaps because New England chests of drawers and desks were so much lighter than their Middle Atlantic counterparts, it was possible to have tall, elegant feet. In any event, case work with noticeably tall feet will probably be from the northern colonies. Looking at the feet it is perhaps the easiest way to tell a New England chest of drawers from a Middle Atlantic chest of drawers.

The tops of Chippendale chests of drawers are usually fastened to the sides of the case by means of a long transverse sliding dovetail, a time-saving feature also seen in some rural New Hampshire chests of drawers. This practice seems to have been limited to the eighteenth century, for after the Revolution most cabinetmakers just dovetailed two slats to the case sides, then fastened the top with screws driven up through the slats. Also by this time, drawer blade dovetails were usually hidden under a covering strip.

When, as was usually the case, the base molding on a chest of drawers or a desk was thicker than the bottom board, there was a problem of accommodating the overlap. In Boston, the normal method was to set the base molding flush with the upper surface of the bottom board, then add filler blocks under the bottom to provide an even surface for the foot blocking. Pull out the bottom drawer and you will see that it slides on the bottom board. Rhode Island cabinetmakers did just the reverse, setting the base molding flush with the lower surface of the bottom board, then resting the drawer on a blade and a pair of slides along the inside of the case.

Pull out the lower drawer on a Boston blockfront or serpentine chest of drawers and not only will you notice that the drawer slides on the bottom of the case, but also that the front base molding is joined to the bottom of the case by a single wide dovetail. This "giant dovetail" is a feature of Boston furniture, and while not found on all case work, is a useful indicator of region when present.

American cabinetmakers in the eighteenth century preferred shaping to carving, probably due to a chronic shortage of skilled labor and an abundance of wood. Nowhere is this more evident than in Massachusetts case work, where the fronts of chests of drawers, chest-on-chests, clothes presses, desks, and desk and bookcases were often shaped or "swelled," either by blocking or with a serpentine curve. This popularity was all the more remarkable in that a shaped front increased the cost by about half again. Swelled fronts are most common in furniture from eastern Massachusetts, but are also seen in pieces from western Massachusetts, Rhode Island, Connecticut, and coastal New Hampshire. A few pieces of New York furniture have blocked fronts. Serpentine-front furniture was produced to some extent in all regions, but was so popular in coastal Massachusetts that a serpentine- or reverse-serpentine-front desk or chest of drawers will probably be from this area.

Before leaving Massachusetts case work, something should be said of bombé furniture, even though you are unlikely to encounter an example of this form outside of a museum or a major auction. Chests of drawers having bombé fronts were produced in Vermont, but in Massachusetts the whole lower portion of the case is swelled as shown in the chest of drawers in figure 11-6F. This very unusual furniture was only produced for about 20 years near the end of the eighteenth century, and then only in Boston and Salem. The distinctive shape is most common in chests of drawers, desks, and desk and bookcases. American bombé furniture is rare, which is little wonder when you consider that the sides of the case had to be worked out of three- or four-inch-thick mahogany boards. The shape was quite common in Europe, but here the swell was made of secondary wood which was then either painted or veneered.

There are other features that can help identify not only Massachusetts furniture, but also, where in Massachusetts a piece may have been made. Not all Boston furniture was production work. John and Thomas Seymour produced superb one-off neoclassical furniture in the first two decades of the nineteenth century, but this exceptional workmanship is rare. The Seymours immigrated from England, and both Seymour and Seymour-type case furniture, as in the chest of drawers in figure 11-16H and the cellaret sideboard in figure 14-2D, may have an English look.

Sliding tambour doors were much in fashion but were difficult to make, and while seen in Salem and Portsmouth, are most likely to be from the Boston area. From Salem, and up along the North Shore as far as Portsmouth, there is a group of furniture in which the cabriole legs are said to be "notched" or "stepped." The leg will have the usual New England sharp edge, or arris, but then instead of a smooth transition to a rounded shape towards the ankle, will have a quite abrupt transition within just an inch or so. In profile, the leg will appear to notch or step in about six inches below the top.

Here also, between Boston and Portsmouth, you are most likely to see the distinctive New England double-tapered leg in which the square, tapering Hepplewhite leg alters angle and tapers in more sharply a few inches above the floor. Normally the transition is signaled by an inlaid cuff of contrasting lighter and darker woods. Another Federal New England feature is the decorative use of a cluster or stack of rings. This is often seen in cookie corners on Sheraton chests of drawers (11-16G), in the legs of Sheraton card tables (18-6E), and in the columns of candlestands (19-2C).

During the first decades of the nineteenth century, it was common in coastal Massachusetts and New Hampshire to vary the color of the banding around drawers with random pieces of lighter wood. The effect is quite striking, and I'm sure was very fashionable, but perhaps is not so much to modern eyes, for from a distance the variegated banding appears to be a poor repair by a very inept cabinetmaker.

Queen Anne and Chippendale case furniture is usually embellished with one or more carved finials, and the shape is region specific. In Massachusetts the favored form was what might be described as an urn and spiral flame, as seen in figure 12-4E. Rhode Island cabinetmakers employed a variety of designs, the most common of which was a somewhat shorter, thicker spiral above a small ball (12-5B).

Seating furniture and tables will be covered later, but here it should be noted that lolling chairs are likely to be from urban areas in Massachusetts, where upholstery and upholsterers were available. Massachusetts Chippendale side chairs are likely to have pierced owl's-eye splats over upholstered seats, cabriole legs with sharp creases, or arris, block and turned stretchers, and club feet with pronounced disks. Armchairs were not favored in Massachusetts, and Massachusetts armchairs are very uncommon. When there is seat reinforcement, it will almost invariably be the nailed triangular pine blocking illustrated in figure 5-6. Throughout New England, the legs on gateleg and tavern tables were most often made with the double-baluster and ring turning pattern shown in the tavern table in figure 20-1A.

Lastly, something must be said about the primary and secondary woods employed in Massachusetts furniture. Much of the better-quality early furniture was made of either black walnut or red cedar, then in coastal areas walnut was employed until supplanted by mahogany in the second half of the eighteenth century. Maple and birch were used everywhere for less expensive furniture, birch mostly in case work, maple in the fashionable Queen Anne chairs. While usually associated with Connecticut and the Connecticut River Valley, cherry is not uncommon in eastern Massachusetts. Except for some use of basswood in Maine and Vermont, the secondary wood in northern New England was almost invariably eastern white pine. South of Massachusetts, you begin to see a mixture of secondary woods, typically white pine in combination with poplar and chestnut in Rhode Island, poplar in coastal Connecticut. Furniture in which the secondary wood is entirely white pine will most likely be from somewhere north of Connecticut and Rhode Island.

Rhode Island

In many ways, this smallest of colonies — and then the smallest of states — is more interesting than the larger, richer, and more populous Massachusetts. Rhode Island covers so small an area that other than Newport and Providence there seem to be no areas of significant furniture production. A piece of Rhode Island furniture will almost surely be from one or the other city. There is another helpful generalization. Before the Revolution, Newport was the major center and the source of most furniture, but was ruined by the conflict and never fully recovered. After the war, production shifted to Providence, which was closer to the inland markets. In a rough way, then, Rhode Island Queen Anne and Chippendale furniture is likely to be from Newport, Hepplewhite and Sheraton furniture from Providence.

Newport has a special place in our survey of New England, for this small Colonial city produced some of America's most singularly beautiful furniture, the likes of which are seen from nowhere else in the 13 colonies, and if I grow a little lyrical in this section, it is not without good reason. Even more remarkably, much of the furniture seems to have been the product of just two intermarried families of Quaker cabinetmakers. However, let's first touch on geography, and then consider the characteristics of Newport furniture. The area influenced by this style center stretched north from Newport to the even smaller city of Providence at the head of Narragansett Bay and south and west into Connecticut's New London County, perhaps 40 miles north to south and 50 miles east to west, about half again the size of the present state. In addition to being seen in New London

County, Rhode Island features are also sometimes seen in pieces from southeastern Massachusetts.

Furniture made in Newport exhibits features that make it easy to identify, even in a roomful of other furniture. In a general way it is conservative, very well made, and modest in scale. The merchants and lawyers of Newport seem to have preferred Queen Anne to Chippendale and to have had little use for the new rococo style that was so fashionable before the Revolution. Newport work seldom has the gilding, fretwork, gadrooning, carved splats, and scrolled bracket feet that were popular elsewhere at this time. To a very considerable extent, cabinetmakers favored a fully developed Queen Anne style and quietly let Thomas Chippendale and rococo pass them by. When they finally did change, after the Revolution, it was to a conservative interpretation of Hepplewhite style, but by this time most trade had shifted to Providence, and there is relatively little of this furniture.

The conservatism in matters of style may also have had some influence on proportions, for while Queen Anne side and wing chairs are quite large and sturdy, case work tends to be smaller than the average run of period furniture. In a display of American high chests of drawers, the Newport example will be quite noticeably the smallest. Nowhere will you see the great big Chippendale desks that were so popular in the Boston area.

Books on American furniture invariably illustrate the beautiful Newport block-and-shell furniture. This singular form of blocking, which alone would have made Newport furniture famous, is largely the providence of two families of cabinetmakers: John Townsend, John Goddard, and about twenty children, cousins, and relatives by marriage. Together, these cabinetmakers pretty much dominated the high end of the Newport furniture trade, developing in the process a whole group of innovations in design and construction that made Newport furniture so unique. Of these, by far the most famous is the idea of terminating the top of blocking with large, carved shells. While neither blocking nor shells were anything new, combining them in this fashion was unique. To add further richness, and perhaps additional Queen Anne curves, the lobes on the large shells curve over on each side as they approach the horizontal as shown in the chest of drawers in figure 11-7C. In addition, the side blocking is carried down into conforming ogee bracket feet, thus providing a graceful termination at each end. In Boston, the blocking is also carried down to the feet, but these are usually straight rather than ogee bracket feet. Before going further, though, it should be mentioned that the block-and-shell motif is not entirely confined to Rhode Island, for as will be noted in the next section, the idea was emulated in the eastern corner of Connecticut in New London County. Here also it should be noted that most all American chests of drawers have four graduated drawers, but those made in Rhode Island and New London County may have just three deep drawers — a configuration often seen in English chests of drawers.

An inherent problem with blocking is terminating the ends, particularly at the top, which is closest to the eye. Boston cabinetmakers solved this problem in chests of drawers by bringing the blocking up to a conforming top that echoed the shape of the blocking. However, this does not work with a slant-front desk, and in pieces made by less-than-skilled hands you will sometimes notice a certain awkwardness at the top of the blocking. The Newport solution was usually to avoid blocking the exterior, and instead incorporate the block and shell motif on inside of the desk, as shown in figure 13-5A.

The combination of block and shell with the distinctive curved lobes was employed in a variety of case work, and in addition to chests of drawers, is seen in dressing tables, chest-on-chests, clock-case doors, and the top-of-the-line, magnificent big desk and bookcases that may have as many as nine carved shells. Even at the time this furniture was very expensive, costing far more than the standard Boston blockfront. Highly prized and beautifully made of the finest mahogany, perhaps a greater percentage has survived in good condition than any other type of furniture. Even so, work of this quality is quite rare. Of the most common form, the bureau table illustrated in figure 12-14A, only about 50 remain today. Probably not many more were ever made. When admiring this grand furniture and the famous family of craftsmen that produced it, we should not overlook the patience and good taste of the people of Newport, or the way they treasured this beautiful furniture. Without their support, the Townsends and Goddards would have been just local makers of Boston-style blockfronts.

However, this discussion of block and shell is something of a distraction, for it leads us away from Newport and Rhode Island features you are far more likely to see, and even here you will not often see them, for although much published, Newport furniture is not all that common. Among design features, you are most likely to notice a solid and conservative ogee bracket foot with a squared pad (11-7A) that is very different from the scrolled bracket feet so often seen in Massachusetts. With this, you are also likely to see the late rococo bail pulls that were much favored in Rhode Island. Even on grand furniture, the top drawers in the upper case are apt to be secured by "Quaker" wooden spring locks, a feature that seems to have appealed to thrifty Quakers everywhere, for these clever locks are also frequently seen in the Delaware Valley. Stop fluting was employed as a decorative treatment almost everywhere on better quality furniture, but was exceedingly popular in Rhode Island, and if you see a chair or table in which the square Marlborough legs are embellished with stop fluting, you are most probably looking at Rhode Island workmanship. While here, it should be mentioned that although ball and claw feet with undercut talons are indeed indicative of Newport workmanship, you will not see these except on the very best quality work. More often, you may see a rather narrow and delicate looking slipper foot that is quite different from the small, rounded Philadelphia slipper foot and the wide, deep New York slipper foot. The other difference is that this foot was employed on tea tables and case furniture rather than on seating furniture.

Rhode Island cabinetmakers also handled the tympanum in a unique manner. No, a tympanum is not an ancient musical instrument. It is the space enclosed by an arch or pediment. Now, so long as high chests and chest-on-chests had flat tops there was no problem, but as soon as cabinetmakers went to a serpentine or bonnet top, the question arose as to how to handle the space between the arch and the upper tier of drawers. Massachusetts cabinetmakers solved the problem by making the center top drawer much deeper than the two flanking drawers, and then generally decorating it with a large shell (12-4E) or a concave scoop (12-4D). The approach taken in Philadelphia was to decorate a deep center drawer with a carved shell and applied leafage (12-8A), or to omit the deep drawer and fill the whole area with applied vine and shell carving. However, Newport cabinetmakers would have none of such rococo frippery. Their solution was to simply to fill this area with a pair of molded panels that conformed to the shape of the arch, as shown in figure 12-5B. This elegantly simple solution was employed on all bonnet tops and is an easy way to spot a piece of Rhode Island furniture. Actually, it would be more correct to say that it is an easy way to spot Rhode Island-region furniture, for these distinctive panels are also seen in adjacent areas of Connecticut and Long Island.

As noted earlier, Newport and Rhode Island furniture is singularly well made, and this high level of workmanship is a help in identification. As a rule, even an average piece will be well made with neatly cut dovetails and a careful selection of woods. Rhode Island cabinetmakers preferred mahogany, but if the customer needed to economize, would usually employ cherry or a nicely figured maple. As in Boston, early Newport Queen Anne formal furniture was made of walnut, but by the time block-and-shell furniture was being produced, mahogany had become the fashionable cabinet wood.

When examining case work, most of us instinctively pull out a drawer to look at the dovetails, and here you will usually see very carefully made, evenly spaced dovetails. The upper corners of desks, where lapped dovetails join the sides to the top, will have a generous number of dovetails. If the dovetails that join drawer blades to the sides of the case are not covered, they will normally be shouldered, then stopped just short of the sides of the case. Often there will be extra structure to assure that box sections remain square: vertical reinforcing strips nailed to the insides of the backs of cases, and cross braces joining the rails of tables.

There are other innovative design and construction features associated with the general high quality of Rhode Island workmanship that are form specific. These will be discussed later in the appropriate chapters. However, because they are such useful indicators and are so easy to spot, we might touch on them here. Usually there is a small gap between the mid-molding and the upper case on chest-on-chests and high chests, but you may notice there will be no such gap in Rhode Island furniture. As described in chapter 11, this is because the mid-molding was usually attached to the upper rather than the lower case, the two being kept in place by a lengthwise cleat on the bottom of the upper case that fits into a corresponding slot in the lower case.

Pull out the lowest drawer in a chest of drawers — or a chest-on-chest or tall chest — and you will see that it slides on a drawer blade and a pair of slides rather than on the bottom of

the case. Then, if you peer under the bottom, you will also see that the foot blocking is glued directly to the bottom board of the case. Elsewhere there will be additional blocking, because the base moldings are normally somewhat thicker than the bottom board of the case. Rhode Island tables were sometimes given little decorative pierced brackets where the legs met the apron, and on good work you will see that these rather delicate rococo embellishments are not only thicker and more solid than they appear, but also, are tenoned into the legs and apron. Elsewhere they were usually just fastened with glue and a couple of small nails or sprigs — and are now missing or restored.

Quite the best-known Rhode Island construction feature is the so-called removable leg that was employed on high chests of drawers, dressing tables, and sometimes on chests on frames. Cabriole-leg furniture seems to have been made this way to facilitate shipment and repair, although such a technique also avoided having the pins visible on the front of the case. In the past it would have been cheaper, and far safer, to ship a high chest of drawers with the rather delicate legs safely tucked into one of the long drawers. Actually, the term itself is not accurate, for the legs were kept in place with blocking and glue, and are not easily removed, although the design would certainly have simplified replacement of a broken leg. The way this was done will be described later, and here we will just note how to spot this construction. If you look at the front of a Rhode Island high chest or dressing table, you will notice that the cabriole legs do not appear to be pinned; that is, there are no pins above the cabriole legs on either side of the drawers. Look more closely and you will see that the legs seem to stop at the bottom of the case, and that the corners of the case have a thin covering strip. Should you be able to see the back of a high chest, you will also notice that the backboard of the lower case is a structural element, being fastened with large dovetails rather than just tacked in place with nails.

For all this discussion of quality and attention to detail, it might be noted that not all furniture that would seem to have been made in Rhode Island is of uniformly good quality. In particular, the standard Rhode Island Chippendale card tables, like that shown in figure 18-2A, may be poorly made. The beds will not be cross braced, the brackets will not be tenoned, and the legs will be just squared rather than stop fluted at the bottom. These card tables may have been cheaply produced for sale in warerooms or may be just survival examples of a very successful design.

Lastly, Rhode Island cabinetmakers employed a variety of secondary woods rather than just the eastern white pine seen in Massachusetts and the northern colonies. Here we begin to see the mix of secondary woods that is characteristic of much Middle Atlantic workmanship. In addition to white pine, you may see poplar, birch, cherry, and chestnut; this is perhaps because Rhode Island cabinetmakers wished to employ the best wood for a particular location, a practice also seen in New York Federal furniture. Chestnut was much favored in southeastern New England, primarily in Rhode Island, but also in adjacent southeastern Massachusetts and eastern Connecticut, where it is frequently seen in drawer bottoms. In Rhode Island, though, it is used everywhere, for drawers, backboards, swing rails, and the blocks or plates under the tops of tea tables and candlestands. Rhode Island drawers typically are all poplar, have poplar sides and chestnut bottoms, or are all chestnut. However, chestnut is such a satisfactory secondary wood that you should not think it equals southeastern New England — any more than cherry equals Connecticut — for it is also seen to some extent in west-central Massachusetts, along the North Shore of Massachusetts, and in Long Island, Philadelphia, and Maryland.

Connecticut and the Connecticut River Valley

In many ways, the flanking New England colonies are more interesting than the larger, central, and more important Massachusetts. Connecticut is no exception. In fact, it is in a class by itself. However, before discussing Connecticut furniture, something should be said about the colony, or perhaps more correctly, the region, for the area encompassed by this remarkable style center covers a lot more acreage than the present state of Connecticut. Some of the different areas and their furniture styles will be discussed later. Here it is sufficient to note that the region covers early settlements along the coast and a string of towns extending up the Connecticut River Valley through western Massachusetts into southern Vermont and New Hampshire — the greater part of settled inland New England prior to the Revolution.

Normally, I touch on cabinet woods at the conclusion of a section, but the use of cherry is so characteristic of Connecticut workmanship that we might start off with a discussion of this prince of cabinet woods. By now you have almost certainly heard somewhere that Connecticut furniture is always made of cherry, and to a remarkable degree this is true, for about five in every six better-quality pieces of furniture are indeed made of cherry, actually black cherry, or more properly, *Prunus serotina*. This preference for cherry is even more remarkable in that much of the remaining sixth comprises such local manufacture as painted furniture and Windsor chairs, for which cherry would not have been suitable. However, before you think that this provides an easy provenance, think again, for the reverse, that furniture made of cherry is always from Connecticut, is anything but true, for this handsome, easily worked wood was used everywhere where mahogany was either too expensive or was not available. It was the favored primary wood in Vermont, is often seen in eastern Massachusetts, is a common alternative to walnut in Delaware Valley corner cupboards, and was frequently used in the South. Perhaps the best way to associate cherry with Connecticut River Valley workmanship is to remember that in this whole area cherry was the favored wood, not just a substitute for better woods. In other inland areas where mahogany would have been expensive or difficult to obtain, cabinetmakers usually employed maple.

Connecticut cabinetmakers seem to have always preferred cherry, for high-style Queen Anne chairs and tea tables were being made of cherry at a time when walnut was still the fashionable wood. This would suggest that a piece of formal furniture, such a high chest, dressing table, tea table, sideboard, or

side chair, if made of cherry, is very likely to be from either Connecticut or the Connecticut River Valley. Interestingly, cherry was often stained up to resemble walnut or mahogany, which would suggest that at least part of its attraction was as a substitute for more costly woods. That it is so pretty to us now is due both to age and because the original finish has so often been removed.

Cabinetmakers also liked doing things a little differently, and in addition to a singular loyalty to cherry, we find all sorts of idiosyncrasies that add much charm to their work. Much of this is perhaps attributable to the rural nature of the colony, but nevertheless, there is still a remarkable vocabulary of design motifs that can help identify Connecticut workmanship. The most obvious, and perhaps the most common, is the scalloping of the tops, aprons, and skirts on all sorts of furniture. While chests of drawers (11-8C), tea tables, and dressing tables (12-11A) having scalloped tops are much published, they are actually relatively scarce, which should not be surprising if we consider the time and difficulty involved in making a molded, scalloped top. Far more common are the reverse curves in the aprons of chests (10-3D) and high chests of drawers (12-6A), which could be easily be cut out with a saw, chisel, and file. Multiple and conspicuous curves are a good indication of Connecticut workmanship.

Connecticut furniture tends to be overdecorated by urban standards, displaying a naive exuberance that adds so much to its charm. The corners on case work are often embellished, either with fluted quarter columns, spiral rope molding, or fluted pilasters, which are sometimes stopped at the bottom. There may be a strip of applied gadrooning across the base of a piece between the feet. Small furniture, particularly light stands, will be decorated with contrasting inlay of local woods, as we see in the charming little stand in figure 19-8D. Icicle inlay was popular throughout the Connecticut River Valley, as well as in Newport and Providence, which would suggest that a table made of cherry with this inlay is probably a Connecticut product.

Unlike those of Massachusetts, the finials do not follow any established pattern, and here you will see all manner of whimsical and innovative creations. For the most part they are products of turning rather than carving. Pinwheels were very popular, and are often seen on case furniture. However, carving a pinwheel is not difficult. Unlike the sophisticated Rhode Island lobed shells, pinwheels are easily laid out and require no particular skill, or for that matter, more tools than a compass and a couple of small, flat chisels. While they were indeed common in Connecticut, they are so easy to carve that they are seen everywhere in New England, principally in Essex County, Massachusetts, and also to the north in rural New Hampshire. For much the same reason, New England furniture is often decorated with simple carved fans.

Connecticut cabinetmakers favored furniture on frames, not so much the high cabriole leg frames that are occasionally seen in all regions, but rather low frames on short bandy cabriole legs that ended in pad feet. These are seen on desks (13-6D), sometimes on desk and bookcases (13-6F), and even on chest-on-chests (11-24F), resulting in that truly wondrous creation, the chest-on-chest-on-frame. New Hampshire cabinetmakers also made some furniture on low frames, but here the primary wood used was usually either maple or birch.

Having touched on the extent of the region, and considered Connecticut cabinetry in a general way, we will look at some specific areas, for not only is it relatively easy to identify Connecticut workmanship, but also to identify where in Connecticut a piece of furniture was probably made. The earliest settlements were along the coast from Bridgeport in the west to Stonington in the east. Just before the Revolution, New Haven was still the largest town in the colony, with over eight thousand inhabitants. Among these coastal communities, those in eastern New London County produced the most distinctive furniture. Here there were a group of large, prosperous towns: New London, Colchester, Stonington, and Norwich. New London is at the mouth of the Thames River, Norwich about 20 miles north at the head of navigation. At this time, the town of Stonington was larger than Hartford.

New London County, tucked up against the southwestern border of Rhode Island, produced furniture with a delightful mix of Connecticut, Boston, Newport, and New York influences. Here we see rural interpretations of Newport block-and-shell furniture (11-8E), as well as detachable legs, slipper feet, and the single center drop favored in high chests of drawers. Bonnet tops have bold dental moldings that follow the curves of the bonnets, and below this have pairs of applied panels in the best Newport style. In New York fashion, case furniture is apt to have ball and claw feet in front, ogee bracket feet at the rear. Primary woods may be either cherry or mahogany, secondary a mix of pine, poplar, chestnut, and for some strange reason, butternut.

For all this, the feature you are most likely to encounter is the distinctive New London County bracket foot. In common with much Connecticut furniture, case work will be supported by large, very solid looking ogee bracket feet. In New London County, the brackets were likely to be embellished with pairs of inward facing wavelike scrolls, as shown in figure 11-8B. This form of scrolling was not unique, but elsewhere the scrolls were usually made to face outward, as was done in New Hampshire. Another aspect of New London furniture is that the sides of the case were carried down behind the facing to support the feet. This made for a very strong foot, but unfortunately, unless the ogee facing was made very thick, gave the feet a somewhat tucked-in look. Unfortunately, this characteristic should be considered no more than another indication of New London workmanship, for like all simple and logical ideas, it is likely to be found anywhere, perhaps more so in New England, where the feet on chests were usually extensions of the sides of the case.

Northwest from the communities of Saybrook and Essex at the mouth of the Connecticut River, there was a group of towns that extended up the river valley through central Connecticut. Today some of the area lies within the city limits of Hartford, but in the eighteenth century, the present capital of Connecticut was but one of a number of prosperous towns along the river valley, beginning with Wethersfield in the south and proceeding north through Hartford to East Windsor, then across the Massachusetts border to Springfield and Northhampton. This is where Eliphalet Chapin, Aaron Chapin, George Belden, and about half a dozen other cabinetmakers were producing distinctive regional furniture in the last decades of the eighteenth century — furniture of what is today called the Chapin Shops or the Chapin School. Eliphalet left Connecticut, apparently to avoid a shotgun marriage, and worked for several years in Philadelphia before returning to East Windsor. The distinctly Pennsylvania look of Hartford-area high chests and dressing tables is usually ascribed to Eliphalet's training, although Connecticut cabinetmakers borrowed so freely from the major style centers that history may give him more credit than is due. In any event, Hartford area cabinet work not only exhibits some Philadelphia influences, but also is notable for its quality and attention to detail. The Connecticut River Valley was probably the richest farmland in New England, and Chapin furniture reflects this prosperity. Interestingly, much of this fine furniture seems to have been produced during the Revolution, probably in part because New England saw little conflict after the unfortunate experience of General Burgoyne in 1777, and in part because the whole area grew rich providing food for the army.

Chapin School chairs are notable in having Philadelphia construction features, New England proportions, and in usually being made of cherry, but they are fairly rare, and you are very unlikely to encounter a side chair like that illustrated in figure 5-21A. Instead, we might consider some features of Hartford-area case work.

In lieu of the built-up enclosed bonnet top, Hartford area furniture is likely to have the scrolled cornice so often seen in the Middle Atlantic, sometimes with an elaborate cartouche and latticework like that illustrated on a Philadelphia chest-on-chest in figure 11-25C, but more commonly with the simpler pierced scrolled pediment shown in figure 12-6C. You may notice that there are neither exposed dovetails nor a covering strip where the drawer blades join the sides of the case. This is because the drawer blades have been fastened with a pair of vertical tenons rather than the usual dovetails. Backboards for such pieces may be set within grooves rather than nailed into rabbets. Also, if you look at the underside of a desk or a chest of drawers, you may see that the feet were not fastened in the normal manner with glue blocks to the bottom of the case. Instead, they were built up as separate assemblies and then either nailed or screwed to the underside of the case. The facings were dovetailed together, usually with mitered dovetails in the front and through dovetails in the back. The latter show clearly if you look at the feet from the rear. This elegant and unusual construction is sometimes seen elsewhere, but in combination with cherry primary wood is an almost certain indication of Hartford-area workmanship. It should be noted that in the Massachusetts portion of the Valley, white pine was the favored secondary wood; in the Hartford area, white pine and poplar; and along the coast, tulip poplar and some yellow pine.

Chapter 3 — The Middle Atlantic Colonies

This chapter will be simpler than the last, for the Middle Atlantic region comprised but four colonies, and of these, New Jersey is of minor significance insofar as furniture is concerned, and Delaware is of even less. Most production was in Pennsylvania and New York, the great majority within the environs of Philadelphia and New York City. We will see that furniture from the Middle Atlantic is very different from that from New England and the South, and better yet, Philadelphia is quite different from New York.

As a general rule, Middle Atlantic furniture is significantly more English than New England furniture, perhaps because of population growth and expansion of trade somewhat later in the colonial period. While the settlement of Jamestown predated Plymouth by over a dozen years, Philadelphia and New York did not exceed Boston in size until the middle of the eighteenth century, and then were swept up in the rococo style so fashionable in England and Europe. During this time Boston had ceased to grow, so much so that by the time of the Revolution, it was by far the smallest of the three urban centers.

New York

New York is an interesting study, for here there were two schools of design and production, though these were not the products of geography as with rural and urban New Hampshire, but rather, the products of period and time — between Colonial New York and Federal New York, and just about at the divide between the eighteenth and nineteenth centuries. Colonial New York was much smaller than the state that now stretches from the Atlantic Ocean to the Great Lakes. Before the Revolution, New York did not extend much beyond the large town of Albany at the head of navigation on the Hudson River. North and west of Albany, the colony was still largely controlled by the native inhabitants and was heavily forested, as Burgoyne found to his dismay in 1777. The majority of the rural population lived either in the Hudson River Valley or on Long Island, which stretched about a hundred miles to the east from New York City. Just prior to the Revolution, New York had a population of about 25,000, half again larger than Boston, but much smaller than Philadelphia.

That New York Colonial furniture is so different from New York Federal furniture, and that so little of the former survives, is mostly due to bad luck — and very bad luck at that. By 1760, New York was the second largest city in America, and from this period there should be much furniture. However, there is so little that for a considerable time it was not even realized that Colonial New York had had a very considerable furniture industry. New York furniture was often confused with Philadelphia and English furniture.

The bad luck was a whole series of misfortunes, commencing with a major fire in 1776 and continuing through another bad fire in 1778, eight years of occupation by the British army during the Revolution, and then the departure of the large loyalist segment of the population in November of 1783. These poor people must have taken everything possible with them, for by this time their cause was lost beyond all hope of recovery. Some of this fine furniture is still drifting back from the United Kingdom and Canada. It is little wonder that high-Style Queen Anne and Chippendale furniture is relatively rare.

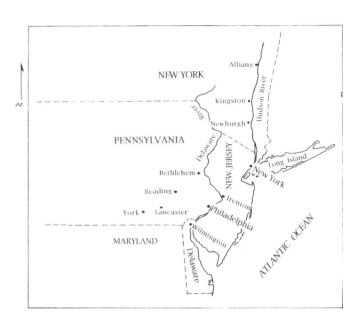

3-1. The Middle Atlantic colonies.

Colonial New York had close ties with England, and New York furniture from this period is notably Georgian in feeling. In fact, it is probably the most English of American furniture. Side chairs exhibit the broad seats and solid stance of English chairs of this period, a feature that is particularly noticeable in Marlborough leg chairs. Cabriole leg chairs are similar to Philadelphia chairs in having slip seats and lacking stretchers. However, the patterns of the splats are often very different, as is the shape of the ball and claw feet (5-1E). When not given ball and claw feet, New York chairs may have been given either Irish drake feet or slipper feet (5-2E). Often the rear legs terminate in small square pads or the oval feet seen in figure 5-16. Seldom will you see block-and-turned stretchers and the disked pad foot that was so popular in New England.

New York Chippendale case work is also distinctive. Probably the most obvious feature, also seen to some extent in New York Federal furniture, is that case work tends to be not only large, but also wide in proportion to depth. The larger case work — chests of drawers, chest-on-chests, presses, desks, and desk and bookcases — is apt to be noticeably big and wide, which is evident if you compare the New York chest-on-chest in figure 11-25A with the Pennsylvania chest-on-chest in figure 11-25B.

In spite of the additional cost, the ball and claw foot was much favored in New York, and ball and claw feet are often seen in chairs, tables, and case furniture. In the last instance, there will often be ball and claw feet in the front and ogee bracket feet in the rear. Massachusetts chests of drawers are also likely to have ball and claw feet, but there will be ball and claw feet all around, and the cases will usually have a blocked or serpentine fronts. Because the ball and claw foot was seldom employed in Philadelphia case furniture, a chest of drawers with ball and claw feet and a flat front will most probably be from New York City.

In addition to ball and claw feet, New York case work exhibits all sorts of English rococo details: chamfered corners, gadrooning, and fretwork just below the top of a chest of drawers or the cornice of a chest-on-chest. These are also seen in Philadelphia, and by themselves are no sure indication of New York workmanship, although New York gadrooning differs from that of Philadelphia by being smooth with no dividing fillets. Middle Atlantic furniture tends to be fitted with full-depth dust boards between the drawers, an English feature uncommon in New England, even on quality work, but normal practice in Philadelphia and New York. In addition, drawer-blade dovetails will normally be hidden behind a covering strip. If you see dovetails on the front of a piece of furniture, and it is not a very rural product, you are probably looking at a New England product.

The chest-on-chest and, somewhat later, the clothespress were favored in New York City. High chests of drawers and tall chests are generally rural products. Many of these are from eastern Long Island due to trade with nearby Connecticut and Rhode Island. That high chests are uncommon is perhaps due to the cultural ties with England, for by the time New York became a significant urban center in the 1750s, the high chest of drawers was long out of fashion in England. Perhaps for the same reason, bonnet tops are seldom seen in New York City furniture. New York chest-on-chests almost invariably have flat tops.

We should also touch on New York tables, which also exhibit distinctive features. The standard Queen Anne or Chippendale drop-leaf dining table has four legs: two fixed legs fastened to the bed of the table, and two swing legs that pivot out to support the leaves. While this is an elegantly simple and economical design, swinging two of the four legs does not make for a very strong and rigid table. In New York, four fixed and two swing legs were preferred, so much so that any six-leg dining table is very likely to be from New York. The large, sturdy dining table in figure 16-4B is typical of New York dining tables, not only in being fitted with six legs, but in having turned rather than shaped cabriole legs and in having ball and claw feet. Some very large dining tables have eight legs, each leaf supported by two swing legs. The New York preference for additional stability and support carries over into neoclassical dining tables and also into card tables, which are likely to have a fifth leg and sometimes even a sixth to support the folding leaf.

Before discussing Federal New York, something might be said about the rural areas adjacent to the city. As noted earlier, the Hudson River Valley was settled as far north as Albany and a little to the west up the Mohawk Valley. Long Island was also settled, in the west by the Dutch from adjacent Manhattan, in the east by people from New England who came south to avoid Puritan rule. Quite the best-known furniture from this whole area is the Hudson River Valley yoke-back chair shown in figure 6-5. Although these chairs are sometimes called Dutch chairs, they would seem to postdate the Dutch settlement of Manhattan. The bread seats and turned cabriole legs have a distinctly Georgian look, suggesting they are perhaps as much English as Dutch.

Among case work there are a considerable number of distinctive regional types, both from New York and from adjacent New Jersey. Long Island has the double-paneled chest (10-5B) and, in the west, in Kings and Queens counties, a large number

of large baroque kasten (15-2A). From New Jersey we see the step-back Hackensack-type cupboards (15-2B) and gumwood clothespresses (11-28E), which were also produced to some extent on Long Island and in the Hudson River Valley. Red gum or gumwood was favored as both a primary and secondary wood throughout this whole region, and its presence is a good indication of New York area workmanship. On Long Island, the primary wood was often apple or cherry, the latter perhaps due to the proximity of Connecticut, which was closer than it would seem in a time when water transport was so common.

The New York kas is easy to confuse with the Pennsylvania schrank, not in the least because the German settlers in Pennsylvania are often referred to as Pennsylvania Dutch. Here we might remember that kasten normally exhibit little variation in form. Although produced for almost a century, most are very much like the kas shown in figure 15-2A; the makers of schranks adapted both to the needs and the times, making them in different sizes and shapes and incorporating elements of later rococo and neoclassical styles.

New York City saw a remarkable recovery with the return of prosperity following the Revolution. This was due to a variety of reasons — a confluence of good luck following years of bad luck — first the opening of the interior of the state to settlement and trade, then a year as interim capital of the United States, and then becoming the financial center of the new nation. Because there were so many famous battles in the Revolution, it is easy to overlook a concurrent and equally bloody conflict, the suppression of the Native American population beyond the coastal piedmont, which opened up vast areas in New York, the Midwest, and the South to European settlement.

In having to start over, largely from scratch and with many people newly rich, New York City was a natural home to the latest English and European styles, beginning with Hepplewhite and progressing rapidly through Sheraton to Empire and Classical — a mix of English Regency and French Empire influences — all overlaid with generous funding and more than a little nouveau riche. As a result, New York neoclassical furniture is quite different from Boston and Philadelphia neoclassical furniture. It exhibits a far greater diversity of forms. Here we see dark, figured mahogany veneers contrasting with brass pulls and cast brass feet or castors. The exposed edges on chairs and tables are enhanced with reeding, the downswept legs on classical tables decorated with waterleaf carving. On high-end furniture we see classical motifs, lyres and harps, carved mythical animals, and furred-front legs ending in paw feet. The New York classical side chair in figure 5-32F is typical of the genre, having a carved lyre back in combination with fur carved front legs and paw feet. Here also, the front of the stiles and the tops of the rails are reeded.

In a general way, Federal New York furniture is somewhat large in scale and well made of the best available cabinet woods. Veneering is almost universally on white pine. Cherry and maple are common for secondary structure where strength is required. Drawers will be all poplar, or white pine with poplar bottoms.

While dark, monochromatic veneer is probably the most noticeable characteristic of New York Federal furniture, there are also a number of design features that can help us identify New York workmanship. The double-elliptical shape shown in the breakfast table in figure 16-13D was much favored for leaves of breakfast and card tables. There are even triple-elliptical tops. This figure also illustrates the standard shape of New York Sheraton foot.

New York pieces, particularly secretaries, dressing tables, and serving tables, frequently have the lower shelf shown in the dressing table in figure 12-15E. While lower shelves are seen elsewhere, they are most common in New York. Classical dining, breakfast, and card tables are often raised on a cluster of four carved colonettes rather than the carved column usually employed on these late Federal tables (16-8D). While colonette tables were not unique to New York, they were so fashionable here as to be a good indication of New York workmanship. Lastly, deeply canted corners were favored and are often seen on New York tables. As with colonettes, they are seen elsewhere and are no more than a suggestion of New York City work.

New Jersey

There is little to say of New Jersey, for even by Southern standards it was very rural, its urban needs apparently met by nearby Philadelphia and New York. Such concentration as existed was in large villages: Princeton, with its small college; Camden, across the Delaware River from Philadelphia; and Hackensack, across the Hudson from Manhattan Island and New York. At the time of the Revolution, Trenton, now the state capital, had a hundred houses, four churches, and a jail. It was built at the head of navigation, at "ye ffalles of ye De La Ware," where there was a head of water to power mills.

From this environment there is not a great deal of furniture, although in the north, just to the west of New York City, were made Bergen County chairs, red gum clothespresses (11-28E), Hackensack-type cupboards (15-2B), and, after the Revolution, a number of fine tall-case clocks. In the south, across the Delaware from Philadelphia, there were made rural interpretations of Philadelphia styles. A significant amount of rural Pennsylvania furniture may actually be from southern New Jersey.

Pennsylvania

Philadelphia was not founded until 1682, about half a century after the Puritans arrived in Boston Harbor. However, it grew rapidly, and by 1750 was the biggest city in America. At the time of the Revolution it was one of the largest cities in the British Empire. Although New York was actually larger than Boston prior to the Revolution, Philadelphia and Boston were the two major style centers in Colonial America. The influence of Philadelphia spread out like the spokes of a giant wheel from the hub in the southeastern corner of Pennsylvania. That New York furniture was so long overlooked is in considerable part due to its similarity to Philadelphia furniture, exhibiting much of the same sort of rococo carving, gadrooning, and fretwork. New York chairs frequently have Philadelphia blocking and through tenoning. Philadelphia-style chairs, high chests, and dressing tables are seen in the adjacent colonies, in New Jersey, Delaware, Maryland,

and Virginia. More rural forms traveled even further. The ubiquitous paneled corner cupboard and painted softwood chest are common in western Pennsylvania and Ohio. Dovetailed walnut dower chests and bracket-foot tall chests move down the Great Waggon Road into Virginia and the Carolinas. Rural interpretations of birdcage tea tables are everywhere, although usually without the compressed ball so fashionable in Philadelphia.

What cherry was to Connecticut, Virginia black walnut (*Juglans nigra*) was to the Delaware Valley, or more correctly, Pennsylvania and much of the South. Here also, a simple rule is inadequate. In early Colonial America, walnut was the fashionable wood, just as it was in England at this time. The popular Boston Queen Anne chairs were usually made of walnut brought up from Virginia. However, with the introduction of mahogany in the middle of the eighteenth century, walnut went out of fashion except in the Philadelphia area, where it remained a favored lower-cost option, and in the South, where walnut and cherry were the woods of choice where mahogany was not available. There seems to have been a lasting affection for this handsome wood, because some very grand furniture, for which cost would not appear to have been a problem, was made of walnut during the third quarter of the eighteenth century. Perhaps it appealed to a people known for their thrift? In any event, because late Colonial furniture is far more plentiful than early Colonial, this continuing popularity has resulted in walnut furniture being likely to be from the Delaware Valley. Whereas in New England a Chippendale chest of drawers would probably have been made of mahogany, maple, or cherry, in Pennsylvania it would probably have been made of walnut. As with cherry, walnut is a suggestion of region if you remember the other factors and do not attribute everything walnut to Philadelphia.

For the most part, Philadelphia chairs are an easy study: Georgian in appearance, without stretchers and with drop seats set between deep rails that are generally through tenoned. Cabriole legs may terminate in the Philadelphia type of ball and claw foot (5-1C), but are more likely to have some form of trifid foot (5-2C). The latter is an excellent identifier of Philadelphia-area work, for while this foot is very common in the Delaware Valley, it is very seldom seen elsewhere. While uncommon in side chairs, blocked feet are often seen in armchairs (8-2D) and card tables (18-4C). With the advent of neoclassicism the blocked foot went out of fashion, but you may see a short, heavy spade foot that suggests a blocked foot that has acquired neoclassical features (18-10A).

Although not immediately evident, the most noticeable characteristic of Delaware Valley case furniture is its sheer weight, this due to a combination of dense walnut, unusually thick case and drawers sides, and dust boards between the drawers. Philadelphia case furniture tends to be heavy, and pieces made by rural workmanship even more so. This weight is seen in the feet of chests of drawers and desks, which usually have very solid-looking bracket feet (11-10A), and in the legs of high chests of drawers, which are noticeably shorter and thicker than their New England counterparts. Seldom will you see a tall, thin cabriole leg. Look under a chest of drawers and you will see the feet have relatively thin facing that covers large, quarter-round vertical blocks.

In addition to stout construction and the use of walnut, Philadelphia-area case work is very likely to have quarter columns. This treatment is so common as to be almost a signature of Delaware Valley cabinetry, the equivalent of the blocked and serpentine front furniture in New England. The use of quarter columns was not limited to high chests and dressing tables; you will see them on a great many chests of drawers, chest-on-chests, tall chests, desks, and desk and bookcases. Like walnut, quarter columns are found elsewhere, particularly in Connecticut, but it is in the Delaware Valley where they become so fashionable as to be seen even on average-grade work.

Pennsylvania high chests of drawers and dressing tables are unusual in that two very different forms were developed, one urban and high style, the other rural and somewhat old-fashioned. The grand Philadelphia high chests of drawers you have probably seen, for they are a high point in American design, being illustrated in virtually every survey of American furniture (12-8A). Note in figure 12-8A that Philadelphia finials are very different from Massachusetts finials, rising from a large urn and having more of a flame shape than the spiral twist favored in New England. While these magnificent high chests garner all the press, far more common are simpler types with flat tops, ball and claw or trifid feet, and of course, quarter columns (12-8B). Both these types of high chests have short, thick cabriole legs very different from those usually seen in New England. However, this is not the end of the matter, for a very different type of high chest and dressing table was also produced in the Delaware Valley. Such chests are distinguished by bold and elegant Spanish feet in combination with unusual two-over-two drawer arrangements in the lower cases (12-8C). Matching dressing tables often have a charming pierced hearts in the centers of the aprons (12-13C). William and Mary Spanish or paintbrush feet are common on New England chairs, and were occasionally employed on tavern tables, but I cannot think of any other area where they are seen on case furniture. Note that the high chest in figure 12-8C does not have quarter columns, and the dressing table in figure 12-13C has fluted, chamfered corners. Quarter columns are indeed very common, but by no means universal.

There are a considerable number — almost a whole vocabulary — of other regional features. In addition to exhibiting the makers' preferences for walnut and quarter columns, the upper cases of high chests and chest-on-chests and the upper registers of tall chests will normally have the three-over-two drawer arrangement seen in the previous illustrations. The high chest in figure 12-8B even has this pattern in the lower case. New York chest-on-chests are more likely to have a single row of three drawers (11-25A). The three-over-two pattern is also seen in New England, but this case work so different from that of Middle Atlantic that there is little chance of confusion. Here it should be noted that upper drawers in desks and chests of drawers are apt to be divided into two smaller drawers, an English feature also seen in Southern furniture. Another English fea-

ture, seen in all regions but perhaps more common in Philadelphia, is a dressing slide between the top and the upper drawer.

The top row of three drawers will very often be fitted with wooden spring locks that are reached through holes in the dust boards. These ingenious locking devices are also seen in furniture made in Newport, which also had a community of Friends, so calling such devices "Quaker" locks may not be inappropriate. However, it should be noted that they were such a logical idea in a time when hardware was so dear that we might expect to see them almost anywhere. As such, they are no more than an indication of Pennsylvania or Newport workmanship.

When a drawer was lipped, it was not really necessary to lip the bottom, and most lipped drawers, while thumbnail molded on all sides, were actually lipped only on the sides and tops. They just appear to have been lipped all around. However, you will sometimes see drawers that have been lipped on all sides, and this practice seems to have been most common in the Delaware Valley. However, as with Quaker locks, lipping all around is no more than a suggestion of Pennsylvania workmanship. The practice is often seen in English case furniture.

The rosette, or bail, pull was much favored in Philadelphia, in part perhaps because its economy, simplicity, and neatness were favored by the Quaker community. While bail pulls are common in rural New England and in Southern furniture, in Philadelphia they are often seen on quality urban furniture. When something grander was desired, cabinetmakers frequently employed the ornate rococo gilded bail pulls so fashionable in England. These gilded pulls, with their ornate gilded rosettes, contribute much to the rococo look of Philadelphia high-style furniture.

There are secondary woods that suggest Delaware Valley workmanship. The most notable is the use of Atlantic white cedar for drawer bottoms, usually in conjunction with tulip poplar for the sides and backs. This soft, aromatic wood is not difficult to identify, for it is easily marked with a thumbnail and is so weak that drawer bottoms invariably run from front to back. The wood is so soft that the back edges of drawer bottoms are apt to be rough and broken out by the teeth of the saw. Sometimes there will be a slight lingering aroma of cedar.

Oak was employed where hardness and strength were required. It is seen in drawer sides, and more commonly, in the swing rails of card tables. Other woods are not so helpful. White and yellow pine were both employed as secondary woods, and among primary woods you may see tiger maple and black cherry; cherry often in rural areas as an alternative to walnut.

Philadelphia-area tea tables are covered at some length in chapter 17, and there is little to add here except to note that square tea tables are rare and that round tea tables normally have dished tops and birdcage mechanisms. The preference throughout the Delaware Valley for tables that both rotated and tilted is remarkable, considering that the mechanism probably added about half again to the cost. Why should a birdcage be so important as to be worth the additional expense? Tilting allowed a table to be set in the corner when not in use, but there would seem to be no particular reason to rotate the top.

The placement of the cleats across the grain assured that the figure of the wood would be set to best advantage. However, a birdcage allowed a round tea table to act as an oversized lazy Susan, suggesting that it might have been normal in the old days to pass something simply by rotating the top of the table. Also, a tea table from the Delaware Valley will normally have a molded collar between the wedge and the lower plate of the birdcage that minimizes wear and allows the top to turn easily. When at afternoon tea, nobody would have to rise to obtain seconds on tea or cakes.

Rural Pennsylvania, principally Chester and Lancaster counties, is very much a school in itself. Actually, it might be seen as several schools. Mile upon mile of rich farmland extends to the north and west of Philadelphia as far as the Allegheny Mountains, and here we find prosperous farms, villages, and large towns: West Chester, Lancaster, and York. In the eighteenth century, Lancaster was the largest inland town in America. The area was settled by a variety of peoples: Quakers from England, Welsh from Wales, and Germans from the Palatinate, the lands bordering the Rhine. From Quakers came rural interpretations of the latest Philadelphia styles; from the Welsh the charming line and berry inlay; and from the Germans the schrank and the lovely dower chests illustrated in chapter 10.

This entire area was organized as a single large Chester County based on the English model by William Penn in 1682, under a charter granted by Charles II, the same Charles for whom Charleston was named. In 1729 the western part was reorganized to form Lancaster County, and in 1789 the southeastern townships were separated to form present-day Delaware County. In common with New England's Connecticut River Valley, the land was fertile and the area very prosperous. Lancaster County was more rural, with a predominately German population, and Chester County was more suburban and middle class, with an English and Welsh community. Every year, the Quakers would attend meetings of the Society of Friends in Philadelphia, which probably contributed to the sophisticated furniture produced in Chester County. It is not easy to separate the average grade of urban and rural Delaware Valley furniture. There are, however, features that suggest Chester County workmanship. In addition to the Welsh vine-and-berry inlay, the sides of the upper cases on high chests and the sides of tall chests are often paneled, either with flat paneling or the fielded panels shown in the tall chest in figure 11-22D. Similar paneling is seen in Lancaster County work. Flat, or more correctly, reverse-fielded, paneling is the most obvious feature of the innumerable poplar, walnut, and cherry cupboards made throughout the Delaware Valley and, thereafter, in western Pennsylvania and Ohio. Chester County is also the source of a group of tall chests with screw-on cabriole legs. This was probably done for much the same reason that Rhode Island high chests have removable legs: ease of transport and ease of repair. Many tea tables and stands follow the Philadelphia practice of both rotating and tilting, but here the lower plate of the birdcage will sometimes be turned and molded as shown in figure 17-8D.

Lancaster County has its own vocabulary, although here there is much overlap with Chester County, perhaps in part because the German population was spread throughout the whole region. At this time about a third of the settlers in Pennsylvania were of German extraction. From here we see the well-known painted dower chests (10-6A), sulfur inlaid walnut dower chests (10-7), and truly massive high chests and scranks. Scrolled bonnet tops from this region are often extravagantly high (11-25D). Backboards, dust boards, and moldings are apt to have been secured with wooden pins, and dovetails wedged with thin slivers of wood. Lastly, Lancaster and Chester counties are most probably the source of many of the transitional Delaware Valley side chairs (5-24K). Throughout this whole area, but perhaps particularly in Chester and Delaware counties, tall chests were very popular. Like other successful designs, they had a long run, successively acquiring Chippendale, Hepplewhite, and Sheraton features. Most were made of walnut, a few of maple or cherry. Often the upper registers have the three-over-two drawer arrangement so commonly seen in the Delaware Valley.

Before ending this section, something needs to be said about the Federal period, for while Boston and New York are better known for their neoclassical furniture, Philadelphia cabinetmakers nevertheless developed distinctive designs and motifs that can help us to identify their workmanship. Unlike New York City and Baltimore, which started smaller but grew rapidly after the Revolution, Philadelphia had a conservative society with fewer new fortunes. Philadelphia also found itself in increasing competition with Baltimore as a seaport, as the entryway to the new lands opening up beyond the mountains. Perhaps as a result, Philadelphia seems to have been a bit slower to accept the new neoclassical styles, avoiding the exuberant furniture seen in New York and Baltimore.

The late Chippendale ladder-back chair continued to be fashionable in Philadelphia to the end of the eighteenth century, acquiring rounded crest rails as a concession to progress (5-26I). The best-known Philadelphia chair to come after these was the racquet-back, with a Sheraton design and a racquet-form splat set between a pair of vertical splats, as shown in figure 5-33C. Not all these chairs have this pattern. However, they have in common the pair of vertical splats and a square Sheraton crest rail that is slightly raised in the center. The other fashionable chair is a square-back with unusual turned and reeded stiles and splats (5-33D). These chairs appear to be unique to Philadelphia.

Perhaps the best-known feature of Federal Philadelphia furniture is the kidney shape seen in many sideboards, card tables (18-10B), and worktables. The curved sides and curved, recessed center combine to suggest a kidney bean, although unlike the vegetable, the back will naturally be flat. During the Federal period, many cabinetmakers moved to Baltimore, and the kidney shape is sometimes seen in Baltimore furniture.

A less well known but equally common feature of Federal Philadelphia is the curved or serpentine ellipse shape used in Sheraton and classical breakfast tables (16-14D, 16-14E). In figure 18-10C we see it again in a Sheraton card table. Note that this table has a standard form of Philadelphia Sheraton foot.

It should be mentioned that in Philadelphia, as elsewhere, popular design features and construction practices carried over into the Federal period. Makers continued to use vertical blocking and through tenoning in chairs and to make furniture of walnut, although walnut was at last giving way to mahogany. The immensely fashionable circular tea table was superseded by the Pembroke table, but all is not lost, for you may still see birdcages fitted on candlestands, even though they are now rectangular Federal stands.

Delaware

Something should be said about Delaware, if only because it was one of the 13 colonies — and also because it is the home of Winterthur. The area was initially settled in the 1630s by a mix of Swedes, Finns, and Dutch. While none contributed to the Delaware furniture seen today, the Swedes brought with them something far more valuable — the log house which provided handy shelter in early settlements throughout much of America. In 1682, the three counties that to this day make up the state — New Castle, Kent, and Sussex — were transferred to William Penn, and although there was later a measure of local control, Delaware remained a sort of annex to Pennsylvania until the beginning of hostilities in 1776. During this time a number of

Quakers moved down to settle the rich farmland, bringing with them Philadelphia fashions in furniture. Wealthy farmers and merchants, most notably Vincent Loockerman, purchased their best furniture in Philadelphia, which was only a short journey away up the Delaware River.

As you would expect from this history, Delaware furniture is very similar to southeastern Pennsylvania furniture. Lacking a label or provenance, there is little to tell them apart. Most are neatly made, with little excessive ornamentation. The relatively few identified Delaware chests of drawers are almost identical to other Delaware Valley work with cove molded tops, quarter columns, and ogee bracket feet. Chippendale chairs are rural interpretations of Philadelphia chairs, with much the same pierced splats, drop seats, and deep rails. Some have the pierced, flaring splat soft often seen in Southern chairs. Although not usually thought of as a Southern state, most all of Delaware lies south of the Mason-Dixon Line. Then, as now, Wilmington was the largest urban center, and most surviving furniture is probably from here. Primary woods were what you would expect, although in addition to walnut, there was considerable use of mahogany and cherry. Secondary woods were usually poplar and pine.

Chapter 4 – The Southern Colonies

The South is by far the largest, and also the most agrarian, of the three regions. The five colonies that composed the Old South — Maryland, Virginia, North Carolina, South Carolina, and Georgia — are perhaps half again larger than New England and the Middle Atlantic region combined. To this day Georgia is the largest state east of the Mississippi. Due to the sheer size of the South, and because there is less demarcation between the furniture produced in the different colonies, we will do things differently and survey this whole vast region on the basis of geography rather than state or colony, covering first the tidewater Chesapeake, then the coastal Low Country, and last, the whole, vast backcountry that lies beyond the fall line of the coastal rivers. There is nothing original in this; it is the same division employed in most all the recent surveys of Southern furniture.

To avoid repetition, we might first discuss Southern furniture in general, particularly the sort of furniture you are most likely to encounter. Although the population of the South at time of the revolution, including slaves, was about equal to the rest of the nation, there were no cities even close to Boston, New York, or Philadelphia in size. The largest, Charleston and Norfolk, at the eve of the revolution were small-to-medium sized, the former about the size of Newport, Rhode Island, the latter about half that. From these cities, though, as well as from Williamsburg, Annapolis, and other smaller entities, there should remain a substantial amount of stylish, formal furniture. But there is not very much. Where did it all go? There is a considerable amount of Southern furniture, but most all is of very rural manufacture. While the Museum of Early Southern Deco-

rative Arts (MESDA) and Colonial Williamsburg have high-style furniture in their collections, remarkably little appears to have survived. For this there are any number of explanations. You will hear that planters purchased furniture through their agents or factors in England, that Southern cabinetmakers had difficulty competing with northern cabinetmakers, that out-of-fashion and neglected furniture soon rotted away in the summer heat and damp, that furniture was lost through lack of maintenance in the economic ruin and poverty that followed the Civil War, and that much other furniture lost its identity after being sent north for sale. All of these are probably true to some extent, particularly the last, for Southern furniture has been shipped north for generations. Only now is some of it coming back home.

However, another factor must be the calamitous history of so much of the South, particularly of the coastal cities. Charleston saw a succession of major fires, two wars, and an earthquake, all interspersed with a series of major hurricanes that flooded this lovely but low-lying city. Norfolk had a terrible fire on New Year's Day 1776, so much so that nine years later it was still described by one observer as a "vast heap of Ruins and Devastation."

During the Civil War, Atlanta, Columbia, and Richmond were burned, and while Charleston avoided this fate, it was heavily shelled and left pretty much in ruins. Throughout much of the South, plantation houses, at the heart of succession and slavery, and probably the home to much fine furniture, were systematically burned. Wherever there was fine furniture was likely to be destroyed. All in all, it is a wonder that any of the better-quality furniture survived.

4-1. The Southern colonies.

The Southern furniture we see today tends to be both rural and stoutly constructed, often showing evidence of long and hard use, suggesting an impoverished agrarian society that had to make do with what little it had. It is apt to be of somewhat atypical design, heavy and very simply made, the sort of work that might be done by a cabinetmaker working very much on his own in a small community with no more than the rough boards provided by the local sawmill, and perhaps more importantly, with a limited set of tools. Even well-made furniture is seldom carved, and ball and claw feet are scarce. The edges of tables and the tops of seat rails tend to be rounded rather than molded, suggesting that molding planes were in short supply. Inlay is often of local manufacture and sometimes poorly made, which would indicate both limited transportation and a lack of fine-toothed saws. Rural Middle Atlantic and New England cabinetry also employed local woods and inlay made up by the cabinetmaker, but it was usually neatly made. Seldom do we get the impression that the artisan simply lacked the right tools for the job. In part this impression of rural naiveté may be due to circumstance — over the years, much of the better-quality furniture may have gone north.

Perhaps more so than in the other regions, there are certain types of furniture associated with Southern workmanship. These will be noted later when we cover the major areas. More generally regional are the primary and secondary woods. Foremost are the hard pines, often identified as yellow pine but actually the whole taeda group, which includes loblolly, longleaf, shortleaf, and slash pine. These are hard pines, heavier, more resinous, and more strongly figured than the soft pines. Although the taeda group is seen in furniture as far north as coastal Connecticut, not until much further south in the Delaware Valley does it become fairly common as a secondary wood, particularly in locations where strength is needed. South

of the Mason-Dixon Line its use was almost universal, both as a primary and secondary wood, and there is little Southern furniture that does not have it somewhere. Painted furniture entirely made of yellow pine will almost always be Southern.

The other common softwood is yellow, or tulip, poplar, which was often used for drawer sides and bottoms. However, this is not much help, for this light, knot-free, easy-to-work wood was used everywhere except in northern New England. More helpful are cypress, mulberry, and magnolia, whose presence are almost sure indications of Southern workmanship.

Walnut, so popular in the Delaware Valley, is seen throughout the South. So common is its use that you will find it in secondary locations, such as drawer slides, where its hardness could be put to advantage. Much Southern furniture is also made of cherry, but this is no help, for this prince of cabinet woods found favor in all regions.

It should be mentioned that rural Southern furniture can be quite remarkably idiosyncratic. In addition to such established forms as hunt boards, bottle cases, sugar chests, and china presses, you will sometimes see furniture the likes of which you have never seen before. You may come across a walnut chest of drawers with a separate desk section on the top, and above this a tall cupboard, the whole structure about eight feet high. This suggests a hot climate in which walnut was abundant, limited production in a very rural environment, and a cabinetmaker working very much on his own — in short, the rural South.

The Chesapeake

We should start with the Chesapeake tidewater, which includes coastal Maryland, Virginia, and northeastern North Carolina, for these were the first areas settled and are the source of most early Southern furniture. While North Carolina does not border the Chesapeake Bay, the northeastern quadrant as far south as Morehead City was settled by immigrants from the Chesapeake Bay, and the furniture is stylistically similar. Within the region were the small urban centers of Norfolk, Williamsburg, Annapolis, and Baltimore, and to the south, Edenton and New Bern in North Carolina.

Although there are exceptions, most surviving Southern furniture does not predate the Revolution. When furniture appears to be older, perhaps William and Mary or Queen Anne in style, and fastened with forged rather than cut nails, it is most likely to be from somewhere in the tidewater area. Very little Low Country furniture predates the Revolution, and the backcountry did not become sufficiently settled as to produce well-made furniture until the last few decades of the eighteenth century.

It is from the Chesapeake, and particularly the small cities, that you are most likely to see Southern Queen Anne and Chippendale furniture. Baltimore produced much furniture, but most all is neoclassical rather than rococo. This will be covered later. Tidewater cabinetry is often described as being neat and plain, that is, well made and conservative, with little ornamentation. In design and construction, it is similar to good-quality rural English workmanship, the sort of work that would be done in a county center or large market town by an apprentice-trained cabinetmaker. The side chair in figure 5-25C, the chest of drawers in figure 11-11A, and the tea table in figure 17-9A are typical of the well-made, conservative furniture produced in the Chesapeake area. Southern chairs usually have drop or slip seats, and very frequently have the upward flaring splat shown in this illustration. When the splat is pierced, it may be stiffened with the little connecting sections shown in figure 5-25B. Box stretchers are usually an indication of rural workmanship, but they were much favored in the South, and are often seen on good-quality formal chairs. Chests of drawers usually have bail pulls and straight bracket feet, and the drawer-blade dovetails will be hidden by covering strips. Some have the peculiarly English flush mitered dovetailed top illustrated in figure 11-11C. Although high chests of drawers are rare, dressing tables were popular. They usually have but a single drawer or a single row of drawers, like the New York dressing table in figure 12-12.

There are other English features seen in Chesapeake, and particularly, in Virginia furniture. Better case work will have dust dividers between the drawers. The bottoms of wide drawers are often split by transverse muntins, a feature seldom seen elsewhere, although in New England you will sometimes see a stiffener nailed to the top of a drawer bottom. The backs of bookcases and clothespresses may be paneled to provide additional stiffness. Normally, feet are supported by a single vertical glue block, but then the grain runs counter to the facing. A better solution, seen in both English and Virginia case work, is to employ a stack of little horizontal blocks. Both dining and dressing tables are likely to have the offset turned cabriole legs seen in the North Carolina table in figure 16-6. This English feature is also seen in New York and Rhode Island dining tables. Six-leg dining tables were also favored. Some have two fixed and four swing legs. When closed, three legs are in parallel at each end, resulting in a very strange-looking table when the leaves are down.

Although nowhere very far from the sea, much stylish furniture was made of walnut rather than mahogany. Furniture made in north coastal North Carolina is understandably walnut, for there are few deep water harbors in this area, but this does not explain why so much good-quality tidewater furniture is made of walnut. Perhaps, as in Philadelphia, it was simply a favored wood; or perhaps the mahogany furniture was purchased in England.

After the capital was moved to Richmond in 1790, Williamsburg settled back into being a small college town, which was ruinous for the local cabinetmakers but has been a blessing for America, for so many of the original dwellings still remained in the twentieth century that it possible to almost completely restore this lovely little Colonial city. New York was also once a charming little city at the foot of Manhattan Island, with handsome brick houses and wide, tree-lined streets, but of this time almost nothing remains.

Annapolis — and Maryland — is a somewhat different case. After the seat of government was moved north from St. Mary's City in 1693, it was never moved again, and until the rise of Baltimore in the latter part of the eighteenth century, Annapolis remained the artistic and cultural center of the tidewater region. As a result, there is a significant amount of Maryland Queen Anne and Chippendale furniture, the greater part of it probably made in either Annapolis or Baltimore. While Maryland was also a tidewater colony, Maryland Colonial furniture is distinctly different from Virginia furniture, most probably because Philadelphia was only a few miles away. Maryland Chippendale furniture is similar to Lancaster County Chippendale furniture in that it suggests a rural interpretation of Philadelphia fashion. High chests of drawers are apt to have unusually high scrolled bonnet tops, and both high chests and dressing tables are likely to be embellished with large shells. On Chippendale chairs, cabriole legs may be given exaggerated curves, and the splats tend to be broad with intricate patterns. Tea tables with Maryland histories look much like their Philadelphia counterparts. Maryland Chippendale furniture is scarce, perhaps because some has been confused with, or passed off as, Delaware Valley workmanship. The Philadelphia influence is so pronounced that it is often difficult to identify.

Annapolis is best known for the work of John Shaw (1745 – 1829), who dominated the local cabinetmaking trade during the last two decades of the nineteenth century in much the way the Townsends and Goddards did in Newport. He is the exception to the rule that Southern furniture is very seldom labeled, for about fifty pieces of furniture have been found with the label of Shaw and Chrisholm or John Shaw. As a result, another fifty or so pieces have been reliably attributed to his shop. Most of his work is both English in form and is at the divide between the rococo and the neoclassical. Here we see square Chippendale- and Hepplewhite-style card tables with wide drawers, similar to card tables then being produced in Philadelphia (18-10A), and Chippendale and Hepplewhite breakfast tables like the Pembroke table in figure 16-15C. The legs on Shaw's tables are usually either square and molded or tapered with the distinctive short ovoid spade feet shown in this illustration. Mr. Shaw seems to have mistrusted conventional glue-block drawer stops, for a characteristic of his work is that drawer sides are extended back to form their own stops. The unusual lobed back on the Hepplewhite side chair in figure 5-34B is identical to those on a set of 24 armchairs made by his shop for the Maryland Senate chamber in 1797. Unlike Virginia furniture, most Annapolis furniture is made of mahogany. Secondary woods are usually a mix: yellow pine in structural locations, tulip poplar for drawers, and white oak for leaf supports and hinge rails where both strength and resistance to wear are desired.

Prior to the Revolution, Norfolk was the largest city in Virginia and, except for Charleston, the largest urban center in the South. Sadly, much of the city burned in 1776 and never fully recovered its position in the economy, for after the Revolution, the center of trade shifted inland to Baltimore. Norfolk Chippendale furniture is now quite rare, apparently as a result of this. However, the city did recover somewhat in the 1790s, and there is a considerable amount of neoclassical furniture. This furniture is very interesting, for not only did the city have to start over from scratch, but the earlier generation of cabinetmakers were replaced by cabinetmakers from New York, Philadelphia, and New England. This new generation brought designs with it, and here we see neoclassical chairs that look much like New York drapery shield-backs (5-32A) and Philadelphia racquet-backs (5-33C), and classical colonette-form tables quite similar to those so fashionable in New York (18-9G).

While these might seem to be products of New York and Philadelphia, there are a number of little differences that indicate Norfolk workmanship. In common with other Southern furniture, walnut may be employed in secondary locations, in this case for seat rails and glue blocks. A Norfolk particularity is the use of a black mastic or pitch as a substitute for ebony in little areas of inlay. Ebony inlay was a fashionable in Regency England, but is uncommon in America, and the use of pitch to simulate ebony seems to be unique to Norfolk. Perhaps, though, it was only logical in a seaport and in the coastal South, where things English had long been fashionable.

We must now discuss Baltimore, which is something of a special case, for while the majority of high-style Southern neoclassical furniture is probably from here, the city is only just in the South, being but 30 miles south of the Mason-Dixon Line. Worse yet, it is not really the Old South. Baltimore began as a cluster of villages near the head of navigation on the Chesapeake Bay. By 1750, it was was equal in size to Annapolis. Thereafter, the city grew rapidly as trade increased with the interior, and by the Revolution had passed Norfolk and Annapolis to become the largest and most important city in the Chesapeake tidewater region. Baltimore continued to grow during the Federal period; by 1820, its population exceeded 60,000.

While Colonial Baltimore furniture is similar to Philadelphia work, Federal Baltimore furniture is very different, although there are still Philadelphia features in the furniture, in part perhaps because of cabinetmakers that moved down to take advantage of the demand for new furniture. Baltimore Federal is a mix of Philadelphia, New York, and English influences. In common with New York, Federal Baltimore was a city with much new money, and here we see use of large figure inlays in the slant fronts of desks, and in the tops and skirts of chests of drawers (11-20A). As is true of New York furniture, the tops and leaves of tables are normally molded, usually with the large triple round molding shown in the dining table in figure 16-9B and in the card table in figure 18-11C. Both of these Federal tables also have the standard type of Baltimore foot and a very distinctive Sheraton leg having little or no taper, and large, somewhat sharp-edged reeding.

As might be expected, Baltimore took to fancy furniture with enthusiasm, and by 1800 was a center of trade in this colorful painted and stenciled furniture. In 1819, Hugh Finlay was employing "nearly seventy men, women, and boys at his Baltimore furniture manufactory." While chairs were the most common product, there were also fancy-form settees, card tables, and window cornices. Unfortunately, nothing in the world of furniture is more ephemeral than delicate, high-style painted furniture, and from what must at one time have been a

vast amount colorful furniture, there now remains mostly just the standard type of Baltimore fancy chair shown in figure 6-9D, with its sharply raked tablet back and unusual triangular section at the rear of the seat rails that serves to tie together the rails, the rear legs, and the back posts. However, more pieces may remain to be discovered, and if you come across an extravagantly decorated settee, pier table, or card table of unusual form, you may be looking at the work of John and Hugh Findlay.

The Low Country

South of New York the difference between land level and sea level, never very great, gradually becomes smaller, slowly diminishing so that by the time one gets down to North Carolina, the highest ground consists of sand dunes like those used by the Wright brothers for gliding tests at Kill Devil Hills. Behind the barrier islands are miles upon miles of cypress swamps. South of Cape Hatteras, from about present day Morehead City to the Florida border, and inland as far as the fall line, is our second Southern region, the Low Country.

Most all there is to say about Low Country furniture can be summarized in one word — *Charleston*. Although there were other centers of production, this lovely city at the junction of the Ashley and Cooper rivers so dominated Low Country taste and style that it must be covered first. Later we will touch on other urban centers, but in terms of furniture, for the most part the story of the Low Country is the story of Charleston.

Charleston, or Charles Towne, as it was known until 1783, was founded in 1680, two years before the Quakers settled Pennsylvania. The combination of an excellent deepwater harbor and access by river to the interior was almost a guarantee of growth and prosperity, and throughout the eighteenth century, the city flourished as a center of trade, as the site of government, and as the summer residence of the wealthier planters. Here, rice and naval stores and, somewhat later, indigo and cotton were warehoused and shipped to European markets. By 1775, Charleston was the fourth largest city in America, and per capita the wealthiest — if one does not count those with no income — the vast number of slaves. From this size and wealth there should remain a very considerable amount of furniture, and yet there is relatively little. At the time of the Revolution, Charleston was slightly larger than Newport, and it continued to prosper right up until the Civil War, yet furniture attributed to Charleston cabinetmakers seldom comes on the market. It is not the case that all the better quality furniture was brought in from England, for the remarkable account books of Thomas Elfe indicate that at least during one eight-year period (1768 – 1775), his shop produced about fifteen hundred pieces of furniture.

That so little remains would seem in large part a function of Charleston's singularly disastrous history. Almost without exception, the small Colonial cities experienced major fires. Some had more than one. However, Charleston is in a class by itself. The city burned in 1740 (300 houses), in 1778 (250 houses), 1796 (500 chimneys), 1810 (200 houses), and also in 1835 and 1861. It was occupied during the Revolutionary War and shelled during the Civil War. As if this were not enough, Charleston is unique among eastern cities in having had a major earthquake, and being periodically flooded by major hurricanes. The wonder is that anything has survived.

Prior to the Revolution, Charleston furniture was similar to that produced in coastal Virginia, both neat and plain and English in style. Much, particularly sets of chairs, was purchased in England. Local cabinetmakers first used walnut, but by 1750 mahogany had been brought up from the Caribbean, and thereafter was the primary wood of choice. During the latter half of the eighteenth century, cabinetmakers thrived, producing furniture for both local use and the inland plantations. Here it should be mentioned that while carpenters were certainly everywhere, there is no record of a cabinetmaker on a plantation, although upon occasion, journeymen may have been sent out to make repairs. Almost no furniture was labeled, probably because Charleston was so small that everyone knew each other. After the Revolution, there arose a "cotton triangle" that eventually proved to be the ruin of the local cabinetmaking industry. Cotton was first shipped to Europe, then freight and immigrants carried to New York, then general cargo to Charleston. With the general cargo came stylish furniture, which could be produced more cheaply in New York. From this time, we see Charleston neoclassical side chairs that but for the secondary woods would seem to be from New York. Similar kinds of "New York" and "Philadelphia" chairs were also produced in Norfolk. In a general way, Charleston furniture prior to the Revolution was English, after the Revolution, New York.

So uncommon is Charleston furniture that there are but two illustrations among the over seven hundred figures in this book. Most of what has survived is either in fine public or private collections or in Charleston antique shops. Prior to the Revolution, chest-on-chests, usually with flat tops like that illustrated in figure 11-26, were favored for storing clothing. After the conflict, with the return of prosperity in the 1790s, clothespresses became fashionable, just as they were in England (11-28G). Both of these case pieces are typical of Charleston workmanship in being well made and having an abundance of decorative trim. They are quite grand. In English fashion, there are full-length dust boards between the drawers, and the full-width drawers usually have transverse muntins across the bottoms. Not infrequently, Charleston chest-on-chests have dressing slides or secretary drawers in either the upper or the lower cases.

Aside from an English or Federal New York appearance, Charleston furniture is best identified by the primary and secondary woods. The city thrived on trade, had an excellent deepwater harbor, and was so close to the Caribbean that mahogany was inexpensive and plentiful. Probate records indicate that even people of moderate means had mahogany furniture in their homes. So available was mahogany that it was used far more generously than was normal, and if you come across a chair with unusually thick mahogany rails, see mahogany casually employed as a secondary wood, or encounter a mahogany bed with the rails also made of mahogany, you are probably looking at Charleston workmanship.

The wood most associated with Charleston is bald cypress. However, this is not as sure an indication of Charleston origin as some would think, for cypress grows all along the coast from Maryland down to Florida, and by itself suggests only the Low Country. However, it is a common secondary wood in Charleston furniture. Here it was often employed for the tops and bottoms of cases, for backboards, dust boards, drawer sides, and drawer bottoms. Perhaps the best indication of Charleston cabinetry is high style in combination with cypress. After the Revolution, vast quantities of eastern white pine were shipped down to Charleston, where it was much in demand for house trim and as a base for veneer. The doors and drawers of the clothespress in figure 11-28G are most probably veneered on white pine. Charleston case work is likely to have a mixture of secondary woods: white pine, poplar, red cedar, a Southern pine, and — of course — cypress.

It should be noted that, in addition to cypress, there are some other cabinet woods that, although minor in importance, are useful indicators of Low Country manufacture. Among these are Southern magnolia (*Magnolia grandiflora*), black mulberry (*Morus nigra*), and red bay (*Persea bobonia*).

Something should be said about the rest of the Low Country, from Wilmington in the north to Savannah in the south. Cabinetmakers in these communities also had access to mahogany, which helps differentiate between Low Country furniture and furniture made further north along the North Carolina coast, where there were few deepwater harbors. For instance, a circular tea table made in Wilmington would likely be made of mahogany, while the same table made further north in Edenton or New Bern might be made of walnut.

Savannah was not founded until 1733, and then grew slowly, hampered both by the general poverty of the settlers and the appalling climate. Three of the first four cabinetmakers to arrive died almost immediately, although they may not have arrived in good health, for the colony was settled mostly by poor people from around London. Not until 1759 was the first wharf built, and the city began to grow. The history of Savannah mirrors that of Charleston, but on a smaller scale. Savannah was also occupied during the Revolution, and then pretty much burned flat in November of 1796. Not until the 1830s did this poor stepsister really began to grow, but by then much furniture was coming down from New York and Philadelphia. Most of what little is identified as being of local manufacture is simple, Federal, and neoclassical. Unlike furniture made in Charleston, pieces made in Savannah show much diversity of both primary and secondary woods. Primary woods may be mahogany, red bay, or magnolia; secondary woods cypress, magnolia, and southern pine.

The Backcountry

By far the largest part of the South is the backcountry, the whole vast area extending inland from the fall line, the head of navigation of the coastal rivers. This includes the piedmont, the plateau from the fall line to the foothills of the Appalachian Mountains, and the land stretching across the mountains into western Virginia, Kentucky, and Tennessee. Although one might think that most settlers came from the coast, moving inland up the meandering coastal rivers, in fact, most people came from the northeast down the Great Wagon Road. The road started in Philadelphia, went west to Gettysburg, then turned southwest down through the Shenandoah Valley of Virginia. Then the road forked, one branch, called the Wilderness Road, going west through the Cumberland Gap into Kentucky, and the other branch continuing south into North Carolina, South Carolina, and Georgia. Settlement followed the path of least resistance, like waves lapping around the end of a sandbar, shifting west and then turning south down the Valley of Virginia into the Carolinas. During much of the eighteenth century, the Great Wagon Road was the most heavily traveled highway in America.

With these settlers came German and Welsh forms of furniture from the Delaware Valley, and in western Virginia and inland North Carolina we see Pennsylvania Dutch paint-decorated chests (10-8A), dovetailed walnut chests (10-8B), and tall chests of drawers (11-23) that could easily have been made in Chester County.

For the most part, backcountry cabinetmakers seem to have worked very much on their own, like rural cabinetmakers everywhere, spending part of their time in farming and house carpentry. There were no schools of cabinetry, and once away from the coastal cities, inland from Baltimore, Annapolis, Norfolk, and Charleston, there were very few communities of artisans that shared design and construction practices. Among the few exceptions was a group of a dozen or so cabinetmakers in the North Carolina piedmont in Davidson, Davie, and Rowan counties. From here, between present-day Winston-Salem and Charlotte, we see distinctive chests (10-8C) and chests of drawers (11-27D) that stand on stout frames with short, squared cabriole legs. Elsewhere, studies of Southern decorative arts have identified furniture that is clearly the product of one or two associated shops, but seldom have the location of the shops or the names of the cabinetmakers been identified.

Rural furniture tends to be overbuilt, and backcountry furniture is no exception. Drawer bottoms are sometimes of such thick stock that they are simply fastened with cut nails driven in from the backs and sides. This may have been because stout construction was preferred, or because the local sawmills did not — or could not — produce thin boards. It is one thing to smooth down a plank, quite another to reduce its thickness. Long after paneled doors went out of fashion, they were common in the backcountry, probably because glass was difficult to obtain. There was much lag in both style and construction. Furniture in Hepplewhite and Sheraton styles continued to be produced right up until the middle of the nineteenth century. You will even sometimes see use of the eighteenth century lipped drawer.

Much of the charm of backcountry furniture lies in the naive and diverse designs. In addition to innumerable huntboards and pie safes, there are many bottle cases, china presses, and sugar chests. Insect-free storage was very necessary, and if you encounter a pie safe that is very nicely made of walnut or cherry and that looks too good for the kitchen, you are probably looking at a Southern pie safe. Sugar chests speak to us of the profoundly rural nature of the backcountry, where visits to town must have been a notable occasion. As you might expect, most are from Tennessee and Kentucky, what was then the most distant backcountry. They exhibit much diversity. In addition to the usual type with a lift top and Sheraton legs (22-3B), there are sugar tables, combination bottle cases and sugar chests, and even a few sugar desks.

While it is often difficult to tell where Southern furniture was made, both the quality of workmanship and the selection of woods can suggest if a piece is from the coast or the backcountry. Such was the state of transportation that very little mahogany made its way inland, and in the backcountry it was very seldom employed, even for veneer as it was in Vermont. On better-quality work, in addition to walnut and cherry, you may see birch, either yellow birch (*Betula alleghaniensis*) or river birch (*Betula nigra*). Drawers everywhere are usually framed in poplar or yellow pine. Budget furniture may be made of tulip poplar, but is more likely to be made of one or another of the Southern pines: loblolly, longleaf, shortleaf, or slash pine. These pines were resistant to insects, easy to work when green, and strong and hard when the wood had seasoned.

This first chapter of furniture covers framed chairs, the sawn, shaped, and carved chairs made by cabinetmakers. It is almost the longest of the chapters on furniture, not only because these chairs survive in large numbers, but also because of the many types from different periods and regions. To assist the reader in locating a specific example, the illustrations are divided first by period and then by region, from earlier to later, and from north to south, commencing with the Queen Anne style in New England and ending with the neoclassical styles in the South. Ladder-back and corner chairs have their own sections in the middle of the chapter. Chairs made prior to the Queen Anne period, including prototypes of the Queen Anne style, are so uncommon that they are simply put together in the beginning. Whenever possible, the other chapters follow this same format, that is, earlier to later and north to south.

The distinction between framed and turned chairs is not always clear, for many rural chairs are a combination of the two, having sawn and shaped crest rails and stiles joined to turned seat rails and front legs. These are included in this chapter because style and region are most clearly exhibited in the backs of chairs, and here these chairs have much in common with the more costly formal chairs.

Although also produced by cabinet and chair makers, stools, chair-back settees, and back stools are not shown because of their rarity among American furniture. Similarly, there are no illustrations of the joiner's wainscot chair, even though it was produced to some extent in all regions. Most of the relatively few American examples are now in public collections. Low slipper chairs are also omitted, not so much because they are uncommon as because they follow the form and style of full-sized chairs, differing only in the length of the legs.

As mentioned earlier, the reader will notice that there are relatively few illustrations of late Federal or classical workmanship, even though many chairs survive from this time. By the 1820s, America had left its colonial past far behind and was very much a single nation, and with this, furniture, and particularly urban furniture, lost most of its regional character. Only a student of this period can discern the small differences in urban workmanship, and even here there is often some conjecture. Similarly, there are few illustrations of rural chairs except those from places where a particular form became so well established as to constitute an identifiable regional type. Much rural workmanship is so simple and logical in design and construction as to have been made almost anywhere by an intelligent carpenter or joiner, and where it was produced can be no more than suggested by the occasional regional motif and the selection of primary and secondary woods.

Chippendale-style chairs typically have pierced vertical splats between the back posts or stiles. Cabinetmakers employed a variety of patterns, many being so fashionable in some cities that they are associated with these urban centers. While these patterns are indeed a quick and useful regional guide, we should always remember to consider a chair in its entirety, for splat patterns that were popular and easy to produce were apt to be copied by many craftsmen, some working far away from where the pattern was most fashionable. In addition, most of the patterns found in American chairs have English antecedents, some adapted from illustrations in books such as Chippendale's *Director*, but most apparently modeled on imported chairs, sometimes for no other reason than to expand an existing set of chairs. Others may have been introduced by immigrant artisans, for to get started, a chairmaker needed both patterns and tools.

Fashionable patterns are more widespread than one might think. For instance, the distinctive owl's-eye splat associated with Boston-area chairs is not only an English pattern, but was used, often in modified form, all up and down the New England coast. It is even found in some Charleston, South Carolina, chairs, although here the inspiration may have come from England. The diamond pattern so often seen in New York chairs was used everywhere: in Philadelphia, Connecticut, Boston, and even in Portsmouth, New Hampshire. Its presence should be no more than a suggestion of New York workmanship. We will also see that simple patterns that are both attractive and easy to lay out may have been produced almost anywhere, and by themselves are no particular indicator of region.

Dozens of different patterns were employed in American chairs. Some combine one or more elements of other designs; others are no more than rural interpretations of fashionable urban designs. While this chapter will illustrate many of the more common patterns, it cannot begin show them all, and the lack of a matching pattern should not imply that the spat has been replaced at some time, or that a chair is not an American product. In addition, the finest-quality chairs, particularly those made in Philadelphia, tend to employ atypical patterns, most probably because the clients requested something special in addition to the extra carving. The splat patterns may be very different from those of the normal run of Philadelphia chairs.

For the most part, American chairs — even those of quality workmanship — were economically made to standard designs. The richly carved high-style chairs seen in fine collections are actually fairly rare, and examples from these sets have usually been published. Should you encounter a really grand American chair, perhaps having an atypical splat pattern or additional carving, that is likely to have been the product of a special order, it is worth some investigation to determine if it might not be part of a documented set.

We may get more help determining region from the smaller elements, particularly the shapes of the crest rail and the feet, for whatever the pattern of splat chosen by the customer, a chair maker would tend to follow local practice in the details of the design. Crest rails will be shown later in the illustrations, but here we will look at feet, for among chairs they speak to us more clearly of region than any other design element.

In all regions, two basic types of foot were employed in Queen Anne and Chippendale-style cabriole leg chairs: a relatively simple pad, club, slipper, or trifid foot that could be fashioned with a saw, lathe, spokeshave, and file; and a carved ball and claw foot that required both experience and a set of carving tools. In urban areas, ball and claw feet were usually the province of carvers, who tended to follow established local patterns. Figures 5-1A – E illustrate the shapes of ball and claw feet typically found in Boston, Newport, Connecticut, New York, and Philadelphia furniture. The ball and claw foot is seldom seen south of the Mason-Dixon Line. We will just touch on these when discussing the Philadelphia-type foot. For further information, and good photo illustrations, I recommend that you consult either Patricia Kane's *300 Years of American Seating Furniture* or John Kirk's *American Chairs*.

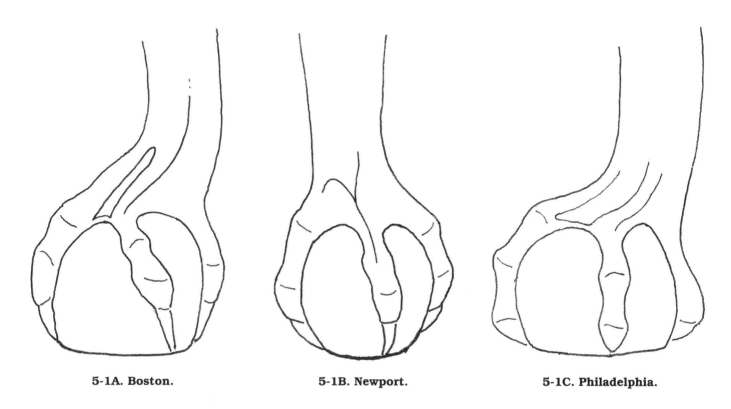

5-1A. Boston. 5-1B. Newport. 5-1C. Philadelphia.

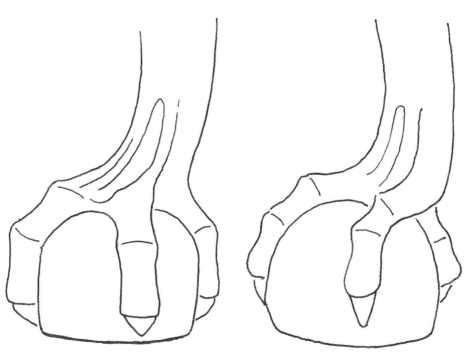

5-1D. Connecticut Chapin type. 5-1E. New York.

Boston, or perhaps more correctly, eastern Massachusetts, is noted for the retracted claw foot in which the side claws are said to be retracted, that is, they slope to the rear of the foot as seen in figure 5-1A. The amount of slope varies with the carver; some are almost straight up and down, while others slant back 30 degrees or more from the vertical. While this is the most obvious feature, there are other ways to identify a Massachusetts foot. So that the claws can rake back across the sides of the ball, they are bunched together at the front of the ball. Aside from being slightly flattened on the bottom, the ball itself is high and rounded and appears to be lightly held by the claws. The talons at the ends of the toes are clearly delineated and tend to be long and slender. While such a foot is popularly associated with Massachusetts workmanship, it is not a sure thing, for it is not unique to Massachusetts. It is found in a few Rhode Island and Philadelphia chairs as well as in English furniture, from which the shape probably originated. Here it might also be noted that the somewhat slapdash workmanship seen in so much Boston-area furniture also infects ball and claw feet. You will see ball and claw feet in which the claws and talons are not well delineated, feet in which the rear claws and talons are just roughed out, and case furniture in which the rear claws and talons are omitted on the back feet, where they would not show.

Newport ball and claw feet are similar to those of Boston in having lightly grasped round balls and moderately long, well delineated talons, although the side claws are not retracted and hence, not grouped together at the fronts of the balls. Often the ball will be noticeably large and round, flattened only slightly on the base as shown in figure 5-1B. On some fine work the talons are undercut; that is, the wood has been carefully removed underneath the talon such that there is an open space between the inside of the talon and the face of the ball. This well-known Newport feature, associated with the Goddard and Townsend families, is actually not all that common and is not even not exclusive to Rhode Island, for it is sometimes seen in both Massachusetts and English furniture, and indeed is a logical refinement for a customer willing to pay a little extra for a nice finishing touch. In any event, talons do not appear to have been undercut on seating furniture, probably because the feet are both relatively small and subject to more that the usual wear and abuse. In addition to the large, round ball, the simplest way to identify a Newport foot is the combination of fairly long talons without the retracted side claws.

Philadelphia ball and claw feet are very different. On a Philadelphia foot, the ball is slightly flattened and tends bulge out between the side claws, suggesting a vegetarian eagle in pursuit of a somewhat overripe tomato (5-1C). The claws are vertical and evenly spaced, the talons noticeably short. Aside from the lack of retraction, perhaps the easiest way to tell Philadelphia from Boston are these stubby little talons. This

distinction is useful, for the great majority of American ball and claw feet will be from either Boston or Philadelphia. In a general way, long, slender talons are not seen south of Rhode Island.

The ball and claw foot carved by the Chapin family of Connecticut is similar in feeling to the Philadelphia foot in having a flattened ball and short talons as shown in figure 5-1D. While it may be derived from the Philadelphia model, it is, in fact, quite different, being smaller, squarish, and having round, well-articulated claws. Note that the ball itself is not fully rounded, being shaped more like an oversized knob. Needless to say, the chair itself will very probably be made of cherry rather than walnut or mahogany. As a group, and a relatively small group at that, Chapin-type ball and claw feet are remarkably consistent in size and shape, which might be expected, as most come from one shop in East Windsor, Connecticut.

Cabriole legs are seldom found in Southern chairs, and ball and claw feet are even less common. There would not appear to be a representative form of ball and claw foot. However, the few extant examples suggest that Philadelphia's lead was generally followed; that is, a Southern ball and claw foot will tend to have a compressed ball and short talons.

Although the ball and claw foot was favored in New York, there does not seem to have developed a single standard form, for in *American Chairs*, John Kirk identifies four different types. However, most that you see exhibit a square, blocky look that is significantly different from the look of Philadelphia work, although each tends to have a somewhat compressed ball and short talons. The foot in figure 5-1E is typical of many in having a rather sharp turn to the ankle such that the middle claw is actually horizontal before transitioning to the first knuckle. Many New York feet are so square in proportion as to suggest a somewhat indolent carver — as if the chair maker had provided a roughed out cube, and then the carver positioned the claws at the very corners so as to remove as little wood as possible.

Club and pad feet are easier to identify, but sometimes tell us less about region. The standard club foot so commonly seen in Massachusetts chairs (5-2A) is also found in Rhode Island, Connecticut, and in the coastal South. Such feet were usually given thin pads or shoes, probably to allow for wear, for dining chairs were set against the walls when not in use and must have been moved almost every day. Even with the addition of this pad, the club feet on chairs are frequently badly worn, the pads appearing now as little more than thin disks. With the advent of the rococo style in coastal Massachusetts, in Boston and Salem, the pads tended to be much thicker, perhaps to add more visual mass to a somewhat larger chair, or perhaps to compensate for the wear that must have been very noticeable by this time. The Massachusetts Chippendale chair in figure 5-19G has these later feet.

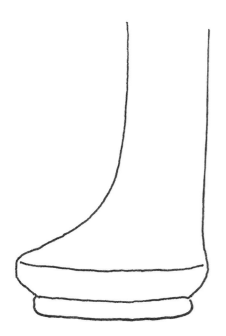

5-2A. Massachusetts club foot.

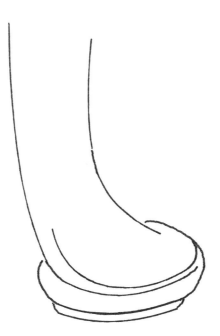

5-2B. Philadelphia pad foot.

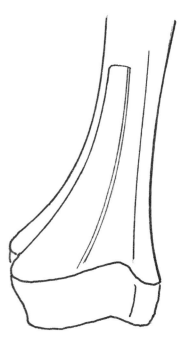

5-2C. Philadelphia trifid foot.

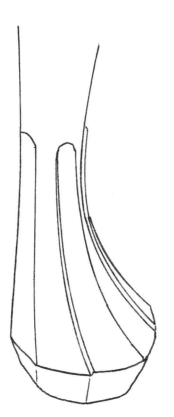

5-2D. Philadelphia trifid foot.

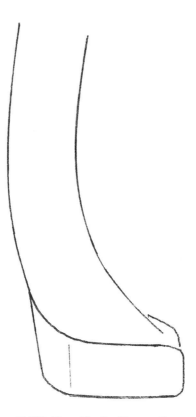

5-2E. New York slipper foot.

Philadelphia chair makers followed a very different route. At first they employed a round pad foot with a distinctive ring in the upper surface (5-2B), then a small rounded slipper foot. Both of these were superseded in the 1750s by a trifid foot (5-2C), a design so popular that it was employed throughout the Delaware Valley until the end of the century, for as long as cabriole leg chairs continued to be produced. Because both the pad and the slipper foot were early developments and relatively short-lived fashions, the great majority of Delaware Valley Queen Anne and Chippendale chairs employ some form of trifid foot. Not all of these feet are as boldly shaped as that shown in figure 5-2C. Sometimes a foot is shaped more like a club, with little more than a suggestion of a three-part division (5-2D). While such a foot is often identified as trifid, it is actually more of a club foot with three flats on the outside edges. On each of these feet, the toes will often be carried upward to suggest a stocking extending about a third of the way up the leg. The earlier slipper foot is also apt to have a tongue extending up the leg. Like much else, this form is not unique to the New World, for very trifid-looking feet — complete with stockings — are found on Irish furniture.

Although set between Boston to the north and Philadelphia to the south, New York cabinetmakers did not often produce club and pad feet. Most Queen Anne and Chippendale cabriole-leg chairs were given ball and claw feet. When a simpler foot was desired, it was generally a deep and wide slipper foot like that shown in figure 5-2E. This distinctive foot is also seen on upholstered chairs and rural case furniture. The slipper foot was employed to some extent in all regions. A short, rounded slipper foot was used in early Philadelphia Queen Anne chairs, but these chairs are so scarce that you are unlikely to see an example outside of a museum collection. More common is the rather narrow, slim slipper foot that was employed in Newport on high chests of drawers and tea tables (17-2C). However, it is very different in shape from the heavy New York slipper foot. Also, it is not seen on seating furniture.

With the advent of the Federal period and the introduction of the Sheraton style, the front legs on chairs were turned and reeded. In urban centers this work was usually done by turners, much the way ball and claw feet were produced by carvers, and for much the same reasons, we see local patterns in the turnings of the legs and feet. Because Sheraton legs are most often seen in neoclassical breakfast and card tables, they are illustrated in figure 16-1 in the chapter on dining and breakfast tables.

Lastly, some note might be made of the Spanish, or paintbrush, foot. This very William and Mary motif is found in both the New England and Middle Atlantic regions, but in very different types of furniture: in New England in a few small tavern tables and a great many rural chairs, and in the Delaware Valley in rural high chests of drawers and dressing tables. While the shape of the foot differs by location, more significant is the use of the foot itself, which we will see when we get to the appropriate furniture chapters.

The way a chair is made also speaks to us of region, for craftsmen everywhere tended to follow locally accepted methods and practices and to employ locally available woods. Before discussing specific chairs, we might consider these methods and practices for they tend to be common to all chairs from a region, whatever the particular design or style of an individual chair. The normal way to construct a chair is to tenon the rails into the stiles and front legs. Today this is almost always done with dowels, but in the past the chair maker would employ mortise and tenon joints. To save time, and to simplify assembly, the tenons were shouldered only on the outside; what is known today as barefaced tenons. A mortise was set in the same amount as the depth of the shoulder such that the outside of the seat rails would be flush with the outside of the legs. The joint was often reinforced with a wooden pin to lock the tenon in place. Stretchers on straight or Marlborough leg chairs were also joined with barefaced tenons, and here again they will be flush with the outside of the legs. Normally the seat rails would be tenoned perhaps two-thirds of the way through the back posts or stiles, but in the Philadelphia region it was common practice to carry the tenon clear through the stiles, an option that cost an additional six pence per chair but provided additional strength and assured the owner that the maker had not slighted on the depth of the mortises. This feature, called through tenoning, or tenoning through the stiles, is particularly useful as a regional identifier, for while sometimes seen elsewhere, it is indicative of Philadelphia-area workmanship. It is also easy to spot, for the ends of the tenons show clearly on the backs of the stiles as shown in figure 5-3.

With the advent of the fully developed Queen Anne style, chair seats are rounded to harmonize with the other curved elements in Queen Anne chairs. In Boston and New York, these compass or balloon seats were made by shaping the side and front rails to produce a curved seat. As before, the rails were then tenoned into the tops of the cabriole legs, and the joint usually reinforced with a pin, as shown in figure 5-4.

However, in Philadelphia, and sometimes in Connecticut, cabinetmakers employed the English method of framing a circular seat. Here the rails were made quite flat and wide, with the required curve being cut on the outside of the rail. The front and side rails were then joined with a wide and relatively thin horizontal mortise-and-tenon joint, the front rail having a mortise at either end to receive the tenons of the side rails. The tops of the cabriole legs were shaped into a stout dowel, which extended up through a hole drilled through the mortise-and-tenon joint, as shown in figure 5-5. This both provided a secure fastening for the leg and locked in the joint. These chairs were fitted with drop seats, and to keep the seats in place, rims were applied to the tops of the rails. In a few instances, the rails of a chair are extra thick, and the rim is worked out of the rails.

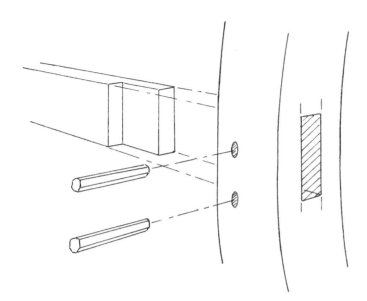

5-3. Through tenoning.

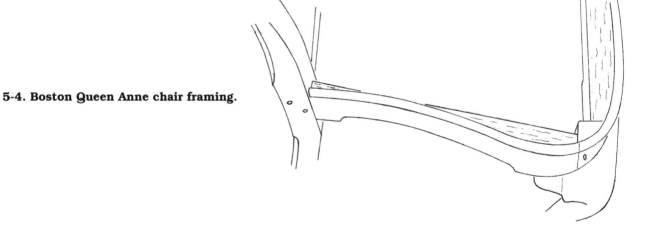

5-4. Boston Queen Anne chair framing.

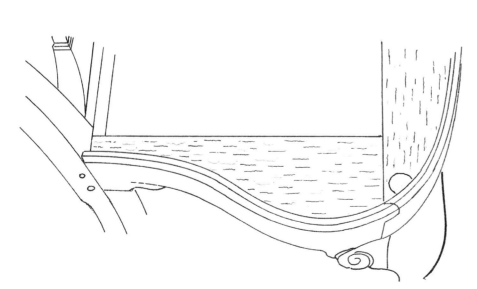

5-5. Philadelphia Queen Anne chair framing.

To maintain a feeling of lightness and delicacy, the rails on a chair were kept relatively thin, and the mortise-and-tenon joints at the stiles required additional reinforcement. This was usually provided by a shaped block called a bracket respond that was glued and nailed to the underside of the rails at the juncture with the rear legs. Sometimes extra strength was obtained by tenoning the respond through the leg. Bracket responds were employed everywhere on both Queen Anne and Chippendale-style chairs, and by themselves are no particular indicator of region, although they are seldom seen on Massachusetts chairs fitted with stretchers, and are very common on Philadelphia Queen Anne chairs due to the lack of stretchers and the shallowness of the rails.

Philadelphia compass seat construction is not difficult to identify if we note the relative thinness of the rails, the way the cabriole legs appear to stop at the rails, and the apparent lack of pins to lock the tenons in place. Lift the drop seat and you will see a square opening formed by the wide, flat rails, and in each front corner, the top of the dowel that fastens the front legs to the seat rails.

When seat rails and tenons are sufficiently thick, there is no particular requirement for extra bracing, nor for additional surface to support a drop seat. However, most good-quality chairs were given additional stiffening on the inside corners of the seat frames, and the way this was done can tell us where a chair was made.

In Boston, and throughout New England, it was normal to use triangular white pine blocks, although in some Rhode Island chairs, the blocking may be chestnut. These were cut with the grain running horizontally and were fastened with glue and then either a pair or two pairs of nails, as seen in figure 5-6. When necessary, a notch would be cut in the corner to clear the tops of the legs and the stiles.

Portsmouth, New Hampshire, Chippendale chairs were sometimes stiffened with diagonal corner braces rather than the usual New England triangular blocking, apparently because some English cabinetmakers settled in Portsmouth in the eighteenth century. For additional strength, the braces were tenoned into the rails and reinforced with nails (5-7). Sometimes there will be seen a mix of reinforcements, cross bracing in the front and triangular blocking in the rear.

Philadelphia blocking is very different. Here the blocking will be quarter round in shape, with the grain running vertically rather than horizontally (5-8). Also, this English form of blocking is not normally reinforced with nails, although there are a few instances where nails or pins were added to provide a little extra reinforcement. The blocking in the front is made up of two pieces to fit around the legs; in the back there may be a filler to pad out the rear rail, as seen in figure 5-8. Normally the front blocking is somewhat larger than the rear blocking. A few Philadelphia chairs have vertical quarter-round blocking in the front and horizontal triangular blocking in the rear, a feature found in many English chairs. Philadelphia chairmakers almost always employed either pine or Atlantic white cedar for blocking, for both are slightly flexible and hold glue well.

Unfortunately, blocking is not as good a regional indicator as we might wish, for either Philadelphia or Boston blocking may be found in New York, Connecticut, and Rhode Island chairs. Southern Chippendale chairs generally follow Philadelphia practice, not only due to Philadelphia's influence, but also because cabinetmakers in the South, particularly along the coast, tended to follow English construction practices.

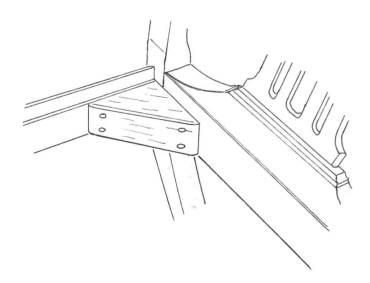

5-6. Massachusetts chair blocking.

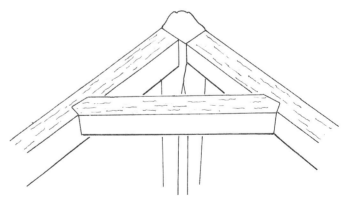

5-7. New Hampshire chair bracing.

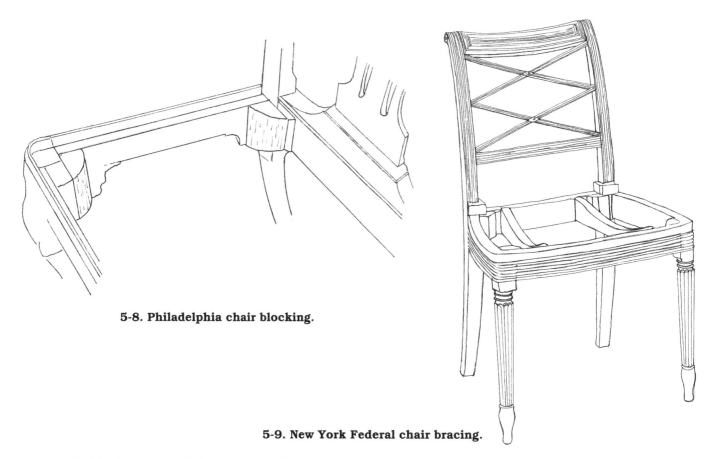

5-8. Philadelphia chair blocking.

5-9. New York Federal chair bracing.

From all this discussion, all that can be said with some certainty is that Massachusetts blocking is very unlikely to be seen in Philadelphia work, and that Philadelphia blocking is rare in Rhode Island and is not found in Massachusetts and New Hampshire.

Following the Revolution the story is more complicated, for the delicate neoclassical chairs of the Federal period were more highly stressed and often required more than just simple corner blocking. Nevertheless, most Boston chairs still retain the traditional triangular blocking, although here and there cross bracing was employed for greater strength. Connecticut chairs may be either quarter-round blocked or cross braced. By this time, New York was both a major city and the center of style, and here we see the greatest innovation. In addition to both quarter-round blocking and cross bracing, New York Federal chairs are very likely to have either one or two medial braces running between the front and back rails as shown in figure 5-9. These were normally used in conjunction with blocking, but sometimes we see a chair having both cross bracing and medial bracing.

Philadelphia was slower to take up the new neoclassical styles, and there was little change in the quarter-round vertical blocking used in Chippendale chairs, although now it was often smaller and composed of a single piece of wood. While it would seem logical that nearby Maryland would follow Philadelphia practice, in fact, Baltimore and Annapolis Federal chairs are more likely to employ the cross bracing so often found in New

York. Charleston chairs may also be cross braced, perhaps due to the influence of New York, for much New York furniture was being shipped south at this time.

Before leaving this subject, it should be noted that blocking and, to a lesser extent, cross bracing, being located at the point of greatest flexing in a chair, are often either missing or replaced. However, it is usually possible to determine the form of the original methods from differences in oxidation, remaining glue, and nail holes. Philadelphia blocking should show traces of old glue and a lighter, less oxidized area that was under the blocking. Boston blocking will show a somewhat larger area of less oxidization, and then either a pair or two pairs of nail holes at each corner. Cross braces were normally mortised into the rails, and here we would expect to find the empty mortises with perhaps small holes where nails had been used for reinforcement.

Secondary woods are a good indicator of region, and the discussions that accompany the illustrations will note the woods we may expect to find in different regions. However, there are a couple of caveats. First off, eastern white pine was so easy to work and held glue so well that it was widely employed in chair blocking and was popular not only throughout New England, but also in the Middle Atlantic in New York City. Secondly, blocking has little surface area, which sometimes makes it difficult to identify. On the other hand, since it is secondary structure, it is easy to obtain an unobtrusive chip from a corner block, drop-seat frame, or seat rail to send out for analysis.

5-10 Massachusetts Cromwell chair. We will begin our survey with the Jacobean-style Cromwell chair. Although chairs, and particularly American chairs with upholstery from the turn of the seventeenth century are fairly rare, a significant number of these early chairs survive. Cromwell chairs were made in limited numbers in Massachusetts, New York, and Pennsylvania. Most are similar to this Massachusetts example, and were probably made in or around Boston. This is a somewhat simplified design; many have additional pairs of ball turnings on the stiles between the upholstered seats and the backs. New England chairs will be maple or of a mixture of woods, most often maple and red oak, but sometimes maple and beech. Similar chairs were produced in Philadelphia, although here they were made of walnut and normally were not upholstered, having an open back and a deep cushion resting on a plank seat. A rare few Boston and Philadelphia chairs have twist turnings. The woods are of interest, for even from this early date we can see the preference for maple in New England and walnut in the Delaware River Valley.

5-11 Massachusetts "Boston" chairs. Among the earliest mass-produced American chairs, and some of the most common, "Boston" chairs were produced in large numbers in the Boston area between 1715 and 1755. They combine elements of both the William and Mary and early Queen Anne styles, and may be described either way in auction catalogs. There are a number of variations among these chairs. We will only consider two. However, they are not difficult to identify, for most have in common overupholstered leather seats and padded leather backs decorated with either one or two rows of brass nails. Some were made with caning rather than leather, but they are rare, for caning was time consuming and expensive in America. Boston chairs were invariably made of soft maple, usually with red oak rails under the seat upholstery.

Figure 5-11A illustrates the earliest form of these Boston chairs. It has a canted back and a flat crest rail set between two turned stiles. There are a few surviving examples that have the carved William and Mary style crest rail seen in early banister-back chairs. They appear to have been quickly superseded by more comfortable designs having spooned or "crooked" backs, for today they are quite rare. Although associated with Boston, this early form is thought by some to have been made in a number of areas, principally New York City.

Far more common are chairs having the shaped crest rail and the reverse-curved Queen Anne back shown in figure 5-11B.

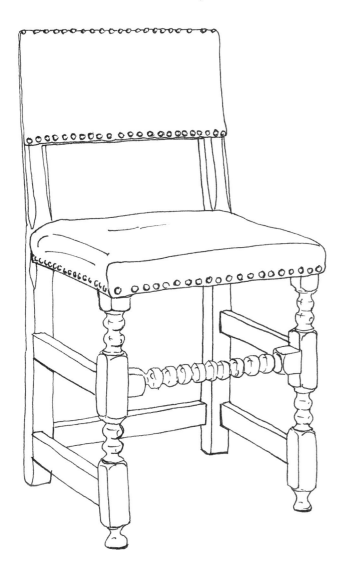

5-10. Massachusetts Cromwell chair, 1650 – 1690.

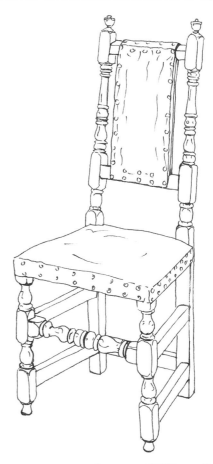

5-11A. Massachusetts William & Mary "Boston" chair, 1710 – 1730.

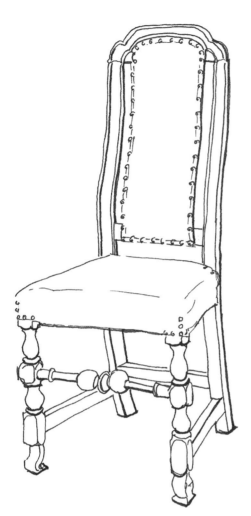

5-11B. Massachusetts Queen Anne "Boston" chair, 1720 – 1760.

There are two forms of crest rails on these chairs, a raised undulating rail with squared-off corners and a flat center section that has a very William and Mary look, and the somewhat later rounded, indented rail shown here that is suggestive of the fully developed Queen Anne style to follow. These crooked-back chairs may have either ball or Spanish feet. The Spanish foot is far more commonly found on the first type of chair.

The fourth type of Boston chair has the traditional Queen Anne round-shouldered yoke crest rail like that shown in the New Hampshire chair in figure 5-12B. These seem to have been made in limited quantities in Rhode Island, most probably in Newport. Like the earliest form, they are also quite rare.

Boston chairs having local histories may turn up far from home, for they were shipped down the coast, particularly to Philadelphia, where they offered more value than locally made chairs. The high production rate could lead to very indifferent workmanship, and there are chairs in which the front legs are not a good match, even though both are original to the chair. Perhaps because a great many were inexpensive export products, most Boston chairs are side chairs rather than armchairs.

5-12 New Hampshire Queen Anne chairs. Although New Hampshire Queen Anne chairs superficially resemble a great many other rural New England Queen Anne chairs, there are significant differences if we consider the details of this common form. The best known were made by the Gaines family of turners who worked both in Ipswich, Massachusetts, and in Portsmouth, New Hampshire. Because these well-known chairs seem to have either served as a model for simpler chairs made by others, or conversely, were perhaps an elaboration of an existing design, we will consider them first.

Gaines-type chairs are attributed to the Portsmouth shop of John Gaines III (1704 – 1743) on the basis of four side chairs owned by a direct descendant, although it is possible that some chairs of this type were actually produced in Ipswich rather than Portsmouth. A Gaines chair has a boldly carved and pierced crest rail and equally boldly carved built-up Spanish feet, as shown in figure 5-12A. In addition, the rush slip seat is set within seat rails that are horizontally shaped with flat arches on the sides and a semicircular drop in the front. The front and rear stretchers are turned, while the side stretchers are sawn. In contrast to the ornate crest, the splat is of simple vase or baluster form, and interestingly, is sometimes quite noticeably asymmetrical.

The more typical New Hampshire Queen Anne chair (5-12B) might be seen as a simplification of this design. The crest rail is still boldly carved, but is not pierced and is of more conventional New England Queen Anne form. The most characteristic New Hampshire feature is the rush seat set within rails, normally with either one or two semicircular drops in the front rail. Although lacking in this example, many New Hampshire Queen Anne chairs have the large, built-up Spanish feet shown in the preceding illustration. That they are not present here would suggest that this may be a late expression of the form. In common with the Boston chairs, and with most rural New England Queen Anne chairs, the primary wood will usually be a soft maple, although some have hard maple elements, and there is at least one recorded chair made of cherry.

5-12A. New Hampshire Queen Anne Gaines-type chair, c. 1730.

5-12B. New Hampshire Queen Anne side chair, 1740 – 1790.

5-13 Massachusetts Queen Anne chairs. So many chairs in the Queen Anne style were produced in Massachusetts that we will consider no fewer than five of the most common types, and then in the next section look at a more fully developed Queen Anne chair that was produced in both Boston and Newport. The standard Boston high-style Queen Anne chair has a yoke crest, flat faced stiles, a simple baluster splat, cabriole legs, and club feet, as shown in figure 5-13A. The curved rails of the compass seat will be tenoned into the tops of the cabriole legs in Boston fashion, as illustrated in figure 5-4. This can be seen, even without even lifting the seat, by the pins used to lock the tenons in place. Except when overupholstered, the front and side rails are reduced in depth by use of a flat arch on the underside of the rail.

Less expensive chairs were given square (actually trapezoidal) seats, and here the front rail was thinned by scalloping (5-13B). The great majority of these chairs are devoid of carving. The design was so popular and became so standardized that today there are a considerable number of assembled sets of nearly identical chairs. Most all these chairs have drop seats that were usually upholstered in leather. A few compass seat chairs are overupholstered as would complement a more expensive chair. Unlike Philadelphia Queen Anne chairs, all but a rare few are fitted with the standard New England block-and-turned stretchers. Normally there will be a simple club foot, although a few have the later thick pad feet seen in eastern Massachusetts Chippendale chairs, and some grander versions were given ball and claw feet.

While the majority of these chairs were made in and around Boston and Salem, they were also produced to the south in Connecticut and to the north in Portsmouth, New Hampshire. Almost identical chairs were made in Newport, differing only slightly in the details of the splats and the stretchers. The fashionable wood of this period was walnut, but it was expensive, and about one in three of these handsome chairs is made of maple, which was stained up to resemble walnut. There are a few Connecticut chairs made of cherry, and some Massachusetts chairs are made from mahogany, for they were produced in parallel with newer Chippendale-style chairs until about 1770. Drop-seat frames are usually either white pine or soft maple, more often the latter.

Rural interpretations of the popular Queen Anne style were produced in enormous numbers throughout New England, primarily in central and eastern Massachusetts and coastal and inland Connecticut. Normally these chairs have a Queen Anne–style back and William and Mary–style front legs, as shown in figures 5-13C and 5-13D. They were produced for almost half a century, from the 1730s until the eve of the Revolution. While we might consider a splat seated in a cross rail to be an indication of rural work, many, if not most, were the inexpensive products of urban shops. Although armchairs tended to be less common in New England, a considerable number of these chairs have arms, and with this, the additional width necessary to accommodate the hips of the sitter. While both these chairs happen to have square sawn back and side stretchers, more often the side stretchers will be turned, and only the back stretcher sawn and rectangular in cross section.

These chairs usually have quickly shaped Spanish feet, not the large, built-up feet so often seen in New Hampshire. A few have either ball or turned pad feet. While normally the front legs terminate in the underside of the rush seat frame, as shown in the side chair, in a few instances the front legs extend above the seat and the rails are mortised into the tops of the legs. Later in this chapter we will see Chippendale interpretations of much the same design. Here it should be noted that, while these simplified Queen Anne chairs were produced all over New England, the form did not travel south of the New York border, and if you see a chair like that shown in figure 5-13C or figure 5-13D, you are very probably looking at a product of New England.

Also, there are a number of hybrid designs having the splat seated in a cross rail in combination with the cabriole legs seen in high-style urban chairs. Normally these inexpensive maple chairs have simple sawn cabriole legs, without applied returns, that terminate in equally simple square pad feet, as illustrated in figure 5-13E.

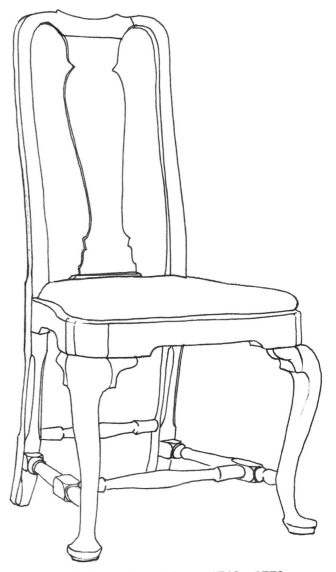

5-13A. Boston Queen Anne, 1740 – 1770.

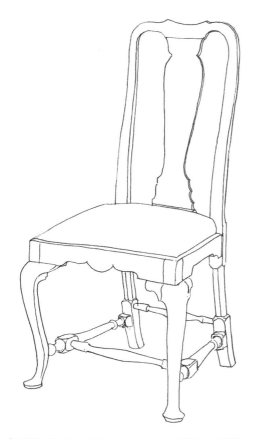

5-13B. Boston Queen Anne, 1740 – 1770.

5-13C. Massachusetts Queen Anne, 1740 – 1780.

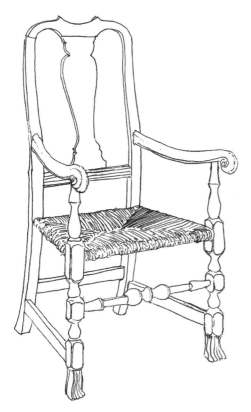

5-13D. Massachusetts Queen Anne, 1740 – 1780.

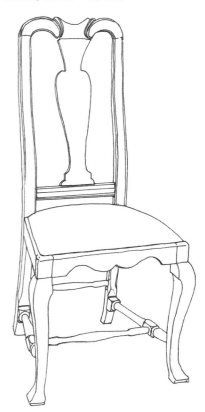

5-13E. Massachusetts Queen Anne, c. 1760.

5-14 Rhode Island Queen Anne chairs. The standard Newport Queen Anne chair is so similar to those of Boston work that we will first look at a more costly chair that was also produced both in Newport and Boston, and then at two chairs having features more often associated with Newport workmanship. Boston and Newport customers wishing the very best could order chairs with a carved shell in the crest rail and the stiles shaped to conform to the curves of the splats (5-14A). Some of these chairs were also given shell-carved knees. Most have club feet. To save a little wood, the stiles were often pieced at the midpoints where the stiles curve in to follow the curves of the splats. Although often identified as Newport work, most of these chairs are now thought to have been made in Boston.

Flat sawn stretchers are historically associated with Newport chairs, even though they were employed everywhere in early Queen Anne chairs. However, they are rarely seen in Massachusetts, so a New England Queen Anne chair with sawn stretchers is likely to be a Newport product (5-14B). Later we will see a Philadelphia Queen Anne chair that was also fitted with flat stretchers. All things considered, flat sawn stretchers are perhaps more a sign of the early Queen Anne style than they are of region.

Far more indicative of Newport workmanship are chairs having the stiles rounded on all sides as shown in the side chair in figure 5-14C. This provides a noticeably elegant and delicate looking back. Like flat stretchers, rounded stiles are unusual in New England Queen Anne chairs, and as such, provide us with another indication of Newport work. They are typical of the quality for which the Newport customer was willing to pay a bit extra.

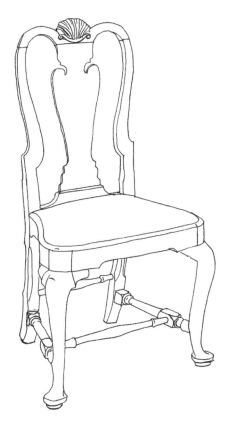

5-14A. Rhode Island Queen Anne, 1745 – 1765.

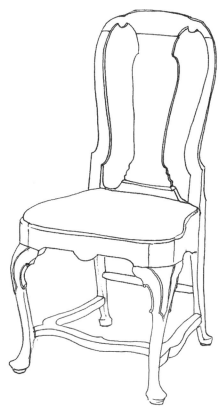

5-14B. Newport Queen Anne, 1730 – 1740.

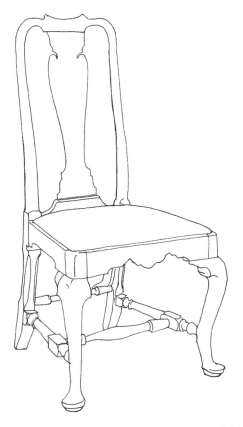

5-14C. Newport Queen Anne, 1740 – 1760.

5-15 Connecticut Queen Anne chairs. Connecticut Queen Anne-style chairs present us with two problems: there are too few to provide a large body of representative work, and they are likely to incorporate Boston, New York, and Philadelphia design elements and construction practices, for Connecticut in the eighteenth century was very rural and lacked a major urban center to provide a focus for production and style. The relatively few high-style Queen Anne chairs that survive are typically rather slim and tall, with narrow backs and somewhat short and narrow seats like the chair shown in figure 5-15A. The splat may be quite noticeably slender and the back will be either canted or will have just a shallow reverse curve. Some chairs lack stretchers and may be through tenoned, and if fitted with compass seats, employ the Philadelphia type of framing. Sometimes, as in this chair, the knee blocks are glued to the face of the seat rails, the rails themselves having been shaped to provide a backing for the blocks. Note that the seat rails have the exuberant scalloping so often seen in Connecticut work. For the most part these chairs will be made of cherry or maple, although there are a few birch and mahogany examples.

Another form of Connecticut chair, produced in both New London County and the lower Connecticut River Valley, has a more Philadelphia Queen Anne splat with a prominent projection or spur about a third of the way up, as we see in figure 5-15B. These chairs have unusual stretcher arrangements. Some have but a single turned stretcher set between the rear legs, but more typically there will be the three stretchers shown in the illustration. Because there is no medial stretcher, there was no need of blocking the side stretchers to receive the ends of the medial stretcher, and these stretchers are just turned rather than block-and-turned.

Rural Queen Anne chairs are very similar to those produced elsewhere in New England, with the exception that they are frequently made of cherry. Also, armchairs may also be given a turned stretcher beneath the arm, as shown in figure 5-15C, a Connecticut feature we will see again when we discuss turned chairs.

5-15A. Connecticut Queen Anne, 1740 – 1760.

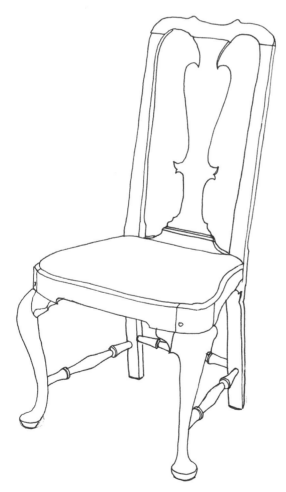

5-15B. Norwich Queen Anne, c. 1760.

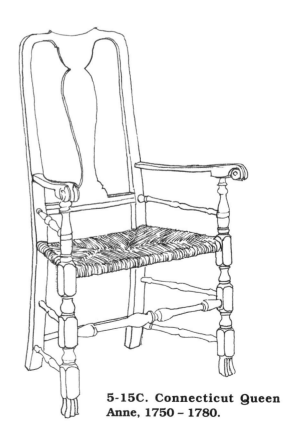

5-15C. Connecticut Queen Anne, 1750 – 1780.

5-16 New York Queen Anne Chair. New York Queen Anne chairs are almost invariably described as being rare — and for good reason, for there are very few surviving examples. However, they are not that difficult to identify so long as they are actually identified as American, for they are very similar to an English George II period chair. Typically, they will seem somewhat shorter and heavier than other American Queen Anne chairs, and the upper halves of the splats will often be pumpkin shaped as shown in figure 5-16. A number of chairs have the tops of the shoes shaped into the cupid's bow shown in this illustration. Most omit stretchers and are given ball and claw feet, although a few have club feet or drake feet, or the deep slipper foot illustrated in figure 5-2E. Often the rear legs taper and terminate in small square or oval pad feet, an English feature sometimes found in Philadelphia and Boston chairs, but most commonly in those from New York. New York compass seat chairs were framed in the Boston manner; that is, the rails were tenoned into the tops of the front legs. In spite of the proximity of the much larger city of Philadelphia, the rails were not through tenoned, although more often than not the joint between the rails and stiles has been reinforced with bracket responds. Most examples are made of walnut, although some will be mahogany and, interestingly, some are made of cherry.

5-16. New York Queen Anne, 1750 – 1760.

5-17 Pennsylvania Queen Anne chairs. In this section we will look at two typical Philadelphia Queen Anne chairs, first an earlier type that is similar in appearance to the standard Boston Queen Anne chair, then the better-known, fully developed Philadelphia Queen Anne chair. Another type of chair that was produced in both Queen Anne and Chippendale styles, the well known Savery chairs, will be discussed when we cover Chippendale chairs.

Early Philadelphia Queen Anne chairs can be confusing, for they are superficially similar to Massachusetts Queen Anne chairs, having much the same tall back, thin solid splat, and yoked crest rail seen throughout New England. They are often fitted with stretchers, although here the stretchers are flat and sawn rather than block and turned, as illustrated in figure 5-17A. The splats of these chairs are also usually very different from the simple baluster form seen in New England, being of a pronounced vase shape, normally with a pair of small curved lobes at the top of the vase. The cabriole legs will terminate in either the early slipper or ringed pad foot, or the trifid foot so characteristic of Philadelphia workmanship.

Far better known is the later Queen Anne chair shown in figure 5-17B. Here the splat is rich and ornate, typically a broad vase shape with projecting lobes or ears in the upper half, then a double swell or a swell and a spur in the lower half. The rails of these chairs are generally through tenoned and employ the standard Philadelphia compass seat construction in which flat seat rails form a square frame into which the front legs are tenoned. The rails appear to be rather thin, and no pinning is visible from the front of the chair. A very fine example will have a recessed break in the front rail that is embellished with a carved shell that complements a carved shell in the crest rail. Often the swells of cabriole legs will have shell or acanthus carvings as shown here. Without exception, these fine chairs have drop or slip seats. Very few have stretchers, and most of those that do will have the sawn stretchers found in earlier Philadelphia chairs. Block and turned stretchers are very rarely found in Philadelphia Queen Anne chairs, although a few have a single turned stretcher between the rear legs. Most chairs have the Philadelphia slipper or trifid foot, a few have ball and claw feet. The great majority are made of walnut, a few are mahogany or maple. Secondary woods are primarily yellow pine and poplar.

With Philadelphia we end our survey of Queen Anne chairs, for there are almost no surviving Queen Anne–style chairs from the colonies south of the Mason-Dixon Line. The rare few that have been discovered seem to have been made in tidewater Virginia. The single published example that I've seen has features common to both Philadelphia and New York chairs and is very English in feeling. Also, you will notice that while we have examined two high-style chairs, there are no rural interpretations to follow, nothing akin to the vast number of surviving rural New England Queen Anne chairs like those shown in figures 5-13C and 5-13D. Why so? Well, I would suggest that the reason is that there were available much superior turned chairs, the Delaware Valley ladder-back chairs, which we will see in the next chapter.

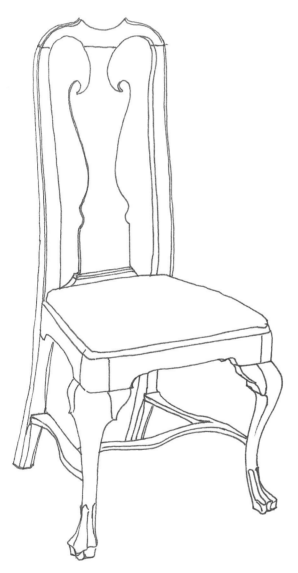

5-17A. Philadelphia Queen Anne, 1730 – 1750.

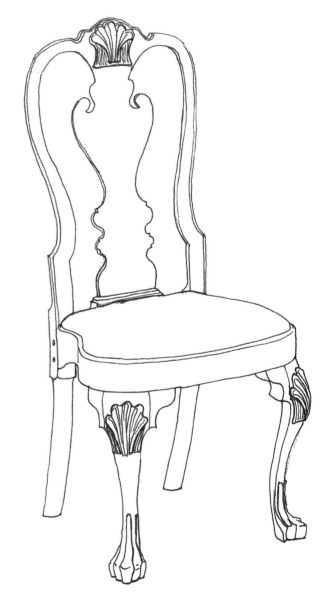

5-17B. Philadelphia Queen Anne, 1740 – 1760.

5-18 New Hampshire Chippendale chairs. In spite of the region's name, New England furniture is usually the least English of American furniture. However, New Hampshire Chippendale chairs are an exception, in large part due to the arrival of a number of English cabinetmakers in the middle decades of the eighteenth century. The most prominent of these was Robert Harrold, whose name first appears in the Portsmouth tax records of 1765 and to whom the chair in figure 5-18A is attributed. Harrold chairs are characterized by intricate splats, unusually wide seats, and the English form of seat reinforcement illustrated in figure 5-7. The complex splat and the rather broad proportions are typical of English chairs of this period. Another English feature seen on armchairs is that the bases of the arm supports scroll out in pairs of front and back volutes as shown in this illustration. When the seats were overupholstered, the front rails were given shallow bows. If this was done, rather than shaping the whole rail, Harrold provided the bows by adding shaped strips of pine to the fronts of the rails. Often the crest rails were decorated with pairs of small spurs on the undersides.

Two other splat patterns, also associated with Robert Harrold, that were fashionable in Portsmouth are shown in figures 5-18B and 5-18C. The first would appear to be a simplified interpretation by another shop, for the crest rail lacks the spurs on the underside, and the pierced splat does not have the little additional decorative fillets that are often seen on Harrold chairs. The second chair is a common English Gothic pattern that was also employed by Joseph Short in Newburyport.

5-18A. Portsmouth Chippendale, 1765 – 1790.

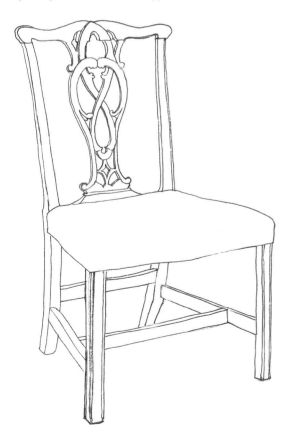

5-18B. Portsmouth Chippendale, 1770 – 1790.

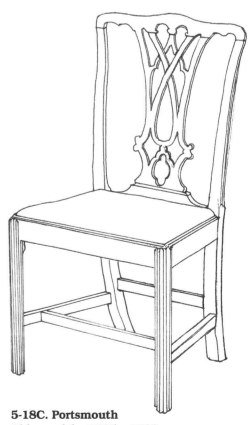

5-18C. Portsmouth Chippendale, 1765 – 1790.

The first two of these chairs are easy studies, for they are patterns that were fashionable in New Hampshire, and at this time, Portsmouth was the only New Hampshire city of any consequence. For a more thorough discussion of this unique group of chairs, and of Portsmouth furniture in general, you might try to locate a copy of *Portsmouth Furniture — Masterworks from the New Hampshire Seacoast*, by Brock Jobe, et al.

Figure 5-18D illustrates another design common to the Portsmouth area. This is an inexpensive version of a popular New Hampshire design. Many of these simple, rugged chairs have box stretchers rather than the medial stretcher shown here. In better-quality chairs, the upward flaring splat will be pierced with connected vertical slots, as shown in the Newport side chair in figure 5-20A. The arched crest rail with the recessed center is another English feature that is also seen in some Southern and New London County chairs. By itself, the shape of this splat tells us little of region, as this pattern was also used in Boston, in Rhode Island, and frequently in the South, but in conjunction with the recessed center crest rail it forms an almost unique Portsmouth type; almost, because there are a few similar Southern chairs, although if from the South they will probably be made of walnut rather than mahogany or birch.

It should be noted that almost all Portsmouth Chippendale chairs have the square Marlborough leg. Whatever the pattern of the splat, a cabriole-leg chair in either the Queen Anne or Chippendale style is unlikely to be from New Hampshire.

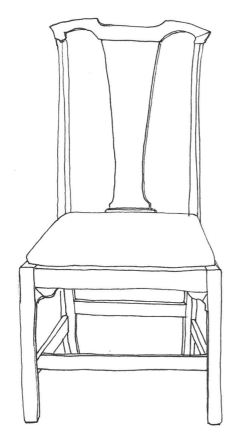

5-18D. New Hampshire Chippendale, 1765 – 1800.

5-19 Massachusetts Chippendale Chairs. There is so much to discuss about Massachusetts chairs that we will spend some time in this section — and will do the same when we get to Pennsylvania, for Boston and Philadelphia were the two major urban centers during the Colonial period, and perhaps 9 of 10, or even 19 of 20, high-style rococo chairs will be from one of these two cities. Although we will see many chairs from other areas, the odds are that a high-style Chippendale chair will be from either Boston or Philadelphia.

Before discussing specific examples, we might first consider the general characteristics of Massachusetts chairs, for they differ significantly from chairs produced elsewhere, particularly those produced in Philadelphia. First off, perhaps one in three will be overupholstered in either fabric or leather, and two in three will be fitted with the very characteristic New England block and turned stretchers. Many will have arrised cabriole legs terminating in either ball and claw or club feet. Most have square seats and are made of mahogany, although there are a significant minority that are transitional in style and construction, having rounded compass seats and being made of walnut. A few are made of birch or cherry. Overupholstered rails and slip seat frames will usually be either soft maple or birch. When the seat rails are reinforced, the blocking will almost always be triangular pieces of eastern white pine that are glued and nailed in place as shown in figure 5-6.

While most chairs were produced in and around Boston, they are all very similar, and chairs from nearby Salem and Newburyport are difficult to tell from those of Boston work. Among the eight illustrations, there is not a single armchair. Armchairs cost about half again more than side chairs, and in budget-conscious Boston they were seldom requested. Just as an upholstered side chair is likely to be a Massachusetts product, so also is an armchair likely to be from somewhere else.

Quite the most common Massachusetts splat design, and probably the best-known pattern among American Chippendale furniture, is the owl's-eye splat shown in figure 5-19A. This enormously popular English design is not only found in central and eastern Massachusetts, but also in Rhode Island, eastern Connecticut, and southeastern New Hampshire. It was the most popular pattern in Boston and Salem. This chair illustrates a number of Massachusetts features: the serpentine crest rail terminates in rather blunt ears, the cabriole legs have a sharp edge, or arris, the knee blocks or brackets are small and flow smoothly up into the seat rails, the legs are supported by block and turned stretchers, and the rear legs are chamfered on all sides.

Figure 5-19B illustrates another common English splat pattern that was popular in the Boston area, and is also seen in a few New York chairs. While the crest rail is suggestive of Portsmouth workmanship, the pattern of the splat and the cabriole legs indicate that this is a Boston or Salem chair. The interlaced splat with the narrow quatrefoil base is also found in Connecticut Marlborough leg chairs, principally those from the Hartford area. Here we might note again that Chippendale-style chairs having the seat overupholstered are not only likely to be from New England, but they will probably be from an urban center where upholsterers were available: Boston, Salem, Portsmouth, or Newburyport.

The next two figures (5-19C, 5-19D) illustrate two other patterns that are not infrequently found in Boston-area chairs, the first on a somewhat atypical Massachusetts chair in which the knee brackets are both large and scroll over instead of being small and flowing up to the seat rail. The rather heavy English-looking splat has a pattern that was popular in the coastal towns north of Boston. It is also seen in Newport and Philadelphia chairs. This chair is also unusual in having extensive carving. Most Massachusetts Chippendale chairs lack any carving other than the shaping of the ears and the ball and claw feet. When a chair has more, it will usually be a fluted shell centered in the crest rail, and maybe some acanthus leaf and scroll carving on the knees. Here again it might be noted that Boston carving is very different from Philadelphia carving, typically being quite shallow and flat, as though the carver was working in haste and was loath to remove any more wood than absolutely necessary.

The second of these chairs (5-19D), while not overupholstered, shows clearly the Boston features of rather thin seat rails, cabriole legs with sharp edges, block and turned stretchers, and retracted toes on the sides of the ball and claw feet. The rails on Massachusetts Chippendale chairs tend to be much thinner than those found in Philadelphia, and often lack the horizontal shaping seen in figure 5-19A.

Note that in this illustration the median stretcher is blocked at the ends. This required additional time to make, but strengthened the join between the median and side stretchers. Although a nice indication of better-quality work, it does little to help us identify region, for it is found in both Massachusetts and Rhode Island chairs.

When a cabriole-leg chair was not given stretchers, the usual practice in Massachusetts was to round and taper the rear legs below the rails, then flare out the legs to form the small, squared feet shown in figure 5-19E. New York chairs may also have squared rear feet, but both the flares and the feet are more pronounced. This chair illustrates one of the few splat patterns that seem to have been taken directly from a design book, in this case Robert Manwaring's *The Cabinet and Chair-Maker's Real Friend and Companion*. Although often illustrated, these Manwaring pattern chairs are actually fairly rare, perhaps in part due to the large center opening, would seem to be inherently weak.

Not all Massachusetts Chippendale splat patterns are as ornate as those we have seen. The simplified pattern shown in figure 5-19F was very popular in chairs made up along the North Shore in Salem and Newburyport. This pierced vase shape will be seen again in a rural New England chair (5-22A), and also in the next section in a Newport compass-seat chair (5-20B). Although the splat pattern suggests no more than New England, the rest of the chair — the serpentine crest rail with blunt ears, the thin seat rails, the arrised cabriole legs ending in pad or club feet, the small knee blocks that flow up to the seat rails, and the block and turned stretchers — are all indicative of eastern Massachusetts workmanship.

Chippendale chairs retaining unpierced Queen Anne–style splats are far more common in the Philadelphia area where they were a very popular form. However, Chippendale-style chairs with solid splats were also produced in Massachusetts as we see from the handsome chair in figure 5-19G. Aside from the solid splat, this is a typical Boston-area Chippendale chair. Chairs with these simpler, less expensive splats were normally given pad rather than ball and claw feet. Note that the splat, while still the baluster form preferred in New England, has been made broader and more curved, both in keeping with the new rococo style and to fill the space between the stiles on a wider chair. While more vase shaped, it is still very different from the common Philadelphia shape shown in the chair in figure 5-24K.

In Massachusetts, the square Chippendale Marlborough leg gradually superseded the cabriole leg toward the end of the eighteenth century and was common after 1785, perhaps because a straight leg was more in keeping with the linear neo-classical styles. Figure 5-19H illustrates one of these chairs, this one having a simplified English splat pattern also seen in Connecticut chairs. The rather strange little fillets at the top of the front legs are sometimes seen on chairs made in Massachusetts. When the front legs are not molded, Boston-area Marlborough-leg chairs often have a single bead worked into the outside edge of each front leg and stretchers. While this chair is very different from the previous cabriole-leg chairs, the overupholstered seat and the serpentine crest rail and blunt ears are typical of Massachusetts workmanship.

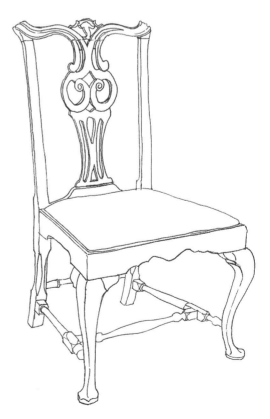

5-19A. Boston Chippendale, 1755 – 1785.

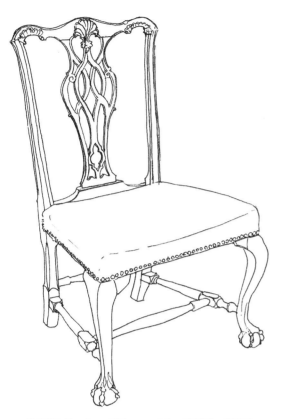

5-19B. Boston Chippendale, 1755 – 1785.

5-19C. North Shore Chippendale, 1755 – 1785.

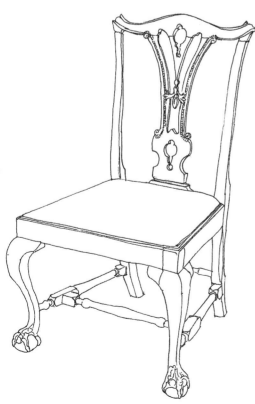

5-19D. Massachusetts Chippendale, 1755 – 1785.

5-19E. Massachusetts Chippendale, 1755 – 1785.

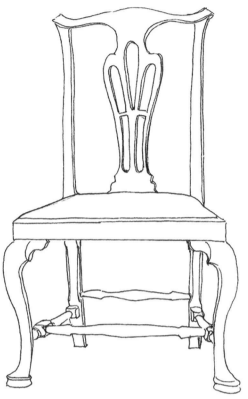

**5-19F. Massachusetts Chippendale,
1755 – 1785.**

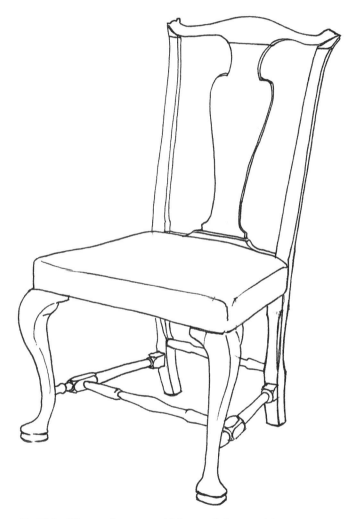

**5-19G. Massachusetts Chippendale, 1755 –
1785.**

**5-19H. Massachusetts Chippendale,
1760 – 1790.**

5-20 Rhode Island Chippendale chairs. Rhode Island, and Newport in particular, appears to have been reluctant to accept the new rococo style, and the Newport Chippendale chairs shown in figures 5-20A and 5-20B are what one might expect from such an environment; each has a simple Chippendale crest rail and very conservative pierced spat, and below, a Queen Anne–style rounded seat. Similar transitional chairs were produced with other splat patterns, most seen elsewhere, particularly in Massachusetts. Whatever the pattern, the best indicator of Newport workmanship is the presence of a compass seat in a Chippendale-style chair, a combination seldom seen in Massachusetts chairs. Due to economic decline following the Revolution, these chairs, while not rare, are not as common as Newport Queen Anne chairs.

Rhode Island Marlborough-leg chairs provide two guides as to origin: the front legs are often molded and stop fluted, and then the center of the crest rail is decorated with a fan shape diagonally cross hatched to form a diamond pattern, each diamond then being embellished with a punched dot in the center (5-20C). Note that this chair retains the conservative and solid look found in earlier Newport chairs. Following the Revolution, Providence outgrew Newport, and this type of chair may have been produced in either city. We will see stop fluted legs again in Rhode Island easy chairs and dining tables.

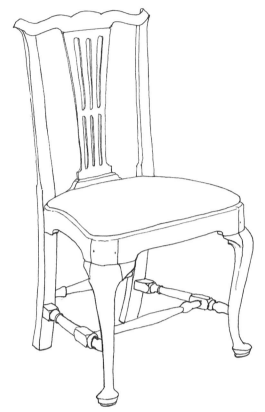

5-20A. Newport Chippendale, 1760 – 1775.

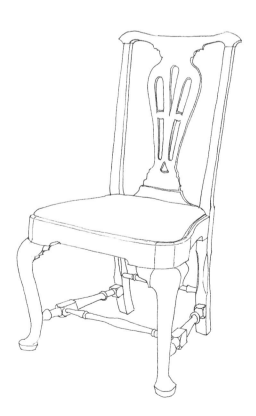

5-20B. Newport Chippendale, 1760 – 1775.

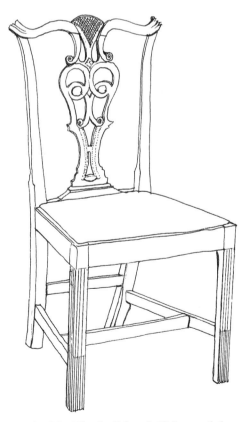

5-20C. Rhode Island Chippendale, 1765 – 1785.

5-21 Connecticut Chippendale chairs. Connecticut Chippendale chairs are far less common than the furniture production of the region would suggest. You will seldom see a formal Connecticut or Connecticut River Valley chair on the market. Although we will discuss two cabriole-leg examples, as in New Hampshire, they tend to have the simpler Marlborough leg. Many employ splat patterns popular in Massachusetts. The great majority — perhaps 9 out of 10 — are made of cherry; the rest are maple, or perhaps mahogany if from near the coast. Secondary woods are usually either white pine or poplar, with some use of chestnut and oak.

Quite the best-known Connecticut Chippendale chairs are those made by the Chapin family of East Windsor, which usually are a medley of Philadelphia, New York, Connecticut, and Massachusetts influences. The chair in figure 5-21A is typical of Chapin work, Philadelphia in overall design and splat pattern, but made of cherry and having an overupholstered seat. Among Chapin chairs you will also see the popular Philadelphia splat pattern shown in figure 5-24B, and the diamond splat so often associated with New York Chippendale chairs. Many have cabriole legs that, in Philadelphia fashion, are not given stretchers. Both cabriole- and Marlborough-leg chairs are likely to be through tenoned and employ the vertical quarter-round Philadelphia blocking, usually reinforced with small nails. Ball and claw feet are similar to those of Philadelphia design, having a flattened ball, vertical claws, and insignificant talons (5-1D). As you would expect, most of these chairs are made of cherry.

More typical of Connecticut production is the side chair illustrated in figure 5-21B. This handsome little cherry side chair also exhibits a mix of features and influences: the cabriole legs with arris and disked pad feet eastern Massachusetts; the square seat rails New York; and the slip seat, stump rear legs, and lack of stretchers Philadelphia. However, the use of cherry and the exuberant serpentine crest rail are very much Connecticut.

The New London County owl's-eye side chair in figure 5-21C illustrates other characteristics of Connecticut chairs. The owl's-eye set high in the splat is a feature of chairs from the Colchester-Norwich area, and is also found in

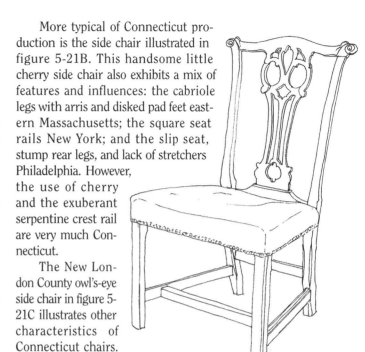

5-21C. New London County Chippendale, 1760 – 1800.

5-21A. Connecticut Chippendale, 1770 – 1780.

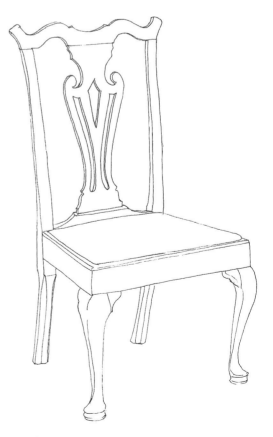

5-21B. Connecticut Chippendale, 1770 – 1790.

chairs with Queen Anne–style crest rails. Other borrowed patterns also tend to have the design focuses set high in the splats. Note that the ears on the crest rail are decorated with the little circular volutes that were so popular in Connecticut. Other Connecticut chairs have ears that resemble tiny mittens with the thumbs facing upward.

5-22 Rural New England Chippendale chairs. Rural New England Chippendale chairs survive in such numbers that we will give them their own section and illustrate three typical examples in figures 5-22A, 5-22B, and 5-22C. While such chairs are popularly associated with rural craftsmen, most are probably actually the budget production of urban shops. All three of these chairs employ simplified versions of spat patterns fashionable in the Boston area. Most of these chairs are made of soft maple, except those from Connecticut, which are apt to be made of cherry. They are normally fitted with inexpensive rush seats. While the first of these chairs is entirely Chippendale in style, many are a combination of styles, most typically having a Chippendale splats and crest rails and William and Mary–style front legs and stretchers. The last example has a rounded compass seat — providing, from top to bottom, a wonderful mix of Chippendale, Queen Anne, and William and Mary styles — all in one small chair! While the Chippendale backs of these chairs are stylistically more recent than the two similar Queen Anne chairs shown in figures 5-13C and 5-13D, all were, in fact, produced concurrently in New England throughout the latter half of the eighteenth century.

5-22B. New England Chippendale, 1770 – 1800.

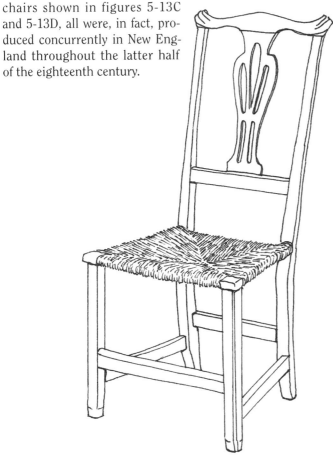

5-22A. New England Chippendale, 1770 – 1800.

5-22C. New England Chippendale, 1770 – 1800.

5-23 New York Chippendale chairs. New York Chippendale chairs are uncommon, and at times, difficult to tell from English chairs. For many years they were confused with Philadelphia workmanship. However, as a group they exhibit a distinctive English flavor and have features that can aid us in identification. First off, they have a markedly early Georgian look, being noticeably shorter and wider than other American chairs, which results in a solid feeling that is particularly evident in Marlborough leg chairs like that shown in figure 5-23C. Cabriole leg chairs are somewhat like Philadelphia chairs in lacking stretchers and having deep seat rails that are usually reinforced with bracket responds. The rails are seldom undercut, which results in a notably square, solid looking seat. Perhaps one in three are through tenoned. Most are made of mahogany, and unlike other cities, the great majority have ball and claw feet, usually the large squared foot illustrated in figure 5-1E. A rare few have club or drake feet.

Although not shown in these examples, better quality chairs may have a strip of carved gadrooning nailed and glued to the base of the front seat rail, a feature also seen in a few Philadelphia chairs. Often the rear legs terminate either in square or ovoid pad feet, a common feature of English chairs. Squared back feet are also seen in Boston chairs, but only when the chair does not have stretchers and the rear legs are tapered as shown in the Manwaring-type chair in figure 5-19E. A few chairs are transitional in style in having compass seats.

The seat rails on New York Chippendale chairs may be reinforced either with Philadelphia type quarter round blocking, or Boston triangular blocking, or with a combination of both, normally the triangular blocks reinforcing the front legs. There are a variety of secondary woods: typically white pine for corner blocks; maple, cherry and poplar for slip seat frames. Over upholstered chairs are apt to have oak rails.

Perhaps the most best known New York Chippendale splat pattern is a diamond shape centered within scrolled strapwork as shown in figure 5-23A. Unfortunately, this pattern is not a good identifier, for it is not only found in some Philadelphia chairs, but was a relatively common pattern in Connecticut and Boston. More indicative of New York workmanship is the "tassel and ruffle" pattern shown in figure 5-23B, and the rather intricate vase form pattern in figure 5-23C, both of which appear to be unique to American chairs produced in New York City. The tassel-back chair is an armchair, and here we see the scrolled eagle-headed arms that were fashionable in New York. This Georgian motif is also seen in a few Boston chairs, but is far more likely to be found on a New York chair.

Lastly, we should note a rural design found on Long Island, but which was probably common to the whole New York area (5-23D). The straight stiles and flat crest rail of this chair are not only similar to the Connecticut Litchfield-type chair, but also, the pierced splat is a design seen all over New England, perhaps what we might expect from an island lying just across a narrow sound from southern New England. Although Chippendale in style, these chairs are probably Federal in production, as is suggested by their relative lightness and linearity.

5-23A. New York Chippendale, 1760 – 1780.

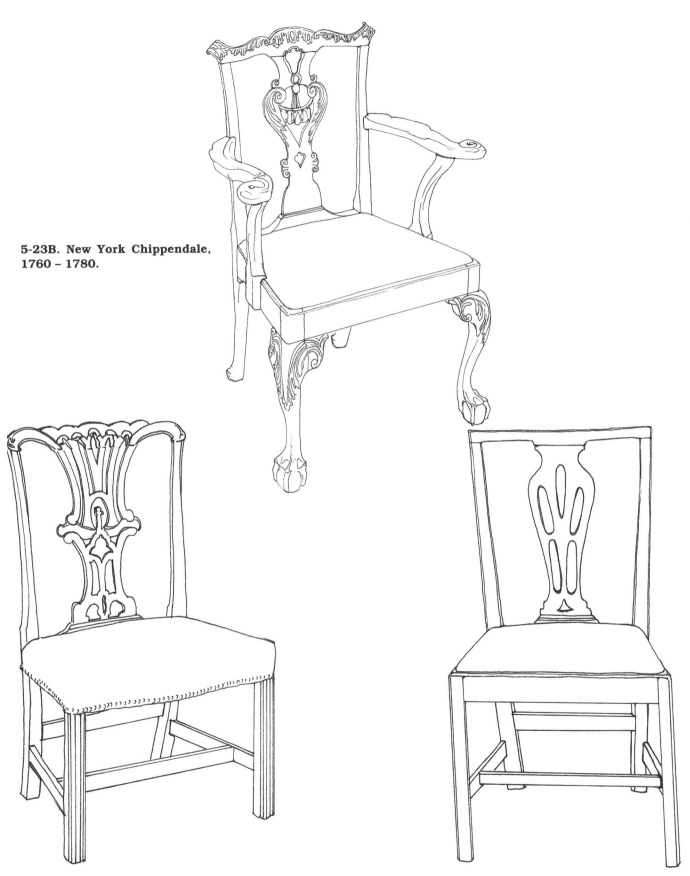

5-23B. New York Chippendale, 1760 – 1780.

5-23C. New York Chippendale, 1760 – 1780.

5-23D. New York Chippendale, 1780 – 1810.

5-24 Pennsylvania Chippendale chairs. Now we have arrived at Pennsylvania, and at Philadelphia, the other major Colonial style center, and again there is much to show you. Philadelphia Chippendale chairs are quite different from the chairs of other areas, and here there is seldom the uncertainty that is associated with New York workmanship. If there is a problem, it is that there is such a profusion of lovely rococo splat patterns that I can only show the more popular and fashionable, and from these suggest what others might look like. Fortunately, they have some common features that can help us in identification.

We might first consider the characteristics of Philadelphia Chippendale chairs. Most will have drop or slip seats, and if given cabriole legs, then omit stretchers. To compensate for the lack of stretchers the rails are made fairly deep, and more often than not, are tenoned through the stiles as shown in figure 5-3. This combination seems to have provided sufficient strength, for Chippendale chairs seldom have bracket responds. The knees on Philadelphia cabriole legs will usually be rounded rather than sharp or arrised. The rails are usually horizontally shaped, that is, cut out to minimize the appearance of depth. I've read that only about one in two Philadelphia Chippendale chairs are through tenoned, but my experience is that this practice was almost universal in the Philadelphia area. However, it is also seen to some extent in New York and Connecticut.

While a few chairs retain Queen Anne pad and slipper feet, most Chippendale chairs will have either the standard Philadelphia form of ball and claw foot (5-1C), or a large trified foot (5-2C). A rare few very grand chairs have Flemish scroll feet. These are the front legs. In marked contrast the rear legs on Philadelphia Chippendale chairs are devoid of embellishment — they curve backward and are simply rounded below the seat rail — what are sometimes called stump rear legs. Even the best quality chairs do not have the shaped back feet found in New York and some Boston chairs. High style Chippendale chairs are normally made of mahogany, others are likely to be made of walnut, which was favored as a lower cost option throughout the Delaware Valley. A few are made of tiger maple.

Slip seat frames are usually either poplar or yellow pine; blocking very often Atlantic white cedar, but also mahogany, poplar, and yellow pine. Blocking will almost always be the vertical built up quarter-round reinforcement illustrated in figure 5-8.

We will start the illustrations with a typical Philadelphia armchair having the splat pattern most often seen in the Delaware Valley (5-24A). Actually, this is not the most common splat, only the most common pierced splat, for later in this section we will see a very popular chair that has a solid splat. The serpentine crest rail shown here is typical of Philadelphia Chippendale chairs, richly carved and terminating in scrolled over ears that are very different from the rather short, blunt ears found in New England chairs. Note that not only the arms, but also the arm posts on this chair are shaped so as to curve in all three dimensions. The curved arm posts are characteristic of Philadelphia armchairs. They are quite unlike two dimensional arm posts seen in New England (5-18A) and New York (5-23B).

Figure 5-24B illustrates another splat pattern often seen in Philadelphia chairs, a pattern also sometimes seen in Newport chairs. Note that this Gothic splat has three vertical ribs with a quatrefoil opening at the base, a common Philadelphia treatment also seen in the next three chairs. Even though the Marlborough legs on this chair are braced with stretchers, the seat rails are still likely to be through tenoned. Large, conservative Marlborough leg side chairs with solid rails and legs were very popular in Philadelphia. This is the first of three you will see in this section. While here it might be noted that there are a rare few Philadelphia Marlborough leg chairs that have blocked feet, and also, a few that lack stretchers. They are very strange looking chairs.

The splat shown in figure 5-24C illustrates another Philadelphia splat design, a pattern that appears to have originated in Philadelphia. Look back at the Massachusetts chair in figure 5-19B and you will see a pattern that looks similar — and yet the overupholstered seat and the block and turned stretchers would immediately tell us that this is not a Philadelphia chair.

The side chair in figure 5-24D illustrates yet another popular pattern, this a more exuberantly rococo expression of the splat shown in figure 5-24B. Note the characteristic stump rear legs and the horizontal shaping of the seat rails seen in so many Philadelphia chairs. This is a very grand chair made by Thomas Tufft with carved back and carved cabriole legs. In event that you have the opportunity to examine one of these high end chairs, you will note that Philadelphia carving is much richer and deeper that the rather flat and shallow carving seen in Massachusetts.

In figure 5-24E we see a Gillingham-type chair, named for Philadelphia chairmaker James Gillingham (1736 – 1781), whose engraved label appears on three chairs having this same trefoil-pierced splat. In lieu of Gothic strapwork, many Philadelphia chairs exhibit a circular opening near the top of the splat. The splat on the following chair (5-24F) is a variation of the popular pattern shown in figure 5-24A. It appears different, but mostly because the center loops are more circular and delineated. Turn back to Massachusetts chairs and you will see that it is superficially very similar to the Boston owl's-eye pattern in figure 5-19A except that the center loops curve up from below rather down from the top, and thus do not have quite the same avian look. Splat patterns are a big help in determining region, but they must be looked at carefully.

The next two illustrations (5-24G, 5-24H) round out this brief survey of high style Philadelphia chairs. The first employs an English splat design that was also popular to some extent in Newport and Massachusetts (5-19C), but here is seen in a very different chair, one with a drop seat, deep rails, and no stretchers. Note that this chair employs the Philadelphia slipper foot more often seen in earlier Queen Anne chairs. The complex looping splat shown in figure 5-24H is quite English in feeling. There will often be a third pair of loops in lieu of the inverted heart shown here. Although the pattern is very different, the splat of the New Hampshire Harrold-type armchair in figure 5-18A is similar in feeling.

More suburban or rural chairs often employ simplified splats that are both strong and relatively easy to lay out, and the pierced vase form splat shown in figure 5-24I is typical of this genre. Chairs like this were made in Reading, then a large town about 50 miles north and west of Philadelphia, although the splat pattern itself is anything but unique to the Reading area, being also found in New Hampshire, Rhode Island and Southern chairs. In this case, though, the deep seat rails, the lack of stretchers and the stump rear legs identify this as a typical Philadelphia area chair.

Early in his long career, William Savery (1721 – 1788) began producing an inexpensive rush-bottom chair. Some of these still retain his label and "Savery" chairs they have been ever since. Although figure 5-24J shows a Savery-type chair with a Chippendale crest rail, he also produced chairs with curved Queen Anne–style yoke crests. These are among the very few Philadelphia area chairs that carry the narrow baluster-form Queen Anne splats that are seen throughout New England. Note that aside from the Chippendale-style crest rail, this chair is very much like the Massachusetts Queen Anne chair shown in figure 5-13E, having similar splat, squared cabriole legs, and square pad feet. It may simply represent a local attempt to meet the Boston competition.

Although we have covered over half a dozen different patterns in pierced splats, the most common Philadelphia Chippendale pattern is not pierced at all, but is instead some variant of the solid Philadelphia Queen Anne splat shown the chair in figure 5-24K. These immensely popular chairs were produced throughout the Delaware Valley for almost half a century, and to some extent in nearby Delaware, Maryland and Virginia. They seem to have provided a lower cost alternative to high style chairs, for perhaps 19 in 20 are made of walnut, and the great majority have trifid rather than ball and claw feet. They were also made with the Philadelphia pad foot, the Philadelphia slipper foot, and a raised or platform pad foot that is reminiscent of New England workmanship.

As you would expect of such a successful form, there is much variation in the shape of the splat, although most all exhibit the same broad, lobed vase shape seen in fully developed Philadelphia Queen Anne chairs. While usually made of walnut, some of these chairs are not budget work at all, having carved shells on the crest and seat rails in addition to ball and claw feet, suggesting a relatively affluent middle class clientele who preferred a solid, conservative chair. Although the retention of the Queen Anne splats would suggest a transitional chair, these chairs are a unique design in themselves, and are not the sort of style transition we saw earlier in Newport Chippendale chairs.

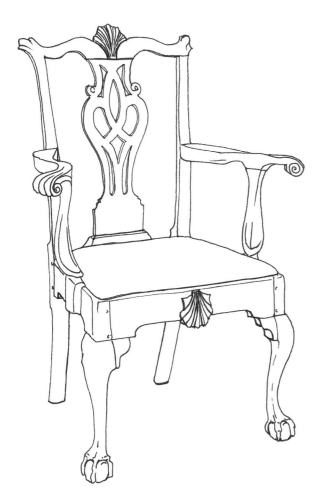

5-24A. Philadelphia Chippendale, 1760 – 1780.

5-24B. Philadelphia Chippendale, 1770 – 1780.

5-24C. Philadelphia Chippendale, 1770 – 1780.

5-24D. Philadelphia Chippendale, c. 1775.

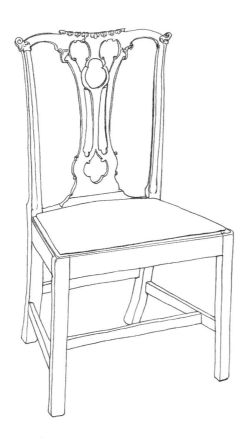

5-24E. Philadelphia Chippendale, 1770 – 1780.

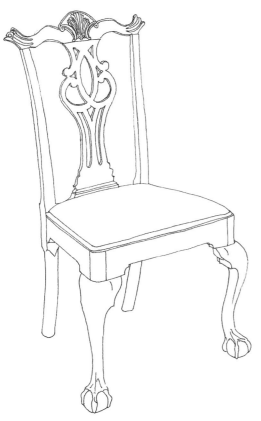

**5-24F. Philadelphia Chippendale,
1760 – 1780.**

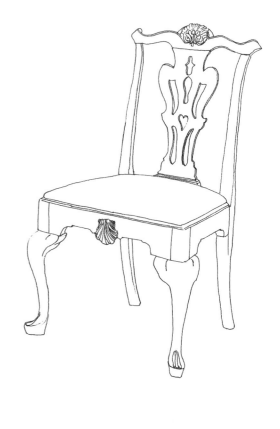

**5-24G. Philadelphia Chippendale,
1760 – 1780.**

**5-24H. Philadelphia Chippendale,
1760 – 1780.**

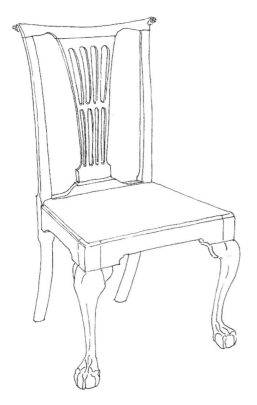

5-24I. Reading Chippendale, c. 1785.

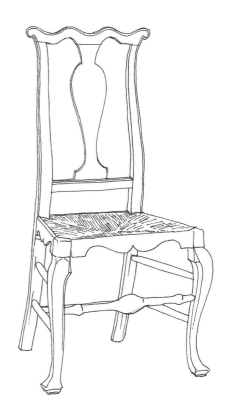

5-24J. Philadelphia Chippendale, 1755 – 1765.

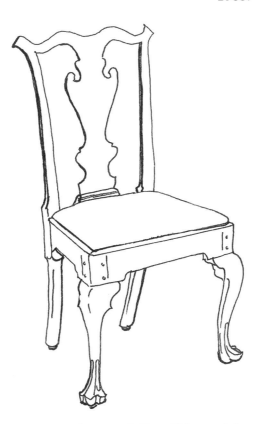

5-24K. Delaware Valley Chippendale, 1750 – 1785.

5-25 Southern Chippendale chairs. In the preceding chapter it was noted that not only is high-style Southern furniture relatively uncommon, but also, prior to the Revolution, there were no major regional schools comparable to Boston and Philadelphia. In addition, there are almost no surviving Southern Queen Anne chairs. Therefore, we will start with Chippendale, and rather than illustrating the products of any particular region, instead discuss Southern Chippendale chairs in general, illustrating three typical examples.

Although uncommon, Southern Chippendale chairs exhibit a number of features that can help in identification. Even if we may not be able to tell exactly where a Southern chair was made, we can tell that it most probably is from the South. First off, Southern chairs tend to be relatively unsophisticated. Most have straight, unmolded Marlborough legs, drop or slip seats, and will be devoid of any more surface decoration than perhaps a little beading or scratch carving. Many have box stretchers. Instead of the usual medial stretcher between the two side stretchers, there will be a stretcher between the front legs. This provides a stronger chair, but at some cost to comfort. Box stretchers are not unique to the South, they are found everywhere in rural chairs, particularly in northern New England, but what makes Southern chairs different is that they are seen so frequently and are not limited to budget work. They are often found on otherwise good quality chairs. Of the three chairs illustrated in this section, two have box stretchers.

Southern chairs frequently exhibit construction peculiarities that indicate an abundance of wood and a limited tool set. In formal chairs, the shoe and the rear seat rail are frequently made of a single piece of wood. Also, there is very little carving, and the tops of the seat rails are often rounded rather than molded, suggesting that the cabinetmaker did not have the molding planes that would have been available to a chairmaker.

A great many Southern chairs are very simple in form and design, having unmolded Marlborough legs, box stretchers, square backs and some form of solid splat like that shown in figure 5-25A. This small walnut chair, thought to have been made in Frederick, Maryland, has a vase shaped splat, although you will more often see an upward flaring splat like that shown in the New Hampshire side chair in figure 5-18D.

By far the most common Southern splat pattern has this upward flaring shape, which if pierced, will be divided into either four or five vertical ribs that are usually stiffened by a connection in the middle as shown in the walnut side chair in figure 5-25B. This pattern is by no means unique to the South; we have seen it in Newport (5-20A) and Pennsylvania (5-24I) Chippendale chairs, but in association with an unsophisticated walnut Marlborough-leg chair, it is suggestive of Southern workmanship. A variation of this splat that is often seen in tidewater Virginia has a heart at the base of the splat as illustrated in figure 5-25C. Although this is a relatively simple chair with box stretchers, it is made of mahogany rather than the more usual walnut. Mahogany is seen everywhere in the South where manufacture is not too far from the sea, particularly in the Chesapeake Bay area and in Charlestown, South Carolina.

When mahogany was not available, Southern Chippendale chairs will usually be constructed of walnut. Slip seats are normally yellow pine, but may also be oak, beech, or walnut. As was noted earlier in the chapter on cabinet woods, the use of walnut as a secondary wood is a good indication of Southern workmanship.

Chairs made south of Philadelphia in Delaware, Maryland, and tidewater Virginia frequently employ either Philadelphia splat patterns, or patterns that are suggestive of Philadelphia workmanship. Aside from these, however, there is little commonality in patterns. Often the splat pattern will appear both somewhat naive and atypical, at times quite unlike anything else you have ever seen.

While too uncommon to justify illustration, there are some other features that may help the reader identify a Southern chair. Chairs made in Delaware, Maryland, and northern Virginia may exhibit Philadelphia characteristics such as deep rails, trifid feet, and through tenons. Maryland chairs are apt to have high backs, very bold ears and intricately pierced splats. Chairs from western Virginia near the Great Wagon Road that led south from Lancaster County may also be through tenoned. Mahogany was so inexpensive in Charleston that the few chairs that survive exhibit a lavish use of the wood, having thick mahogany rails, and even mahogany corner blocks.

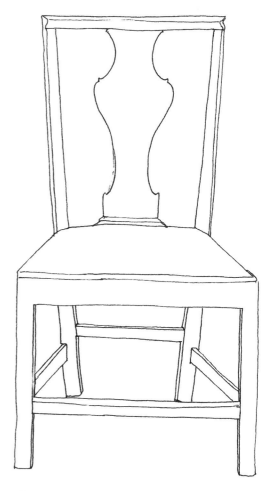

5-25A. Maryland Chippendale, 1770 – 1810.

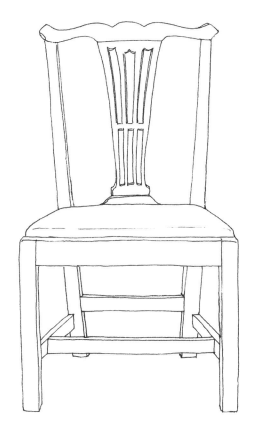

5-25B. Southern Chippendale, 1770 – 1800.

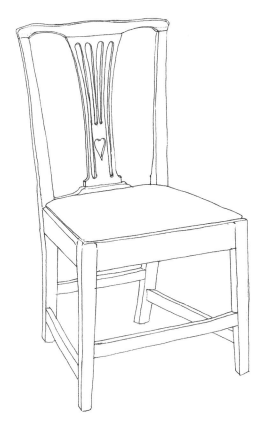

5-25C. Virginia Chippendale, 1770 – 1800.

5-26 Ladder-back chairs. Ladder-back, or ribbon-back, chairs are a late Chippendale style, and might be thought of as a transition between the rococo and the neoclassical. Although they commonly are given the Marlborough leg we associate with Chippendale, most American ladder-backs actually post-date the Revolution, being produced between 1780 and 1800, and in rural areas, as late as 1810. They were quite popular in New England from southern New Hampshire to Connecticut; and then in Philadelphia and south into Maryland. Not as many were produced in New York, the most fashionable Federal city, nor in the South, with the exception of Maryland.

As a general rule, ladder-backs continue in the regional preferences established prior to the Revolution. New England chairs, even somewhat rural products like that shown in figure 5-26A, will usually be overupholstered, while Philadelphia chairs will have the bowed slip seats illustrated in figures 5-26G and 5-26H. Philadelphia was slow in accepting the new neoclassic styles, and ladder-back chairs were popular right up until the end of the century, even though they lose even a suggestion of Chippendale style ears and acquire the rounded crest rails shown in figure 5-26I. Those having the draped pierced splats illustrated in figure 5-26H appear to be unique to Philadelphia. While often ascribed to the shop of Daniel Trotter, they seem to have been a popular Philadelphia type.

There are a few Philadelphia area ladder-backs that have tapered legs, no stretchers, and over upholstered seats — features seen in later Philadelphia Federal chairs. By this time walnut is long out of style and most ladder-backs are made of mahogany, although in northern New England inexpensive chairs may be made of soft maple or birch.

The most popular splat pattern in both Massachusetts and Philadelphia is the single braced loop shown in figures 5-26A and 5-26G. While the backs on these two chairs appear very similar, in Boston the splat will usually be either flush or carved in low relief, while in Philadelphia the overlap of the loop and the bracing is normally more clearly delineated such that the center of each splat clearly shows as a loop that is braced on either side. This greater depth might be expected, for it was noted earlier that Massachusetts carving tends to be flat and shallow, and Philadelphia carving deep and bold. Even when fitted with stretchers, Philadelphia ladder-backs like that shown in figure 5-26G are more often than not through tenoned. This chair also has the neoclassical Hepplewhite leg that is often seen in ladder-back chairs.

Figure 5-26D illustrates an unusual serpentine splat pattern found in a number of chairs made in Portsmouth, New Hampshire, and along the North Shore of Massachusetts. Better-quality Portsmouth chairs of this type will be framed and over upholstered, and the middle half of each splat may be pierced to provide a lighter looking splat. This undulating pattern is also seen in English chairs and was probably introduced in Portsmouth by immigrant cabinetmakers. Similar chairs, but with splats having only a single undulation (5-26E), were produced in Colchester, Connecticut, possibly by Samuel Loomis. Interestingly, they are sometimes made of mahogany rather than cherry.

Almost without exception, ladder-backs have either straight Marlborough or tapering neoclassical legs, not only because they are late Chippendale in style, but also because the linear shape of these legs compliments the square shape of the back. However, there is a small group of ladder-backs with cabriole legs that appear to have been produced in coastal Essex County, Massachusetts (5-26F). Although chairs from a number of sets survive, the design does not seem to have been a success, for they are quite rare. In common with some other New England ladder-backs, these chairs have only three horizontal splats, or more correctly, two splats and a conforming crest rail. This form is not unique to Massachusetts, for similar cabriole leg chairs, but with four rather than three horizontal splats, are found among English furniture. Some of these unusual ladder-backs have the serpentine splats illustrated earlier in Portsmouth and North Shore chairs (5-26D), which would tend to confirm Essex County as the source.

5-26A. New England Chippendale, 1780 – 1800.

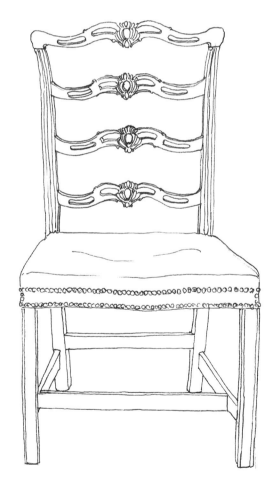

5-26B. Boston Chippendale, 1780 – 1800.

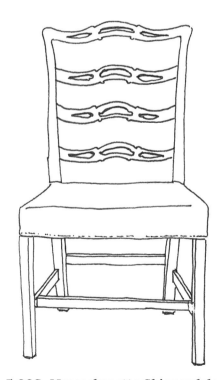

5-26C. Massachusetts Chippendale, 1780 – 1800.

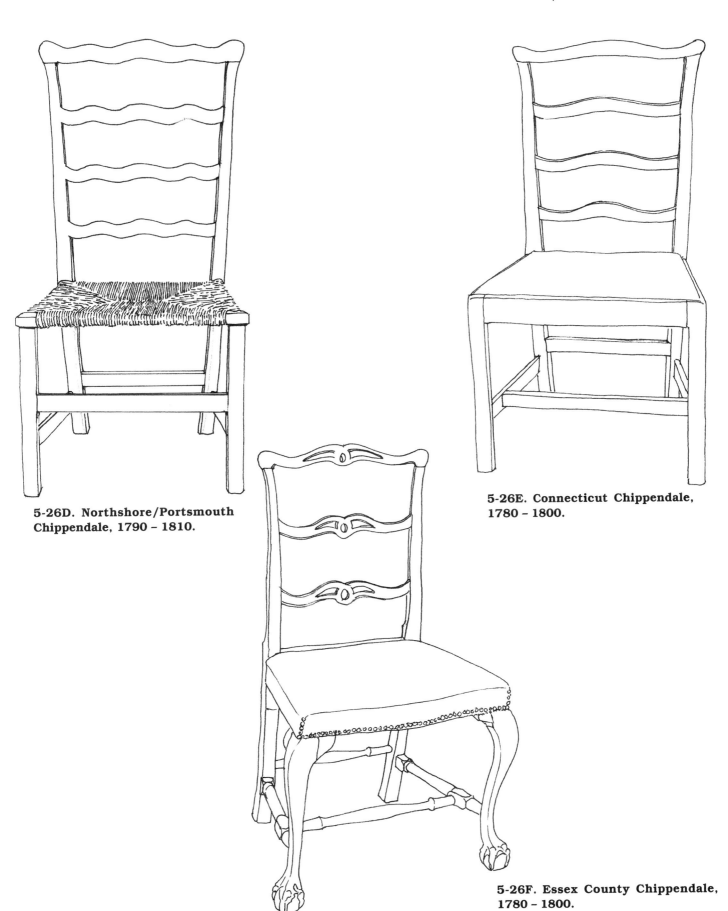

5-26D. Northshore/Portsmouth Chippendale, 1790 – 1810.

5-26E. Connecticut Chippendale, 1780 – 1800.

5-26F. Essex County Chippendale, 1780 – 1800.

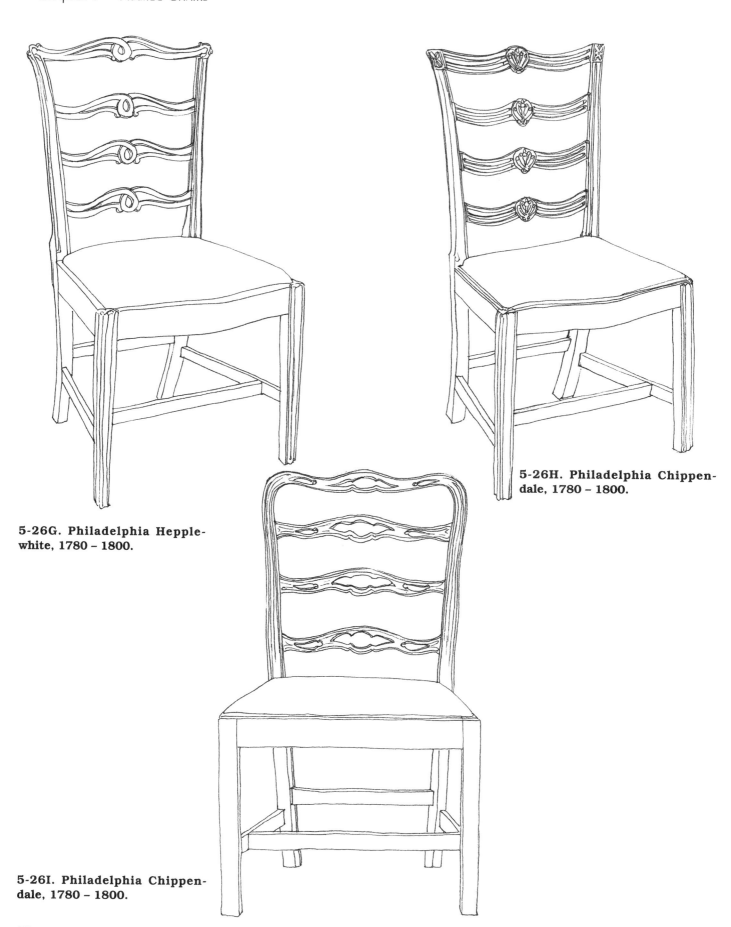

5-26G. Philadelphia Hepple-white, 1780 – 1800.

5-26H. Philadelphia Chippen-dale, 1780 – 1800.

5-26I. Philadelphia Chippen-dale, 1780 – 1800.

5-27 Corner chairs. Before surveying neoclassical chairs, we should discuss corner chairs, for after the rococo, and after the Revolution, they went out of favor, and except in rural areas, out of production. Although long gone, they are not difficult to identify, for they employ many of the same style and design features as side chairs and can be dated and identified as to region in much the same way. Called roundabouts in the North and corner or smoking chairs in the South, they were often used at desks and secretaries where the low arms allowed the writer to draw the chair under the open lid. The support provided by the encircling arms and the four square leg arrangement also made them useful as close-stools, and many were fitted with chamber pots, usually with an extra deep skirt to hide the pot.

Historically, corner chairs appear to have been considered somewhat utilitarian furniture and were seldom given the full treatment often seen in high-style dining chairs. Corner chairs having cabriole legs and pad or ball and claw feet all around are quite rare. Generally they lack any sort of carving and only the front leg is shaped rather than turned. They were a popular form in New England, and far more survive from here than from any other region.

Figure 5-27A illustrates quite the most successful design, the standard Boston Queen Anne corner chair with a compass seat, cabriole front leg, club foot, and block and turned cross stretchers. Cross stretchers were a popular feature in Boston and northeastern New England. We will see them again in a Marlborough leg corner chair. The side and rear legs on these handsome chairs will almost always have either a button foot or the small turned foot shown in this example. As with Queen Anne side chairs, corner chairs produced in Newport are almost identical. Similar chairs were also made to some extent in Connecticut.

On later Chippendale chairs cross stretchers were sometimes omitted if the rails were sufficiently deep as shown in figure 5-27B. Note that this chair has a compressed version of the Massachusetts splat pattern shown in figure 5-19H, and that the front leg has the characteristic thick pad foot found in Boston and Salem Chippendale chairs. To allow even wear all the way around, the button feet on the side and rear legs are themselves given little pads. The same thing was done when a small turned foot is used.

Although less common, New England Chippendale corner chairs were also made with straight Marlborough legs as illustrated in figure 5-27C. Note again, that while square rather than turned, this solid looking corner chair has been given cross stretchers. This is a better-than-average-quality mahogany chair. Most of these chairs will be made of maple, cherry, or birch. Chippendale corner chairs tend to employ Queen Anne splats, perhaps to save a little money on a utilitarian product, and maybe also because it was difficult to work in an attractive pierced pattern in the narrow space between the seat and the arm rail.

There are so many surviving rural New England corner chairs that we will consider three examples, the first another Marlborough leg chair, but this time a rural product having box rather than cross stretchers (5-27D). This rush seat chair employs the same serpentine splat we saw on Portsmouth and North Shore chairs, and probably comes from the same area. That it is made of birch also suggests an origin in northeast New England.

Turned chairs are not covered until the next chapter, but here we might step ahead and consider the standard turned corner chair that was produced throughout New England. Most all of these chairs are made of soft maple with rush seats and either one or two rows of turned box stretchers as shown in figure 5-27E. They are so budget a chair that they frequently dispense with horizontal splats. These chairs also seem to have been produced as far south as coastal Connecticut and the Hudson River valley, for there are some having the trumpet turned front leg and pad foot so often seen in chairs from this area.

As you would expect, rural corner chairs frequently emulated the patterns of rural side chairs. The New England corner chair shown in figure 5-27F has the same charming mix of William and Mary and Chippendale elements we saw earlier in a rural New England Chippendale chair. It employs the same splat pattern and has much the same turnings and stretchers as illustrated in figure 5-22B.

South of New England the corner chair seems to lose popularity in rural areas, for surviving New York, Philadelphia, and Southern corner chairs are, almost without exception, sawn and shaped chairs made of either mahogany or walnut. Although more conventional chairs were produced, the best-known New York design is something of an oddity, having a quadrant front resting on three cabriole legs (5-27G). Even without this regional peculiarity, the deep slipper feet on this chair would suggest New York workmanship.

Pennsylvania Queen Anne and Chippendale corner chairs tend to be far more heavy and solid looking than those made in New England. The majority are made of walnut and are very obviously commode chairs, being given deep rails to hide the chamber pot like that shown in figure 5-27H. Usually they have either a trifid foot in the front, or trifid feet all around. Most are through tenoned, many double tenoned due to the extreme depth of the rails. There are a few Connecticut corner chairs that also have through tenoning. Those with compass seats will be framed in the same manner as Philadelphia Queen Anne chairs.

Southern corner chairs are very scarce. Most of the few that survive are conservative in design, having either Marlborough legs, or turned legs with a single cabriole leg in front. A rare few have cabriole legs all around. In common with other Southern chairs, secondary woods are most likely to be walnut or yellow pine. However, you need not worry too much as to these details, for you are very unlikely to encounter a Southern corner chair. I have seen only two at auction in 20 years.

5-27A. Massachusetts Queen Anne, 1750 – 1790.

5-27B. Massachusetts Chippendale, 1760 – 1790.

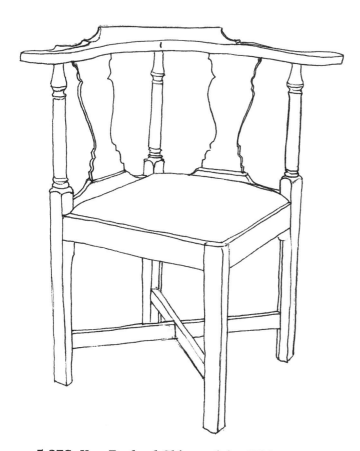

5-27C. New England Chippendale, 1760 – 1790.

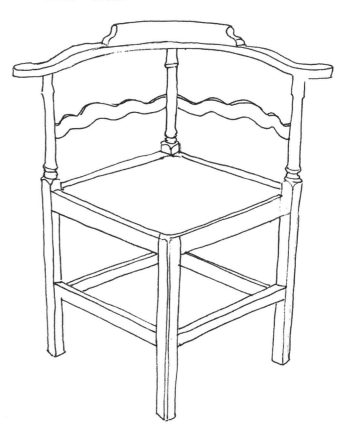

5-27D. New England Chippendale, 1770 – 1800.

5-27E. New England, 1770 – 1810.

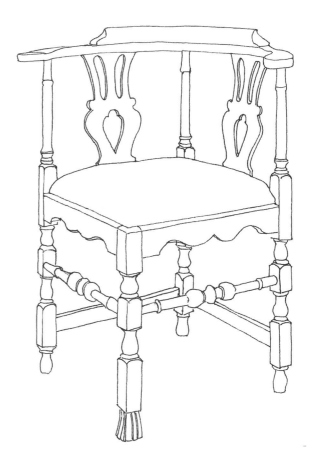

5-27F. New England Chippendale, 1750 – 1780.

5-27G. New York Queen Anne, 1750 – 1775.

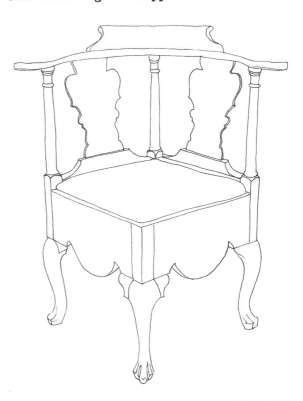

5-27H. Pennsylvania Queen Anne, 1750 – 1790.

5-28 New Hampshire neoclassical chair. Lastly, we will cover neoclassical Federal chairs, again starting in New Hampshire and proceeding down the coast. This section and those that follow differ in two respects. After the Revolution, the center of style shifted from Philadelphia and Boston to New York City, and here we see the most innovation and variation; and secondly, these chairs are easier to identify in terms of design and form than in selection of materials and details of construction, so I will place more emphasis on the types of chairs made in different regions.

The square-back chair shown in figure 5-28 is one of a number of high style chairs that were fashionable in Portsmouth at the turn of the century. While probably made by others, these chairs are often attributed to Langley Boardman (1774 – 1833) on the basis of a set of three chairs that descended in his family. This is the simplest and perhaps least costly of a group of similar fine chairs attributed to the shop of Mr. Boardman. Others have a veneered central vase shaped splat, or oval openings in the vertical splats, or the arching crest rail shown in the Massachusetts chair in figure 5-29D. Whatever the

design of the back, Boardman chairs are characterized by fine workmanship, a feeling of delicacy, and reeding on the crest rail, the stiles, and the stay rail. Normally there will also be small, square carved rosettes at the corners where the crest rail is joined to the stiles. Neoclassical square-back chairs are not unique to New Hampshire. Side chairs with similar backs were produced to a limited extent in Philadelphia, and in a little bit we will see the same shape in a chair made in Connecticut, but in this case a chair much simpler in execution than this high style urban product.

Before going further, there is a matter of terminology. Normally furniture having square, tapering legs, or outswept French feet, is considered to be Hepplewhite in style. However, neoclassical side chairs are an exception, for a chair with a flat crest rail is usually identified as Sheraton, even though it may have tapering Hepplewhite legs. In the following sections you will see many of these chairs, which to be correct will be identified as Sheraton in style. To some extent, they exhibit the mix of styles so often seen in American furniture.

5-28. Portsmouth Sheraton, c. 1800.

5-29 Massachusetts neoclassical chairs. In Massachusetts, the preference for over upholstery continued into the Federal period, although by now this feature was less notable because urban chairs everywhere tend to be upholstered. More significantly, Massachusetts chairmakers remained partial to the use of stretchers, which by this time were seldom seen elsewhere except on the somewhat delicate shield-back chairs. Aside from a few chairs made by the Seymours, most Massachusetts side chairs have either tapering Hepplewhite or curved saber legs. Sheraton legs are common on New England couches, but for some reason, are seldom seen on side chairs. Although neoclassical chairs are lightly framed and tend to be highly stressed, in New England chairmakers continued to employ the horizontal triangular nailed blocking so often seen in Chippendale chairs (5-6). While mahogany was now almost universally used in urban furniture, some northern New England chairs continue to be made of birch.

Following a brief period after the Revolution when ladderback chairs were in vogue, neoclassical shield-back chairs became very fashionable in Massachusetts. So many were produced in and around Boston and Salem that we should consider three of the more common designs: the first with downward facing sheaf of wheat carving at the top of the splats (5-29A), the second with inlaid oval paterae in the splats (5-29B), and the last, a common treatment in which the splats are uncarved and simply flare out at the top (5-29C). The inlaid paterae on the second example would suggest a Boston origin, for Salem chairmakers favored carving over inlay. While very popular in the Boston area, these designs are not unique to Massachusetts. Chairs similar to the first two were also produced to some

extent in New York and Philadelphia, although here they are far less common and are more likely to omit stretchers.

With the advent of the Sheraton style at the turn of the century, square-back chairs with arching crest rails come into fashion, being particularly popular in Salem. The three most common Massachusetts forms of these chairs have thin vertical splats that either curve over at the top to form a series of interleaved Gothic arches (5-29D) or, like many Massachusetts shield-backs, fan out at the top (5-29E), or crisscross to form a lattice shaped back (5-29F). Better-quality Salem chairs often have a rectangular carved tablet centered in the crest rail as shown in figures 5-29D and 5-29F.

By the second decade of the nineteenth century, American furniture began to lose its regional identity, and nowhere is this more evident than in the common saber leg chair. In the average grade of these chairs there is little to distinguish them from the products of Boston, New York, and Philadelphia. Here the best indication of region may be in the secondary woods. Typically the front and back seat rails are made of a hard wood double tenoned into the side rails and then faced or veneered with mahogany. In Massachusetts, the rail under the veneer will be birch or perhaps soft maple; in New York, probably ash; and in Philadelphia, very often oak.

Also, in the more expensive and fashionable chairs we sometimes find significant regional preferences. In Boston there are two candidates: the tablet-back chair shown in figure 5-29G and the somewhat later classical drapery-back chair shown in figure 5-29H. Both of these designs appear to be unique to the Boston area.

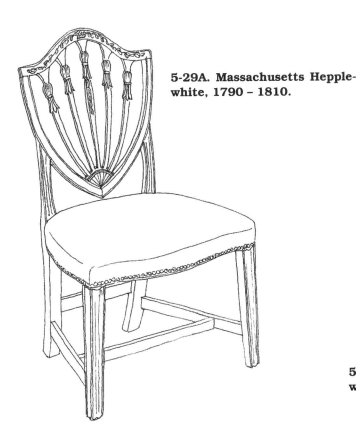

5-29A. Massachusetts Hepplewhite, 1790 – 1810.

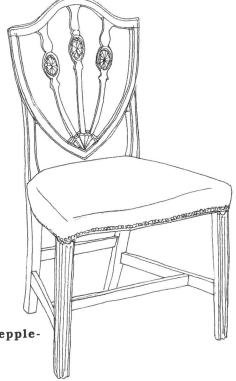

5-29B. Boston Hepplewhite, 1790 – 1810.

5-29C. Massachusetts Hepplewhite, 1790 – 1810.

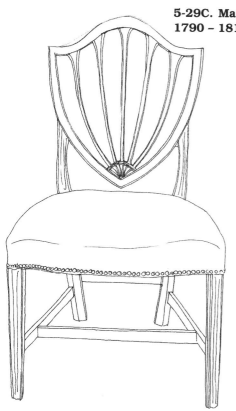

5-29D. Salem Sheraton, 1800 – 1810.

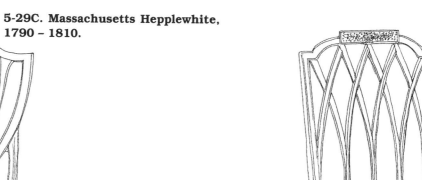

5-29E. Massachusetts Shera-ton, 1800 – 1810.

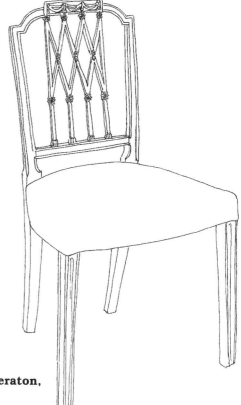

5-29F. Salem Sheraton, 1800 – 1810.

5-30 Rhode Island neoclassical chair. After the Revolution, Providence grews to be the principal urban center in Rhode Island, and it is from here that most Federal Rhode Island chairs originated. The best known of these have an arched crest rail above a kylix and swag or festoon pattern splat, as shown in figure 5-30. In shield-back chairs the lower portion of the splat is then usually composed of the five vertical bars seen in this illustration. Chairs having a kylix and swag pattern were also made to a limited extent in Massachusetts.

While I've shown you a shield-back chair, more often Rhode Island kylix and swag chairs employ the simpler, more conventional pierced splat like that shown in the following Connecticut chair (5-31A), although in this case the lower part of the splat will often be occupied by two large, downward facing carved bellflowers rather than the pattern of vertical bars. Interestingly, a number of these Rhode Island chairs are through tenoned, a practice that may have wandered over from nearby Connecticut, or may have been felt necessary due to the light neoclassical framing.

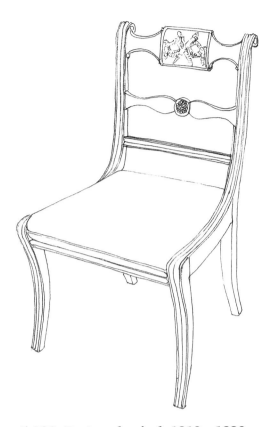

5-29G. Boston classical, 1810 – 1820.

5-29H. Boston classical, 1810 – 1820.

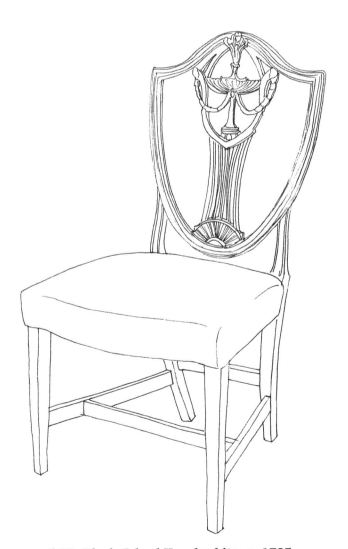

5-30. Rhode Island Hepplewhite, c. 1795.

5-31 Connecticut neoclassical chairs. Just as the state of Rhode Island produced a single well known pattern of neoclassical Federal chair, so also Connecticut produced another. This is the urn-back pattern illustrated in figure 5-31A. Many of these distinctive chairs are attributed to the Hartford firm of Samuel Kneeland and Lemuel Adams on the basis of a 1793 bill of sale for a set of six to a Mrs. Dickerson. Although a number of these chairs retain Chippendale crest rails or, like this chair, have Marlborough legs, the delicate curved splat with its central urn are very much Adam and neoclassical. These chairs were also popular in Rhode Island, and perhaps half are from this state. The simple neoclassical splat pattern had wide appeal, and there are many simpler versions with rush seats, and having the splat seated in a cross rail rather than a shoe and seat rail as shown here. Urn-backs were made of mahogany, cherry and birch. Mahogany would suggest an urban location, cherry Connecticut rather than Rhode Island. Chairs with a similar curved

splat, but with a pattern of three Prince of Wales feathers in lieu of the central urn, were made in New York City.

Before leaving Connecticut we might discuss a distinctive group of chairs produced in and around Litchfield, Connecticut. These "Litchfield" chairs, as shown in Figure 5-31B, are characterized by straight stiles, a flat crest rail, and splats that usually flare slightly from bottom to top to offset the flare of the stiles. While similar in form to the Boardman type chair shown in Figure 5-28, they are a far more rural product. Litchfield chairs are usually made of cherry, with some mahogany and walnut examples, and are transitional in style in that they may have either the Marlborough leg or the Hepplewhite leg shown here. Although a flat crest rail is a Sheraton feature, it would be difficult to associate these chairs with this style. They are often identified as Chippendale in auction catalogs. A few of these distinctive chairs seem to have been produced just across the Sound in nearby Long Island.

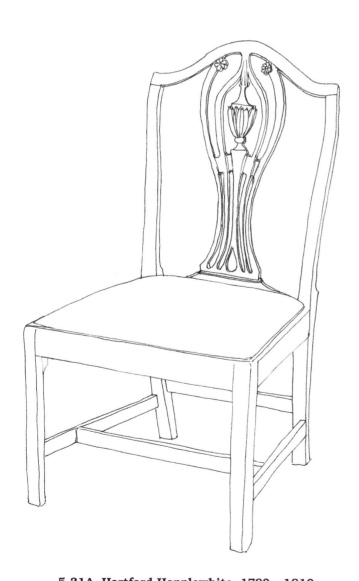

5-31A. Hartford Hepplewhite, 1790 – 1810.

5-31B. Litchfield Hepplewhite, 1780 – 1810.

5-32 New York neoclassical chairs. During the Federal period the city of New York produced more different types of chairs than any other American urban center. While I will show you the major types that illustrate the wide range of designs, I cannot begin to show the dozens of interesting variations in New York seating furniture. New York Federal chairs could easily be the subject of a whole chapter. In terms of style, Federal New York was the most up to date American city, and the style of side chairs rapidly passed through Hepplewhite and Sheraton to Empire and classical. In the illustrations that follow you will see one Hepplewhite, two Sheraton, and three classical chairs.

Federal New York was a wealthy city, and as a group, side chairs are distinguished not only by their individuality, but also by the general quality of workmanship. In addition to the use of hard, dense mahoganies, the seats are carefully framed, sometimes with blocking or diagonal corner braces, but often with one or two front to back medial braces as shown in figure 5-9. Sometimes there will be both corner braces and a medial brace. Seat rails are commonly ash, medial braces usually red gum or cherry. Many chairs have spade feet, a common feature in English furniture, but seldom seen in Philadelphia chairs and found only on better quality Massachusetts chairs.

Shield-back chairs were not as popular in New York as in New England, and the only high-style shield-back that was produced in quantity employs the draped swag pattern shown in Figure 5-32A. While this chair has stretchers, New York shield-backs frequently lack stretchers, and then often have spade feet, features less common elsewhere. Unfortunately, this singularly pleasing neoclassical motif is not unique to New York City, for the draped swag is also seen in a few Philadelphia, Rhode Island, and Massachusetts chairs.

The most common type of high style New York Sheraton chair has a square back enclosing a draped, pierced urn that is topped with three Prince of Wales feathers as illustrated in figure 5-32B. The middle third of the flat crest rail is raised in the center, a New York feature also seen in Slover and Taylor–type chairs (5-32C). This treatment is distinctly different from the arched crest rails typically seen in Massachusetts Sheraton chairs. Note that both of these chairs lack stretchers and have spade feet.

Perhaps the most handsome and best-known New York Federal chair has an X-shaped splat and a crest rail that scrolls over at the top as shown in figure 5-32D. Scroll-backs were made in a variety of designs, some with a double X-shaped splat, others with carved or brass paw feet, still others with a curving curule-form base. However, most are simpler with the single X-shaped splat and the turned, reeded legs shown here. The turned foot that swells out at the top and then tapers in toward the bottom is a very characteristic New York shape that we will see again and again in tables and case work.

The better grade of New York saber leg chair tends to be heavier and wider than comparable Boston chairs, and there will often be a continuous line of reeding extending from the top of the stiles to the bottom of the feet as seen in figure 5-32E. While this chair has a simple reeded horizontal splat, New York saber leg chairs often have richly carved splats with Federal or classical motifs such as eagles or cornucopia. High-style classical chairs may have harp or lyre splats, then rather strange looking carved hairy legs that terminate in paw feet (5-32F). Although frequently illustrated, these distinctive chairs were expensive and are not common.

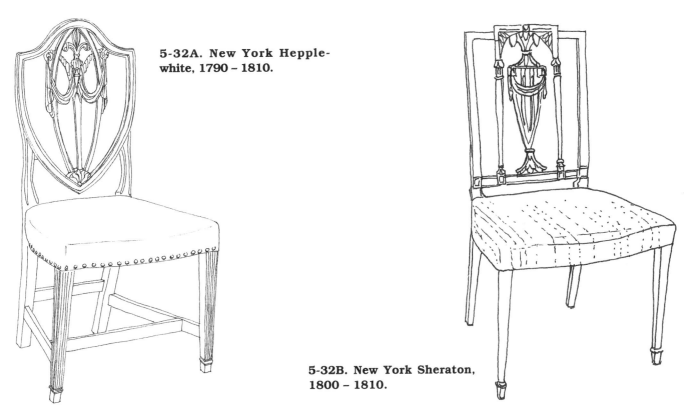

5-32A. New York Hepplewhite, 1790 – 1810.

5-32B. New York Sheraton, 1800 – 1810.

5-32C. New York Sheraton, 1800 – 1810.

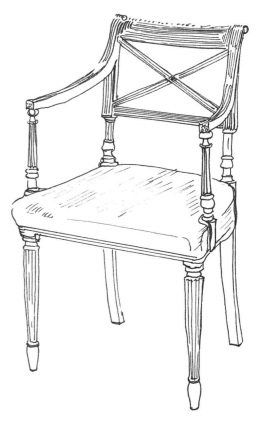

5-32D. New York classical, 1805 – 1815.

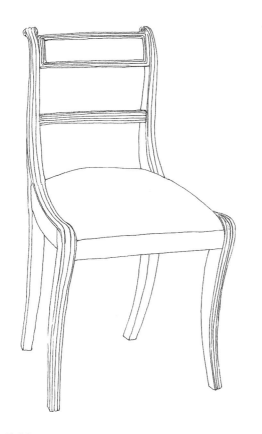

5-32E. New York classical, 1810 – 1820.

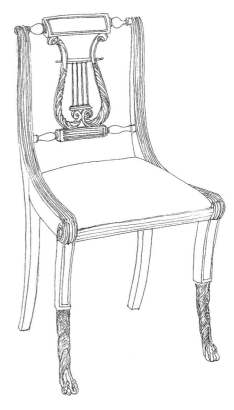

5-32F. New York classical, 1810 – 1820.

5-33 Philadelphia neoclassical chairs. Philadelphia Federal chairs are quite different from New York and Boston chairs, although by now even in Philadelphia walnut has finally given way to mahogany; and also, fashionable side chairs are far more likely to be overupholstered. Neoclassical spade feet are uncommon, but what you may see is a truncated spade shape reminiscent of the blocked feet so often seen in Philadelphia rococo furniture. As before, the preference for vertical blocking continued, and when original blocking survives, it will usually be the same built-up vertical pine or poplar blocking that was used before the Revolution (5-8). Philadelphia, and Southern, chairs often employ oak as a secondary wood for slip-seat frames and the rails on overupholstered chairs. Through tenoning also continues to be used in Philadelphia chairs. While not illustrated in this section, there are a considerable number of high-style overupholstered Philadelphia side chairs that have rounded or compass seats.

During the period when shield-back chairs were so fashionable in New England, the ladder-back was still popular in Philadelphia, and this may be the reason Philadelphia shield-back chairs are not common. Those that you see are generally somewhat fuller and wider than New England shield-backs. They normally have the same bowed slip seats so often seen in Philadelphia ladder-back chairs; and then have a shield that is rounded rather than pointed on the bottom as shown in figure 5-33A. Most are fitted with stretchers. Shield-backs having rounded bottoms were made everywhere, but are rare in New England and uncommon in New York. They are most likely to be from either Philadelphia or Baltimore. Here it should be noted that *shield-back* is a modern term; in the past, these chairs were called urn-backs when the bottoms of the shields were rounded and vase-backs when the bottoms of the shields were pointed.

Heart-back chairs might be considered an elegant variation of the shield-back, having an elliptical, heart shaped back and crest rail instead of the usual pierced splat and arched crest rail. They were produced to some extent in all urban centers, but are most common in the Middle Atlantic and the upper South. A heart-back chair will usually be from either New York or Baltimore, perhaps from Philadelphia. Although the side chair illustrated in figure 5-33B was identified in the auction catalog as being from either "Philadelphia or New York," the lack of stretchers, the reeded legs, and the spade feet would indicate the latter. The heart-shaped design of the backs of these chairs precludes significant variation in the pattern of the central splat, but in a general way a carved splat suggests a New York or Philadelphia chair, an inlaid splat a Baltimore chair. Here also it might be noted that molded legs are common in Philadelphia, rare in Baltimore.

Quite the best-known Philadelphia Federal chair is the racquet-back type shown in figure 5-33C, so-called because the pattern of the splat resembles an early wooden tennis racquet. Racquet-backs are actually just the best known of a whole group of similar Philadelphia chairs having pairs of vertical splats, slightly raised square crest rails, then pierced and carved designs between the splats. In many respects they resemble the New York draped urn chairs (5-32B), although they are very

unlikely to have spade feet. As would be expected with such a popular and fashionable design, a few racquet-backs were made both in New York and in nearby Maryland.

Another regional favorite was a square-back chair having carved and reeded stiles and spindles as illustrated in Figure 5-33D. These are usually identified as Haines-Connelly chairs because they resemble chairs made by cabinetmakers Ephraim Haines and Henry Connelly. Better-quality examples may have carved rectangular tablets where the leg is squared to meet the seat rail, a feature we will see later in a Philadelphia sofa. The design is somewhat unusual among Federal chairs in that it appears to be unique to the Philadelphia area. Mr. Haines is famous for having made a set of these chairs entirely out of ebony for the merchant and banker Stephen Girard. Note that even at this late date some high-style Philadelphia chairs continued to be given slip seats. The turned feet on this chair are a standard Philadelphia pattern that we will see later in card tables.

Philadelphia saber leg chairs tend to be more restrained than New York chairs, more in keeping with the simpler lines of many Boston chairs. Typically the stiles and legs are not reeded and the crest rails overlap and extend beyond the stiles as shown in figure 5-33E. Oak was a popular secondary wood in Philadelphia, and the front and back seat rails are often mahogany veneered over oak.

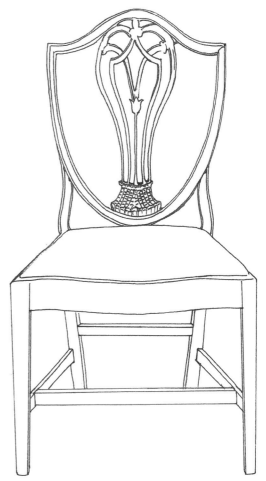

5-33A. Philadelphia Hepplewhite, 1790 – 1810.

5-33B. Middle Atlantic Hepple-white, 1790 – 1810.

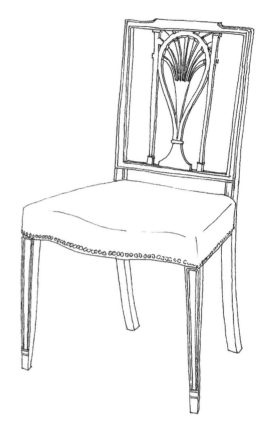

5-33C. Philadelphia Sheraton, 1800 – 1810.

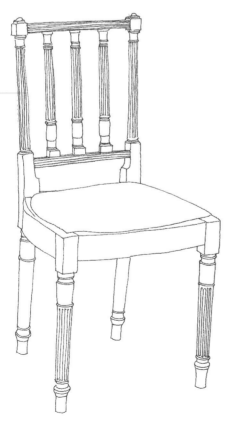

5-33D. Philadelphia Sheraton, 1800 – 1815.

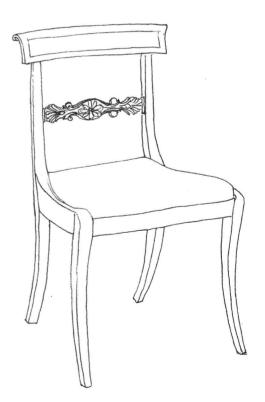

5-33E. Philadelphia classical, 1810 – 1820.

5-34 Southern neoclassical chairs. South of the Mason-Dixon Line stylish side chairs in Hepplewhite and Sheraton styles were produced in the urban centers: Baltimore, Annapolis, Norfolk, and Charleston. Because none of these cities, with the possible exception of Baltimore, developed into a major style center, it is not as easy to determine where a Southern neoclassical chair was made. Many are adaptations of fashionable New York and Philadelphia designs; others seem to have been taken from English models, or simply devised by the chairmaker. Even quite high style chairs sometimes give an impression of limited production. However, even if we have trouble with a specific location, there are features that help identify a Southern Federal chair. Chairs made in the South, and in Baltimore in particular, differ from Philadelphia workmanship in that they often employ the diagonal open bracing seen in New York side chairs. The front legs are seldom molded. Over-upholstered seat rails are frequently ash, but may also be oak or poplar. By this time, mahogany was the norm for fashionable urban furniture. However, this was not always so in the South, and a good-quality Hepplewhite or Sheraton chair fashioned of walnut will most probably be of Southern origin.

While they were fashionable in England, oval-back chairs were difficult to make and are rare in America. Aside from a handful of high-style painted chairs produced in Salem, most are from either Philadelphia or Baltimore, more likely the latter, where the design was very fashionable. The oval-back chair in figure 5-34A is a typical Baltimore product. The unusual teardrop-shaped piercing of the spats is also seen in Baltimore shield-back chairs.

Often, Southern chairs exhibit atypical splat patterns like the handsome lobed-back Hepplewhite chair shown in figure 5-34B that was made by John Shaw in Annapolis about 1790. The chair is very similar to a set of 24 armchairs he made for the Maryland Senate Chamber in 1797. An atypical pattern of this sort in combination with the use of oak or yellow pine secondary woods is suggestive of Southern workmanship.

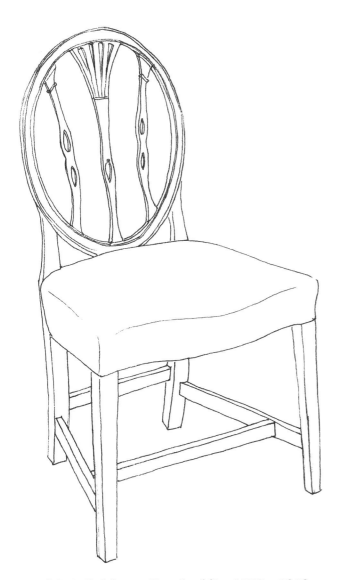

5-34A. Baltimore Hepplewhite, 1790 – 1810.

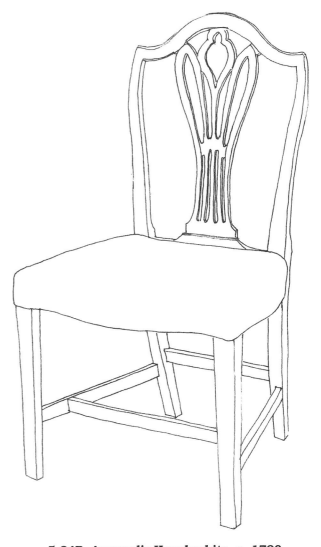

5-34B. Annapolis Hepplewhite, c. 1790.

Turned chairs present us with more than the usual problems in regional identification, if only because they are so easy to make. Almost anyone with a lathe and a basic set of tools can produce a serviceable chair. From the earliest days of our country, simple turned chairs were made everywhere, and unless exhibiting some feature unique to a region, tell us little of their origin. Nor is the choice of materials likely to be much help, for in all regions they were made of soft maple with ash rails and stretchers, although in the South the horizontal members tend to be hickory rather than ash. Compounding the problem is the lack of secondary woods, and that, for the most part, there are few significant differences in construction. This suggests that we must look to details of form and design in determining where a turned chair was produced, focusing on regional schools with significant production, on those chairs we are both likely to see and be able to identify.

Throughout the Colonial period turned chairs were produced in dozens of little shops all up and down the Atlantic coast. They were the product of turners, an ancient craft that predates the seventeenth century joiner and the eighteenth century cabinetmaker. The interchangeable parts of turned chairs were perfectly suited for mass production, and they were produced by the thousands at a cost of no more than four or five shillings each. John Underwood of Boston is recorded as having made over 6,000 chairs between 1734 and 1736. Probate records tell us of turners leaving hundreds of posts and stretchers awaiting final assembly and painting. Turned chairs were well suited to withstand the rigors of Colonial transportation, and were shipped all up and down the coast. Boston chairs were being sold in Maryland by the third quarter of the seventeenth century. This suggests that the provenance of a long family history may not indicate the region of manufacture, much the way that most Restoration chairs were made in London even though they have been in American homes for almost three hundred years.

Again we will begin in the north and proceed south, but this time by type rather than style, for turned chairs do not conveniently divide into style and period, into William and Mary, Queen Anne, and Chippendale. The reader will see more examples of New England than Middle Atlantic and Southern chairs, in part because these chairs have been the subject of much study, and in part because the New England colonies produced an unusual number of productive regional schools. There appear to be far more surviving turned chairs from New England than from any other region. A relatively sophisticated turned chair lacking any particular regional characteristic is more likely than not to be from somewhere in New England.

Before starting, something might be said about the dates that accompany the illustrations in this chapter. By their very nature, turned chairs are difficult to date, and rather than being too specific, I have tried to provide an estimate of the whole period range of the type, although the examples are somewhat better than average, and would tend to be earlier rather than later. Slat-back chairs, in particular, present a problem in dating, for in addition to seeing much hard use, they continued to be made right up through the nineteenth century, and indeed, are still in production. The reader should be very careful when confronted with an "old" slat-back chair.

6-1 New England Carver chair. Very early turned chairs from all regions are usually turned all over, that is, they lack the flat splats and shaped arms seen in most turned chairs, as though the turners that made them had nothing more to work with than a pole lathe to turn the posts and spindles and a few augers to drill the circular mortises. Most are from the first centers of population, eastern Massachusetts and coastal Connecticut. The popular name comes from a chair owned by John Carver, governor of the Plymouth Colony. Similar chairs, but with additional rows of vertical spindles under the arm rests and between the stretchers, are called Brewster chairs, after William Brewster, the first minister of the colony. They are very rare.

The most notable characteristic of these early chairs is the massive turned posts, which are often 2½" or more in diameter. Most exhibit no more decoration than turned spindles, mushroom handholds on the front posts and decorative finials on top of the stiles as shown in figure 6-1. Typically the back is composed of an upper turned rail, then a single tier of three turned vertical spindles set between two horizontal members. A few have four vertical spindles; some have two tiers of spindles. There is much variation in the shape of the spindles, but in New England they tend to include some form of symmetrical double baluster and ring, which might be seen as an early expression of the New England preference for symmetrical turnings.

Although Carver-type chairs are most often from coastal New England, similar chairs were made in all regions from Massachusetts down to New Jersey. Southern examples are exceedingly rare. The earliest New England chairs were made of different woods — poplar, oak, maple, and ash, but with time tend to be maple with ash seat lists and stretchers. These "great chairs" were at first only armchairs, but later there are side chairs. Although they look to be very early, most surviving examples are probably eighteenth rather than seventeenth century. New England examples survive in considerable numbers, suggesting that they must once have been extremely common. These are even assembled sets of side chairs. The great majority have seen much wear and survive in poor condition, frequently missing finials, mushroom handholds, one or more stretchers, and perhaps several inches in height.

If not missing, the front stretcher of one of these early turned chairs will be

6-1. New England Carver-type, 48" h, 1660 – 1700.

set close to the floor. If not restored, it will also be well worn, silent testimony to us — three hundred years later — of how appallingly cold and drafty houses were in winter.

6-2 New England slat-back chairs. Slat-back chairs came into use about the turn of the seventeenth century. At first they were very similar to Carver chairs, except that the back spindles were replaced by simpler and more comfortable splats. Usually the slats sweep up from the sides to meet a flat top as illustrated in figure 6-2A. Normally the top slat will be slightly deeper than the other two. These early slat-backs are sometimes identified as southern New England, although Jobe and Kaye illustrate an almost identical chair made in either Boston or Salem, and indeed, they were probably produced everywhere that Carver-type chairs were produced, in eastern Massachusetts and coastal Connecticut. Some were also made in adjacent New York.

Within just a few years, in the first quarter of the eighteenth century, New England slat-backs lose their massive framing and become both lighter and elegantly tall, reminiscent of the Early Baroque or William and Mary styles, similar in feeling to the fashionable Restoration chair illustrated in the next section. While three or four splats are the norm, some chairs may have five or even six splats. Figure 6-2B illustrates one of these handsome early slat-backs. Note that they retain the turned arms seen on Carver chairs. This is not as budget a chair as it might seem, for to produce the large handholds, the front posts had to be laboriously turned down from a three- or four-inch billet. Sadly, these bold handholds tend to crack and chip, and a great many have been cut off.

The most common type of eighteenth century New England slat-back has either three or four arched splats set between maple posts decorated with a finial and a single ball turning between each splat. By now armchairs have acquired more comfortable sawn and shaped arms that rest on the top of the posts. The splats are almost invariably flat across the bottom, and on better work slightly graduated with the thickest at the top. On many examples the top splat is significantly thicker and is a different shape, curving down at the ends as shown in figure 6-2C. This may have been done to provide a little additional strength, for you will notice that many early slat-backs are missing the top of the upper slat.

By now the design of these chairs has become standardized, and in New England the finials will usually be a stack of turnings with a ball and nipple at the top, then one or two smaller rings below, as shown in the armchair in figure 6-2C and the side chair in figure 6-2D. These finials are very different from the tapering turnings seen in early chairs (6-1, 6-2A) and are also different from the finials we will see later on Middle Atlantic chairs. Inexpensive slat-back chairs were produced throughout New England for well over a century, the form becoming so standardized that later examples are difficult to date. In common with turned chairs everywhere, many are probably a lot newer than wear and early form would suggest.

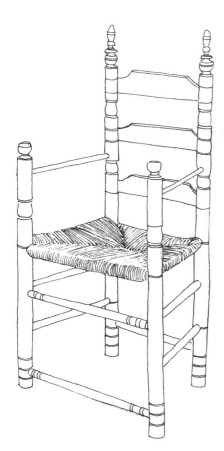

6-2A. New England slat-back, 48" h, c. 1700.

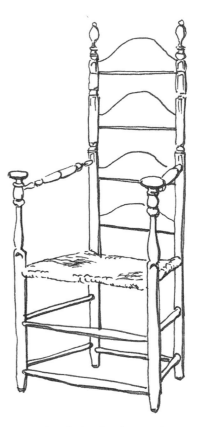

6-2B. New England slat-back, 47" h, 1690 – 1720.

6-2C. New England slat-back, 1740 – 1780.

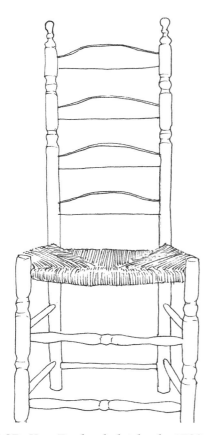

6-2D. New England slat-back, 1760 – 1820.

6-3 Banister-back chairs. We will start this section with a chair that is neither American nor banister-back but nevertheless should be included, not only because chairs like this are seen at Americana auctions, but also because this style is believed to have been the inspiration for the innumerable banister-back chairs produced in America. These high-backed William and Mary chairs are known as Restoration chairs, after the restoration of the English monarchy in 1660. Typically they have the caned seat and back and the carved stretcher and crest rail shown in figure 6-3A. There is a large gap under the stay rail, and the seat rails are not decorated because the seat had a thick cushion. Many chairs have simpler turned front legs rather than the elaborate Flemish scroll illustrated here. Originally called cane chairs, they were made in London and exported to America by the thousands. Because of the amount of carving, and because caning was labor intensive and is somewhat delicate, very few caned chairs were produced in America. While the best quality chairs are made of walnut, most will be beech stained up to look like walnut, or painted black to imitate ebony.

To provide a lower cost alternative, local turners substituted decorative turnings for much of the carving, split balusters for the caned back, and woven rush for the caned seat. Baluster was later corrupted to banister, and today these chairs are called banister-backs. We will look at six examples, all but one from the Northeast, for while enormously popular throughout New England, they are uncommon in the Middle Atlantic and rare in the South. When you see a banister-back chair, you are most likely looking at a New England chair. This section will help you tell where in New England the chair might have been made.

The earliest American banister-backs, and those most similar to their London prototypes, typically have carved crest rails, squared back legs, block and compressed vase turned front legs, and single ball-and-ring turned front stretchers like the example in figure 6-3B. These William and Mary–style chairs were made from Boston eastward to Salem and northward up to coastal New Hampshire. Although they are early chairs, and more expensive than slat-backs, a surprising number turn up at auctions. They seem to have been very fashionable in their time.

Far more common is a simplified chair that is turned all over, the crest rail shaped with a saw rather than carved, and the legs cylinder and ball turned with a double row of stretchers as shown in figure 6-3C. This late example has turned legs, but some of these chairs retain the squared rear legs, vase and block turned front legs, and the single front stretcher seen in earlier chairs. A few have Spanish, or paintbrush, feet. While there are innumerable local variations, more often than not the crest rail will have either a single arch or the double arch shown here. Note that the finials are identical to those on New England slat-back chairs. These inexpensive banister-backs are very common. They were made all over New England, and unless there is a feature to suggest a particular region, there is little to tell us when or where a banister-back was made, except, of course, that it was most probably made in New England. Note in these illustrations, that when turned, the pattern of the balusters will almost always mirror the turnings of the posts or stiles.

However, one such feature is the unusual "staghorn" or "fishtail" crest rail seen in banister-back chairs produced in Essex County and adjacent Portsmouth, New Hampshire (6-3D). The rather strange-looking rail is not all that tells us where this chair was made. The noticeably drooping handholds also suggest a chair made in or near Portsmouth. On inexpensive chairs, the sawn arms are typically scrolled over at the ends to provide a handhold, but here they often have a pronounced droop, almost as though the wood has melted a little.

Connecticut furniture tends to be distinctive, and Connecticut banister-backs are no exception. Quite the best known are the "heart and crown" chairs like that shown in figure 6-3E. These much published chairs were produced in a number of western coastal towns between 1725 and 1820, primarily Norwalk, Stratford, Milford, and Gilford. The design is attributed to the shop of an English immigrant, Thomas Salmon, who settled in Stratford in 1719. The distinctive crest rail might be seen as a rural interpretation of the carved crests in Boston chairs. This handsome chair illustrates a number of other Connecticut features: the intermediate stretchers under the arms, the square molded splats, and the symmetrical ring and ball turnings on the front stretchers. The crest rail is the focal point of decoration on a banister-back chair, and if you see a banister-back with an unusually bold or whimsical crest rail, you may be looking at a Connecticut chair.

Another Connecticut feature concerns the turned and split half-round spats in these chairs. Normally they are positioned for most comfort, that is, the flat side facing the back of the sitter. However, some chairs from Connecticut and the Connecticut River Valley have the splats reversed so that the curved side faces the sitter's back, which provides a more visually interesting — but perhaps somewhat less comfortable — chair.

Another type of Connecticut banister-back has an inverse-arched crest rail (6-3F). These chairs, sometimes described as yoke-back, banister-back chairs, were also produced on Long Island, and were very popular in the Hudson River Valley. They are a relatively late form of banister-back, replacing the William and Mary heart and crown chairs in the third quarter of the eighteenth century. They normally have the square molded splats shown in this illustration.

Banister-back chairs were far less successful in the Delaware Valley, perhaps because Philadelphia was settled later than Boston, and by the time they were being produced, their rather old fashioned William and Mary design was already being superseded by the more comfortable and elegant ladder-back chairs we will see in a little bit. Pennsylvania banister-back chairs are very different from New England banister-backs, being very solid looking with a rather heavy back in which square molded splats are typically set within a molded frame as shown in the large armchair in figure 6-3G. Note that the arched crest rail rests on top of the posts, a feature of Philadelphia and New York chairs that is seldom seen

in New England. The front legs employ the same cylinder and ball tuning and elongated tapering ball foot seen on early Philadelphia-area Windsor chairs.

Here it should be noted that as a general rule, the crest rails on banister-back chairs made in New England are flat across the bottom, while those from the Middle Atlantic colonies are arched. There are a few Connecticut chairs that are the exception. However, these are very much New England products, for not only is the crest rail set between the posts, but

6-3A. London William & Mary Restoration chair, 50" h, c. 1700.

6-3B. Massachusetts William & Mary banister-back, 48" h, 1710 – 1750.

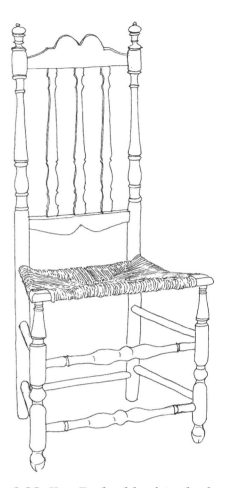

6-3C. New England banister-back, 42" h, 1750 – 1810.

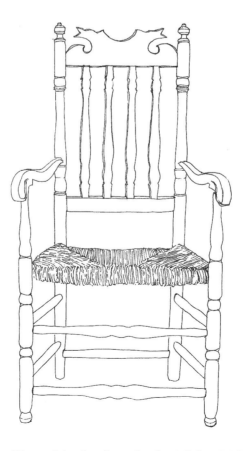

6-3D. New Hampshire banister-back, 44" h, 1740 – 1770.

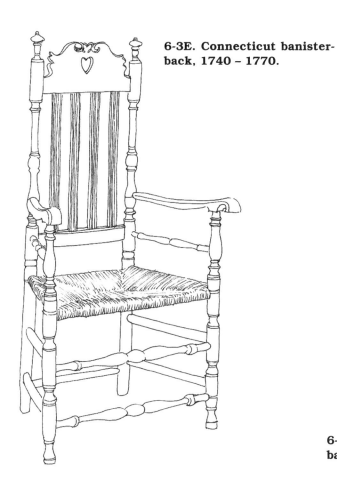

6-3E. Connecticut banister-back, 1740 – 1770.

6-3F. Connecticut yoke-back banister-back, 1770 – 1800.

6-3G. Delaware Valley banister-back, 48" h, 1730 – 1750.

also, they are so vertical and lightly framed that there is no mistaking them for Middle Atlantic workmanship.

6-4 Connecticut fiddle-back chair. Turned chairs normally have open slats mounted horizontally between the back posts, or balusters mounted vertically between crest and stay rails. The Connecticut fiddle-back chair in figure 6-4 and the following New York yoke-back chair are exceptions. The solid fiddle-shaped splats on these chairs are rural interpretations of the then-popular Queen Anne style. Fiddle-backs were produced with a wide variety of crest rails, most commonly the inverse arch shown here, or an exaggerated serpentine rail having Chippendale ears that rests on top of the posts, or a curved Queen Anne–style crest similar to that seen on the following yoke-back chair. Although fiddle-back chairs are usually associated with western coastal Connecticut, they were also produced up the Connecticut River Valley and across the sound on Long Island.

6-5 New York yoke-back chair. Quite the best-known turned chair in the Queen Anne style is the New York or Hudson River Valley yoke-back chair illustrated in figure 6-5. These popular chairs were produced over a wide area in and around New York City: the Hudson River Valley, northern New Jersey, Long Island, and coastal Connecticut. In the past they were often called York chairs because they came from New York, and even today are sometimes referred to as Dutch chairs because New York was originally a Dutch colony. Although the Queen Anne yoke-form crest rail and solid splat are what first catch the eye, what makes these chairs most distinctive are the broad seats and the heavy trumpet turned cabriole legs and pad feet. Fiddle-back chairs may also have the same yoke crest rail, which gets its name from the wooden yoke used to harness a pair of oxen. Like many rural chairs, yoke-backs retain elements of earlier styles, in this case the William and Mary ball and ring turned front stretcher.

Connecticut yoke-backs are thought to differ slightly in having double-ball turnings at the top of the posts and in lacking a central disk between the ball turnings on the front stretcher, but as there are documented Long Island chairs with these same features, this may be more a sign of Connecticut influence than a sign Connecticut workmanship. A better indication might be the presence of a somewhat vertical looking chair in combination with a relatively narrow splat. As befits a very successful design, there are all sorts of little variations. Some New York chairs have serpentine Chippendale crest rails, and some Long Island chairs have inverted splats, that is, the widest part of such a chair's splat is at the bottom.

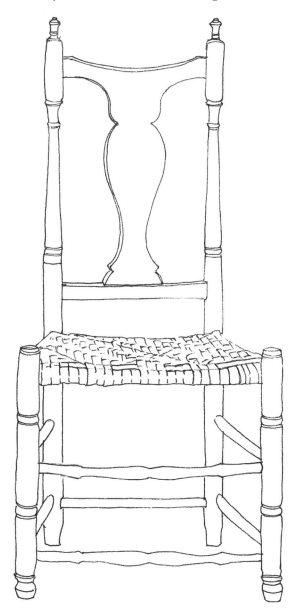

6-4. Connecticut fiddle-back, 1790 – 1810.

6-5. New York yoke-back, 41" h, 1760 – 1820.

6-6 New Jersey slat-back chair. The armchair in figure 6-6 is representative of a large group of early slat-back chairs produced in central and northern New Jersey and, to some extent, in New York and Long Island. These typically have single ball turnings on the posts between both the slats, single ball turnings between the stretchers on the front legs, and two sausage-turned front stretchers. Normally there will be either three or four graduated and fairly deep slats that are flat on the bottom and evenly curved across the top. Some slats are given a small nipple in the center as shown in this illustration. Most of these chairs have the distinctive finial shown here, a ball and nipple above a single ring. In lieu of the ball foot shown here a number of these chairs have the tapered ball or "blunt arrow" foot like that which we saw in a Delaware Valley banister-back chair, and which we will see again in Philadelphia Windsors.

Somewhat similar chairs were made just to the north of New York City in Bergen County. These later chairs are generally smaller in scale, but retain the single ball turnings on both the posts and front legs. Many have tapered rear feet, which in this instance may be a sign of nineteenth century workmanship.

6-7 Delaware Valley ladder-back chairs. Normally, turned chairs having horizontal slats are termed slat-backs, and cabinet-maker's chairs with horizontal splats are termed ladder- or ribbon-backs, but the lovely slat-backs produced for almost a century in the Delaware Valley are so elegant that they are almost invariably known as ladder-backs. These chairs are easy to identify, for not only is the design unique, but also, there is relatively little variation within the form — almost as though nothing could be done to improve on a perfect chair. The armchair in figure 6-7A and the side chair in figure 6-7B are typical of these fine chairs, having round or acorn finials, multiple arched slats, undercut arms, tapered rear feet, and bold front ball feet joined by a single large ball and ring turned stretcher. In common with early New England armchairs and New York yoke-back chairs, the front legs were often turned down from extra thick stock, in this case to provide for the distinctive ball feet. To allow for wear, a stout button is left below the balls on the front feet. Typically there will be four to six slats. A few even have seven. Most slats are arched on both the top and bottom and are graduated in thickness toward the top. They may be quite delicate and thin as seen in figure 6-7B. Unlike most turned chairs, these chairs were generally made entirely of maple rather than a mixture of maple and ash or maple and hickory, and were sometimes varnished rather than painted. While side chairs tend to be elegantly tall and thin, armchairs may be large and heavy, a characteristic of rural southeastern Pennsylvania work that we will see later in Delaware Valley case furniture. Some, probably late survivals, have two turned stretchers between the front legs rather than the single ball and ring stretcher shown in these illustrations. These wonderful chairs were produced all over the Delaware Valley, including adjacent southern New Jersey.

6-8 Southern slat-back chair. It is difficult to illustrate specific types of Southern turned chairs because the region appears to have produced only relatively small and scattered regional schools. Unlike

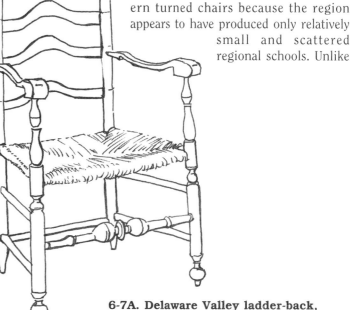

6-6. New Jersey slat-back, 44" h, 1730 – 1780.

6-7A. Delaware Valley ladder-back, 42" h, 1730 – 1810.

the New England and Middle Atlantic colonies, there are not large bodies of similar chairs. However, the chair shown in figure 6-8 is in many ways typical of Southern turned chairs and can provide us with a model of what to expect. Although the shape of the finials with a ball above a single ring is suggestive of New Jersey workmanship, and the ball turned front feet are reminiscent of Delaware Valley ladder-backs, there is little to tell us where this chair was made. The atypical pattern of the slats and the front stretchers seem to be the work of a rural craftsman working on his own. The arms are also typical of those found on Southern chairs, having a simple sawn shape and being set rather high above the seat. Sometimes the arms will be turned, but unlike those seen in early New England chairs, they are apt to extend over the arm posts, terminating in a barrel shape that provides both a handhold and sufficient stock to receive the post tenon.

In common with many Southern turned chairs, the back posts are turned at both ends; that is, there are finials at the top and then turnings at the bottom that usually match the turned feet on the front legs. Sometimes the back legs were given additional turnings, something almost never seen in other areas. North of the Mason-Dixon Line, the back legs were typically left in the round with nothing more than perhaps a taper at the bottom.

Most Southern turned chairs are made of soft maple with hickory for the seat lists and stretchers, but you may also encounter oak, ash, cherry, walnut and mulberry. The sturdy armchair in figure 6-8 is made of walnut, something you will almost never see except in the South. The presence of either walnut or mulberry in an inexpensive turned chair is indicative of Southern workmanship. Actually, the presence of mulberry in any furniture is indicative of Southern workmanship.

6-7B. Delaware Valley ladder-back, 44" h, 1730 – 1810.

6-8. Southern slat-back, 43" h, 1730 – 1760.

6-9 Fancy Chairs. Fancy chairs do not have a natural home, for they are not of any one type, and may be of sawn and shaped, or turned, or Windsor construction. However, since the great majority are turned chairs, and rather late turned chairs at that, we will discuss them at this point. The name itself is not a twentieth century appellation. Paint-decorated chairs have always been called fancy chairs.

Paint-decorated chairs appeared after the Revolution, initially in the major urban centers as high-style painted furniture in the new neoclassical Adam style. The idea was very popular, and within a few years both turned and Windsor chairs were being decorated with delightful little scenes painted on the crest rails or on tablets mounted between the back posts. By the second decade of the nineteenth century, economical versions were being produced, the skilled hand work replaced by quick, inexpensive stenciling, and soon Lambert Hitchcock's Connecticut factory was producing a thousand chairs a month. Needless to say, quite the best and most charming work is from early on, when chairs were still being individually hand painted.

Determining region in a fancy chair is not easy, for they were both a late development and were made everywhere, although very few seem to have been produced south of Baltimore. The problem is somewhat simpler in the earlier chairs that tend to mimic features found in formal side chairs. The New England chair in figure 6-9A has a back similar to a Massachusetts classical tablet-back chair. Turned legs that curve out to button feet are found in many fancy chairs from this region.

There are more paint-decorated chairs from New York than from any other region. In common with other New York Federal chairs, they come in a wide variety of designs. As a group they tend to have rush compass seats, a shape also seen in many New England chairs. However, the chair shown in figure 6-9B is an easy study, for not only is the back reminiscent of a great many New York scroll-back chairs, but also, it has very recognizably New York feet.

If auction records are any indication, Philadelphia produced very little paint-decorated furniture. It may be that fancy chairs had little appeal in a city that was already slow in accepting the new neoclassic style. The same was not true in rapidly growing Baltimore, where painted furniture was greeted with enthusiasm. There are so many surviving Baltimore fancy chairs that we might consider two typical examples, the first an early version with a painted tablet in the crest rail and a simplified version of the X-shaped splat seen in many New York chairs, and which indeed, might well be of New York influence (6-9C). As seen here, these handsome chairs typically have caned rather than rush seats that are slightly bowed on the front and sides. The shape of each of the lower front legs, with a notch that serves to delineate the foot, seems to be a unique Baltimore feature.

The design most commonly associated with Baltimore fancy chairs has a caned seat, a sharply raked tablet back and a rather strange looking triangular section at the rear of the seat rails that serves to tie together the rails, the rear legs, and the back posts as shown in figure 6-9D. These Empire-style chairs are often attributed to the shop of John and Hugh Finlay, although they were produced by a number of shops.

6-9A. New England fancy, c. 1815.

6-9B. New York fancy, 34" h, 1805 – 1815.

6-9C. Baltimore fancy, 1805 – 1815.

6-9D. Baltimore fancy, c. 1825.

With luck, you will have little difficulty telling where a Windsor chair was made, for not only were different types of Windsors popular in each region, but also, production was much standardized and there are marked regional differences in the turnings of the legs and the spindles. Unless the chair is a late product, or a rural one of a kind effort, it is usually possible to identify at least region in a Windsor chair. Because they were frequently made on speculation for sale elsewhere, Windsors often carry the stamp, brand, or label of the maker on the bottom of the seat, and today there is probably more detailed information on their manufacture than any other type of furniture. However, the problem we encountered in high-style chairs also afflicts Windsors — the later the chair, the less easy the identification.

The first American Windsors were made in Philadelphia in the 1740s, and for the next 30 years, Philadelphia chairmakers dominated the trade before manufacturing spread up the coast. Production began in New York City just prior to the Revolution, but did not really get going until the economy recovered in the early 1790s. Prior to the Revolution, New England production was limited to a relative few low and comb-back Windsors made in Rhode Island, most probably in Newport. Elsewhere, Philadelphia Windsors were so common that they were often just called "Philadelphia chairs", much the way the early leather-backed chairs produced in Massachusetts were called "Boston" chairs. A very early Windsor, whatever its family provenance, is likely to have been made in Philadelphia.

In determining region, we should first consider regional characteristics that can help to us tell where a chair was made, the distinctive features that may be found in any Windsor chair produced in a particular region. Enormous numbers of Windsor chairs were made during the last quarter of the eighteenth and the first half of the nineteenth century, and this mass production led to much standardization in the major centers of production: Philadelphia, New York City, coastal Connecticut, and eastern Massachusetts. Manufacturing was not limited to the original colonies. In the early years of the nineteenth century production spread south through the Carolinas, west into Ohio and Kentucky, and north through Vermont and Maine and into eastern Canada. Although these later Windsors are not as easy to place, here and there you may be lucky and find one that still retains the maker's label.

The best indication of region lies in the type of chair and in the shaping of individual elements in the design. Different types of Windsors will be covered in a little bit, but here we might first consider the shaping of the legs. The first Philadelphia Windsors had a distinctive cylinder-and-ball leg that would seem to have been borrowed from the Delaware Valley ladder-back chair discussed in the preceding chapter. The foot at the base of the cylinder will usually be either a somewhat elongated ball or the blunt arrow shown in the Philadelphia comb-back chair in figure 7-1A, although in many of these early Windsors the feet are so worn that only the top of the foot remains. Similar looking legs were used on Rhode Island Windsors prior to the Revolution, but these lack the well defined baluster and ring turnings and the cylinder section is quite short and bowed in the center as we see in the Rhode Island low-back in figure 7-2B.

Cylinder-and-ball legs were difficult to turn and could not be trimmed to suit the height of the user, and by the 1760s were replaced by a tapered leg more suitable to mass production. Thereafter, tapered legs of one type or another were employed in all regions until being superseded by bamboo turnings with the advent of the neoclassical style after the Revolution. Most all tapered legs have the same basic turning sequence. At the top will be a short baluster that rests on a small ring, and below this, a longer baluster that rests on another small ring; then below this a compressed ball resting on top of a conical lower section that tapers to the foot. The differences between the tapered legs produced in different areas are not all that evident, and are difficult to describe without the aid of very good illustrations. Here I would suggest that the reader consult Charles Santore's *The Windsor Style in America — 1730 – 1830*, and in particular the lovely Portfolio of Drawings at the front of the book.

There are other regional practices that suggest where a chair was made. The low-back and early comb-back chairs made in Philadelphia and Rhode Island have sawn arms that are joined together in the back by a center section. In Philadelphia the center section is set between and overlaps the back ends of the arms. In Rhode Island the arms curve around to meet at the center of the back, and then are joined to a crest section that rests on the arms. Here also the arms are somewhat thicker and the arm posts and spindles do not penetrate the arms.

Normally the posts that support the arms on a Windsor chair will be turned to a pattern that emulates and harmonizes with the turnings on the legs. However, some makers followed the English practice in using the sawn "ram's horn" arm supports illustrated in figures 7-1B and 7-5C. While this is occasionally seen in New England, ram's horn supports are fairly common in Philadelphia Windsors, sometimes in comb-back chairs, but more often in bow-back armchairs.

Outside of Philadelphia, particularly in and around Lancaster County, it was common practice to employ different turnings on the front and back legs; the earlier cylinder and blunt arrow legs were on the front and the newer tapered legs on the back, as shown in the handsome sack-back Windsor in figure 7-4B. This treatment was popular right up until the turn of the century, even though cylinder-and-ball legs were by this time long out of fashion in Philadelphia. It is seen on fan-back, sack-back, and bow-back chairs.

The backs of New York continuous-arm and bow-back Windsors tend to have pronounced rakes; that is, they have very noticeable backward slants. In addition, the spindles on New York City chairs are shaped so that they swell very slightly from the bottom to a maximum diameter about a third of the way up from the seat, then taper gently in towards the top.

Connecticut Windsors have a number of features that make for fairly easy identification. The spindles usually have a small swelling or bulb about a third the way above the seat, which unlike New York spindles, seems to have been done more for decoration rather than to provide additional strength. This swelling is occasionally seen in Massachusetts and Rhode Island chairs, but is most common in eastern Connecticut. Connecticut Windsors also generally lack the seat groove, or "rain gutter," that is usually found in front of the spindles, and the legs do not penetrate the seat. In common with other furniture made in Connecticut, Windsor chairs may exhibit slightly odd or individualistic features. This is particularly noticeable in the crest rails on comb-back and fan-back chairs, which lend themselves to innovation, and here you may see an exuberant curve or perhaps little carved pinwheels in lieu of the more usual volutes. Many Connecticut chairs were produced in the eastern part of the state in New London County by the extended family of Ebenezar Tracy (1744 – 1803).

Windsor chairs were normally made of a mixture of woods chosen for their particular attributes, a relatively soft wood for the shaped seat, then easily turned maple for the legs and tough hickory and oak for framing the back and spindles. However, in Rhode Island it was not uncommon to make Windsors of a single wood, and if you see a Windsor made entirely of maple or chestnut, you are probably looking at a Rhode Island chair.

Early Rhode Island low-back and comb-back Windsors often have the same block and turned cross stretchers that we saw earlier in a Massachusetts Queen Anne corner chair, but to add a little confusion, these stretchers were also employed on a rural Connecticut Windsor in the Garvan collection. As noted earlier, the sawn arms on these chairs are constructed very differently from those made in Philadelphia. Also, the spindles on Rhode Island chairs are often given a little decorative baluster or vase shaped turning across the back as is seen in figures 7-1D and 7-2B. Otherwise, Rhode Island Windsors are similar to Windsor chairs produced by the Tracy family in omitting rain gutters and not having the legs pierce the seat.

Although a large number of Windsors were produced in Massachusetts, they lack distinctive features and are not easy to describe. Most are identified as simply being from New England. Perhaps the best indication of a northern New England origin is the use of white pine in the seat of a chair that does not seem to be from either Connecticut or Rhode Island.

Windsor chairmakers everywhere tended to use the same basic woods in their chairs, usually maple for the legs, then hickory, ash, and oak for the arms and backs. However, the seats echo regional preferences in secondary woods, and here we can obtain an idea of where a Windsor was made. Chairmakers in northern New England, Massachusetts, New Hampshire and Maine normally used white pine. Early Rhode Island chairs are apt to have either soft maple or chestnut seats, later chairs will have either white pine or chestnut. The seats of Connecticut chairs may be yellow poplar, white pine or chestnut, chestnut if from the eastern part of the state. Some Connecticut and Rhode Island chairs have ash seats. South of Connecticut most Windsors have popular seats, although a significant number of New York chairs and a few Delaware Valley chairs have pine seats. Basswood or linden was sometimes used in rural New York and New England, most commonly in Connecticut, western Massachusetts and southern Vermont.

This brief discussion has covered only the more common and noticeable regional differences. There are many other more subtle indications of region in the shape of the backs, seats, handholds, and stretchers of Windsor chairs that are beyond the scope of this survey, but are discussed and illustrated at length in the two excellent books on Windsor chairs by Charles Santore, and in the magisterial study of Windsors by Nancy Goyne Evans. Both books also contain appendices that list Windsor chairmakers, and if you are so fortunate as to find a brand or label on the bottom of a chair, you should be able to identify at once where it was made.

Before discussing the various types of Windsor chairs, it might be noted that a variety of terms are used to describe them, and that many, such as *bird-cage*, *arrow-back*, and *thumb-back*, are based on design features rather than the overall form of the chair. There are also variations in the description of different forms, particularly between comb-backs and fan-backs, sack-backs and bow-backs. Here we will follow the terminology employed by Mr. Santore in *The Windsor Style in America*. In *American Windsor Chairs*, Ms. Evans employs somewhat different terms, identifying comb-backs as high-backs, rod-backs as square-backs. Her book is particularly helpful in identifying the later Windsors, and in Windsor production in outlying regions.

7-1 Comb-back Windsors. The first Philadelphia Windsors were comb-back armchairs, and to this day, more than half of the surviving comb-backs are from somewhere in the Delaware Valley. While rare in New York, many were also produced late in the century in New England, particularly in Connecticut and Rhode Island. Therefore, we might consider four comb-backs: two from Pennsylvania, one from Connecticut, and one from Rhode Island.

Early Philadelphia comb-backs have great wide D-shaped seats and cylinder-and-ball legs, much like the low-back Windsor in figure 7-2A. Later comb-backs are less beamy and often employ the more tapered ball foot shown in figure 7-1A, perhaps because it was noticed that a ball left no room for wear. The makers of ladder-back chairs in the Delaware Valley avoided this problem by leaving a stout button below the ball. As noted earlier, ram's horn arm supports are often from eastern Pennsylvania, and in figure 7-1B we see these in a Philadelphia comb-back Windsor. This is probably a somewhat later chair, for it employs the tapered leg that was introduced in the 1760s.

The best of Connecticut comb-backs exhibit a cheerful exuberance in the shaping of the crest rail and the splay of the legs (7-1C). Note here also that the spindles have a slight swell below the arm rail, a feature not seen in the two previous Delaware Valley chairs. Rhode Island comb-backs will be somewhat more conservative, and usually are given oval seats. The comb-back in figure 7-1D also has the inward curve in the taper of the lower legs and the baluster turnings in the spindles that are characteristic of Rhode Island Windsors.

7-1A. Pennsylvania comb-back, 1760 – 1775.

7-1B. Pennsylvania comb-back, 1770 – 1780.

7-1C. Connecticut comb-back, 1780 – 1790.

7-1D. Rhode Island comb-back, 1780 – 1790.

7-2 Low-back Windsors. Although frequently seen today as firehouse chairs, in the past low-back Windsors appear to have enjoyed only an early and limited popularity, for period examples are not common. Like most other Windsors, the design originated in Philadelphia, and perhaps two out of three are from this area. Figure 7-2A illustrates an early Philadelphia low-back with cylinder and ball legs and the same great, wide D-shaped seat seen on early comb-back Windsors.

Of the relatively few New England low-backs, many — or perhaps most — will be from Rhode Island like the chair shown in figure 7-2B. Rhode Island low-backs often have these block-and-turned X-form stretchers, a common feature in English Windsors that is also seen in New England corner chairs. Note that while this chair might be said to have cylinder and ball legs, they are quite unlike the Philadelphia cylinder and ball shape. This chair is also uncommon in having an upholstered seat, a feature more often seen in continuous-arm and bow-back Windsors. Like the previous Rhode Island comb-back, there is a row of little vase shaped turnings across the bottom of the spindles, a suggestion of the attention to quality and detail that is so characteristic of Rhode Island workmanship.

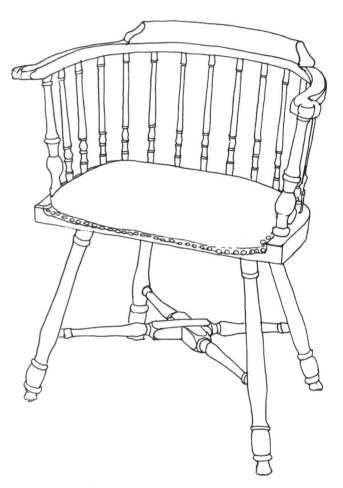

7-2B. Rhode Island low-back, 1760 – 1770.

7-2A. Philadelphia low-back, 1750 – 1770.

7-3 Fan-back Windsors. While the fan-back Windsor also originated in Philadelphia, the number of surviving examples suggests that they became as fashionable in New England as in Pennsylvania. For some reason, they were seldom produced in New York. The name comes from the shape of the back, in which the posts and spindles fan out from the seat. They are the first American Windsors without arm rails, and to provide additional support for the back, many of these chairs are given two extra spindles or braces that run diagonally from the crest rail to a rectangular projection or tailpiece at the back of the seat as shown in figure 7-3A. These chairs are often called brace-backs, even though fan-back in form. To be accurate, one might call them brace-back fan-back Windsors. Later we will see brace-back bow-back Windsors.

The addition of a tailpiece presented the chairmaker with a structural problem, for the normal practice of having the grain of the seat run crosswise could not be used because the narrow tailpiece would then have a cross grain. The simplest solution was to have the grain of the seat run from front to back, but this both wasted wood and required very wide boards. While this was often done, in Philadelphia some Windsor chairmakers would lay out the seats to have the grain run diagonally so that the tailpiece would have a diagonal rather than a cross grain. In New England the solution was to have the seat grain run crosswise as before, then to mortise in a separate tailpiece, the grain running front to back. Sometimes the center spindle in the back is passed through the tailpiece to lock in the joint.

Fan-back armchairs are fairly rare, although some were produced in Philadelphia and in coastal New England. Superficially they resemble comb-backs, except that the arm rail does not extend across the back of the chair. Often the back posts are squared at the junction of the arms to provide a solid bearing surface, although this has not been done on the elegant Philadelphia armchair shown in figure 7-3B. Note that the back of this chair is also braced, even though the arms provide additional support.

The way in which the arms are joined to the posts can help tell us where the chair was made, for if fastened with a wooden pin the chair will probably be from the Philadelphia area, and if fastened with a rosehead nail, then probably New England.

That both of the illustrated chairs are brace-backs should not imply that most fan-backs are braced. Actually, no more than about one in five are given this additional stiffening.

7-3A. New England fan-back, 1770 – 1780.

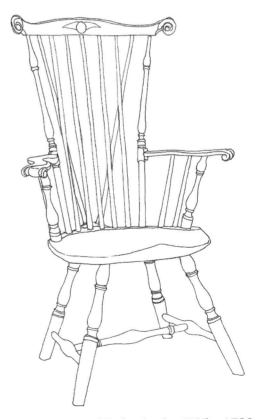

7-3B. Philadelphia fan-back, 1765 – 1780.

101

7-4 Sack-back Windsors. By far the most the most common Windsor armchair is the sack-back shown in figures 7-4A and 7-4B. First produced in Philadelphia in the 1760s, it was being produced everywhere following the Revolution, particularly in New England. By that time, Windsor chairmaking was becoming standardized, and it is not always easy to determine region with this very successful design. The popularity of sack-backs led to much local production, and you will often see remarkably ama-teurish-looking rural versions. It might be noted here that in common with most all comb-backs and all low-backs, all sack-back Windsors are armchairs, so it is not necessary to call a sack-back Windsor a sack-back Windsor armchair.

In addition to regional differences in the shaping of the legs and spindles, there are some features that can help to tell us where a sack-back was made. Philadelphia and New York chairs tend to be rather square and solid-looking with not a great deal of splay in the legs. Being a relatively early design, some Philadelphia chairs retain the three piece sawn arm rail that was employed in Philadelphia low-backs and early comb-backs. A number of Philadelphia sack-backs have mahogany arms, sug-gesting that early Windsors were not always budget chairs. Lancaster County sack-backs, as well as fan-backs and bow-backs, may have cylinder and ball or blunt arrow front legs and tapered back legs as shown in figure 7-4B.

7-4B. Lancaster County sack-back, 1780 – 1790.

7-4A. Philadelphia sack-back, 1770 – 1790.

7-5 Bow-back Windsors. Bow-back Windsors are also very common and also were made just about everywhere, and here again we need to look at the legs and spindles to determine region. The bow-back shown in figure 7-5A was made by Ebenezer Tracy in Lisbon, Connecticut. That it is a Connecticut, or possibly a Rhode Island chair, is suggested by the swell in the spindles.

The first bow-backs were produced in Philadelphia shortly after the Revolution, and here we see the first use of bamboo turned legs and spindles. While bamboo turned legs are found everywhere on later bow-backs, a bow-back with bamboo turned spindles is most likely to be from the Delaware Valley.

In common with fan-back side chairs, bow-backs can use additional back support, and except for those made in Philadelphia, are very apt to be brace-backs. Due their sharply canted backs, New York bow-backs are very often braced. That brace-backs are rare in Philadelphia may be because so many bow-backs from this area have arms which provide additional support for the back. Only in Rhode Island do we also see large numbers of armchairs (7-5B). Note in figure 7-5B that the baluster turned spindles and incurved lower legs that are so commonly seen in Rhode Island Windsors. The arms on these fine chairs are usually made of mahogany.

Figure 7-5C illustrates a Philadelphia bow-back armchair with bamboo turned spindles and the ram's horn arm supports characteristic of this region. The arms of this chair will most probably be fastened to the bow with a mortise and tenon joint.

7-5A. Connecticut bow-back, 1780 – 1800.

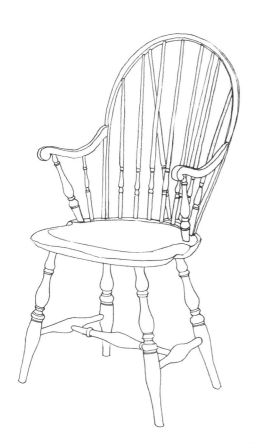

7-5B. Rhode Island bow-back, 1780 – 1800.

7-5C. Philadelphia bow-back, 1790 – 1820.

7-6 Continuous-arm Windsor. The continuous-arm Windsor is not only uniquely American, but is the only major type that was not initially produced in Philadelphia, having been developed in New York in the 1780s. From here production spread north through New England to as far as Massachusetts, but very seldom south to Philadelphia and the Delaware Valley. The complex curved bow that forms both the arms and back on these chairs required real skill to form and most of these chairs came from the centers of Windsor production: New York City, eastern Connecticut, Rhode Island, and eastern Massachusetts. In common with bow-backs, continuous-arm Windsors from New York are apt to be brace-backs and have a pronounced rake to the back. The pronounced swells in the spindles on the continuous-arm Windsor in figure 7-6 suggest the chair was probably made in Connecticut.

7-7 Rod-back Windsors. Rod-backs were the first nineteenth century Windsors, and also the first in which the new fashion of bamboo turnings was integrated into the entire chair such that the back posts, spindles, legs, and stretchers were all bamboo turned. Most are fitted with inexpensive box stretchers and have three bamboo turnings in the legs, the middle housing the front and back stretchers and the bottom housing the side stretchers. Some Philadelphia rod-backs have but two bamboo leg turnings and retain the H-stretchers normally seen on Windsors, and while this is occasionally seen elsewhere, a rod-back with H-stretchers is probably from Philadelphia.

Although some early rod-backs have only a single crest rail, the most common design is the double rail "birdcage" Windsor shown in figure 7-7A in which every second spindle is stopped at the lower rail. These Windsors were produced everywhere in great numbers, and by themselves are no particular indication of region.

The other common form of rod-back has a solid crest rail that rests on top of the posts (7-7B). In New England, and to some limited extent further south, this crest rail was notched or stepped, probably emulating the stepped crest rail found in high style Sheraton chairs of this period. These "step-down" Windsors were extremely popular and were made all over New England, particularly from Massachusetts north into New Hampshire and Maine.

Rod-back Windsors were made everywhere, although relatively-few seem to have been produced in New York and Rhode Island. Sadly, by now it is becoming difficult to tell where a Windsor was made.

7-6. Connecticut continuous-arm Windsor, 1780 – 1800.

7-7A. Birdcage rod-back Windsor, 1800 – 1820.

7-8 Arrow-back Windsor. Arrow-backs are a late development of the rod-back Windsor, the name derived from the arrow-shaped spindles. The posts on these chairs are usually flattened, starting about a third the way above the seat and then tapering over at the top. Because of the taper, they are often called thumb-backs. By the 1820s and 1830s, fewer significant regional differences remained among Windsor chairs, and most arrow-backs are simply identified in auction catalogs as being either from New England or the Middle Atlantic, New England if the seat is made of pine, and the Middle Atlantic if the seat is made of poplar.

By now seats have lost much of their shaping, and the pretty bamboo turnings have been superseded by even simpler ball turnings. Sometimes these turnings can tell us where an arrow-back originated. The ball-cylinder-and-ball shape of the feet on the arrow-back in figure 7-8 was popular in the Philadelphia area. We will see it again later in Sheraton card tables.

7-7B. Step-down rod-back Windsor, 1800 – 1820.

7-8. Pennsylvania arrow-back, 1820 – 1840.

7-9 Balloon and tablet-back Windsors. If you see a late Windsor with either a solid or pierced splat in lieu of turned spindles, you are most probably looking at a chair made in Pennsylvania. The best known of these chairs have the wide curved or balloon back shown in figure 7-9A. The other type has turned posts which are topped with a deep crest rail, and are called tablet-backs. Quite the most distinctive Pennsylvania tablet-backs employ the pierced lyre-shaped "boot-jack" splat illustrated in figure 7-9B. They are often called boot-jack chairs.

By the second quarter of the century there are a bewildering variety of Windsors, for in addition to arrow-backs, balloon-backs, and tablet-backs, we see crown-tops, roll-tops, and slat-backs. The best single source on these many late Windsors is Nancy Goyne Evans's *American Windsor Chairs*. This is quite the best place to look up a nineteenth century Windsor. However, the book is expensive, and you might first try to locate a copy in the reference section of your local public library. If they don't have it, see if you can badger them into purchasing a copy. Tell them every decent library has a copy of this excellent reference book.

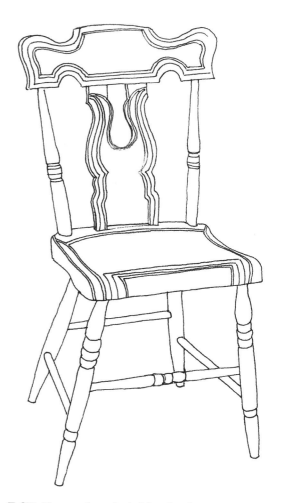

7-9B. Pennsylvania tablet-back, 1840 – 1850.

7-9A. Pennsylvania balloon-back, c. 1860.

7-10 Writing-arm Windsor. Writing-arm Windsors also would seem to be uniquely American. Most are comb-backs like the chair shown in figure 7-10, but there are also low-back, rod-back, bow-back, and arrow-back models. While occasionally produced in the Middle Atlantic, most are from New England, particularly Connecticut; and of the Connecticut chairs, the majority are from the shop of Ebenezar Tracy. The idea of a writing arm may indeed have originated in Connecticut. Although lacking in this example, many of these Windsors have little drawers under the writing surface and under the seat for paper and ink, suggesting that they saw very regular use, and perhaps were seen as a low-cost alternative to a desk.

7-11 Windsor settees. Settees were often produced en suite with sets of chairs, and generally reflect the same regional preferences for type and design that we see in chairs. If we can identify region in a chair, then we can probably identify region in a similar settee. Prior to the Revolution, the most common settees are low-backs with tapered legs produced in and around Philadelphia, like that shown in figure 7-11A. A few of these have the early cylinder-and-ball or blunt arrow legs.

Quite the most common surviving Pennsylvania settees are nineteenth century tablet-backs (7-11B). The median splat above a row of turned spindles shown in this illustration is found everywhere in late Windsors, and by itself is no particular indicator of region. Many of the nineteenth century Pennsylvania settees have the boot-jack splats that we saw earlier in a Pennsylvania tablet-back Windsor side chair (7-9B).

Rod-back settees were made in all regions, but were especially popular in New England. The step-down rod-back in figure 7-11C is typical of a great many produced throughout New England. In New England, when the crest rail does not rest on the top of the posts, it tends to be between them, while in the Middle Atlantic it is more likely to be in front, as shown in the tablet-back Windsor in figure 7-9B. New England settees tend to be lighter and more delicate-looking than Middle Atlantic settees. Also, settees were not popular in New York, and if a settee appears to be a product of the Middle Atlantic, maybe having a poplar seat, then it most probably was made somewhere in or around Philadelphia.

7-10. Connecticut writing-arm, 1780 – 1800.

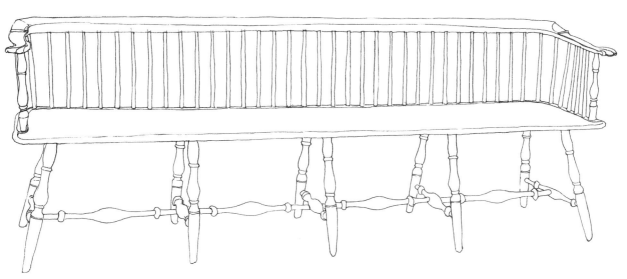

7-11A. Pennsylvania, 31" h x 80" l, 1765 – 1780.

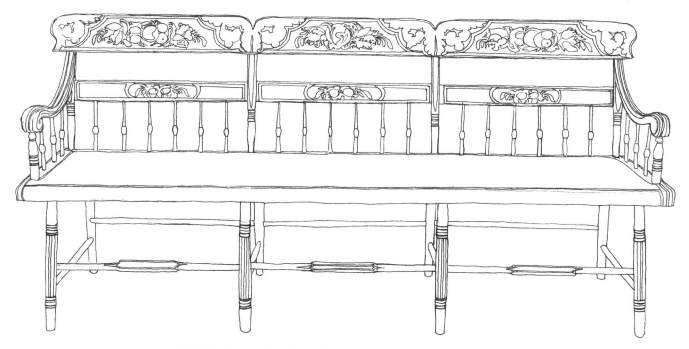

7-11B. Pennsylvania table-back settee, 1820 – 1850.

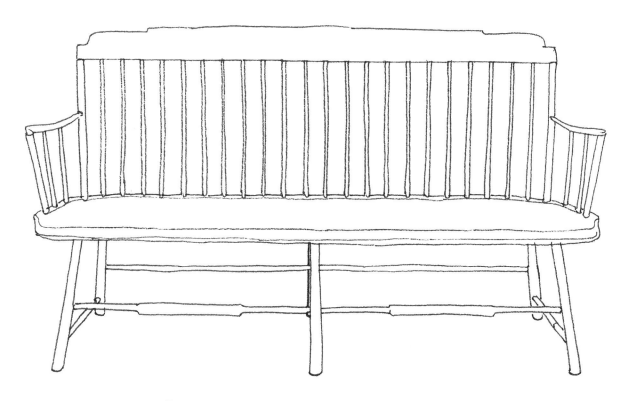

7-11C. New England rod-back settee, 1810 – 1830.

This will not be a long chapter, for in the past, upholstery fabric was hand woven and fairly expensive, and upholstered furniture was relatively rare. Even after the Revolution, fabric covered chairs were only seen in the more prosperous homes. In addition, upholstered chairs provide less opportunity for innovation — there are only a limited number of ways to shape the legs, the arms, and the back of an upholstered chair. Nowhere is there the freedom of design in the carving of a crest rail and in the shaping of a splat.

Nevertheless, determining region is less of a challenge than it might seem, for while an upholsterer normally finished and marketed the final product, the frame of an upholstered chair was made by the same craftsmen that made high style framed chairs, and here we see the same secondary woods, construction practices and design features found in other chairs of the period and region. Not only do the shape of the legs and feet follow regional preferences, but also, local construction practices carry over into the framing, and again we see the cross bracing employed in New Hampshire, the triangular blocking used throughout New England, and the through tenoning so common in the Delaware Valley. In all regions chairmakers employed the same familiar and available secondary woods, and the frame of an upholstered chair can tell us much about region.

It is also a help to remember that upholstered furniture can only originate where both upholstery fabric and upholsterers were available. Rural chairs are seldom upholstered, and when there is some fabric, it will usually be no more than the covering on a slip seat which involved no particular experience and required a minimum of material. A Massachusetts over-upholstered chair will probably be from somewhere in or around Boston or Salem, or up along the North Shore in Newburyport, a New York chair from New York City, or possibly Albany, and a Pennsylvania chair from Philadelphia.

Because there are fewer forms to consider, upholstered chairs will be covered in just two sweeps down the Atlantic seaboard: first upholstered easy or wing chairs, then upholstered open armchairs. Lastly, we will take a brief look at two Empire-style bergere chairs and a Campeche chair. Although I will show you two chairs that are believed to have been made in the South, upholstered chairs from this region are very rare. Unless there is a family history, this region should be your last consideration in determining region.

8-1 New England easy chairs. We will start off with an easy chair in the William and Mary style made in Boston in the first decades of the eighteenth century. Although an early chair, and a very early upholstered chair, a number survive, perhaps because they are so stoutly constructed, many being given the three transverse stretchers shown in figure 8-1A. Similar chairs have turned rather than Spanish feet or omit the front stretcher or have squared cabriole legs. Most are made of soft maple, although as is typical of early furniture, they may have other secondary woods such as oak and chestnut. The arms are unusual for Colonial New England in that they scroll over across the top, then scroll out across the base in Philadelphia fashion.

Scrolled-over arms went out of fashion in New England in the 1730s, and thereafter, until about 1790, New England easy chairs almost always had arms that were flat across the top and then scrolled out in front, as shown in figure 8-1B. Here we see the standard New England Queen Anne easy chair that was so popular a design that it continued to be produced right up into the last decade of the eighteenth century, perhaps a decade after the Revolution. Like the equally successful Boston Queen Anne chair, these handsome easy chairs saw little change in almost half a century of production. In addition to vertically scrolled arms, they typically have an arched crest rail, a flat or slightly rounded front seat, block-and-turned stretchers, and pad or club-footed cabriole legs. Some chairs have the thick pad under the foot that is associated with the Chippendale style in coastal Massachusetts.

The front and side seat rails will be joined by mortise-and-tenon joints, usually the side rails tenoned into the front rail, but sometimes the reverse, the front rail tenoned into the side rails. The front legs are then joined to the rails with either a dovetail tenon at the outside corner where the front and side rails meet, or a square tenon through the center of the mortise-and-tenon joint.

Normally the front legs and stretchers are walnut, the rear legs and stiles a soft maple stained up below the fabric line to resemble walnut. A few chairs are entirely maple or employ birch for the rear legs and stiles. Sometimes the seat rails are made of birch, although usually the entire frame is soft maple, the conical arm supports white pine.

While the great majority of these chairs have block-and-turned stretchers, a rare few have straight or serpentine sawn stretchers, or omit the stretchers altogether. On a few the rear legs are chamfered both above and below the stretchers, a feature not seen on New York easy chairs with block and turned stretchers.

So successful was the Queen Anne style in these chairs that relatively few have the Chippendale ball and claw foot that came into fashion in the 1760s. Ball and claw versions are usually made of mahogany, and here the rear legs will also be made of mahogany. This may have been done because they were made for a wealthier clientele, or perhaps because maple could not be stained up to effectively resemble mahogany.

In Rhode Island, a conservative Chippendale design with Marlborough legs was also fashionable during the late Colonial period (8-1C). Most of these handsome chairs are thought to have been produced in Newport rather than Providence. While this chair has the vertically scrolled New England type of arm, and the stop-fluted legs that were so popular in Rhode Island, others of this type have horizontally scrolled arms and molded legs, this perhaps reflecting a New York influence.

Easy chairs continued in popularity in America after the Revolution, but were modified to be more in keeping with the new Hepplewhite and Sheraton styles. Everywhere the arms now scrolled over and the wings became separate elements attached to the outsides of the arms as shown in figure 8-1D. The legs were somewhat lighter square Marlborough legs, tapered Hepplewhite-style legs, or turned Sheraton legs. The arm scrolls were smaller and the whole feeling was lighter and more neoclassical. Even in New England, stretchers may be omitted. By this time, there was less regional diversity —much less difference between a Federal New England easy chair and a Federal Middle Atlantic easy chair. Here we may need to examine secondary woods and construction to determine region. While most easy chairs were now made of mahogany rather than of walnut, in New England you may see birch that has been stained up to resemble mahogany. The secondary woods are likely to be either birch or soft maple. When the rails are stiffened, we would expect to see nailed triangular blocking.

While Sheraton easy chairs with turned front legs were made to some extent in New England, the Hepplewhite style seems to have been the more favored for easy chairs. This suggests that a Federal Sheraton easy chair is more likely to be from New York or Philadelphia.

Before leaving New England we might note a small group of easy chairs produced in northern coastal Massachusetts and Portsmouth, New Hampshire that are distinguished by the unusual squared serpentine rear leg illustrated in figure 8-1E. Some of these chairs have cabriole rather than Marlborough legs. Others have the English type of cross bracing that is seen in Portsmouth side chairs. Both features probably reflect the presence of English cabinetmakers in Portsmouth.

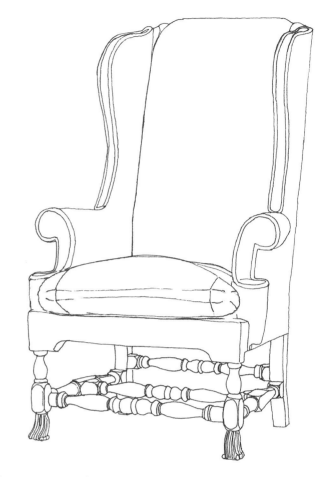

8-1A. New England William & Mary, 49" h, 1720 – 1740.

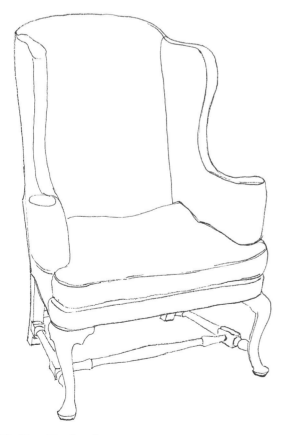

8-1B. New England Queen Anne, 47" h, 1740 – 1790.

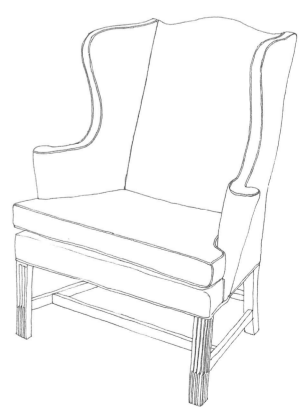

8-1C. Newport Chippendale, 45" h, 1765 – 1790.

8-1D. New England Federal Chippendale, 1780 – 1800.

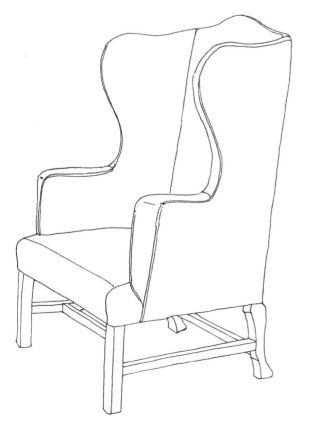

8-1E. Coastal New England Chippendale, 1770 – 1800.

8-2 Middle Atlantic easy chairs. New York furniture from the Colonial period is not common, and easy chairs are unusual. Probably only Southern easy chairs are more rare. Most of the few surviving New York chairs share a mixture of English, Boston, and Philadelphia features. Although you may never encounter one, they are sufficiently distinctive that we might consider two examples.

Both Queen Anne and Chippendale easy chairs are similar to New York side chairs in exhibiting the broad proportions of early Georgian furniture. Arms may either scroll out in New England fashion, or scroll over as was customary in Philadelphia. Although vertically scrolled arms are somewhat more common in New York easy chairs, the Queen Anne chair in figure 8-2A is recognizably a New York product when we consider the generous width of the seat and the very characteristic large, squared slipper foot. Here it might be noted that the seats on New York easy chairs are generally flat across the front in the manner of New England easy chairs.

In figure 8-2B, we see a more typical New York easy chair. This large mahogany chair exhibits the amalgam of Georgian, Boston, and Philadelphia features so often seen in New York chairs. The general proportions are early Georgian; the block and turned stretchers New England; and the scrolled and richly carved front legs Philadelphia. At first glance the turned stretchers would suggest a New England chair, but the square, blocky ball and claw feet are very different from Massachusetts retracted claw feet. Many New York easy chairs do not have stretchers. In addition, they are more likely to be made of mahogany rather than walnut. The secondary woods are usually white or red oak, white pine, and tulip poplar.

Philadelphia Queen Anne and Chippendale easy chairs are very different from their New England counterparts. With a few rare exceptions, the arms scroll over rather than out, horizontally rather than vertically, and the legs are not fitted with stretchers as we see in figure 8-2C. Typically there will be a pronounced bow in the front seat rail. A few have tapering back legs and ovoid feet in lieu of the rounded stump legs shown here. Most Philadelphia chairs are made of mahogany and have the carved legs and ball and claw feet. There are a few Queen Anne style chairs with cabriole legs and either slipper or trifid feet. These chairs, perhaps budget products, are usually made of walnut. They might been seen as an easy chair version of the immensely popular solid splat, trifid foot Chippendale chairs of this period. While Philadelphia Chippendale easy chairs are often illustrated — Winterthur seems to have almost a dozen of them — they are not as common as their New England counterparts, perhaps because in milder Philadelphia there was less reason for such expensive furniture.

The seat rails on Philadelphia easy chairs are similar to those found in Philadelphia Queen Anne chairs in that they are made with relatively wide boards, and the front and side rails are fastened together with a lapped joint. This method of joining the rails is also found in Connecticut and Rhode Island easy chairs, which helps to distinguish them from Massachusetts workmanship. As we might expect, the side rails in Philadelphia easy chairs are frequently tenoned through the stiles, even though the additional quality implied by this type of joint would not show under the fabric, and in any event, would hardly seem necessary in an easy chair.

Although not as well known, easy chairs with both square Chippendale legs and tapered Hepplewhite legs were also made in Philadelphia. Perhaps the most regionally distinctive have the English blocked Marlborough legs so often found in Philadelphia area furniture (8-2D). Blocked feet are sometimes seen in New England, but are so uncommon that a table or chair with blocked feet is most probably from Pennsylvania.

Another type of easy chair that appears to be unique to Philadelphia is a Federal design with an upright curved back that flows around into the wings as seen in figure 8-2E. The wings on these circular or barrel-back chairs may also curve such that they transition smoothly into the circular back. Some of these easy chairs have turned rear legs, an unusual feature seldom seen outside of Philadelphia.

The secondary woods found in Philadelphia easy chairs do not follow the uniform and consistent pattern of secondary woods found in New England easy chairs, and here we often find a mix of woods: white or red oak, walnut, cherry, ash, soft maple, white or yellow pine, and tulip poplar. Sometimes even the left and right seat rails, or the left and right stiles, will be of different woods, giving the impression that Philadelphia cabinetmakers gave little thought to framing, employing any wood that was suitable and available.

The great majority of Federal Sheraton easy chairs are from the Middle Atlantic, perhaps because of the popularity of the Hepplewhite lolling chair in New England, and we might end this section with a typical New York Federal easy chair (8-2F). In addition to the choice of secondary woods, the legs of a Sheraton chair can suggest the place of manufacture if they happen to follow established New York and Philadelphia turning patterns. In the front legs of this chair we see the same turning employed in the feet of a great many New York chairs and tables.

Although there is little documentation, easy chairs in the Sheraton and Hepplewhite styles seem to have been made in Baltimore and Annapolis. In the Winterthur collection there is a Baltimore easy chair with unusual outscrolled and downward sloping arms that may be a characteristic of Baltimore chairs. Should you come across a wing chair with yellow pine or tulip popular rails, it may be a product of one of these cities.

8-2A. New York Queen Anne, 45" h, 1740 – 1770.

8-2B. New York Chippendale, 1750 – 1780.

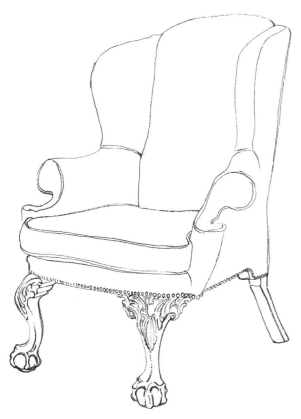

8-2C. Philadelphia Chippendale, 1750 – 1790.

8-2D. Philadelphia Chippendale, c. 1770.

8-2E. Philadelphia Sheraton, 48" h, 1800 – 1815.

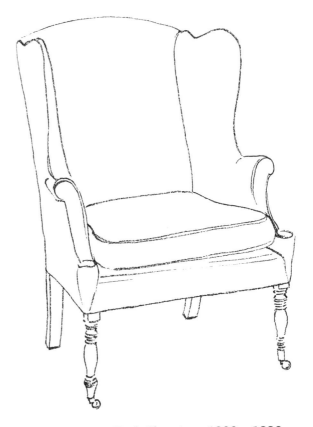

8-2F. New York Sheraton, 1800 – 1820.

8-3 Southern easy chairs. Easy chairs produced south of the Mason-Dixon Line, and particularly, south of Baltimore and Maryland, are so scarce that it is difficult to illustrate a representative example. While I will show you two chairs, they do no more than suggest what we might look for. Nor is it easy to determine specific region, or even to state with certainty that an easy chair is Southern. In the auction catalogs from which these illustrations were selected, the cabriole leg easy chair shown in figure 8-3A was identified as "probably Southern," the Marlborough-leg chair in figure 8-3B as "possibly Virginia." Both exhibit the neat and plain construction characteristic of much Southern furniture, being well made but having little ornamentation. The cabriole-leg chair has just simple pad feet, the Marlborough-leg chair none of the usual molding on the front of the legs. Both chairs have outscrolling arms, a New England feature seldom seen south of New York City, but which is very common in Southern easy chairs. Some cabriole-leg chairs have the oval pad rear feet seen in English and New York chairs. Aside from a general simplicity and stylistic questions, such as the lack of block and turned stretchers on what appears to be a typical New England cabriole leg easy chair, the choice of secondary woods is perhaps the best indication of Southern workmanship, and here you may see cherry, walnut, yellow pine, tulip poplar, and in coastal South Carolina, bald cypress.

8-3A. Southern Queen Anne, 1760 – 1770.

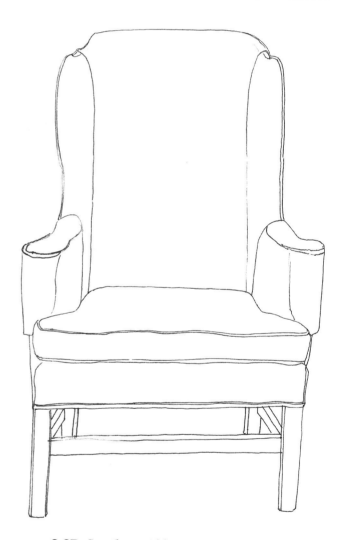

8-3B. Southern Chippendale, c. 1770.

8-4 Massachusetts Chippendale open armchair. Upholstered armchairs, or more correctly, open armchairs, were produced in limited quantities prior to the Revolution. Although made in all regions, they are so scarce that we will confine ourselves to the most common form, and then just touch on another type. Open armchairs are common among English furniture where they are called library armchairs. American examples are generally simpler in execution and somewhat lighter in appearance, usually lacking carving and pierced stretchers, having higher backs, and of course, employing local secondary woods. Most are from either Massachusetts or Rhode Island and have the serpentine crest rail, upholstered arms and molded Marlborough legs shown in figure 8-4. Rhode Island chairs frequently have stop-fluted legs. There are a few grand high-style Philadelphia examples with carved handholds and carved and blocked Marlborough legs.

In addition, a small group of open armchairs in the Queen Anne style were produced in Massachusetts. These typically have high backs with flat or slightly arched crests, unupholstered serpentine arms, cabriole legs ending in pad or club feet, and block-and-turned stretchers. They resemble the Joseph Short type lolling chair shown in figure 8-5B, but have cabriole rather than Marlborough legs. In design, and in secondary woods, they are much like the standard New England Queen Anne easy chair.

8-5 New England lolling chairs. Earlier it was noted that following the Revolution, easy chairs acquired neoclassical features. In much the same way, the open armchair evolved into a lighter, high-backed chair with thinner arms and slender, tapered legs. For a long time, these neoclassical chairs have been called Martha Washington chairs after one purportedly owned by the first First Lady, although the original name of lolling chair is now returning to general use. These handsome upholstered chairs became enormously popular throughout New England, many hundreds being made between 1785 and 1820. Lolling chairs are unique to America, and indeed are our single contribution to the furniture of this period. We will look at three New England examples.

Most lolling chairs were produced in coastal New England, particularly in and around Boston. They typically have high backs with serpentine crests, unupholstered arms, and tapered Hepplewhite legs joined with stretchers, as shown in figure 8-5A. Normally the arms have moderate bows, and the faces of both the arm posts and the legs are molded. The posts usually curve down and out to meet the front legs, although sometimes they are given a reverse curve and terminate either on the top or the outside of the side rails. The front legs are occasionally inlaid with bellflowers, or are given the double taper so often seen in New England card tables. A few omit stretchers. Most are made of mahogany with birch or soft maple frames, although a few are made of cherry, maple, or birch, which was usually stained up to resemble mahogany. Typically the seat rails are reinforced with the triangular pine blocking found in side chairs throughout New England. A few are reinforced with open braces.

Not all open armchairs made a complete transition to the neoclassical. A number of Federal lolling chairs retain the square Marlborough leg. These may also have upholstered arms. While they resemble open armchairs, they were produced after the Revolution and usually exhibit somewhat more neoclassical proportions.

While these are by far the most common types of New England lolling chair, two variations should be mentioned. The first was produced in Essex County and up along the coast in Portsmouth, New Hampshire. These chairs have distinctive outscrolling arms that extend beyond the junction with the arm posts as shown in figure 8-5B. Lolling chairs of this type are often ascribed to Joseph Short of Newburyport, although he was probably only one of a number of makers of these handsome chairs.

As with other lolling chairs, the arm posts on these chairs may be joined to the front legs, or to the top or side of the rails. When a post terminates on the outside of the rail, there will sometimes be a decorative scroll at the base as shown in this illustration. These scrolls, a feature of Newburyport area furniture, are also found in Portsmouth Chippendale armchairs. Similar chairs made in Portsmouth are apt to have the seat rails cross braced in the English manner. Naturally, they are credited to the shop of Robert Harrold.

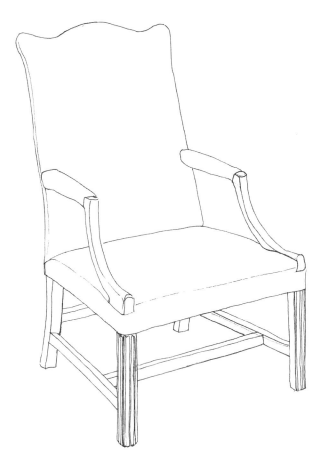

8-4. Massachusetts Chippendale open armchair, 1760 – 1785.

The second variation is likewise ascribed to an individual, in this case Lemuel Churchill of Boston. These chairs are distinctively different from the normal lolling chair, lacking stretchers and having serpentine arm posts that curve over to meet the tops of the legs and high-bowed backs that flare out toward the tops as seen in figure 8-5C. Unlike the preceding chair, they are so consistent in their design that they may indeed be the product of a single maker.

A few lolling chairs were produced with slip seats rather than the normal overupholstery. They seem to have been made this way so that the chair could be fitted with a chamber pot, a feature more often seen in easy chairs which have seat cushions to hide the covers of the pots.

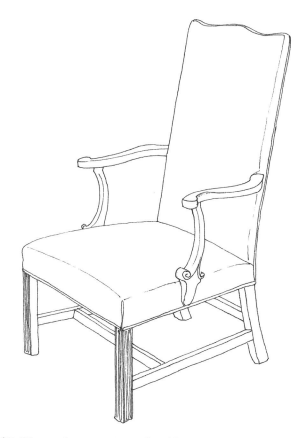

8-5B. Massachusetts Hepplewhite, 42" h, 1785 – 1805.

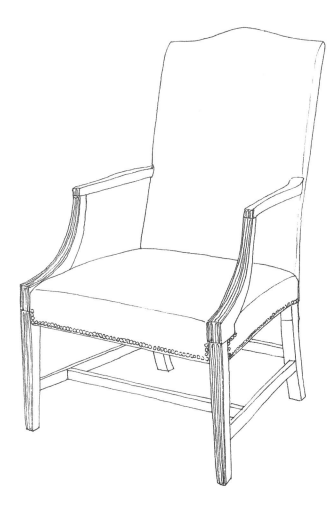

8-5A. Massachusetts Hepplewhite, 1780 – 1820.

8-5C. Massachusetts Hepplewhite, c. 1805.

8-6 Middle Atlantic lolling chair. Lolling chairs are not only unique to America, they are also pretty much unique to northern New England. For some reason, their popularity did not extend very far south of Massachusetts, and examples from New York and Philadelphia are fairly rare. The Philadelphia chair illustrated in figure 8-6 is what we might expect from this area, being somewhat wider and less vertical than the typical Massachusetts chair. The design is also somewhat old fashioned; the arms retain their upholstery and the legs do not have a neoclassical taper. In form, this chair is very similar to both the Massachusetts Chippendale open armchair that we saw earlier, and also to the simpler sort of English library armchair. Here we might examine construction and secondary woods to determine region — and possibly nationality. New England lolling chairs are usually framed up with birch and soft maple, and the seat is reinforced with triangular blocking. A Philadelphia chair of this period is likely to employ oak, ash, cherry, and tulip poplar, and the side rails are likely to be tenoned through the stiles. The frame of a library armchair will usually be made of beech. It will very often have some worm damage.

8-7 Bergere chairs. Bergere is a French term for an upholstered chair with a low, curved back. American examples are not common, perhaps because of the difficulty in framing the curved back. Production of these high-style chairs seems to have been limited to the major urban centers — Boston, New York, and Philadelphia. Most appear to be from New York and are Empire in style, which might be expected, for by the first decades of the nineteenth century New York was both very style conscious and was rapidly becoming the largest and wealthiest city in America. Figure 8-7A illustrates a typical New York City Empire bergere with an exposed mahogany frame, turned and reeded legs, and scrolled over handholds. In common with much New York Federal furniture, these chairs are quite large in scale. They are not really bergere chairs, for the back does not curve down and around as shown in the next illustration. Instead, the back will usually be either gently rounded as shown here, or square across like the back of a Federal sofa.

While there may be fewer Massachusetts bergeres, they are far better known, this because of a set of 30 chairs made in 1797 by George Bright for the Senate Chamber of the new Massachusetts State House. The mahogany bergere in figure 8-7B is either one of these celebrated tub chairs or a very similar Boston example; similar, because this chair lacks the brass swiveling castors seen on the State House chairs. Philadelphia bergeres are similar in design and scale to Boston bergeres except that their front legs exhibit local turning patterns, and the squared section where the front legs join the seat rail is sometimes decorated with a carved tablet. Some Philadelphia bergeres have turned rear legs, a feature seldom seen outside of Philadelphia.

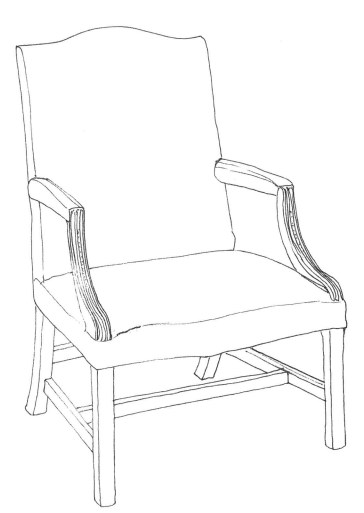

8-6. Philadelphia Chippendale, 42" h, 1770 – 1790.

8-7A. New York Empire bergere, 1800 – 1830.

8-8 Campeche chair. Lastly, there is an unusual type of easy chair that will be discussed with upholstered chairs, even though it is mostly a sawn and shaped chair, more the product of the cabinetmaker rather than the combined efforts of cabinetmaker and upholsterer. This is the Campeche chair illustrated in figure 8-8. Most American Campeche chairs are armchairs and are made of walnut. While considered a Southern form, these chairs are as much Caribbean as they are Southern, for they were also produced in the West Indies. In the collection at Winterthur is a mahogany armchair that appears to have been made in New York, although it might have been produced for export. The name itself seems to have come from the city of Campeche on the west coast of the Yucatan peninsula. That the armchair shown here is an American product — and also a product of the South — is suggested by the use of walnut. A Campeche chair made in the Caribbean would probably be made of a tropical hardwood. Most of these unusual but comfortable chairs were probably made in the first half of the nineteenth century. Neoclassical chairs with the same "Grecian cross" form of leg were being produced in New York during the second decade of the nineteenth century.

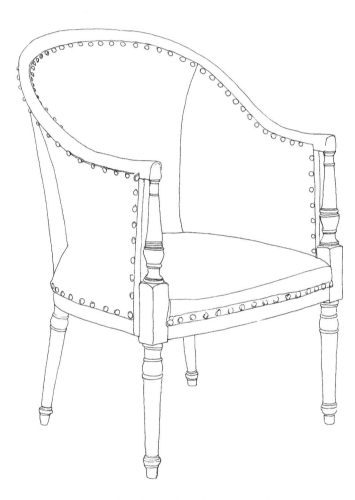

8-7B. Boston Sheraton bergere, c. 1800.

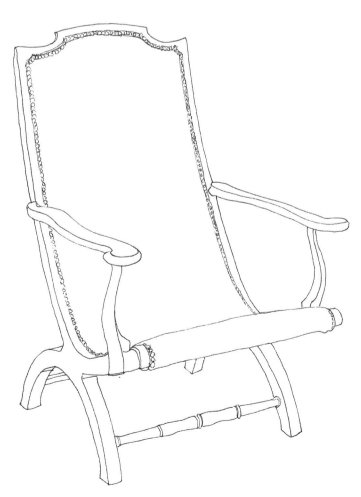

8-8. Campeche chair, 1800 – 1850.

This chapter will also be short, for upholstered sofas were even more costly than upholstered chairs, and are correspondingly less varied and less common. American Queen Anne settees are very rare, and there are no more than a relative handful of Chippendale sofas that predate the Revolution. Sofas did not become common until well into the Federal period when the economy was rapidly expanding and more people were able to afford upholstered furniture. By the late Federal or classical period, sofas were found in many homes, but by that time there were fewer regional differences among American furniture, and it is not always easy to determine the source of a classical sofa.

For the most part, the local secondary woods and regional construction methods that carried over into the making of easy chairs are also seen in sofas. These are particularly useful in determining the source of sofas. In a general way, the stiles, rails, and medial braces of Massachusetts and New Hampshire sofas will be made of birch or soft maple, in New York of ash or poplar, and in Philadelphia of poplar or red oak. Medial braces in New York sofas are frequently made of cherry, as they are in Federal chairs. In common with easy chairs, the frames of Philadelphia sofas are apt to employ a wide variety of woods, and in addition to poplar and red oak, we may also find birch, yellow pine, and soft maple. The presence of yellow pine or poplar would also suggest a Southern origin, most probably Baltimore. Seat bracing is also regional: Massachusetts sofas tend to have triangular nailed blocking, and New York and Philadelphia, glue blocking or cross braces. The seat rails on Philadelphia sofas are apt to be through tenoned.

The reader will notice that this survey ends in Federal Baltimore, for below the Mason-Dixon Line there are almost no surviving sofas from any period. This is probably due to a combination of factors: the rural character of the South, the lesser popularity of upholstered furniture in a hot climate, and in particular, the years of grinding poverty that followed the Civil War. Most of the value of a sofa is in the fabric, and once that is gone, there is little worth saving.

9-1 Camelback sofas. The first sofa produced in significant quantities in America was a standard Chippendale design having high outward-scrolling arms and a sweeping serpentine or camelback crest. Although made to some extent in all urban centers, camelback sofas seem to have been most popular in Philadelphia, and here, as shown in figure 9-1A, the legs were often given the blocked feet so often seen in furniture from the Delaware River Valley. In some the back is a separate frame that rests in slots in the back legs, which then is screwed to the rear of the arms and seat rail. This probably was done to simplify upholstering. However, this construction was neither a Philadelphia innovation nor an assurance of Philadelphia workmanship, for the same feature is found in English sofas of this period.

In common with easy chairs, camelback sofas continue in fashion well into the Federal period; here they also acquired neoclassical features, becoming lighter and being given tapering legs in the new Hepplewhite style. They were produced in all regions, and are as likely to be from New York or New England as Philadelphia. The New York sofa illustrated in figure 9-1B is typical of these later camelback sofas. The back on this sofa appears excessively high because the sofa is missing its thick seat cushion.

There are few obvious regional differences among late camelback sofas, although in New York they are apt to have spade feet, and in Connecticut they are likely to have cherry legs and stretchers. On others it may be necessary to examine construction and secondary woods to determine region.

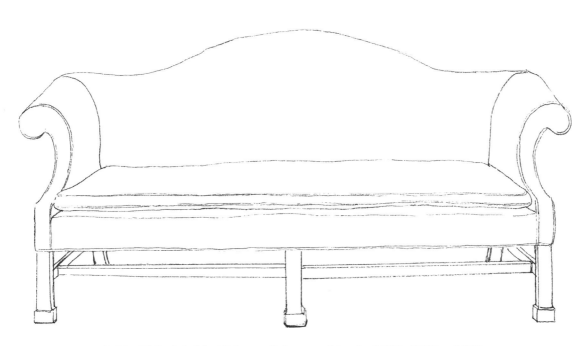

9-1A. Philadelphia Chippendale camel-back, 89" 1, 1760 – 1800.

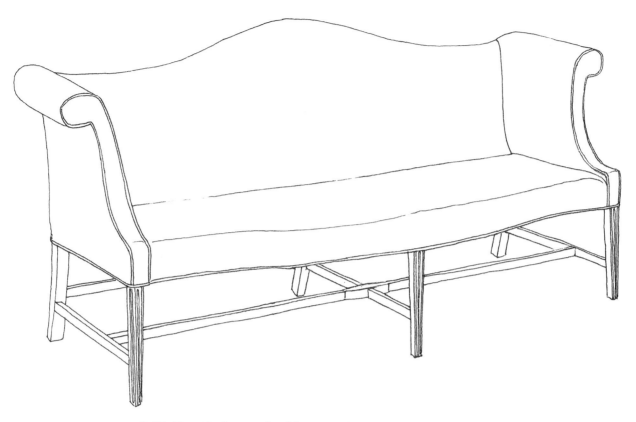

9-1B. New York Hepplewhite camel-back, 87" l, 1780 – 1810.

9-2 Federal cabriole sofas. American sofas with curved or cabriole backs are not common, perhaps because they were more expensive than the conventional square-back sofa, being difficult to frame and upholster. Cabriole-back sofas are also somewhat earlier and usually have Hepplewhite legs, which when made in New York were apt to be given spade feet. Most are from either Boston or New York.

We will look at two examples, the first probably made in Massachusetts about 1790 (9-2A), the second produced a few years later in New York (9-2B). The former sofa is more representative of the type, having a fully upholstered back with no exposed wood other than the molded Hepplewhite legs. The New York sofa is one of a small group of high-quality New York cabriole sofas, and is typical of New York Federal sofas in having the arms and back bordered in mahogany. The spade feet also suggest New York City workmanship.

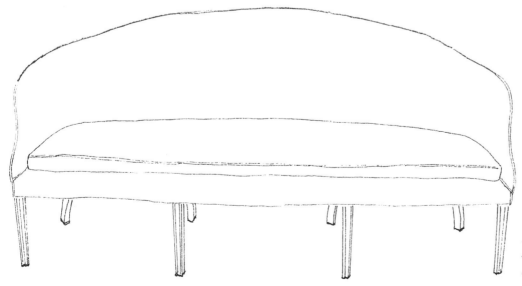

9-2A. New England Hepplewhite cabriole, 38" h x 78" l, c. 1790.

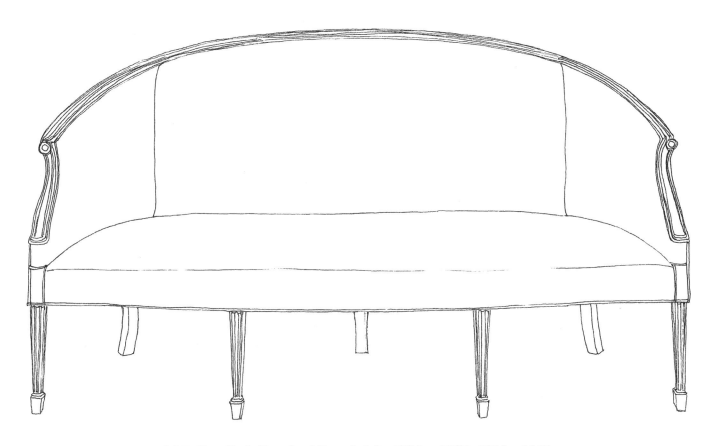

9-2B. New York Hepplewhite cabriole, 39" h x 72" l, 1800 – 1815.

9-3 Federal square-back sofas. Federal neoclassical sofas with square backs are so common that we will look at almost a dozen examples from New England, New York, Philadelphia, and Baltimore. In most of these sofas the front legs are carried up past the seat rails to form arm posts which terminate in scrolled over handholds. The great majority are Sheraton in style with turned and reeded legs, and here the shape of the legs and feet can suggest where the sofa was produced.

Not all front legs on square-back sofas carry up to arm posts. Simpler, less costly sofas were made in New England with the Hepplewhite legs and stretchers seen in later camelback sofas, but with the high serpentine back and scrolled over arms replaced by a more linear neoclassical shape (9-3A). While still somewhat Chippendale in form, and sometimes identified as such, these inexpensive sofas postdate the Revolution, and were produced right up into the first decade of the nineteenth century. The rather high arms and resulting boxy appearance are typical of New England Federal sofas.

Figures 9-3B and 9-3C illustrate two of the more common designs among many Massachusetts square-back sofas. Typically these have turned front legs that continue upward to form bulbous turned and reeded arm posts. There will be a pronounced opening between the posts and the front edges of the arms. Very often, as seen in both these illustrations, the frame will be decorated with inlaid rectangular tablets of figured birch or maple where the leg is squared to meet the front and side rails. Some-

times the entire crest rail will be veneered in light woods. Such a treatment would suggest the North Shore of Massachusetts or Portsmouth, New Hampshire, where light wood inlays were very much in fashion.

On better work the legs of these sofas will be reeded and given brass castors. The tops of the arms and the crest rail may be exposed, although this is not as common as in New York. When there is a mahogany crest rail, it will often be curved on the sides, and then be raised in the middle to enclose an inlaid rectangular panel of lighter wood as shown in figure 9-3C. In the best quality Salem work this panel is often decorated with a carved basket of fruit and flowers. The carving will normally have a star-punched background. Note in both these figures that while the arms sweep down to the handholds, the sweep is rather shallow and the arms are quite high. These deep arms may not be so much a question of style as a reflection on the bitter New England winters.

A few Federal sofas have the outswept saber legs seen in so many late Federal chairs. Most all are thought to be from Massachusetts, which would suggest that a saber-leg sofa could be assigned to either Boston or Salem.

Before leaving New England, we should look at one of a group of unusual sofas or settees made in Portsmouth, New Hampshire (9-3D). These have open arms, the openings being filled with a variety of decorative spindles. The inlaid rectangles of lighter woods in the crest rail of this handsome settee are typical

121

of North Shore and New Hampshire tastes. Although these settees appear to have been produced relatively late in the Federal period, they retain the lightness of the best neoclassical workmanship.

New York Federal sofas, like New York Federal chairs, are characterized by a general high quality of workmanship. Usually both the arms and crest rails are exposed mahogany, and the crest rails are frequently decorated with carving. Most often a crest rail is divided into three elongated rectangular tablets embellished with carved swags, bowknots, reeds, and ears of wheat within each tablet. The ends of the arms are often shaped in three dimensions, curving in and down toward the handholds. A front seat rail is generally reeded and bowed at the ends, then tenoned into the front of the leg posts as shown in figure 9-3E. A few sofas have overupholstered seat rails. While sofas of the type shown in figure 9-3E are frequently attributed to the shop of Duncan Phyfe, they were a standard form produced in a number of shops. One is labeled by Michael Allison. That these sofas were produced in considerable quantity again illustrates the wealth of Federal New York, for with the carved crest rails, three-dimension shaped and reeded arms, curved and reeded front rails, and then reeded legs with brass casters, they must have been expensive pieces of furniture.

When the front seat rail of a New York sofa is flat and tenoned into the side of the posts, the squared section of the post may be either carved or left plain, but will not be inlaid with a lighter wood as was normal practice in New England. Exposed rails and arms are normally reeded, a feature often seen in New York chairs of this time. Most New York sofas have exposed crest rails; a square-back sofa having a fabric crest rail will most probably be from either New England, or possibly, Pennsylvania. Most New York sofas have turned and reeded Sheraton legs; a few have inlaid Hepplewhite legs, and a few the carved animal paw feet seen in high-style chairs. The feet on Sheraton legs generally follow the standard New York pattern of a pronounced swell at the top of the foot, then terminate in brass castors as shown in figure 9-3E. Lastly, the arms exhibit a more pronounced down sweep than is found in Massachusetts. They avoid the boxy look seen in many New England sofas.

Before leaving New York City we should look at a lighter, and in some ways, more elegant sofa (9-3F). Sofas of this type differ from the more common Duncan Phyfe type in having raised, carved rectangular tablets centered in the crest rails, straight rather than incurved arms, carved tablets on the squared sections of the posts, and upholstered seat rails that are tenoned into the sides of the leg posts. Some have Hepplewhite rather than Sheraton legs. These sofas are also frequently attributed to the work of a single shop, that of the firm of Slover and Taylor, but this may be no more than an educated supposition, for I am not aware of any labeled examples.

Although neoclassical sofas are not nearly as common in Philadelphia as in New York, we will again consider two examples, the first attributed to the Haines-Connelly School (9-3G), the second a more typical Philadelphia-area sofa (9-3H). Both have turned and reeded legs that terminate in standard Philadelphia Sheraton feet. Hepplewhite legs are rarely seen in Philadelphia sofas, perhaps because Philadelphia was slow to adopt the new neoclassical styles. Hepplewhite may have been out of fashion by the time these sofas began to be produced in Philadelphia.

In common with Haines-Connelly type chairs, the Haines-Connelly type sofa, with its unusual incurving carved arm posts, appears to have been unique to Philadelphia. In other respects, this sofa, with its exposed crest rail and down curving arms, is similar in form to New York sofas.

The second sofa is more typical of Philadelphia sofas, although again it is not unlike New York City workmanship. Note, however, that while the seat rail is bowed, it is a shallow bow. The ends of the rail are tenoned into the sides rather than the fronts of the leg posts. Also, the rail is veneered rather than reeded. The squared section of the post is then decorated with carving set within a rectangular tablet, a feature seen in some New York sofas, but not in New England. The same carving is seen in Philadelphia chairs. While this sofa is fitted with brass casters, they are not nearly as common in Philadelphia as in New York. The overall impression is that of a conservative and somewhat budget conscious New York product.

Perhaps the most striking aspect of Philadelphia sofas is how few there seem to be in comparison to New York City sofas. Should you encounter a neoclassical square-back sofa without any particular regional characteristics, but one that is definitely not a New England product, it will most probably be from New York City.

Lastly, we should consider a Southern neoclassical sofa, and here the most likely candidate will be a square-back sofa from Baltimore. At first, glance, the sofa in figure 9-3I, with its reeded downswept arms and bowed seat rail, would seem to be a New York product. However, it is very different, although the reeded arms and veneered seat rail are probably New York and Philadelphia influences. The large reeding on the crest rail is similar in feeling to the large triple round molding seen in many classical Baltimore dining and card tables. More characteristic of Baltimore are the legs with their oversize outset reeding and ring turned feet. In addition, the exuberant reeded melon shape in the arm supports is quite unlike the restrained baluster seen in Middle Atlantic and New England sofa.

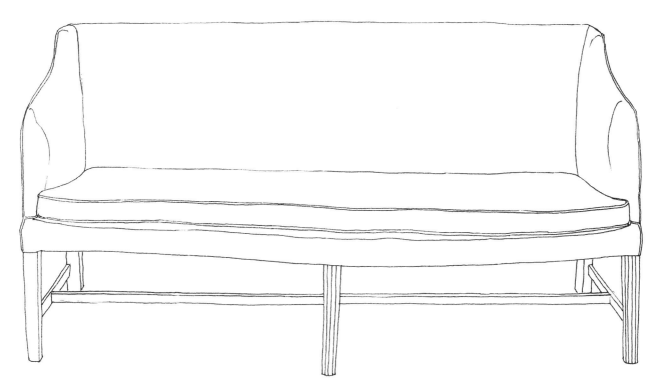

9-3A. New England Hepplewhite, 37" h x 75" l, 1780 – 1810.

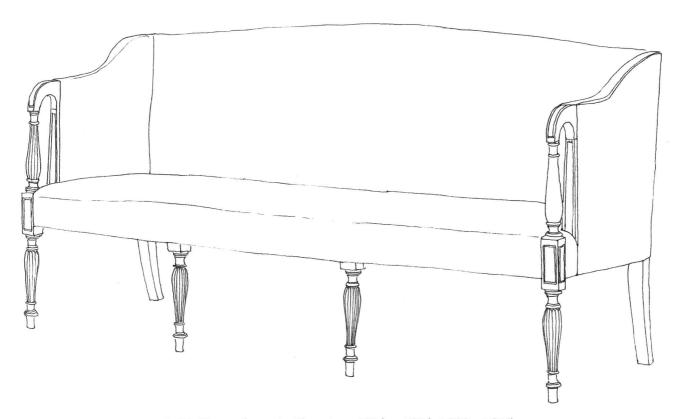

9-3B. Massachusetts Sheraton, 36" h x 72" l, 1800 – 1815.

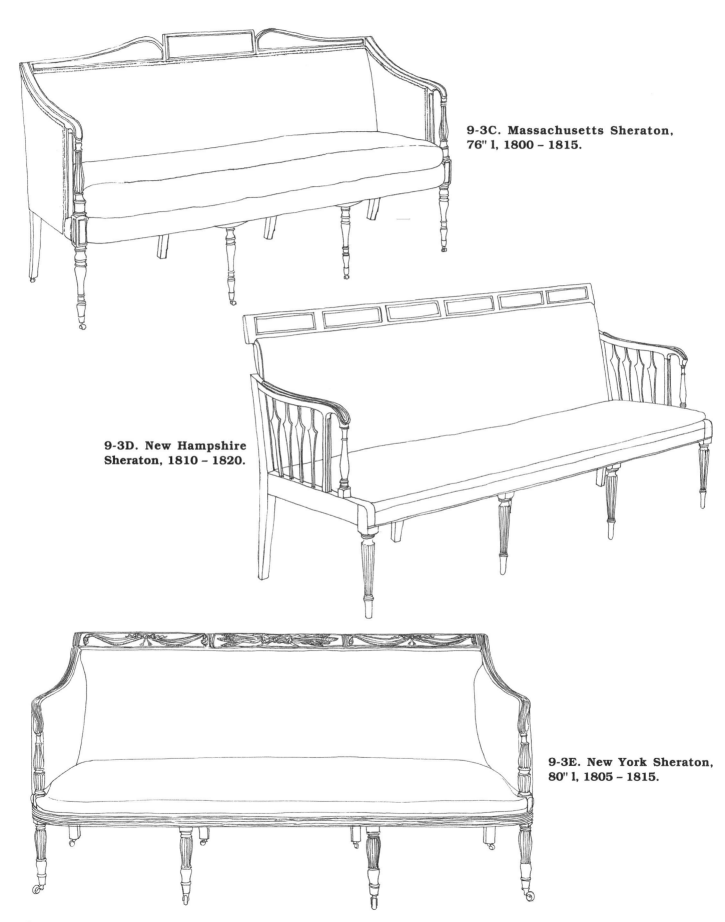

9-3C. Massachusetts Sheraton, 76" l, 1800 – 1815.

9-3D. New Hampshire Sheraton, 1810 – 1820.

9-3E. New York Sheraton, 80" l, 1805 – 1815.

9-3F. New York Sheraton, 78" l, c. 1805.

9-3G. Philadelphia Sheraton, 75" l, c. 1815.

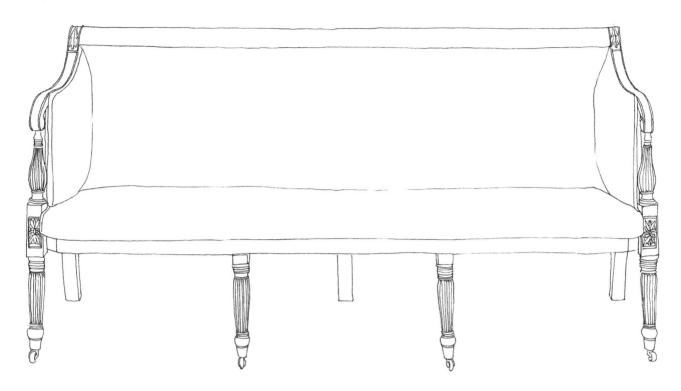

9-3H. Philadelphia Sheraton, 1800 – 1810.

9-3I. Baltimore Sheraton, 1800 – 1810.

9-4 Classical sofas. We will just touch on classical sofas, for by the second decade of the nineteenth century, there were precious few regional differences among upholstered urban furniture. Even scholars have difficulty identifying late Federal sofas, and it is not unusual to find one of these sofas cataloged as being from "Philadelphia or Baltimore," or identified simply as "American." The easiest to identify tend to be the earliest that still retain some fashionable neoclassical features. Massachusetts sofas are apt to have the spiral-carved rails and arm supports found in many New England classical table legs (9-4A). The crest rails on the best Salem work frequently incorporate carved baskets of fruit

or grapevines on a star-punched background. New York sofas tend to have the reeded seat rails and arm supports seen in New York square-back sofas, and if given the ubiquitous classical paw feet, then either carved eagle's wings (9-4B) or cornucopia on the legs. The crest rails on early models may retain the three elongated carved tablets that we saw earlier in a Sheraton square-back sofa. Later rectangular tablets tend not to have carving and simply scroll over. Philadelphia classical sofas either by — or of the School of — Anthony Quervelle can be distinguished by elaborate openwork carved scroll and leaf returns on the legs (9-4C). Note that all three of these sofas are very similar in general form.

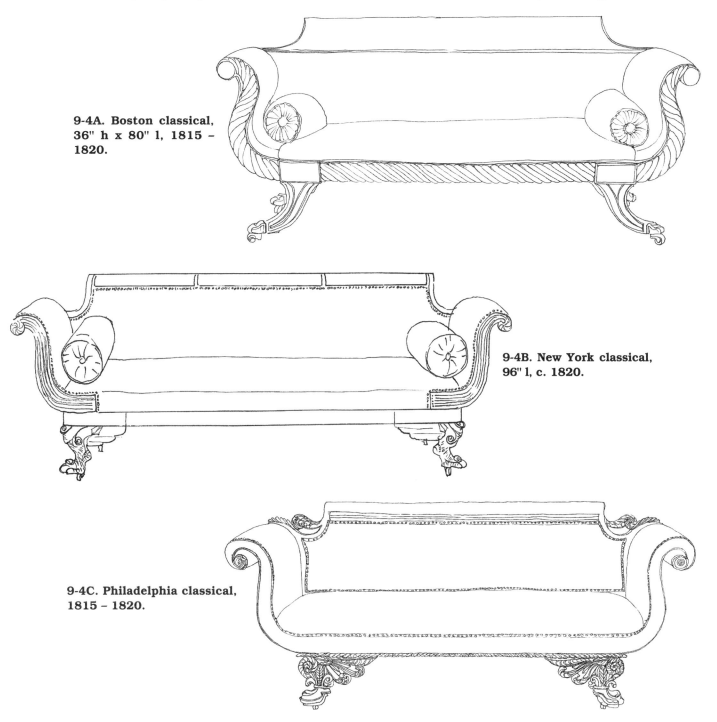

9-4A. Boston classical, 36" h x 80" l, 1815 – 1820.

9-4B. New York classical, 96" l, c. 1820.

9-4C. Philadelphia classical, 1815 – 1820.

Chapter 10 – Chests and Chests over Drawers

This first chapter on case furniture covers chests and chests over drawers, that is, lift-top chests and lift-top chests having one or more drawers each underneath the bin. It is a logical place to start, not only because chests are the simplest case furniture, but also because they are by far the oldest type of case furniture, already ancient when Europeans first settled in America.

Although now seen mostly in children's bedrooms as containers for toys, and elsewhere as mothproof summer storage for woolens, chests were once the primary furniture for storing linens and clothes. Except in the South, chests survive in enormous numbers. Well into the nineteenth century they were quite the most common case furniture. This was a time when most people had no more than a few sets of clothes, perhaps two for work (the second for Monday wash) and one for Sunday best, and for this a good-sized chest was quite adequate. Small personal items were kept in a lidded till just under the top, which is usually located on the left side, suggesting that right-handed people preferred the till on the left and left-handed people preferred it on the right.

Chests resist positive identification. Except for the early Pilgrim Century chests, which have been intensively studied, and those whose decoration has been associated with a particular individual or area, they are difficult to place more closely than region. While paneled chests were the provenance of the joiner, and dovetailed chests required some measure of cabinet-making experience, the simple six-board variety required no more tools than those available to the carpenter, and could be made anywhere suitably wide planks were available — which was almost everywhere. However, there are marked regional differences, and it is usually not difficult to tell if a chest is from New England or the Middle Atlantic or the South.

Most chests were made of softwood and painted. Many are grain painted, or are decorated with a pattern of vines and flowers, or divided into panels enclosing flowers and mythical animals. The illustrations in this chapter are at some disadvantage here, for not only are pen and ink drawings a poor venue for painted furniture; but also, paint is infinitely flexible in color and pattern, and among paint decorated chests there are far too many local schools to ever be covered in a single chapter. However, in design, materials, and construction, a chest can tell us much about where it may have originated. If you need further help, I would suggest Dean Fale's *American Painted Furniture 1680 – 1880* or Cynthia Schaffner and Susan Klein's *American Painted Furniture*. These two books illustrate, in color, dozens of painted chests from all regions.

The great majority of chests are rural products and exhibit the style lag so often seen in country furniture. The William and Mary ball foot and the Queen Anne or Chippendale bracket foot were used on chests well into the nineteenth century, and thereafter, Empire feet were employed until at least the middle of the century. Large chests complete with William and Mary style base moldings and ball feet were being produced in Ohio in the 1850s. Aside from the early New England paneled chests, there is so much overlap that I will simply cover chests by region, commencing first with New England, then the Middle Atlantic, and finally the South; beginning with the earliest New England

Jacobean paneled chests and ending with the advent of Empire, which in some ways brings us back to where we started, for once again we see chests with lathe turned feet.

10-1 New England paneled chests. New England is an appropriate place to start, for no other region produced so many chests and chests over drawers in such diversity in design and construction. We will begin with the joiner's paneled chest, the first New England case work to survive in significant numbers. While these Jacobean style chests were produced to some extent in all regions, most surviving examples are from New England, from coastal Massachusetts, Connecticut, and the Connecticut River Valley. Later we will see other paneled chests, but in general, if you encounter a chest constructed of thin panels set within grooved stiles and rails, and if it appears to be very old, you are most probably looking at a chest from somewhere in New England.

Early paneled chests were the product of the joiner who split oak into billets to form rails and stiles. These were given mortise and tenon joints and grooved on the inner edges to hold the panels. Normally the stiles extend down to provide feet. The joints are locked with oak pins. In Massachusetts, the top was usually a single wide board of very hard pine stiffened by cleats at the ends and hinged at the back with forged snipe hinges. The source of the hard pine has been the subject of endless speculation, but now it is thought to have been pitch pine (*Pinus rigida*), a heavy, soft resinous pine that becomes exceedingly hard as the wood seasons and the resin dries out. Except for a few Connecticut and Pennsylvania chests, the top will be made of a single board. In England and in Europe, where wide boards were not as available, tops were usually paneled.

Normally the front of these chests will be divided into three or four panels, although there are a few with five. Many are quite simple, having no more decoration than a little molding worked into the stiles and rails as seen in the chest in figure 10-1A. When more was desired, the front panels might be given geometric moldings and the stiles and rails decorated with ebonized split spindles and egg-shaped bosses as shown in the Essex County chest in figure 10-1B. The spindles and bosses were just glued on, and often have been lost over the years. Many of these old chests are but a fragment of their former glory, retaining only portions of the geometric moldings.

The other treatment was to decorate the front panels with shallow carving as shown in the Massachusetts chest in figure 10-1C. This type of carving was particularly fashionable in Connecticut and in coastal Essex County, Massachusetts. These Pilgrim Century chests have been the subject of much study, and sometimes it is possible to identify the maker from the design of the carving. Although made of oak, or a mix of oak and pine, these "joyned" chests are not as massive as they would seem, for the panels themselves are quite thin.

Quite the best known early paneled chests are a considerable group that was made in the Connecticut River Valley between Hartford, Connecticut, and Deerfield, Massachusetts, between about 1680 and 1740. Today they are known as Hadley chests, from one identified in Hadley, Massachusetts, although they might more accurately be called Connecticut River Valley chests. The Hadley chest is unusual in the amount of carving; the entire face of the chest, the rails, the stiles, and the panels are covered with shallow carving, as shown in figure 10-1D. While now usually missing, this carving was then highlighted with red, black, or green paint applied to the raised, that is, uncarved, surfaces.

Hadley chests often carry the initials of the owner, but these seem to have been hope chests rather than dower chests, for the initials that have been identified are those of young women. So well documented are these chests that they are sometimes identified simply by the carved initials. The chest shown here would be the "RD" Hadley chest. Most of the 150 or so surviving chests are actually chests over drawers, each having one and sometimes two drawers worked in under the bin, as shown in this illustration.

While too rare to warrant illustration, it might be noted that slightly earlier, somewhat similar "sunflower"-type chests were made just to the south in Wethersfield, Connecticut. These normally have spindle-decorated stiles and two drawers faced with the egg-shaped bosses shown earlier. The name comes from the distinctive tulip and sunflower carving on the panels, although there is some thought that the sunflowers are actually stylized Tudor roses. Interestingly, the tops of both Hadley and sunflower chests are usually made of a hard pine of the taeda group, for Southern yellow pine grew north into the Connecticut River Valley. Also, some early Connecticut chests have tops made of oak, so an oak rather than a pine top is not a sure indication of English workmanship.

Although these paneled chests and chests over drawers are now very old, they are surprisingly common, a tribute perhaps to the almost indestructible oak frame and mortise and tenon construction, and also perhaps because a large old chest could always find use in the barn. That many of these early chests are now lacking their feet and lower drawers suggests this very environment.

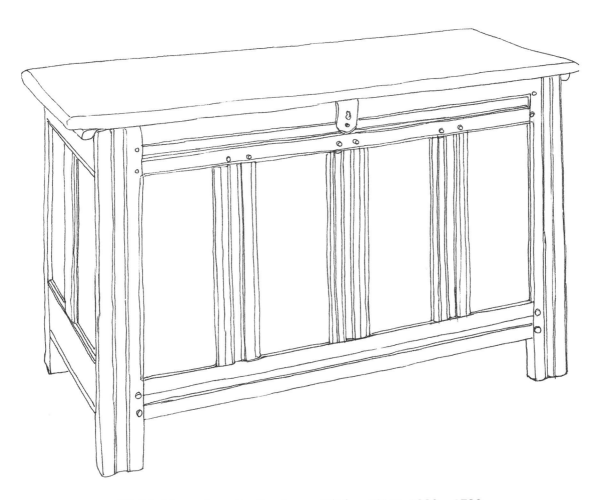

10-1A. Massachusetts Jacobean, 25" h x 43" w, 1660 – 1720.

10-1B. Massachusetts Jacobean, 31" h x 55" w, 1680 – 1720.

10-1C. Massachusetts Jacobean, 27" h x 44" w, c. 1700.

10-1D. Massachusetts Hadley-type Jacobean, 37" h x 45" w, 1680 – 1740.

10-2 New England ball-foot chests. While New England William and Mary ball-foot chests of drawers are uncommon, stylistically similar chests over drawers survive in considerable numbers, in part because many are not as old as they would seem, for they continued to be produced right up into the middle of the eighteenth century. The form is region specific, for tall ball-foot chests over drawers would appear to be unique, or perhaps almost unique, to New England. Most are made of pine, some with maple drawer fronts, and a few entirely maple. The turned feet will normally be maple or ash. There is considerable variation among these old chests, and here we might consider three examples.

Unlike many later New England chests over drawers, the upper section is almost always faced with simulated drawers. Normally this was done by carrying the William and Mary style convex single- or double-arched moldings that frame the real drawers upward to simulate two additional drawers as shown in figure 10-2A. The illusion was completed by giving these drawers their own brass pulls and escutcheons. They were so neatly integrated into the design that it is easy to find oneself foolishly tugging at a dummy drawer.

This example has bun feet all around, but more often than not, you will notice that the cabinetmaker saved a little time and money, and perhaps provided a little more strength, by turning only the front feet. The rear feet were formed by simply extending the sides of the case under the base molding, as is evident in the Connecticut chest over drawers in figure 10-2B. While a common feature of early New England casework, this economy is not unique to this time or place, for is found in both chests and chests of drawers from all regions well into the nineteenth century. Also note here that the upper "drawer" is divided into two smaller drawers. While this English feature is more common in Middle Atlantic and Southern furniture, it is also seen in early New England case work.

Most ball-foot chests over drawers have two simulated drawers over two real drawers, but you will also see three over two, two over three, and even two or three simulated drawers over one real drawer. An alternative arrangement seen on early New England chests over drawers is to have the two simulated top drawers divided by a narrow surface which carries uppermost escutcheon (10-2C). Sometimes this area is given its own set of pulls to simulate a small center drawer.

Note that the turned feet on these three chests are all very different in shape and size. These early chests were rural one of a kind products. They lack the standardization that comes with urban production, and in the feet you will see a wonderful variety of fanciful turnings.

10-2A. New England William & Mary, 41" h x 37" w, 1730 – 1750.

10-2B. Connecticut William & Mary, 41" h x 36" w, 1730 – 1750.

10-2C. New England William & Mary, 41" h x 37" w, 1700 – 1730.

10-3 New England six-board chests. When wide boards are cheap and available, the easiest way to made a chest is to simply nail four boards together for the sides and add a fifth board for the bottom and a sixth for the top. To avoid nailing into end grain, the end boards have the grain running vertically. These are carried below the bottom of the case and given a decorative arch to provide feet as shown in figure 10-3A. On somewhat better work the top is molded and the feet have curved facings so as to resemble bracket feet. The top was normally stiffened and restrained from warping by nailing a pair of cleats across the ends. This makes a very serviceable chest, and in New England where wide white pine boards were abundant, these six-board chests were probably the most common form of case furniture.

Six-board chests were produced in America in vast numbers for almost two hundred years, starting in the last decades of the seventeenth century and continuing until factory-made furniture was available everywhere at the close of the nineteenth century. Early New England chests are noticeably long and narrow in proportion. They usually have some decorative molding or scratch carving worked into the front as seen in figure 10-3B. The front corners are often embellished with chip carving of the sort that might have been made with a small chisel or a penknife. Here you will also see the heads of the old rose-headed nails that fastened the case together. Some of these early chests have oak end panels. Connecticut Valley examples are apt to be made of yellow pine.

Although far less common, there are a number Pilgrim Century six-board chests over drawers. These usually have a single long drawer that laps over the end boards as seen in the early Connecticut chest in figure 10-3C. This chest is typical of many early chests in having lost the wooden drawer pulls. Note that both of these chests are the most basic possible six-board design. The legs lack even the simple facings shown in figure 10-3A.

With the exception of the chests over drawers discussed in the previous section, lift-top chests with ball feet are not common in New England. However, the base molding associated with the William and Mary style is found on many New England six-board type chests, particularly in the higher chests over drawers. Connecticut produced the most distinctive of these transitional chests. Typically these are quite tall, with two drawers under a deep bin, high feet, and boldly curved aprons (10-3D). Most have brass pulls on the simulated drawers. These chests were made of both pine and poplar. Some have cherry drawer fronts.

Six-board type chests with stacked drawers, that is, drawers arranged one above another as in chests of drawers, were produced throughout New England. Most are made of softwoods, principally white pine and tulip poplar. They were always painted, often with colorful grain painting. Of all furniture types, chests and chests over drawers are the most likely to be grain painted. So common are these late eighteenth and early nineteenth century chests that we might look at two examples, the first a red-painted single drawer chest that could be from anywhere in New England (10-3E); the second a far grander chest over drawers from Maine in which the two simulated drawers are so neatly integrated with the two real drawers that it is easy to think that one is looking at a conventional four-drawer chest of drawers (10-3F). Here it might be noted that the shape of the feet and aprons on better-quality New England chests can tell us something of region, for they tend to emulate those found on chests of drawers.

Similar chests with stacked drawers were also produced to some extent in New York, including eastern Long Island. There are a few from Pennsylvania, although here they usually have separate bracket feet. However, for the most part, a chest with stacked drawers will be from somewhere in New England.

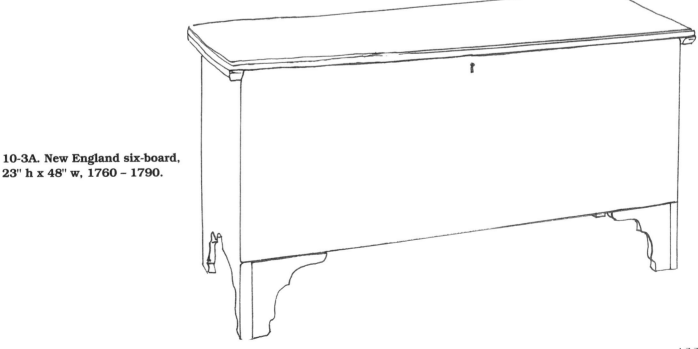

10-3A. New England six-board, 23" h x 48" w, 1760 – 1790.

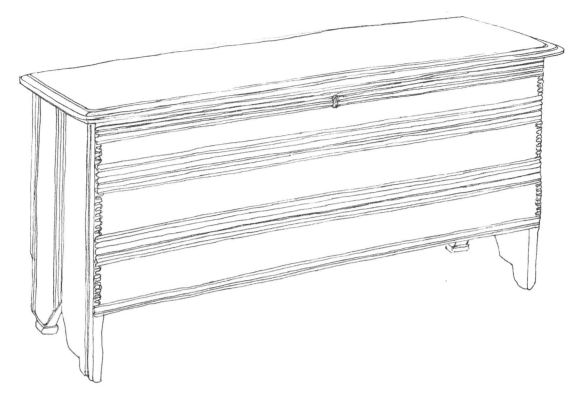

10-3B. New England Pilgrim Century, 24" h x 50" w, 1680 – 1720.

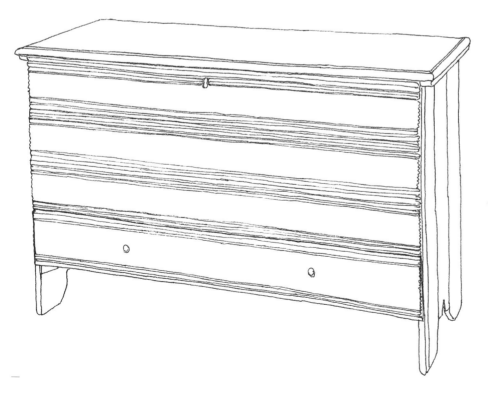

10-3C. Connecticut Pilgrim Century, 48" w, c. 1700.

10-3D. Connecticut, 49" h x 36" w, c. 1780.

10-3E. New England, 1800 – 1830.

10-3F. Maine Hepplewhite,
35" h x 40" w, c. 1820.

10-4 New England bracket-foot chests. While not nearly so common as the six-board type, there are a substantial number of New England chests and chests over drawers with bracket feet. These resemble six-board chests except that they have separate built-up base molding and straight bracket feet as shown in figure 10-4A. As befits a better-quality chest, the top will usually have applied moldings on the sides and front rather than nailed cleats across the ends. Note again, that on both this chest and on the following chest over drawers, that the shape of the feet are similar to those found on New England chests of drawers.

New England bracket-foot chests over drawers tend to emulate chests of drawers of the same period (10-4B). A few of these chests are made of maple, but the majority are pine as befits an essentially budget product. Many are of simple nailed construction. Most New England examples will have two simulated drawers over two real drawers, but three over two are not uncommon, and there are a few that emulate tall chests

with three simulated drawers over three real drawers. It is a mystery how anyone was able to find anything at the bottom of so deep a bin.

Although seldom identified as such, both these New England bracket-foot chests are Chippendale in style. To differentiate these styles of chests from the six-board type, and because we will shortly see some Sheraton and Empire style chests, we might identify them in this fashion.

Before leaving New England, it should be noted that in New England, and particularly in New Hampshire and Connecticut, it is not unusual to see case furniture raised on short cabriole legs in the Queen Anne style. Often these will be mounted on a separate frames. The same form is occasionally seen in chests over drawers, although seldom will there actually be a separate frames. The tiger maple two-over-two chest over drawers in figure 10-4C is an example of this uncommon type. While this chest is not made of cherry, the scalloping of the apron is suggestive of Connecticut workmanship.

10-4A. Massachusetts Chippendale, 24" h x 48" w, c. 1790.

10-4B. New England Chippendale, 51" h x 39" w, 1770 – 1800.

10-4C. New England Queen Anne, 50" h, 1750 – 1780.

10-5 Middle Atlantic paneled chests. Although New York City was actually founded a few years before Boston, the colony grew very slowly, and there are only a handful of surviving New York Jacobean paneled chests. The Delaware Valley also produced very few of these chests — not so much for lack of population as for relatively late settlement, for Philadelphia was not founded until the early 1680s. By that time, paneled construction was being superseded by dovetailed panels in the new William and Mary style. So few early paneled chests survive from the Middle Atlantic that there are seldom the establish types we saw in New England. This suggests that if you encounter a very old paneled chest unlike anything illustrated in this chapter, and the top is not paneled in European fashion, you might consider the Middle Atlantic, particularly if it is made of walnut.

However, we might look at two later paneled chests that exist in sufficient numbers so as to be encountered by the collector or dealer, the first a Sheraton, or perhaps Empire, expression of the standard Delaware Valley lift-top chest (10-5A). The

reverse fielded panels on these chests are the same sort of paneling we will see later on nineteenth century Delaware Valley cupboards.

More interesting are the distinctive double-paneled chests made on Long Island (10-5B). These paneled chests over drawers are unusual both in their form and in their continuing popularity, for they were produced successively in William and Mary, Chippendale, and Hepplewhite styles for over a century, being fitted first with ball, and then bracket, and finally, French feet. The chest shown in figure 10-5B is of better-than-average quality, for it is made of tiger maple rather than the more usual pine or poplar.

Here, as in most Middle Atlantic paneled chests, the paneling is as much for decoration as it is for structure. These chests were produced a century or more after paneled furniture went out of favor, and are of very different construction than the New England joined chests illustrated in section 10-1.

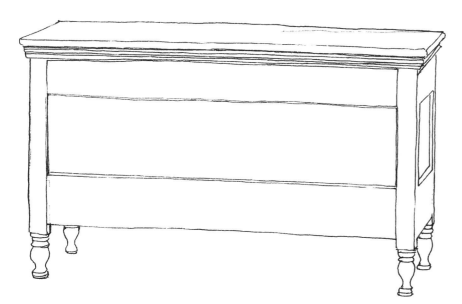

**10-5A. Pennsylvania Sheraton,
25" h x 42" w, c. 1820.**

10-5B. Long Island Chippendale, 38" h x 42" w, 1750 – 1800.

10-6 Middle Atlantic painted chests. We will cover Middle Atlantic paint-decorated chests and chests over drawers in just one section, for while a great many survive, they exhibit far less diversity in construction and form than those produced in New England. The most noticeable differences between New England and Middle Atlantic chests, particularly those made in southeastern Pennsylvania, are their larger size and more solid construction. They are generally much bigger and heavier than New England chests, having thick sides, heavy drawers, and enormous blacksmith locks. As in other case work, the weight is reflected in the shape of the feet, which you can easily see if you compare the New England bracket-foot chests in figures 10-4A and 10-4B with similar Pennsylvania chests in figures 10-6A and 10-6C. Rural Pennsylvania case work tends to be both overlarge and overbuilt, and chests are no exception.

The other major difference in Delaware Valley chests is that the drawers are almost always arranged side by side rather than stacked. Most of the earlier chests are of dovetail construction and have an applied base molding and straight bracket feet. Somewhat better models may have ogee bracket feet. A few have old fashioned William and Mary ball feet. They are made of either eastern white pine, yellow poplar, or yellow pine.

Quite the best known of these are the paint-decorated dower chests made in the German communities to the west of Philadelphia. The chest in figure 10-6A is a fine example of this type. The bright polychrome designs on the front and sides of are usually set within square or arched painted panels. There has been much research into the craftsmen that painted these delightful chests, and it is often possible to associate a chest with an artist. This one is attributed to Daniel Otto, who not surprisingly is known as the "Flat Tulip" artist.

Similar paint-decorated chests were produced in the counties north and west of Philadelphia and, to a lesser extent, by Dutch and German immigrants in New York's Montgomery and Schoharie counties just to the west of Albany. In general, when not given a decorative design, these pine and poplar chests were either grain painted or painted a bright overall color. Paint darkens with time, and most are now far less colorful than when new.

Not all Delaware Valley chests are this large and pretty — or now this expensive. You are far more likely to encounter a grain-painted chest having turned Empire feet (10-6B). Frequently, the original graining will have been either stripped or overpainted. These later lift-top chests tend to be smaller, and among them are a large number of children's chests and storage boxes. The ball feet shown on this chest are a common Pennsylvania turning. The large chest over drawers in figure 10-6D has very similar feet.

Many of these polychrome chests were given two or three drawers under the bin as seen in figure 10-6C. When there are drawers, the mass of the chest will usually be broken by the addition of a small midmolding just above the drawers, although later chests tend to omit this refinement. This is a much larger chest than the small illustration would suggest, being almost 51" wide and 31" high — an inch or so higher than a dining table. Later Pennsylvania chests over drawers have turned rather than bracket feet, and are perhaps more Empire than Sheraton in style (10-6D). These were often grain painted.

10-6A. Pennsylvania Chippendale, 24" h x 51" w, 1803.

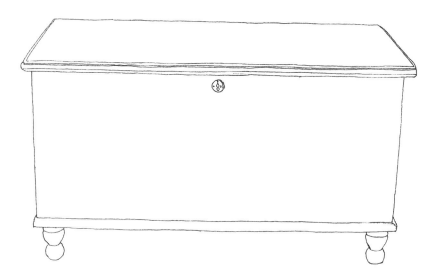

10-6B. Pennsylvania Empire, 24" h x 42" w, 1830 – 1840.

10-6C. Pennsylvania Chippendale, 31" h x 51" w, c. 1820.

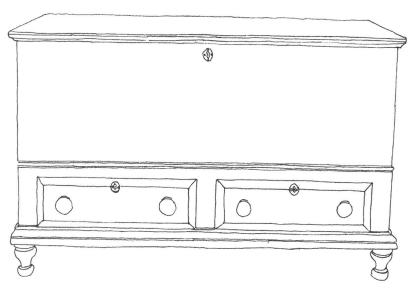

10-6D. Pennsylvania Empire, 33" h x 47" w, c. 1830.

10-7 Middle Atlantic hardwood chest. Most chests and chests over drawers are rural budget products, fashioned of softwoods and lacking any carving or inlay. A few are maple, which was probably stained up to resemble mahogany. However, there is a notable exception, and we will conclude the Middle Atlantic, and Pennsylvania, with what are probably the most developed lift-top chests, the grand walnut dower chests made to the north and west of Philadelphia in Montgomery, Chester, and Berks counties. Unlike Hadley chests, these large, dovetailed chests were dower, or dowry, chests, and often have a bride's married initials, or marriage date, or both, inlaid on the front, as is seen in figure 10-7. Much in keeping with other Delaware Valley work, these chests have a broad, solid English or German look quite unlike that of New England chests. They are also noticeably larger than New England chests. Some are very large indeed.

One of the most interesting characteristics of these chests is the way in which decoration is incorporated into the construction. The moldings on the top and base, and the facing on the bracket feet, are often fastened with wooden pins. This may been done as an economy, or perhaps as a superior method of fastening, but in either event, the dark end grain of the pins provides a pleasing accent to the lighter color of the moldings. The case sides were dovetailed, and sometimes also the bracket feet, and here again there is a decorative element, for the cabinetmakers almost always employed through dovetails which show on the front of the chest. Not only are there often more dovetails than needed, but in addition, they are sometimes given fanciful shapes. In any event, lapped or half-blind dovetails could easily have been employed if it were desired that they not show on the front. They were not beyond the knowledge or skill of the craftsmen, for the drawers under the bin are constructed this way. Another characteristic of this area is that the dovetails may be wedged with thin slivers of wood.

Most of these handsome chests are fitted with three drawers set below a small midmolding. Many have the ogee bracket feet shown in this illustration. A few retain the earlier ball foot. Most are made of walnut, although there are a few cherry examples.

Before leaving the Middle Atlantic, it should be noted that the dovetailed bracket-foot chests that were so popular in southeastern Pennsylvania are not confined to this area. Very similar chests, usually made of softwoods and painted, were produced to the north in New York state, to the west across the Appalachian Mountains, and to the south as far down as North Carolina, and then westward into eastern Tennessee. A few similar chests over drawers were produced in New England, but these are very clearly products of New England, having a single wide drawer above typical New England bracket feet. In the next section we will see that hardwood chests like that shown here followed settlers down the Shenandoah Valley into North Carolina.

10-7. Pennsylvania Chippendale, 30" h x 48" w, 1784.

10-8 Southern chests. This will not be a long section, for in comparison to New England and the Middle Atlantic, there are not a great many Southern chests. There are very few paneled chests, and more puzzling yet, not as many of the simple six-board variety as might have been expected from an agrarian society. This may be due to the summer heat and damp. An old chest put out in the barn, even if made of resistant yellow pine, would probably not last very long.

We will therefore consider just four chests, one from Virginia, two from North Carolina, and one that might have been produced almost anywhere in the South. The first two are similar to chests made in southeastern Pennsylvania, in large part because they were made by immigrants who moved south along the Great Wagon Road through the Shenandoah Valley. The first chest is one of a group attributed to Johannes Spitler, who worked in Shenandoah County in the early years of the nineteenth century (10-8A). The case is dovetailed and pegged in Pennsylvania fashion. It is not known whether Mr. Spitler actually made these chests, or was just the painter. Most Southern paint decorated chests are from western Virginia, and appear to have been made by German immigrants.

The second example is one of a group of walnut chests made in the North Carolina piedmont (10-8B). The use of walnut, the dovetailed case, and the dovetailed feet all suggest southeastern Pennsylvania, but the curious reversed scrolls on the bracket feet hint at a rural cabinetmaker working on his own. Most Southern walnut chests are fairly simple, although there are a few with the sulfur inlay seen in figure 10-7. They seldom have the ogee bracket foot found on many Pennsylvania chests.

Earlier we saw a New England chest on frame with cabriole legs, and now we might look at a Southern chest that fits the same description, but that is very different in design and execution. The chest on frame in figure 10-8C is one of a group of similar chests and chests of drawers produced in Randolph and Rowan Counties just to the south of present day Winston-Salem. This is a budget effort, made of yellow pine and fastened with cut nails. In chapter 11, you will see a far more sophisticated inlaid walnut chest of drawers from the same area. Note that while this chest indeed has cabriole legs, they are of a very simplified form, most all the curve being on the outside of the leg. This simplification is common in rural chests. Other chests and chests of drawers from this area are far better made, having dovetailed cases and being made of walnut or cherry.

Dovetailed bracket-foot chests were produced everywhere in the South. The painted lift-top chest in figure 10-8D is typical of these chests. Two features of the chest suggest Southern workmanship: the overall simplicity of execution, particularly the very basic arched bracket feet, and the yellow pine primary wood. Although hard pine grew as far north as Connecticut, a painted chest made of yellow pine will most probably be a Southern chest.

Lastly, it might be mentioned that as a group, Southern chests tend to be relatively new. Of the four chests illustrated in this section, only the last might have been produced in the eighteenth century, and even it is most probably Federal rather than Colonial.

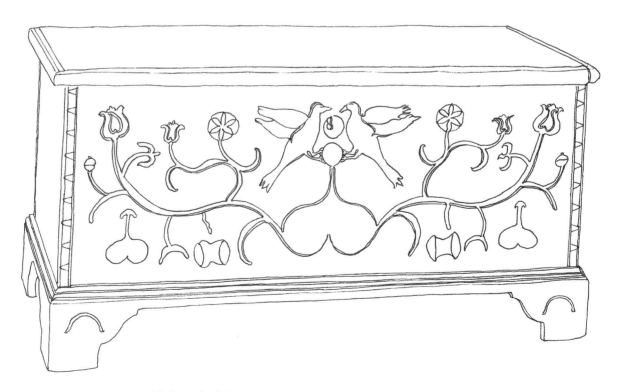

10-8A. Virginia Chippendale, 24" h x 49" w, c. 1800.

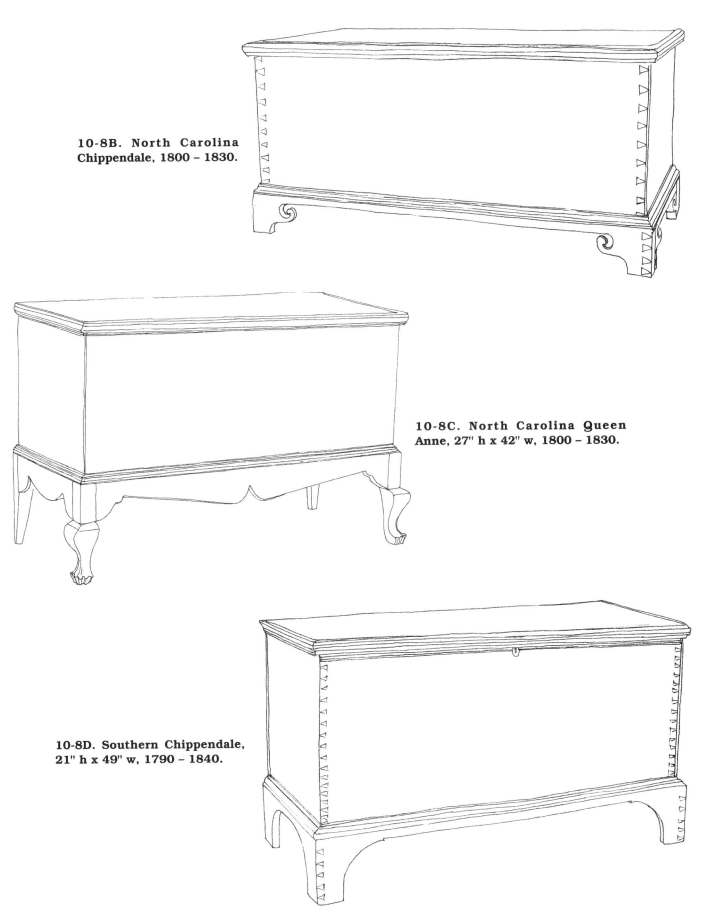

10-8B. North Carolina Chippendale, 1800 – 1830.

10-8C. North Carolina Queen Anne, 27" h x 42" w, 1800 – 1830.

10-8D. Southern Chippendale, 21" h x 49" w, 1790 – 1840.

Chapter 11 – Chests of Drawers

This second chapter on case furniture will survey the chest of drawers and its near relatives, the tall chest, the chest-on-frame, the chest-on-chest, the clothespress, and that ultimate in stacked case work, the chest-on-chest-on-frame. Drawers are little more than open boxes with pairs of handles on the fronts that move back and forward on slides. The name comes from the way they are accessed — they are "drawn out" through the front of the case. In the eighteenth century, they were often called cases of drawers — and they are just that, rectangular cases housing sets of drawers. Except for some early production, the drawers were usually graduated in depth, the deepest at the bottom, the shallowest at the top. Horner notes that in Philadelphia, the chest-on-chest was identified in probate records as a "chest upon chest," a "double case of drawers," or simply as a "case upon case."

Chests of drawers are far less stressed than chairs, and aside from the feet and the brasses, generally survive pretty much intact. Their construction engenders a long life, for normally the sides, the tops and bottoms, and the drawer dividers or blades are all dovetailed together. But for Jacobean and William and Mary types, they have never lost their utility or gone out of fashion, and large numbers survive, some even dating to the last decades of the seventeenth century. Because there are so many from different periods, we will cover them in three groups, first those in the early Jacobean and William and Mary styles, then those in the Queen Anne and Chippendale styles, and lastly, those produced after the Revolution in the neoclassical Hepplewhite and Sheraton styles. To facilitate regional comparison, the relatives are given their own sections.

There is so much style lag in American furniture, and particularly in case work, that styles do not match historical periods. We will see William and Mary ball-foot chests of drawers made half a century after the reign of William and Mary, and Queen Anne cabriole leg chests of drawers that actually post-date the Revolution. Among case furniture, only the neoclassical styles are more or less true to their period.

11-1 New England paneled chests of drawers. With rare exceptions, Jacobean paneled chests of drawers will be from New England. New York had only a small population and Pennsylvania was not settled until the end of the seventeenth century, by which time the joiner's paneled case work was being superseded by the cabinetmaker's dovetailed furniture. However, a few survive, and if you see an early paneled chest of drawers constructed of walnut, you are looking at a product of the Middle Atlantic, most probably southeastern Pennsylvania.

Most paneled chests of drawers are from either coastal Massachusetts or Connecticut. We will consider two that appear very different and yet are similar in design and construction. The first is a high-style Jacobean chest of drawers in which the drawer fronts are decorated with applied geometric moldings flanked by split turned spindles (11-1A). Typically the drawers will not be graduated and pattern of the moldings varies with the depth of the drawer. Sometimes the case will be made in two sections, each having a pair drawers. That the feet on this large chest lack character and seem a bit small is for good reason. They have been restored.

The second example is simpler, and somewhat later, for by now all the drawers have the same moldings and are graduated in the normal manner with the shallowest at the top and the deepest at the bottom (11-1B). Frequently only the front feet are turned, the rear being simply an extension of the stiles as shown here, a treatment similar to that seen in New England ball-foot chests over drawers. Most of these chests are made of red oak and have yellow or white pine tops. Some employ cedar as a secondary wood. They tend to be very heavy, not only due to the oak, but because the drawers were hung from rails and had to have very thick sides to allow a slot for the rail.

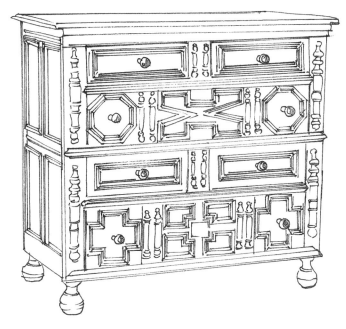

11-1A. Massachusetts Jacobean, 40" h x 39" w, 1670 – 1690.

11-1B. Massachusetts Jacobean, 39" h x 39" w, 1680 – 1720.

11-2 New England William and Mary chest of drawers. New England William and Mary ball-foot chests of drawers are something of an anomaly, for they are both uncommon and seldom of the quality found to the south in the Delaware Valley. That most were made of softwoods and simply nailed together may account in part for their scarcity, for originally they must have been quite common. They are usually made of pine and either painted or paint decorated as shown in figure 11-2. Some are a mixture of maple and pine, a few are all maple, and a rare few have the crotch walnut veneered drawers that we will see in the next chapter. Nearly all have four tiers of graduated drawers. About half have the top drawer divided into two smaller drawers, a feature more common to Middle Atlantic and Southern case work, but also seen in early New England desks and chests of drawers.

11-2. Massachusetts William & Mary, 40" h x 35" w, c. 1730.

145

11-3 Pennsylvania William and Mary chest of drawers. Quite the most successful William and Mary style ball-foot chests of drawers were produced in Philadelphia and surrounding Delaware Valley. Almost without exception these handsome dovetailed chests are made of walnut and have the two over three drawer arrangement shown in figure 11-3. Some have just ball feet in the front, and a few have the paneled ends we will see later in early tall chests from this region. This very fine example with a built up molded top was probably made in Philadelphia. The two upper drawers that lack escutcheons may be fitted with wooden spring locks.

11-3. Philadelphia William & Mary, 45" h x 43" w, 1720 – 1740.

11-4 New England Chippendale chest of drawers. So many chests of drawers in the Chippendale style were produced in New England, that before surveying the individual colonies, we should consider a representative example. Bracket-foot chests are usually identified as being Chippendale, and sometimes as Queen Anne, although a great many probably post-date the Revolution and might more honestly be identified as Federal. The maple chest of drawers in figure 11-4 is typical of a great many produced throughout the region. Most will have a rectangular molded top and bracket feet. A lesser number have curved ogee bracket feet. Often there will be a sharp downward point or spur on the inside face of the brackets, although this feature is found everywhere and is no particular indicator of region. However, the rather high, bold stance of this chest of drawers is characteristic of New England workmanship.

This chest is typical of rural New England case furniture in that there is no attempt to cover or stop the dovetail joints that fasten the drawer blades to the sides of the case. They are simply through dovetailed and left to show on the front and sides. Most all of these chests of drawers have four long graduated drawers, although a split top drawer, that is, two short drawers over three, is not unknown, particularly in earlier work.

These chests were made throughout the northeast and frequently have no more regional attribution than New England. However, one made of maple or birch is most likely a product of northern New England, quite possibly rural New Hampshire. Similar chests of drawers made of cherry are more likely be from the Connecticut or the Connecticut River Valley, and if made with poplar rather than white pine drawers, then coastal Connecticut. The use of chestnut for drawer bottoms or backboards would suggest Rhode Island or vicinity.

11-4. New England Chippendale, 33" h x 39" w, 1770 – 1800.

11-5 New Hampshire Queen Anne and Chippendale chests of drawers. To survey New Hampshire we will consider two chests of drawers, one typical of rural workmanship, the other of urban. The first is a cabriole-leg Dunlap-type chest from south-central New Hampshire (11-5A). Here there seems to have been an affection for the old-fashioned Queen Anne cabriole leg, for when we consider tall chests and chests-on-frames, we will see this same leg again. Grander examples of these chests have carved base moldings and rather naive ball and claw feet that lack the lower halves of the balls, not too unlike the elongated paw feet seen on New England tea tables. Interestingly, you may also see the Boston type of sliding dovetail used to join the tops to the sides of the cases. As you would expect, the primary wood will be either maple or birch, secondary wood eastern white pine. The chest in this illustration is a combination of maple and birch. For some reason, perhaps because it was available and easy to shape, knee brackets are often made of basswood.

Rural New England cabinetmakers, like rural cabinetmakers everywhere, would emulate urban features when it could be done cheaply with the available tools. Sometimes they would bow the top of a straight-front chest of drawers in imitation of the fashionable bowfronts found on city furniture. A similar approach seen in southern New Hampshire was to serpentine the top, perhaps to suggest the elegant serpentine-front chests then being produced just to the south in Massachusetts. The molded top on this chest of drawers has been given these fashionable curves. Later we will see a Connecticut chest of drawers with an even more pronounced scalloped top.

Although New Hampshire is largely rural, high-style urban furniture was being produced in Portsmouth long before the Revolution. Among chests of drawers, perhaps the best known in the Chippendale style is a Federal serpentine-front chest whose design seems to have come from Salem, where there were similar chests of drawers made with canted corners (11-5B). While this chest has conforming bracket feet, the high stance, the string inlay, and the ring pulls are very much neoclassical. The drawers are mahogany veneered over white pine. Normally there will be short dustboards behind the drawer blades. Some of these handsome chests have spruce backboards; a wood seldom used elsewhere in American furniture. These chests are often attributed to the shop of Langley Boardman (1774 – 1833) based on a bill of sale to James Rundlet in 1802. The price was $28.00 dollars.

11-5A. New Hampshire Queen Anne, 38" h x 41" w, 1790 – 1810.

11-5B. Portsmouth Chippendale, 36" h x 43" w, 1795 – 1810.

11-6 Massachusetts Chippendale chests of drawers. Here there is much to discuss, for Massachusetts, and particularly coastal Massachusetts, produced an enormous amount and variety of case work. A chest of drawers that is clearly urban and from New England will most likely be from somewhere in the Boston area. However, before discussing specific examples, we should discuss Boston construction methods, for as in all urban centers, there were standard practices that can help us identify region.

Boston cabinetmakers had an elegantly simple method of fastening the tops on chests of drawers, but one that required some experience and the right tools. They would cut a half dovetail along the top edges of the sides of the case and a corresponding pair of slots on the underside of the top, stopping just short of the front edge. The top was then tapped on from the front. While this sliding dovetail is also seen to some extent in New Hampshire, it is a good indicator of Boston workmanship. It is easy to spot when you note the lack of blocking or slats under the top, and the half dovetail showing at the back of the case.

After the Revolution, most Boston cabinetmakers employed the more normal method of fastening the top by first dovetailing two slats to the sides of the case, then fastening the top to the slats with screws driven up from below. The cost of hardware was less by this time, and perhaps also this was a better method on neoclassical chests where the top was often made of mahogany veneered on white pine.

When the base molding is thicker than the bottom board, as it usually is, the cabinetmaker is faced with the problem of accommodating the overlap. In Boston, the normal method was to set the base molding flush with the upper surface of the bottom board, then add filler blocks under the bottom to provide a flush surface for the foot blocking. The bottom drawer would then slide directly on the bottom of the case. Rhode Island cabinetmakers did just the reverse, setting the base molding flush with the lower surface of the bottom board, then because of the overlap, adding a pair of slides along the inside of the case to carry the bottom drawer.

Pull out the bottom drawer on a Boston blockfront or serpentine chest of drawers and not only will you notice that the drawer slides on the bottom of the case, but often that the front base molding is joined to the bottom of the case by a single wide dovetail. This "giant dovetail" is a feature of Boston casework, and while not found on all blockfront and serpentine chests made in Boston, is a useful indicator when present.

It should be noted that quantity production did not always go hand in hand with quality, and even on what would have been relatively expensive mahogany furniture you may encounter signs of hasty work. It is not unusual to see rather sloppy dovetails on a grand blockfront chest of drawers. The drawer runners were usually set into shallow dadoes or grooves, and then held in place with nails. They were often nailed throughout their length with little apparent thought for shrinkage, and there are many split case sides where the runners resisted the normal contraction of the sides of the case.

In New England, furniture having shaped or "swelled" fronts was very fashionable. When one considers the additional labor and cost, the number of blocked or serpentine New England chests of drawers is truly astonishing. Case furniture having a shaped front will most probably be from somewhere in New England, most likely from coastal Massachusetts. Chests of drawers with bowed fronts were made everywhere, but if blocked or serpentine, then New England is the most probable source. Serpentine front chests of drawers were made in Philadelphia, and also to some extent in the South, but these are rare in comparison to New England production.

However, before discussing this case work, we should look at a chest of drawers with a flat front. While not rare, there are not many examples, and surprisingly few that predate the Revolution. Most people seem to have used chests or chests over drawers, and when there was more money to spend, it appears to have gone into chests of drawers with shaped facades. The simple birch North Shore chest of drawers in figure 11-6A is typical of these, and while it has a molded top and bracket feet, it is quite probably Federal rather than Colonial. As such, it exhibits the style lag so often seen in American furniture. Not all Massachusetts Chippendale chests are so rococo in style. Somewhat later, more urban models are neoclassical in all but the bracket feet, having square tops, cockbeaded drawers, veneered drawer fronts, and oval brasses.

Blockfront furniture first appears in Boston in the late 1730s, the earliest documented example being a desk and bookcase signed by Job Coit in 1738. Thereafter, blocking remained popular until almost the end of the century when the rococo style finally gave way to neoclassicism. It was so much the fashion that Boston-area cabinetmakers blocked all sorts of furniture: chests of drawers, chest-on-chests, bureau tables, desks, desk and bookcases, and clothespresses. Rural artisans went a step further and blockfronted highboys and lowboys, generally with rather strange results. While we associate blockfronting with Boston, blocking was employed all up and down coastal New England, from Portsmouth in the north to Connecticut in the south. There was some blocking in New York City, and a few pieces from Virginia. Except for Connecticut, where cherry was preferred, block-front furniture will almost always be made of mahogany. So many of these elegant chests of drawers survive that it is easy to forget that in their day they were expensive high style furniture, costing about half again more than an ordinary chest of drawers.

Blocking may be either flat or curved. Flat blocking, blocking that is flat across the front with an abrupt rounding at the edges is associated with earlier work, perhaps 1750 – 1780. Portsmouth blocking also tends to be flat, although the few pieces attributed to this city may all be early work. Connecticut blocking is also flat, and here again it is not clear this is due to period or the more rural workmanship.

Later in style and more common is blocking in which the face of the block is rounded as shown in the chest of drawers in figure 11-6B. Chests with either form of blocking may have straight or ogee bracket feet. A few with rounded blocking have ball and claw feet, a somewhat later feature which we see in a serpentine front chest (11-6E). The pronounced downcurving point or spur on the faces of the foot brackets are seen on many Boston pieces. The other common Boston-area pattern, seen in figure 11-6C, is a dip or smaller spur, then above this a small half-round just before the bracket meets the base molding.

While block fronts occupy center stage, the great majority of New England chests of drawers with shaped fronts are not blocked. Instead, they are either a serpentine or reverse-serpentine shape. The serpentine bows in from each side and then out toward the center; the reverse-serpentine swells out from each side and then in toward the center. In this it resembles a shallow oxbow, and reverse-serpentine chests are often called oxbow chests. There are so many variations among these popular chests of drawers that we might look at three common Massachusetts types. Later will see similar, but significantly different Rhode Island and Connecticut interpretations of this popular form.

Most often these chests of drawers have reverse-serpentine front shown in figure 11-6C. Some, particularly if reverse-serpentine, have the ends of the drawers blocked or squared as shown here. This was probably an extra cost feature. Roughly half have ogee rather than straight bracket feet.

Also fashionable, but less common, are serpentine chests of drawers. These are usually somewhat later and often have late rococo bail pulls, or neoclassical Hepplewhite pulls, and stamped oval escutcheons as seen in figure 11-6D. Other serpentine chests tend further to the neoclassical, and while retaining bracket feet, have string inlay edging the drawers and foot facings, and Sheraton rosette or ring pulls. A few have canted corners, although this must have been an expensive option, for while made in all regions, they are fairly rare.

A common option, particularly on reverse-serpentine chests of drawers, are ball and claw feet (11-6E). Although one would

think that this would be an early feature, it is frequently seen on the later Federal chests, and as such, may simply reflect of a rising prosperity. We will see in a bit that in New England, even Federal bowfront chests were given ball and claw feet. Note that the ball and claw feet in figure 11-6E are very much in Massachusetts fashion, with retracted claws and long talons. The shell carved center drop would suggest this chest is from the North Shore, probably either Salem or Newburyport. Other case work from this area may have a rounded convex scallop shell in the center drop.

Serpentine and reverse-serpentine front chests were produced all over New England, usually of mahogany in Massachusetts, but also of birch, maple, and cherry; frequently maple and birch in New Hampshire, and normally cherry in Connecticut and the Connecticut River Valley. Secondary woods will usually be white pine in the Boston area, then north into New Hampshire, and in the Massachusetts portion of the Connecticut River Valley. To some extent, birch is to northern New England what walnut is to the Delaware Valley.

Before leaving Massachusetts chests of drawers, some mention should be made of the bombé form, although you are unlikely to see a piece of bombé furniture except at a major auction or in a museum collection, and a very fine collection at that. These magnificent chests of drawers (11-6F) are a high point in Massachusetts rococo furniture. Produced in limited numbers in Boston and Salem, they must have been very expensive, for the swelled sides are worked out from a single thick mahogany plank. To a lessor extent, the bombé form is also found in chest-on-chests, desks, and desks and bookcases. As grand as this chest seems, it is not the top of the line, for some examples have ball-and-claw feet, and a few have both swelled sides and swelled fronts.

11-6A. Massachusetts Chippendale, 33" h x 35" w, 1770 – 1800.

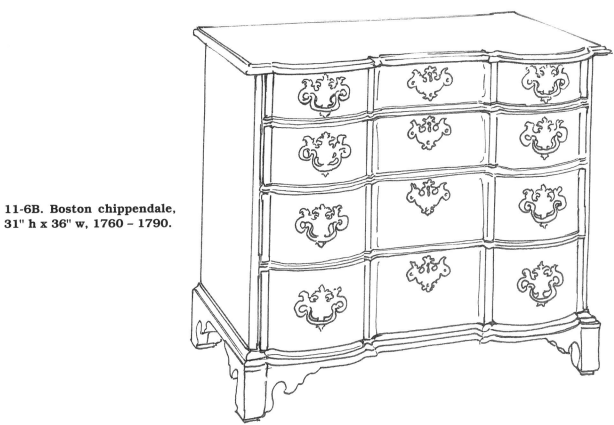

11-6B. Boston chippendale, 31" h x 36" w, 1760 – 1790.

11-6C. Massachusetts Chippendale reverse-serpentine, 31" h x 37" w, 1770 – 1800.

11-6D. Massachusetts Chippendale, 37" h x 42" w, 1770 – 1810.

11-6E. Salem Chippendale, 34" h x 36" w, 1770 – 1810.

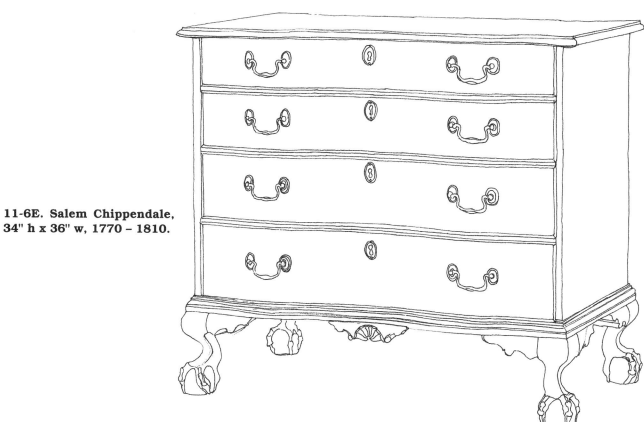

11-6F. Boston Chippendale, 33" h x 37" w, 1760 – 1790.

11-7 Rhode Island Chippendale chests of drawers. This section will be an easy study, for Rhode Island furniture is distinctive, and chests of drawers are no exception. The most common form is a four drawer chest with molded top and ogee bracket feet (11-7A). While this chest is similar to many other New England Chippendale chests of drawers, there are a number of features that tell us it is a Rhode Island product. The most obvious are the conservative ogee bracket feet that terminate in a squared pad. They are quite unlike the bracket feet illustrated in the previous section.

At the bottom of the case, in Rhode Island fashion, the base molding will most probably be set flush with the underside of the bottom board. Take out the bottom drawer and you will see that it rests on a pair of slides rather than, in Boston fashion, on the bottom of the case.

The drawers of these chests will usually be chestnut, or have poplar sides and chestnut bottoms. The backboards are also likely to be chestnut. Here it might be noted that while chestnut was a favored secondary wood in Rhode Islands and environs, it is not a positive identification, for this stable, easily worked wood was often used elsewhere, not only in New England, but also sometimes in the Middle Atlantic and the South.

Most of these chests of drawers are fitted with conservative, transitional bail pulls and oval Hepplewhite escutcheons. Many are made of cherry, which may reflect a Connecticut influence, or may simply have been favored as a less expensive option.

The next example is a fine serpentine chest of drawers made in Newport about 1790 (11-7B). While not evident in this small illustration, this chest is most beautifully made with selected mahogany and very neatly cut dovetails, almost as though made by Shakers half a century later. Such fine cabinet work alone would suggest Newport. As might be expected, the drawer bottoms are chestnut and the feet are the standard Rhode Island form; and again, the chest is fitted with bail pulls, which judging from the number of examples, seem to have been favored in Rhode Island. While the third serpentine bracket-foot New England chest of drawers we have seen, this form is not unique to New England, for serpentine-front chests were made everywhere in urban centers, often with canted corners when something extra was desired. There are documented examples from Portsmouth, Salem, Boston, New York City, Philadelphia, Baltimore, Norfolk, and Charleston.

Lastly, we will look at one of the block and shell chests of drawers for which Newport is famous, although as with bombé furniture, you are unlikely to encounter an example outside of a museum (11-7C). This striking combination of block and shell was produced in limited quantities in Newport and Providence — and emulated in Connecticut's New London County. While the design is most often seen bureau or dressing tables, it is also found on Rhode Island chests of drawers, tall clock cases, chest-on-chests, and magnificent big desks and bookcases.

In the unlikely event that you encounter a piece of this furniture, it is possible to tell where it was made. While there are a number of subtle differences between Newport and Providence workmanship, there are two that are easy to spot. If the convex shells are carved from the solid wood rather than glued on, and on some pieces, if simulated lipping is carved on the drawer fronts, the piece was made in Providence. It is a mystery why Providence cabinetmakers went to this extra work on furniture that was already very labor intensive.

11-7A. Providence Chippendale, 36" h x 39" w, 1780 – 1800.

**11-7B. Newport Chippendale,
33" h x 35" w, c. 1790.**

**11-7C. Newport Chippendale,
33" h x 36" w, c. 1765.**

11-8 Connecticut Chippendale chests of drawers. Connecticut exhibits all sorts of interesting case work, for the naive exuberance with which Connecticut cabinetmakers approached their trade often resulted in some very original chests of drawers. However, before going further, something again should be said about cherry, for you have probably heard somewhere that cherry is Connecticut, or perhaps that a furniture made of cherry will always be from Connecticut. Well, it's not true.

Cherry grows all up and down the Atlantic seaboard, particularly inland from New York south to West Virginia. It was used in almost all regions, either from choice or as an inexpensive substitute for mahogany. Furniture made of cherry is found from Vermont to Georgia, and by itself, is no particular indication of region. What suggests Connecticut, and the Connecticut River Valley, is the use of cherry on first-class furniture, although this may not be what one would consider urban high style furniture. Thus, when we see a very nice rural cherry high chest, dressing table, or chest-on-chest, we are likely to be looking at Connecticut workmanship. However, this is not a hard and fast rule, for elsewhere first-class furniture was occasionally fashioned of this prince of cabinet woods. Among the very grand Providence block and shell desks and bookcases, there is at least one that is made of cherry. Nor is Connecticut limited to cherry, for there are a significant number of Connecticut chests of drawers made of maple; and mahogany was often used near the coast, particularly in New London County.

Secondary woods are also not always consistent, but nevertheless can offer some guidance. Furniture made in the Connecticut River Valley, including western Massachusetts and southern Vermont, normally will have white pine as a secondary wood, although here there is also some use of basswood. Further south you will see either pine or poplar, or a mix of both. In the eastern corner of Connecticut near to Rhode Island, you will sometimes find chestnut. Chestnut is also found in southeastern Massachusetts, again perhaps due to the proximity of Rhode Island.

A good way to spot Connecticut workmanship is to note the use of cherry in combination with some embellishment to the facade of the chest. When there was a little extra to spend you will typically see quarter columns, and frequently also a row of simple gadrooning applied to the underside of the base molding as shown in figure 11-8A. This chest of drawers is typical of Connecticut work, not only in these embellishments, but also in the rather vertical proportions and the use of ogee rather than straight bracket feet. Perhaps two of every three Connecticut Chippendale chests of drawers have ogee bracket feet. These may be similar to the restrained Rhode Island foot, or to a Boston foot with a downcurving spur, or sometimes a Boston foot with an extended, curved spur. Cabinetmakers in New London County often reversed the scroll to face inward, and then, for good measure, added another scroll (11-8B). This treatment was not all that unusual, for you will frequently see bracket feet on Connecticut furniture embellished with somewhat naive curved scrolls. Note that multiple scrolled returns are not unique to Connecticut. We saw them on a Dunlap type chest of drawers (11-5A), although here the scrolls faced outward rather than inward. All in all, overly large scrolls are probably more a sign of rural workmanship than an indication of region.

The other feature seen in New London furniture is that the sides of the case are carried down behind the facing to support the feet. If you were to tip the chest in figure 11-8B on its back, you would see that the sides of the front and back feet behind the facing is provided by an extension of the case sides. This construction makes for a very strong foot, but can result in a somewhat tucked in look unless the ogee facing is made very thick. Sadly, this innovative method is not unique to either New London County or New England.

When there were insufficient funds to block or to serpentine the front of a chest of drawers, something might have been done with the top, and quite often you will see Connecticut chests in which the tops have been given large overhangs, have been bowed across the fronts, or have been given oxbow or serpentine shapes. The ultimate expression of this practice is the scallop top, of which the chest shown in figure 11-8C is actually a rather modest example. Although Connecticut furniture is well known for scalloping, it is actually not very common, probably because laying out, sawing, and molding these tops required considerable time and labor.

Most chests of drawers with shaped fronts are of the reverse-serpentine shape so popular in Massachusetts. To a much lessor extent you will also see serpentine and blockfront chests of drawers. Either are likely to be embellished in some manner, and you will often see bold, overhanging tops, quarter columns, and gadrooned base moldings. The cherrywood reverse-serpentine chest of drawers in figure 11-8D is also typical of Connecticut workmanship in being rather tall in proportion to width, a feature noted earlier in this section.

This chest has another feature that is probably unique to Connecticut, and to case work made in and around Hartford. Note that the ogee feet are both large and have a pronounced outward splay. Tip this chest on its back and you will see that the feet are not fastened with glue blocks in the normal manner. Instead, they have been built up as separate assemblies and then simply nailed or screwed to the bottom of the case. Were you to take apart one of the front feet you would see that the two facings are fastened together either with mitered dovetails or a rebated miter joint, and then joined to a chamfered quarter-round plate or block by tenons cut into the straight sides of the block. The facing and back of the rear feet are likely to be joined with through dovetails. Some of these blocks are triangular or cut off square to form a polygon shape. In any event, the whole assembly was simply nailed or screwed to the bottom of the case. So standardized are some of these feet that there is some conjecture that they may have been fabricated separately, as a sort of cottage industry, and then supplied to cabinetmakers as required.

Due to their unique construction these chests of drawers are sometimes called quadrant-base chests. You will also hear them referred to as "Belden" chests after George Belden (1770 – 1838), who signed a chest of drawers and a secretary having these feet. Not all this work was done in Hartford, for there are documented examples from as far north as Greenfield, Massachusetts.

While here, that is, in the vicinity of Hartford, we must discuss the case work produced by Eliphalet and Aaron Chapin, George Belden, and about half a dozen other area cabinetmakers; what is often called the Chapin Shops or the Chapin School. This furniture, all cherry with white pine secondary, is characterized by a general high quality of workmanship. In addition to platform or quadrant-base foot construction, the drawer blades will be fastened to the sides of the case with vertical double tenons rather than the usual dovetails. Look where the blades meet the case and you will see that there is neither a dovetail showing on the front, nor a covering strip to hide a dovetail. In addition, the backboards may be set in grooves in the sides of the case rather than simply nailed into rabbets.

The tops on chests of drawers will be fastened with screws to a full width pine subtop which is butted to a top drawer blade and dovetailed to the sides of the case. If the chest has a reverse-serpentine front, pull out a drawer and you will notice that the inside of the drawer front has not been cut away in the usual manner, that is, parallel with the outside. Instead, it will have been scooped out in a slope such that the top is cut away in the normal manner, but the bottom has been left straight. Because of this, you will see that bail posts have deep pockets and the drawer bottom is straight across the front edge. Also, the sides of the drawers may be given a curved bead on the outside edges.

The two previous sections concluded with a well-known furniture form you are unlikely to ever see in a shop or at an auction, and we will close Connecticut in much the same way. For well-off customers, New London County cabinetmakers would provide block-front furniture in the best Boston manner, and for really well-off customers, block and shell furniture in the best Newport manner. While the chest of drawers in figure 11-8E resembles the Newport chest of drawers in the previous section, it is quite different, not only in the use of cherry and in the ball and claw feet, but in design and construction details, and in the overall larger size. Note that instead of the conservative Rhode Island ogee bracket foot, there are short cabriole legs, and then a whole row of little scrolls inside the legs. Were this a side view, you would also note that there are only two ball and claw feet. The rear of the case is supported by a pair of large ogee bracket feet, a feature also seen in New York Chippendale furniture. This unusual chest of drawers is a nice illustration of the medley of local idioms and style elements from other regions that so characterizes, and adds so much charm to, Connecticut furniture.

11-8A. Connecticut Chippendale, 41" h x 38" w, 1770 – 1810.

11-8B. New London County Chippendale, 34" h x 38" w, c. 1780.

11-8C. Connecticut Chippendale, 34" h x 33" w, 1780 – 1810.

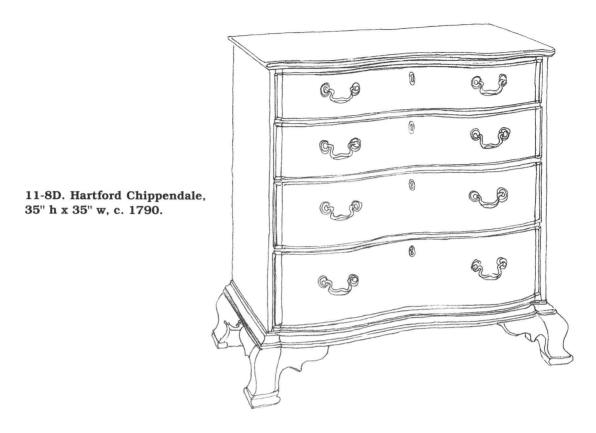

**11-8D. Hartford Chippendale,
35" h x 35" w, c. 1790.**

**11-8E. New London County
Chippendale, 35" h x 40" w,
1770 – 1790.**

11-9 New York Chippendale chests of drawers. There are so few surviving New York chests of drawers in the rococo style that we will consider but two, the first a somewhat Georgian chest that predates the Revolution, and the second a more typical early Federal product. New York produced very little case furniture that was transitional in style, for when New York City became wealthy and started to grow following the Revolution, furniture was ordered in the latest neoclassical Hepplewhite and Sheraton styles. There was not the gradual transition seen in New England where chests of drawers in Queen Anne and Chippendale styles continued to be produced right up into the early nineteenth century. In addition, chests of drawers appear to have been seldom made in rural areas. Dean Failey's excellent book on Long Island furniture illustrates dozens of chests, chests over drawers, high chests of drawers, presses, and kasten, but only a single chest of drawers, and this a Federal example in the Hepplewhite style.

New York Colonial chests of drawers are easy to spot, for seldom will you see a flat-front mahogany chest of drawers given ball and claw feet (11-9A). New York Chippendale case work rarely has the swelled fronts that were so fashionable in New England. This small chest has two other New York features: the strip of applied gadrooning across the base, and the square, blocky New York ball and claw feet. Many of these very rococo chests of drawers have ball and claw feet in front and ogee bracket feet in the rear, a feature only seldom seen else-where. That this chest appears rather tall is only because the case is only 34" wide. Unlike New York chest-on-chests, New York Colonial chests of drawers are apt to be rather small, more in the scale of English bachelor's chests. Like other New York furniture produced before the Revolution, these fine mahogany chests have a distinctly Georgian appearance. The fluted, chamfered corners and gadrooning on this chest are also seen in Philadelphia, but in Philadelphia, chests of drawers never have ball and claw feet.

Figure 11-9B shows an early Federal New York chest of drawers. While the bracket feet are heavier than what one would expect from New England, what really suggests New York workmanship is that the case is unusually wide in proportion to its depth, in this example 40" wide. Later in this chapter we will see the same characteristic in a New York chest-on-chest. Both of these chests are made of mahogany and most probably have pine and poplar secondary, white or yellow pine for the structural members, and tulip poplar for the drawer sides and bottoms.

In common with other Middle Atlantic case work, there most likely will be dust boards between the drawers. They are fairly good indicators of region, for New England cabinetmakers seldom fitted them except on some of the best-quality work, while in the Middle Atlantic, dust boards are found on even average-quality furniture. Also, from New York south, the drawer blade dovetails are usually hidden.

11-9A. New York Chippendale, 33" h x 34" w, 1760 – 1780.

11-9B. New York Chippendale, 33" h x 40" w, c. 1780.

11-10 Pennsylvania Chippendale chests of drawers. Although produced in a rich and populous region, Pennsylvania chests of drawers exhibit remarkably little diversity in either form or construction, and in this section there are just three. Before looking at these, however, we might consider Delaware Valley Chippendale chests of drawers in general, for they have a number of features that help in identification. While only the first chest of drawers has been given quarter columns, this enhancement is exceedingly common in Delaware Valley case work, not only in southeastern Pennsylvania, but also in adjacent regions in New Jersey, Delaware, Maryland, and Virginia. So universal is this feature that should you see a chest of drawers with fluted quarter columns, you are most likely looking at Delaware Valley workmanship. To some extent, quarter columns are what the swelled front was to New England, a fashionable addition when there was something extra to spend. Generally they were made up of three sections: a turned capital, a turned and fluted column, and a turned base. One complete assembly would provide enough parts for two chests. Even though produced in quantity, they must have been a fairly costly option, not only because of the additional time and material for making the columns, but also for the framing around the columns and the addition of drawer glides, for the drawers could no longer be guided by the sides of the case.

Not all chests of drawers with embellished corners were given quarter columns. An alternative, and perhaps slightly less expensive option, was a chamfered, fluted corner. This treatment, sometimes called a fluted lamb's tongue corner, is also seen in Maryland and New York furniture.

Both Pennsylvania and Southern furniture are associated with walnut, and while American black walnut is a good indicator of Southern workmanship, we need to be careful with Pennsylvania. Walnut is indeed the most common primary wood in Delaware Valley case work, but it is by no means the only wood. About one in four chests of drawers will be made of mahogany, and one in five will be of cherry. Mahogany would suggest an urban shop, most likely in Philadelphia itself; cherry either a more rural environment or the wish to spend a little less money. Among local woods, cherry is second only to walnut in the Middle Atlantic, and is often seen in chests and chests of drawers. In particular, we need to be careful to distinguish between Connecticut and Pennsylvania when looking at a cherrywood chest of drawers fitted with quarter columns.

Secondary woods in Delaware Valley chests of drawers are usually yellow pine and tulip poplar, pine for the top and bottom of the case and the backboards, poplar also for backboards and for drawer sides and bottoms. What makes this formula different from that of New York is the frequent use of Atlantic white cedar for the bottoms of drawers. It is also sometimes seen in backboards. Due to the softness of the wood, cedar drawer bottoms usually run from front to back — the shortest span across a full-width drawer. Cedar is simple to identify. The wood is so soft it is easily marked with a thumbnail, and there may still be a faint lingering aroma of cedar. Also, a cut across end grain — such as the back of a drawer bottom — will often look coarse and broken out due to the softness of the wood.

By far the most common Philadelphia-area Chippendale chest of drawers will be made of walnut and have four long drawers flanked by quarter columns as seen in figure 11-10A. Most all are raised on very solid and conservative ogee bracket feet, and necessarily so, for with the generous use of walnut and the dust dividers between the drawers, they are very solid chests. Some are remarkably heavy. Look under the bottom and you will see that the feet are usually backed with a single large curved glue block.

These chests of drawers have a solid, substantial appearance quite different in feeling from New England work. Part of this is due to the additional mass of the quarter columns, but perhaps more is due to the design of the top. Typically the top will have a moderate overhang which is molded on the front and sides, or has applied moldings, and then is given a cove molding just under the top. This molding helps to give the top depth and integrate it with the case. It is often seen on Pennsylvania William and Mary chests of drawers, but was also the normal treatment on high quality Rhode Island chest of drawers. Cove moldings are seldom seem on New England chests of drawers, even on the grandest furniture, in part because of the prevalence of shaped fronts, and also perhaps due to a preference for a greater overhang on a top. Only among early Pennsylvania chests of drawers do we find the bold, projecting tops seen on so much New England furniture.

Everywhere you may sometimes see a piece of case furniture in which the top, or even the entire upper section, extends back two or three inches so as to rest flush against the wall; this because the case below must be set out to clear a chair rail. This feature is commonly seen in Philadelphia chests of drawers, and as such, is an indicator of Delaware Valley workmanship.

The walnut chest of drawers shown in figure 11-10A is typical of a good-grade Philadelphia chest of drawers. Better-quality chests are made of figured mahogany and given elaborate gilded rococo bail pulls. Sometimes there will be a writing slide or a fretwork frieze just under the top of one of these. Bail pulls were favored in the Delaware Valley.

While a great many Philadelphia-area Chippendale chests of drawers were given quarter columns and ogee bracket feet, not all were made this way, and we might consider the exception. The handsome little chest of drawers in figure 11-10B has a somewhat New England look, but the use of walnut and the cove molding just under the top immediately suggest the

Delaware Valley. Here the top has a slight overhang and the corners have been notched, a little extra that was very popular in the Delaware Valley. We will see notched corners in the next chapter on a Philadelphia dressing table. Remove one of the top drawers and you will most probably see that there are full depth dust dividers between the drawers. This chest has lipped drawers, and here you may also notice that they are lipped all around, that is, on all four sides. The normal method was to lip drawers only on the top and sides, then thumbnail mold them all around, but on some case work the drawers are also lipped on all sides; and this technique, also seen in English furniture, is more common in the Delaware Valley than in New England.

This chest of drawers illustrates another feature of Middle Atlantic case work. Instead of the four long drawers seen in so much American furniture, the upper drawer has been divided into two smaller drawers. Although this is seen in early New England case work, it is far more common in the Middle Atlantic and in the South. About one in ten Pennsylvania chests of drawers has this two-over-three drawer arrangement.

Here it should be noted that the fronts of the drawers on chests of drawers made in Chester County may be decorated with a charming line and berry inlay. Typically the lines are formed with a series of compass arcs, and at the end will be a compass formed tulip, or three little circular berries, or both. The clusters of berries are themselves distinctive, for normally two will be of a lighter wood, and one darker. All of this inlay stands out very nicely against the darker walnut of the case. However, line and berry furniture is much prized and seldom comes on the market.

Following precedent, we will again close a section with an historically important form that you are unlikely to ever encounter outside of a museum. Earlier it was noted that high-quality serpentine-front chests of drawers were made everywhere, and the chest shown in figure 11-10C is Philadelphia's contribution to this group. As suggested by the heavy ogee bracket feet, these are large chests. Some are massive. The example in the Garvan Collection at Yale University is 41" high and almost 5' long. The broad canted corners are normally fluted as shown here, although in at least one example the corners are decorated with fretwork. In typical Philadelphia fashion, these chests have bail pulls. The best known, and perhaps the only makers, of these English pattern chests were Jonathan Gostelowe and Thomas Jones. These grand serpentine-front chests were to Philadelphia what the bombé was to Boston — something out of the ordinary and a bit flashy for the customer who could afford the very best.

11-10A. Pennsylvania Chippendale, 35" h x 40" w, 1760 – 1790.

11-10B. Pennsylvania Chippendale, 35" h x 37" w, 1760 – 1790.

11-10C. Philadelphia Chippendale, 38" h x 48" w, 1770 – 1790.

11-11 Southern Chippendale chests of drawers. While it may not seem altogether fair and balanced, we will cover the whole of the South in one section. This is due both to the scarcity of Chippendale chests of drawers and the relatively few urban centers producing standard types of case furniture. As noted earlier, the South was overwhelmingly agrarian prior to the Revolution, and with few exceptions, did not have the major style and production centers that tell us where something was made, that tell us at a glance that a chest is from Boston or Philadelphia, Newport or New York. By themselves, Southern chests of drawers are not difficult to identify. The problem is in determining where they were produced.

In general, Southern case work exhibits conservative styling and simple, solid construction. Framing is apt to heavy with thick boards and generous use of materials, which are suggestive of rural workmanship and a low production rate. Pull out a drawer and you will generally see thick drawer sides fastened with a minimum of dovetails, except in pieces made near the ocean. The primary wood will usually be walnut, and to a lesser extent, cherry. The drawers, the tops and bottoms of the case, and the backboards, are very likely to be yellow pine. In English fashion, backboards may be set vertically rather than horizontally, and on better work you are apt to see dust dividers between the drawers. Secretary drawers were fashionable, and

they are seen in chests of drawers, chest-on-chests, and clothespresses. Even on rural work, the drawer blade dovetails will generally be hidden under a covering strip. None of the chests of drawers in this section have exposed dovetails, although all are probably the products of small rural shops. However, they all postdate the Revolution, a time when everywhere dovetails tended to be hidden.

While there are exceptions, particularly in museum collections, Southern case work tends toward a rural simplicity, often very notably so. Not only is stock heavier than necessary, but workmanship frequently lacks the quality seen in other regions, even among rural furniture. Inlay is often somewhat crude, as though the craftsman turned out only a few pieces each year and had to make do with a very limited tool set. New England and the Middle Atlantic were also very rural at this time, but produced significantly better-quality furniture. It may be that because the sheer size of the backcountry, and the general lack of industry, that the Southern cabinetmaker simply lacked the basic tools — fine dovetail saws, a good set of planes, and a variety of chisels — to do neat cabinet work.

We will start with the most common form of Southern Chippendale chest of drawers, a walnut chest with a flat front, four graduated drawers, bail pulls, and rather conservative straight bracket feet (11-11A). Although identified as being from Virginia, there is little to suggest where in Virginia, although the use of walnut rather than mahogany would suggest somewhere inland. Walnut was so abundant that in addition to being used as a primary wood, you are apt to see it in secondary locations where a strong wood could be used to advantage, particularly in drawer sides and drawer slides.

Much Southern furniture can be located no closer than general area, and such is the case of the large chest of drawers in figure 11-11B, which although almost certainly Southern, has little to suggest a specific area of manufacture. The general simplicity of execution, the use of walnut and yellow pine, and the thick drawer sides all suggest Southern workmanship. The English two-over-three drawer arrangement is often seen in Southern chests of drawers. Ogee bracket feet are uncommon in the South, which would suggest this chest might have been made in the vicinity of Philadelphia, perhaps in northern Virginia.

Note that the position of the brasses is not quite correct, being centered on the posts rather than the pulls. On the bottom drawer, even the posts are not centered. Oddly positioned brasses are often seen in rural workmanship, and are not indicative of any particular region. However, they do suggest a small operation with limited production.

Case furniture having the top set flush with the sides is fairly common in England, but rare in America, most probably because there was no shortage of cabinet wood, and because this construction requires a very carefully mitered dovetail joint where the top meets the sides. However, a number of chests of drawers were made this way in tidewater Virginia, and this is probably the source of the walnut chest illustrated in figure 11-11C. Note that aside from the sophisticated dovetail joint this chest of drawers is a very rural product with simple bracket feet and neoclassical brasses that are too small for the case. They are most likely all that the cabinetmaker had on hand.

While Southern case work tends to be difficult to assign to a particular area, and even more so to a particular individual, we will conclude this section with a chest of drawers so unusual that it is easy to identify. Southern furniture can be noticeably idiosyncratic, and perhaps nowhere is this more evident than in the marvelous furniture made by John Shearer. An immigrant from England, Mr. Shearer worked in and around Martinsburg, West Virginia, at the turn of the eighteenth century. This was before the Civil War, when Martinsburg was still part of the Old Dominion. The serpentine chest of drawers in figure 11-11D is but a modest example of his wonderful cabinetry. Other case work employs stop-fluted quarter columns, tambour doors, and perhaps most remarkably, inlayed political statements that would seem to reflect his homeland ("Britannia Rules," "God Save the King," etc.). Mr. Shearer favored a shallow serpentine front with wide blocked ends. This shape is found not only in chests of drawers, but also in his pier tables, desks and secretaries. Perhaps because the deep blocking left no flat for the pulls, or because Mr. Shearer liked to be different, they are often set vertically as shown here. Whatever the reason, the result is very distinctive furniture.

11-11A. Virginia Chippendale, 39" w, 1780 – 1810.

**11-11B. Southern Chippendale,
36" h x 40" w, 1790 – 1810.**

**11-11C. Virginia Chippendale,
36" h x 42" w, c. 1800.**

11-11D. West Virginia Chippendale, 41" w, c. 1800.

11-12 New England neoclassical chest of drawers. We will begin a last sweep down the coast with the introduction of neoclassical styles during the economic recovery that followed the Revolution, that is, about 1790 or thereabouts. This time we will start further north, for Vermont has now filled up with people, and Maine will soon separate from Massachusetts to become its own state.

First we might consider a typical Federal New England chest of drawers (11-12). These inexpensive four-drawer chests were made everywhere in New England, usually of local hardwoods. Many are very simple, having no more than scratchbeaded drawer edges and the straight French feet shown here. Better-quality chests will have cockbeaded drawers and built-up outward sweeping feet. By now, even in rural work, the drawer blade dovetails were often hidden, either under a covering strip, or by stopping the dovetail slot just short of the front of the case.

These Hepplewhite-style chests of drawers can seldom be assigned to any particular location. As noted earlier, though, a chest made of maple or birch is most likely a product of northern New England. Similar chests of drawers made of cherry, maybe with poplar rather than white pine drawers, are more likely be from southeastern New England, possibly Connecticut. The use of chestnut for drawer bottoms or backboards would suggest Rhode Island or vicinity.

11-12. New England Hepplewhite, 39" h x 39" w, 1790 – 1830.

11-13 Vermont neoclassical chests of drawers. The Connecticut River flows up through western Massachusetts into Vermont, and from this there appears to have come to Vermont the preference for cherrywood that so characterizes the Connecticut River Valley. But this was not the only foreign influence, for adjacent rural New Hampshire seems to have provided a liking for figured maples; and coastal New Hampshire the practice of veneering drawer fronts with light maple or birch, then cross-banding the edges with a dark contrasting mahogany.

As a result, Vermont chests of drawers are apt to be made of cherry and have maple or birch veneered drawer fronts edged with mahogany, as shown in figure 11-13A. They resemble coastal New Hampshire and North Shore chests of drawers but that the case is made of cherry rather than birch or mahogany. Typically they also have rather thin unmolded tops and simple, straight French feet, sometimes with the notch or step shown in this illustration.

Basswood was much favored in Vermont. For some reason, perhaps because it was available and easily worked, Vermont cabinetmakers often employed this soft, light colored wood for drawers and backboards. When a chest was to be painted or grain decorated, it was often made entirely of basswood, even though white pine would have provided a more stable and stronger base. It may be that, by the early years of the nineteenth century, wide pine boards were becoming difficult to locate. Basswood was also employed as a primary and secondary wood in northern and inland Maine, and perhaps for the same reason.

We have seen that urban areas each seemed to produce one unusual and costly form of furniture: the bombé in Boston, the block and shell in Newport, and the overly large serpentine chests of drawers in Philadelphia. Vermont's contribution to this genre is a Hepplewhite chest of drawers having a bombé front (11-13B). However, you are also unlikely to come across this most famous of Vermont case work, for only about half a dozen seem to have been produced, and of these few, one is in Winterthur, another is in the Bennington Museum, and a third is in the Henry Ford Museum. The form most probably came upriver from Connecticut where there are some bracket-foot examples. Note that while there is a superficial resemblance to Boston bombé case work, these chests of drawers are much simpler, for only the fronts are swelled, rather than both the fronts and the sides.

11-13A. Vermont Hepplewhite, 35" h x 43" w, 1805 – 1820.

11-13B. Vermont Hepplewhite, 36" h x 40" w, 1810 – 1820.

11-14 Maine neoclassical chest of drawers. In the early years of the nineteenth century Maine was still very rural, and aside from some furniture produced in Saco on the extreme southeast coast, it appears to have produced little high-style furniture. The most common Maine chests of drawers are late Sheraton or Empire in style, having backsplashes and two small drawers on the tops of the cases, then four graduated drawers and turned legs, as seen in figure 11-14. Most are made entirely of white pine, although inland you may see basswood employed for drawer bottoms and backboards. At this time grain painting was very popular, and Maine case work is notable for its imaginative and fanciful decoration. A boldly grain-painted chest of drawers is likely to be from New England, and north of Massachusetts, most probably either Maine or Vermont.

11-14. Maine Sheraton, 51" h x 43" w, c. 1840.

11-15 New Hampshire neoclassical chest of drawers. In the first two decades of the nineteenth century, cabinetmakers in the small, prosperous city of Portsmouth produced a large group of notably colorful chests of drawers. These typically had bowed drawer fronts veneered with a light-colored wood: bird's-eye maple, flame birch, or tiger maple. To frame the drawers and provide contrast, the edges were then cross banded in a darker mahogany, and on the more striking examples, divided by further crossbanding into either two or three panels (11-15). A few have neoclassical ovals set within the center panels. Below these there will usually be a rectangular tablet or dropped panel centered in the apron. These distinctive dropped panels are a handy identifier, for they are seen on much Portsmouth-area furniture. A word of caution: neoclassical case work frequently has some inlay in the center of the apron. Sometimes this is a panel of lighter wood, an ellipse, or perhaps a diamond shape. What suggests Portsmouth is the rectangular panel.

It should be noted here that Massachusetts bowfront chests of drawers, particularly those from the North Shore, are apt to have some New Hampshire features: mahogany edged drawer fronts veneered in light maple or birch, or a rectangular tablet in the apron, or sometimes both. While these are associated with New Hampshire workmanship, the inspiration probably traveled north rather than south.

Although the facade is what first catches the eye, these chests have other features that characterize Portsmouth area workmanship and that can help us to identify more conservative less spectacular chests of drawers. The cases are raised on notably high French feet, which normally are given a small spur on the inside. The feet often flair out at the bottom to form the small, squared toe shown in this illustration. The rear feet are apt to be supported across the back by large, dovetailed, diagonal braces. Pull out the second drawer and you will often see that the case has been stiffened across the middle with a thick, wide, crosswise board set into the slots that carry the drawer slides. Although usually described as a dustboard, it may be open at the front and back, and is far more of a brace than a dustboard.

While these colorful chests of drawers appear to be made of mahogany, often the only mahogany is in the trim around the drawer fronts. The top and sides of the case will be birch stained up to resemble mahogany. Similar chests of drawers were made southward along the North Shore of Massachusetts, and at least 40 miles to the northeast in Saco, Maine.

11-15. Portsmouth Hepplewhite, 38" h x 40" w, 1800 – 1815.

11-16 Massachusetts neoclassical chests of drawers. We again will consider a number of Massachusetts chests of drawers, for the diversity in forms that characterized the Colonial period continues into the Federal. There is also a continuing preference for shaped case work, but with the advent of the neoclassical, chests of drawers are more apt to be bowed or swelled rather than blocked or serpentined.

Chests of drawers having curved or bowed fronts, "round front bureaus," as they were described in price books, are among the most common Federal furniture, so ordinary and middle class that they are seldom represented in museum collections. They were produced in quantity throughout New England, particularly in the northern tier of states: Massachusetts, New Hampshire, and Vermont. Fewer are from Rhode Island and Connecticut, this perhaps due to the small size of Rhode Island and the Connecticut preference for cherry. Curved fronts are usually veneered, and cherry seldom exhibits the decorative figure preferred for a veneer.

Bowed fronts were normally built up of softwood blocks, which were glued together, then leveled and veneered. As a general rule, in New England the blocking will be white pine, and in the Middle Atlantic and the South, poplar. However, there are many exceptions, for white pine is both stable and holds glue well, and it was used as far south as Charleston as a ground for veneer.

There are so many Boston area bowfront chests of drawers that we might first consider three produced prior to the advent of the Sheraton style: a conservative bowfront that retains the Chippendale bracket foot (11-16A), the far more common form with French feet in the new Hepplewhite style (11-16B), and a truly transitional chest of drawers that combines the neoclassical bowed front with a molded top and Chippendale ball and claw feet (11-16C). This last example is an easy study, for ball and claw bowfront chests of drawers appear to be unique to New England, and more specifically, to Boston and the North Shore, with a few from coastal New Hampshire.

Here it should be noted that Massachusetts case work had an unusually long transition between the rococo and neoclassical styles. In fact, for about two decades it is a complete muddle as older forms slowly acquire neoclassical features. This is seen in these three chests of drawers. Although bowed fronts are normally thought of as being neoclassical, and I have placed these with neoclassical chests of drawers, the first retains the old fashioned bracket feet, the second is up to date with a square, unmolded top and Hepplewhite French feet, and the third is rococo or Chippendale in everything but the bow front.

As you would expect, bowfont chests of drawers with bracket feet are somewhat earlier than those with neoclassical French feet. About half have the earlier molded tops, and a number retain the equally early ogee bracket feet. They also tend to be lower, lacking the height so often seen in neoclassical case work. The bracket-foot chest of drawers illustrated in figure 11-16A is a later example, and is more typical of the neoclassical influence in New England, having a thin, slightly molded top, string inlay on the front of the drawers, and oval neoclassical pulls. In common with neoclassical chests of drawers, it is also more square in proportion, being 40" wide and 37" high.

Far more common among Massachusetts bowfronts, and more common in New England generally, are bowfront chests of drawers with the neoclassical French feet (11-16B). The more fashionable may have a squared toe at the base of such a foot, and many have the additional stiffening behind the rear feet shown in this illustration. Although such bracing is associated with Portsmouth workmanship, it is a common feature, particularly when a chest has rather high legs.

Chests of drawers in the Sheraton style with turned legs were so popular in northern New England that we will look at four common types: a high-style Boston chest with an attached dressing mirror (11-16D), an urban chest with the less common flat front (11-16E), the well-known Salem type with carving at the top of the stiles or colonettes (11-16F), and one of the ubiquitous late Sheraton chests of drawers with spiral-turned stiles (11-16G). We will also see a Seymour-type chest of drawers, but these are so scarce that you may never see one at auction.

Raising a chest on thin legs poses a structural problem, for no longer is it possible to simply glue the feet to the bottom of the case. The obvious solution, long seen on highboys, is to extend the structure of the legs up the sides of the case, and the best way to do this on a chest of drawers is to set the legs out a bit so they do not have to be cut away for the drawers. The extension of the turned legs, the stiles or colonettes, then terminate at the top of the case with a round cookie shaped pad. Although described in museum collections as chests of drawers with outset corner columns, or three quarter-round stiles, or engaged colonettes, they are everywhere simply called "cookie corner" chests.

To avoid having the case appear top heavy on the rather thin legs, most of these chests have either a very shallow bow, or more commonly, the swelled or flattened D-shape shown in figure 11-16E. Many rural products have straight fronts, although this is no particular indication of rural workmanship, for high-style cookie corner chests with straight fronts were made in Boston (11-16F). Here it should be mentioned that for a short period it was fashionable to decorate the mahogany banding around the drawers with alternating sections of lighter wood, which today gives the impression that the banding has been extensively and poorly repaired. This unusual decorative effect seems to have been limited to coastal Massachusetts and New Hampshire.

High-style Sheraton chests of drawers will most probably be from Boston, Salem, or perhaps Newburyport. On better work, the colonettes were normally turned and then reeded as shown in figures 11-16D and 11-16E. In common with other fine case work, the small drawers below the mirror in figure 11-16D are likely to be made of mahogany. With time the legs and colonettes become thicker, and better quality work, particularly in Salem, is apt to have extensive carving under the circular pad. The carving on the Salem chest of drawers in figure 11-16F is often ascribed to the hand of Samuel McIntire, although he was but one of at least half a dozen carvers active in Salem at this time.

There is no end of different colonette turnings on these chests, and it is sometimes possible to locate a chest on the basis of the turnings. One such example is a large group of North Shore chests in which the lower legs have the distinctive cylinders, compressed balusters, balusters, and double ring turnings shown in figure 11-16G. The spiral turnings are more an indication of lateness than region, for they are also found on much Connecticut furniture. They speak more to us of technological development, for economical production requires lathes with spiral turning attachments. Note that the top of the colonettes are decorated with the stacked rings that are often seen in Federal New England furniture.

Cookie-corner chests of drawers were made to some extent everywhere, mostly in northeastern New England, eastern Massachusetts, and coastal New Hampshire. A few are from Rhode Island, almost none from Connecticut. To a much lesser extent they were produced in New York, although these have so many New York features that there should be no confusion as to origin. Like a great many successful designs, cookie corners are not even American, and you will often see them in English antique shops. Here the chests of drawers may resemble the somewhat English-looking Boston chest of drawers illustrated in figure 11-16H, which is similar to those made by John and Thomas Seymour. These chests are notable for the shallow arched skirts or aprons that curve down at the ends to support the legs. Those from the Seymour's shop will be most beautifully made with the very best of veneers and inlays. Later, in the chapter on sideboards and serving tables, we will see a similar arched skirt in a small Boston cellaret sideboard (14-2F).

11-16A. Massachusetts Chippendale, 37" h x 40" w, 1780 – 1800.

11-16B. Massachusetts Hepple-white, 38" h x 39" w, 1790 – 1810.

11-16C. Massachusetts Chippen-dale, 32" h x 40" w, c. 1790.

11-16D. Boston Sheraton, 73" h x 43" w, 1810 – 1820.

11-16E. Boston Sheraton, 38" h x 42" w, 1810 – 1820.

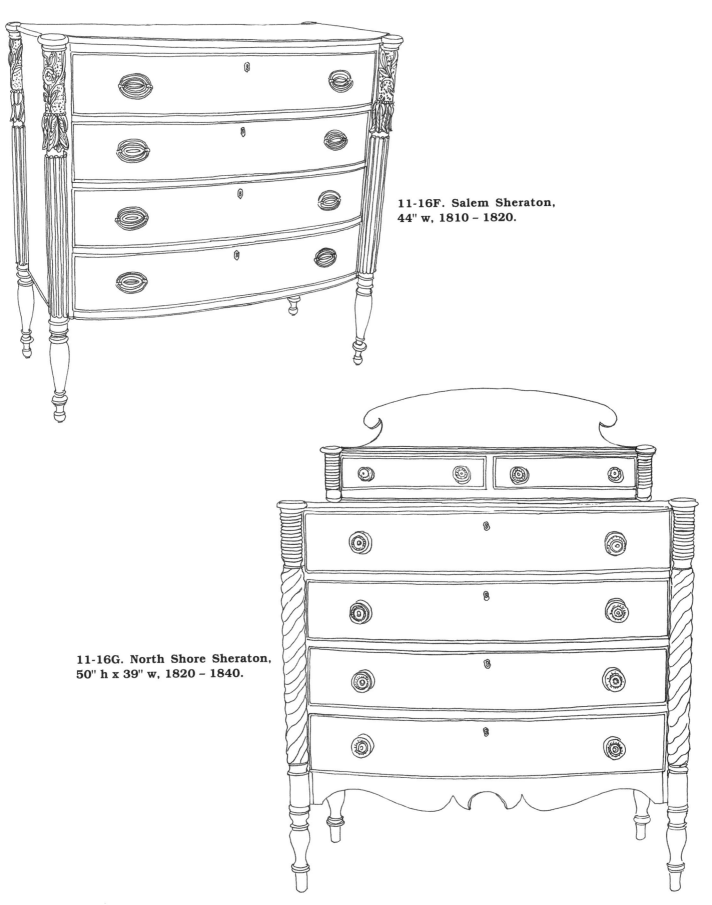

**11-16F. Salem Sheraton,
44" w, 1810 – 1820.**

**11-16G. North Shore Sheraton,
50" h x 39" w, 1820 – 1840.**

11-16H. Boston Seymore-type, c. 1810.

11-17 Connecticut neoclassical chest of drawers. Neoclassical chests of drawers from Connecticut and Rhode Island are little different from others of New England workmanship and can perhaps be best identified by the retention of local features: the use of poplar and chestnut as secondary woods in Rhode Island and eastern Connecticut, the use of poplar in coastal Connecticut, and the preference for cherrywood in Connecticut, and also up the Connecticut River Valley through western Massachusetts. Connecticut bowfront chests of drawers tend to retain the quarter columns that we saw in earlier in a Chippendale chest of drawers.

In addition to usually being made of cherry, a Connecticut chest of drawers is very likely to have a little extra decoration here and there, perhaps an oval or diamond shaped inlay of lighter wood centered in the top, a double band of line inlay on the front and sides edges of the top, some decorative inlay on the drawer fronts, a band of line inlay across the top of the apron, or, quite frequently, some inlay on the face of the bracket feet as shown in figure 11-17. A cherry chest of drawers may or may not be from Connecticut, but if there is also some slightly naive additional decoration, then it is very likely to be from the Connecticut River Valley. The Valley continues up through western Massachusetts, and here you are apt to see cherry case work with a distinctly Massachusetts look about it, particularly in Sheraton chests of drawers.

11-17. Connecticut Chippendale, 40" w, 1800 – 1820.

11-18 New York neoclassical chests of drawers. New York Federal chests of drawers may be a problem, for among the average grade of work it is not always easy to differentiate between New York City and Philadelphia. The authors of auction catalogs nimbly skirt the question by identifying many chests of drawers as simply being Middle Atlantic. However, we will try to do a little better, and hopefully will be able to direct you toward one city or the other.

The best known neoclassical New York chests of drawers have a deep drawer above three smaller graduated drawers (11-18A). The example shown here, in which the upper drawer is decorated with a pair of diamond shaped satinwood inlays flanking a large oval inlay, would most probably be attributed to New York cabinetmaker Michael Allison on the basis of a number of labeled examples. Michael Allison labeled much of the work from his shop, and should you be examining a well made Middle Atlantic chest of drawers, it is worth a look to see if his label is not inside a drawer.

Similar chests of drawers were made throughout eastern New York and Northern New Jersey, most much simpler than this urban product. A few appear to have been made in Maryland, maybe by New York cabinetmakers that had moved south in search of more opportunity. The deep drawer was probably used for the large hats and bonnets that were fashionable at this time. In some, these drawers are fitted with butler's desks. Like much New York case work, these chests of drawers tend to be large and rather wide in proportion to their depth.

High-style New York Federal chests of drawers frequently have the rather delicate-looking outswept French feet shown in figure 11-18B. Often there will be either two or three top draw-ers. Sometimes the top drawers are separated by the rectangular satinwood panel or reserve shown here. The panel itself may be a working drawer. Chests of drawers similar to this are also labeled by Michael Allison.

As we see in figure 11-18C, in New York the new Sheraton style was interpreted very differently. Here we have a cookie corner chest of drawers quite unlike anything produced in New England. The deep flat-front case is raised on short reeded legs, which terminate in brass ball feet. It is quite large, 44" high and almost 49" wide. In keeping with New York Federal fashion, the drawer fronts are single slabs of dark, rich mahogany veneer without either light-wood stringing or cross banding. The chest has the two-over-three drawer arrangement frequently seen in New York case work. Similar chests will have a deep top drawer. At times the sides will be paneled, and this may have been done as much to avoid the danger of splitting as to economize on mahogany, for these large chests of drawers were not budget products.

In general, Federal chests of drawers from New York City will be both large and well made, almost always of mahogany, the drawer faces veneered with richly figured mahogany, sometimes with a string of holly inlay. Most have flat fronts devoid of any shaping or carving. The legs often have brass ball feet; sometimes carved or brass paw feet. Veneering will usually be on a base of eastern white pine. Drawers are commonly made of tulip poplar. Pull out the top drawer and you will see there are full depth dividers between the drawers. New York Federal case furniture generally lacks the contrasting veneers and feeling of lightness seen in that from in New England, and does not have the bowed fronts and inlay we will see further south.

11-18A. New York Hepplewhite, 46" h x 45" w, 1800 – 1810.

11-18B. New York Hepplewhite, 41" h x 44" w, 1790 – 1810.

11-18C. New York Sheraton, 44" h x 49" w, c. 1815.

11-19 Pennsylvania neoclassical chests of drawers. While bowfront chests of drawers were not common in New York, they were very popular in Pennsylvania, and I will show you three examples. However, we might first consider a typical straight-front chest of drawers made in eastern Pennsylvania (11-19A). These can often be identified by earlier features that have been adapted to the new neoclassical taste. In addition to a continuing use of walnut, you may see a simplified line and berry inlay worked into the drawer fronts, or line-inlaid quarter columns or chamfered corners. The chest of drawers illustrated in figure 11-19A is made of walnut. The chamfered corners are line-inlaid with a lighter wood, line inlay having replaced the earlier rococo fluting.

The bowfront chest of drawers in figure 11-19B also is a continuation of earlier traditions, having the fluted quarter columns and the large ogee bracket feet so often seen in Pennsylvania Chippendale chests of drawers. It is different, though, for in addition to the neoclassical brasses and the bow front, there is no longer a cove molding below the top, and perhaps more significantly, the chest is made of mahogany, for even in Pennsylvania walnut is finally giving way to this more fashionable cabinet wood. This chest is also newer than you might think, for it carries the signature of Philadelphia cabinetmaker William Trotter, Jr., and the date of June 1801. Massachusetts was not the only state to have a slow transition to the neoclassical.

The second bowfront chest has acquired further neoclassical features: a straight-edged top decorated with line inlay, inlaid vase-shaped escutcheons, outswept French feet, and perhaps most interestingly, an oval patera centered in the skirt (11-19C). While this chest of drawers was identified in an auction catalog as Middle Atlantic, the figure inlay in the center of the skirt suggests that it was made in Philadelphia rather than New York. Although the French feet are nicely proportioned, if you look back to a similar Massachusetts bowfront chest of drawers (11-16B), you will note that they are not nearly as tall and do not have the little squared toes at the bases of the feet.

The last bowfront is Sheraton in style, but very different from the cookie corner chests we saw in New England, and to a lesser extent, in New York. Here the legs again extend up the sides of the case, but they are not outset as in New England (11-19D). On some the stiles are molded on the front so as to resemble pilasters. Aside from the typical Pennsylvania turnings of the feet, there is nothing particularly regional in this design. Simpler versions with straight fronts were made everywhere, and in the next section we will see a Southern example.

It might be noted that while bowfront chests of drawers from the Delaware Valley were seldom made of walnut, they are not all mahogany, for many are made of cherry, sometimes in combination with mahogany. This was not always a question of economy, for the handsome inlaid chest in figure 11-19C is made of cherry, and the chest in figure 11-19D is of a figured maple. It might also be noted that in most of these chests, the drawer fronts will be blocked up with poplar rather than white pine.

11-19A. Pennsylvania Hepplewhite, 37" h x 41" w, 1790 – 1810.

11-19B. Philadelphia Chippendale, 37" h x 44" w, 1801.

11-19C. Middle Atlantic Hepplewhite, 37" h x 40" w, 1790 – 1820.

11-19D. Pennsylvania Sheraton, 41" h x 40" w, c. 1825.

11-20 Southern neoclassical chests of drawers. There are many surviving Southern neoclassical chests of drawers, but again, unless there is a signature or some family history, it may not be easy to determine the location of manufacture. To some extent the primary woods can help, for by this time mahogany was employed almost everywhere it was available, and this can suggest region. One would expect that better-quality furniture made in eastern Maryland, tidewater Virginia, and coastal North and South Carolina to be made of mahogany, while further inland, cabinet-makers would have to make do with either walnut or cherry. An urban chest of drawers made of mahogany will most likely be from either Baltimore, Annapolis, Norfolk, or Charleston. It is very unlikely to be from either Salem or Charlotte.

The popularity of the bowfront in Philadelphia area extended across the Mason-Dixon Line to nearby Maryland, and there are a considerable number of bowfront chests of drawers with Maryland provenances. However, they are newer in style, for while some have quarter columns, none seem to retain the old-fashioned molded top and ogee bracket feet that continued to be employed in Philadelphia. Aside from somewhat greater use of yellow pine, it is not always easy to tell the difference between a Maryland and a Pennsylvania bowfront chest of drawers. However, should you encounter one with an extravagant amount of inlay, perhaps a large oval patera centered in the top, or an oversize fan in the skirt (11-20A), you are very probably looking at Baltimore workmanship. Look back at figure 11-19C and you will see a far more restrained handling of figure inlay. It should be noted that while most Southern bowfront chests are from Maryland, a considerable number of walnut and cherry bowfront chests of drawers were produced in Tennessee and Kentucky, where this neoclassical design seems to have been very fashionable. Should you encounter a relatively simple bowfront chest of drawers made of cherry or walnut having much yellow pine among the secondary woods, it may be a product of the Southern backcountry.

Earlier it was noted that serpentine chests of drawers were produced everywhere in urban areas. This is also true of the South, where high quality serpentine front chests were made in Baltimore, Norfolk, and Charleston — everywhere there was the money and the skill. The Baltimore serpentine-front chest of drawers in figure 11-20B is unusual in having French feet which gives it a distinctly English appearance. Most American serpentine chests of drawers have either straight or ogee bracket feet. However, this might be expected, for in terms of style, Colonial New York and Federal Baltimore were the most English of American cities. In addition to French feet, Southern serpentine chests are apt to exhibit atypical features such as decorative inlay worked into canted stiles that flank the drawers. So inexpensive was mahogany in Charleston that some serpentine drawer fronts were not veneered in the normal manner, but instead were cut from single thick boards.

Southern Hepplewhite chests of drawers are not very different from the Southern Chippendale chests of drawers covered in section 11-11. Normally they will be rural, will be somewhat overbuilt, and will employ yellow pine as a secondary wood. Most will be made of either walnut or cherry, or will be made of mahogany if made in an urban center near the coast.

They are quite common, and we might look at two very different designs. The Rowan County, North Carolina, chest of drawers in figure 11-20C is typical of Southern production in the decades following the Revolution. It has the deep bonnet drawer that we saw in a New York Federal chest of drawers, but which is no particular indicator of region, for these drawers are seen everywhere. More indicative of Southern workmanship is the neat appearance in combination with the general simplicity of execution. There is a single row of stringing across the apron. The drawer fronts are decorated with a little stringing having invected, or in-curving, corners. Although this pattern is seen in all regions, it is particularly common in Southern furniture, perhaps because it could be laid out with no more than a depth gauge and a compass.

The second Hepplewhite chest of drawers is a more interesting subject, for it exhibits so many of the features seen in rural Southern case work. At first glance, the four-drawer flat-front bureau in figure 11-20D would seem a typical Federal product, but if we saw it in person we would immediately realize that it was not from New England — and most probably not from the Middle Atlantic either. The walnut case and the tulip poplar drawers suggest Pennsylvania, except that the cabinet-maker seems to have been working with a remarkably limited set of tools. Although given a little neoclassical stringing, the drawer fronts are not veneered. The fans at the corners are crudely made up of local woods, then glued into quarter-round depressions chiseled into the corners of the drawers. In common with Southern case work, the drawer blade dovetails have been given a covering strip. These are fastened with wooden pins, which suggests the cabinetmaker, or the cabinetmaking tradition, came from the Delaware Valley. The chest might be from the Valley of Virginia or the North Carolina backcountry. Now look at the scalloped apron or skirt. The center section is of typical form, but then there are strange little rococo-like scrolls tucked in at the corners where the skirt joins the leg. The pattern is attempted with less success on the sides of the case, where there is not enough room for all the curves. The whole effect is of limited production and a craftsman working very much on his own without other examples or the help of peers from which to develop standard harmonious shapes. Were this chest to be examined more closely, you would probably see that although the drawers are made of poplar, the structural members, the bottom of the case, and the drawer slides are of a hard Southern pine.

Sheraton-style chests of drawers with flat fronts and paneled ends were produced in all regions, but here we might look at a Southern example, not only because such chests are particularly common in the South, but because they are just the sort of pieces that may have lost their Southern provenance if sent north for sale. The chest of drawers in figure 11-20D is typical of a large number of Sheraton chests of drawers produced throughout the South in the first decades of the nineteenth century. Most are made of walnut or cherry, with poplar or yellow pine secondary. Often there will be a little inlay worked into either the stiles or the fronts of the drawers. Note that the oval pulls are somewhat old-fashioned; they are more Hepplewhite than Sheraton. Were this an urban product, it would probably be fitted with either flush ring pulls or the raised embossed knobs illustrated in figure 11-19D.

It should be noted that the great majority of surviving Southern case work is relatively new. Very little survives that was made prior to the Revolution. The chests of drawers in this section are all typical of Southern workmanship, and yet not one is Colonial. Most are not even early Federal.

11-20A. Baltimore Hepplewhite, 36" h x 40" w, c. 1810.

11-20B. Baltimore Hepplewhite, 38" h x 46" w, c. 1810.

11-20C. North Carolina Hepplewhite, 45" h x 44" w, 1800 – 1810.

11-20D. Southern Hepplewhite, 41" h x 37" w, c. 1820.

11-20E. Southern Sheraton, 44" h x 42" w, c. 1825.

11-21 New England tall chests of drawers. In a land in which good cabinet wood was everywhere, the tall chest of drawers proved an irresistible attraction. For the fractional cost of a little extra wood and the time required to assemble two or three additional drawers, a cabinetmaker could provide almost as much storage as a chest-on-chest. Better yet, if the upper surface were above eye level, there would be no need for a carefully leveled and molded top. A simple cornice molding would do just as well. As a natural result, tall chests of drawers were produced almost everywhere in America, particularly in northern New England and the Delaware Valley.

For the most part, tall chests of drawers are rural products and often can be identified no closer than region, although sometimes there are clues that can help us determine a specific area. First we might consider two typical New England tall chests of drawers, then look at some others having local features. Tall chests are rural or semirural products. I have never seen a documented example from either Boston or Philadelphia, or one made of mahogany, even though they were produced near major urban centers.

The typical New England tall chest will have five or six graduated drawers above straight bracket feet as shown in figure 11-21A. A few have French feet; a rare few, ogee bracket feet. Most are made of maple with white pine drawers and backboards. Others will be birch, pine, or cherry, or sometimes apple, butternut, or sycamore, or a mixture such as maple and pine — any suitable and available wood. While splitting the top drawer into two

smaller drawers is commonly associated with Middle Atlantic case work, about one in four New England tall chests has a divided top drawer — or what appears to be a divided top drawer, for frequently the front of the drawer is shaped to resemble two or three small drawers. One popular treatment was to divide the top drawers into three sections, with a little carved fan in the center "drawer," as seen in figure 11-21B.

New Hampshire cabinetmakers favored the decorative economy of false drawers, and it is not unusual to see case work in which both upper and lower drawers have false fronts. The red-washed birch New Hampshire tall chest of drawers in figure 11-21C is a admirable example, for the pinwheel carved drawer and the four small flanking drawers at the top of the case are but a single deep drawer. Unfortunately, there is nothing unique to New Hampshire in this particular drawer arrangement, for you will shortly see the same idea in a Connecticut tall chest.

Earlier it was noted that New Hampshire residents had an affection for the Queen Anne style, which we saw in a Dunlap-type chest of drawers with cabriole legs (11-5A). Tall chests of drawers were given the same treatment. Aside from a number of Dunlap School examples, the best known are the work of Peter Bartlett of Salisbury, New Hampshire, who is believed to have made the six-drawer tall chest shown in figure 11-21D. Later we will see a similar Queen Anne style desk attributed to Mr. Bartlett. Note that the legs on this chest differ from Dunlap work in being more angular and having knees with clear arris, and then having a pronounced pad under the feet, much the same shape seen in the late Chippendale Massachusetts chairs. Bartlett-type chests also lack the whimsical carving so often seen on the base molding of Dunlap case work. A number of these bandy-leg tall chests have separate frames.

The woods employed in New Hampshire are remarkably consistent. When not painted white pine, most all case work will be maple or birch or a combination of both. Drawers and backboards are almost invariably white pine.

Massachusetts tall chests are not particularly distinctive, although the majority of tall chests identified simply as being from New England may actually be from this most populous New England colony. However, Rhode Island tall chests are not difficult to identify. In addition to the presence of chestnut, we see a quality of workmanship not usually seen in New England. Tall chests made in Rhode Island are sometimes cherry, but are usually maple, and very often tiger maple — what might be expected in a better-than-average product. The dovetails joining the top of the case will frequently be hidden, either by a raised cornice molding, or a raised molding and dovetails covering the case, or a finished top fitted within a raised molding, as shown in figure 11-21E. When none of these are done and the dovetails are left to show, the top will still be neatly finished. Often the upper drawer will be split or will be shaped to resemble three drawers, with a carved fan in the center drawer as seen earlier. At the bottom of the case, the base molding will be set flush with the lower surface of the bottom board. Pull out the bottom drawer and you will see that it rests on a pair of slides rather than on the bottom of the case.

On very tall chests, you will sometimes see the three-short-over-two-short drawer arrangement that was so popular in the Delaware Valley. These may also be fitted with the wood spring "Quaker" locks so often seen in Pennsylvania cabinet work. One might speculate that the use of Quaker locks in both areas is due to the presence of Quaker cabinetmakers in both areas, but this simple locking mechanism is such a logical method to economize on hardware that it might be found anywhere.

The tall chest was not as popular in Connecticut as it was further north, but this is more than made up for by variety and visual interest, and I will show you two fairly typical examples. The first is what is called a semitall chest, a chest that has five tiers of drawers but is only a little over 40" high (11-21F). These are fairly common among Connecticut furniture, but are not unique to Connecticut, nor even to New England, for in the next section we will see two Delaware Valley examples. While this is

a simple, inexpensive painted chest, it illustrates the divided upper drawer and pronounced cornice molding typical of these chests. It gives the impression they may have started out life as the upper section of a highboy or chest-on-chest, which they did not. Better quality semi-tall chests will be made of cherry and may be enhanced with quarter columns or fan carving in a top drawer. A number employ the five drawer pattern illustrated in the next figure.

The second Connecticut tall chest of drawers (11-21G) is of a more conventional height. It has the same grouping of upper drawers that we saw simulated in New Hampshire, a pattern that was popular in Connecticut and which you will see again in a Connecticut highboy. Although this distinctive pattern is most often seen in New England case work, it is not unique to the region, for there are Delaware Valley tall chests made the same way. The popularity of this somewhat odd configuration is perhaps due to the layout, for the square center drawer provides a perfect location for a carved pinwheel or fan.

11-21A. New England Chippendale, 52" h, 1780 – 1810.

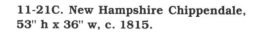

11-21B. New England Chippendale, 55" h x 36" w, 1780 – 1810.

11-21C. New Hampshire Chippendale, 53" h x 36" w, c. 1815.

11-21D. New Hampshire Queen Anne, c. 1810.

11-21E. Rhode Island Chippendale, 44" h x 36" w, 1760 – 1790.

11-21F. Connecticut Chippendale, 43" h x 40" w, c. 1780.

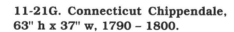
11-21G. Connecticut Chippendale, 63" h x 37" w, 1790 – 1800.

11-22 Middle Atlantic tall chests of drawers. South of Connecticut the tall chest of drawers lost popularity to such an extent that it was never, or almost never, produced in New York and northern New Jersey. Dean Failey's book on Long Island does not show a single tall chest of drawers. In New York, and also in northern New Jersey, the chest-on-chest and the clothespress were employed when additional storage was desired.

Not until we get down to Pennsylvania and the Delaware Valley does the tall chest of drawers return, and it is here that it becomes most fully developed. This is where we see good primary woods and fine case work in what in New England was often a budget product. These grand big tall chests of drawers were produced over so long a period, and survive in such quantities, that we will look at a number of examples in different styles. In their best rococo form, they stand about 5½' high on large ogee bracket feet, have generous built-up molded cornices, and quarter columns flanking their full lengths (11-22A). There are two common drawer patterns: the three short over two short over four or five long shown here, or three short over four, five, or even six long. Sometimes there is a small, square drawer tucked in between the two short drawers. A rare few have the five drawer grouping in the upper case that was so popular in New England.

Not every customer desired quarter columns, and many good-quality tall chests do not have them. Neither are all tall chests flat topped, for there are a few with the scrolled tops, carved rosettes, and turned finials seen on many area highboys. Some also have high-style fire gilt rococo brasses, suggesting that, at least in the Delaware Valley, not all tall chests were products of rural shops.

A Delaware Valley tall chest, in common with the lift-top chests discussed in the last chapter, tends to be large, heavy, and very stoutly constructed. Drawer sides are thick and the bottoms are often set into dadoes or slots all around, rather than the usual practice in which dadoes are on only the front and sides, the drawer bottom being inserted from the rear. Wooden pins are employed to fasten dust boards and backboards. To help carry the weight of the case, the sides of the case may continue behind the bracket feet all the way to the floor. What appears to be separate ogee feet is just a facing.

Very often the short upper drawers were fitted with wooden Quaker locks, and although frequently now missing, you will see the remains of the locks on the underside of the drawers. Although they may seem to be no more than a thrifty substitute for a regular metal lock, there were practical advantages. A high-up lock is difficult to use, and also, a short drawer has little room for both a pull and an escutcheon. It is thought that tall furniture was given short drawers in the upper registers because these drawers were normally accessed by being lifted out and set down on a flat surface. One would not want to have to reach up and lift out a full-width drawer.

It might be noted here, that like much else, the three over two drawer arrangement so favored in Delaware Valley case work is by no means unique to the Delaware Valley. It is also seen in

New England, although here tall chests will not be so massive; the primary wood is likely to be maple, and the top tier of drawers may actually be a single drawer faced to simulate three.

Most all these tall chests were made of walnut, although later there was more use of cherry and, sometimes, maple. Secondary woods that you'll see are most likely to be either pine or poplar. Drawers will sometimes be bottomed front to back in Atlantic white cedar. In common with lift-top chests, a date and the initials of the owners will sometimes be inlayed in the top drawers, suggesting that these chests may have been made as dower furniture.

After the Revolution, the tall chest continued in popularity, acquiring French feet and neoclassical brasses (11-22B). There are other neoclassical influences that we can see: the cornice became simpler, the escutcheons are apt to be ivory or light wood inlay, the drawers may be cockbeaded rather than lipped, and there will often be a little string inlay on the front of the drawers, as shown here. Most omit quarter columns. Instead you may see chamfered corners with a little line inlay. Many of these later chests, perhaps even the majority, are made of cherry rather than walnut. A few are tiger maple.

Such was the popularity of the tall chest in the Delaware Valley that they continued in production well into the nineteenth century, and you will even see survival examples in the Sheraton style (11-22C). Note that while this cherry tall chest retains the same three-short-over-five-long drawer arrangement seen in the previous illustration, it is similar in many ways to the Pennsylvania Sheraton bowfront chest of drawers in figure 11-19D, having the same construction, paneled ends, and leg turnings. On this tall chest, the stiles are molded on the front so as to resemble pilasters.

Tall chests with fielded paneled sides are thought to be from northeast of Philadelphia in Chester County, but as similar chests are credited to Lancaster County, paneling may be more a sign of rural workmanship than location. That the walnut tall chest shown in figure 11-22D may also be an early product is suggested by the small Queen Anne style bat-wing brasses and the straight bracket feet. In some Chester County tall chests, the upper tiers of small drawers will be curved or arched across the tops.

Semitall chests were fairly common in the Delaware Valley, and before moving south we will take a look at two regional examples. Although the tall chest in figure 11-22E is very similar to the standard Pennsylvania walnut chest of drawers, it is made of pine and poplar, then grain painted to resemble walnut. While Chippendale in style, it is Federal rather than Colonial. In spite of the use of pine, poplar and paint, the maker took the time and effort to give it the fluted quarter columns and ogee bracket feet seen in traditional — and by this time very old-fashioned — Chippendale-style tall chests of drawers.

Delaware Valley case work tends toward the massive, and nowhere is this more evident than in the brown-painted cherry semitall chest of drawers shown in figure 11-22F. While actually a few inches smaller in both height and width than the preceding example, the early bracket feet give it a well-deserved massive look. Similar chests were produced in Berks County, which lies about an hour's drive to the northeast of Philadelphia. Note that there was no effort to hide the joint where the drawer blades were fastened to the sides of the case. Instead we see the simple through dovetails employed in so much rural New England case work.

Most of these Delaware Valley semitall chests of drawers are about 4' high and employ the two-short-over-four-long drawer pattern shown here. Others will mimic full-height chests, with three short drawers over two short drawers over three long drawers.

11-22A. Delaware Valley Chippendale, 64" h x 40" w, 1760 – 1790.

11-22B. Delaware Valley Hepple-white, 65" h x 44" w, 1790 – 1810.

11-22C. Delaware Valley Sheraton, 66" h x 41" w, 1830 – 1840.

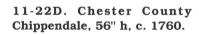

11-22D. Chester County Chippendale, 56" h, c. 1760.

11-22E. Delaware Valley Chippendale, 50" h x 40" w, 1790 – 1810.

11-22F. Delaware Valley Chippendale, 47" h x 37" w, 1760 – 1810.

11-23 Southern tall chest of drawers. Although very seldom, if ever, produced in coastal areas, the tall chest of drawers was quite popular in the backcountry, the design having come south with settlers from Lancaster and surrounding counties. Although lacking quarter columns, the walnut tall chest in figure 11-23 would seem to be a Delaware Valley product, but it was probably made in North Carolina, where Pennsylvania-type tall chests were especially fashionable. Although made of walnut, the secondary wood is a yellow pine, and it is fastened entirely with cut nails. These factors suggest both a rather late date and a source other than the Delaware Valley. Some North Carolina tall chests have pitched pediments similar in shape to that shown in the Philadelphia chest-on-chest in figure 11-25E.

11-23. North Carolina Chippendale, 66" h x 44" w, c. 1800.

11-24 New England chest-on-chests. Chest-on-chests were made in all regions, but there are areas where they were very uncommon. They were popular in the coastal South, but were seldom made in the backcountry. While you would think that this very English furniture type would be most fashionable in the more English of the colonies, they were also fashionable in New England, particularly in New Hampshire and Connecticut. It may be that in rural areas they were considered both easier to construct and provided more storage than a high chest of drawers. A cabinetmaker who could produce a serviceable chest of drawers could most probably also make a chest-on-chest, particularly as it did not require a finished top.

While we will see some grand urban versions, the great majority of New England chest-on-chests are rural products. In common with tall chests of drawers, they may lack any particular feature to suggest an particular area of manufacture, and we must rely on the primary and secondary woods to get an idea of where they might have been produced. The most common New England chest-on-chest has a flat top, five long drawers in the upper case, four drawers in the lower case, and scrolled straight bracket feet as shown in figure 11-24A. Most are made of maple or birch and are of very simple construction with the drawer blade dovetails simply tenoned through the sides of the case. Some have but three drawers in the lower case.

Bonnet-tops were much the fashion in New England, and although they were more of a challenge to the cabinetmaker, and maybe added another third to the cost, there are many rural examples. The bonnet-top in figure 11-24B is a very basic model. Many have a fan in the deep center drawer, a pair of flanking finials, and simple rosettes at the top of the scrolls. Aside from being produced in New England, It is difficult to tell where either of these chest-on-chests were made. The wood can help a little. Maple was used everywhere, but particularly in southern New Hampshire, as also was birch. Cherry is found everywhere, but was most popular in the Connecticut River Valley. Among secondary woods, white pine is most likely north of Boston, poplar in coastal Connecticut, and chestnut in Rhode Island, the eastern corner of Connecticut, and southeast Massachusetts.

Although most New Hampshire customers opted for the basic bracket foot chest-on-chest, when there was a little extra to spend it was often spent on the cabriole legs shown in figure 11-24C. This again is a simple version. Other chests of this type will have the five drawer grouping seen in New Hampshire tall chests, and again, these drawers may be simulated. Dunlap School chest-on-chests will have the deep, fancifully scrolled skirt that we will see in the next chapter in a Dunlap high chest. A number of these tall chest-on-chests are on frames, that is, they are chest-on-chest-on-frames. A few are given rather provincial-looking ball and claw feet. In common with New England practice, and particularly in New Hampshire, there has been no attempt to hide the drawer blade dovetails, which extend through the sides of the case. While these very rural chest-on-chests are Queen Anne in style, many of them postdate the Revolution.

Having seen three rural New England chest-on-chests, we might now consider two urban examples. The first is one of a number of similar chest-on-chests made in the Boston area, that is, Boston, Charlestown, Salem, and up along the North Shore (11-24D). Most are made of mahogany and have white pine as a secondary wood, although there are a few walnut, maple, and birch examples. The commonality lies in the upper case: a bonnet top surmounted by either a central urn and spiral finial, or three urn and spiral finials; a carved-shell deep drawer with two smaller flanking drawers, and a pair of fluted pilasters on either side of the drawers. The lower case may be either blocked, as shown here, or reverse-serpentine or flat across the front; below this may be straight bracket feet, ogee bracket feet, or, sometimes, ball and claw feet. A reverse-serpentine lower case would suggest a chest produced not earlier than the 1780s. The chest-on-chest shown here is unusual in having a dressing slide, a feature found everywhere on quality work, but more commonly seen on Middle Atlantic and English chest-on-chests.

Rhode Island bonnet-top chest-on-chests, like Rhode Island chests of drawers, are an easy study, for in both design and construction they are quite unlike anything produced in any other region. Starting at the top, you will notice that the Newport chest-on-chest in figure 11-24E has a closed bonnet, that is, the opening behind the scrolled top is covered with a thin board. Not all Rhode Island pieces have this feature, but it is often seen in Newport. More striking yet is the handling of the tympanum, the recessed area underneath a pediment, in this instance the space between the topmost drawers and the molding on the bonnet. In the two preceding bonnet-top chest-on-chests this area is partly filled with a deep drawer, but in Rhode Island, and to some extent in adjacent eastern Connecticut, the tympanum is instead decorated with a pair of molded applied panels. While here, note also that there are no escutcheons on the upper pair of drawers. Even though this is an expensive mahogany chest, these drawers are probably secured by wooden spring locks.

Construction is also very different. Pull out a drawer and you will notice very neatly cut dovetails. You may also see a vertical reinforcing strip nailed to the inside back of the case. Newport cabinetmakers took particular care that box structures remained square. For all this quality workmanship and attention to detail, Newport cabinetmakers typically left the drawer blade dovetails exposed where they joined the sides of the case. However, they were neatly shouldered and stopped just short of the side of the case.

Usually there will be a small gap between the upper and lower sections on a chest-on-chest, because the upper section rests within and is held in place by the midmolding, which is nailed and glued to the top of the lower section. Newport cabinetmakers did just the opposite. They fastened the midmolding to the upper case, the bottom of the molding flush with the bottom of the case. Then, to keep the upper case in position, they made the top board of the lower case in two sections, with a wide gap between them. Lastly, they nailed a cleat to the bottom of the upper case that fitted neatly into the gap, so that the upper case could not shift in any direction. You can spot this unique construction when you notice that there is no gap at the midmolding. Normally, shrinkage will leave a very noticeable gap between the upper and lower cases on a chest-on-chest.

The lower case of this chest-on-case is much what we would expect on a Rhode Island product. Pull out the bottom drawer and you will see that it rests on a pair of slides rather than resting on the bottom of the case. The lower edge of the base molding will be flush with the underside of the bottom board. Notice that the ogee bracket feet are the same standard, conservative pattern that we saw earlier on Providence and Newport chests of drawers.

While we have been discussing a fine bonnet-top chest-on-chest, simpler flat-top chest-on-chests were made in much the same way. They also employ the same primary and secondary woods favored in Rhode Island, mahogany when the best could be afforded, otherwise cherry or a figured maple, then eastern white pine and chestnut as secondary woods.

Earlier when discussing chests of drawers it was noted that Connecticut cabinetmakers approached their trade with a singularly naive exuberance. The additional surface area and unused top provided by the chest-on-chest gave full reign to this proclivity, and there is no end to the diversity of this form. While we will look at two examples, what is shown here does not begin to cover the many local idioms and ideas borrowed from Boston, Newport, New York, and Philadelphia. Here you may see flat, scrolled, pedimented, and bonnet tops, every size and form of carved fan, large and small straight and curved pinwheels, straight fluted or spiral-twist quarter columns, fluted pilasters, tympanum panels, and gadrooned base moldings. A rather strange-looking chest-on-chest that is made of cherry is very likely to be from either Connecticut or somewhere up the Connecticut River Valley.

A chest-on-chest-on-frame will almost always be from either Connecticut or New Hampshire; Connecticut if made of cherry, New Hampshire if made of maple or birch. The Connecticut chest-on-chest-on-frame in figure 11-24F is a grand example of this form. The lower case rests on a low frame supported by short cabriole legs on pad feet. Usually the skirt of one of these pieces will be given some decorative shaping. Chest-on-chest-on-frames were more expensive furniture, and the lower and upper cases will usually be embellished with fluted or spiral turned quarter columns and have either carved fans or pinwheels in the deep top drawers. Note that the upper case employs the five-drawer grouping that was so popular in New England. In Connecticut there was no standardization in the finials as there was in Massachusetts, and here you are very likely to see unusual and whimsical shapes, many, like these, produced by turning so as to avoid the complication and cost of carving.

While bonnet tops were very fashionable in Connecticut, a large number of simpler flat top chest-on-chests were also produced. The cherry chest-on-chest in figure 11-24G is typical of Connecticut workmanship in that we see a combination of standard and atypical features. The dentil molding under the cornice, the three top drawers with a carved-fan center drawer, and the five-over-three drawer configuration is found in many Connecticut chest-on-chests. However, the lower case is most unusual. Here the cabinetmaker seems to have wished to emulate high chests by having a second, somewhat larger fan in the

lower case, and to do this he shaped the top drawer in the lower case to resemble three drawers, then carved a large fan in the center. To complete the illusion, he even added a small pull at the bottom of the fan. The bracket feet are also unusual, for not only is the facing atypical, but the feet have been given slight outward bows or curves. Normally Connecticut chest-on-chests will have ogee bracket feet. There are a few chests with straight bracket feet, and about one in four will have the short cabriole legs that were so popular in New Hampshire.

Connecticut chest-on-chests are almost always made of cherry. This may be because customers with extra to spend selected the favored wood, or perhaps because chest-on-chests of maple or birch are seldom identified with Connecticut.

11-24A. New England Chippendale, 77" h x 39" w, 1770 – 1790.

11-24B. New England Chippendale, 89" h x 39" w, c. 1780.

11-24C. New Hampshire Queen Anne, 77" h x 41" w, c. 1780.

11-24D. Massachusetts Chippendale, 86" h x 42" w, 1760 – 1800.

11-24E. Newport Chippendale, 88" h x 40" w, 1760 – 1790.

11-24G. Connecticut Chippendale, 73" h x 39" w, 1760 – 1800.

11-24F. Connecticut Queen Anne, 90" h x 40" w, c. 1780.

11-25 Middle Atlantic chest-on-chests. To continue down the eastern seaboard in an orderly manner, we will start this section with a New York City chest-on-chest, although you are unlikely to encounter one of these, for they are scarce. However, their relative rarity is more than offset by their standardization. Once you have seen one New York Chippendale chest-on-chest, you have, in a sense, seen them all. Most have either two or three short drawers over three long in the upper case, and then four long in the lower case. In common with both Philadelphia and English practice, there may be fretwork frieze on the front and sides of the upper case just below the cornice, and the top drawer in the lower case is sometimes divided into two smaller drawers. The corners of the upper case, and sometimes the lower case, will almost always be chamfered and fluted as shown in figure 11-25A.

Most New York Chippendale chest-on-chests will have ball and claw feet all around, or else ball and claw feet in front and ogee bracket feet in the rear. Frequently there will be the line of applied gadrooning under the base molding. Although ball and claw feet in themselves are unusual on American chest-on-chests, what may first catch the eye is the proportions, for they tend to be both large and unusually wide in relation to their depth, a feature also seen in New York Chippendale desks and desk and bookcases.

In New York there was a preference for flat facades of rich woods, and we see this expressed in chest-on-chests, where aside from some restrained embellishment at the edges of the case — a fretwork frieze, chamfered corners, and some gadrooning — there is no surface decoration. Even on the best work there are neither blocked nor serpentine fronts, nor carved fans, nor bonnet tops.

In common with New York chests of drawers, most all chest-on-chests are made of mahogany, and except for Atlantic white cedar, have much the same mix of secondary woods seen in Philadelphia: white pine, yellow pine, and poplar.

Not until we reach Philadelphia and its environs do we find variation in chest-on-chests, but even here they tend follow a standard pattern, and we should consider this first. Perhaps nine of ten southeastern Pennsylvania chest-on-chests are made of walnut, have a flat top, quarter columns on both upper and lower cases, ogee bracket feet, and the three-over-two drawer pattern seen in figure 11-25B. Similar versions may be made of cherry rather than walnut, omit the quarter columns, or have only two deep drawers in the lower cases. A few have straight bracket feet. While this chest has the three-over-two drawer arrangement seen in so many Delaware Valley tall chests, often there will just be three short drawers over four long drawers in the upper case.

In common with much Delaware Valley case work, these popular chest-on-chests tend to be both large and heavy, not the least because they are made of walnut and normally were given full dust boards. The chest in figure 11-25B is 6½' tall, but it is not unusual to see examples 7' high. Although these chests are popularly associated with southeastern Pennsylvania,

they were also produced to some extent in adjoining regions, in south New Jersey across the Delaware River from Philadelphia, and to the south in nearby Maryland.

When further embellishment of a chest was desired, it was obtained primarily by enhancing the top, not by shaping the facade as was done in New England, and here we see three different approaches. The first is a grand Philadelphia mahogany chest-on-chest with an elaborately carved cartouche, a pierced latticework tympanum, and then a very English fretwork frieze (11-25C). Below this there are cockbeaded drawers and flame gilt rococo brasses. A less costly version will be made of walnut rather than mahogany, employ a simple carved flame finial in lieu of the cartouche, have a solid tympanum, omit the fretwork frieze, and have lipped drawers and standard Chippendale brasses. Whatever the relative grandeur, they all employ the English practice of constructing a pediment as a separate assembly that rests on top of the case. In England this was done to minimize shrinkage and to simplify construction and repair, but in Philadelphia it may also have been a necessity, for these grand high-style chest-on-chests are about 8' high.

Outside of Philadelphia, the normal practice was to omit the horizontal cornice molding and the separate pediment and to simply extend the face of the case upward, as shown in figure 11-25D. To fill a portion of the tympanum, the center drawer was deepened as was done in New England, although here the face of the drawer was often left uncarved. The extravagantly high scrolled bonnet is a common feature — almost a signature — of rural Delaware Valley furniture. This large walnut chest-on-chest illustrates two other features seen in Delaware Valley case work. First, the corners of the upper and lower cases are chamfered and fluted rather than having fluted quarter columns; and second, the top drawer in the lower case is divided into two smaller a drawers, a feature often seen in English, and also Southern, chest-on-chests and chests of drawers.

Note in each of these examples that the waist molding is not flush with the lower case but instead is a built-up assembly that extends well beyond the front and sides of the lower case. Also, while these chests are often described as bonnet-tops, most are actually scroll-tops, for the curved top is usually not enclosed.

Broken, or "pitched," architectural pediments are occasionally seen on high-style desks and bookcases, particularly on those made in Boston, but this very Georgian feature was seldom employed on chest-on-chests except in Philadelphia, where it had some limited popularity (11-25E). In common with other Philadelphia chest-on-chests, these broken pediment chests are quite high and the pediment is a separate assembly. Note that this chest has the brush-shaped flame finial that was fashionable in Philadelphia.

All but the most grand Pennsylvania chest-on-chests were constructed of walnut, even though mahogany was in use in Philadelphia as early as 1720. Poplar or yellow pine was used for the top, bottom, and backboards of the cases, poplar was usually used for drawers, and sometimes oak was used for drawer sides and runners.

11-25A. New York Chippendale, 72" h x 48" w, c. 1770.

11-25B. Pennsylvania Chippendale, 84" h, 1760 – 1800.

11-25C. Philadelphia Chippendale, 92" h, 1760 – 1775.

11-25D. Pennsylvania Chippendale, 95" h, 1760 – 1790.

11-25E. Philadelphia Chippendale, 94" h x 43" w, 1760 – 1775.

11-26 Southern Chippendale chest-on-chest. Although the South is usually thought of as being very English, there are surprisingly few surviving chest-on-chests. This may be because the clothespress had superseded the chest-on-chest in England by the time there was a significant requirement for large case furniture in the South, and the need for additional storage was met by clothespresses rather than chest-on-chests.

As mentioned in the previous section, the standard Pennsylvania chest-on-chest was produced to the south of Philadelphia, and should you encounter a somewhat rural version of one of these chests, possibly with fluted chamfered corners rather than fluted quarter columns, and much yellow pine among the secondary woods, you may be looking at a Maryland product.

The other likely origin is Charleston, South Carolina, where chest-on-chests were popular and from which the English looking chest-on-chest in figure 11-26 most probably originated. It is suggestive of the south-to-north trade in antique furniture that this large mahogany chest-on-chest was offered for sale at an auction in northern New England.

In addition to having a generally English look, this chest is typical of Charleston chest-on-chests in having chamfered and stop-fluted corners on both upper and lower cases. Other examples omit the chamfer on the lower case. Grander versions may have carved chamfers, a fretwork frieze on front and sides, and a scroll top with the elaborate pierced latticework tympanum we saw on a stylish Philadelphia chest. In common with both Philadelphia and English case work, there will be dust dividers between all drawers. Sometimes there will be a dressing slide or a secretary drawer in either the upper or lower case.

Aside from the English appearance, Charleston workmanship is probably best identified by the use of primary and secondary woods. Mahogany was easily shipped up from the Caribbean and was relatively cheap and plentiful in coastal South Carolina, and if you see it used extravagantly, you are likely to be looking at a piece of Charleston furniture. It is a good base for veneer, and on the best work you may see a figured mahogany veneered on mahogany. You may also see scraps of mahogany employed in secondary locations, in glue blocks, drawer slides, and drawer stops.

The other characteristic of Charleston furniture is the use of bald cypress. Cypress grows along the coast from Maryland down to South Carolina, but is best known as secondary wood in Charleston, where it was employed for the tops and bottoms of cases, for backboards, dustboards, drawer sides, and drawer bottoms. High-style furniture containing cypress will generally be a Charleston product. We need to be careful here, though, for after the Revolution, so much eastern white pine was shipped down from New England that cypress was largely supplanted as a secondary wood in the best-quality furniture.

11-26. Charleston Chippendale, 69" h x 42" w, c. 1780.

11-27 Chests on frames. While chests of drawers on frames are by no means rare, there are not many regional forms, and in this section we will consider just a few of the more common types. First, it might be noted that most any chest of drawers having cabriole legs may be given a separate frame. Both the Dunlap-type chest of drawers illustrated in figure 11-5A and the Bartlett-type tall chest of drawers in figure 11-21D were sometimes constructed as chests on frames.

New England chests of drawers on frames vary in the designs of the frames, although if the apron is not flat across the bottom, there will usually be some form of the double scallop shown in figure 11-27A. Some Rhode Island chests on frames are made in the Newport manner with the removable legs described in the next chapter. Connecticut chests, in addition to being made of cherry, are very apt to have extravagantly scalloped aprons. Most are made of maple, have five or six drawers, often with the split top drawer shown here, and stand on cabriole legs that end in small pad feet. A few have a single, shallow drawer in the frame.

Chests on frames are far more prevalent in the Philadelphia area, and in common with the area's tall chests, are both consistent in general design and are a somewhat more developed form. We might look at two typical examples, the first with rather high legs and a two-over-four drawer arrangement (11-27B), and the second with a drawer in the frame and the three-over-two drawer pattern seen in so much Delaware Valley case work (11-27C). While the aprons on these two chests have a somewhat similar pattern, there does not seem to have been any particular standard shape, and you will see a wide variety of patterns.

Neither of these chests have quarter columns, which, for some reason, are seldom seen anywhere on chests on frames. Aside from the lack of quarter columns, they are typical of Delaware Valley work, being made of walnut with full dust boards and Philadelphia trifid feet. A few Delaware Valley chests on frames have carved-shell knees and ball and claw feet — features usually found on high-style furniture. There a rare few examples with the early William and Mary–style trumpet-turned legs.

In common with the tall chest, these walnut chests on frames were made throughout the area, not only in southeastern Pennsylvania, but also to the west in southern New Jersey and to the south in Maryland and Virginia. They are so common that one cannot but help wonder at their popularity. Was it that raising the case off the ground provided easy access to the lower drawers, or that it kept these drawers away from inquisitive little children, or maybe that it kept the contents clear of the ever- present vermin? It would be a little upsetting to take out your best waistcoat for a Christmas dance, only to find that it had become home to a family of field mice.

While Southern case work tends to be difficult to assign to a particular area, we will conclude this section with a chest on frame so atypical that it is easy to identify. The unusual inlaid walnut chest in figure 11-27D is one of a group of chests of drawers and chests on frames that were made in North Carolina in Randolph and Rowan counties, just to the south of present-day Winston-Salem. This example has short, squared cabriole legs all around; others from this area have cabriole legs in front and tapered Hepplewhite legs in the rear. While most have simple blocked feet, here we see unusual trifid feet whose concept most probably came down from Pennsylvania via the Shenandoah Valley.

11-27A. New England Queen Anne, 60" h x 33" w, 1760 – 1790.

11-27B. Pennsylvania Queen Anne, 65" h x 41" w, 1740 – 1790.

11-27C. Pennsylvania Queen Anne, 66" h x 41" w, 1740 – 1790.

11-27D. North Carolina Queen Anne, 48" h x 40" w, 1800 – 1830.

11-28 Clothespresses. In America, the clothes or linen press never achieved the popularity enjoyed by the tall chest and the chest-on-chest. Even though they were produced everywhere except in rural northern New England, and were particularly fashionable in the coastal South, we can cover them in just one section. Unlike chest-on-chests, clothespresses are a relatively late form and do not exhibit much diversity, and aside from the selection of primary and secondary woods, there is not all that much difference between the average product of New England and the average product of the Middle Atlantic. To determine where a clothespress was made, we sometimes have to look for regional characteristics.

An example of this would be one of a small group of clothespresses produced in and around Boston. Although very different in layout from a chest-on-chest, the press illustrated in figure 11-28A is obviously a Massachusetts product if we look back at the Massachusetts bonnet-top chest-on-chest in figure 11-24D, for it has the same urn and spiral finials, the same fluted pilasters on either side of the doors, and the same blocked lower case. Some of these clothespresses are also fitted with a dressing slide. Behind the doors of most presses you will see either shelves or slide-out trays, but here there will usually be a set of five graduated drawers. It is a mystery why these grand, big mahogany clothespresses were given both doors and drawers.

Perhaps Boston only grudgingly accepted the new English style, and still insisted on drawers in both upper and lower cases?

While clothespresses do not seem to have been produced in Vermont or New Hampshire, they enjoyed considerable popularity in Connecticut, and here we might look at an example (11-28B), although, aside from the use of cherry, there is no standard form. Other Connecticut presses will have three drawers in the lower cases; either French, ogee bracket, or ball and claw feet; sometimes bonnet tops; and often the flanking quarter or spiral columns that are so often seen in Connecticut case work. Note that the doors of this clothespress are set well in from the sides of the case, suggesting that behind them there is nothing more than a set of fixed shelves.

The clothespress was more popular in the Middle Atlantic and the South, although to a lesser extent in Philadelphia, which suggests that a good-quality press made of mahogany is most likely to be from either somewhere in or near New York, or from the coastal South — Baltimore, Annapolis, eastern Virginia, and quite possibly, Charleston, South Carolina. The handsome mahogany New Jersey press in figure 11-28C is typical of the fashionable neoclassical presses produced in New York and northern New Jersey at the turn of the nineteenth century. Less urban and stylistically earlier are presses from a considerable group of bracket-foot presses made in both Pennsylvania and New Jersey (11-28D). These are characterized by bold cornice moldings, either straight or ogee bracket feet, chamfered and fluted corners in the upper case, and the complex scroll at the top of paneled doors. They are likely to be made of walnut or cherry rather than mahogany, and of red gum if from northern New Jersey. A number are attributed to Matthew Edgerton, who had a shop about 25 miles southwest of New York City in New Brunswick, New Jersey.

The best-known Middle Atlantic clothespresses are the gum-wood presses made in rural communities surrounding New York City, to some extent on Long Island and up the Hudson River Valley, but mostly in northern New Jersey. Although there are many variations, they are usually made of red gum, have large, overhanging cornice moldings above a pair of arched, paneled Queen Anne style doors that are flanked by applied, fluted pilasters as shown in figure 11-28E. On some the pilasters are flat and have arched tops that echo the shape of the paneled doors. If you turn ahead to the chapter about cupboards, in figure 15-2B you will see much the same fluted pilasters on a New Jersey Hackensack cupboard. The lower cases on these presses are usually given three deep drawers. Often the top drawer is split, as shown here. As you would expect, there is a fair amount of local diversity in these presses. Other area presses may be made of cherry or maple rather than red gum, have more complex scrolled arches in the doors, like those shown in figure 11-28D, be given fluted chamfered corners rather than applied pilasters, have second pairs of doors in the lower cases, and have curved ogee rather than straight bracket feet.

The clothespress was fashionable in the coastal South, and we will close out this long chapter with two examples, one from eastern Virginia, the other most probably from Charleston. Although produced everywhere to some extent, most presses were made near the coast, where English influence was most pronounced — eastern Maryland, tidewater Virginia, and Charleston, South Carolina.

The press in figure 11-28F is typical of clothespresses produced in tidewater Virginia. This is a better-than-average-quality example, being made of mahogany and having a secretary drawer behind the two upper "drawers" in the lower case. It perfectly exhibits the English "neat and plain" look that was so favored in the Chesapeake region. Less expensive presses are usually made of walnut and quite often have but two tiers of drawers in the lower cases. Secondary woods are mostly yellow pine. To stiffen the large opening, the back of the top section frequently is paneled. While most clothespresses were constructed in two sections and have doors above and drawers below, a number from this region have but a single section with a pair of doors. They are usually about 4½' high.

A good indication of tidewater Virginia workmanship is the way in which the trays are supported. The normal method is to have them move back and forth on slides attached to the sides of the case. Chesapeake area cabinetmakers had a more elegant solution. They cut pairs of dadoes into the case sides, and then simply extended the bottoms of the trays so that they fit into these slots. This both omitted the need for supporting slides and restrained the tray from tipping if pulled out a bit too far.

Clothespresses were very fashionable in Charleston, and we will finish with a grand high style press that was probably made in Charleston about 1790 (11-28G). By this time in Charleston the native cypress had been largely replaced by white pine, most likely because it was readily available and provided an excellent ground for veneer, and in a large case piece like this you will probably see not only white pine, but also a mixture of other woods — poplar, red cedar, maybe a Southern pine — and in addition, perhaps some cypress. Unlike most Southern presses, Charleston clothespresses will always be made of mahogany, and probably very choice mahogany.

11-28A. Massachusetts Chippendale, 90" h x 42" w, 1760 – 1800.

11-28B. Connecticut Chippendale, 86" h x 48" w, c. 1790.

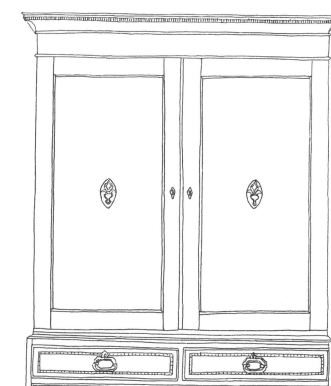

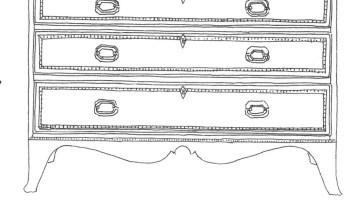

11-28C. New Jersey Hepplewhite, 88" h x 48" w, 1790 – 1810.

**11-28D. Middle Atlantic
Chippendale, 1780 – 1800.**

**11-28E. New Jersey Chippendale,
77" h x 46" w, 1780 – 1800.**

11-28F. Virginia Chippendale, 92" h x 48" w, 1780 – 1810.

11-28G. Charleston neoclassical, 97" h x 48" w, c. 1790.

For the first time among case furniture we encounter — and cannot wiggle around — a question of terminology. Why should this chapter be called High Chests of Drawers and Dressing Tables rather than Highboys and Lowboys? The reason is simple. *Highboy* and *lowboy* are relatively modern terms. They were not used in eighteenth century, and in this time of historical correctness there is an effort to return to original terms in describing old furniture. Probate records variously identify the highboy as a "standing chest of drawers," a "case of drawers," a "chest of drawers," or simply "drawers," the lowboy either as a "chamber table" or just a "table," although these terms in themselves may be abbreviated, for in moving from room to room writing out a list of contents, there would be a natural tendency toward brevity. In any event, those who write about furniture now call highboys and lowboys high chests of drawers and dressing tables, and as auction houses have begun to follow their lead, we should do so also, even though the terms are less picturesque — and your friends may think you are putting on airs when you proudly show them your recently acquired "Massachusetts Queen Anne high chest of drawers."

Aside from this, high chests of drawers and dressing tables are an easy study, for their heyday was at a time when regional differences were still very evident, and then they went out of fashion before American furniture becomes so difficult to place. Seldom in an auction catalog or museum publication will you see a high chest or dressing table identified as "probably New England" or "New York or Philadelphia." Identification is made easier yet by marked regional preferences. Dressing tables were rarely made in New Hampshire and infrequently in Newport and New York City, and there are relatively few high chests from New York and almost none from south of the Mason-Dixon Line. Most high chests and dressing tables are from either New England or the Delaware Valley, and these two areas are so far apart that their products are normally quite different.

High chests and dressing tables are a particularly interesting study because they so often incorporate the stylistic features of their regions. Here we see the distinctive New York club foot, the Philadelphia trifed foot, the North Shore ridged or stepped knee, and the complete vocabulary of Connecticut decorative motifs. They were so enormously popular that production in rural areas did not end with Chippendale and the Revolution. On Long Island, Nathaniel Dominy V was making high chests of drawers in the last decade of the eighteenth century. If examining a rural high chest, you might check to see if the backboards are not fastened with the cut nails that came into use in the 1790s.

In the second half of the eighteenth century, the high chest of drawers and its accompanying dressing table were very fashionable throughout the New England and Middle Atlantic colonies. There appear to be far more surviving high chests from the 1740 – 1780 period than chests of drawers. They seem to have been an expression of middle class affluence, for they are listed not only in the probate records of doctors and lawyers, but also in the homes of shopkeepers and craftsmen. In this they were stylistically late, for by their heyday in America they

had been superseded in England by chest-on-chests and bureau tables. This popularity may be in part because America in the middle years of the century was becoming very prosperous, and in part because the abundant maple and hard cherry led to really elegant high chests and dressing tables. These two woods, in addition to mahogany, encouraged the lightness and the verticality so favored in American furniture.

This time we will move down the coast in two passes, halting at the Mason-Dixon Line because there are so few Southern high chests and dressing tables. We will first take a brief look at the William and Mary style, then an extended survey of Queen Anne and Chippendale, for these two styles are so similar in high chests and dressing tables that it is more useful to discuss them as a unit. Although high chests and dressing tables were frequently produced and sold en suite, we might discuss them separately, for they seldom are found together, and you will most likely be trying to identify either one or the other. This chapter also covers two related forms of bedroom furniture: the bureau table and the chamber table. While they survive in considerable numbers, they exhibit too little diversity to rate a chapter of their own.

12-1 William and Mary high chests of drawers and dressing tables. When you see a high chest of drawers or dressing table with the distinctive trumpet turned legs and flat, curved stretchers of the William and Mary style, you are most likely looking at a product of coastal New England. You are also likely to be looking at considerable restoration, for the legs are secured with no more than glue blocks, and both legs and stretchers have often been restored.

The majority of American William and Mary high chests were made in and around Boston in the first half of the eighteenth century. Typically they have two short over three long drawers in the upper case and three short drawers in the lower case as shown in figure 12-1A. Below these there will be rather thin trumpet turned legs and ball and pad feet. Some have blind frieze drawers worked into the cornice moldings, or second tiers of drawers in the lower case. They are smaller than this illustration might suggest. Most are quite diminutive, typically not more than a few inches over 5' high.

This pen and ink drawing also does not illustrate the most striking feature of these high chests — the boldly figured burl-walnut veneer found on better-quality urban work. Unlike English high chests, the veneering is limited to the front of the case, the apron, and the front of the drawers. The sides may be walnut, but are more likely to be either maple or pine stained up to harmonize with the veneer. Simpler high chests omit the veneer and have maple, pine, or poplar cases, which were probably originally stained to resemble walnut, the fashionable wood of the day. A rare few are japanned. A cherry case would suggest Connecticut origin.

For the most part, the delicate looking legs are turned from soft maple, although some are made of aspen. Veneering will be on eastern white pine. The drawers will usually also be white pine. In southern New England, there may be yellow pine and poplar.

A number of high chests of drawers in the William and Mary style were produced in New York, mostly in and around the city and to the east on Long Island. They are similar in appearance to New England high chests, but differ in that they are seldom veneered and have three rather than two short drawers at the top of the upper case. Sometimes the small center drawer in the lower case will be divided into two drawers. The case will be either pine or red gum, the legs either ash or maple.

There are very few surviving Philadelphia William and Mary high chests of drawers, in part because Philadelphia was founded over half a century after Boston — and perhaps also in part because the additional weight of a walnut case made them even more liable to collapse. This may be why New England William and Mary high chests so often have pine or poplar cases, even though the legs are usually maple. In either event, Philadelphia William and Mary high chests have two attributes that make for easy identification: both the legs and the cases are normally made of solid walnut and are not veneered, and there is a noticeable separation or division between the small drawers in the lower cases as seen in figure 12-1B. Both the upper and lower cases are normally dovetailed. The dovetails in the upper case are covered at the top by the cornice moldings and the bottom by the midmoldings, but because the cases are not veneered, the dovetails will show on the sides of the lower case. This chest also has paneled ends, a feature of early southeastern Pennsylvania furniture that we saw previously in a Chester County tall chest (11-22D). In a few instances, the small drawers in the lower case have a figured walnut veneer, and also, they are apt to have a double set of pulls. Secondary woods are usually yellow pine with Atlantic white cedar drawer bottoms. A rare few are made of eastern red cedar.

Although different in form and scale, New England William and Mary dressing tables are similar to the region's high chests, having maple legs, then either a pine or maple case with walnut veneer on both the front and the top. The somewhat delicate veneer on the top is often either missing or has been restored. Unlike high chests, they are fitted with X-stretchers to allow room for the sitter's legs as shown in figure 12-1C. A rare few are made entirely of walnut in the Philadelphia manner. Some have walnut veneered or stained birch sides, a few others aspen legs. Secondary wood will mostly be eastern white pine.

Philadelphia-area dressing tables are easy to identify for much the same reason that Philadelphia high chests are easy to identify: both the legs and the case are made of walnut and not veneered, and there is a noticeable separation or division between the small drawers as shown in figure 12-1D. Because the case is not veneered, the dovetails that join the horizontal boards of the case are exposed on the sides of the case. In addition, just under the top there is usually a cove molding, a feature also seen in Philadelphia Chippendale dressing tables. As before, secondary woods are usually yellow pine with Atlantic white cedar drawer bottoms. Note that although similar in execution, the leg turnings on these Massachusetts and Pennsylvania high chests and dressing tables are actually quite different in shape.

Lastly, it might be noted that you can tell something of the relative age of William and Mary furniture by the single or double half round applied moldings that often flank the drawers. In England, where the furniture crafts were more formally established, and William and Mary furniture style was made in quantity, it is possible to date case work by the shape of these molding. The earliest, the single half-round molding, was introduced about 1670, and was out of fashion by about 1710. Most of the William and Mary furniture made in America employs the later double half-round or double-bead molding that was fashionable in England between about 1700 and 1740. Even allowing for some lag in style, particularly in more rural areas, American case work fitted with single half-round moldings would probably date not much later than the second decade of the eighteenth century — assuming, of course, that the craftsman had access to a double-bead molding plane, and a single half-round molding was not simply the product of expediency.

12-1A. Massachusetts William & Mary, 62" h x 37" w, 1700 – 1730.

12-1B. Pennsylvania William & Mary, 65" h x 42" w, 1700 – 1730.

12-1C. Massachusetts William & Mary, 30" h x 34" w, 1700 – 1730.

12-1D. Pennsylvania William & Mary, 29" h, 1700 – 1730.

12-2 New England Queen Anne high chests of drawers. There are so many surviving New England Queen Anne high chests of drawers that we might start with two very common, almost generic, examples. The first is a somewhat earlier type in that there is but a single tier of drawers in the lower case (12-2A). In this aspect it resembles a William and Mary high chest. The other similarity is the pronounced transition between the lower and upper case; there is a large built-up midmolding and the upper case is set well inside the lower. Usually there will be two short over three long drawers in the upper case. Some retain the William and Mary–style blind frieze drawer worked into the cornice molding. Perhaps the most noticeable aspect of these early Queen Anne high chests is that the additional length of the legs due to the lack of a long drawer in the lower case often gives them a somewhat leggy look.

Most all these early New England high chests are made of local woods, generally maple, but also cherry or a combination of woods, often a pine case with maple legs and perhaps maple drawer fronts. The high chest in figure 12-2A has a pine case and maple legs.

Far more common are rural high chests with two ranks of drawers in the lower cases as shown in figure 12-2B. This is the standard layout seen in most high chests, and might be considered the more fully developed form. Here there are two basic drawer configurations. The first, shown here, has three

drawers, two deep drawers that flank a somewhat wider shallow middle drawer, below a shallow long drawer. The apron is gracefully arched in the center to handle the space under the drawer. The other solution was to have a row of three deep drawers below the long drawer, often with a carved fan in the middle drawer. By this time it was less common to split the top drawer in the case, and more often than not, there will just be five long drawers in the upper case.

With few exceptions, the cabriole legs on both these high chests end in pad feet, often with the small turned pads or disks under the feet shown in figure 12-2A. A few have narrow slipper feet or squared cabriole legs that terminate in squared feet. These high chests are made of local woods, again generally maple, but also tiger maple, cherry, birch, or sometimes a combination of woods, usually walnut and maple. Secondary woods are similar to those seen in New England chests of drawers: white pine around Boston, west into the Massachusetts portion of the Connecticut River Valley, and north into New Hampshire; pine or poplar in coastal Connecticut and Rhode Island, and chestnut in and around Rhode Island.

12-2A. New England Queen Anne, 70" h x 42" w, 1730 – 1760.

12-2B. New England Queen Anne, 73" h x 39" w, 1740 – 1800.

12-3 New Hampshire Queen Anne high chests of drawers.
In this section we will look at two New Hampshire high chests, one much published, the other more typical and considerably more common. The best-known of these are the elaborately decorated high chests of drawers made by the Dunlap family in south central New Hampshire. Most are attributed to the shop of Major John Dunlap in Bedford, New Hampshire, and indeed may be, for they are remarkably consistent in details of design. They have large cases with elaborate fans and basket-weave cornices, and carved aprons decorated with pairs of shells flanking pairs of whimsical S-scrolls as shown in figure 12-3A. In typical New Hampshire fashion, what appears to be three bottom drawers is but one large carved-fan drawer. Note that the decorative elements are all clustered together at the top and bottom of a very high stack of drawers.

Most New Hampshire high chests are far less elaborate but nevertheless exhibit some Dunlap influences. Typically such a chest has five rows of drawers in the upper case and, more often than not, three rows in the lower case, the bottom drawer with a large carved fan in the center. Below this, the apron will often be decorated with a pair of simplified S-scrolls. Again, the three bottom drawers are likely to be but one, and if there are three complimentary short drawers at the top of the upper case, as shown in figure 12-3B, these also may actually be but one. It is unusual to have three tiers of drawers in the lower case of a high chest of drawers, and this, more than anything else, gives the New Hampshire high chest its unique appearance. In design and proportion, it is very similar to the New Hampshire cabriole-leg chest-on-chest we saw in the preceding chapter. On some high chests, the lower cases are so deep and the legs are so short that there is no clear distinction between them and chest-on-chests. Not all these high chests have three drawers in the lower cases, but if not, there are generally other features, such the S-scrolls, that will suggest New Hampshire workmanship.

Salem cabinetmakers had significant influence in rural New Hampshire, and it is not unusual to see Salem features in New Hampshire high chests. Cabriole legs usually have sharp edges, or arris, and they sometimes, in the Salem manner, about a third of the way down, make rapid transitions to rounded lower legs. These rather strange looking "stepped" knees are found in furniture made along the North Shore. The other Salem influence lies in the shape of a piece's apron, which may be reverse-curved and at the center have a pair of small inward scrolled drops or volutes like those shown in figure 12-4E.

Most New Hampshire high chests are made of maple, often figured maple. A few, including at least one attributed to Major Dunlap, are of cherry. For some reason, perhaps lack of strength, birch was seldom employed, even though it is often seen in other New Hampshire furniture. The secondary wood will almost invariably be eastern white pine.

12-3A. New Hampshire Queen Anne, 83" h x 42" w, 1780 – 1790.

12-3B. New Hampshire Queen Anne, 77" h x 35" w, 1780 – 1800.

12-4 Massachusetts Queen Anne and Chippendale high chests of drawers. In this section there is more to illustrate, for much of the population and the wealth of New England was concentrated in eastern Massachusetts, in and around Boston, and northeastward along the coast through Salem, Marblehead, and Ipswich.

The cabriole leg first came into use on high chests and dressing tables in the 1730s, but at first there was little change in the case itself, which continued to be walnut veneered, although it had become more common to employ crotch rather than burl veneers. Most of these early Queen Anne high chests have two short drawers over three long in the upper case and a long drawer over three short drawers in the lower case, although some omit this lower long drawer or divide it into two short drawers as shown in figure 12-4A. Typically the front of the drawers are bordered with a diagonal herringbone veneer. This is an early example, for there is a concealed drawer in the large built-up cornice molding, the herringbone edged drawers are bordered with applied double-bead moldings, and there is a broad midmolding between the upper and lower cases. Later high chests of this type, produced around the middle of the century, differ little from later work aside from the veneering on the drawer fronts. By this time a substantial amount of walnut was being brought into Massachusetts, and these urban high chests typically have walnut legs and cases.

By the middle of the eighteenth century the bonnet-top was becoming fashionable, and later Massachusetts high chests with flat tops are generally budget products made of local woods, sometimes walnut or cherry, but more generally maple, which was then stained up to resemble walnut or mahogany. The maple flat-top high chest shown in figure 12-4B is typical of a large number of high chests produced in Massachusetts during the last half of the century. Most have five graduated long drawers in the upper case; others will have the top drawer split, or the popular grouping of five small drawers seen everywhere in New England. The majority have one long drawer above three deep drawers in the lower case, and then a fan carved in the center drawer. The flattened arches between the two drops are typical of Boston workmanship, but this became a popular treatment throughout New England, particularly in Connecticut, and we have to look further to determine location of manufacture. Here the exposed drawer blade dovetails and the arrised cabriole legs suggest a shop outside of Boston, then the small step or hock in the ankle just above the foot suggest somewhere up along the North Shore.

With the exception of Rhode Island, Connecticut, and to some extent, the Connecticut River Valley, New England bonnet-top high chests of drawers will be products of coastal Massachusetts. If through design or construction you can eliminate these other areas, then with a rare few exceptions, the piece will be from eastern Massachusetts. We will examine three very typical Massachusetts bonnet-top high chests, two made in or near Boston and one probably made in Salem.

The first illustrates the old adage that the best work is often done early in a period, even though a pen and ink drawing does not do justice to the grand Queen Anne walnut veneered bonnet-top high chest of drawers illustrated in figure 12-4C, which was probably made in Boston about the middle of the century. The veneered drawer fronts are both crossbanded and inlaid with stringing, and then visually divided by veneer to give the impression of pairs of short drawers flanking escutcheon panels. This division is carried downward to the long drawer in the lower case, which is also divided, but here into two separate drawers. Aside from the striking use of veneer, the most characteristic feature of the early Queen Anne is the shell inlay in the lower and upper cases. What might appear in this illustration to be carved shells are actually fan-shaped contrasting inlays of alternating light and dark woods. Other high chests of this period have carved and gilded shells. Later we will see a Boston dressing table with the same type of inlay.

In common with a great many New England high chests of drawers, all these high chests have a turned disk under the pad foot. While this may have been done to provide for wear, it is more likely that it was done to give more visual size and depth to a somewhat small foot.

Veneering goes out of fashion by the middle of the century, and most Boston area bonnet-top high chests are made of solid woods, first walnut and then mahogany, for by the 1760s mahogany was becoming the fashionable wood. The mahogany high chest of drawers in figure 12-4D is a typical product of this time. That it was produced either in or near Boston is suggested by the flattened arches flanking two drops in the apron and the rounded cabriole legs. In Boston fashion, the drawer blade dovetails are hidden by a thin covering strip, and in lieu of carved shells, the center drawers at the top and bottom of the case are decorated with a simple and attractive concave scoop — an economy that seems to have been very popular with Boston customers.

Bonnet-top high chests of drawers produced in Salem and up along the North Shore in Essex County superficially resemble Boston workmanship, but there are significant differences. Starting at the top, for some mysterious reason Salem cabinetmakers often extended the backboards on the upper case to enclose the rear of the bonnet. Perhaps they felt the bonnet looked better when thus enclosed, or perhaps they felt that the bed chamber wall should not show behind the bonnet?

On good work, Boston cabinetmakers would cover the drawer blade dovetails with a thin strip of wood, but in Salem the blade dovetails were not normally hidden, although on good furniture they were stopped so as to not show on the sides of the case.

As noted earlier, in Boston and elsewhere it was common to give the apron three flattened arches set between the two drops, and indeed, the last three high chests have all had this shape, even though the first (12-4B) was most probably made on the North Shore. However, in Salem the drops were usually omitted and the apron instead would simply have a series of reverse curves. The most distinctive of these patterns has bold reverse curves that flank a small pair of inward facing drops or volutes shown in the Salem high chest in figure 12-4E. Between these there is often a little diamond shaped cutout. On later chests the volutes may be pinwheel carved.

In common with chairs made in Salem, the cabriole legs on high chests usually have sharp edges, or arris, and this treatment may have been seen as somewhat more economical than the careful rounding practiced in Boston. Another feature, also seen in chairs, is that about a third of the way down each leg there will be a rapid transition, or step, from the arris to the rounded lower leg. While this elegant Salem high chest has ball and claw feet, there is no particular area associated with ball and claw feet, for while uncommon on New England high chests, they are found on Boston, Rhode Island, and Connecticut pieces. Major John Dunlap even employed them on occasion, although here they have a very rural look. Although ball and claw feet are usually identified as later in style than pad feet, in most cases the difference is more in the purse of the customer than in the time of manufacture, for during the second half of the eighteenth century, the pad foot and the ball and claw foot were produced concurrently.

Somewhere mention should be made of the way the returns, or knee blocks, are attached, particularly as they are easy to examine on the front of a high chest or dressing table. The usual method was to attach them under the apron with glue and nails, but in Boston, the North Shore, and the upper Connecticut River Valley, that is, all across Massachusetts, it was more common to attach them to the face of the apron. Naturally, the apron had to be shaped to match the curve of the return. While this is only a small indication of region, it has the virtue of being easy to observe.

12-4A. Boston Queen Anne, 72" h x 39" w, 1730 – 1750.

12-4B. North Shore Queen Anne, 73" h x 38" w, 1740 – 1800.

12-4C. Boston Queen Anne, 87" h x 41" w, 1740 – 1760.

12-4D. Boston Queen Anne, 74" h x 38" w, 1740 – 1790.

12-4E. Salem Chippendale, 84" h x 40" w, 1750 – 1790.

12-5 Rhode Island Queen Anne high chests of drawers. Among New England high chests of drawers and dressing tables, the work of Rhode Island cabinetmakers, and in particular, the products of the small city of Newport, are a special case, although you are unlikely to see an example outside of a major auction, and even here they are not common. Massachusetts and Connecticut high chests abound, and there are a fair number of New Hampshire examples, but you will seldom see a Rhode Island high chest of drawers. However, they are so different in both scale and construction from other high chests that they are easy to identify, and in the happy chance that you encounter one set out in the back of a barn, we might consider the two most common types.

Aside from the unusual slipper feet, early Newport high chests of drawers resemble other rural New England high chests. They have much the same drawer arrangement: two or three short drawers over three long drawers in the upper cases and one long over three short in the lower cases (12-5A). Not until you take a closer look will you realize how different they are. Most early New England high chests are either walnut veneered or maple stained to resemble walnut, or perhaps a stained-up mixture of maple and pine, but Newport cabinetmakers avoided veneer and favored the best of woods, and these high chests will be made of tiger maple, walnut, or quite frequently, mahogany, even though mahogany was just coming into use at this time.

The construction of the lower case of one of these will also be very different from that of other New England high chests of drawers, or for that matter, from high chests of drawers anywhere. The normal method of framing the lower case of a high chest was to extend the legs upward to the top of the case and then tenon the front, sides, and back into the legs. The joints were then usually pinned for additional strength, and if you look at the lower case of an American high chest, you will frequently see these pins.

Although this is a logical and strong construction, it has two drawbacks: the sides of the case are prone to split because the horizontal grain of the sides is at right angles to vertical grain of the legs and, worse yet, to replace a broken leg the entire case must be disassembled. Newport cabinetmakers had a very different approach. They first dovetailed the front, sides, and back of the lower case together to form a box structure. Then the legs were fashioned with about an inch step back at the shoulder such that the post could pass up the inside of the case. To provide sufficient lateral support, the posts would extend about half way up the lower case. The legs were then secured with pairs of long glue blocks set against the posts on the inside of the case. The step at the shoulder of the cabriole legs actually carried the weight of the chest; the glue-blocked posts simply kept the legs vertical and in place. In event that a high chest was shipped, the legs and glue blocks could simply have been placed in a drawer for assembly on site. Should a leg be broken, it was not difficult to replace.

The dovetails that joined the lower case were lapped at the front and back so that they would not show on the sides. Then a thin strip of matching wood covered the dovetails at the front. Normally this blends in so neatly that it looks as though the legs extend up the sides of the case, but if you look closely you will see that what appears to be an extension of the leg is but a covering strip. Also, there will be no pins to strengthen the joint. If you look at the back of the case you will see the dovetails that join the lower case. Finally, it should be noted that this sophisticated method of construction migrated to some extent to adjacent eastern Connecticut and eastern Long Island. Removable legs are a good indication of Newport workmanship, but are not a guarantee of Newport workmanship, for they are also seen in some Boston furniture.

As you would expect, the bonnet tops on Newport high chests have the same distinctive form seen earlier in a Newport bonnet-top chest-on-chest (11-24E). Cabinetmakers normally employed either a deep drawer or carving to fill the tympanum, the recessed area underneath the pediment, but in Newport the fashion was to treat this area with a pair of applied molded panels, as shown in figure 12-5B. This treatment is an excellent indicator, for it was only used in Rhode Island, and to some extent in adjacent eastern Connecticut.

The upper cases of Newport high chests normally exhibit three Rhode Island features: there may be a vertical reinforcing strips nailed to the inside back of the case; the drawer blade dovetails will be exposed but neatly shouldered, and will stop short of the sides of the case, and the midmolding will be fastened to the upper rather than the lower case. Here we might simply restate what was said in the previous chapter concerning Newport chest-on-chests. Normally there will be a visible gap between the upper and lower cases of a high chest because the upper section rests within, and is held in position by, the midmolding, which is nailed and glued to the top of the lower case. However, Newport cabinetmakers did just the opposite. They fastened the midmolding to the upper case, the bottom of the molding flush with the bottom of the case. Then, to keep the upper case in position, they made the top board of the lower case in two sections with a wide gap between them. Lastly, they nailed a cleat to the bottom of the upper case that fitted neatly into the gap so that the upper case could not shift in any direction. You can spot this unique construction when you notice that there is no gap at the midmolding.

The lower case of the bonnet-top high chest illustrated in figure 12-5B will be made in that same fashion described earlier. On most of these somewhat later high chests there will be single large shells worked onto the centers of the aprons below shallow middle drawers, this instead of deep drawers and pairs of complimentary carved fans in the upper and lower cases as was common elsewhere in New England. Not every high chest has this distinctive shell. Others in this group omit the shells in favor of deeply scrolled aprons flanking single center drops. This high chest is unusual in that it has pad feet all around, for most of these Newport chests have ball and claw feet in front and pad feet in the rear. Others have ball and claw feet all around. When there are ball and claw feet, the talons on the feet may be "open," that is, cut out behind; this is a neat little quality touch that is sometimes seen elsewhere, but which was particularly fashionable in Newport.

While not evident in this illustration, Newport bonnet-top high chests of drawers are significantly smaller than other New England bonnet tops. In a row of New England high chests of the same period, they will be quite the smallest. Also, it should be noted that both bonnet and flat-top high chests made in Newport tend to have a high stance, that is, the lower case will be tall in relation to the upper case. In the high chest shown in figure 12-5A, the upper case is actually a bit shorter than the lower case, and in figure 12-5B it is also shorter if we discount the height of the bonnet. In each chest there are but four rows of drawers in the upper case.

Most of the later Newport high chests are made of mahogany. A few are walnut. Secondary woods are typically a mix, often yellow poplar and white pine, and almost always some chestnut, often in the sides and bottoms of the drawers.

It should be noted that not all Rhode Island high chests are made in the Newport manner. Should you encounter a conservative, nicely made flat-top high chest framed in the normal way, perhaps made of cherry or a figured maple, with some chestnut in the drawers or backboards, you are probably looking at a product of either Rhode Island or somewhere in the vicinity. Also, some Newport features, the removable legs and the molded panels in the tympanum, migrated to nearby areas, and are sometimes seen in southeastern Massachusetts, eastern Connecticut, and eastern Long Island.

12-5A. Newport Queen Anne, 72" h x 38" w, 1745 – 1770.

12-5B. Newport Queen Anne, 88" h x 39" w, 1755 – 1780.

12-6 Connecticut Queen Anne high chests of drawers. The high chest of drawers was popular in Connecticut, and if you encounter a New England high chest made of cherry, you are very likely looking at a product of Connecticut or somewhere up the Connecticut River Valley. In this section we will consider three representative examples: a flat-top high chest, a bonnet-top high chest, and a product of the Chapin School.

The majority of Connecticut flat-top high chests of drawers are made of cherry and have some carving on the drawers, usually large fans worked into the deep center drawers of the lower cases. A common adjunct is a grouping of five drawers at the top of the case, with a pinwheel in the deep center drawer as shown in figure 12-6A. Pinwheels, or sunbursts as some now call them, are often seen in Connecticut case work, perhaps because one can be so easily laid out with a compass. However, they are so simple a decoration that they are also seen elsewhere in New England, particularly in Essex County, Massachusetts, and in nearby New Hampshire. Other Connecticut high chests have single fans in the top registers, or pinwheels both top and bottom, or in Newport fashion, shells centered in the aprons. Note that the fan shown in this illustration is much simpler than the sophisticated curved lobe shell produced in Newport.

There is no single dominant apron pattern in Connecticut high chests, and in addition to the flattened arches so popular in Boston, you will see the row of reverse curves shown here, and quite often, the pair of deep reverse curves flanking a smaller pair of linked curves as shown in the next figure. These linked curves are also seen in this high chest, that is, the high chest in figure 12-6A. Similar high chests produced near the coast in Stonington and New London counties may have nautical motifs in the aprons, most notably fish and lobster tails, which if not handled with restraint (as is too often the case) can produce rather strange-looking furniture.

While most all Connecticut bonnet-top high chests are made of cherry, the same is not true for the less costly flat-tops, of which about one in four are maple. Secondary woods will typically be either yellow poplar or white pine, with some use of aspen. This is not much help except that we might remember that poplar is seldom found north of Connecticut. Here it might be noted yet again that while cherry was very popular in Connecticut, something made of cherry was not necessarily produced in Connecticut. Cherry was used everywhere it was available, and not always as an inexpensive substitute for walnut or mahogany. The Dunlap high chest in figure 12-3A is made of cherry, as is some first class Rhode Island and Pennsylvania case work. Cherry was often employed in the South, even though walnut was abundant. A fair amount of the "Connecticut" furniture in private collections is probably not from Connecticut.

Bonnet-top high chests were very fashionable in Connecticut, and there are a large number of surviving examples. Typically the apron will have either the flattened arches so popular in Boston, or the pair of reverse curves shown in figure 12-6B. Above this will usually be a large fan in the lower case, then an equally large fan, or perhaps a pinwheel, in the upper case. When there are two fans, there will often be a small pinwheel just below the center finial, as shown here. Bonnet and scroll tops are often exaggerated in rural work, and some Connecticut chests have very high bonnets. There are examples with a complete additional drawer worked into the tympanum.

High chests and chest-on-chests were usually embellished with finials at the centers and flanks of the bonnets. Boston-area cabinetmakers favored covered urns topped by tight corkscrews. Newport chests tend to have simpler, more open corkscrews, and both the plinths and the urns are apt to be larger and may be fluted. As you would expect, Connecticut cabinetmakers employed a wide variety of finials: various forms of corkscrews, stylized flames, and a multitude of individualistic turnings when no carvers were available.

In the preceding chapter we noted the distinctive work of a group of about half a dozen Hartford-area cabinetmakers, notably Eliphalet Chapin, Aaron Chapin, and George Belden. In addition to chests of drawers, they produced a small number of Chippendale ball and claw scroll-top high chests of drawers in what might be seen as a Connecticut interpretation of the best Philadelphia manner. This design has an elaborately carved cartouche and a pierced latticework tympanum like that shown in the chest on chest in figure 11-25C. Because these have been much published — and also, very seldom come on the market — we might consider instead a simpler product of the same school that has Connecticut features but nevertheless is quite different from the usual Connecticut work. The lower case of the cherry high chest in figure 12-6C is similar to many other Connecticut high chests, although the off-center positioning of the pinwheel in the center drawer is somewhat unusual. However, the upper case is very different. In lieu of a fan or pinwheel in the top center drawer, there are two applied interlaced vines and above these an open strap-work pediment flanking an opening that once probably held a cartouche. Note that because there is a scrolled pediment rather than the usual built-up enclosed bonnet, this is more properly a scroll-top high chest of drawers. It is very different from the bonnet-top high chest. This scrolled pediment is also seen in the bookcase tops of Hartford-area desks. It is thought to be a slightly later, somewhat more neoclassical interpretation of the basketweave pediments seen in the best of Eliphalet Chapin's work.

12-6A. Connecticut Queen Anne, 69" h x 39" w, 1750 – 1800

12-6B. Connecticut Queen Anne, 81" h x 39" w, 1760 – 1790.

12-6C. Connecticut Queen Anne, 81" h x 40" w, 1780 – 1800.

12-7 New York Queen Anne high chests of drawers. New York high chests of drawers are not uncommon, although by the second half of the eighteenth century, the chest-on-chest and, somewhat later, the clothespress, were more fashionable in New York City. This is probably why most New York high chests are rural products made of local woods: cherry, maple, walnut, and quite often, the red gum or gumwood that was so favored in clothespresses. New York high chests made of mahogany, having canted fluted corners, or with ball and claw feet are quite rare. There are no bonnet or scroll-top versions, and very few with even the simplest fan and pinwheel carvings of the type so popular in New England. The impression is of a form that never developed beyond a standard design.

Most New York high chests have three short drawers over three or four drawers in the upper cases, then two rows of drawers in the lower. Often the upper drawer in the lower case of such a chest is split as shown in figure 12-7. Early versions have wide midmolding and the upper cases set well inside the lower, a feature also seen in early New England high chests and probably in early high chests everywhere. New York high chests also tend to exhibit the somewhat broad proportions seen in much New York furniture. However, quite the most noticeable feature of these rather ordinary high chests lies in the feet, which are usually the New York type of wide, blunt slipper foot, which could be worked out by rural cabinetmakers without the use of either lathes or sets of carving tools.

High chests seem to have been most popular on Long Island, perhaps due to trade with nearby Connecticut and Rhode Island. Chests attributed to cabinetmakers in Oyster Bay have curious scalloped aprons consisting of pairs of deep, exaggerated reverse curves that flank central drops; this perhaps a rural interpretation of Newport workmanship.

12-7. New York Queen Anne, 75" h x 39" w, 1740 – 1770.

228

12-8 Pennsylvania Queen Anne and Chippendale high chests of drawers. Not until we get down to southeastern Pennsylvania and nearby southern New Jersey, and to some extent adjacent Maryland, do we again encounter a large number of high chests and dressing tables. But here they are very different from the New England product, being generally larger and more solid in appearance. High stance and delicate-looking legs are seldom found south of Connecticut and adjacent Long Island. In this section we will examine three typical Delaware Valley high chests of drawers: a large, high-style carved Philadelphia high chest of the type seen in museum collections; a simpler, and far more common, trifid foot design; and an example of the Spanish-foot high chests that seem to be unique to the Delaware Valley.

The Philadelphia Chippendale high chest of drawers is generally judged to be the grandest of American furniture, which might be expected, for by the middle of eighteenth century high chests of drawers were much in fashion — and Philadelphia was by far the largest and most wealthy American city. The high chest in figure 12-8A is typical of these magnificent creations. There are two basic facades: that shown here with matching carved drawers in the upper and lower cases, and a second in which the carving in the upper case is centered in the tympanum above a row of three short drawers. Although frequently identified as bonnet tops, most of these high chests do not have an enclosed hood and might more properly be identified as scroll-top high chests of drawers. A few have the broken or pitched architectural pediment that we saw earlier in a Philadelphia chest-on-chest. Most of these high chests have some form of the covered urn and flame finial that was common in Philadelphia. While these grand high chests are large by New England standards, they are modest in comparison to some imitative rural versions produced in Lancaster County.

These urban high chests are firmly within the Chippendale period, most being made of mahogany and having ball and claw feet. The method of carving might be considered an example of Quaker thrift. To provide sufficient depth without excessive smoothing or very thick mahogany, the shell is carved into the front of the drawer. Then the surrounding acanthus foliage is carved separately and glued to the face of the drawer.

More typical of Delaware Valley workmanship, and far more common, is the type of high chest shown in figure 12-8B. Most are made of walnut, a number are maple, and a few are mahogany or cherry. This chest has the popular trifid feet, but you will also see ball and claw feet, Spanish feet, slipper feet, and sometimes simple squared pad feet whose only apparent merit is that they must have been easy to produce. Often the knees of the legs, particularly on chests with trifid feet, will be embellished with carved shells.

While Delaware Valley chests of drawers are notably consistent in design, the same is not true for these fashionable high chests of drawers. In addition to differences in primary woods and type of feet, they may have the quarter columns shown here, simpler chamfered and fluted corners, or quite frequently, neither. The lower case sometimes has but a single tier of draw-

ers, and a few have but a single deep drawer. Here the lower case repeats the popular three-over-two pattern of the upper case. Note in this figure that the upper two rows of drawers in the upper case are not given escutcheons. They are probably secured with the thrifty wooden spring or Quaker locks so often found in Delaware Valley case work.

For all their individual differences, both these high chests of drawers are very typical of Pennsylvania case work, being similar to the Delaware Valley chests of drawers, tall chests, and chest-on-chests discussed in the preceding chapter. There is the same three-over-two drawer arrangement in the upper register, and both upper and lower cases are flanked by the ever-popular quarter columns.

However, there is also an unusual group of high chests having Spanish, or paintbrush, feet that were produced throughout southeastern Pennsylvania and in nearby southern New Jersey. Many of these rural high chests have the two-over-two drawer arrangement in the lower case shown in figure 12-8C. The best of them have high undercut carved feet with the pronounced cuffs illustrated here. Some have extravagantly curved cabriole legs. Later we will see a companion dressing table with the same two-over-two pattern of drawers.

The Spanish foot, a William and Mary feature, is a handy identifier, for with the exception of a rare few early New England dressing tables, it was seldom used elsewhere in case work. Spanish-foot chairs are common in New England, and there are a few early Spanish-foot tavern and dressing tables, but if you see a high chest with Spanish feet, you are most likely looking at a high chest made somewhere in the Delaware Valley.

The secondary woods in these three high chests are what you would expect from the Delaware Valley: yellow or tulip poplar, white and yellow pine, and often Atlantic white cedar for the bottoms of drawers. In common with other case work from this region, there will normally be full dust boards between the drawers.

With Philadelphia and the Delaware Valley we come to the end of the Middle Atlantic region, but not quite to the end of high chests of drawers, for the influence of Philadelphia extended across the Mason-Dixon Line into Maryland and Virginia. Here we find two distinct interpretations of the Philadelphia high chest, one produced in Maryland, the other in the Virginia backcountry.

Most Maryland high chests were probably produced in or near Baltimore, which at this period was a small but rapidly growing city. This small group of high chests is characterized by chamfered, fluted corners on the upper and lower cases, and then large carved shells with curved lobes, not always just centered in top and bottom drawers, but also in the aprons and at the top of the tympanums. The woods that were used are similar to those used in Philadelphia: mahogany or walnut primary, and yellow and white pine, poplar, Atlantic white cedar, and also oak secondary.

The other small group of Southern high chests seems to be from around Frederick County in the northwest corner of Virginia. These reflect a somewhat more rural Delaware Valley influence, being usually made of walnut or cherry with secondary woods of poplar and yellow pine. The few surviving examples suggest a preference for the traditional Delaware Valley quarter column.

12-8B. Delaware Valley Queen Anne, 75" h x 39" w, 1750 – 1790.

12-8A. Philadelphia Chippendale 90" h x 47" w, 1760 – 1790.

12-8C. Delaware Valley Queen Anne, 75" h, 1740 – 1790.

12-9 Massachusetts Queen Anne dressing tables. The second part of this chapter will start with Massachusetts, for while high chests of drawers were fashionable in New Hampshire, there are no more than a handful of dressing tables. This may be due the rural character of much of the colony. In general, there are relatively few dressing tables of rural manufacture, perhaps because the women in farming communities had less occasion to use dressing tables. Most were made in urban centers or in well established towns, and for this reason are generally easier to identify.

Therefore, we might start with Massachusetts dressing tables, and more specifically, tables produced in eastern Massachusetts, in and around Boston, and to the east and north in Salem and Essex Counties. Dressing tables from western Massachusetts tables will be discussed with Connecticut and the Connecticut River Valley. Here, then, we will see three eastern Massachusetts dressing tables: two early walnut veneered tables, then a fully developed form that would seem to have been produced by the hundreds.

At first, Queen Anne Massachusetts cabriole-leg dressing tables continue the William and Mary practice of veneering the case and top with figured walnut. What seem to be the earliest are characterized by tripartite aprons, each having two small arches flanking a high central arch, as shown in figure 12-9A. Between the arches is a pair of turned acorn drops. The drawers are normally edged with herringbone veneer, and the top row of drawers is usually divided into two, and sometimes three, smaller drawers. Some retain the William and Mary–style double half-round moldings around the drawers. The legs are often rather thin and delicate, and may have pronounced bows. Many of the same features are present in William and Mary dressing tables, the only significant changes being the curved cabriole legs and the second rows of drawers, and of course, the completely different method of construction.

Within just a few years the high central arch of the table, and the shallow drawer above it, were replaced by a deep middle drawer. This was decorated with either a carved, gilded shell or a fan of contrasting inlays of alternating light and dark woods (12-9B). In addition, there will often be charming inlaid compasses of light and dark woods on the sides and top of the case. These dressing tables were made when walnut veneer was losing favor to solid walnut. Some tables are veneered; others, like that illustrated in figure 12-9B, are made of solid walnut with the new thumbnail molded lipped drawers.

From this there evolved a standard form of Massachusetts dressing table that proved so successful that it not only remained in production for almost half a century, but was emulated elsewhere, particularly in Connecticut. This table is essentially a simplification of the previous Queen Anne form, the veneering replaced by solid walnut, the gilding and inlay by the carved, recessed fan shown in figure 12-9C. As before, the apron is composed of three flattened arches divided by a pair of drops — the same shape seen in Massachusetts high chests. Note that the apron is blocked in at the center to conform to the shape of the fan.

Within this standard form there are variations which can sometimes tell us where in Massachusetts this type of dressing table was made. In lieu of a carved fan, Boston customers often selected the simple and attractive concave scoop shown on the bonnet-top high chest in figure 12-4D. Salem dressing tables can be identified by the arrised legs, sometimes with the peculiar notch or step where the arris transitions to the rounded lower leg. Other Salem area dressing tables omit the acorn drops and have instead reverse curved aprons with small pairs of volutes and diamond-shaped cutouts in the centers that are similar to those shown in the high chest in figure 12-4E. Some dressing tables omit the carved fans. This may have been done to save a little money, for in addition, these tables also often lack rails above the top drawers. This saves more labor than you might think, for without a rail there is also no need for a pair of kickers to keep the drawer from pitching down when opened. Unfortunately, this economy is no particular indication of region, for dressing tables from both Connecticut and the South sometimes lack top rails.

Ball and claw feet are found on a few New England dressing tables, but again this is of little help, for these feet seem to have been produced everywhere for customers wishing to spend a little extra. There are examples from coastal Massachusetts, Connecticut, and the Connecticut River Valley in western Massachusetts. Feet with retracted side talons would suggest Massachusetts, perhaps Boston or Salem.

Most Massachusetts dressing tables are made of walnut with white pine secondary. A few, particularly those with the somewhat later ball and claw feet, are made of mahogany. Others will be cherry, maple, or a mix of maple and walnut.

12-9A. Massachusetts Queen Anne, 31" H, 1730 – 1750.

12-9B. Boston Queen Anne, 28" h, 1750 – 1760.

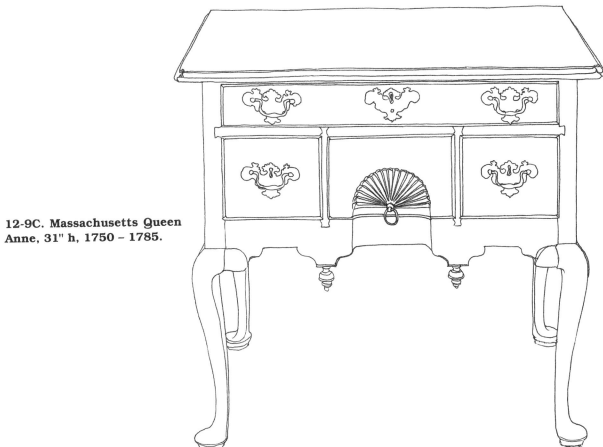

12-9C. Massachusetts Queen Anne, 31" h, 1750 – 1785.

12-10 Rhode Island Queen Anne dressing table. Rhode Island dressing tables are fairly scarce, and Rhode Island should probably be your last thought when trying to place a New England dressing table. Nevertheless, these tables are not difficult to identify. Some emulate the standard Massachusetts model, but differ in the use of poplar and chestnut for secondary woods and in being fitted with removable cabriole legs. A few have the same carved-shell type of apron that we saw earlier in a Newport bonnet-top high chest (12-5B). For some reason, these often have slipper feet rather than ball and claw or pad feet, suggesting they may not have been made en suite with the more prevalent high chests.

However, what seems to be the most common Rhode Island dressing table is clearly a companion to the earlier type of Newport high chest of drawers illustrated in figure 12-5A. These have the same slipper feet, removable legs, and high arched aprons that characterize the high chests. The apron will be decorated with either the single center drop employed in many high chests, or the pair of drops shown in figure 12-10. Note that this rather delicate-looking dressing table has the same high stance we saw earlier in Newport high chests of drawers.

12-10. Rhode Island Queen Anne, 31" h, 1750 – 1770.

12-11 Connecticut Queen Anne dressing tables. There is so much variation among Connecticut dressing tables that it is not easy to select a representative example. Instead, we will consider three typical designs, and then provide some other information to help you identify a Connecticut product.

Quite the most noteworthy Connecticut dressing tables are the scallop-top tables produced in the upper Connecticut River Valley, even though most are actually from Massachusetts rather than Connecticut, being made in the area where the Connecticut River flows south through western Massachusetts. These are characterized by boldly curved or scalloped tops like the one shown in figure 12-11A. Other than these tops, they are fairly standard Connecticut Valley dressing tables. The bonnet-top high chest shown in figure 12-6B has the same apron shape as, to a lesser extent, do both the next two Connecticut dressing tables. While much illustrated, there are not many of these singular dressing tables, perhaps because they never enjoyed more than a limited rural popularity, and perhaps also because scalloping the top required considerable extra labor.

Far more common are the two dressing tables shown in figures 12-11B and 12-11C. These are typical of a great many produced in Connecticut during the last half of the eighteenth century. They differ mostly in the depth of the middle drawers and in the location of the carved shells. In the first, the shell is in the lower middle drawer; in the second it is located, Newport fashion, in the center of the apron. Note that all three of these tables have the same pair of deep reverse curves in their aprons. Other Connecticut dressing tables have the flattened arches and acorn drops that were so favored in Massachusetts high chests and dressing tables (12-9C).

Look at the back of a Connecticut dressing table and you may see that not only does the top overhang the case, but it also is molded across the back, that is, finished on all four sides. Some Connecticut dressing tables have the tray tops that are so often seen in Connecticut candlestands.

Connecticut dressing tables tend to be larger and higher than normal for dressing tables. It is not unusual for them to be 33" or 34" high rather than the 28" to 30" seen in most dressing tables. Some are so large that they would seem to be the lower sections of small high chests. The dressing table illustrated in figure 12-11B is over 33" high and 35½" wide.

With few exceptions, Connecticut dressing tables will have the small pad feet shown in these three examples. A rare few have ball and claw or Spanish feet. Most Connecticut dressing tables are made of cherry, but occasionally you will see maple, walnut, or mahogany. Secondary woods are usually either white pine or poplar, but sometimes also aspen and oak.

12-11A. Connecticut Queen Anne, 32" h, 1760 – 1790.

12-11B. Connecticut Queen Anne, 33" h, 1750 – 1790.

12-11C. Connecticut Queen Anne, 30" h, 1750 – 1790.

12-12 New York Chippendale dressing table. While there are but a handful of surviving New York dressing tables, they are usually not difficult to identify, for they tend to follow the English practice of having but a single row of drawers beneath the top as shown in figure 12-12. The other English feature is the turned cabriole legs, in this case terminating in the typical square, blocky New York ball and claw feet. Other New York dressing tables have conventional sawn and shaped cabriole legs, but the same single rows of drawers and ball and claw feet.

In common with other New York Chippendale furniture, the primary wood will most probably be mahogany.

Here it might be noted that among the few surviving Southern dressing tables, a number have much the same English configuration: a single row of either one, two, or three drawers, and then turned cabriole legs. Here though, the primary wood will probably be walnut rather than mahogany, the legs will most likely end in simple offset turned pad feet, and there will likely be some yellow pine among the secondary woods.

12-12. New York Chippendale, 27" h, c. 1760.

12-13 Pennsylvania Queen Anne and Chippendale dressing tables. Dressing tables were enormously popular throughout the Delaware Valley, and while we will consider three typical examples, there are innumerable variations in drawer arrangement, apron shape, and foot design. What they have in common, though, is a solid, substantial appearance that is very different from New England workmanship. Early Queen Anne dressing tables are less heavy looking than later Chippendale models, but even here you will seldom see a delicate cabriole leg terminating in a small pad foot.

Quite the most illustrated are the grand, high-style dressing tables made in Philadelphia in the last few decades before the Revolution. These usually employ the complete vocabulary of the Philadelphia Chippendale style: fluted quarter columns, elaborately carved deep center drawers, large ornate rococo brasses, cabriole legs with shell or acanthus carved knees, and ball and claw feet as shown in figure 12-13A. This figure illustrates two other features often seen in Delaware Valley dressing tables: the front corners of the top are given notches or cusps, and there is cove molding just under the tops, which serves to provide additional depth to balance the deep cases. Even though by this time mahogany was the fashionable wood, the majority of these big dressing tables were made of walnut.

Notching a top avoids sharp corners and is a nice little decorative touch. In a time when nights were very dark, notched corners were a good idea. They were also a token of affluence — a sign of extra work. In themselves, notched corners are no particular indicator of region, for they are found on furniture from everywhere except New York and the South. However, they were unusually popular in Pennsylvania, and if you see notched corners on a table, you are likely to be looking at Delaware Valley workmanship.

Far more common among Delaware Valley dressing tables are modest, middle-class versions like that shown in figure 12-13B. Typically they have the one-long-over-three-short drawer arrangement and the deep trifed feet shown here. There are innumerable variations in drawer layout, case, and feet. This example has the most common drawer pattern — one long over three short drawers, with an arched apron below the shallower middle lower drawer, but you may also see an extradeep middle drawer like that shown in the preceeding figure, or a deep arch in lieu of a middle drawer. Some may have but a single row of drawers. More often than not the corners of the case will be square and not embellished, but if something extra is done, it will usually be fluted chamfering rather than quarter columns. Every type of Philadelphia foot was used, most commonly the large trifid foot shown here, but also ball and claw, slipper, and the club-shaped paneled stocking foot. Although generally less massive

than high-style tables, these dressing tables are nevertheless a very recognizable Middle Atlantic product, being deeper across the front and sides than similar New England dressing tables. The great majority are made of walnut, but sometimes you will see tiger maple or cherry.

When discussing Connecticut high chests of drawers it was noted that Hartford-area cabinetmakers, notably Eliphalet Chapin, emulated Philadelphia fashion in high chests and dressing tables. Most of these are well documented, but if you happen to come across what appears to be a Pennsylvania dressing table with quarter columns, a cove-molded top, and ball and claw feet, but with a New England fan in the middle lower drawer and constructed of cherry with white pine secondary, you may be looking at a Chapin dressing table.

Early Philadelphia cabriole-leg dressing tables had high, elegant William and Mary–style Spanish feet and a distinctive four-square, two-over-two drawer arrangement. Although soon out of fashion in Philadelphia, they remained a popular form in rural southeastern Pennsylvania, and in nearby southern New Jersey, for at least another quarter of a century. Earlier we saw a high chest of this type (12-8C). The dressing table in figure 12-13C is a later product, for it has acquired broad Chippendale proportions. Note that the Spanish feet are very different from New England workmanship, having prominent cuffs at the ankles, and also that it has the notched top and chamfered corners seen in so much Delaware Valley case furniture.

The secondary woods in these three dressing tables are what you might expect from this region: tulip poplar, white pine, yellow pine, sometimes oak, and often Atlantic white cedar for the bottoms of drawers.

12-13A. Philadelphia chippendale, 31" h, 1760 – 1780.

12-13B. Delaware Valley Queen Anne, 30" h, 1750 – 1780.

12-13C. Delaware Valley Queen Anne, 29" h, 1740 – 1770.

12-14 Bureau tables. In addition to high chests of drawers, this chapter should cover other types of dressing furniture — bureau, chamber, and dressing tables. *Bureau table* is another word that fell into disuse and that has been resurrected. The modern term is *kneehole desk*, which is not entirely a misnomer, for in England, bureau tables often had writing slides, and in America the top drawer was sometimes fitted with a writing compartment. However, bureau tables seem to have been primarily employed as dressing tables, the small drawers that flank the center opening being used for powder, combs, brushes, kerchiefs and gloves. Actually, the recess for the knees and the small flanking drawers would seem to make them more comfortable than the dressing tables seen in the previous sections. On some Boston tables the prospect doors and cupboards can be removed, apparently because they were used for storing wigs.

While three American bureau tables are shown, the only one you are likely to encounter is one of the handsome block-fronts made in Boston during the last half of the eighteenth century. Bureau tables were produced in all the major Colonial urban centers, but never were very common. There are no more than a scattered few from the South, and no more than a relative handful from either Philadelphia or New York. The best known are the famous Newport block-and-shell bureau tables, of which about fifty are known (12-14A). It is a mystery why the citizens of this small city lavished such affection on such an expensive form of furniture. The majority of these truly remarkable little bureau tables even have carved shells on the recessed cabinet doors, where they would hardly show in dimly lit rooms. They are the most common of Newport block-and-shell furniture.

Middle Atlantic bureau tables are not only uncommon, but also may be difficult to place. Some, like the table in figure 12-14B, are quite simple, lacking the tray drawer above the kneehole opening and a pair of feet in the front. Most are made of mahogany, a few of walnut. Better-quality Philadelphia tables may have quarter columns. Block-front furniture is rare in New York, but there is a small group of very grand New York bureau tables with blocked fronts and ball and claw feet all around — two on the backs and four across the front. They are a visual delight.

Quite the most common American bureau tables are the standard Boston block-front type. With a few rare exceptions, they are consistent in form: round blocking under conforming tops, four straight bracket feet across the fronts, and arched paneled cabinet doors below shallow tray drawers, as shown in figure 12-14C. Most are made of mahogany with white pine secondary. A few are walnut. Some may have been made in Rhode Island. Why the bureau table was so fashionable in this least English of American cities is another mystery. Perhaps these pieces were sold in conjunction with the elegant clothespresses that were being produced in Boston at this same time?

12-14A. Newport Queen Anne, 30" h, 1760 – 1795.

12-14B. Middle Atlantic Chippendale, 32" h, c. 1780.

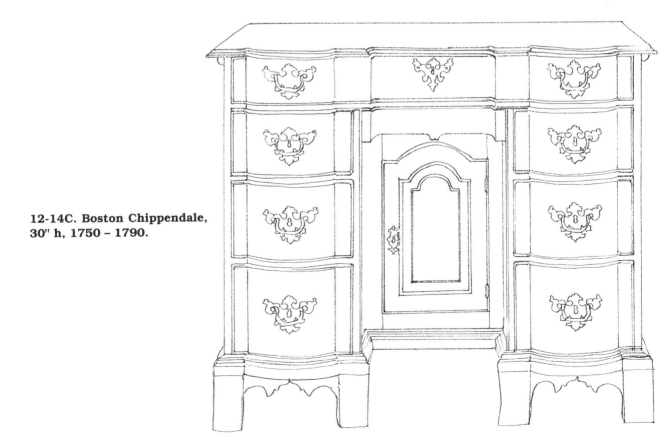

12-14C. Boston Chippendale, 30" h, 1750 – 1790.

12-15 Neoclassical dressing and chamber tables. Federal neoclassical dressing and chamber tables so differ from their Queen Anne and Chippendale counterparts that we will give them their very own section, and because there are not all that many, we will also simply put them together in this final section.

Following the Revolution, dressing tables in the new Hepplewhite and Sheraton styles became fashionable everywhere, particularly in New England and principally in northern New England: Massachusetts, New Hampshire, and Maine. There are many examples, and we might first look at two common rural versions, although these differ chiefly mostly in the number and placement of the drawers (12-15A, 12-15B). Most are fitted with the scrolled splashboards shown in these two illustrations. When there is a second row of drawers, it will usually be in the form of two small glove drawers just under the splashboard. Some have dressing mirrors rather than splashboards. The majority are made of softwood, principally pine; others are mahogany and mahogany veneer, or tiger maple, sometimes with contrasting mahogany veneered drawers. Most are either grain painted or painted and then stenciled. A few are beautifully paint decorated. While some have tapered Hepplewhite legs, the great majority have the later turned Sheraton leg. There is no end of different fanciful leg turnings, suggesting that here local cabinetmakers did their own turning.

It is difficult to tell where these simple dressing tables were made. The secondary woods can suggest general areas. White pine would indicate northern New England and the upper Connecticut River Valley; tulip poplar, somewhere further south. By this time it was becoming more common to label furniture, and a number of these dressing tables carry the name of the maker or the warerooms where they were sold.

Location of manufacture is less a question among a group of formal dressing tables made up along the North Shore and just across the border in Portsmouth, New Hampshire. Visually they resemble a federal neoclassical card table until you notice that there is no folding leaf. Usually there will be a wide single drawer in the apron, and sometimes a conforming glove box on the top as seen in figure 12-15C. The glove box may be a separate assembly, and if so, may be given a little dressing mirror. While these dressing tables resemble Massachusetts area card tables, being much the same width and depth, they tend to be a few inches higher. Most are made of mahogany, but there are some lovely paint decorated examples. A few have Hepplewhite rather than Sheraton legs.

Less common, but from the same area, is a group of Sheraton dressing tables that are identified as chamber tables in price books. There are two forms of the chamber tables. One has a serpentine or bowed front with an arched skirt flanking a pair of drawers The other, more common, has two full-length drawers and a either a flat front or the serpentine front shown in figure 12-15D. In scale and form these resemble an oversized Federal card table with two rows of drawers. The chamber table shown here is early. Later versions acquire the unfortunate thick carved and spiral turned legs so frequently seen on late Federal Salem card tables. When we get to the chapter on sideboards, we will see much the same form employed in dining rooms as serving tables.

Perhaps the most common high-style dressing tables are the Sheraton tables produced in New York City during the second decade of the nineteenth century (12-15E). They are notably consistent in scale and form: an attached dressing mirror above a rectangular case having two rows of drawers, reeded legs stiffened by a thin, wide shelf, and very often, brass ball and cup feet. A few have the front-to-back curule legs sometimes seen on New York classical chairs. These tables are very typical of later Federal New York, large in scale and having flat surfaces decorated with rich, dark mahogany veneer. The deep, low shelf is often seen in New York City case work. Later we will see the same shelf in a secretary and a serving table.

12-15A. New England Sheraton, 34" h, 1820 – 1840.

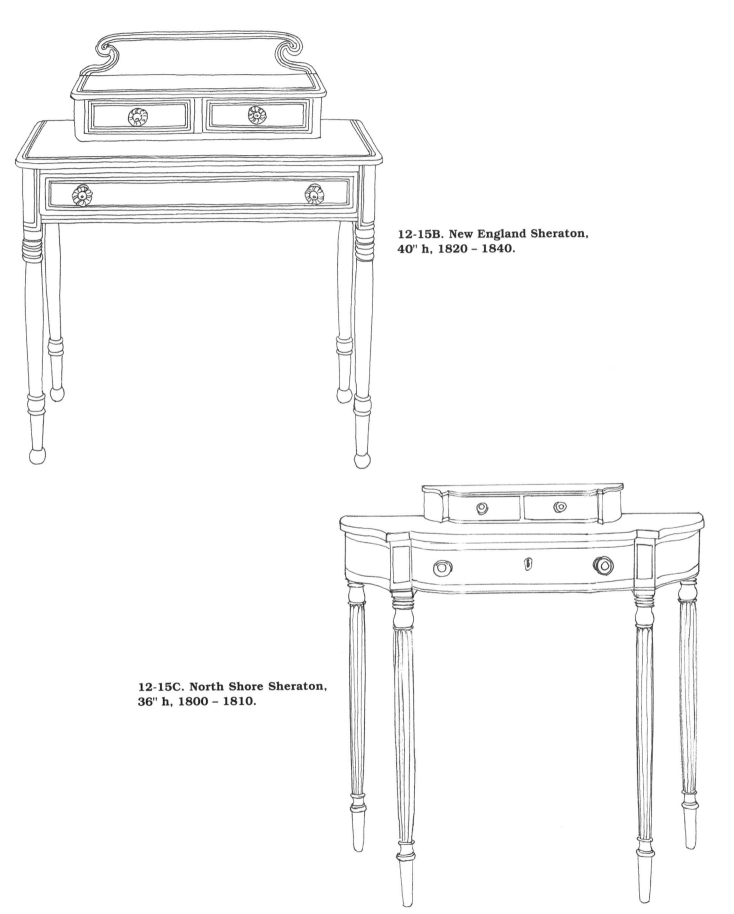

12-15B. New England Sheraton, 40" h, 1820 – 1840.

12-15C. North Shore Sheraton, 36" h, 1800 – 1810.

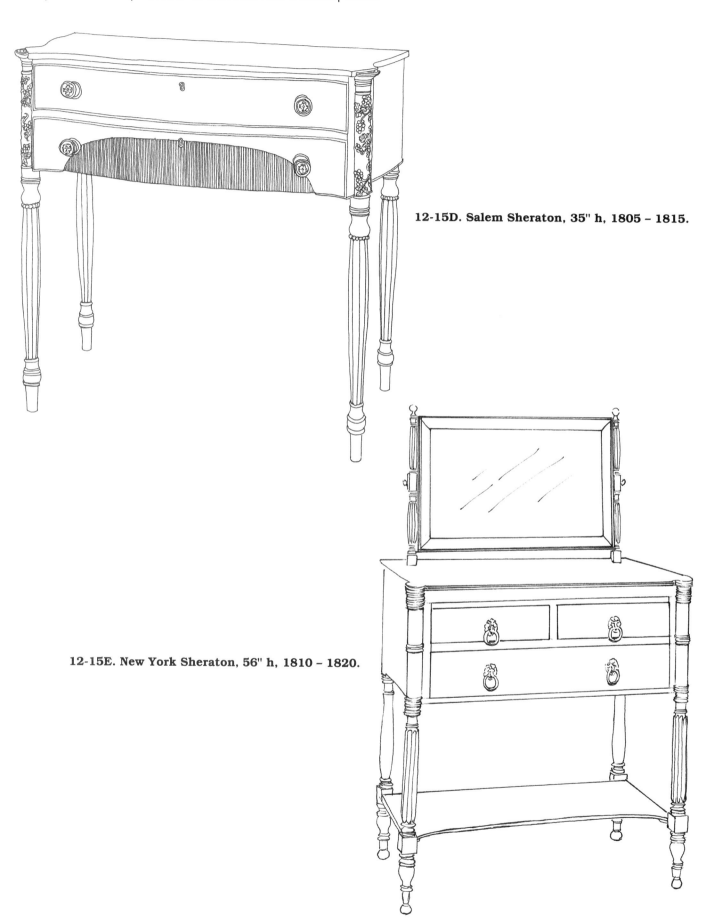

12-15D. Salem Sheraton, 35" h, 1805 – 1815.

12-15E. New York Sheraton, 56" h, 1810 – 1820.

Again we will begin with a question of terminology, but this time a simpler question, for desks have always been called desks, although the term once referred to any flat writing surface. However, what we now call a secretary was then a desk and bookcase, and not unreasonably so, for in the past they were always separate components, and a purchaser might well have ordered a desk "and a bookcase" from the cabinetmaker. The terms *secretary* and *secretary bookcase* were introduced from England in the 1780s to describe a new type of desk in which a deep drawer was fitted with the little drawers and pigeonholes. The front then folded down to provide a writing surface, and the drawer itself pulled out about half way to provide the necessary leg room. Today these are often called butler's desks, and sometimes butler's secretaries when fitted with bookcase tops, even though it is unlikely that in America they were often used by butlers. In this chapter they will be identified by the terms most often employed in auction catalogs — *butler's desks* and *secretary bookcases*.

However, this is not the end of the problem, for cabinetmakers in New England developed a desk having a relatively narrow writing flap that folded out to rest on two short pulls. The pigeonholes and little drawers were then either placed in a separate section or put behind the bookcase doors. What do we call this popular form? It is something of a hybrid — neither a slant-front desk nor a secretary. There seems to be no one answer, for you may see them described as a "secretary," a "ladies' writing desk," or a "lady's desk"; and if fitted with sliding tambour doors, as "tambour desk" or "tambour lady's desk"; and when given a bookcase top, then "secretary," "ladies' secretary," "desk bookcase," and "secretary bookcase." In this chapter I identify them as "secretary" or "secretary bookcase," with the addition of "tambour" if given tambour doors. There are far too many examples to have been the exclusive provenance of New England ladies. However, this is not the end of the matter, for when we get to Massachusetts neoclassical desks there are several other designs, but we will cross that bridge when we get there.

For the most part Americans preferred the slant-front desk, even though they had gone out of fashion in England well before the end of the eighteenth century. In the past such desks were often called fall front desks, perhaps to distinguish them from desks having the writing surfaces hinged at the tops. While we will see a number of different types of desk in this chapter, about 19 in 20 American desks will be the traditional slant-front.

When considering region in a desk, do not hesitate to look back to the chapter about chests of drawers, for a slant-front desk is most often no more than a writing section atop a chest of drawers, and there are innumerable regional similarities between the two.

In this chapter we will first take a brief look at an early William and Mary desk, then survey desks and desk and bookcases in two groups, first Queen Anne and Chippendale, then the neoclassical Hepplewhite

and Sheraton styles produced after the Revolution. Cylinder-fall desks, which were produced to a limited extent in all regions, will be discussed briefly at the very end.

13-1 New England William and Mary desk. Most William and Mary ball-foot desks are from New England, the great majority from eastern Massachusetts. Wherever made, most are similar to the desk shown in figure 13-1. The interior is normally recessed in the center to leave room for a sliding cover over a storage well, this in lieu of a shallow top drawer. The slides, or lopers, that support the lid will be almost square in cross section. Although a split-top drawer is more common in Pennsylvania and the South, it is also seen in early New England case work. This desk is a fine example with a nicely fitted interior. Many New England examples are far simpler. They are also usually made of local woods: pine, maple, and cherry. Others, probably urban products, are made of walnut or a mixture of maple and walnut. There are a few grand Boston-area desks in which the lids and drawer fronts are veneered in burled walnut, the same treatment seen in New England William and Mary high chests and dressing tables.

While William and Mary ball-foot desks are most commonly from New England, they were produced in all regions. New York examples are apt to be made of red gum, or bilsted as it was then called, a wood that was also favored for kasten and clothespresses. Philadelphia desks are likely to be solid walnut with poplar, with yellow pine or white cedar secondary. A rare few of these early desks have bookcase tops.

13-1. New England William & Mary, 39" h, c. 1730.

13-2 New England Chippendale desk and desk and bookcase. There are an extraordinary number of surviving rural New England desks, in part because the Puritans encouraged education so that everyone could read the Bible. The number is all the more remarkable in that even simple desks were relatively expensive, requiring thin stock and additional labor to fabricate the pigeonholes and little drawers. This leads to a first suggestion: a rural slant-front desk is most likely to be from somewhere in New England, particularly if the secondary wood is white pine.

Although there are so many local variations that it is difficult to show a truly representative example, the desk and desk and bookcase in figures 13-1A and 13-2B are typical products of the northeast, and might have been made in any small town in New England. By the middle of the eighteenth century, most slant-front desks were no longer made with wells under the writing surfaces. Instead, a desk from this period will have deep, thin lopers with a shallow drawer in between, and below this a set of graduated long drawers. There is no standard pattern in the interior of these desks, although the stepped interior illustrated in figure 13-2A, with two rows of drawers below a row of pigeonholes, is popularly thought to be an earlier feature; and placing the drawers above the pigeonholes, as shown in the second figure, is thought to have come later, perhaps postdating the Revolution. The broad horizontal openings seen in many of these desks were for account ledgers or daybooks. Most have very simple interiors, lacking the concealed pilaster drawers and prospect door normally seen in urban desks, and often even the central prospect drawer shown in these two illustrations.

It is difficult to date these rural desks, for most retain the early straight bracket foot, probably because it was so easy to make. Here you might look for neoclassical pulls and cut nails tacking in the drawer bottoms and fastening the backboards. In common with rural workmanship, the drawer-blade dovetails will usually be left to show, and will often show through the sides of the case. These desks are typically fashioned of local woods, most commonly of maple, but also of cherry and birch, and sometimes of apple and sycamore. Some are made of walnut. These were probably made near the coast, where walnut would have been available. The desk and bookcase in figure 13-2B is made of birch, suggesting manufacture somewhere in northern New England, and the little pinwheel cut into the prospect drawer either Essex County, Massachusetts, or nearby coastal New Hampshire.

Secondary woods can help identification. White pine would point to northern New England, including the upper Connecticut River Valley; tulip poplar, to coastal and western Connecticut; and chestnut, to Rhode Island and vicinity.

13-2A. New England Chippendale, 41" h, 1760 – 1810.

13-2B. New England Chippendale, 78" h, 1780 – 1810.

13-3 New Hampshire Queen Anne desk. Earlier it was noted that the Queen Anne style was favored in New Hampshire. This is evident in desks, which are likely to be given cabriole legs. There are two similar types of desk. The first is a slant-lid version of the Dunlap chest of drawers illustrated in figure 11-5A. Better-quality desks of this type will have carvings on the base moldings, and the small interior drawers will be decorated with little carved fans.

The other desk is the Bartlett-type shown in figure 13-3. Although also very much Queen Anne in style, these desks are not nearly as old as they look, for they postdate the Revolution. Many were produced in the first decades of the nineteenth century. This one is attributed to Peter Bartlett (1788 – 1838), who worked in Salisbury, a town just to the northwest of Concord in central New Hampshire. In addition to the cabriole legs, a Bartlett-type desk has two other characteristics: the lid is somewhat deeper and the interior writing section is noticeably higher than normal, and the interior is very ornate for a rural desk, often having pilaster drawers on either side of a stack of blocked prospect drawers. Queen Anne style desks were also popular in Connecticut, although here the legs may be fastened to a separate frame, and the primary wood will very likely be cherry.

In addition to the old-fashioned legs, New Hampshire work can be inferred from the selection of primary and secondary woods. Most of these desks are made of either maple or birch — often tiger maple and wavy birch. Drawers and backboards will usually be white pine.

13-3. New Hampshire Queen Anne, 44" h, c. 1805.

13-4 Massachusetts Chippendale desks and desk and bookcases. Massachusetts, and particularly coastal Massachusetts, produced a great deal of case work. A New England desk or desk and bookcase that is clearly an urban product will most likely be from somewhere in the Boston area. Here also we should remember that in urban centers the craftsmen tended to follow certain construction methods, and to some extent a Boston-area desk can be identified by the way it is made. If you turn back to section 11-6, you will read how Boston cabinetmakers constructed the base molding and feet on chests of drawers. The same methods were employed on desks.

Another similarity is the remarkable New England affection for shaped case work, for just as Massachusetts chests of drawers are likely to have serpentine or blocked fronts, so also are desks. All but one of the five Massachusetts desks and desk and bookcases in this section have curved fronts.

Not all Massachusetts desks have shaped fronts, and we might start off with a flat-front desk that could have been made almost anywhere in coastal Massachusetts (13-4A). The symmetrical interior with the central stack of blocked and carved prospect drawers is typical of better-quality New England workmanship. A number of similar mahogany desks carry the label of Benjamin Frothingham of Charlestown, Massachusetts, which was then a separate town just a hop and a skip across the Charles River from Boston. These desks may have been made for customers desiring good desks, but for whom blocking was felt to be too expensive or ostentatious. Blocking probably added about a third again to the cost of a desk.

Blockfront desks, like that shown in figure 13-4B, were the height of fashion in the two decades prior to the Revolution. Most were produced in and around Boston and Salem; a few were made in coastal New Hampshire, Connecticut, and Rhode Island. With these high-end desks we see the standard Boston interior pattern of a central prospect door flanked by a pair of pilastered document drawers, then a pair of pigeonholes above a small drawer, then at the sides a stack of small, blocked drawers. The prospect door and the top drawers at the ends are decorated with carved fans. Often the second row of drawers will be set back, or "stepped," as shown in the blockfront desk and bookcase. Desks of this type usually have straight bracket feet, but you also see ogee bracket and ball and claw feet. In a few examples the blocking is carried up into the lids of the desks, although here it was obtained by scooping out the center of the lid, then adding shaped panels on either side. This is sometimes thought to be a Salem feature. For those who wanted something special, there were also made a rare few bombé desks and desk and bookcases similar to the bombé chest of drawers illustrated in figure 11-6F.

By far the most common Massachusetts Chippendale desks are the large oxbow or reverse-serpentine desks like that shown in figure 13-4B. Although rococo in style, most of these desks were produced after the Revolution. Together with a great many similar serpentine-front chests of drawers, they are a notable example of style lag in American furniture. Many are obviously transitional, being fitted with Hepplewhite round or oval pulls. The small interior drawers are often given a little neoclassical inlay.

These large desks were so fashionable that they were produced to some extent all over New England, in eastern Connecticut, western Massachusetts, and coastal New Hampshire. I find their most striking feature the simple interiors that usually lie within the grand cases. Even when made of mahogany, they are normally far grander on the outside than the inside. The interior layout shown in this figure is typical of these popular desks. That the drawers are placed above the pigeonholes would suggest this desk might date to the turn of the century.

Many of these large desks have ball and claw feet. Most others have ogee bracket feet, although you will sometimes see straight bracket or neoclassical French feet. A few have ball and claw feet in front and ogee bracket feet in the rear, an arrangement also seen in New London and New York case furniture. The use of Chippendale-style ball and claw feet on these handsome desks is again perhaps more a reflection of rising prosperity than an early date of manufacture. They are likely be made of mahogany when from coastal Massachusetts, maple or birch when from New Hampshire, and cherry when from Connecticut or western Massachusetts.

There are two basic designs of Massachusetts Chippendale secretaries: an earlier type in which the bookcase doors have a Queen Anne arch (13-4D), and the more common form in which the doors are square with a serpentine border (13-4E). Usually the doors are paneled, but some have mirrored doors, an English feature seen only in New England in Boston furniture. Most of these high-end Chippendale desks and bookcases have scrolled or bonnet tops with tight corkscrew finials. The doors will be flanked by the fluted pilasters seen in Massachusetts chest-on-chests and clothespresses. Another fashionable treatment, particularly on the later reverse-serpentine front desks, is a pitched pediment like that shown on a Philadelphia Chippendale chest-on-chest (11-25E). A few reverse-serpentine-front desk and bookcases are transitional in nature, having bookcase doors with geometrical neoclassical glazing. Note that the imposing desk and bookcase in figure 13-4D has the same stepped interior layout seen earlier in the blockfront desk. Open the bookcase doors and there will probably be vertical partitions to hold ledgers, testifying to a time in which these imposing desk and bookcase were very much at the center of a gentleman's business activity.

13-4A. Massachusetts Chippendale, 42" h, c. 1780.

13-4B. Massachusetts Chippendale, 41" h, c. 1760 – 1780.

13-4C. Massachusetts Chippendale, 44" h, 1780 – 1810.

13-4D. Massachusetts Chippendale, 90" h, 1760 – 1780.

13-4E. Massachusetts Chippendale, 78" h, 1770 – 1800.

13-5 Rhode Island Chippendale desk and desk and book-case. Although Rhode Island is hardly 50 miles from Boston, Rhode Island Chippendale desks are so different that they are not difficult to identify. Whatever the individual features, Rhode Island workmanship is so unlike Boston workmanship that there should be little question of identification. Here you might first review section 11-7, Rhode Island Chippendale chests of drawers, noting the Rhode Island method of fastening base moldings, the very characteristic conservative Rhode Island ogee bracket foot, and that chestnut will likely be found among the secondary woods.

The desk shown in figure 13-5A is typical of good-quality Newport work. In addition to the standard Rhode Island feet, the interior differs from the normal Massachusetts pattern in not being stepped and lacking the document drawers on either side of the central prospect door. If scale permitted, you would also see that lobes of the small carved shells are curved in Newport fashion. For all their quality, Rhode Island desks almost never have document drawers. This three shell mahogany desk would probably have been top of the line. Simpler versions will have but a single shell carved into the prospect door, simpler yet uncarved prospect drawers, and straight bracket rather than ogee bracket feet.

Rhode Island desks have another distinguishing feature.

For some reason, perhaps to clear the users' knees on a moderate-size desk, many do not have the deep lopers that by this time were found on most desks. While the desk in figure 13-5A has normal lopers, on many Newport desks the lopers, although still rectangular in cross section, will only be about half this depth, even though there is ample room on either side of the top drawers for deeper lopers.

It might also be noted that straight-front desks were favored in Rhode Island. There are no more than a handful of Rhode Island desks having serpentine, reverse-serpentine, or blocked fronts. When something extra was desired, money was spent on the interior. This differs from Massachusetts practice, where many desks have costly shaped fronts and then very simple interiors.

There are surprisingly few Rhode Island desk and bookcases, and but for the famous block and shell form, no well-known types. Here we need to look for Rhode Island features. That the desk and bookcase in figure 13-5B is a Rhode Island product is immediately suggested by the shape of the feet and the applied panels that decorate the tympanum. Rhode Island desk and bookcases also tend to have the rather old-fashioned fielded paneled bookcase doors shown here. Although Chippendale in period, this desk, like much Rhode Island case work, is very much Queen Anne in feeling.

13-5A. Newport Chippendale, 41" h, 1760 – 1780.

13-5B. Rhode Island Chippendale, 91" h, c. 1780.

13-6 Connecticut Queen Anne and Chippendale desks and desk and bookcases. The individuality and naive enthusiasm that so characterizes Connecticut workmanship is also seen in Connecticut desks. While we will look at some typical examples, there are far too many local variations to do justice to the remarkable work of this small colony, and again we might review what was said earlier in regard to Connecticut case work.

As discussed in Chests of Drawers, there are a number of features that indicate Connecticut workmanship. The first, obviously, is the use of cherry in combination with white pine or tulip poplar. With this comes a penchant for a little additional decoration: boldly shaped aprons, ogee rather than straight bracket feet, some pinwheels here and there, quarter columns along the sides of the case, and fan inlay at the corners of drawers and desk lids. In addition, Connecticut case work often exhibits Massachusetts, Rhode Island, and New York influences, and this is particularly evident in desks and desk and bookcases. Here you may see Massachusetts serpentined bookcase doors, New York gadrooning, and in New London County, features borrowed from adjacent in Rhode Island.

The desk in figure 13-6A has little decoration, although here the use of cherry and the ogee bracket feet would suggest a Connecticut provenance. However, the pronounced outward splay of the feet indicates that this is an example of the quadrant-base furniture made in the Hartford area. Look back at figure 11-8D and you will see similar feet in a chest of drawers. This desk is also unusually wide in proportion to its depth, which might reflect a New York influence.

Figure 13-6B is another Connecticut desk, this one with the same rather vertical proportions often seen in Connecticut chests of drawers. Here we can also determine the location of manufacture with reasonable certainty, for the oversize ogee bracket feet with the inward facing scrolls are typical of New London County case work. Look back again to the section on Connecticut Chippendale chests of drawers, and in figure 11-8B you will see similar feet and scrolls. More interesting yet, the case is flanked with pilasters that for some reason are stop-fluted in the center. This may be a rural interpretation of the stop-fluting so popular in nearby Rhode Island.

Desks on frames were produced to some extent in all regions, but nowhere was the form as popular as it was in Connecticut, from where come not only a significant number of surviving desk-on-frames, but even desk-and-bookcases-on-frames, which might be seen as the literary counterpart of the Connecticut chest-on-chest-on-frame. Here we see two different approaches. The first, and perhaps the earliest, employs a high cabriole-leg frame on which rests a desk section and a drawer (13-6C). Sometimes the drawer will be in the desk section, as shown here; at other times it will be within the frame, and occasionally there will be drawers in both sections. The other form of desk-on-frame employs a low frame resting on short cabriole-legs, and above this a conventional desk having four graduated drawers (13-6D). Note that both these desks have the elaborately scalloped aprons so often seen in Connecticut furniture. In addition to desk-on-frames, there are a number of Connecticut desks with short cabriole legs and pad feet. However, they differ from New Hampshire cabriole-leg desks in having Connecticut features and being made of cherry rather than maple or birch.

We should not end without illustrating a Connecticut desk and bookcase, but this is something of a problem, for the colony did not have a Boston or a Newport to provide a guide in style, and there is no standard type. Instead, we will consider two fairly typical examples, and then note other features you are likely to see in Connecticut work. The first is a simple flat-top desk and bookcase with the rather bold cornice and large blocked ogee feet often seen in Connecticut case work (13-6E). The second is a type that may be unique to Connecticut, a desk-and-bookcase-on-frame (13-6F). Note that the swan's-neck pediment terminates in a pair of applied pinwheels. Shaped tops were very popular in Connecticut, and many desk and bookcases have either bonnet or scroll tops. Here we are likely to see extravagantly arched tops similar to those produced in rural Pennsylvania, or the open strapwork pediment found in Hartford-area high chests of drawers. While both of these desks have simple rectangular bookcase doors, you will see almost every shape; the most common is rectangular, but also the Queen Anne tombstone arch, the serpentine border so popular in Boston, and a hybrid with a single arch spanning both doors, the left portion at the top of the left-hand door, the right portion at the top of the right-hand door.

Without an urban center to provide guidance, the interior layout of Connecticut desks can perhaps most charitably be described as eclectic. On better work, though, particularly on desk and bookcases, there will usually be vertical document drawers on either side of the prospect doors or prospect drawers. These are usually either fluted or have applied turned pilasters.

13-6A. Hartford Chippendale, 42" h, c. 1790.

**13-6B. New London County
Chippendale, 47" h, c. 1780.**

13-6C. Connecticut Queen Anne, 39" h, 1740 – 1760.

13-6D. Connecticut Queen Anne, 40" h, 1750 – 1770.

13-6E. Connecticut Chippendale, 80" h, 1760 – 1790.

13-6F. Connecticut Queen Anne, 86" h, 1750 – 1770.

13-7 New York Chippendale desk. There are not many sur-viving New York City Chippendale desks, and even fewer desk and bookcases, but before moving down to Pennsylvania, I will show you a representative example. New York Chippendale desks are not difficult to identify, for not only are they consis-tent in form, but also, they very much relate to other New York Chippendale case work. Even if there were no illustrations in this section, you should have no problem with identification. The imposing desk in figure 13-7 is a typical New York product. Note that it is both large and wide in proportion to its depth, features often seen in New York case work. Most desks are about 46" wide. Other New York features are the strips of applied gadrooning across the fronts of the case, and the use of ball and claw feet in front and ogee bracket feet in the rear.

New York desks are typical of Middle Atlantic workmanship in that you will seldom see case furniture with blocked or ser-pentine fronts, and almost never flat-front mahogany desks with ball and claw feet. That this desk is a New York rather than a Philadelphia product is suggested by the ball and claw feet, which were seldom employed in Philadelphia case furniture. Like much other New York Colonial furniture, these fine desks have a distinctly Georgian appearance.

13-7. New York Chippendale, 45" h, c. 1770.

13-8 Pennsylvania Chippendale desks and desk and bookcases. Earlier it was noted that there was relatively little diversity among Pennsylvania chests of drawers. This is also true of desks and desk and bookcases. Compared with Massachusetts, the other major Colonial center of production, there are not many different designs. Here we will see but two desks and two desks and bookcases, and in form, they are all quite similar.

The standard Pennsylvania Chippendale desk will be made of walnut, have a flat front, and more often than not, the ogee bracket feet shown in figure 13-8A. This desk has two other features sometimes seen in Delaware Valley desks: in lieu of lopers to support the lid there will be a pair of candle drawers, and the second drawer is split, an English feature that also occurs in some early New England and in many Southern desks. Splitting this drawer would have been particularly useful in a desk, for it allowed a user to access a drawer without having to push back from the desk.

The desk in figure 13-8B has the fluted quarter columns so often seen in Delaware Valley case work. Here also we see the typical Pennsylvania interior layout: at the center a Queen Anne–style arched prospect door flanked by a pair of deep document drawers, then on each side four valanced pigeonholes with two pairs of small drawers beneath. The small drawers often have curved fronts and blocked ends. Usually the document drawers are simply fluted as shown here, but you will also see built-up pilasters, applied turned columns, and simulated book splines. On quality work, the prospect door will have a carved shell that is flanked by rows of identical shells in the little valance drawers. Lancaster County desks often have large, elaborate shells centered in the prospect doors. Desks oftentimes held valuables, and many Delaware Valley desks have secret compartments; usually in the form of a nest of little drawers tucked in behind the prospect door.

The most notable aspect of Pennsylvania desk and bookcases is their height, probably in part because ceilings were higher in a warmer climate. This is evident when you compare the New England desk and bookcase in figure 13-2B with the Pennsylvania desk and bookcase in figure 13-8C. In the latter, the bookcase section is as high as the desk section. The scroll-top desk and bookcase in figure 13-8D is fully 8' high, even though a relatively budget product with a simple interior and straight bracket feet. High-style desk and bookcases are similar in form to this example, although there will be additional embellishments: more elaborate interiors, large shell and applied acanthus leaf carvings in the tympanums, and usually ogee bracket feet. A few have the architectural pitched pediment seen earlier in a Philadelphia chest-on-chest (11-25E). Bookcase doors are usually either rectangular or arched, as shown in these two illustrations.

For the most part, Delaware Valley desks and desk and bookcases will be made of walnut. Even grand high-end desk and bookcases are very often walnut. Other primary woods are cherry and maple, particularly figured maple. Secondary woods are what you would expect: tulip poplar, white pine, yellow pine, and Atlantic white cedar.

As a general rule, Philadelphia-area case work employs thicker stock than Boston-area case work, which is quite noticeable in desks in which the sides of the cases are exposed under slant lids. Normally the sides of a Delaware Valley desk will be a quarter inch or so thicker than the sides of a comparable New England desk. Some Delaware Valley desks are extraordinarily heavy.

13-8A. Pennsylvania Chippendale, 41" h, 1760 – 1790.

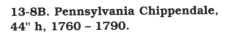
13-8B. Pennsylvania Chippendale, 44" h, 1760 – 1790.

13-8C. Pennsylvania Chippendale, 90" h, 1760 – 1790.

13-8D. Pennsylvania Chippendale, 96" h, 1760 – 1790.

13-9 Southern Chippendale desk and desk and bookcase. South of the Mason-Dixon Line, desks and desk and bookcases are far less common. Worse yet, the South had fewer major regional centers like those that now make it so easy to identify a Boston, Newport, New York, or Philadelphia desk. In this section we will see a Chippendale desk and desk and bookcase. Both are made of walnut and were probably produced in Virginia, but in material and form they could have been produced almost anywhere south of Pennsylvania.

The walnut desk in figure 13-9A is a fair example of the neat and plain construction and design favored in the South. Although neatly made, including having covered drawer-blade dovetails, it lacks any ornamentation other than the conservative shaping of the bracket feet. Pull out a drawer and you are likely to see that the sides and bottom are made of either poplar or yellow pine, and also, that it is heavily constructed. Also, in English fashion, the backboards of such a piece may run vertically, and there may also be dust dividers between the drawers.

The Virginia desk and bookcase in figure 13-9B is another example of the well-made and conservative furniture so favored in the South. This rather tall bracket-foot walnut desk has another feature often seen in Southern desks, the split second drawer that we saw previously in a Pennsylvania desk. The back of this bookcase, also in English fashion, may be paneled to provide additional stiffness. Although this Chippendale desk and bookcase is probably Federal rather than Colonial, it does not have the neoclassical glazed doors that were becoming fashionable in the North.

Southern desks are generally made of walnut, sometimes cherry, and occasionally birch, although this may be river birch (*Betula nigra*) rather than the yellow birch (*Betula alleghaniensis*) used in New England. A mahogany desk will likely have been made somewhere near the coast, perhaps Baltimore, Annapolis, Norfolk, or Charleston. Secondary woods are usually either poplar or yellow pine, sometimes red cedar, and if near the coast, then also bald cypress.

13-9A. Virginia Chippendale, 40" h, 1770 – 1800.

13-9B. Virginia Chippendale, 85" h, 1770 – 1790.

13-10 New England neoclassical desk, desk and bookcase, and secretary bookcase. There are so many rural New England desks from the Federal period, that is, from about 1780 to 1840, that we might begin our second sweep down the coast with a brief look at three typical examples. The first two are simply updated models of the generic New England Chippendale slant-front, bracket-foot desks illustrated in section 13-2. The third is a rural version of a fashionable new neoclassic desk.

For the most part the standard four-drawer slant-lid desk continued to be popular, acquiring only more up-to-date oval brasses, some neoclassical string inlay, and Hepplewhite French feet (13-10A). Sometimes the old bracket-foot construction was retained, the feet just being canted out a little and reshaped to suggest outswept French feet. The cherry slant-front desk in figure 13-10A is a good identifier of this type, for it carries the label of Samuel S. Noyes of East Sudbury, Massachusetts. Note that use of the high, thin French foot provides a lighter, more linear neoclassical appearance.

The desk and bookcase also remains largely unchanged, although in addition to updated brasses and Hepplewhite feet, the desk in figure 13-10B has some stringing and the neoclassical oval inlay that was so enormously popular in the Federal period. By this time, construction was somewhat more sophisticated, perhaps because of the greater availability of woodworking tools, and the drawer blade dovetails will normally be hidden. America was wealthier and the roads had gone from being awful to just plain bad, so that inland there was more use of mahogany and mahogany veneers, although most rural New England desks were still made of local woods: maple, cherry, and birch.

In addition to these traditional slant-lid designs, you are very likely to encounter rural versions of the popular neoclassical secretary bookcases being produced in Massachusetts and New Hampshire (13-10C). Behind the doors, you will see the pigeonholes and little drawers that originally were hidden behind curtains mounted inside of the doors.

13-10A. New England Hepplewhite, 45" h, c. 1810.

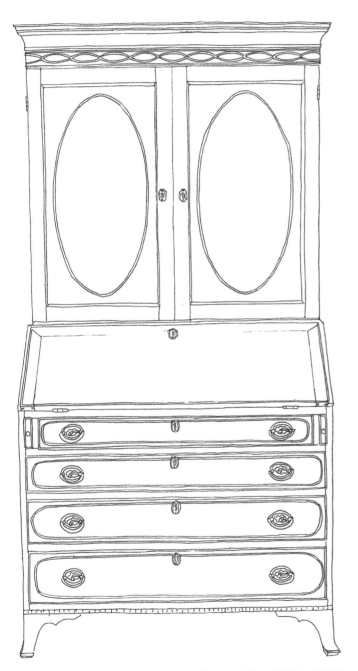

13-10B. New England Hepplewhite, 86" h, 1790 – 1810.

13-10C. New England Sheraton, 70" h, 1810 – 1830.

13-11 New Hampshire neoclassical secretary and secretary bookcase. The chapter on chests of drawers noted that New Hampshire Federal neoclassical furniture was distinguished by drawer fronts of light veneers that were framed by darker woods. The same is true of desks. If you see a secretary or a secretary bookcase having drawers veneered in flame birch or tiger or bird's-eye maple, with an edging of mahogany, you are probably looking at a product of New Hampshire or the adjacent North Shore of Massachusetts. The pen and ink drawings in this book do not do credit to this quite spectacular case furniture.

Here we will first consider a simpler interpretation of this style in a fall-front desk veneered in bird's-eye maple (13-11A). Note that while the fall front is edged in mahogany, in the case just the drawer blades and stiles are veneered to obtain the same effect. While this secretary, or perhaps more correctly, fall-front desk, is most probably from rural New Hampshire, similar but less-colorful Sheraton secretaries might be from

anywhere in New England. Employing the fall front to cover the interior of the desk was a common economy.

More typical of New Hampshire is the fashionable Portsmouth secretary bookcase shown in figure 13-11B. Here we see many of the elements of Federal Portsmouth workmanship: the three-part veneered drawer fronts of light wood framed by darker mahogany, the rectangular panel in the apron, and the high French feet with the small squared toes. The sides of the case of such a piece are likely to be birch stained up to resemble mahogany.

Although not shown in either of these illustrations, desks produced north of Boston are apt to be given a pair of deep bottle drawers on the lower outside corners of the case. We will see them when we get to sideboards. Whether in a desk they were used for keeping ledgers — or for keeping something stronger — I will leave to the reader.

13-11A. New Hampshire Sheraton, 50" h, 1810 – 1820.

13-11B. Portsmouth Hepplewhite, 64" h, c. 1810.

13-12 Massachusetts neoclassical secretaries and secretary bookcases. With Massachusetts we come to quite the longest section in this chapter, and for good reason, for the coastal area of this most populous New England state witnessed almost an explosion in different types of desks in the decades following the Revolution. Here we will see desks with fold-out writing flaps, secretary drawers, and tambour doors, and will see one in which the case itself folds out to support the writing surface.

Quite the most common design of Federal Massachusetts secretary has a relatively narrow writing flap supported on two deep lopers (13-12A). Above this is a separate section that accommodates the small drawers and pigeonholes. Some have a bookcase on top of this section. There are many variations on this popular design: Sheraton rather than Hepplewhite legs, two long drawers rather than the three shown here, and sometimes a row of small drawers above the doors. Many have four long drawers and are suggestive of chests of drawers with French feet, as shown in the next figure. Both these types of secretaries are sometimes called tambour desks, which they are not, or ladies' desks, which they may have been. The inlay of a lighter wood on the legs and stiles of this secretary suggests that it might have been made either on the North Shore of Massachusetts or, possibly, in Portsmouth, New Hampshire. Similar secretaries were produced as far north as southern Maine, but for some reason, far fewer were produced to the south in Rhode Island and Connecticut.

Massachusetts secretary bookcases are similar in form, although, often as not, the small drawers and pigeonholes were placed behind the bookcase doors, which were then fitted with curtains (13-12B). Often these small secretaries have arched or Gothic doors rather than the simple diagonal pattern shown here. Note that this handsome little secretary has the high outswept French feet favored in New England. Also, by now neoclassical urns have superseded rococo corkscrew finials. Usually they were made of brass rather than wood, similar to those seen on Federal clocks. These handsome secretary bookcases enjoyed a long period of popularity, and there are many classical examples (13-12C), although they could be from most anywhere in New England. Providing a writing surface by use of a narrow fold-out writing flap was seldom employed south of New England, although in the next section you will see the same design in a New York secretary bookcase. There are documented examples of similar desks made in Wilmington, North Carolina, and Charleston, South Carolina. That both these cities are located on the coast would suggest that local cabinetmakers may have been emulating venture cargo examples.

Quite the most lovely and best known of neoclassical Massachusetts secretaries are the delicate little tambour desks made in Boston in the first decades of the nineteenth century (13-12D). On the secretary shown here, the small drawers and the pigeonholes are hidden behind tambour doors that slide back into the sides of the cases. Some very fine examples made by John and Thomas Seymour have inlay set directly into the tambour shutters. Most have no more than two long drawers in the cases, which contributes to their light and graceful proportions. A rare few have additional incurved triangular storage sections on the tops of the cases. Tambour doors require real skill to make, and most tambour desks are from either Boston or Salem. They are uniquely American, for in England the tambour action is only found in cylinder-top desks. Here also it should be noted that, in a general way, vertical tambour actions are New England, horizontal tambour actions Middle Atlantic and England. However, do not forget "general," for John and Thomas Seymour made some cylinder-fall desks with horizontal tambour lids. But then, they had recently arrived from England.

The English form of desk having a deep secretary drawer fitted with little drawers and pigeonholes never achieved any great popularity in America, and production was primarily limited to urban centers. The Massachusetts secretary bookcase shown in figure 13-12E is this type of desk, but otherwise is a typical New England product, for it has the same pediment and high outswept French feet that we saw in the preceding Massachusetts secretary bookcase. In the next section we will see a similar Middle Atlantic secretary bookcase.

Among Massachusetts desks, perhaps the most unusual are the small secretaries in which the fronts of the tops swing up and over to provide the writing surfaces, as illustrated in figure 13-12F. In form, these unusual little desks are basically just enlarged versions of the common lap desk such as was employed by Thomas Jefferson to draft the Declaration of Independence. Most are small in scale and are thought to have been used by women. There is also some thought that their size made them suitable for voyaging, and for this reason they are sometimes called captain's desks. Indeed, if made with solid rather than veneered cases, perhaps with separate frames, they may have gone to sea. Not all are as small as this example. Somewhat larger versions may have separate sections on the top, like that shown in the secretary in figure 13-12A. A few are in the form of full-size secretaries with bookcase tops. Most have Sheraton rather than the Hepplewhite legs shown here. While of an unusual design, they enjoyed considerable popularity in New England. A few were made in Baltimore, but differ from New England examples in not having white pine secondary wood and in employing the heavily reeded Sheraton legs that were fashionable in Baltimore.

Breakfront bookcases and breakfront secretaries were produced only in limited numbers, and then only in the larger urban centers, and are fairly rare among American furniture. The relatively small gentleman's secretaries made in Salem are the most notable examples, and even here there are no more than perhaps a dozen surviving examples (13-12G). In form this secretary is a little break-front bookcase raised on short legs and fitted with a secretary drawer. For all their size and apparent fragility, a number seem to have been made as venture cargo, for one turned up in Charleston, South Carolina, and even more remarkably, another was found in Capetown, South Africa.

By this time, mahogany had long supplanted walnut as the fashionable cabinet wood, and aside from some upper Connecticut Valley workmanship, most all Massachusetts secretaries and secretary bookcases, even budget products, will be made of mahogany or mahogany veneered on eastern white pine. Drawers and backboards will also be white pine. On the best-quality work the small drawers may be made of mahogany, and sometimes also, the long drawers will be veneered on walnut. The use of white pine in northern New England is more help than it may seem, for a considerable amount of furniture was sent south as venture cargo, and in both Pennsylvania, and in the South, you will sometimes see local interpretations of Massachusetts Federal secretaries and secretary bookcases. Here, though, you will probably also see the use of walnut, cherry, tulip poplar, and Southern hard pine.

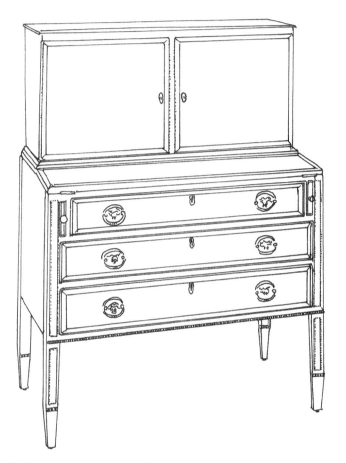

13-12A. Massachusetts Hepplewhite, 52" h, 1800 – 1820.

13-12B. Massachusetts Hepplewhite, 78" h, 1800 – 1820.

13-12C. New England classical, 84" h, 1820 – 1840.

13-12D. Boston Hepplewhite, 42" h, 1790 – 1810.

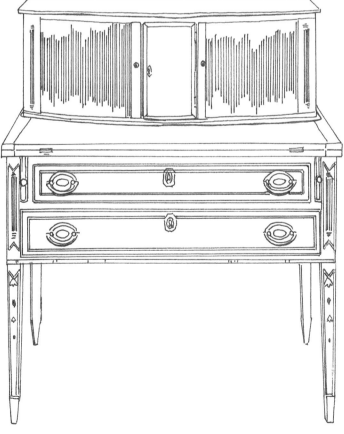

13-12E. Massachusetts Hepplewhite, 78" h, 1800 – 1810.

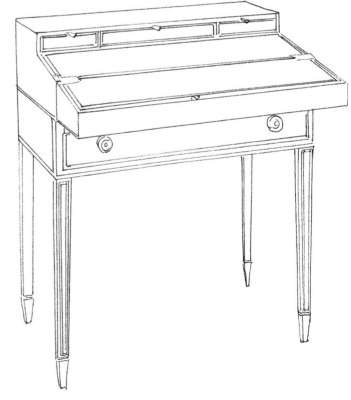

13-12F. Massachusetts Hepplewhite, 34" h, 1790 – 1810.

13-12G. Salem gentleman's secretary, 87" h x 67" w, 1790 – 1810.

13-13 New York neoclassical secretaries and secretary bookcases. New York, and in particular, New York City, is something of a muddle, for here there is no preeminent type of neo-classical desk. While I will show you a number of secretaries and secretary bookcases, only one immediately suggests that it is a product of New York City, and this because of a feature that has little to do with function but is frequently seen on other late Federal New York furniture. Perhaps the best help in identifying a New York desk or secretary is to keep in mind the characteristics of New York City Federal furniture: high-quality workmanship; a preference for the latest, most fashionable styles; and the use of dark mahogany veneers. Case work is noticeably dark and monochromatic — very different from the walnut and string inlay seen in Pennsylvania and the light, contrasting veneers found in Massachusetts.

In this section we might proceed from small to large, beginning with a delicate little New York ladies' secretary (13-13A) and a similar secretary bookcase (13-13B). Desks of this scale are rare in American furniture. Although most all are from urban centers — Baltimore, Philadelphia, New York, Providence, and Boston — they seem to have been particularly favored in New York. That both of the small desks shown here are from New York is evident in the straight reeded legs and the very characteristic New York Sheraton feet. The feet on the secretary bookcase are ended out, with the brass ball caps that are frequently seen in better-quality New York furniture. These charming and very feminine desks speak to a time before the telephone and the Internet when so much communication was by means of short notes.

Even in stylish New York, desks with secretary drawers had only limited acceptance, although they are more frequently seen here and in the South than elsewhere in America. That the secretary bookcase in figure 13-13C is most probably from New York City is suggested by the flat top, the ornate door glazing, the scalloped apron, and the French feet, which are very different from those seen in Massachusetts. The mahogany veneered desk and bookcase in figure 13-13D was also made in New York City, perhaps for a conservative customer, for by this time slant-front desks were going out of fashion in New York, and bookcase doors were more likely to be glazed. The very delicate-looking outswept Hepplewhite feet are characteristic of New York City furniture. Elaborate swan's-neck crests are also seen in northern New Jersey.

Lastly, I will show you a type of classical secretary and bookcase that immediately suggests New York City because of the low shelf set between the legs (13-13E). In the previous chapter we saw the same rectangular cookie-corner case, Sheraton legs, and low shelf in a New York dressing table, and in the next chapter we will see the same basic form employed as a server. Note that this is one of the few instances in which the narrow New England writing flap is seen south of Boston.

As mentioned earlier, perhaps the most striking aspect of New York City Federal case work is the use of flat panels of dark, figured mahogany veneer. These were usually laid on eastern white pine, which provided an exceptionally good base for veneer. Backboards and drawers will usually be made of yellow or tulip poplar.

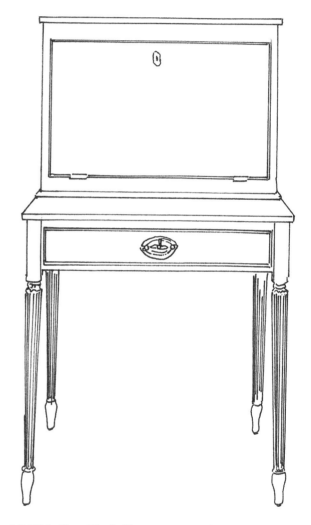

13-13A. New York Sheraton, 49" h, 1800 – 1810.

13-13B. New York Sheraton, 77" h, 1800 – 1810.

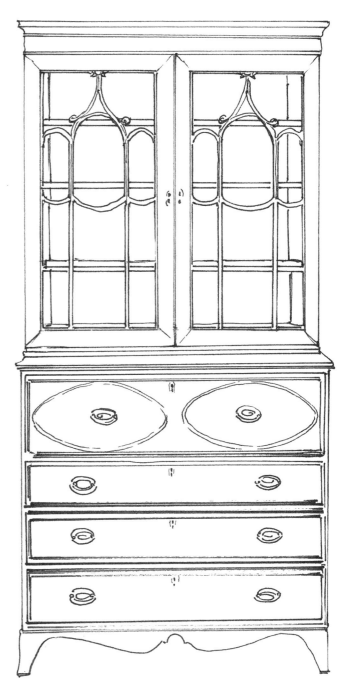

13-13C. New York Hepplewhite, 83" h, 1790 – 1810.

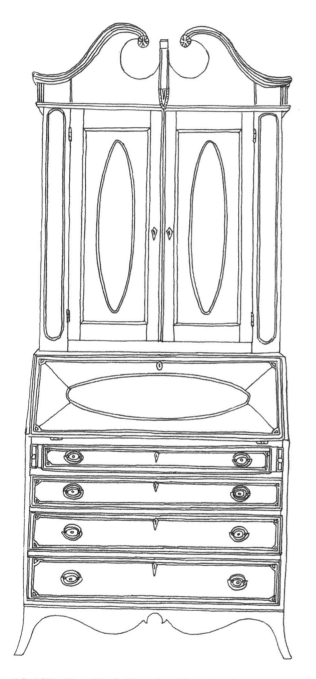

13-13D. New York Hepplewhite, 85" h, c. 1800.

13-13E. New York classical, 62" h, 1820 – 1830.

13-14 Pennsylvania neoclassical desks. Philadelphia was slow to embrace the new neoclassical styles that became so fashionable in New York and Baltimore, and this is particularly evident in their secretaries, or perhaps more correctly, their desks, for the two examples shown here are little more than updated versions of the Pennsylvania Chippendale desks seen in section 13-8. Desks with secretary drawers and cylinder-fall fronts also enjoyed some popularity, but for now we will consider a desk most probably made in Philadelphia and a simpler example from southeastern Pennsylvania.

The desk in figure 13-14A is typical of conservative Philadelphia cabinet work in the decades following the Revolution. In form, this desk is much like the Pennsylvania Chippendale desk seen earlier, having the same basic interior arrangement and the quarter columns flanking the case. However, when we note the French feet, the stringing that borders the front of the document drawers, the prospect door, and the long drawers, we realize this is a later neoclassical product. Also, the curved and blocked fronts of the interior drawers have been replaced by the flat surfaces favored in the new style.

The walnut desk in figure 13-14B is a simpler rural product, but again it has been updated with Hepplewhite feet and a little stringing across the apron and around the drawers, although it still retains the by now old fashioned bail brasses that were so popular in Pennsylvania. Here the standard Pennsylvania interior omits the document drawers, and in a sign of lateness, the little drawers are on the top and the pigeonholes are on the bottom.

Most of these desks continued to be made of walnut, or sometimes cherry, even though by this time mahogany had replaced walnut in all the other urban centers. Secondary woods were generally yellow pine, white pine, or tulip poplar.

13-14A. Philadelphia Hepplewhite, 40" h, c. 1800.

13-14B. Pennsylvania Hepplewhite, 45" h, 1800 – 1810.

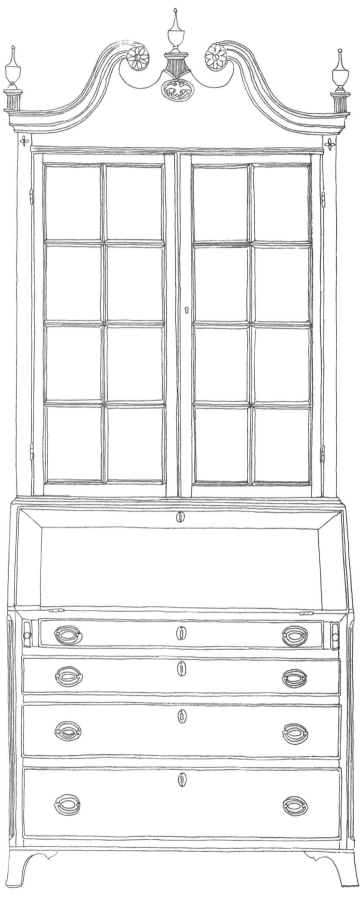

13-15 Southern neoclassical desk and bookcase. Desks produced in the South after the Revolution may also be confusing. In Baltimore, secretary bookcases were made in the very latest fashions, while elsewhere desks and desk and bookcases were simply upgraded with some neoclassical features, much as we have seen in Pennsylvania.

Here we will look at a desk and bookcase made in Virginia about the turn of the century. The very high walnut slant-front desk in figure 13-15 is not veneered and retains the old fashioned lipped drawers, but has been updated with urn finials, a little neoclassical inlay in the scroll top, glazed doors, oval brasses, and French feet. The glazing is not the geometric or Gothic pattern normally seen in neoclassical desks and bookcases, but is a simple rectangular pattern more appropriate to a cupboard or a window. The impression is of a cabinet-maker familiar with fashioning double-hung windows.

Secretary drawers are fairly common in all sorts of Southern furniture, and if you encounter a rather strange-looking desk and bookcase fitted with a secretary drawer and made of walnut or mahogany, you are most probably looking at a rural Southern secretary bookcase.

13-15. Virginia Hepplewhite, 100" h, c. 1800.

13-16 Cylinder-fall desks. Desks having the writing surfaces, small drawers, and pigeonholes covered by rotating cylinders were made to some extent in all regions, although very seldom south of Baltimore, which might be expected, for fabricating a smoothly operating cylinder would require both experience and a fine set of tools. These desks are variously called cylinder, cylinder-top, and cylinder-fall desks, but I use the latter simply because I like the old-fashioned sound of the word.

Here in this last section we will briefly consider three examples that span the east coast from Massachusetts down to Baltimore, commencing with what may be the most common type, one of a significant group of Sheraton cylinder-fall desk and bookcases made in the Boston area (13-16A). For the most part they are similar to this example, although some lack the lower long drawer and the row of small drawers above the cylinder fall. Others have a neoclassical pediment like that shown in the Massachusetts secretary bookcase in figure 13-12B.

The next significant center of cylinder-fall production is New York City. That the cylinder-fall desk in figure 13-16B is most probably from New York is suggested by the size of the case, the use of large sheets of mahogany veneer that are taken right up to the edges of the drawers without the usual banding, and the pronounced outsweep of the French feet.

Fewer cylinder-fall desks seem to have been produced in Philadelphia, even though a tambour cylinder-fall desk and bookcase was made here by John Aitken for George Washington in 1797. Instead, we might end this section, and this chapter, with a fine example of a Baltimore cylinder-fall desk (13-16C). Baltimore Federal furniture is noted for its generous use of inlay, and if you see a mahogany veneered desk with an unusual amount of line and figure inlay, you are likely to be looking at Baltimore workmanship. In a cylinder-fall desk, the focus of the design is the cylinder, and here it has been decorated, in the best Baltimore fashion, not only with a large neoclassical ellipse, but also with a very large figural inlay.

13-16A. Massachusetts Sheraton, 75" h, 1800 – 1820.

13-16B. New York Hepplewhite, 48" h, 1790 – 1810.

13-16C. Baltimore Hepple-white, 44" h, 1790 – 1810.

Chapter 14 – Sideboards and Serving Tables

This will be a relatively short chapter, for the cellaret sideboard, that is, the modern form of sideboard having a deep drawer, or cellaret, to hold wine bottles, was not produced in America until after the Revolution and the return of prosperity in the 1790s. Since then, cellaret sideboards have never gone out of production, although our survey will end with the classical style in the 1820s, hardly three decades after their introduction. For all their modernity, a great many period examples survive, for they have never ceased to be practical, and in their time were exceedingly fashionable. Together with the lolling chair and the gaming table, the cellaret sideboard is the signature of Federal period furniture.

As a group, cellaret sideboards can be difficult to place, for by the Federal period American furniture had lost much of its regional identity. Worse yet, they are a new form, and there is no prior history to help us in identification. Unlike so much other furniture, there are no neoclassical updates of existing regional forms. Even among museum collections you will sometimes see a lovely cellaret sideboard identified only as being "American."

It has been my practice to discuss secondary woods in the individual sections, but here we might review them before turning to specific examples, for they can help in identifying a form that has fewer other regional attributes. First off, remember that eastern white pine not only provides an excellent base for the veneering employed in neoclassical furniture, but also that large amounts were shipped as far south as Charleston, South Carolina. That a sideboard has some white pine among its secondary woods does not mean that the sideboard was made in New England. However, that all, or most all, of the secondary structure is white pine does indicate central and northern New England: Rhode Island, Massachusetts, New Hampshire, Vermont, Maine, and the Connecticut River Valley. Vermont sideboards may have some basswood. South of this area, tulip poplar was the preferred wood for drawers and backboards, although stronger woods were generally used in the framing. Rhode Island sideboards are likely to include some chestnut, principally in drawers and backboards. Sideboards made in New York usually have some maple, ash, and cherry in the framing, the same woods seen in New York Federal chairs. From New York City south there was an increasing use of the hard Southern pines, even though in most regions white pine was still preferred as a base for veneer. In North and South Carolina, yellow pine was often the only secondary wood used. Maryland furniture is apt to employ some oak where additional strength is required. In common with urban New York, Charleston case work employs a variety of secondary woods, and here you may see both white and yellow pine, tulip poplar, Southern red cedar, and cypress. The large veneered doors in sideboards are prone to warping, and you will often see the veneer laid on a hardwood base. John and Thomas Seymour would veneer these doors on mahogany, which was not just simple extravagance, for among its many virtues, mahogany is an excellent base for veneer.

The fronts of sideboards are usually curved to lessen the mass of the case, and it is tempting to associate different shapes with different regions. To some extent this is true, and in the sections that follow these will be noted when applicable. However, it

is not a good idea to assign region simply on the basis of shape without checking that the secondary wood conforms with your assessment. In *Charleston Furniture*, E. Milby Burton illustrates over a dozen Charleston sideboards, many of which from shape alone might be attributed to New York, Rhode Island, Massachusetts — and the United Kingdom. This is particularly significant when we remember that in the twentieth century, much old Southern furniture was sent north to obtain a better sale price.

Because cellaret sideboards are confined to the Federal period and are all neoclassical in style, we will cover them in a single sweep down the coast, commencing in northern New England with a small Vermont sideboard and ending in the South with a pair of huntboards. This will be followed by two brief sections on serving tables and china presses, which, ironically, are often easier to place than their larger brethren.

14-1 Vermont neoclassical sideboard. Small "half" sideboards were popular in rural areas north of Boston, and we might start with an example produced in Vermont in the first decades of the nineteen century (14-1). Some of these are in the form of butler's desks, the top drawer folding down to reveal pigeon holes, small drawers, and a writing surface. The flanking bottle drawers seen here are often at the top of the case. Most of these sideboards are made of cherry, which might be expected, for not only is Vermont well inland, but also, it is at the top of the Connecticut River Valley. The use of cherry is unusual in sideboards, for by now mahogany was everywhere the fashionable wood. After we leave the Connecticut River Valley, we will see no primary wood but mahogany until well south of the Mason-Dixon Line, and here again, most examples will be from areas where mahogany would not have been available.

The inlaid diamond in the center of the upper drawer is a feature often seen in Vermont case work, perhaps because the shape was easier to execute than an ellipse. The drawers may be made of bass or whitewood. These small half sideboards enjoyed a long run, and there are Hepplewhite, Sheraton, and classical examples.

14-1. Vermont half sideboard, 40" h, 1810 – 1820

14-2 Massachusetts cellaret sideboards. In the last chapter it was noted that Federal Massachusetts was unusual in the variety of secretaries produced in the state. The same is true of sideboards, and here we will see a number of different sizes and shapes, many but variations on the cookie-corner design so enormously popular in New England. For the most part, Massachusetts sideboards are conservative in the use of veneers and inlay. There is little use of light wood veneers, of figured birch and maple, except in some high-style Boston work, and in sideboards produced up along the North Shore. In this respect, Massachusetts sideboards have more in common with those from Philadelphia than with those from New York City and Baltimore.

By far the most common type of Massachusetts cellaret sideboard has the D-shaped front shown in figure 14-2A. Frequently the facade will be broken by setting the center section between the two inner legs is out or in a few inches. Sometimes the middle drawers will be tambored. Even so, the D-shape tends to give them a very recognizable, and somewhat unfortunate, heavy and stocky appearance. Similar sideboards were made all over New England, and in other regions, particularly in New York, although New York cabinetmakers usually alleviated the heavy look by deeply recessing the center sections below the middle drawers. However, that this sideboard is from New England, and most probably from Massachusetts, is suggested both in the restrained decoration and in the double-tapered legs.

Less common in Massachusetts, but by no means rare, are serpentine-front sideboards like that illustrated in figure 14-2B. Again, we see a restrained use of veneer and inlay that is unlike New York workmanship. Also, if you pull out a drawer you will notice that it is made of eastern white pine rather than tulip poplar. Many of these sideboards also have the center recessed below the top middle drawer.

With the advent of the Sheraton style, the outset cookie corner was applied to sideboards, particularly in Boston and northeastern Massachusetts. The solid rectangular sideboard in figure 14-2C was most probably made in Salem or somewhere up along the North Shore. Although in this example the reeding is carried all the way up the stiles, you may also see the acanthus leaf carving at the top that was so popular in Salem. To minimize the boxy look of a large, rectangular case, on better work the center section was sometimes serpentined as shown here, or else given a shallow arch across the bottom. By this time knife boxes had gone out of fashion, and many of these somewhat later Federal sideboards have a pair of small, square silver drawers just above the bottle drawers.

At the top end of Massachusetts workmanship is a small group of tiered Sheraton sideboards, many of which are attributed to the workshop of John and Thomas Seymour (14-2D). Some of these grand high-style cellaret sideboards have additional splashboards above the concave superstructures. The deeply arched center, which does much to lighten the appearance of such a massive sideboard, is a feature more often seen on English sideboards, and may reflect the Seymours' English background.

Small sideboards are more common in New England than in any other region, perhaps because of older housing stock and somewhat smaller dining rooms. We will look at two examples, the first a standard type made in Salem (14-2E). The carved leafage at the top of the columns is popularly associated with Salem workmanship, but is so common that it was probably produced by many area shops. Typically these small four-leg sideboards have the swelled fronts also seen in New England Sheraton chests of drawers. This is an average example; a somewhat better-quality piece will have a pair of bottle drawers, and then sometimes a pair of silver drawers above them.

The second small sideboard was most probably made in Boston, this because of the complex and sophisticated facade, the interrupted fluting on the columns, and the arched skirt associated with the work of the Seymour family (14-2F). Earlier we saw a similar skirt on a Boston chest of drawers.

14-2A. Massachusetts Hepplewhite, 43" h, 1790 – 1810.

14-2B. Boston Hepplewhite, 38" h, c. 1795.

14-2C. Massachusetts Sheraton, 42" h, 1800 – 1810.

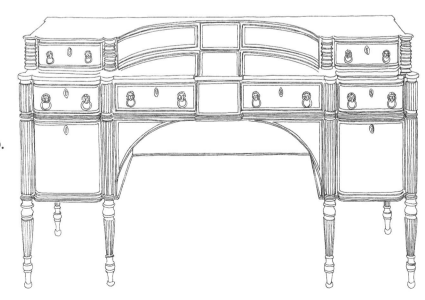

14-2D. Boston Sheraton, 55" h, c. 1810.

14-2E. Salem Sheraton, 43" h, 1810 – 1820.

14-2F. Boston Sheraton, 40" h, 1800 – 1815.

14-3 Rhode Island cellaret sideboard. As you might expect, Rhode Island cellaret sideboards are similar to fashionable Boston models, and here you will see both D-shaped and serpentine-front sideboards, perhaps differing in having some chestnut among the secondary woods. Instead of illustrating one of these, I will show you a charming small rectangular sideboard whose design appears to be unique to Rhode Island, one of the few instances in which an average grade of cellaret sideboard is found only in one area. These little sideboards are usually attributed to the shop of Thomas Howard (1744 – 1833), although they seem to have been made by more than one shop. The sideboard in figure 14-3 may have been ordered to a budget or be the product of another shop, for it lacks inlay on the legs and, more significantly, the crossed branch and leaf inlay in the center of the apron that is a characteristic of the Howard shop.

14-3. Rhode Island Hepplewhite, 39" h, 1790 – 1810.

14-4 Connecticut cellaret sideboard. Sideboards do not seem to have been particularly fashionable in Connecticut, and there are not a great many surviving examples. There are also few standard forms, although the D-front and the serpentine-front popular in Massachusetts are apt to be seen in Connecticut and up the Connecticut River Valley in western Massachusetts. What is different, however, is that away from the coast, the case will commonly be made of cherry. This is helpful, for aside from huntboards, sideboards were almost invariably made of mahogany and mahogany veneer. If you see a sideboard with a cherry case, you are most probably looking at a sideboard produced somewhere within the Connecticut River Valley.

The somewhat rural sideboard in figure 14-4 is typical of this production, although it should be stressed that there is no typical Connecticut sideboard. However, the cherry case and the oversize and rather naive urns squeezed into the stiles suggest Connecticut workmanship. Note that the case is not serpentine, nor is it really rectangular, for there is a shallow bow worked into the center — a feature seen in Connecticut sideboards.

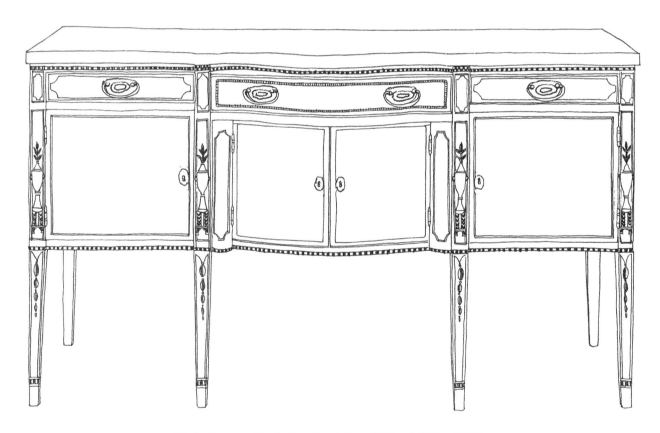

14-4. Connecticut Hepplewhite, 42" h, 1800 – 1810.

14-5 New York cellaret sideboards. As a group, New York cellaret sideboards are distinctive and usually not difficult to identify. With the possible exception of Charleston, New York was the wealthiest city in America after the Revolution, and this is reflected in its fashionable dining room furniture. Here we see large, very high-quality sideboards in the latest neoclassical fashion. The facade of such a sideboard will be veneered with carefully chosen veneers and decorated with light-wood banding around the drawers, string-bordered ellipses of contrasting veneers, pictorial and fan inlay, and strings of bellflowers both on the stiles and extending down the legs. When the curve of the front breaks at the inner legs, the legs are likely to be shaped to conform to the angle of the case. A very high-quality sideboard, in which the sides and bottoms of the drawers are made of tulip poplar, is likely to be a product of New York City.

Having said that New York sideboards were made to the latest fashion, we will start with an example of an unusual group of early New York cellaret sideboards that are transitional in form — having both rococo and neoclassical elements in the design. The sideboard in figure 14-5A is typical of this group, some of which carry the label of Thomas Burling, whose long career spanned both Colonial and Federal America. The late rococo bail pulls may appear to be replacements, but they are not, for when this large sideboard was made, they were still very much in style. Many of these Burling-type sideboards have straight fronts rather than the bowed front shown here, although in both types the center doors are recessed as shown in this illustration.

New York sideboards are most likely to have either the serpentine front with the recessed center shown in figure 14-5B, or the more complex elliptical front shown in figure 14-5C, which was described in price books as having an "elliptic middle and ogee on each side." Note in the former that the legs appear very delicate for so large a case. On some New York, sideboards they will taper almost to points. Here it might be noted that a rare few sideboards made in Connecticut, New York, and Baltimore have eight legs each, that is, they have six legs on the front. In New York this is seen in large elliptic-front sideboards in which there will be legs on both sides of the bottle drawers.

Just as serpentine-front sideboards were produced in Massachusetts, so also D-front sideboards were made in New York, and here we might show an example, for it illustrates the differences between Massachusetts and New York workmanship. The cellaret sideboard in figure 14-5D was made in New York City about 1805. Although similar in shape to the Massachusetts sideboard in figure 14-2A, it is far richer in detail, having the top edged in light-wood inlay, the doors and drawers decorated with light-wood string inlay and contrasting veneer, and the stiles and legs embellished with oval, carrot-shaped, and bellflower inlays. The left-hand center door has even been given a little inlaid key surround to balance the keyhole on the right-hand door. Again, the drawers and backboards will most probably be fashioned of poplar rather than the white pine one would expect to see in Massachusetts.

Rectangular sideboards having flat fronts were produced in all regions, and by itself, this shape is little help in identification. However, the form enjoyed considerable popularity in New York, and we will illustrate an elegantly simple example that has been embellished with large circles of contrasting veneer on the doors and strings of husk inlay on the legs (14-5E). Again, note the delicate-looking slightly outswept Hepplewhite legs. Here it might be noted that Sheraton legs are very seldom seen on early Federal New York cellaret sideboards, perhaps because the fashionable thin and delicate look would prove fatal in a turned leg. A sideboard with turned and reeded legs will most probably be a product of either Massachusetts or Pennsylvania, and then probably Boston or Philadelphia, where full-time turners would have been most available. Some Baltimore sideboards also have Sheraton legs.

Having just stated that New York sideboards rarely have Sheraton legs, I will show you an exception, although the double, or two-pedestal, sideboard shown in figure 14-5F is so unlike the normal cellaret form that there is little chance of confusion. With time there was need for additional storage, and with this came an unfortunate deepening of the case, first at the ends as we see here, and then across the entire front, as shown in the next illustration. These large sideboards were produced to some extent in Boston, but were most common in New York, and if you see such a sideboard, you are very probably looking at a New York product. In typical New York fashion, most are fitted with brass toe caps. Others have the paw feet seen on so much classical furniture. A few pedestal-end sideboards were also produced in Baltimore.

We will end with a typical example of one of the many surviving New York classical sideboard. By this time there is less variation among sideboards, although Massachusetts sideboards may retain cookie corners, and sideboards made in Philadelphia are apt to have recessed centers backed by large fixed mirrors. The sideboard in figure 14-5G is typical of many New York Classical sideboards in the rectangular stepped splashboard with the flanking brass rails. Many have pineapple shaped finials at the corners and steps of the splashboard.

14-5A. New York Hepplewhite, 39" h, c. 1790.

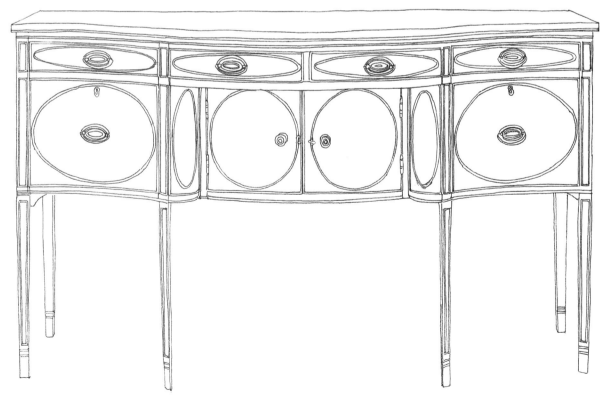

14-5B. New York Hepplewhite, 43" h, 1790 – 1810.

14-5C. New York Hepplewhite, 41" h, 1790 – 1810.

14-5D. New York Hepplewhite, 39" h, 1790 – 1810.

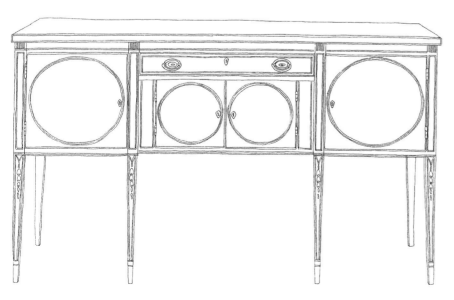

14-5E. New York Hepplewhite, 40" h, 1790 – 1810.

14-5F. New York Sheraton, 54" h, c. 1815.

14-5G. New York classical, 53" h, 1810 – 1830.

14-6 Philadelphia cellaret sideboards. The easiest way to identify a Philadelphia sideboard is by the pronounced kidney shape induced by the rounded ends and the recessed center. Most will have curved ends in combination with incurved centers, like that shown in figure 14-6A. In some the center section is simply recessed, in others there will be a shallow serpentine like the one shown here. The kidney shape was very fashionable in Federal Philadelphia, and we will see it again in card and work tables.

Early Philadelphia sideboards are of typical Hepplewhite style with square tapered legs, light mahogany veneers, stringing,

and pictorial inlays. Somewhat later sideboards, like this sideboard, which is attributed to Ephram Haines, tend to follow New York fashion in being darker and more monochromatic, but unlike New York, in having turned and reeded Sheraton legs.

Many Philadelphia sideboards have rounded ends and then but four legs as seen in figure 14-6B. Although you would think that four legs would be employed only on small sideboards, many of these unusual sideboards are full size, that is, about 6' long. While most fashionable in Philadelphia, the kidney shape, and the use of four rather than six legs, is also seen in Baltimore.

14-6A. Philadelphia Sheraton, 40" h, 1800 – 1815.

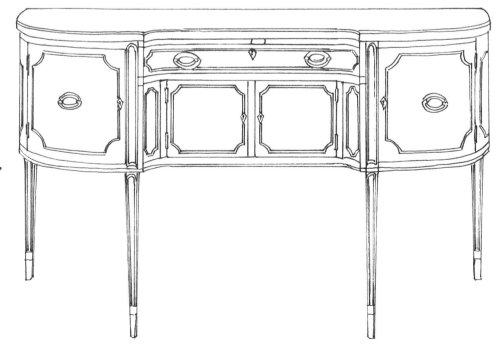

14-6B. Philadelphia Hepplewhite, 40" h, 1790 – 1810.

14-7 Southern cellaret sideboards and huntboards. In surveying the many sideboards and huntboards produced in the South, we will look at four typical examples, although there is so much variation that it is difficult to show other than representative types. However, there are a number of features that may suggest Southern origin. The first, obviously, is the use of hard Southern pine in the framing. If you find a considerable amount of yellow pine in the blocking, the drawer supports, the bottom of the case, and the backboards, you are most probably examining a Southern sideboard. Maryland sideboards are also apt to incorporate some oak; Charleston sideboards, cypress and red cedar. Maryland sideboards may have the spade feet and arched centers that are common in English sideboards. The large fronts of sideboards are perfect venues for decorative inlay, particularly the extensions of the legs that carry up to the undersides of the tops. If you see atypical inlay here, and perhaps also on the door or drawer fronts, you are probably looking at small production, and this is most likely to be from somewhere in the South. Also, high-style mahogany veneered and inlaid cellaret sideboards will probably be from an urban center near the coast, if not Baltimore, then Annapolis, Norfolk, Wilmington, or Charleston.

Having said all this, let's look at some sideboards and huntboards, first a Baltimore example, if only because there appear to be more surviving sideboards from Baltimore than from any other Southern city. In the previous section it was noted that Baltimore cabinetmakers often emulated fashionable Philadelphia kidney-shape designs, so instead we will look at a serpentine-front sideboard, a form that was also popular in Baltimore (14-7A). That this sideboard is a Maryland product is suggested by the spade feet, and that it is a Baltimore product is suggested by the enthusiastic use of stringing and pictorial inlay. The larger drawer and door fronts are decorated with oval stringing, the smaller with large oval paterae, the stiles with elongated bookend inlays and somewhat smaller paterae, and the legs with strings of bellflowers. There is hardly any room for further decoration! Not shown here, but in keeping with a general enthusiasm for decoration, the legs of many Baltimore sideboards have wide cuffs of light woods.

The simplest type of cellaret sideboard will have a square, rectangular case supported by tapered Hepplewhite legs, to which has been added perhaps no more decoration than an inlaid circle or a single band of light-wood stringing around the drawers and doors. As you might expect, many Southern sideboards are of this type. The rather handsome Delaware sideboard in figure 14-7B is a typical example. Similar cellaret sideboards were made throughout the South, generally of mahogany where it was available, and otherwise of walnut or perhaps, cherry. Secondary structural members will usually be a Southern pine. Drawers may be poplar rather than pine. Here it might be noted that Southern sideboards seldom have Sheraton legs, perhaps because it was difficult to obtain the services of turners in rural areas.

Huntboards come in every conceivable shape and size, which might be expected of a vernacular form produced by many rural cabinetmakers over an enormous region. However, most have one of two forms: a high buffet table fitted with two drawers (14-7C), or a much simplified cellaret sideboard (14-7D). In general, they will be made of either Southern pine, walnut, or a combination of both. Most have rather thin and elegant tapered Hepplewhite legs. They are typically a little over 40" high, reputedly to keep dogs away from the food. But then, this is about normal for any sideboard. In common with other rural furniture, huntboards are difficult to date, although the early neoclassical style would suggest that most were produced in the first decades of the nineteenth century.

14-7A. Baltimore Hepplewhite, 37" h, c. 1800.

14-7B. Delaware Hepplewhite, 39" h, c. 1800.

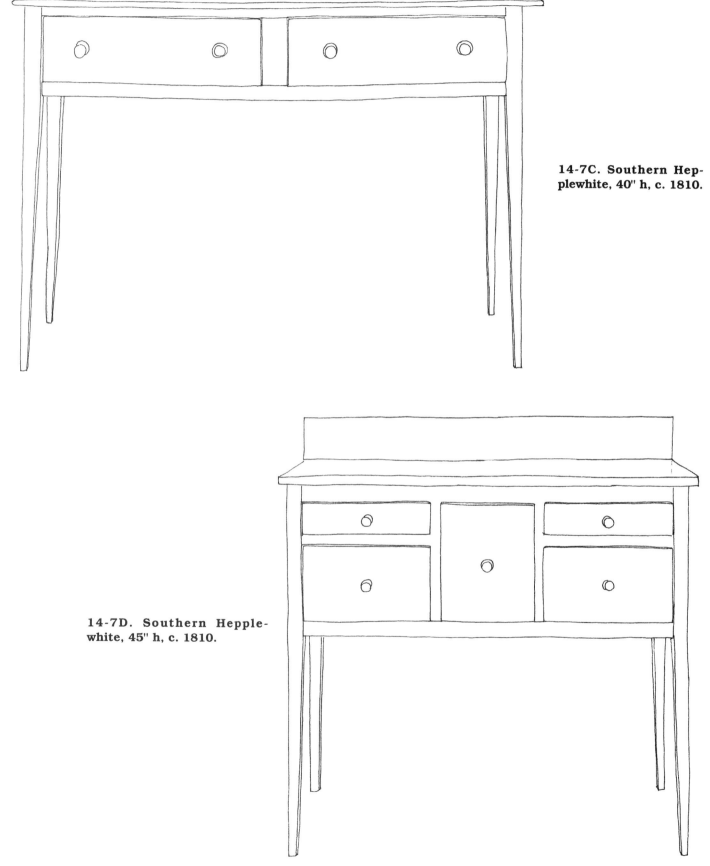

14-7C. Southern Hepplewhite, 40" h, c. 1810.

14-7D. Southern Hepplewhite, 45" h, c. 1810.

14-8 Serving tables. Serving tables, or servers as they were called, can be difficult to correctly identify, for many are very similar to the dressing and chamber tables we saw in chapter 12. In price books they are often listed as chamber tables, suggesting that more than a few of the serving tables in auction catalogs may actually have been made for use in the bedroom. Those that we know for certain that were intended for the dining room are the rare few having marble tops so as not to be damaged by spilled wine.

Tables intended for the dining room rather than the bedroom tend to be somewhat wider than the normal 36" of chamber tables. The server in figure 14-8A is typical of a group of Massachusetts serving tables, being a little over 38" long. Most of these have bow or serpentine fronts and the outset cookie corners that were so fashionable in Federal Massachusetts. Note that the columns of this handsome server also have the stacked rings that are seen in much New England furniture.

When space is limited, a chest of drawers provides an alternative to the sideboard, particularly if cupboards were substituted for some of the drawers. The server in figure 14-8B is of this type. That this server was made in Connecticut is suggested not only by the cherry case, but by the outward splay of the

large ogee bracket feet. Turn back to chapter 11, to figure 11-8D, and you will see the same feet in a Hartford-area chest of drawers. Look under the bottom of such a piece and you will probably observe that, in the Hartford manner, the feet were constructed as separate assemblies and then simply nailed or screwed to the bottom of the case. The inventive combination of the long drawers of a chest of drawers with the storage of a cellaret sideboard again illustrates the innovative nature of Connecticut cabinetmakers. It also shows how even a fairly rare form of furniture can be identified if we remember the characteristics and preferences of different areas and regions.

As you would expect, the dining rooms in wealthy Federal New York City had need of additional storage and serving space, and here we have the most common form of server (14-8C). These standard New York servers are typically almost square, about 3' wide and 3' high. Most have the brass ball and cup feet seen on much of the smaller New York case work of this period. If this serving table looks familiar, it is for good reason, for we have previously seen the same shape in a New York dressing table, and much the same form in a classical New York secretary and bookcase.

14-8A. Massachusetts Sheraton, 33" h, c. 1810.

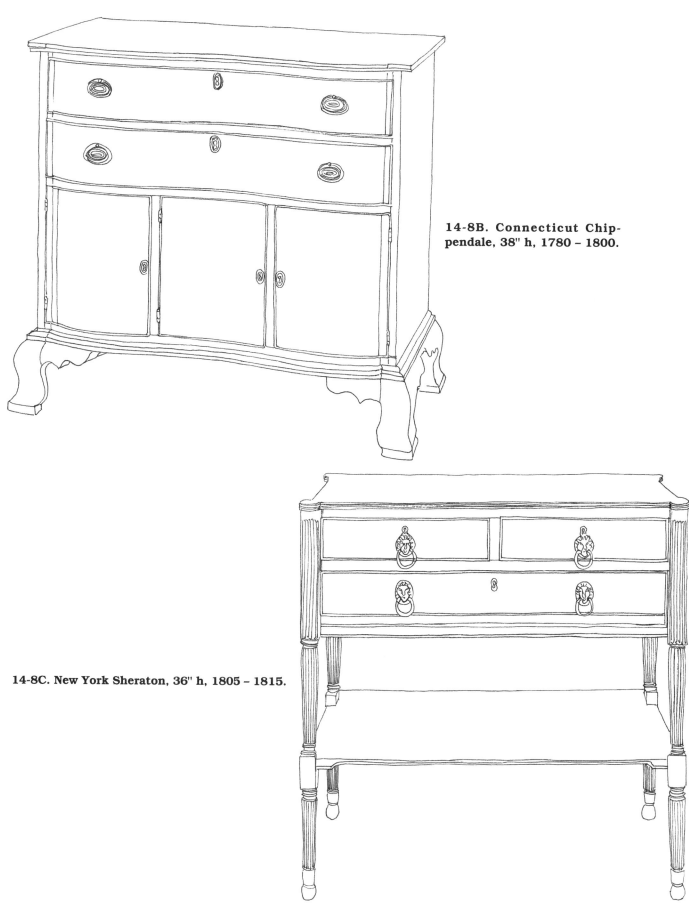

14-8B. Connecticut Chippendale, 38" h, 1780 – 1800.

14-8C. New York Sheraton, 36" h, 1805 – 1815.

14-9 Southern china press. In every survey of furniture, there are some things that do not fit conveniently in any particular chapter. One is the chest of drawers with the bookcase top in figure 14-9. In the South such pieces are called china presses. They were particularly popular in northeastern North Carolina, but were also produced to some extent in Virginia and Tennessee. Most are made of either walnut or cherry, as is to be expected from better-than-average furniture produced in the rural South. They appear to have been dining-room furniture, some clearly so, having a pair of cupboard doors under the upper drawer in the lower case. Combinations of chests of drawers and bookcases are not unique to the South. While most common here, they were produced to some extent in all regions, particularly in rural areas, perhaps because they were easy to make and required less wall space than a sideboard or huntboard.

14-9. North Carolina Hepplewhite, 89" h, 1800 – 1820.

Chapter 15 – Cupboards and Wardrobes

This last chapter on case furniture surveys the cupboards used for storing linens, china, and pewter in the kitchen and dining room, and the kasten and schranks for keeping linens and clothing in the bedroom. In the past, people had far fewer possessions, and for these, one or two large cupboards were quite adequate. This was a time before kitchens were fitted with rows of built-in cupboards and bedrooms had walk-in closets the size of small rooms. The place where people now hang their clothing would have been a bedroom for half a dozen little children.

Cupboards tend to be utilitarian furniture. With few exceptions they resist the positive identification of more formal case work. They seldom can be placed more closely than state or, perhaps, county. Aside from those with the rare signature, none are labeled. We will see that in New England they were for the most part built-in furniture, often the products of carpenters rather than cabinetmakers. Not until we get down to the Middle Atlantic and, in particular, eastern Pennsylvania, do we commonly find really well-made cupboards. Like much vernacular furniture, cupboards exhibit both style lag and hard wear. Many are a lot younger than their replaced hinges and worn paint would suggest.

Here again, keep in mind the normal range of softwoods employed in furniture. One would expect to see some white pine in Pennsylvania and New York, then more in Connecticut, and much more from Massachusetts north into New Hampshire, Vermont, and Maine. Both tulip poplar and yellow pine are seen in coastal Connecticut, then increasingly so the further south one goes. Delaware Valley cupboards are typically a mix of both, with perhaps white cedar in the drawer bottoms. South of Pennsylvania there will be the Southern hard pines, although drawers may be tulip poplar. A cupboard made entirely of yellow pine will most probably be from somewhere in the South. There are also local preferences: basswood in northern New England, chestnut in Rhode Island and vicinity, and bald cypress in coastal North or South Carolina.

In this chapter, we will work down the coast in three big steps: first New England, then the Middle Atlantic, and lastly, the South; lingering the longest in the Middle Atlantic, which tended to produce both the best-quality and most attractive cupboards. Hanging cupboards are briefly covered in the chapter on miscellaneous regional furniture.

15-1 New England cupboards. The salient point to remember about New England cupboards is not that they are generally made of eastern white pine — which they indeed are — but that most were originally built into the sides and corners of rooms. If you see a cupboard that lacks feet, or in which the feet seem to have been added at a later date, you are likely to be looking at a product of New England. If the cupboard is made of tulip popular rather than white pine, then perhaps from rural New York.

For historical consistency, and little else, we might start with the earliest cupboards, the court cupboards made in Massachusetts and Connecticut in the last decades of the seventeenth century. *Court* is the French word for "short," and this

may simply describe a cupboard of less-than-normal height. The Jacobean cupboard in figure 15-1A is typical of the rare few that are not now in museum collections — a somewhat budget design that has probably seen considerable restoration. Not all of these large cupboards are from the Pilgrim Century; paint-decorated survival forms were produced in Connecticut well into the eighteenth century. Very few are seen outside of New England. While frequently listed in Virginia probate records, there are only two surviving Southern examples.

Simple pine step-back cupboards with paneled doors like that shown in figure 15-1B were produced all over New England. Most were originally built-in furniture and either lack feet, as seen here, or have simple feet worked into the base. On some, the upper section of each slopes to the back, perhaps to avoid a top-heavy look, or perhaps to keep the doors closed without the necessity of a latch. Many have been altered to be more attractive and useful in modern homes. Some have acquired base moldings and low bracket feet; in others, the doors have been removed to provide open shelves.

Large step-back cupboards, or pewter dressers as they are sometimes called, were produced to some extent in all regions. Figure 15-1C illustrates one of a group of pine cupboards from coastal Massachusetts, most probably from the North Shore. Later, we will see a similar cupboard from Pennsylvania, but far more carefully made and fashioned of walnut rather than white pine.

Early New England houses had massive central chimney stacks with fireplaces opening into almost every room. Often a pair of narrow cupboards flanked the fireplaces. While many of these houses are gone, the cupboards have survived. The handsome eighteenth century example in figure 15-1D is typical, being no more than about 2' wide. The high feet are unusual, for most of these cupboards were built in and do not have proper feet. The lack of an apron under the door suggests that the feet may have been shaped at a later time.

Corner cupboards were popular in New England, and we might look at three common types: a rather narrow cupboard with paneled doors (15-1E), a larger cupboard with an arched opening and scalloped shelves (15-1F), and what is called an architectural cupboard that was once part of a grand house (15-1G). Open the doors of the first cupboard and you will most probably see the scalloped shelves shown in the other two examples. Most New England cupboards of this period have paneled doors, wood being much less expensive than glass. The cupboard shown in figure 15-1F has possibly lost its paneled doors. Better-quality cupboards of this type may have built-up semicircular interiors. These are sometimes called barrel-backs, for when seen from the rear the framing resembles the narrow staves of a barrel. Architectural cupboards, many far grander than the relatively modest example in figure 15-1G, may be from any region. Those from the Delaware Valley and south across the Mason-Dixon Line, will most probably be made of tulip poplar or yellow pine. Note that all three of these cupboards are both made of pine and lack feet. They all were originally built into the corners of rooms.

Not all New England cupboards are utilitarian and made of softwoods, and we will end this section with a grand cherry corner cupboard made in or near Hartford, Connecticut (15-1H). This cupboard is a product of the Chapin School of cabinetmaking. If you look back to the chapter about high chests of drawers, in figure 12-6C you will see the same open strapwork pediment on a Chapin-type high chest.

Although not illustrated here, later New England cupboards from the Federal period are more likely to be freestanding, to have reverse-fielded panels and glazed doors, and to be made of hardwoods, usually either cherry or maple. They are not much different from the Federal Middle Atlantic cupboards we will see in the following section.

15-1A. Massachusetts court cupboard, 65" h x 50" w, c. 1690.

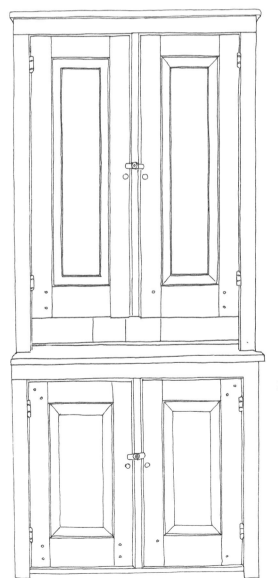

15-1B. New England step-back, 81" h, 1800 – 1820.

15-1C. Massachusetts step-back dresser, 88" h x 73" w, 1740 – 1790.

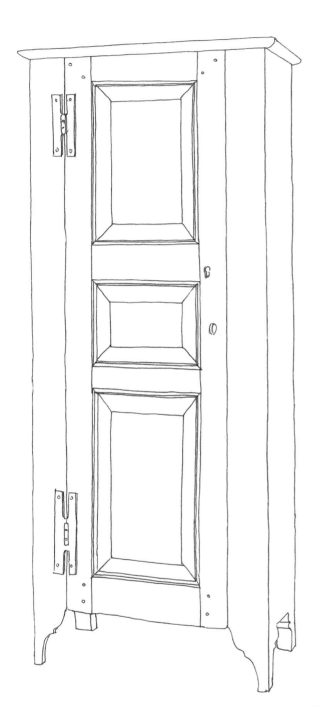

15-1D. New England chimney, 67" h x 27" w, 1740 – 1780.

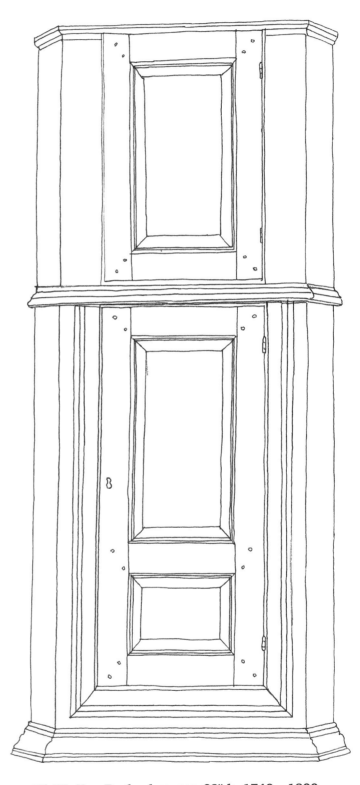

15-1E. New England corner, 83" h, 1740 – 1800.

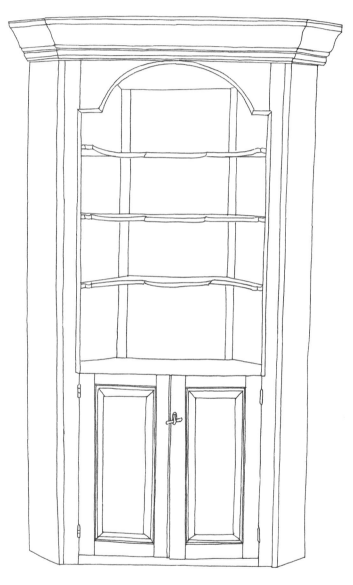

15-1F. New England corner, 88" h, 1740 – 1800.

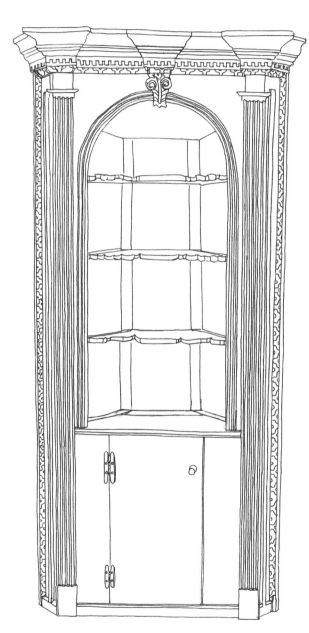

15-1G. New England architectural corner, 90" h, 1740 – 1800.

15-1H. Connecticut corner, 88" h x 44" w, 1780 – 1800.

15-2 Middle Atlantic cupboards. The Middle Atlantic is a fun study, for this region produced the most interesting, and generally, the best-quality cupboards. As noted earlier, the distinguishing characteristic of Middle Atlantic cupboards is that most were designed as freestanding units. They usually have shaped feet and are reasonably well made, often of pine or poplar, but frequently of local hardwoods: cherry or walnut, or sometimes maple or butternut. As a group, they are far more likely to have been made by cabinetmakers than carpenters.

Here there is much to see. We will start with two cupboards from rural areas around New York City, then move down to eastern Pennsylvania and the Delaware River Valley. Quite the best known New York cupboards are the large baroque kasten, most of which were produced in the Dutch settlements in Kings and Queens counties on western Long Island. These distinctive multipart wardrobes are notable not only for their northern European appearance, but also for their consistency of form, for while produced for almost a century, they never lost their baroque style. Unlike other case furniture, there are almost no adaptations to the newer rococo and neoclassical fashions. Although there are a few smaller and simpler versions, most are very similar to that shown in figure 15-2A. Almost all have outsized built-up cornices, large paneled doors with flanking rectangular panels, single tiers of either one or two drawers flanked by diamond-shaped moldings, and massive ebonized ball feet — usually just in the front. In general, kasten are just as large as they appear to be in this illustration, 6' – 7' high, 5' – 6' wide. Like the Pennsylvania schranks, they can be taken apart to be moved. Often the large feet are separate assemblies. Most are made of local woods, or a mix of local woods: pine, poplar, cherry, or the red gum so often seen in New Jersey clothespresses.

On a more reasonable scale are a considerable group of pine step-back cupboards produced in and around Hackensack, New Jersey. Hackensack is in Bergan County just to the west of Manhattan. The most obvious features of these cupboards are a pair of square candle drawers that flank a central long drawer, and below these, molded rectangular panels as seen in 15-2B. Under the cornice there will usually be a row of reeding, and then on either side of the glazed doors much the same reeded pilasters that we saw in a New Jersey clothespress. Corner cupboards from this area typically lack the candle drawers, but usually have the same pilasters.

In a general way, schranks are the Pennsylvania equivalent of the New York kasten. Both originated as baroque designs in northern Europe, and for this reason are superficially similar. However, schranks were initially produced by the Germans who settled Lancaster County rather than by the Dutch who settled New York, and because of this, there are major differences. The most obvious is that shranks not only exhibit much diversity, but also, that the form accommodated over time to changing tastes and fashions. While there is no standard design, the schrank illustrated in figure 15-2C is typical of these large wardrobes. Normally the upper case will have a pair of paneled doors on either side of a fixed panel; the lower case, either one or two tiers of drawers, and if the latter, then usually the three-over-two arrangement so favored in the Delaware Valley. The large case will rest on either the dovetailed straight bracket feet shown here or on ball feet, ogee bracket feet, or, sometimes, neoclassical French feet. In common with other Germanic Pennsylvania furniture, dovetails are left showing as decorative elements, as seen here on the bracket feet. The backboards and moldings are likely to be fastened with wooden pins, and the tenons may be wedged.

Like kasten, schranks are large, sometimes extraordinarily so. Although the schrank in figure 15-2C is about average size, it is over 7' high and 6½' wide. A number are distinctly architectural in form, with plinths in the lower section, and above them, outset fluted pilasters extending clear up to the cornices. Some have a solid Georgian appearance with brass H-hinges, bail pulls, and quarter columns flanking the cupboard doors, suggesting they might have been produced outside Lancaster County for English or Welsh customers. Like the Pennsylvania tall chest, the form migrated south with settlers from southeastern Pennsylvania, but probably not as far as the tall chest, which traveled clear down to North Carolina. However, there are documented examples from the Shenandoah Valley of Virginia.

In the previous section we saw a Massachusetts pewter dresser, and here we might look at a Middle Atlantic interpretation of the same form, for the differences between the two are characteristic of the differences between New England and Middle Atlantic cupboards. The Pennsylvania open-top cupboard in figure 15-2D has proper feet — it is not the built-in cupboard shown in figure 15-1C. More significantly, it is made of walnut, a wood far too expensive in New England to have been employed in utilitarian furniture. The charming "lollipop" terminals are also seen on New York and Southern cupboards. In general, the Pennsylvania cupboard (if this cupboard is indeed from Pennsylvania, for similar cupboards were also produced in the South) is a better-made product.

The two most common features of Pennsylvania cupboards are glazed doors and reverse-fielded paneling. By the turn of the century, that is, about 1800, the lower cost of glass and the increasing wealth led to far more use of glazing in utilitarian furniture, and as a result, a great many Delaware Valley cupboards have glazed doors. Paneling also becomes much thinner, perhaps because sawmills are now able to produce thin hardwood boards. Whatever the reason, the typical panel has become quite thin, with no more than a shallow bevel around the edge, and this bevel, apparently lacking any decorative value, is reversed and placed on the inside. Doors paneled in this manner, with the bevel or fielding on the inside, are said to be reverse fielded.

Having said this, we will start with an earlier Pennsylvania glazed-door step-back cupboard having fielded paneling on the lower doors (15-2E). The widely spaced fluting on the upper and lower cases is seen in many of these imposing cupboards. Many have pairs of small candle drawers worked into the base of the upper section. Note that in typical rural Pennsylvania fashion, the case has been fastened with small wooden pins. These grand big walnut cupboards have served as prototypes for a great many simpler versions to come.

Far more common are somewhat smaller cupboards of the same basic form. A cupboard of this type will have the same glazed doors and distinctive arched opening or recess at the base of the upper case, but reverse-fielded paneled doors in the lower case (15-2F). Not all Pennsylvania step-back cupboards have this handy recess — handy because it provides a level surface on which to set cups and plates as they are put in and taken out the cupboard. These popular cupboards continued to be made well into the nineteenth century, acquiring neoclassical features and more neoclassical proportions. They were produced clear up into the middle of the nineteenth century and as far west as Ohio. There are many Sheraton and empire examples like that shown in the next figure (15-2G). Note that this rather narrow cupboard has much the same incised fluting seen in the early step-back cupboard. Many of these later cupboards are made of cherry rather than walnut. Less expensive versions will be of painted-up pine or poplar.

Of Pennsylvania and Delaware Valley corner cupboards there is a legion, and I will show you four representative examples. Depending on width, there will normally be one or two glazed doors in the upper case and one or two paneled doors with reverse fielding in the lower case. Sometimes there will be a row of short drawers in the lower case. Better-quality early cupboards will be made of walnut; later cupboards are as likely to be of cherry. Less expensive cupboards will be of pine, poplar, and sometimes butternut.

Cupboards with paneled doors in both their upper and lower cases tend to be earlier, and are not nearly as common as those with glazed doors. Most are made of walnut. The handsome cupboard in figure 15-2H is typical of the simpler sort of paneled Pennsylvania cupboard. Although the broad cornice and H-hinges give it a distinctly Chippendale appearance, the reverse-fielded paneling suggests that it dates from after the Revolution.

Pennsylvania glazed-door corner cupboards may have either arched or rectangular doors. We will look at three common types. The walnut cupboard in figure 15-2I is probably the earliest of this group, having fielded paneling and scrolled bracket feet. Often the arched doors are complemented by a scrolled molded pediment (15-2J), a feature also seen in many Southern cupboards. Note that this tall cupboard, which was most probably made in southeastern Pennsylvania, has become neoclassical in style, and that the cupboard doors are reverse fielded.

The most common Pennsylvania corner cupboard has a single square glazed door in the top section, then two reverse-fielded paneled doors in the bottom, as seen in figure 15-2K. Some wide cupboards will have pairs of glazed doors, and sometimes there will be short drawers in the lower cases. Note that all these cupboards have proper feet. None were built-in furniture.

Corner cupboards continued to be made well into the century, generally of pine or poplar, and they were often grain painted. Some acquire very strange-looking ball feet which are not early and William and Mary, but rather, are late and Empire.

15-2A. New York kas, 75" h x 72" w, 1720 – 1800.

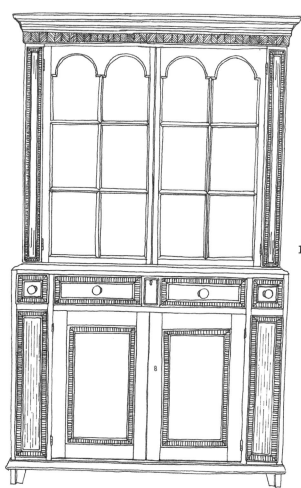

15-2B. New Jersey–Hackensack type, 87" h x 52" w, 1800 – 1810.

15-2C. Pennsylvania schrank, 88" h x 78" w, c. 1770.

15-2D. Pennsylvania dresser, 86" h x 63" w, c. 1770.

15-2E. Pennsylvania step-back, 89" h, 1760 – 1790.

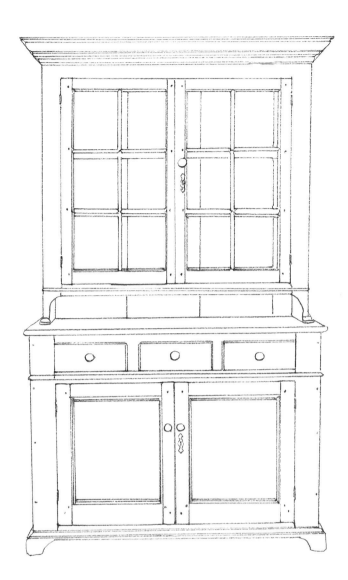

15-2F. Pennsylvania step-back, 86" h x 51" w, 1800 – 1840.

15-2G. Pennsylvania Sheraton, 88" h x 50" w, 1830 – 1840.

15-2H. Pennsylvania Chippendale, 85" h x 45" w, c. 1800.

15-2I. Pennsylvania Chippendale, 83" h x 46" w, 1770 – 1790.

15-2J. Pennsylvania scroll-top, 95" h x 42" w, 1800 – 1810.

15-2K. Pennsylvania corner, 83" h, 1810 – 1820.

15-3 Southern cupboards. For the most part, Southern cupboards are not hard to identify, but they can be very difficult to place if lacking provenance or have been moved far from their place of origin. However, there are a number of features that help tell us that a cupboard was produced south of the Mason-Dixon Line. The most obvious is the use of a Southern pine. A cupboard made entirely of yellow pine will very probably be from somewhere in the South.

Earlier it was noted that people moved south from Pennsylvania by way of the Shenandoah Valley to settle in the Virginia and Carolina backcountry. With them went their furniture styles. Thus, if you see a cupboard similar to one of the Pennsylvania cupboards illustrated in the previous section, but which does not seem to be from the Delaware Valley, even though it has a distinctly Delaware Valley look, you are likely to be looking at a Southern cupboard.

Heat — and bugs — are very much a part of the South, and this is reflected in Southern cupboards. Rooms tended to have high ceilings, and if you encounter a cupboard that is 7½' or 8' high, you are probably looking at a product of the South. For ventilation, and perhaps to discourage insects, it was common for furniture to be fitted with pierced tinned panels. Pie safes were made everywhere, but if you see a well-made cupboard with tinned panels, perhaps made of cherry, you are again most probably looking at a product of the South. In Tennessee, two-part step-back cupboards with glazed doors in the upper section and tinned panel doors in the lower were known as Jackson presses.

In surveying Southern cupboards, we will see a group of representative examples, although I use the term pretty loosely, for there is so much variation that it is difficult to select truly representative cupboards. Instead, we will look at four better-than-average examples that exhibit features seen in a great many cupboards produced in the South. The first is a simple but neatly made corner cupboard (15-3A). That this is a product of the South is suggested by the use of walnut, the 7½' height, and the make-do half-moon inlay in the apron. The upper doors are divided into two panels, the same arrangement we saw in a Southern desk and bookcase. In some of these cupboards the upper panels are pierced tin.

Scroll-top cupboards were popular throughout the South, and we might look at two different approaches, the first a budget product in which a scalloped pediment with a little dentilled molding has been added to enhance a rectangular cupboard (15-3B), the second a cupboard having a proper swan's-neck pediment and a pair of glazed doors (15-3C). The first cupboard has a feature often seen in Southern cupboards: a single short drawer centered between the upper and lower sections. Note also that the apron seems more the product of enthusiasm than experience. The second cupboard has small dark ovals inlaid on the paneled doors, then an incongruous light-wood fan centered in the apron. Both these cupboards are over 8' high. All three have neoclassical feet and reverse-fielded paneling, and probably date from the first decades of the nineteenth century. They are all made of walnut.

Lastly, we might look at a form of corner cupboard that may

be unique to the South. This is the "turkey-breast" cupboard in which the front was bowed out, usually to a shallow point so that the doors themselves did not have to be rounded. The pine Kentucky corner cupboard in figure 15-3D is unusual in that the entire front has been given a shallow bow. Most turkey-breast cupboards have glazed doors and are from the tidewater region, either Delaware or the eastern shore of Maryland or Virginia.

One more note: in spite of often being quite high, Southern cupboards tend to be of single piece construction, although the upper and lower sections may be visually divided by applied moldings, as shown in figure 15-3B. All of the cupboards illustrated in this section are single units.

15-3A. Southern Hepplewhite, 91" h x 41" w, 1800 – 1830.

15-3C. Southern Hepplewhite, 98" h x 53" w, c. 1805.

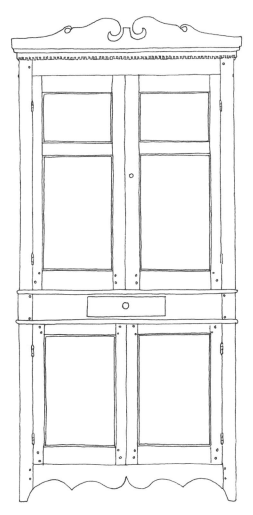

15-3B. Kentucky Hepplewhite, 100" h x 50" w, 1800 – 1820.

15-3D. Kentucky turkey breast, 86" h x 42" w, 1800 – 1830.

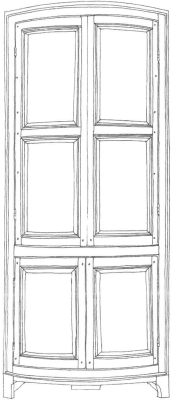

311

Chapter 16 – Dining and Breakfast Tables

Having first surveyed seating furniture, then case work, we come at last to tables. The four chapters that follow cover the common types, proceeding from largest to smallest, commencing first with dining and breakfast tables, then tea tables, card tables, and candlestands and worktables. Those that do not fit any particular category are covered in an additional short chapter on tavern and farm tables.

Though a table's primary purpose is sometimes obvious from its size or form, the principal function of many old tables is not at all clear. In his book on the many tables in the Garvan Collection at Yale, David Barquist neatly sidesteps this problem by simply identifying these as "tables." In truth, tables served a multitude of functions. Paintings show card tables being used for writing and set between windows to act as pier tables. Candlestands had tilt tops, not only so that they could be set aside, but also so that they might serve as fire screens. Everywhere small tables were used for writing, sewing, and informal meals.

Cabriole leg tables were made by the same artisans that made cabriole leg chairs, and the club and trifid feet on these tables reflect the same regional preferences. Ball and claw feet were shaped by the same carvers that carved the feet of chairs and chests of drawers, and here again we see the same regional forms. This helps in identification, for tables tend to be quite similar. The more common shapes of ball and claw feet are illustrated in figures 5-1A – E, the more common club, pad, and trifid feet in figures 5-2A – E.

With the introduction of the Sheraton style, tables acquire turned and reeded legs. In urban centers these were often provided to cabinetmakers by full-time turners. These professionals tended to produce standardized turned and reeded legs that would meet the needs of many customers, and it is often possible to associate particular patterns of turnings with certain urban centers. For simplicity we will consider just the feet, for these are easier to understand and are a good indication of region. The more common of these patterns are illustrated in figures 16-1A – H.

These regional patterns are most applicable to card tables, somewhat less so to breakfast tables, and much less so to dining tables which have heavier legs. Although urban shapes, they are often seen in surrounding rural areas where cabinetmakers probably did their own turning. In reference to these figures, some comments are in order. The very common New York inverted baluster shape (16-1E) is sometimes also seen in New England. The North Shore pattern with the distinctive swell in the foot (16-1D) is seen in both Salem and Portsmouth tables. New England Federal furniture often exhibits a pattern of thin stacked rings, which is seen in figures 16-1A and 16-1D. Similarly, the compressed ball so fashionable in Philadelphia is suggested in all three of the Philadelphia examples. Ball and tapering shaft patterns similar to that in figure 16-1H are also seen in New England. Dining and card tables in all regions, particularly later tables, are apt to have small balls at the bases of the feet.

With the advent of the neoclassical style came the return of decorative inlays, and it is possible to infer from the patterns of stringing and banding, and the design of pictorial inlays, where a table was made. Inlays are particularly useful in identifying the better-quality Hepplewhite dining and breakfast tables, which often have inlaid tablets at the tops of each leg and then inlay extending down the legs. While regional patterns of inlay are beyond the scope of this book, some characteristic inlays will be noted in the coming sections. For illustrations of regional patterns, I would suggest that the reader consult Montgomery's *American Furniture — The Federal Period*, and Hewitt, Kane, and Ward's *The Work of Many Hands: Card Tables in Federal America, 1790 – 1820*. Neither of these long-out-of-print books is inexpensive, but the former should be available in your local library.

Aside from tables built around a pillar or column, most tables have a top, a bed, and four or more legs. The bed is the box section that supports the legs and forms the junction between them and the top. Normally this is composed of four rails that are tenoned into the tops of the legs. The top is then fastened to the rails. One or more drawers may be fitted within the bed. Tables have little in the way of secondary woods except for blocking used to fasten the tops, the fixed and swing rails, and the sides and bottoms of drawers. However, these can help us determine origin, and in the coming sections I will note them when appropriate.

There are so many surviving dining tables that we will first cover William and Mary gate-leg tables, then Queen Anne and Chippendale tables, and finally, the neoclassical tables produced after the Revolution. Breakfast tables are treated separately.

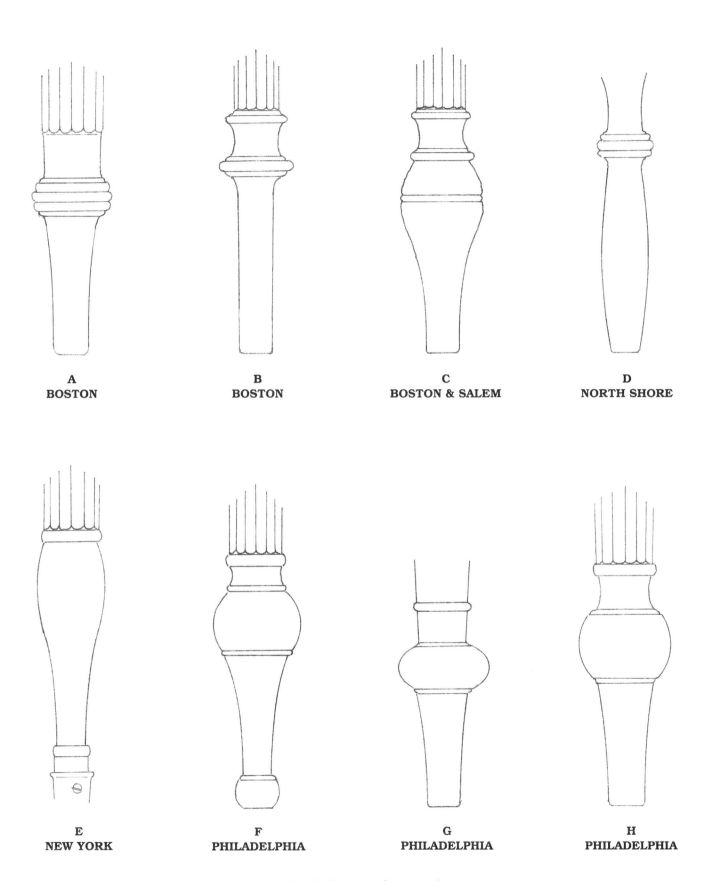

A	B	C	D
BOSTON	**BOSTON**	**BOSTON & SALEM**	**NORTH SHORE**

E	F	G	H
NEW YORK	**PHILADELPHIA**	**PHILADELPHIA**	**PHILADELPHIA**

16-1. Regional Sheraton foot turnings.

16-2 William and Mary gate-leg dining tables. Gate-leg tables were produced in all regions. The term itself is modern. In probate records they are identified as "oval," "turned," or "drop-leave" tables. They served a variety purposes, and are found in a wide range of sizes from diminutive breakfast or tea tables to large double-gated dining tables with two swing legs under each leaf. For the most part they were made by the same artisans that produced the innumerable eighteenth century turned chairs. Because so many are the product of rural turners rather than urban joiners, most are difficult to place more closely than region and colony. Thus we will see examples from Massachusetts and Pennsylvania, but not from Boston and Philadelphia.

New England gate-leg tables typically have double-baluster turnings separated by a ring as shown in figure 16-2A. Note that the balusters are a mirror image, the lower element is reversed to provide a symmetrical turning. The swing gates and stretchers normally have the same pattern, although here the balusters are compressed to fit within the lesser space. The double-baluster pattern is seen in a great many northeastern tables, and is a signature of New England workmanship. We will see it again in the chapter on tavern and farm tables. Now having said this, it should be emphasized that many New England gate-leg tables — about one in four — employ other patterns. That a gate-leg table does not have double-baluster turnings does not mean that it was not made in New England. As you would expect, the earlier the table, the bolder and more atypical the turnings, as is shown by the grand, big early-Massachusetts gate-leg table in figure 16-2B. Early Rhode Island tables are also very different, having the double ball-and-column pattern shown in Figure 16-2C. Most gate-leg tables have small bun or ball feet. A rare few New England gate-leg tables have carved Spanish feet, a feature also seen in English tables.

Many New England gate-leg tables are made of walnut or have maple legs and walnut tops. Others are entirely maple, sometimes tiger maple. There is also some use of birch and sycamore. Drawers will usually be white pine, perhaps with chestnut bottoms if from Rhode Island or vicinity. The frequent use of better woods, particularly imported walnut, may be a historical anomaly. In the past most New England gate-leg tables probably had inexpensive maple legs and white pine tops and leaves, but far fewer of these have survived.

New York gate-leg tables are likely to be made of gumwood, which in New Yok was favored as an inexpensive substitue for walnut, and later, for mahogany. In addition, they exhibit a variety of turnings. Some have urns and balusters, others the Pennsylvania form of ball and baluster. The large New York gate-leg table in figure 16-2D has but a single elongated baluster. This rather stocky maple table may not be as early as it would appear, for the leaf hinges have the later rule joint rather than the earlier bead-and-groove joint seen in figure 16-2A. You will also see butt joints on gate-leg tables, but these may be as much an indication of rural workmanship as they are of early date.

Not until we reach Pennsylvania is there another large group of gate-leg tables, and here again we have another standard turning — the ball and baluster combination shown in figure 16-2E. Often the ball is more compressed and the baluster more elongated than shown here. Most of the surviving tables are made of walnut. The drawers will usually be poplar, sometimes with white cedar bottoms. These tables usually have short drawers at both ends rather than the single deep drawers seen in New England tables. In common with much other Middle Atlantic furniture, they tend to appear heavier and more solid than New England tables. A delicate-looking gate-leg table will most probably be from somewhere in New England. Also, Middle Atlantic turnings, particularly those from Pennsylvania, will often be decorated with shallow grooves at the widest points of the turnings. The scrolled apron seen in figures 16-2D and 16-2E does not seem to be characteristic of region, although it may be an indication of better-than-average and, perhaps, earlier workmanship.

In common with New York tables, Southern gate-leg tables do not exhibit a standard turning pattern that can help us in identification. However, the simple columnar turning shown in the North Carolina table in figure 16-2F is seen in many Southern — and English — gate-leg tables. The other English feature seen in many Southern tables is that the stretchers and lower gates will be left square and not partially turned as shown here. As you might expect, this table is made of walnut with yellow pine drawer sides and bottom. As was noted earlier, walnut was so available in the South that it is seen in secondary locations, and the gate frames on these tables are apt to be walnut.

The drawer on this table is rather crudely made, but in gate-legs this is not any particular indication of either rural or Southern workmanship, for most of these tables were made by turners, and the drawers are apt to lack dovetails. Gate-leg tables were made to some extent throughout the South. Should you find bald cypress among the drawer woods, the table will most likely be from coastal North or South Carolina.

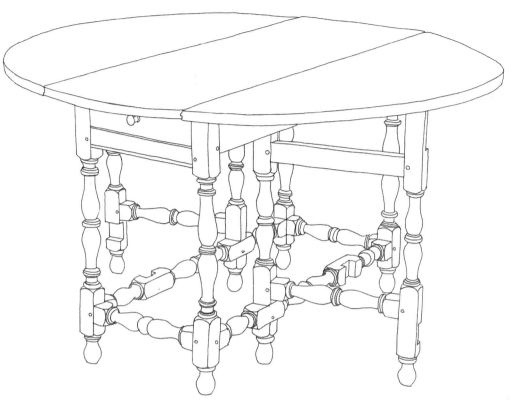

16-2A. Massachusetts William & Mary, 1740 – 1760.

16-2B. Massachusetts William & Mary, 1700 –1740.

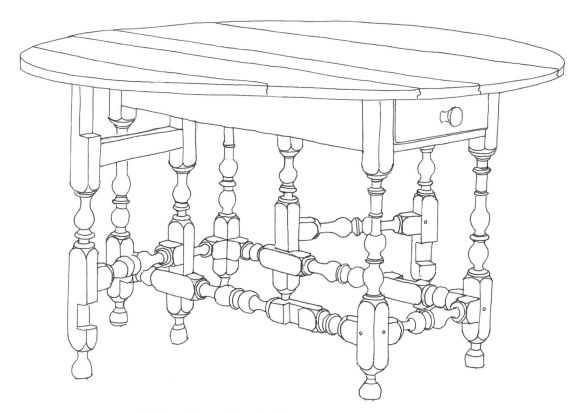

16-2C. Rhode Island William & Mary, 1690 – 1710.

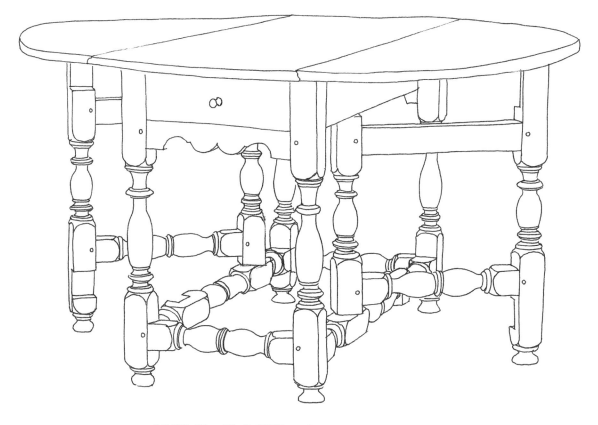

16-2D. New York William & Mary, 1720 – 1760.

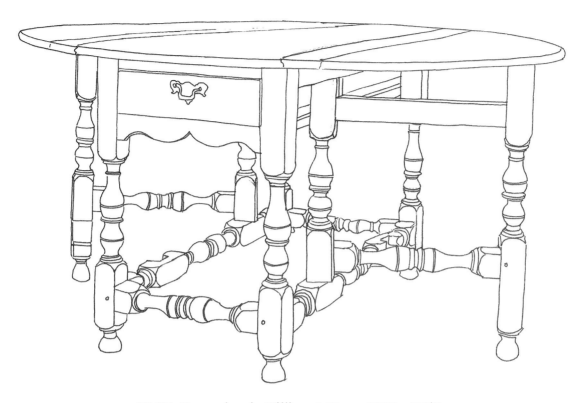

16-2E. Pennsylvania William & Mary, 1700 – 1750.

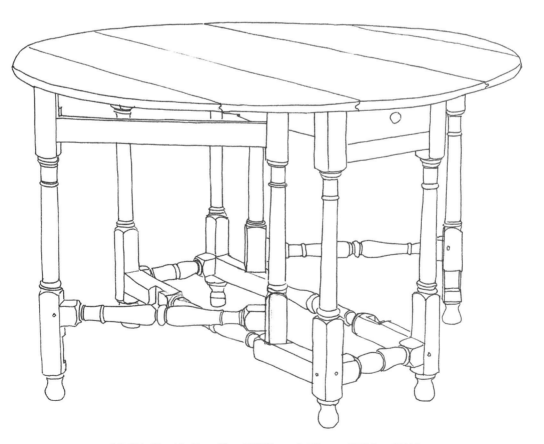

16-2F. North Carolina William & Mary, 1720 – 1740.

16-3 New England Queen Anne and Chippendale dining tables. In this section we will see over half a dozen New England cabriole and Marlborough-leg drop-leaf dining tables. While it is not difficult to assign a dining table to New England, determining the place of manufacture is not always so easy, for Queen Anne–style and Chippendale-style tables were produced throughout the northeast, and a great many of them speak to us of nothing more than region.

We might start with the form you are most likely to see, a Queen Anne cabriole-leg table with two fixed and two swing legs. These handsome tables were enormously popular for almost half a century, and there is hardly a New England auction that does not have one or two among the lots. Many are very much budget products, with a straight skirt and either simple squared legs or the offset turned legs shown in figure 16-3A. Better-quality tables will have scalloped skirts and shaped cabriole legs (16-3B). Later tables were often given square tops, not only to provide larger surfaces, but also so that a pair of tables could be butted together to create a single large dining table (16-3C). Many of these were probably once sold in pairs. Note that the edges of the leaves do not have the usual ovolo or ogee molding, but instead have been left square so that two tables could be butted together.

The offset turned legs shown in figure 16-3A are frequently associated with Rhode Island and New York workmanship, but seem to have been employed almost everywhere, with the possible exception of southeastern Pennsylvania, as an alternative to shaped cabriole legs. They are frequently seen in southeastern New England, particularly in Rhode Island. Should you encounter a neatly made table with these legs and perhaps made of tiger maple rather than maple, and also with a dovetailed-in stiffening brace across the underside of the bed, and maybe also with chestnut swing rails, you are most probably looking at a Rhode Island table.

Most of these Queen Anne tables are made of maple, but you will also see birch, a combination of maple and birch, cherry, and if better-quality work, then mahogany. Cherry tables are often associated with Connecticut or the Connecticut River Valley, but cherry was used elsewhere in New England as a less costly substitute for mahogany, and by itself does not mean that the table was made in Connecticut. Square-top tables, like that in figure 16-3C, are likely to be mahogany, and if so, will probably be from coastal Massachusetts. Note that this table has the large disks under the pad feet that are associated with the rococo style in New England. While this handsome Massachusetts table is Queen Anne in style, the use of mahogany and the prominent disks under the feet suggest it is a late example of the style.

With the advent of rococo, these fashionable tables frequently acquired the ball and claw feet shown in figure 16-3D. As you might think, most of these more expensive tables are made of walnut or mahogany and are from coastal Massachusetts, the Boston-Salem area. Note that the feet on this table have the retracted claws so often seen on Massachusetts Chippendale chairs.

Following the Revolution, the straight Marlborough leg found some favor in New England, maybe because it was more in keeping with the linear look of the incoming neoclassical styles (16-3E). Most of these tables are relatively inexpensive, the only decoration being some molding on the legs. For perhaps the same reason, many are made of cherry rather than mahogany.

To save time and effort, New England cabinetmakers often employed finger rather than knuckle hinges on drop-leaf tables. This reduced cost, but required the fixed and fly rails to be separated by spacers to allow the fingers to pivot. This is a handy identifier, for you can detect the separation by just reaching under a table. Also, the swing rails on New England drop-leaf tables will normally be either maple or birch, and for some reason, more often the latter.

Dining tables with ball and claw feet were also produced in Rhode Island, but these are very different from Massachusetts workmanship. Here we see the conservatism, the quality, and the attention to detail that so characterizes Newport cabinetry. More often than not these fine mahogany tables have the earlier oval top, which elsewhere is seldom seen in association with ball and claw feet (16-3F). The cabriole legs are distinctively sharp edged — almost square in cross section — and have the Newport form of ball and claw feet. On some very fine tables the talons are undercut, that is, there are openings between the insides of the talons and the faces of the balls.

For all their quality, these tables were costly and are relatively rare. The Rhode Island dining table you are far more likely to see is a drop-leaf Chippendale design with the square, stop-fluted Marlborough legs that were so fashionable in Rhode Island (16-3G). Although less expensive, these tables are also very well made. Look under the top of one and you will usually see neatly made knuckle hinges, and that the bed has been stiffened with cross braces dovetailed into the rails. Typically there will be three braces under the top and two on the underside of the bed. These were evidently felt necessary to assure that the bed of the table did not twist. On most dining tables of this period the tops are fastened with rows of glue blocks, but on these tables the tops are instead fastened with screws driven up through the undersides of the braces. Here it might be noted that Southern drop-leaf tables also may be cross braced, but there will usually be a single brace set diagonally so as to avoid the swing rail hinges.

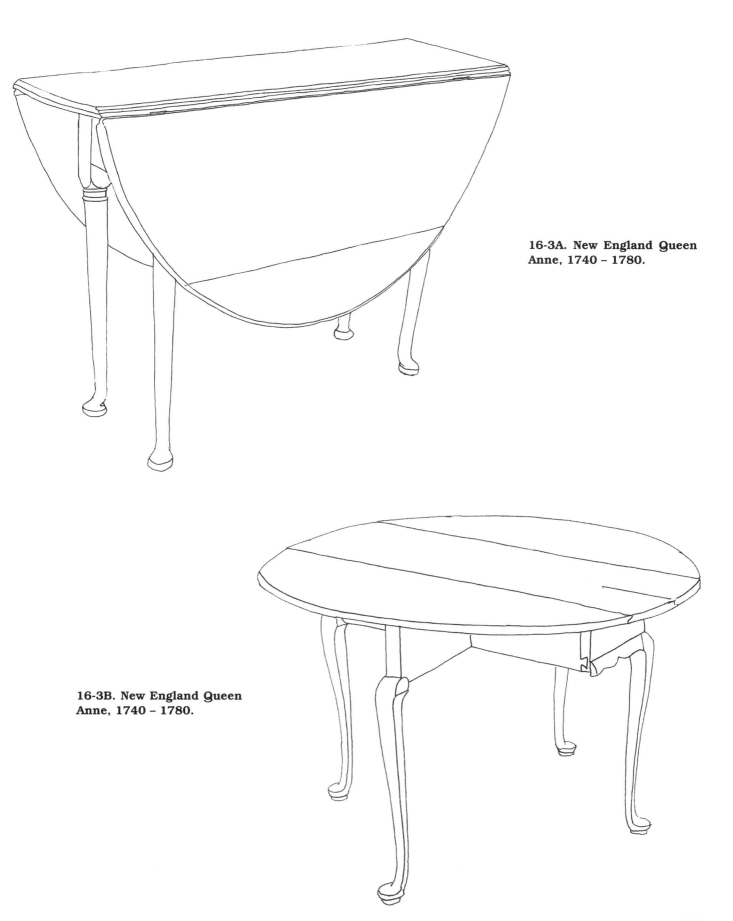

16-3A. New England Queen Anne, 1740 – 1780.

16-3B. New England Queen Anne, 1740 – 1780.

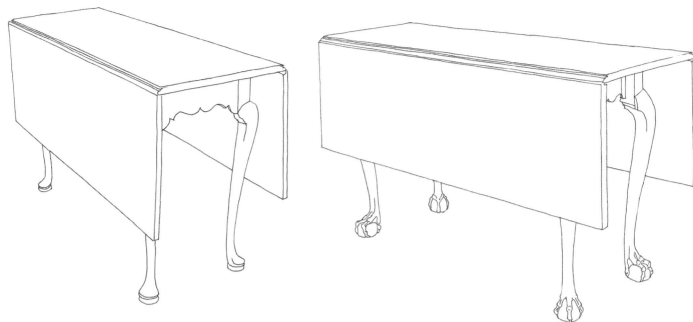

16-3C. Massachusetts Queen Anne, 1770 – 1790.

16-3D. Massachusetts Chippendale, 1780 – 1800.

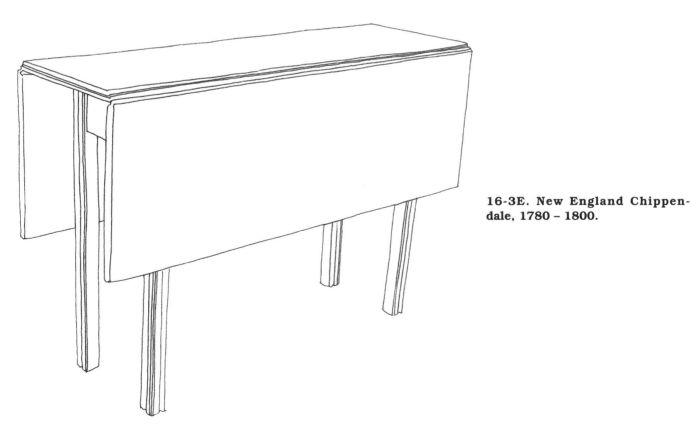

16-3E. New England Chippendale, 1780 – 1800.

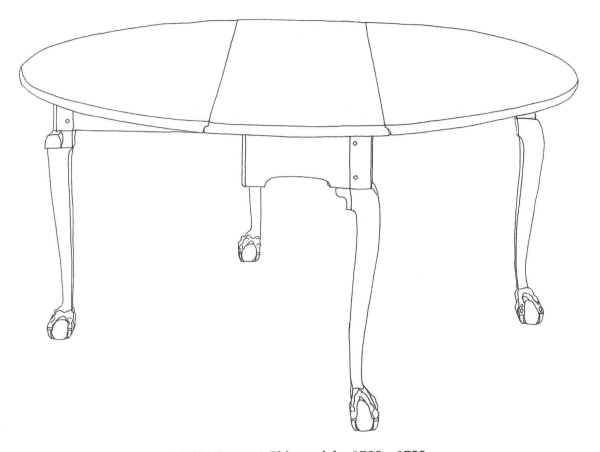

16-3F. Newport Chippendale, 1760 – 1780.

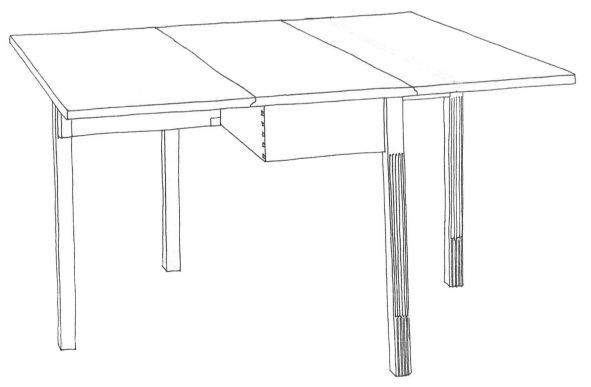

16-3G. Rhode Island Chippendale, 1760 – 1790.

16-4 New York Queen Anne and Chippendale dining tables. Although New England dining tables were covered in a single section, Pennsylvania and New York dining tables are so different that we should give each its own part. Surviving New York dining tables are not at all common, and you are unlikely to encounter one. However, they are quite distinctive, and we will look at three examples. While a great many New York tables have four fixed and two swing legs, not all do, and we might start with a somewhat rural cherrywood dining table with the more usual combination of two fixed and two swing legs (16-4A). Otherwise, this is a very typical New York product with turned cabriole legs and deep New York slipper feet.

More typical of New York workmanship are the large six-leg ball and claw mahogany dining tables produced in New York City (16-4B). As large as this table shown is, the square edges of the top suggest that it was once but one of a pair. A few of these dining tables are so large that they have two swing legs under each leaf. While dining tables having six legs are usually from New York, they were also produced in the South, and there are a rare few from Boston and Pennsylvania. However, if you see a dining table with four fixed and either two or four swing legs, you are most probably looking at a table made in New York City.

Perhaps because four fixed legs provides a more stable platform or a more rigid bed, many six-leg New York dining tables are fitted with a deep drawer. Here also it might be noted that the term *turned cabriole legs* is something of a misnomer, for while these legs lack the knees or shoulders usually associated with cabriole legs, many are sawn and shaped rather than lathe turned. That they were not considered economical is indicated by the great many that have carved ball and claw feet.

Not all New York tables have either six legs or turned cabriole legs. A number, like that shown in figure 16-4C, are of conventional Chippendale form with two fixed and two swing legs, shouldered cabriole legs, and ball and claw feet. That the table shown is a New York table is suggested by the flat leaf carvings at the top of the legs and the shaping of the feet. New York ball and claw feet are not all to a pattern, and here you might wish to review the illustrations in John Kirk's *American Chairs*. Although it is distinctive, the simple semicircular cutout in the apron of this table is no particular indicator of origin, for it is also seen in many Pennsylvania tables.

While the first of these tables is made of cherry, New York dining tables are usually made of mahogany. There are a few walnut examples. Swing-rail woods are often maple, but you may also see chestnut, oak, and the cherry that was so favored as a secondary wood in neoclassical chairs. The sides and bottoms of drawers will normally be tulip poplar.

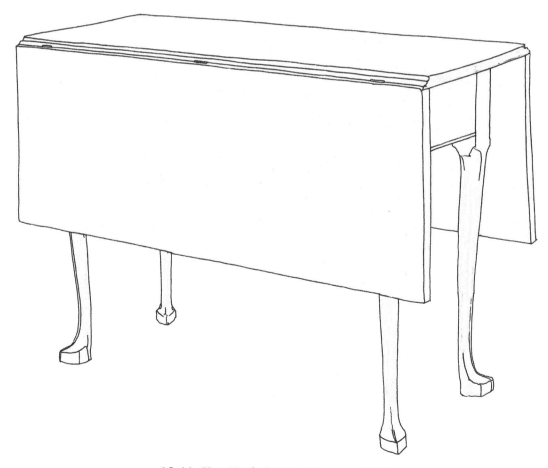

16-4A. New York Queen Anne, c. 1760.

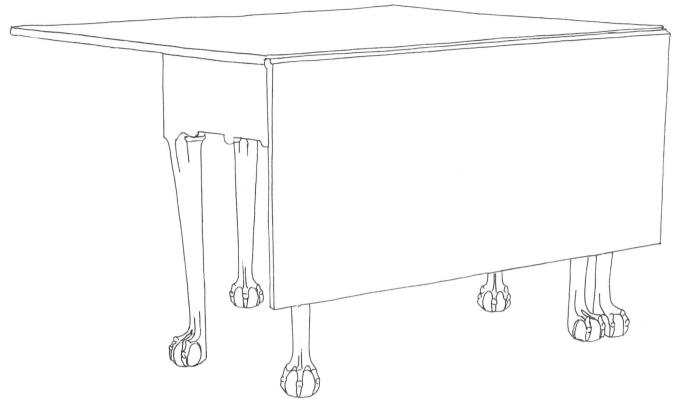

16-4B. New York Chippendale, 1760 – 1780.

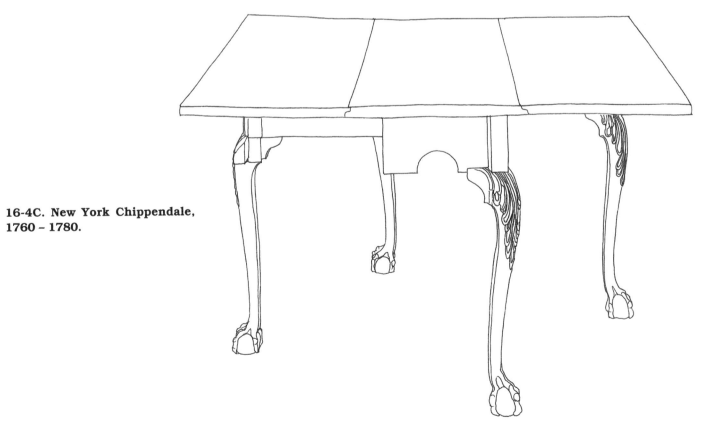

**16-4C. New York Chippendale,
1760 – 1780.**

16-5 Pennsylvania Queen Anne and Chippendale dining tables. Here we will also see three Middle Atlantic drop-leaf dining tables, but these are very different from New York workmanship. As you might expect, many Pennsylvania dining tables have the trifid feet that were so enormously popular in the Delaware Valley (16-5A). In addition to the trifid feet with well delineated toes shown here, you may also see other Philadelphia feet that are illustrated in chapter 5, particularly a round pad foot with a distinctive ring in the upper surface, and the trifid foot that is shaped like a club with little more than a suggestion of a three part division. As previously noted, the semicircular curve in the apron of this table is not unique to the Delaware Valley. However, what is characteristic is the presence of deep cutouts in the end aprons.

Not all large mahogany dining tables are from New York, as is shown by the grand big Philadelphia table in figure 16-5B. Here we see the Philadelphia type of ball and claw foot discussed in chapter 5, but even without looking here, there are three other features that immediately suggest a Pennsylvania table: the deep double arch in the apron, the invected or notched corners of the leaves, and fact that the apron is not flush with the legs, but instead is slightly inset. This last feature is also seen in New York dining tables, and might more properly be considered a Middle Atlantic feature. In addition to the semicircular and double-arch cutouts seen in these two figures, you may also see a cupid's-bow shape.

Drop-leaf dining tables with straight Marlborough legs were also made in the Delaware Valley, sometimes with the molded legs so common in New England (16-3E), but more often with the English blocked feet that were so fashionable in Philadelphia (16-5C). In keeping with the rectilinear form of these tables, the apron of such a table is normally uncurved, decorated only with the small applied molding across the bottom as shown in this illustration. Some of these handsome tables have drawers in the beds.

Whereas most New York dining tables are made of mahogany, most Pennsylvania tables are made of walnut, with some use of cherry. Only very grand Philadelphia tables, like that shown in figure 16-5B, are likely to be made of mahogany. The inner rails on Pennsylvania tables will usually be either tulip poplar or yellow pine, the outer and swing rails oak.

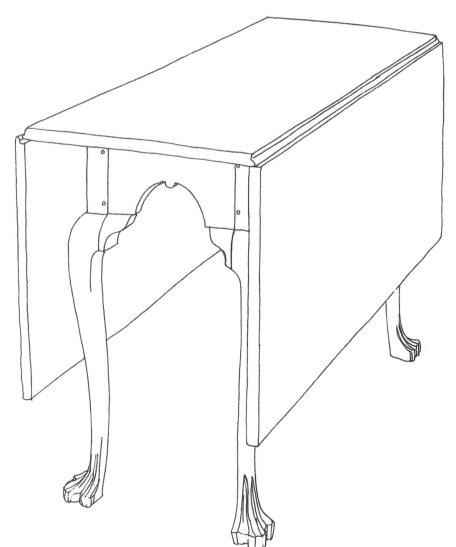

16-5A. Pennsylvania Queen Anne, 1750 – 1790.

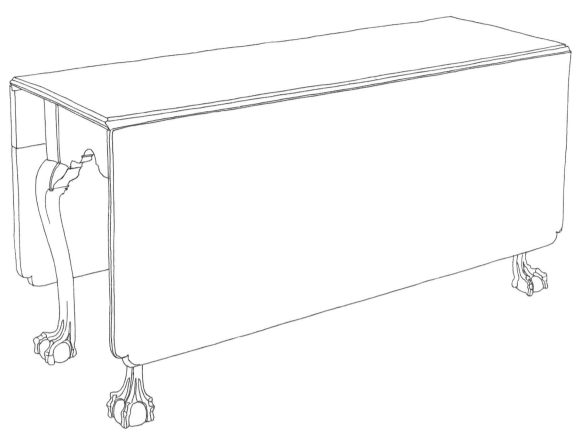

16-5B. Philadelphia Chippendale, 1760 – 1775.

16-5C. Pennsylvania Chippendale, 1770 – 1790.

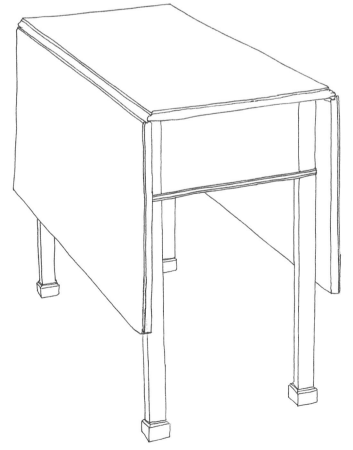

16-6 Southern Queen Anne drop-leaf dining table. South-ern Queen Anne dining tables are something of a conundrum, for not only are they fairly scarce, but also, there are too few to illustrate common designs. While I will show you a table repre-sentative of Southern craftsmanship, it is difficult to illustrate the sort of standard form that we have seen in Rhode Island, New York, and Philadelphia. For the most part, Southern dining tables tend to be well made but have little ornamentation, the "neat and plain" manner that was favored in the South. There are very few with ball and claw feet, and more often than not, they have the simpler offset turned cabriole legs shown in the Virginia or North Carolina walnut six-leg table in figure 16-6. Straight Marlborough legs are also seen, usually without mold-ing and with no more decoration than small edge beads.

Six-leg tables are fairly common. In addition to the normal form of swing leg shown in figure 16-6, there is a kind of six-leg table from Virginia and adjacent northeastern North Carolina that has a stationary leg in the middle of the end apron and two flanking legs that swing out to support the leaves. The result is a very strange-looking table with the leaves down, but quite a use-ful and comfortable table with the leaves up.

Many Southern dining tables are cross braced, but unlike those from Rhode Island, a typical table normally has but a sin-gle brace, and this usually runs diagonally across the bed so as to clear the hinges of the swing legs.

Most Southern dining tables are made of walnut, but you will also see cherry and mahogany. Secondary woods will usually be oak and yellow pine.

16-6. Southern Queen Anne, 1760 – 1790.

16-7 New England neoclassical dining tables. Now we return to New England and begin a second pass down the eastern seaboard, this time surveying the neoclassical styles that become fashionable in the half century following the Revolution. Although dining tables in these new Hepplewhite and Sheraton styles sometimes carry earlier dates, the great majority cannot have been produced much earlier than the 1790s when the federal government was established and the economy finally recovered from a long postwar depression. By this time, American furniture had lost much of its regional character, and many Federal dining tables lack any particular regional feature.

The most common New England Hepplewhite dining table has a square top and two swing legs like that shown in figure 16-7A. A few have the double tapered legs so often seen in New England card tables. Most are made of maple, birch, or cherry, a few of mahogany. Similar tables were made in all regions, and to to try to determine where a piece was made, we should consider the primary and secondary woods. Middle Atlantic and Southern tables are likely to be made of either cherry or walnut, more often the latter. The inner rails on Delaware Valley tables will usually be either tulip poplar or yellow pine, the swing rails oak. Secondary woods on Southern tables will be either oak or yellow pine. In a Southern table you may also encounter walnut swing rails. As was noted earlier, a Southern dining table is apt to be stiffened with a single diagonal medial brace.

Sheraton drop-leaf dining tables were also produced in all regions, and again you may need to examine the secondary woods. Many are quite large formal tables made of mahogany. The leaves tend to be deeper and there will often be separate pairs of legs to support the leaves, as shown in the New England dining table illustrated in figure 16-7B. If the table appears to be an urban product, you might check the shape of the feet against those illustrated in figure 16-1. In rural New England, ball turned feet were often employed in lieu of coasters, although this was also done in Pennsylvania. The spiral leg turnings on this table are frequently seen in New England, but are more a sign of increasing mechanization than region.

In both design and use, these tables are no more than stylistic upgrades of the Queen Anne and Chippendale drop-leaf dining tables that we have seen in previous sections. The legs swing in the same way, and the leaves are stored the same way. More indicative of the neoclassical style are the two- and three-part extension tables that became fashionable in the 1790s. These also have swing legs and drop-leaves, but there are usually four fixed legs at the corners and, except for the optional third center section, normally only one swing leg and one drop leaf in each section. Two and three-part extension tables were produced in all regions, and they can be difficult to identify unless there is some defining regional characteristic. The three-part table in figure 16-7C is typical of many Hepplewhite tables produced in New England. Most are made of mahogany, a few of cherry. Unless there is some distinctive regional inlay, then aside from the secondary woods, there is little to tell us were this sort of average-grade table was made.

Extension tables in the slightly later Sheraton style, with semicircular or D-shaped ends, were also produced in all regions, and while these usually lack any distinctive inlay, we may get some assistance from the turnings of the legs and feet. The tapered reeded legs and single ball foot pattern shown in figure 16-7D are sometimes seen in Massachusetts, although the ball is more normally composed of stacked rings as shown in figure 16-1A. Unfortunately, seldom in New England do we see anything like the standardization present in New York, perhaps because so many dining tables were made outside of Boston.

Lastly, I will show you an uncommon but singularly elegant solution to the problem of extending a dining table to support the leaves. Here there is no fixed top, but rather, a center section and two large leaves that are supported by all four legs, which pivot on a floating rectangular frame (16-7E). Some of these tables have tapered fluted columns rather than the ring-turned columns shown here. A few may have been produced — or more likely, just labeled — in New York. In England they are called Cumberland-action tables. They are so unusual that one wonders if the design was not brought to Boston by John and Thomas Seymour.

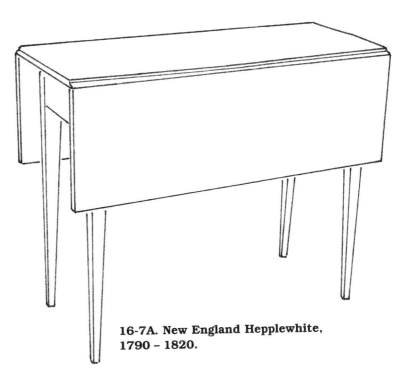

16-7A. New England Hepplewhite, 1790 – 1820.

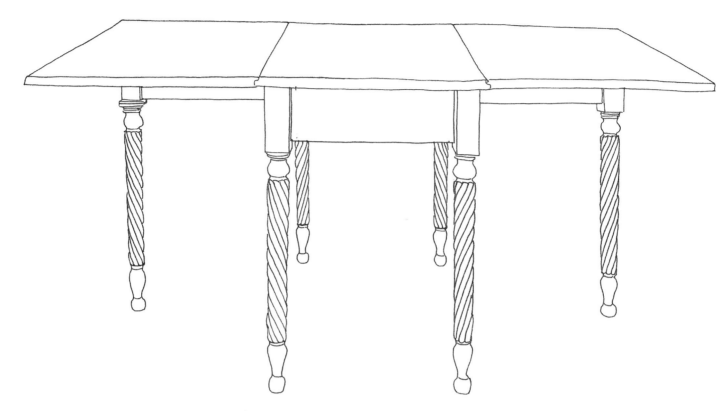

16-7B. New England Sheraton, 1820 – 1830.

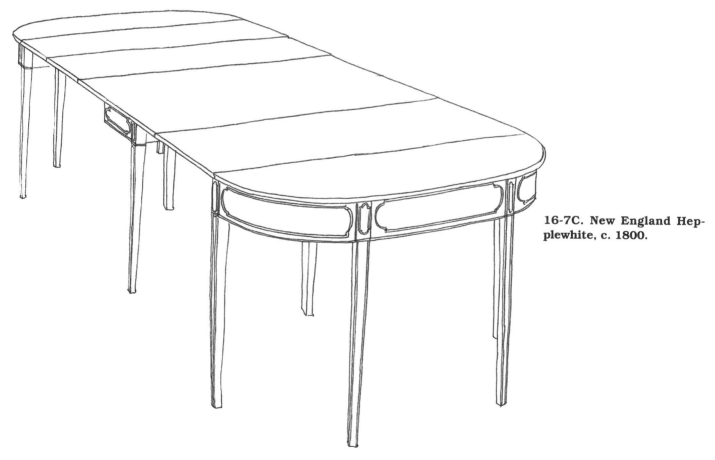

16-7C. New England Hepplewhite, c. 1800.

16-7D. Massachusetts Sheraton, 1800 – 1810.

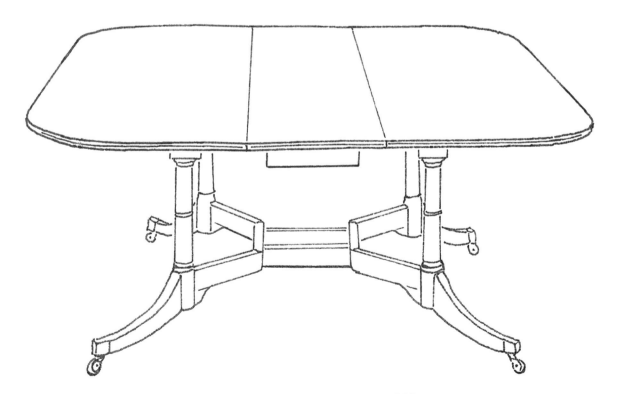

16-7E. Boston classical, 1810 – 1820.

16-8 Middle Atlantic neoclassical dining tables. As you might think, the wealth of Federal New York is reflected in its dining tables. After all, what is the advantage of being rich if you cannot show off your wealth, and what better way to do this than hosting a large dinner party? A really grand dining or banquet table, of perhaps somewhat unusual form, is very likely to be from New York City.

However, we will start with a fairly standard Sheraton drop-leaf dining table, but one that can be associated with New York by its six legs and its use of brass ball and cup feet (16-8A). This large square table may once have been one of a pair. While not evident in this small illustration, it is a very good quality table with the dense mahogany and the dark, monochromatic look so favored in Federal New York. Here also it might be noted that New York dining tables tend to be Sheraton rather than Hepplewhite in style, perhaps because the latest styles were favored, and in America, the Sheraton style arrived right on the heels of Hepplewhite. In keeping with the general quality of New York City work, most dining tables are fitted with either brass swiveling castors or brass ball feet.

Canted corners were much favored in New York, and in figure 16-8B we see a two-part extension table of this type. Other New York dining tables are likely to have D-shaped ends. Whatever the shape of the top, the feet of New York Sheraton dining tables often have the characteristic inverted baluster turning shown in figure 16-1E. Although this is a two-part table, a great many New York extension tables are three-part, which, again, is probably a reflection of the general wealth of the city.

Pedestal, or pillar-form, dining tables appear in England at the end of the eighteenth century, but most American examples date from the first quarter of the next century, and are either Empire or classical in style. These large dining tables were very fashionable in England, and most of those that you see are English rather than American. As a general rule, an American example, like the New York table in figure 16-8C, will retain a shallow apron or bed under the top, perhaps to add depth to a thin top, to hide the leaf supports, or to give the top additional stiffening. Similar pedestal tables were produced in America in limited numbers in all the major urban centers, primarily in Boston, New York, and Baltimore. The carved fluted urns on the pedestals in figure 16-8C are often seen in New York tables.

Among the most elegant New York extension dining tables are those in which each section is raised on small columns or colonettes (16-8D). Later we will see the same design in an equally handsome New York card table. Aside from the novel form, that this is a New York City product is immediately suggested by the canted corners and the leaf-form carving used on the down-curving legs. This distinctive acanthus-leaf carving is also seen on a great many New York breakfast and card tables.

In the previous section we saw a relatively small accordion-action dining table (16-7E). Now we will look at a really grand Philadelphia example (16-8E). Very large accordion-action banquet tables are rare in America furniture, and I illustrate one here more for historical completeness than in expectation that you will ever need to identify one. Similar large accordion-action banquet tables were produced in New York City, but here the top is normally supported by a pair of acanthus-carved colonettes rather that the pair of scrolls shown here.

Before leaving the Middle Atlantic, something should be said about Philadelphia two- and three-part extension tables. The conservatism and style lag characteristic of Philadelphia Federal furniture is also seen in dining tables, and not only does Hepplewhite seem to be as common as Sheraton, but also, there will usually be no more inlay than perhaps a little stringing in the apron and legs. Most are visually similar to the average grade of New England Hepplewhite and Sheraton extension table illustrated in figures 16-7C and 16-7D. However, the swing rails will probably be made of either red oak or yellow pine rather than maple or birch, and the feet may be one of the Philadelphia-area patterns shown in figure 16-1. Actually, the Massachusetts dining table in figure 16-7D could easily be from Philadelphia.

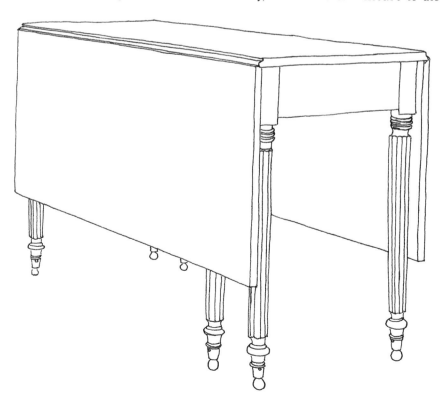

16-8A. New York Sheraton, 1800 – 1810.

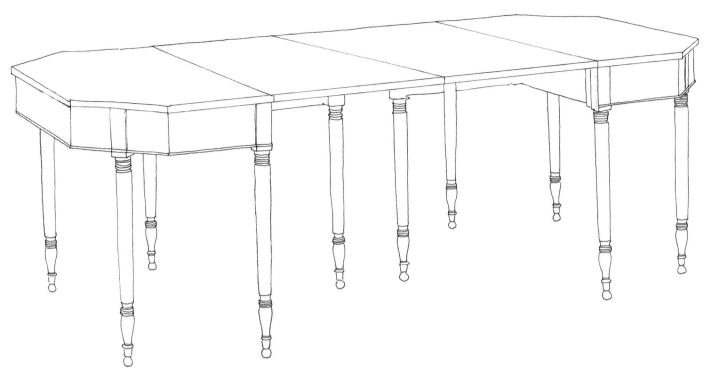

16-8B. New York Sheraton, 1800 – 1810.

16-8C. New York classical, 1810 – 1820.

16-8D. New York classical, 1805 – 1815.

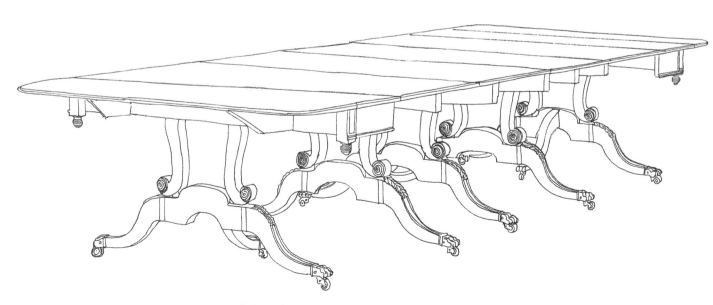

16-8E. Philadelphia classical, 1810 – 1820.

16-9 Southern neoclassical dining tables. Neoclassical dining tables produced in the South are also difficult to illustrate, for not only are they not common, but also, there is no large body of similar work. As a rule, they tend to be of standard form and well made, but with a minimum of decoration, very much the neat and plain construction seen in so much Southern furniture. For the most part they are Hepplewhite in style, most probably because square tapered legs do not require lathes or the services of turners. Rural drop-leaf tables are often made of either cherry or walnut. Blocking is likely be yellow pine, and you may see walnut used for leaf supports and swing rails. Extension tables are usually only two-part, and are mostly products of coastal Maryland and Virginia. A few extension tables are made of walnut, a wood seldom used elsewhere for neoclassical multiple-part dining tables. The Maryland table in figure 16-9A is unusual only in that it is a three-part table.

For the most part, a Southern dining table that is not neat and plain, like that shown in figure 16-9A, will have been made in Baltimore. Here we find high-style mahogany Hepplewhite extension tables decorated with string inlay, oval pictorial inlays at the top of the legs, and often, single rows of inlaid bellflowers extending down the legs. Because Boston and Philadelphia dining tables tend to be conservative, and New York dining tables tend to be Sheraton rather than Hepplewhite in style, such a table is likely to be from Baltimore. When there is bellflower inlay, the middle petals are likely to be considerably longer than the two side petals, and they may be separated by a light wood dot.

Baltimore cabinetmakers also produced distinctive Sheraton dining tables. These late Federal tables are unusual in that the edges of the tops have pronounced double or triple round molding, and the legs have large, somewhat sharp-edged reeding, often with little or no taper from top to bottom, as seen in figure 16-9B. Later we will see a very similar Baltimore card table.

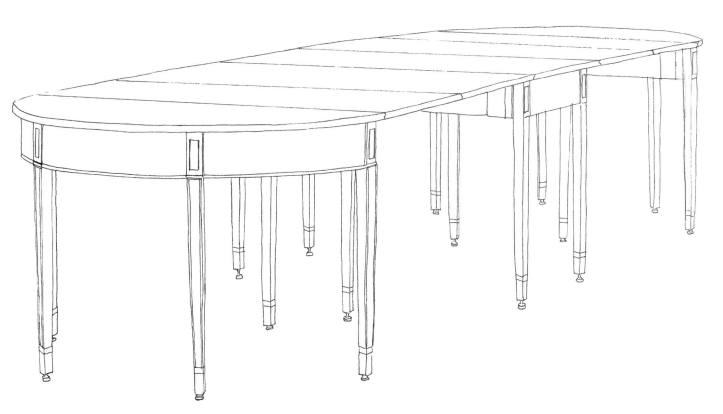

16-9A. Maryland Hepplewhite, 1790 – 1810.

16-9B. Baltimore Sheraton, 1815 – 1820.

Breakfast Tables

Tables with folding leaves of a size suitable for breakfast are too modest a topic to rate their own chapter, but they need to be covered, and since we have been discussing dining tables, this seems as logical a place as any. While I will show you a charming little Queen Anne drop-leaf table, most are of the Pembroke type that was introduced in England about 1750, the first reputedly made at the request of a countess of Pembroke. This was a new type of drop-leaf table. Rather than swinging legs that support the leaves, the leaves are supported by hinged brackets or flies mounted on the side rails. On larger tables there may be two flies under each leaf.

Unlike many words used to describe furniture, *Pembroke* is not a modern term. In price books, Pembroke tables were also identified as breakfast tables, which both confirms their function and is the name now used in many auction catalogs. Most American Pembroke tables postdate the Revolution and are Federal rather than Colonial, even if they retain rococo features. As noted earlier, the Marlborough leg remained in favor after the Revolution, perhaps in part because it was compatible with the new linear neoclassical style.

There is a considerable similarity between Federal Pembroke tables and Federal card tables, particularly in the shaping of the leaves. In the sections that follow, you will see a number of regional features that are common to both breakfast and card tables.

16-10 Massachusetts breakfast tables. We will start with one of the diminutive Queen Anne drop-leaf breakfast tables that were fashionable in eastern Massachusetts before the Revolution. In form, this type of table is but a scaled down version of the popular Queen Anne dining table. Sometimes you will see tables of this kind identified as tea tables, and indeed, they could have served either purpose. These charming little swing-leg tables may have either the oval top shown in figure 16-10A or the square-top seen in the later Queen Anne dining tables. Also in common with the larger dining tables, some square-top tables have ball and claw rather than pad feet. As a general rule, those with oval tops will be made of walnut, and those with square tops of mahogany. These charming little breakfast or tea tables were made to some extent throughout coastal New England, in New Hampshire, Rhode Island, and Connecticut. Rhode Island examples are apt to have offset turned legs. A rare few square tables have but a single swing leg and a single folding leaf.

Massachusetts is something of an anomaly, for the standard elliptical or oblong Pembroke table so associated with the neo-classical style does not seem to have been popular in Boston. The best examples of these tables are from the western part of the state in the Connecticut River Valley, and these probably reflect Connecticut tastes.

The most common form of Massachusetts Hepplewhite Pembroke table has a square top with inset rounded or ovolo leaves, the same shape seen in Massachusetts card tables (16-10B). Insetting rounded corners an inch or so is such a logical decorative treatment that we might expect to see it elsewhere, and

indeed, similar tables were not only produced throughout New England, but also in New York City and adjacent northern New Jersey. However, New York tables are so different that it should not be difficult to tell which is which. New England models will generally be conservative, and if not made of mahogany, then cherry or birch with white pine drawers. New York tables will usually be much flashier products, almost always made of mahogany with generous use of inlay to outline the curve of the leaves. The drawers will be either made of tulip poplar, or will have white pine sides and poplar bottoms. Some New England tables have the double tapered legs that are so often seen in New England.

Massachusetts Sheraton Pembroke tables do not have a signature form, although conservative tables with elliptical leaves and hidden veneered frieze drawers were fashionable in Boston in the first two decades of the nineteenth century. While the delicate legs and brass castors of the table in figure 16-10C suggest this table was produced in Boston, there is nothing particularly unique about the shape of the leaves, which are found elsewhere in New England and New York. Some Boston tables have the unusual concave apron seen in the next illustration. Similar Pembroke tables with figured maple or flame birch veneered drawer fronts were made in Portsmouth, New Hampshire.

All urban centers produced classical pedestal form breakfast tables, and the average grade can be hard to identify, but not so some of those made in the Boston area. These have the distinctive concave ends illustrated in figure 16-10D. This seems to have been done to provide a little extra room to those sitting at the ends of the tables.

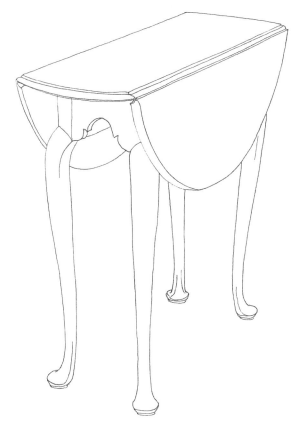

16-10B. Massachusetts Hepplewhite, 1790 – 1810.

16-10A. Boston Queen Anne, 1750 – 1780.

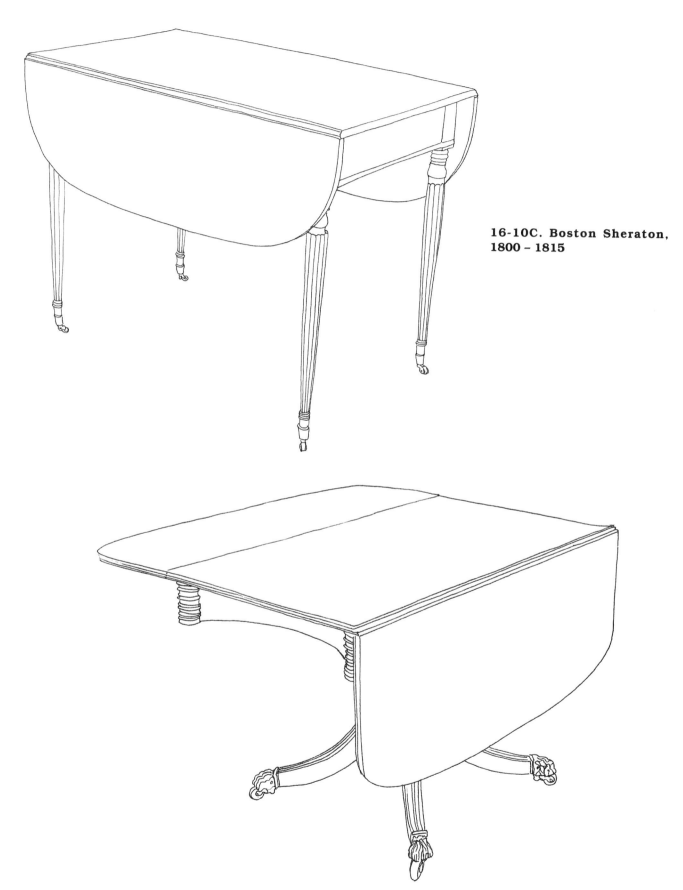

**16-10C. Boston Sheraton,
1800 – 1815**

16-10D. Massachusetts classical, 1815 – 1825.

16-11 Rhode Island breakfast tables. In this section we will see three Rhode Island breakfast tables, but none whose form is unique to Rhode Island. This suggests that the best way to spot a Rhode Island Pembroke table is to keep in mind the characteristics of Newport and Providence workmanship: fine quality with attention to detail, conservative design, and some chestnut among the secondary woods.

The conservative nature of Rhode Island Pembroke tables is typified by the square-top mahogany Chippendale table shown in figure 16-11A. Some of these tables have the stop-fluted Marlborough legs so often seen in Rhode Island Chippendale furniture. Similar square-top tables with flat stretchers were produced in Connecticut, but these are usually not as sophisticated, and also, are apt to be made of cherry rather than mahogany. Almost identical tables with pierced stretchers were made up along the North Shore of Massachusetts and in Portsmouth, New Hampshire. Makers of Portsmouth tables sometimes followed the English practice of joining the stretchers to the legs with screws and small iron angle brackets. Normally the stretchers on these tables are simply tenoned into the legs.

Beginning in Rhode Island, we see more examples of the classic form of Hepplewhite Pembroke table having the curved ends and conforming oblong top illustrated in figure 16-11B. With this comes a greater use of pictorial inlay, which in New England tables typically consists of "bookends" at the top of the legs, then either tapering icicles or single rows of bellflowers down the sides of the legs. These tables were also fashionable in Connecticut and western Massachusetts, although here they are usually made of cherry rather than mahogany, and there may be different pictorial inlays: not only bookends, icicles, and bellflowers, but also paterae, vines, and leaves, and sometimes paterae centered in the tops and the leaves. Similar tables were made to the north in Portsmouth, New Hampshire, leaving one to wonder why they were not more fashionable in Boston.

Although in decline after the Revolution, Newport nevertheless continued to produce some very fine furniture. Among the best work are elegantly simple Pembroke tables like that shown in figure 16-11C. Complete and balanced in every respect, it would be hard to find a more perfect small table. In Newport fashion, the bed of this table is stiffened with cross-braces, and the top is fastened with screws driven up through the braces. Note that while this and the previous table are both Federal and neoclassical, in keeping with conservative Rhode Island tastes, they are fitted with the late Chippendale-style bail pulls. Lastly, it might be mentioned that the Sheraton style does not seem to have been fashionable in Rhode Island. All the tables we have seen are either Chippendale or Hepplewhite in style.

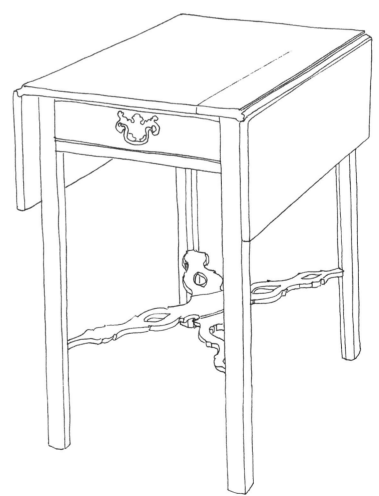

16-11A. Rhode Island Chippendale, c. 1780.

**16-11B. Rhode Island Hepplewhite,
1790 – 1810.**

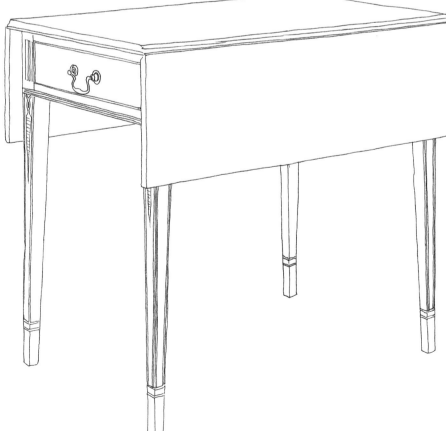

**16-11C. Newport Hepple-
white, c. 1790.**

16-12 Connecticut breakfast tables. Connecticut furniture is usually an interesting study, and breakfast tables are no exception. We will look at four area Pembroke tables, the first two clearly Connecticut products, the third from either Connecticut or western Massachusetts, and the fourth only possibly from Connecticut, but included here because they are too common a New England type to neglect, and this seems as good a spot as any to discuss them.

Pembroke tables with vertical serpentine cross-stretchers like those shown in figure 16-12A were popular in the Connecticut River Valley, but are seldom seen elsewhere in New England. Better models have serpentine rather than square tops, the most expensive both pierced stretchers and the ovolo porringer corners illustrated in figure 16-12B. Later I will show you a very different Pennsylvania breakfast table with serpentine leaves.

While serpentine tops are associated with Connecticut, Pembroke tables with serpentine tops were made throughout New England, perhaps because when a shaped table was desired it was simpler to serpentine just the top rather than to curve both the top and the end aprons. Many of these tables are rural products made of cherry, maple, and birch. Cross-stretchers are usually omitted unless the legs are unusually delicate. The Hepplewhite table in figure 16-12C is a better-than-average example of this common type, better than average because the entire top has been curved and outlined with stringing, and the legs have been embellished with paterae and icicles. The double taper of the legs tell us this table is most likely a product of New Eng-

land; the cherry wood and the generous use of inlay suggest the Connecticut Valley.

Square Hepplewhite Pembroke tables are both easy to construct and are inherently handsome, particularly if the frequently rather delicate legs are given more visual balance by the addition of simple X-form cross stretchers (16-12D). These tables were particularly popular in New England, but were also produced in other regions: New York, the South, and in Pennsylvania, where square tables were very much in fashion. Aside from what can be inferred from the use of primary and secondary woods, there may be very little to tell these tables apart. A mahogany table could be from anywhere, but is probably from somewhere near the coast; a maple or birch table would suggest inland New England, cherry the Connecticut River Valley, and walnut most likely either Pennsylvania or the South. New England tables will usually have white pine drawers, New York tables either poplar drawers or white pine drawers with poplar bottoms, Pennsylvania either poplar, or a mix of hard pine, poplar, and white cedar. Hinge rails on New York tables are apt to be cherry.

Before leaving New England, it should be noted that New York City influenced Pembroke table design in adjacent Connecticut, and it is not unusual to see elements of fashionable New York design in tables from this area. Here you may see Connecticut tables with the leaves having canted corners, or double elliptics, or with the distinctive stepped serpentine shape that was popular in New York (16-13B).

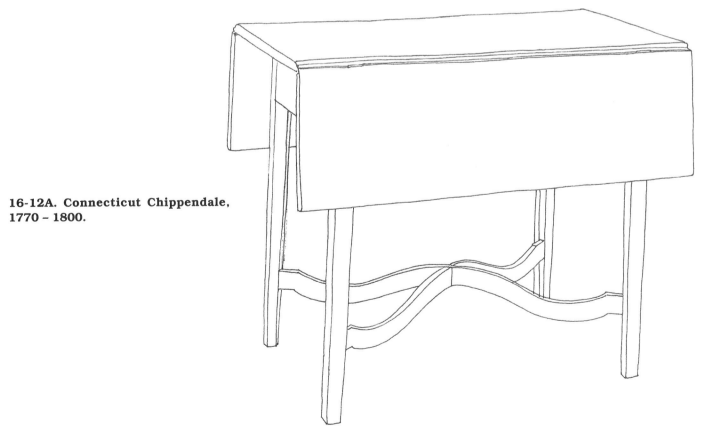

16-12A. Connecticut Chippendale, 1770 – 1800.

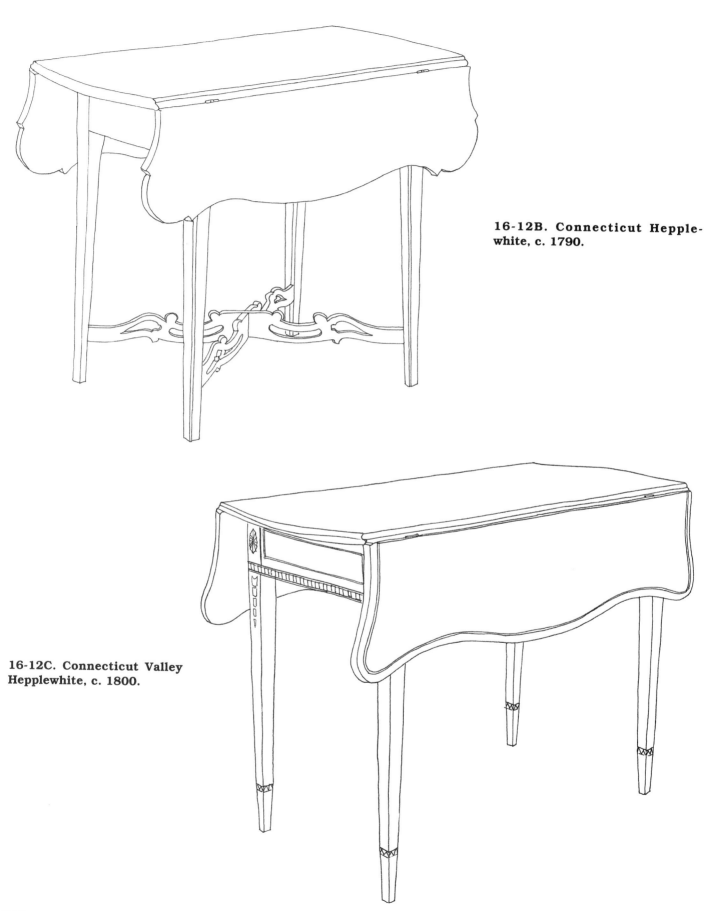

16-12B. Connecticut Hepplewhite, c. 1790.

16-12C. Connecticut Valley Hepplewhite, c. 1800.

16-12D. New England Hepplewhite, 1800 – 1810.

16-13 New York breakfast tables. New York breakfast tables are an attractive subject. Not only are there many surviving examples, but also, they exhibit a whole vocabulary of designs, some very different from the products of other areas. If any one trait characterizes New York furniture, it is that of wealth. New York Federal furniture tends to be generous in scale, well made of the best cabinet woods, and with ample hardware. A somewhat large neoclassical Pembroke table made of select mahogany and mahogany veneers is likely to be from New York.

Elliptical or oblong Hepplewhite Pembroke tables were the very height of fashion in early Federal New York. The best quality tables are distinguished by an almost extravagant use of inlay, and indeed, they provide the perfect venue to display the inlay patterns associated with the Hepplewhite style. The table in figure 16-13A is typical of New York workmanship, having the top and leaves decorated with both stringing and edging, then an ellipse in the drawer front, inlaid paterae at the top of the legs, bellflowers down the fronts and sides of the legs, and banded cuffs of lighter woods. In New York fashion, the bellflowers are separated by looped stringing. Unlike those in Connecticut and Rhode Island, New York cabinetmakers employed the latest neoclassical oval, ring, and rosette pulls. Not all these tables were produced in the city. Somewhat simpler versions were made in adjacent northern New Jersey.

Hepplewhite tables with square ends were produced in a wide variety of shapes, sometimes with simple square, canted, or elliptical leaves, but more often with the ovolo rounding popular in Massachusetts or the double elliptic shape we will see later in a Sheraton table, but also, with the unusual stepped serpentine-shaped leaves seen in figure 16-13B. This complex serpentine form, a combination of ovolo corners and an elliptical center, may be unique to New York City. Although this is no more than an average quality New York table, the drawer front, the top, and the leaves are bordered with stringing, and there are inlaid diamonds at the top of the legs.

Not all New York Hepplewhite breakfast tables are as grand as these two, and before going on to a Sheraton Pembroke table, I will show you a more modest effort having the stepped elliptical leaves sometimes seen in New York tables (16-13C). When identifying the average grade of New York work, it is helpful to remember the secondary woods favored by New York cabinetmakers. Drawers are usually poplar, or white pine with poplar bottoms. Where more strength is required, in drawer slides and hinge rails, you are apt to see white pine and cherry, often white pine side rails and beech or cherry hinge rails. Veneer will almost invariably be laid on a base of white pine.

With the advent of the Sheraton style there was a significant change in New York furniture. In lieu of light wood stringing and pictorial inlay, we see dark veneers and carving. The leaves on Pembroke tables are likely to be the double-elliptic shape seen in so many Federal New York tables (16-13D). Note that the feet on this table are of a standard New York inverted vase form.

New York pedestal-form breakfast tables are also distinctive. A table of the best quality will have a fluted urn at the base of the column, then leaf-carved downswept legs with brass claw casters as shown in figure 16-13E. Usually there will be small turned drops under the corners of the top. This example has the popular double-elliptic leaves, but you will also see elliptical leaves, canted corners, and even triple-elliptic leaves. The upper surfaces of the legs will sometimes be left plain or will be molded rather than carved.

Before leaving New York it might be noted that colonette-form breakfast tables, much like the dinner table shown in figure 16-8D, were also produced in New York City. Colonettes and canted corners are a handsome combination, and these breakfast tables often have these corners. In chapter 18 you will see a very similar card table. The colonette form is not unique to New York City, for there are a few Boston colonette breakfast or library tables, although here you are unlikely to see canted corners, and the carving on the top of the legs will be very different from New York practice.

16-13A. New York Hepplewhite, 1790 – 1800.

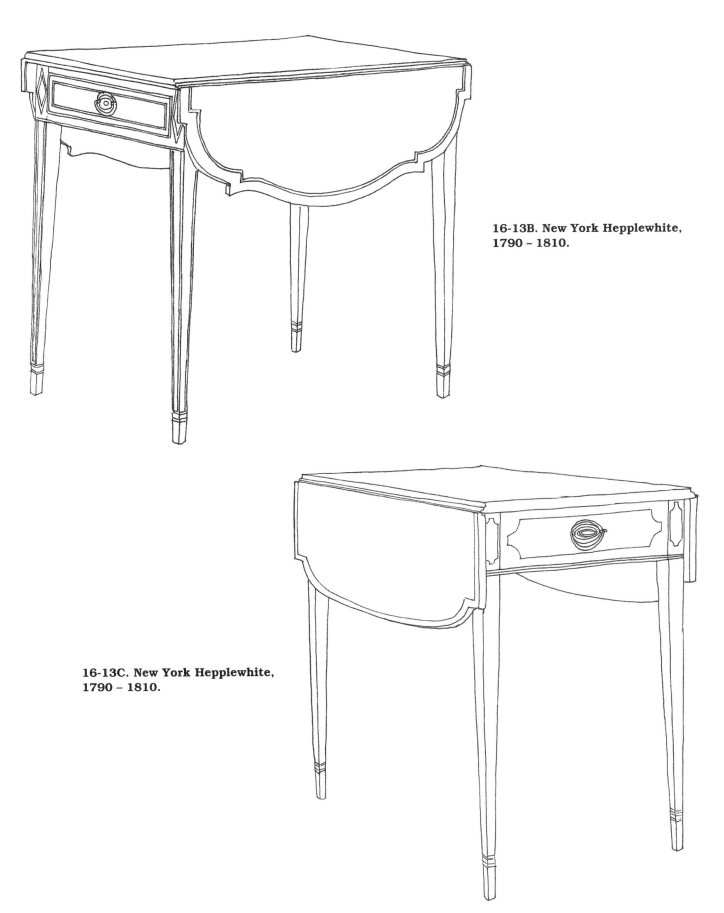

16-13B. New York Hepplewhite, 1790 – 1810.

16-13C. New York Hepplewhite, 1790 – 1810.

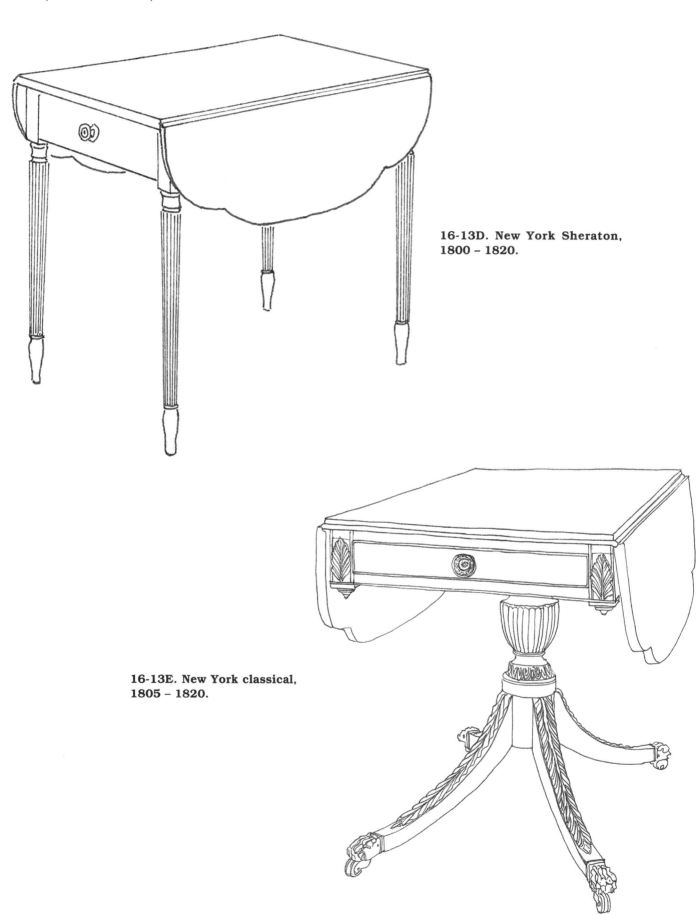

**16-13D. New York Sheraton,
1800 – 1820.**

**16-13E. New York classical,
1805 – 1820.**

16-14 Pennsylvania breakfast tables. Although Philadelphia and New York are less than a hundred miles apart, Philadelphia Pembroke tables are very different from New York Pembroke tables, so much so that you are far more likely to confuse a Pennsylvania table with a New England table than you are with a New York table. New York City was quick to accept the new neoclassical styles following the Revolution, while Philadelphia and the Delaware Valley, even more than New England, continued to employ the rococo. Indeed, so conservative are Pennsylvania breakfast tables that those made before the advent of the Sheraton style are usually identified as Pembroke tables rather than breakfast tables.

Pennsylvania Chippendale-style Pembroke tables are so common that we might look at two typical examples, the first table without stretchers but with little rococo-style fillets under the apron (16-14A); the second table with the distinctive serpentine stretchers often seen on these tables (16-14B). Both of these tables have the Marlborough legs and blocked feet so often seen in Philadelphia Chippendale furniture. Better-quality tables may be given rows of gadrooning under the aprons, others will have the straight pierced stretchers seen on English library armchairs. After the Revolution these popular tables acquired a lighter, more linear neoclassical look, and but for the Marlborough legs, may look like the New England table illustrated in figure 16-12D.

In Philadelphia, fashionable tables finally transition to neoclassical and acquire tapering Hepplewhite legs, spade feet, and serpentined tops like that seen in figure 16-14C. However, they retain bail pulls. Most Chippendale-style tables are made of either walnut or mahogany, and a few are made of cherry. Later tables, like that in figure 16-14C, will usually be made of mahogany.

It might be mentioned here that there are surprisingly few Philadelphia Pembroke tables with elliptical or oblong tops. The classic form of Hepplewhite Pembroke table so popular elsewhere does not appear to have been popular in Pennsylvania. Also, there seem to be almost no surviving New York Pembroke tables in the Chippendale style, that is, with square tops and Marlborough legs, even though they must once have been fairly common; so if you encounter such a table, and it does not seem to be a New England product, then it is most likely to be from southeastern Pennsylvania. However, there is another possibility. Square Pembroke tables with either Marlborough or Hepplewhite legs were made everywhere, and should you encounter an unadorned but neatly made example, it may not be from either New England or the Middle Atlantic. It may be from the South.

For some reason, Philadelphia Sheraton breakfast tables appear to be less common than Chippendale and Hepplewhite types, but to be complete, we will look at a very nice example (16-14D). In form these tables are not unlike New York Sheraton tables, but they will have Philadelphia legs and feet, and often the pleasing serpentine corners shown in this illustration.

Classical Philadelphia breakfast tables can be identified by the unusual trestle-form base in which the legs are set parallel to each other as shown in figure 16-14E. Although structurally different, this arrangement is similar in form to the legs in the Philadelphia accordion-action dining table illustrated in figure 16-8E. While not showing in this illustration, the pedestals on this table are braced by a pair of transverse turned stretchers that are doweled through the base of the pedestals. The ends are then hidden under a pair of turned or carved roundels. Note also that the leaves on this table are much the same shape as those of the previous Sheraton breakfast table. Later we will see the same distinctive elliptic front and serpentine corners in a Philadelphia card table. Look under the leaves and you are likely to see that the outer rails and hinged brackets are made of oak.

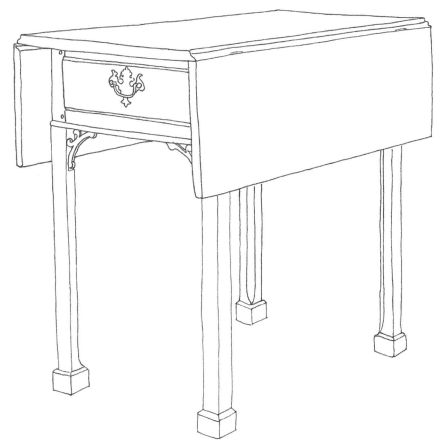

16-14A. Pennsylvania Chippendale, 1770 – 1790.

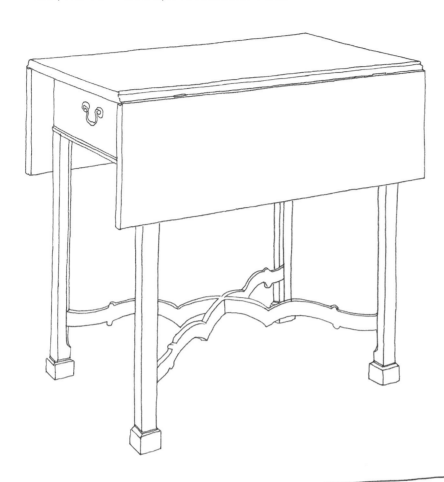

16-14B. Pennsylvania Chippendale, 1770 – 1790.

16-14C. Philadelphia Hepplewhite, 1790 – 1810.

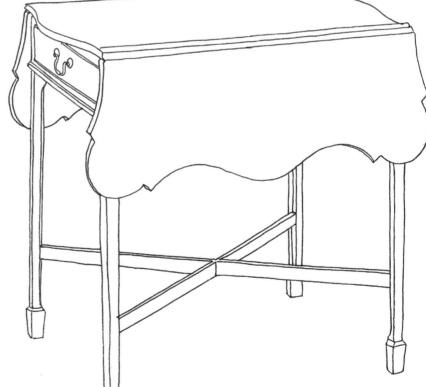

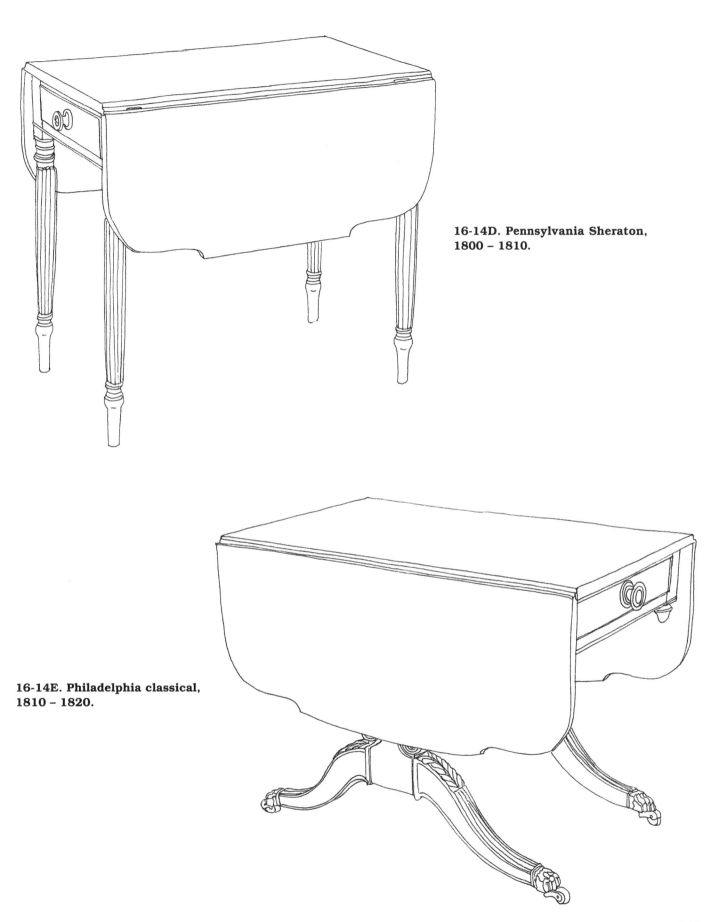

16-14D. Pennsylvania Sheraton, 1800 – 1810.

16-14E. Philadelphia classical, 1810 – 1820.

16-15 Southern breakfast tables. There are a considerable number of surviving Southern breakfast tables, and we might consider four examples. Normally, they fall into two categories: sophisticated urban tables, principally made in Baltimore, but also in tidewater Maryland and Virginia and south in Charleston, South Carolina; and more rural products that might have been produced in almost any area. When considering Southern breakfast tables, keep in mind that not only are Pennsylvania designs found in adjacent Maryland, but also, that after the Revolution much New York furniture was exported to the South, particularly to coastal communities. The Pennsylvania type of Pembroke table was made in Maryland, and the New York inverted-vase-form foot is found in Charleston furniture. The other aspect of the export trade is that a breakfast or card table that has been in a Southern family for many generations may not be of Southern manufacture.

The urban Southern furniture you are most likely to encounter will have been produced in Federal Baltimore, and here we might show two examples, first one of the elliptical breakfast tables that were fashionable in Baltimore at the turn of the century (16-15A). While these tables are amply decorated with inlay in New York fashion, there are significant differences between them and tables made in New York. They are apt to be somewhat large, the tops and the leaves will have square edges, and the bellflowers on the legs are likely have elongated central petals. In lieu of bookends at the tops of the legs, you may see either paterae or hollow cornered rectangles with ovals in the centers. However, the most striking aspect of these large Pembroke tables is that many do not have the usual single drawer. In the space normally occupied by a drawer there will be a cross or medial brace set at a slight diagonal between the sides. These tables typically also have unusually thick built-up aprons.

The other Baltimore breakfast tables you may see are large classical pedestal tables (16-15B). Like similar New York tables, these are typically well made, with generous use of mahogany and brass-paw coaster feet. Most have rather heavy reeding on down-swept legs. Were the leaves of this table up, you would most probably see that the column has a prominent carved urn like that shown in figure 18-11D. In New York fashion, the edges of the tops of these tables will usually be reeded.

Although you are very unlikely to encounter an Annapolis table, we will look at one, for they are very different from those of Baltimore workmanship, reflecting as they do the older, more settled tradition of the tidewater South. The breakfast table in figure 16-15C is attributed to the shop of John Shaw on the basis of the unusually thin top, the distinctive serpentine shape of the leaves, and the unusual, rather stubby ovoid spade feet. While you may never see one of these tables, remember that a nicely made mahogany Hepplewhite breakfast table with spade feet and restrained use of light wood stringing and inlay might be from tidewater Maryland or Virginia. The drawer will probably be poplar, the inner rails perhaps yellow pine, and the outer and fly rails red oak.

Neat and plain breakfast tables were made everywhere in the South, and before ending we might look at the sort of Pembroke table you are most likely to encounter. The cherry Hepplewhite table in figure 16-15D was probably made in Virginia, but could have been made almost anywhere in the South, or for that matter, almost anywhere east of the Mississippi during the first decades of the nineteenth century. To determine if such a table is actually Southern, we might consider the primary and secondary woods. If the table is not mahogany, it will most likely be either walnut or cherry, but also sometimes river birch or cypress, and if a very rural product, then a hard Southern pine. The drawer will most often be made of yellow pine, but you may also see some use of walnut or cypress, perhaps walnut drawer sides or a cypress drawer bottom. Walnut was so common in the South that on mahogany tables you may find it employed in secondary locations where a hard wood was required, such as drawer runners, hinge rails, and fly rails. Atypical secondary woods are frequently indications of Southern workmanship.

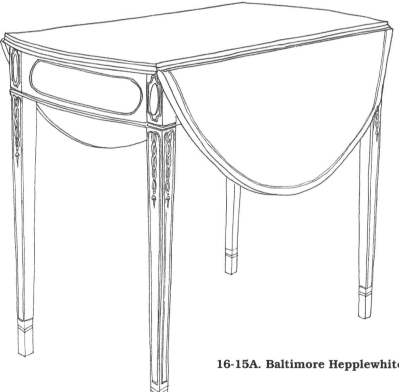

16-15A. Baltimore Hepplewhite, 1790 – 1810.

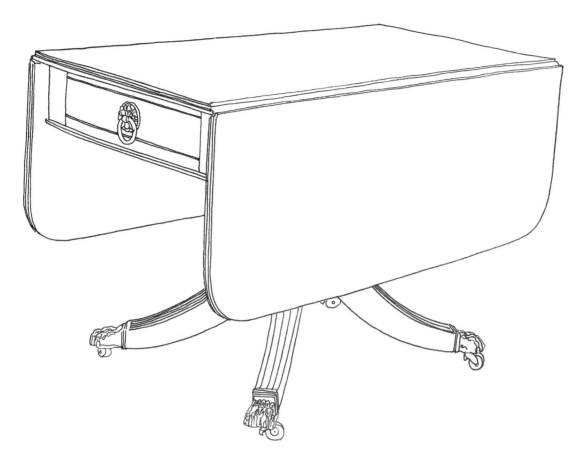

16-15B. Baltimore classical, 1815 – 1820.

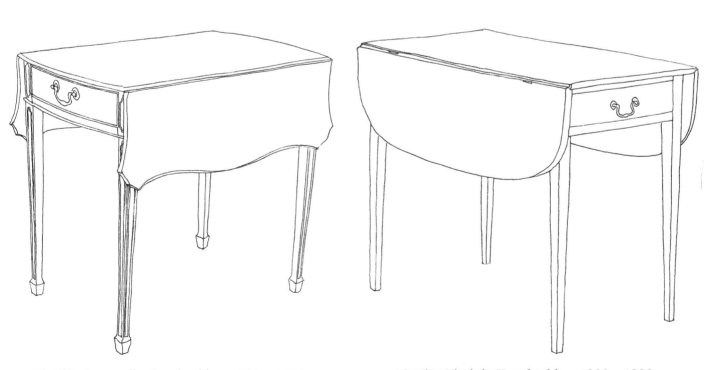

16-15C. Annapolis Hepplewhite, 1790 – 1810.

16-15D. Virginia Hepplewhite, 1800 – 1820.

Chapter 17 – Tea Tables

Although breakfast tables were covered in the same chapter as dining tables, tea tables should have their own chapter. So many survive that there is not an Americana auction anywhere that does not have at least a few from which to choose. They are of two basic forms: those having a square bed and standing on four legs, and those having a column or pillar and supported by three cabriole legs. Either may have a round, square, or serpentine top. So different are these two forms that here we might depart from custom and rather than proceeding by style and region down the coast, survey first the square bed tables, then the pillar tables.

In the previous chapter there was a question of terminology — whether or not small Queen Anne–style drop-leaf tables should be identified as breakfast tables or tea tables. A similar problem afflicts other small occasional tables. How are we to separate tea tables from tavern or tap tables? Small Queen Anne cabriole leg tables are usually considered tea tables, but what about the great many New England tables having oval or porringer tops and offset turned legs? Here I will resort to the beloved practice of the bureaucrat — the arbitrary ruling — and classify these as tea tables, this because so many are too finely made, or are too delicate, to have been intended for public use; and because, whatever their original purpose, such tables should be discussed together, and this is as good a spot as any. Similar small stretcher-base tables, which are more suitable for the rough and tumble of a tavern, are classified as tavern tables. These are covered in a later chapter on tavern and farm tables.

Tea tables lie firmly within the Queen Anne and Chippendale traditions, appearing in the 1740s, then losing favor with the advent of the neoclassical at the end of the century. Although survival examples continued to be made into the early years of the nineteenth century, tea tables did not transition to the neoclassical. Instead, they seem to have been supplanted by the newer Pembroke table. As with chairs and dining tables, there remains the question of Queen Anne and Chippendale. Here we will follow precedent and simply identify all tea tables as Queen Anne unless given some form of ball and claw foot, remembering though, that in America, Queen Anne–style furniture continued to be produced parallel with Chippendale, and that these terms serve mostly to identify style, and not even very well at that. A simple Queen Anne pillar tea table is as likely as not to date from the early years of the nineteenth century.

In urban centers pillar tea tables were a joint effort of the cabinetmaker, who shaped, assembled, and leveled the top; the turner, who turned the columns; and the carver, who carved the ball and claw feet and, on better-quality tables, also carved the knees and columns and scalloped the tops. So popular were these tables that it appears that both the legs and columns were made up to standard shapes and sizes, then purchased by cabinetmakers as required. The dished tops of tea tables and candlestands were made on lathes, and the turnings had to be very carefully done, not only to obtain level surfaces, but also so as to not break out the rather thin raised edges. In some areas, particularly in Philadelphia, where these tops were the norm, this may also have been its own specialty.

The term *tea table* is not recent. Although pillar-type tea tables were sometimes identified as "pillar and claw," "claw," or "snap tables" in England, in America they were usually just called "tea tables," sometimes with the added notation "round." Because not all these tables have circular tops, I will follow the terminology employed in many auction catalogs and identify them as tilt-top tea tables. Likewise, square cabriole-leg tea tables will be called tray-top tea tables.

17-1 Queen Anne turned-leg tea tables. There are so many tea tables with turned tapering legs that we might look at five examples. The great majority are from New England, but they were also produced to some extent in the South. The most common New England table will have an oval top and the offset turned legs seen in figure 17-1A. Usually the apron will be flat, with the integral bracket responds shown here, but you may also see curved aprons and flat aprons without bracket responds. Often there will be small turned pads under the feet. In advertisements these tables are usually identified as being produced between 1740 and 1760, but they were such a successful design that they probably continued in limited production until the end of the century.

Figure 17-1B illustrates a simpler oval-top New England tea table. This maple and pine table not only has a flat apron without responds, but also, its splayed legs do not have the usual offset turned feet. When legs are not offset turned, they often have button feet, sometimes with pads beneath to compensate for wear. Button feet were commonly employed on thin turned legs to minimize wear, and are not region specific. They are the sort of simple, logical idea that might be found in any region.

The great majority of New England tea tables have oval tops. The next most common shape is the porringer top shown in a Rhode Island table in figure 17-1C. Rhode Island tea tables, like much Rhode Island furniture, are notable for their quality and attention to detail. Note that the bracket responds on this table are given a little step to break the curve, a nice little touch often seen in Rhode Island tea tables. This table is made of mahogany, but you will also see a figured maple. Elsewhere in New England, tea tables were made of local woods, most commonly maple, but also of cherry and birch, or a mix of woods. An all-cherry table would suggest either Connecticut or the Connecticut River Valley; birch, northern New England, perhaps New Hampshire. Budget products, like the table in figure 17-1B, usually have maple legs and pine tops. While walnut is often found in New England furniture, it was seldom employed in tea tables, and if you encounter a simple walnut table, perhaps with a square top, turned legs, and button feet, you may be looking at a Southern table.

A substantial number of New England tea tables have rectangular tops (17-1D). When this is the case, there is often a small drawer in the apron. Square tea tables were popular in Rhode Island, and this maple table, with a little step in the bracket responds and an elegantly thin mahogany top with notched corners, is most probably from Rhode Island.

Normally I have avoided the fine and the rare as being too uncommon to justify inclusion in a survey, but the tea table in figure 17-1E is too interesting to ignore. A handful of these elegant little three-leg tables were made in Rhode Island, probably early in the third quarter of the eighteenth century. This is a far finer table than may be evident in the small pen and ink illustration. It is made of mahogany, and the circular top has been dished on a lathe. Because of the triangular bed, the top of each leg has also been turned. Small three-leg tables, but of very different design, were also produced in New York and Connecticut.

17-1A. New England Queen Anne, oval top, 27" h, 1740 – 1770.

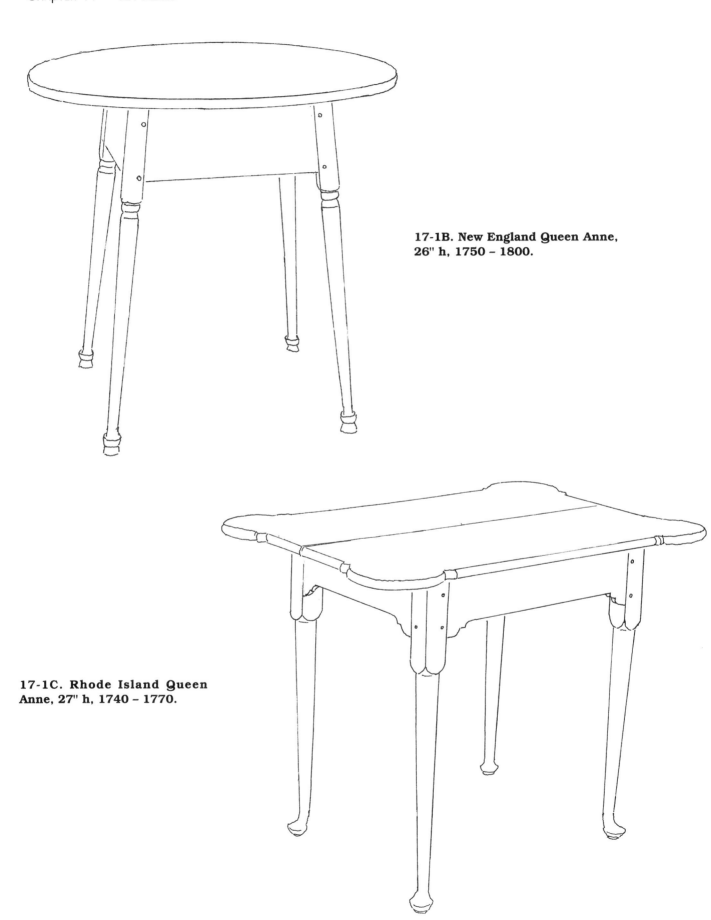

17-1B. New England Queen Anne, 26" h, 1750 – 1800.

17-1C. Rhode Island Queen Anne, 27" h, 1740 – 1770.

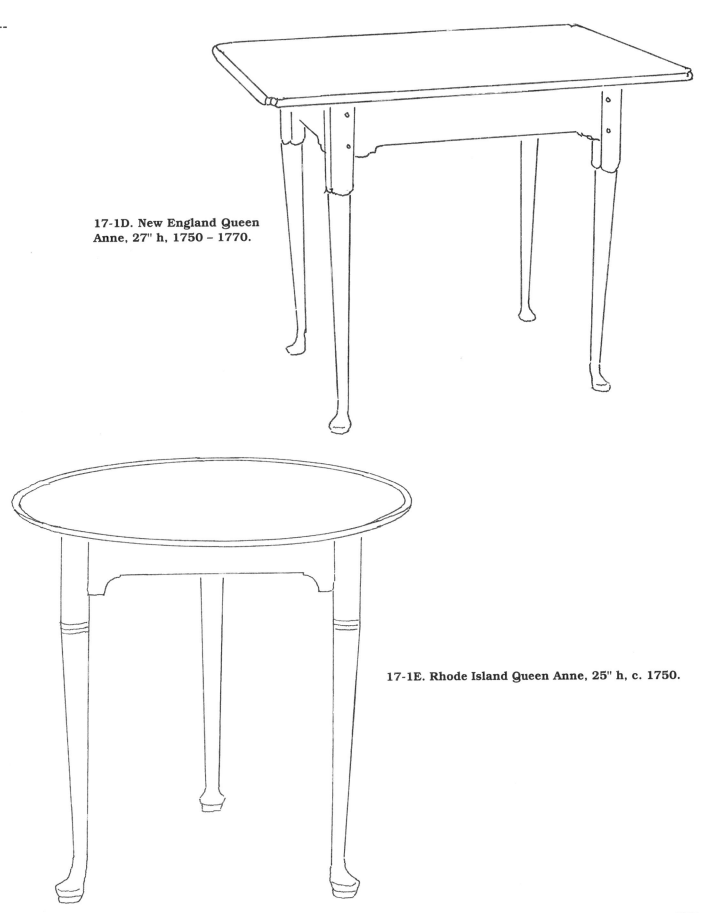

17-1D. New England Queen
Anne, 27" h, 1750 – 1770.

17-1E. Rhode Island Queen Anne, 25" h, c. 1750.

17-2 Queen Anne cabriole-leg tea tables. Here we will consider two very different forms of cabriole-leg tea tables: a cabriole-leg version of the table covered in the previous section, and the stylish tray-top tables so often seen in magazine advertisements and fine collections. Tea or china tables with straight Marlborough legs and raised fretwork galleries around the tops are omitted because they are so rare among American furniture. Those few that you see are likely to be English.

Before discussing tray-top tea tables, we should look at an elegant little maple table that was probably made in eastern Massachusetts (17-2A). This small table is essentially a cabriole-leg version of the tea tables illustrated in the previous section. Most of these charming little tables have square tops, often with drawers in the aprons. Sometimes the top will be notched, or there will be an applied raised molding around the top. In common with much rural work, there are no brackets at the top of the thin cabriole legs.

The great majority of the more formal tray-top tea tables were produced in New England, and as most are probably from eastern Massachusetts, we might consider one of these first. The standard type has rounded cabriole legs with pad feet and a bowed serpentine apron like that shown in figure 17-2B. While there is no particular pattern to the apron, they are normally conservative and restrained. There will usually be small turned disks under the pad feet. This is a very fine Boston table with notched corners in the tray top and delicate C-scrolls on the insides of the legs. Some tables have candleslides worked into the ends. Most tray-top tables are made of walnut or mahogany; a few are made of maple. The blocking under the tops will be white pine.

Newport tray-top tea tables are so completely different from other New England tea tables that there is little chance of confusion. The design is very consistent: a straight, bowed apron with small knee brackets shaped into the ends, then squared cabriole legs terminating in slipper feet (17-2C). The squared cabriole legs harmonize with the unadorned rectangular shape of the top. Most of these tables are made of mahogany. A few have drawers in the aprons or are made of the tiger maple that was favored in Rhode Island.

Although adjacent to Rhode Island, Connecticut tray-top tea tables are more similar to Massachusetts tables, except that the primary wood is likely to be cherry rather than walnut or mahogany. In addition to being cherrywood, the table in figure 17-2D has a somewhat rural appearance: the apron is a bit deep, the pad feet are large and flattened, and the scalloping at the base of the apron is so deep that it has been pieced out. While similar to the Massachusetts table in figure 17-2B, it is a very different table. Connecticut patrons liked to have something extra, and Connecticut tables are apt to have ball and claw feet.

As you might expect, some Connecticut tea tables have scalloped tops similar to that shown in the chest of drawers in figure 11-8C. While these are often published, they are actually fairly rare, and you are very unlikely to see one outside of a museum. However, should you encounter a cabriole-leg tea table with a scalloped top made of cherry, you are most probably looking at a tea table made in the Connecticut River Valley.

New York tray-top tea tables are uncommon, but are not so rare that they should be neglected. The cherrywood table in figure 17-2E could easily be attributed to New York on the basis of the New York slipper feet and the characteristic flat apron with lobed ends and single center drop. However, the very delicate cabriole-legs with the sweeping curves at the ankles suggest Connecticut, as does the use of cherry. This elegant table may actually have been made in western Connecticut near the border of New York.

High-style carved ball and claw tea tables were produced in both New York and Philadelphia, but are exceedingly rare. Therefore we might look at a simpler table with feet having Pennsylvania stockinged trifid form, in this case the trifid form that is shaped more like a club, and has no more than a suggestion of a three-part division (17-2F). Note that because the apron of this table is not bowed, the cabriole legs have been given returns.

There are only a few surviving Southern tray-top tea tables — too few to illustrate a representative example. These are mostly from tidewater Virginia. What you might keep in mind, though, is that an atypical tea table fashioned of either mahogany or walnut, perhaps with some Philadelphia features, could be a product of the South. Here you might check what type of wood has been used in the blocking that secures the top to the rails.

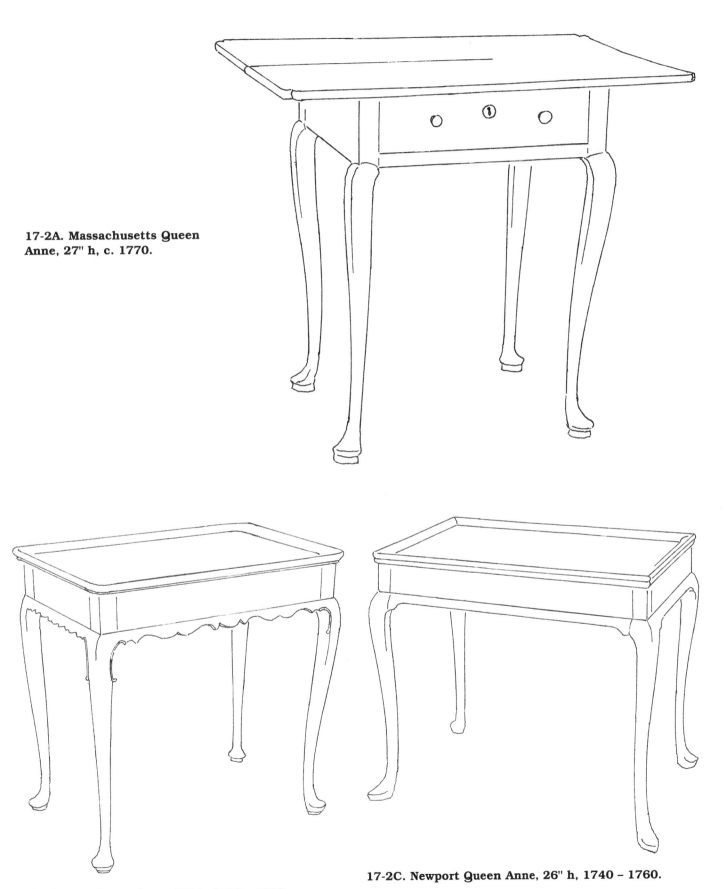

17-2A. Massachusetts Queen Anne, 27" h, c. 1770.

17-2B. Boston Queen Anne, 26" h, 1740 – 1760.

17-2C. Newport Queen Anne, 26" h, 1740 – 1760.

355

17-2D. Connecticut Queen Anne, 27" h, 1750 – 1770.   **17-2E. New York Queen Anne, 27" h, 1750 – 1775.**

17-2F. Pennsylvania Queen Anne, 28" h, 1750 – 1780.

17-3 New Hampshire Queen Anne tilt-top tea table. The square tray-top tea table was most popular in New England, but even here went out of fashion prior to the Revolution. Not so the pillar-form tea table, which continued in production in all regions right up into the early years of the nineteenth century. So many of these tables survive that we will give each colony its own section. (Colony because the states were still colonies at the time these tables became so fashionable).

A pillar tea table has three principle components: the top, the pillar or column, and the cabriole legs; and in the following sections we will see that all three can serve to tell us where a table was made. In addition, the shaping of the cleats under the top, the juncture between the top and the column, and the method of joining the legs to the column also vary among the colonies. There are no components of these enormously popular tables that do not help tell us where they were made.

The first table we will consider is easy to identify, for it is constructed in an unusual manner. Normally the legs on a tea table or stand are fastened to the column with blind dovetail joints. Dovetails were cut at the inner ends of the legs, then the legs were slid into matching slots cut into the bottom of the column. Because the joint is somewhat fragile, a Y-shaped iron brace is normally fastened to the base of the column. However, in New Hampshire, and occasionally elsewhere, it was common practice to fasten the legs with mortise-and-tenon joints; the legs were tenoned into a hexagonal base, as shown in figure 17-3. Because this joint does not lock in place, it is usually pinned. Note that the legs on this very rural table are not tapered; they are flat-sided to the width of the mortise-and-tenon joint. As you would expect, most of these simple Dunlap-type tea tables are made of maple or birch or a combination of the two. Later we will see the same construction in New Hampshire candlestands.

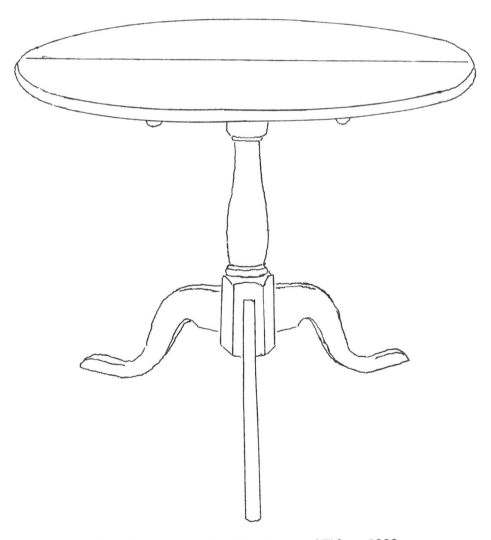

17-3. New Hampshire Queen Anne, 27" h, c. 1800.

17-4 Massachusetts Queen Anne and Chippendale tilt-top tea tables. In this section we will first touch on the general characteristics of New England pillar-form tea tables, then discuss three Massachusetts examples. For the most part, New England tea tables are very different from Middle Atlantic and Southern tables. Although we will see some exceptions, the top of such a table is usually molded or rounded, the knees are left plain, and there will not be the birdcage mechanism that allows the top to both rotate and tilt. A table with a dished or scalloped top, carving on the knees, and a pillared box under the top, will almost always be from somewhere south of Massachusetts.

If the number of illustrated examples are any indication, quite the most fashionable type of Massachusetts tea table has a serpentine top with molded edges, a spiral-carved urn at the base of a straight column, and the rather thin, elongated ball and claw feet shown in figure 17-4A. In spite of the additional cost, these "rat's-paw" feet are found on a great many Massachusetts tea tables. These very popular tables were also made with square tops, sometimes with notched or cusped corners. Less costly tables may not have carving on the urns, or may omit the ball and claw feet. Local versions of these tables were also produced in New Hampshire, Rhode Island, and Connecticut.

When not given a rat's-paw foot, Massachusetts tea tables usually have bold, elongated pad feet on thin platforms. Tables from the North Shore are likely to have pointed feet with pronounced ridges across the tops as illustrated in figure 17-4B. These "snake feet" are also seen in southern New Hampshire.

Otherwise, a foot will normally have a pronounced crease, or arris, across the tops and this may extend for the length of the leg. Also, on North Shore table the urn at the base of the column is likely to be uncarved and may be tighter and more cylindrical in shape.

Not all Massachusetts tea tables have the urn and column pillar shape shown in these two figures — an urn at the base of a tapering cylinder. A small number of high-end Boston tables have the fluted column shown in figure 17-4C. This is a very fine mahogany table; not only has the column been fluted, but also, the legs are carved and there are large ball and claw feet. There is nothing unique about the shape of the column. It is seen in many English tables, and in the following section we will see it again in a Newport table.

Most Massachusetts tilt-top tea tables are made of mahogany, perhaps in part because the additional cost of the material was somewhat offset by being able to fashion the top of of a table from a single wide piece of very stable wood. This is suggested by the fact that in New England tilt-top tables are seldom made of walnut, even though at this time walnut was still being employed in other New England furniture. However, where money was to be saved, or there was a preference, New England tea tables were also made of cherry, maple, or birch; cherry probably in the Connecticut River Valley, but also in eastern Massachusetts; maple and birch north of Boston. Whatever the primary wood, the block or plate at the top of the pillar will usually be maple or birch.

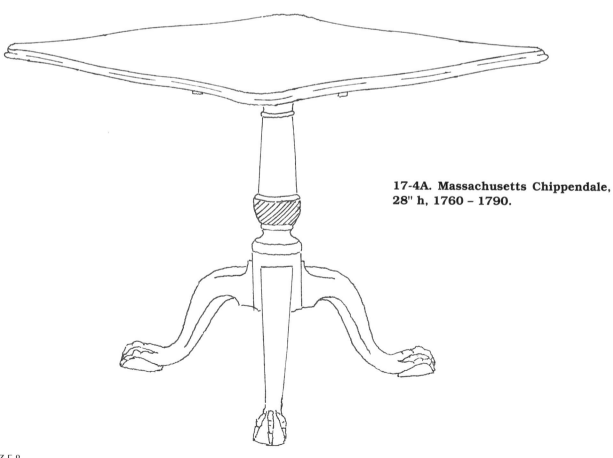

17-4A. Massachusetts Chippendale, 28" h, 1760 – 1790.

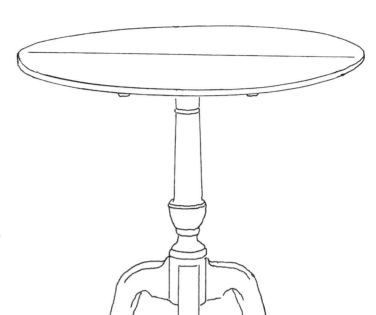

17-4B. Massachusetts Queen Anne, 28" h, 1740 – 1770.

17-4C. Boston Chippendale, 29" h, 1760 – 1790.

17-5 Rhode Island Queen Anne tilt-top tea tables. Rhode Island tea tables are not all that common, but are so different from Massachusetts products and exhibit so much variety that we will look at three examples. Prior to the Revolution, Newport was the leading city in Rhode Island, and a large proportion of the relatively few Rhode Island tea tables are likely to be from Newport.

Aside from a general quality and attention to detail, perhaps the most distinctive feature of the Newport tilt-top tea table is the shape of the column, notably the elegantly simple "gun barrel" turning shown in figure 17-5A. While popular in Newport, it should be noted that columnar turnings are common on English tables, and are also seen on Philadelphia and tidewater Virginia pieces. Other Newport characteristics include the shapes of the legs and feet. Cabriole legs often have rather soft curves without the sharp bends at the ankles and the high knees seen elsewhere. The feet, when not carved, are bulbous and rounded. These features are also seen on many English tables of this period, although the latter are usually fitted with birdcage mechanisms and have simple flush tops with rounded edges.

Rhode Island cabinetmakers employed a variety of turnings in tea tables, most often that of the tapered column illustrated in figure 17-5A, a Rhode Island interpretation of the Massachusetts spiral turned urn and column, or the simple baluster and ring pattern shown in figure 17-5B. Both of these tables have the dished tops common in Newport tea tables. Note that in the typical attention to detail, the cleats have been reduced in depth at the ends to show as little as possible under the top. Also, the bottoms of the columns have not been relieved with little rounded notches or scallops as was normally done in pillar-form tables. Lastly, look at the feet in the figure 17-5B. Here within the approximate contours of the typical bulbous Newport feet there are attenuated ball and claw feet, all the more unusual in that they have five claws each rather than the usual three. These rather strange looking ball and claw feet are unique to Newport.

Even on a tea table it was necessary to reinforce the bottom of the column to keep the dovetail mortises from splitting out. To avoid this problem, Rhode Island cabinetmakers sometimes employed the English method of joining the legs to the column with a triangular block or plate, what is known as a platform base. The somewhat rural Rhode Island tea table in figure 17-5C has this distinctive construction. Aside from this feature and the characteristic legs, the table is unusual for Rhode Island in having a birdcage mechanism and lacking a dished top.

While most Rhode Island tea tables are made of mahogany, a few, improbably, are made of walnut; perhaps to save a little cost, or perhaps for a conservative customer. Quite often the block under the top will be chestnut rather than the maple or birch seen in most New England tables.

17-5A. Newport Queen Anne, 28" h, 1760 – 1790.

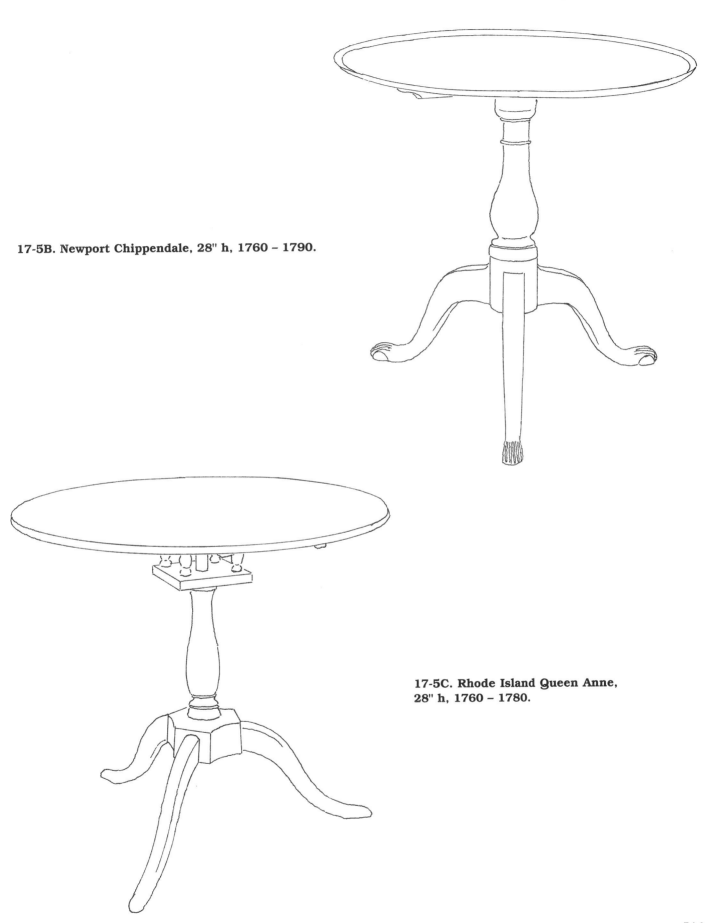

17-5B. Newport Chippendale, 28" h, 1760 – 1790.

17-5C. Rhode Island Queen Anne, 28" h, 1760 – 1780.

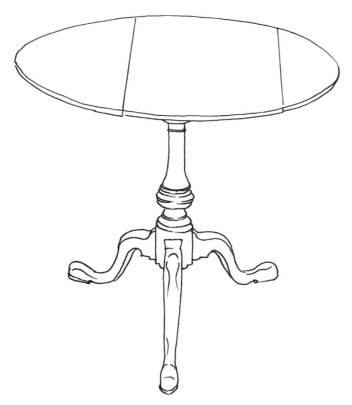

17-6A. Connecticut Queen Anne, 28" h x 38" dia., c. 1785.

17-6 Connecticut Queen Anne tilt-top tea tables. A Connecticut tea table typically exhibits a mix of elements from other regions. The columns of such tables are a case in point. Here you may see local interpretations of the Philadelphia compressed ball, the Massachusetts urn and column, and the Newport gun barrel column, and in typical Connecticut fashion, some so peculiar that you wonder what in the world the turner was thinking of. When not ball and claw feet, the feet are similar to elongated Massachusetts pad feet, sometimes with rounded rather than pointed ends. Others have legs and feet similar to those on the Newport table in figure 17-5A. Most tea tables are made of cherry and are fitted with birdcage mechanisms, sometimes with the turned and molded collars so often seen on Pennsylvania tables. The combination of birdcage and cherry in a rural tea table is a good indication of Connecticut workmanship.

Perhaps the most published Connecticut tea tables are those made in the Hartford area by the Chapin family. These usually have some form of the ball column so popular in Pennsylvania, either a well-delineated compressed ball like that shown in figure 17-8A, or a far more flattened ball at the base of a flaring column as illustrated in figure 17-6A. Note that this table has the rounded Newport-type pad feet. Many of these tables have ball and claw foot, and here you will see the Connecticut type of foot similar to that illustrated in figure 5-1D. The top may be dished or scalloped, but more often is simply rounded, often curving under so as to suggest a dished top, but without the complication of a raised edge.

Many Connecticut tea tables have a markedly rural appearance, having naive turnings and birdcage mechanisms with excessively large plates or overly tall colonettes. Most are made of cherry, the top made up of two or three boards. The large tea table shown in figure 17-6B is a typical example. The column has the large bowl shape favored in Connecticut stands, the tops of the legs have the deep cutouts seen in New York tables, and the feet are the elongated Massachusetts type, but here with rounded ends.

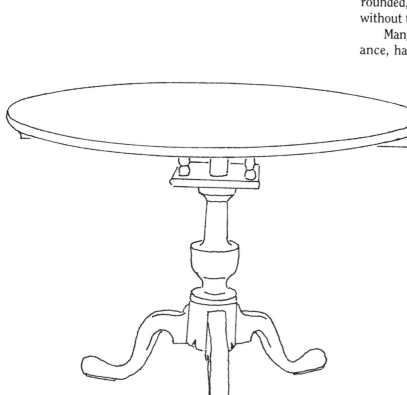

17-6B. Connecticut Queen Anne, 27" h, 1780 – 1800.

17-7 New York Chippendale tilt-top tea tables. New York tea tables are fairly scarce, but nevertheless survive in significant enough numbers to justify illustrating the two most common forms. Like much New York rococo furniture, they have a distinctly English look about them and might easily be mistaken for late George II or early George III workmanship. As a group they are not particularly impressive; usually made of mahogany, but with plain, rounded tops, baluster or cup turned shafts, uncarved legs, and ball and claw or rounded pad feet. Unlike Philadelphia tables, they do not have collars under the birdcage keys. As was noted in chapter 5, ball and claw feet were much favored in New York, and they are far more frequently seen on tea tables than the additional time and expense would suggest.

The most common type of New York tilt-top tea table has the somewhat heavy baluster-form pillar illustrated in figure 17-7A. This is usually balanced by a narrow ring at the top of the column and a second ring at the base of the baluster. Often the ball and claw feet will have the square, blocky look seen in New York chairs. A number of these tables carry the label of Thomas Burling, whose label is also seen on sideboards.

The other form of New York tea table has the cup and flared shaft shown in figure 17-7B. Note that the legs on these tables are deeply undercut below the knee. Both have ball and claw feet in typical New York fashion, but if given pad feet, you will normally see a rounded foot on a solid platform. Most New York tea tables have round tops with simple, rounded edges in English fashion, but there are some with square molded tops, and a rare few with carved legs, fluted columns, and scalloped, or "piecrust," tops.

17-7A. New York Chippendale, 28" h, 1760 – 1790.

17-7B. New York Chippendale, 29" h, 1760 – 1790.

363

17-8 Pennsylvania Queen Anne and Chippendale tilt-top tea tables. This will be quite the longest section, for circular tea tables were exceedingly popular throughout the Delaware Valley, and here there is much to discuss. As noted earlier, tea tables were a joint effort of the cabinetmaker, the turner, and the carver. Such was the demand that turners appear to have produced columns on speculation, for there are Philadelphia newspaper advertisements for "mahogany and walnut table columns." Carvers probably also produced standard ball and claw legs. To fill an order for a table, a cabinetmaker might obtain ball and claw legs from a carver, the column from a turner. Not only are there are tables made of different woods, but also, the butt ends of legs sometimes do not exactly match the curve of the base of a column, although here the shoulders of the dovetail may have been undercut to assure a quick fit. Most Pennsylvania tables have dished tops, and this lathe work may also have been a specialty.

When a table was fitted with a birdcage mechanism so as to both tilt and rotate, the top was kept in place with a small wedge that passes through a square slot in the top of the column and bears on the upper surface of the lower plate. However, as the top was turned, the bottom of the wedge rubbed against the plate, and not only did the wedge become worn, but also, it tended to come loose. The solution was to insert a loose collar between the wedge and the lower plate. This would minimize the wear and make the top easier to turn. Normally these collars were turned on a lathe and were given an attractive molded edge. This refinement is a good indicator of Delaware Valley workmanship, for it was seldom employed elsewhere. The only American exception I'm aware of is Connecticut, where collars are seen on some better-quality tea tables, most probably in emulation of Philadelphia fashion.

There are three basic patterns of Philadelphia turnings: a compressed ball and column, a stout baluster shape, and a carved vase form under what might be described as a ruffled canopy or ring. The latter is quite rare and only seen on some of the best work. There are also a few grand tables having stop-fluted columns reminiscent of Newport or English workmanship. However, about two out of every three tables will have the well known compressed ball shape shown in figure 17-8A. This is an average grade table with a dished top and ball and claw feet. Better quality may have a scalloped top, carved legs, and then maybe some carving on the ball, and fluting on the column. Note that the birdcage is fitted with a molded collar. The compressed ball pattern was enormously popular throughout the Delaware Valley, and indeed, is almost the signature of Pennsylvania pillar form tables. There are many variations in this pattern. At times the ball is more flattened; at other times almost circular. We will see the same form later in Philadelphia candlestands. Like much else in American furniture, the ball and column pattern is an English import, and that a table has this shape of column does not guarantee that it is from Pennsylvania — or is even American.

The other common Delaware Valley pattern has a large baluster above a ring as seen in figure 17-8B. This is a better than average quality table with a scalloped top and leaf carved legs. So fashionable were these circular tables in Pennsylvania that an unusual number — perhaps one in ten — have these time consuming and expensive tops. Almost all other Pennsylvania tables have dished tops, which provided an edge stop at a fraction the cost of scalloping.

These fashionable tables were produced throughout the Delaware Valley and surrounding areas: in southeastern Pennsylvania, southern New Jersey, Delaware, and Maryland. There are local variations, and we might look at two; the first a table probably made in Lancaster County in which the column has a pronounced separate ring below the baluster (17-8C), the second a Chester County table in which the bottom plate of the birdcage is turned and molded (17-8D). This unusual feature has some logic, for the curve of the plate compliments the curve of the top. Like almost everything else, it is not a certain indicator of Chester County workmanship, for it is sometimes seen in New England. There are also a few Connecticut tables with octagonal bottom plates. Note that the little birdcage pillars on this table are higher than necessary, a idiosyncrasy often seen on rural tables. Connecticut tables are apt to have excessively tall colonettes. Both of these tables have pad feet, which in Pennsylvania is usually bulbous and rounded as shown in Figure 17-8D.

In addition to the prevalence of dished tops, Pennsylvania tea tables are notable for the use of walnut. About one in two will be made of this wood, even though this involved a built up top. All the tables illustrated in this section are made of walnut, even the grand table with the scalloped top and carved knees, for which the additional cost of mahogany would not seem to have been a major concern. As with other Delaware Valley furniture, there is considerable use of cherrywood, and here again, that a table is made of cherry does not mean that it is from Connecticut. Although unusual, a few Delaware Valley tea tables are made of maple.

Lastly, it might be mentioned that because Delaware Valley tilt-top tables were normally fitted with rotating mechanisms, they are invariably round rather than square. South of New England, you are very unlikely to see a square tea table.

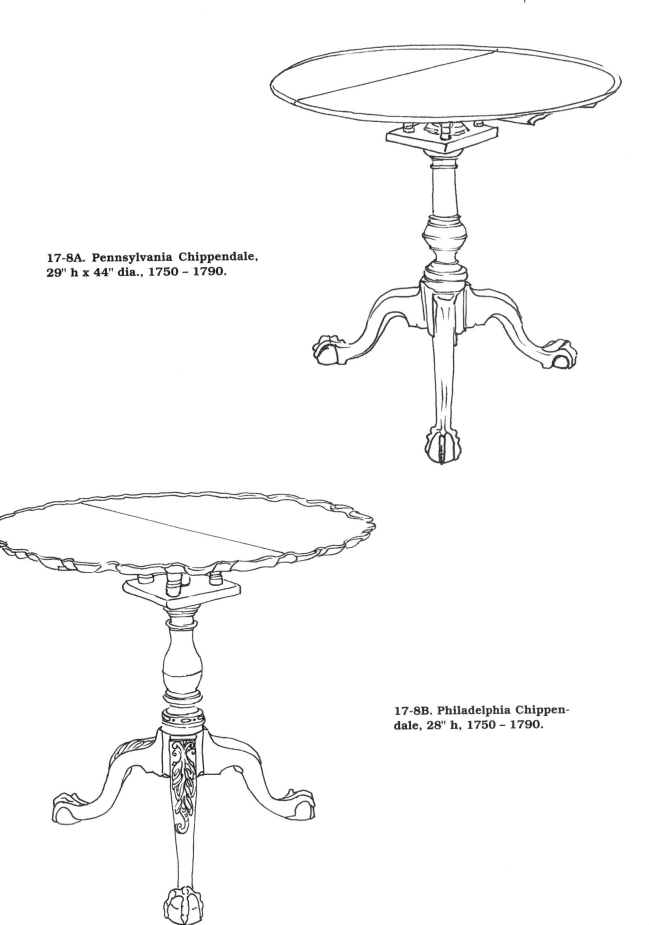

17-8A. Pennsylvania Chippendale,
29" h x 44" dia., 1750 – 1790.

17-8B. Philadelphia Chippendale, 28" h, 1750 – 1790.

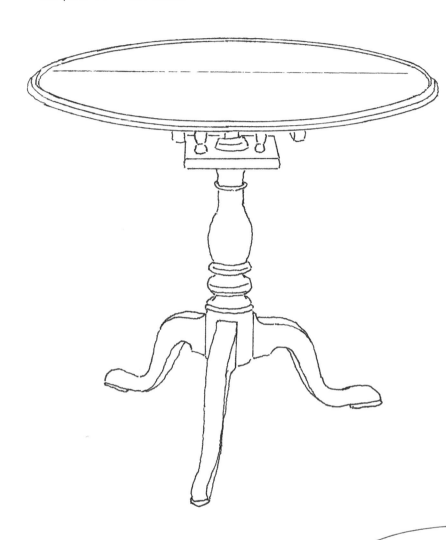

17-8C. Lancaster County Queen Anne, 35" h, c. 1780.

17-8D. Chester County Queen Anne, 28" h, c. 1780.

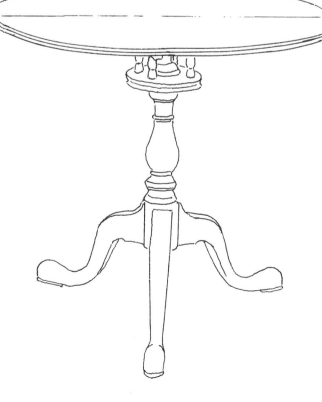

17-9 Southern Queen Anne tilt-top tea tables. Tilt-top tea tables were made in all regions, and the South is no exception. While we will consider just two examples, they are by no means rare. Although there are some very fine tea tables with scalloped tops, leaf-carved legs, and ball and claw feet in museum collections, for the most part Southern tea tables are relatively simple, Queen Anne in style with rounded tops and pad feet like the Wilmington, North Carolina, table in figure 17-9A. Southern tea tables exhibit no particular pattern in the columns, and you may see the Massachusetts spiral-carved urn, the Newport column, the New York cup and flared shaft, and the Pennsylvania baluster. These patterns are probably as much derived from English prototypes as borrowed from the Northern colonies.

Many Southern tea tables are fitted with birdcage mechanisms, and here you may see unusual turnings in the pillars between the plates. In some tables the plates are not separated by pillars; but, the birdcage is a small dovetailed box with open ends, a feature also seen in provincial English tables.

The Chowan County table in figure 17-9B is fitted with one of these solid box mechanisms. Note that this North Carolina table has unusual little carved roundels under the curve of the legs.

Both these tables are made of mahogany, as are many Southern tables from coastal areas. You will also see walnut and sometimes cherry, particularly when some distance from the sea. Because most Delaware Valley tilt-top tables have either scalloped or dished tops, and walnut was seldom employed north of Pennsylvania, a tilt-top tea table made of walnut or, perhaps, cherry, with pad feet and a flat top with rounded edges — perhaps with an atypical column — may well be of Southern manufacture.

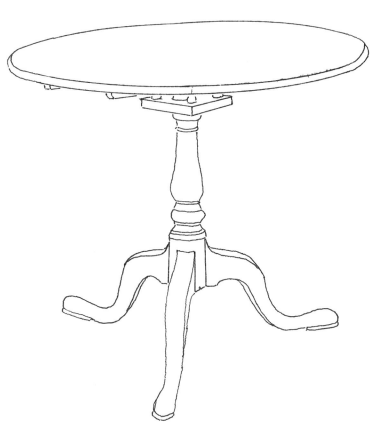

17-9A. North Carolina Queen Anne, 31" h, c. 1770.

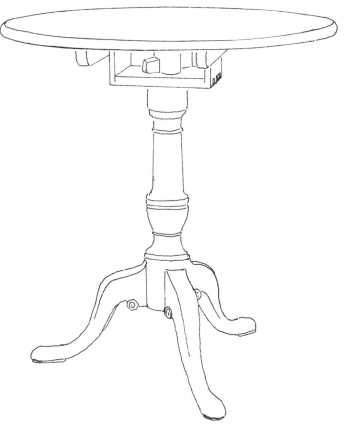

17-9B. North Carolina Queen Anne, 28" h, 1760 – 1780.

Chapter 18 – Card Tables

Until now we have seen tables that are set up either by raising a pair of drop leaves or by bringing down a tilting top. Now we will survey tables that are unique in having a single large leaf that folds over and rests on the top of the table when not in use. These card, or gaming, tables are an old form, first appearing in the William and Mary period at the turn of the seventeenth century, then continuing to be produced in baroque, rococo, and neoclassical styles until the eve of the Civil War — for almost 150 years. Whatever the style, they all operate in the same basic fashion. Each has a single large folding leaf that conforms to the shape of the top and rests on the top when that table is not in use. Normally the top, the leaf, and the apron are all of the same shape.

While we will see some earlier examples, the great majority of American card tables postdate the Revolution. Then they became very popular, so much so that of those you see in shops and at auctions, almost all will be Federal rather than Colonial, neoclassical rather than rococo. In spite of their rather light construction, there are so many surviving Federal card tables that one gets the impression that Americans celebrated their independence by playing cards every single day except, of course, on the Sabbath, which would have been sinful. A more sensible explanation is that not only were they the height of Federal fashion, but also, their lightness and portability made them useful for a variety of uses, not just for playing cards, but also for light meals, writing, and sewing. Folded and set against walls or under mirrors, they made inexpensive pier tables.

Card tables were usually sold in pairs, sometimes in double pairs. So popular were they in Federal America that a great many, perhaps most, seem to have been made on speculation for sale in retail shops or warerooms. This is probably why they often carry labels, initials, or signatures. Analysis of labeled and signed tables indicate that cabinetmakers tended to specialize in certain types of tables. For instance, John Dunlap II tended to make tables having square sides and elliptic fronts; Jacob Forster was inclined to make semicircular tables.

Of necessity, this discussion is limited. There is only so much that can be covered in a chapter, and in the bibliography there are suggestions for further reading. Here Federal card tables are something of a special case, for among the many books devoted to periods and regions, there is one remarkable little volume that deals only with Federal card tables, and should you seek further information, there is no better source than *The Work of Many Hands: Card Tables in Federal America, 1790 – 1820* by Benjamin A Hewitt, Patrica E. Kane, and Gerald W. R. Ward. This wonderful study covers every facet of Hepplewhite and Sheraton-style card tables: regional design and construction details, leg turning patterns, secondary woods, and inlays and patterns of veneering. That is the good news. The bad news is that this slim volume, published in conjunction with an exhibition of Federal card tables by Yale University in 1982, had only one limited printing. While copies can sometimes be found on the Internet, they are very expensive. However, should you be able locate a copy, perhaps in a major area library, you might discretely copy a few of the more informative pages. I'm sure you will not be the first.

In the following sections, particular note is made of the shapes of the tops and leaves of card tables. This is a good starting point, for shape is both helpful in determining identity and comes most immediately to the eye. Because a shape fashionable in one area is often seen in other areas, I then branch into regional construction details and secondary woods for further identification. However, this approach has its limits, for among the thousands of surviving Federal card tables, there are innumerable shapes. Hewitt, Kane, and Ward identify no less than twenty-six, but there are probably as many more again to be found among hundreds of inventive cabinetmakers. This chapter can only illustrate the more common regional patterns. Should you encounter another shape, you might try to locate a copy of *The Work of Many Hands* and see if a similar example is illustrated there, and if so, where it might have been made.

Most card tables were designed for four players and are within an inch or so of 36" wide. A few seem to have been planned for additional players, or to double as dining or side tables, and are 40" – 42" wide. More commonly, you will encounter smaller tables that are only about 30" wide. These unusual sizes are not region specific, although most are urban products. Diminutive card tables seem to have been particularly favored in Rhode Island, for a significant number of the standard Rhode Island card tables like that illustrated in figure 18-2A are less than the normal 36" width.

Because card tables were produced for so long, and in so many styles, this survey is divided into two parts: first a short review of tables made prior to the Revolution in the Queen Anne and Chippendale styles, then a more extensive survey of the great many neoclassical tables produced after the Revolution. Here you will notice that the same regional preferences in the shape of the leaves on breakfast or Pembroke tables are also seen in card tables. The top of a New York card table is likely to be much the same shape as the top of a New York breakfast table.

18-1 Massachusetts Queen Anne and Chippendale card tables. Gaming tables with projecting circular corners were the height of fashion in the middle years of the eighteenth century, and although you are very unlikely to encounter one of these grand "turret-top" tables, we might look at both a Boston and a Philadelphia example because they illustrate the differences in the development of the same form in the New England and Middle Atlantic colonies. The Boston table in figure 18-1A is much lighter and more delicate in feeling than the similar Philadelphia table illustrated in figure 18-4A. Typically the legs will be rather slim and the knees uncarved, and the legs will terminate in pad feet raised on shallow disks. Unlike a Federal card table, a Queen Anne or Chippendale table will often have a drawer in the apron, which in a Boston table will usually be relatively small. While not unattractive, the neoclassical pull on this drawer is a later addition.

Somewhat more common are Massachusetts Chippendale tables having the projecting square corners shown in figure 18-1B. This is the standard form of Massachusetts rococo card table, easier to make than a turret-top, and yet still providing the outset corners on which to set candles. The square facade of this table is reminiscent of the blocking so fashionable in Massachusetts during this period. Most of these tables have ball and claw feet, often in conjunction with some carving on the knees. Most all are made of mahogany. The glue blocks that fasten the top will normally be white pine.

18-1A. Boston Queen Anne, 1740 – 1760.

18-1B. Massachusetts Chippendale, 1750 – 1780.

18-2 Rhode Island Chippendale card tables. Rhode Island furniture tends to be both distinctive and conservative. This is also true of card tables, where cabinetmakers employed a restrained design that is not only unique to Rhode Island, but also, does not appear to have been produced anywhere else, not even in England. In common with other Rhode Island furniture, there is relatively little variation once a successful design has been developed, and the table in figure 18-2A is typical of a great many Rhode Island card tables in the early federal period. Most have a shallow serpentine front and sides with blocked ends, a row of gouged notches on the folding leaf, and small pierced brackets where the legs meet the apron. This table has molded legs, but you will often see the stop-fluting that was so fashionable in Rhode Island. Similar tables, made of cherry, were sometimes made in Connecticut. These distinctive card tables are quite the most common New England Chippendale style card tables, and perhaps for good reason, for most all are federal rather than colonial — and as such, are part and parcel of the vast numbers of card tables produced after the Revolution. They are typically a few inches narrower than the normal 36". The table shown here is only 33" wide. A significant number are no more than 24" – 30" wide. Why diminutive card tables were favored in Rhode island is a question I'll leave to the scholars.

Not all Rhode Island card tables have serpentine fronts and sides. Many retain the notched edges and pierced brackets, but then have simpler straight sides like the table shown in figure 18-2B. Although the brackets on this table are a rococo feature, the rather slender Hepplewhite legs are very much neoclassical. This is a budget effort, better quality may have inlaid patera and line inlay on the legs. While this table has the notched edges that were so popular in Rhode Island, you will also see molded and rounded edges. Rhode Island card tables seldom have the wide drawer so often seen in square card tables, probably because the beds of these tables were often cross-braced. Some Newport tables avoid this problem by having a small drawer worked into the end.

That square card tables were fashionable in Rhode Island does not mean that a square New England table will always be from Rhode Island, for they are such a logical approach to the requirement for a conservative and moderately priced card table that they might be made anywhere. Square card tables with Marlborough or Hepplewhite legs and full width drawers were also produced in coastal Massachusetts and New Hampshire. However, these will lack the notched edges and pierced brackets seen in Rhode Island tables.

18-2A. Rhode Island Chippendale, 1770 – 1790.

18-2B. Rhode Island Hepplewhite, 1780 – 1800.

18-3A. New York Chippendale, 1760 – 1775.

18-3B. New York Chippendale, 1760 – 1775.

18-3 New York Chippendale card tables. Middle Atlantic Chippendale card tables are very different from New England products, being heavier and more Georgian in appearance. Although pre-Revolutionary New York card tables are fairly rare, we nevertheless will consider two examples, for both illustrate features often seen in New York tables. The first is the classic form of New York rococo card table with serpentined front and sides, gadrooned apron, five carved cabriole legs, and ball and claw feet (18-3A). Although the outset square corners, the cabriole legs, and the ball and claw feet are also seen in Massachusetts tables, this card table is very different, not only in the gadrooned apron and shaping of the facade, but in the use of a separate fifth swing leg. The carved knee blocks at the tops of the cabriole legs also differ from New England practice in that they do not flow smoothly up into the apron as seen in figure 18-1B. Serpentine-front tables seldom have a drawer in the curved front. In lieu of this, many New York card tables have a small drawer in the rear behind the swing rail.

As in other regions, a customer might request a moderately priced table, and the square card table in figure 18-3B might have been the result. That this table was produced in New York is suggested by the rather solid, Georgian appearance, the turned cabriole legs, and the large, blocky ball and claw feet. Somewhat more costly versions of these tables will have shaped cabriole legs and applied gadrooning across the front and sides. Whatever the quality, New York rococo card tables are almost invariably made of mahogany and have ball and claw feet.

18-4 Pennsylvania Chippendale card tables. Turret-top card tables were produced in New York, but they are very rare, and we will instead consider a Philadelphia table, although even these are so uncommon that you are unlikely to see one outside of a museum. While the Philadelphia turret-top table in figure 18-4A is the same basic shape as the Massachusetts turret-top table in figure 18-1A, it is very different in proportion and detail. Starting at the top, the apron is deeper and has an applied strip of gadrooning on the front and sides, the legs are thicker and more curved, the knees are deeply carved, and the legs terminate in typical Philadelphia ball and claw feet. New York turret-top tables are very similar, although the few I've seen do not have drawers in the front, perhaps because it was thought wiser to keep playing cards and counters in little drawers behind the swing rails where they would be out of the reach of inquisitive children.

Whatever the region, turret-top card tables are fairly rare. In Philadelphia, the standard Chippendale cabriole leg card table will be rectangular in shape as shown in figure 18-4B. As was noted earlier when surveying Pembroke tables, square tables were favored in Pennsylvania. While gadooning is not as common in Philadelphia as it is in New York, it is generally seen in the aprons of these fashionable rococo tables. Most Pennsylvania card tables of this period have the full-width drawer shown in this and in the following illustration. While card tables are usually made of mahogany, which is far and away the most fashionable wood in the last half of the eighteenth century, a number of these tables are made of walnut, which suggests that if you encounter a walnut Chippendale card table, it is likely to be from Pennsylvania.

Quite the most common Philadelphia card table, and probably the most common of all surviving rococo card tables, is the square table with blocked Marlborough legs produced in and around Philadelphia in the latter half of the eighteenth century. The table in figure 18-4C is the basic model of these popular tables. Most have the pierced brackets shown here. More expensive may have applied gadrooning in lieu of the half round molding at the base of the apron. These standard card tables are often made of walnut. So successful were square card tables that the form carried over into the Federal period, and later we will see a neoclassical version of the same basic table.

Similar tables were also made to some extent in New York. These differ from Philadelphia tables in usually not having a drawer and normally being made of mahogany. In New York fashion there is also likely to be a small drawer tucked in behind the swing rail.

Not all Philadelphia card tables are square, and before turning to Federal card tables, we might take a brief look at a high-style serpentine-top card table that was fashionable in Philadelphia just prior to the Revolution (18-4D). While not rectangular in shape, the gadrooning, the carved, pierced brackets, and the full-width drawer are very much in the Philadelphia taste. These grand tables are a perfect expression of the rococo style. They would have been equally at home in English drawing rooms.

The drawers in Philadelphia Chippendale card tables will normally have tulip poplar sides and backs and white cedar bottoms. The swing rails are very likely to be red oak, although oak is also seen in New York and Southern tables.

This survey of Queen Anne and Chippendale card tables ends at the border with Maryland, for Southern card tables that predate the Revolution are very rare. However, there are a few Maryland tables similar to the basic square Philadelphia type. These might be identified by somewhat atypical design features, and also perhaps because they employ yellow pine blocking.

18-4A. Philadelphia Chippendale, 1750 – 1770.

18-4B. Philadelphia Chippendale, 1750 – 1780.

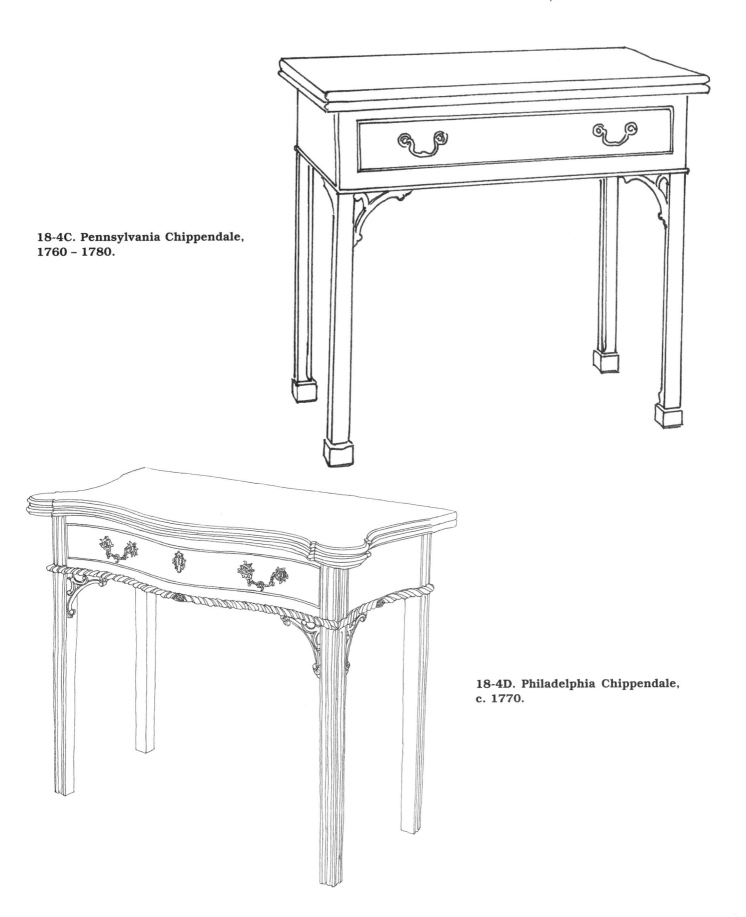

18-4C. Pennsylvania Chippendale, 1760 – 1780.

18-4D. Philadelphia Chippendale, c. 1770.

18-5 Northern New England neoclassical card tables. We will begin neoclassical card tables with four tables produced in northern New England, that is, north of the border of Massachusetts in New Hampshire, Maine, and Vermont. The first is a simple red-painted rural table that was perhaps made in New Hampshire, but could have been produced in almost any small town in America in the first decades of the nineteenth century (18-5A). That this particular table is from New England, and also from somewhere north of Boston, is suggested by the birch primary wood, which was particularly favored in New Hampshire.

Many of these country tables do not operate in the manner normal to a card table. Instead of the folding leaf being supported by a swinging rear leg, all the legs are fixed and the top swivels on an offset wooden pivot so that the leaf rests on the bed of the table. Also, the leaf will be fastened to the top with inexpensive cast-iron butt hinges rather than the usual brass card table hinges that are fastened to the corners of the leaves. Swivel-top card tables came into use with the introduction of the pedestal-type card table in the second decade of the nineteenth century, but are also likely to be found vernacular tables.

Here it might be noted that rural New England card tables are typically made of local hardwoods: birch, cherry, or maple. That a card table is made of cherry does not mean that it is from Connecticut. When there is a drawer, it will usually be made of white pine if north and west of Boston, perhaps poplar to the south along the coast. The swing rails will usually be either birch or soft maple, sometimes white pine or cherry, and chestnut if from Rhode Island. Later we will see that different woods were favored in the Middle Atlantic and the South.

Next we might look at another rural card table, but a more sophisticated example, with a bowed inlaid front and nicely turned Sheraton-style legs. The birch table in figure 18-5B was probably made in either Maine or Vermont in the second decade of the nineteenth century. This is a more rural table than it may seem in this drawing, for the workmanship is of the simplest kind and the folding leaf has been attached to the top with a pair

of small butt hinges. We will see the unusual cone shape at the top of the legs again in the next chapter in a Maine light stand (19-8B). Here it might be noted that Federal card tables produced in small New England communities such as Concord, New Hampshire, and Saco, Maine, are surprisingly sophisticated in the use of veneered inlay. Not only were thin veneers of figured woods available, but there was the skill to properly prepare the ground and lay the inlay. This skill may have come from journeymen moving north from Massachusetts to find employment in these growing communities.

The best known New Hampshire Federal card tables are those having the square ends and shallow elliptic front shown in figure 18-5C. Sometimes these elegantly simple tables are attributed to the shop of John Dunlap II (1784 – 1869), on the basis of a labeled cherrywood table in the Garvan Collection. This table is made of maple, which was sometimes used in New Hampshire for card tables, but was seldom used elsewhere. The elliptic front was popular throughout northern New England, and many of these tables were produced in Massachusetts, often with reeded Sheraton legs. A few were made in Rhode Island and New York. New Hampshire tables frequently have a three-part light wood facade of veneered figured birch or maple, often with an oval rather than a rectangle in the center. As you would expect, rural New England card tables are likely to be made of local woods, have simple facades, and be more stoutly made than urban card tables.

Another form of card table associated with New Hampshire has a facade that is flat at the ends, then swells, or bows, in the center. In the next section we will see much the same shape in a Sheraton table, but here we will consider a distinctive Portsmouth version with tapered legs and small canted corners (18-5D). In price books, these rather strange tables are described as "square with elliptic front, canted corners." Whatever the shape of the sides or the type of leg, the feature to watch for in northern New England tables is the elliptic bow in the center of an otherwise flat front.

18-5A. New England Hepplewhite, 1800 – 1810.

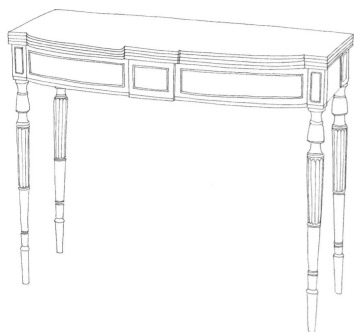

18-5B. New England Sheraton, 1815 – 1820.

18-5C. New Hampshire Hepplewhite, 1800 – 1820.

18-5D. Portsmith Hepplewhite, 1800 – 1815.

18-6 Massachusetts neoclassical card tables. This will be a longer than usual section, for the great majority of Federal New England gaming tables were produced in Massachusetts, most of them probably in and around Boston, then east and north up the coast through Salem and Newburyport. Should you be baffled by what appears to be a New England card table, and reduced to the sorry expedient of simply guessing where it was made, coastal Massachusetts would not be a bad choice. It might also be noted that Massachusetts and New York exhibit the greatest diversity among Federal card tables. Although a great many card tables were produced in Philadelphia and Baltimore, these two cities produced a limited number of fashionable designs.

Here we should pause to consider central and northern New England Federal card tables in general, for whatever the particular shape, they have a number of common features that will suggest Massachusetts, New Hampshire, and Maine workmanship, even if the specific location is not clear. As a group, they tend to be economically and lightly constructed, perhaps not altogether different from the rather casual construction seen in Boston blockfront chests of drawers. The rails are apt to be thin. When curved, they are either made from single boards sawn to shape or made up from one or two laminates. The ovolo quarter-round corner seen on many Massachusetts tables (18-6B) was usually made by slitting a thin board with a row of parallel saw cuts about a quarter inch apart so that the board could be bent without breaking. The saw cuts were then filled with glue and reinforced with coarse muslin glued to the back of the apron.

Normally, card tables made in New England will have three fixed legs and one flyleg that swings out to support the leaf. The flyleg, when closed, simply butts up against inner rail. South of Massachusetts the top of the flyleg is usually given a little shelf, so that when closed it fits under the back rail and helps support the bed of the table.

The fly or swing legs on a Massachusetts or New Hampshire table usually pivot on square finger hinges. Because these project from the surface when the leg is swung, the inner and outer rails must be separated by thin filler blocks. This construction is also seen in some Providence, Rhode Island, card tables. Also, New England card tables seldom employ medial braces to stiffen the bed of the table. Lastly, to provide some additional support to the leaf, and to help keep it level with the top when open, there will often be little beveled tenons on the back of the top that fit into corresponding mortises in the edge of the leaf. These tenons are seldom seen in New England tables. These little construction differences are easy to spot; all you have to do is to look at the back of the table, feel under the rail for a gap between the inner and outer rails, and swing the flyleg out a few inches

The card table most indicative of Massachusetts workmanship has the elliptic front and serpentine ends shown in figure 18-6A. These very popular tables were primarily made in eastern Massachusetts — in and around Boston, up along the North Shore in Salem and Newburyport; and then in adjacent Portsmouth, New Hampshire. The form does not seem to have traveled south of Boston, although a few were produced in Rhode Island. So successful was this design that it carried over

into the Sheraton style, and many of these card tables have turned and reeded legs rather than the double tapered leg so often seen in northern New England. On better work there will usually be a three part facade between the two front legs, often with the central ellipse shown here. This also is a good indication of New England workmanship, for three part facades are seldom seen elsewhere. If you turn back to chapter 12, you will see the same serpentine ends and elliptic front in a North Shore dressing table.

The Hepplewhite card table in figure 18-6A has the double tapered leg that was so fashionable in northern New England. However, there is another form of this double taper. Furniture produced in and around Boston will sometimes have what might be called squat taper legs. With this kind of leg, the inlaid cuffs are set very low on the leg, and then there is about a two inch tapered section under the cuffs. The double taper is there, but it is much compressed. The result is rather heavy looking and not particularly attractive, and it does not seem to have been very successful. However, therein lies its value to us, for it is only seen in furniture made in and around Boston. If you come across these feet, you are looking at Boston workmanship.

The three shapes of card tables most popular in the Boston area were those having serpentine ends and elliptic front, those with ovolo corners, and those of a circular or demilune shape. We have seen the first. Next we will look at the second, a simpler table with square ends, a flat front, and ovolo corners (18-6B). This is a budget example: the facade and the corners are single panels of mahogany veneer, and there is no inlay other than geometric tablets at the top of the legs and a little stringing at the base of the apron. Better-quality tables will usually have three part facades like that shown in the previous illustration, or a single part facade decorated with a large ellipse. A number of these tables have a separate fifth swing leg. Most all have Hepplewhite legs, often with the double taper shown in Figure 18-6A. Square card tables with ovolo corners were produced to some extent in all regions. Later we will see a New York example. This corner treatment is often seen in Massachusetts and New York breakfast tables.

The third form of Boston card table is more of a challenge, for circular or demilune card tables were produced in all regions, and among the average grade of table there are few obvious differences. The table in figure 18-6C is typical of somewhat better-quality Massachusetts demilune tables, having the facades bordered with string inlay, then an oval patera in the center of each facade. Other tables of this type may be decorated with paterae and bellflowers on the legs. However, many have no more decoration than a little stringing, and are not all that different from similar Middle Atlantic card tables. To identify a Massachusetts table, remember that conservative design was favored in Boston, that a Massachusetts table will usually have a single swing leg that does not support the bed of the table, that the swing leg will pivot on a square finger hinge, and therefore, the inner and outer rails will be separated by thin filler blocks. In addition, there will seldom be medial bracing, and the swing rail will almost always be either maple or birch.

A card table with elliptic front and serpentine ends, like that shown in figure 18-6A, may have either Hepplewhite or Sheraton legs, but with the introduction of outset corner columns, the shape of the top was altered to provide short flat surfaces on either side of the round leg. In price books these tables were defined as "square with elliptic front, half-elliptic ends, ovolo corners." In addition to the flat surfaces on either side of the corner columns, the ends are now half-elliptic rather than serpentine in shape. The table in figure 18-6D is a less expensive example with the apron veneered in tiger maple. In other tables the facade is divided into either three or five panels; five if each flat is given its own treatment. A few Salem tables have raised carved panels in the centers of the aprons. Tables of this type were produced to some extent in Boston, but were especially popular up along the North Shore. Note that the facade of this table is very similar to the facade of the New Hampshire table with canted corners that was illustrated in the previous section.

Quite the most common form of Massachusetts cookie-corner card table has both serpentine front and sides, or is, as identified in price books, "square with serpentine front, serpentine ends, ovolo corners over colonettes." The table in figure 18-6E is typical of a great many of these tables with the three-part facade that is so often seen in northern coastal New England. There are many minor variations in this very successful design. Boston tables are apt to have the skirts or folding leaves edged by half-round lunette inlay; Salem tables leaf carvings at the tops of the front legs. These card tables were produced in and around Boston, then northward along the coast as far as Saco, Maine. In common with card tables having elliptic fronts and serpentine ends, they were seldom produced south of Boston, although there are a few Rhode Island examples.

Here it might be noted that light wood veneers are seen everywhere in these popular Massachusetts card tables. Unlike case work, they should not be associated just with Portsmouth and North Shore workmanship.

With the advent of the late Federal, or classical, period, Massachusetts card tables become both heavier and more diverse, and we will end this long section with two of the better known forms of these tables, the first a Sheraton table that was very popular in the Salem area, the second a Boston expression of the rampant classicism so often seen in this period.

Among New England cities, Salem had an unusual affection for the carving employed with the Sheraton style, and nowhere is this more often seen than in the somewhat heavy-looking late Federal card tables fashionable in Salem in the 1820s (18-6F). These tables typically have serpentine ends and fronts, often with the outset elliptical center shown here. In addition to the carving at the tops of the legs, the legs on many of these tables have additional leafy, bell-shaped carvings just below the aprons. Later versions become simpler, carving giving way to ring turning and spiral-carved tapering legs. While the carving on these lushly decorated tables is often attributed to Samuel McIntire, so many survive that it is obvious that he must have been but one of at least half a dozen or more carvers working in the Salem area.

While the Hepplewhite and the Sheraton styles were inspired by the classical world, the classical, or classical revival, style that followed employed a far more literal interpretation of Greek, Roman, and Egyptian motifs, and everywhere we see klismos, or sabre, legs; paw feet; harps; and cornucopia. Among card tables the most common expression of this style is stringed lyres, probably because the shape so perfectly lent itself to a pedestal table. The lyre-base table in figure 18-6G is a handsome example of a common type of Boston table. In Boston fashion, the strings are simulated with dark wood inlay. Other Boston tables may employ brass rods for the strings.

18-6A. Massachusetts Hepplewhite, 1790 – 1810.

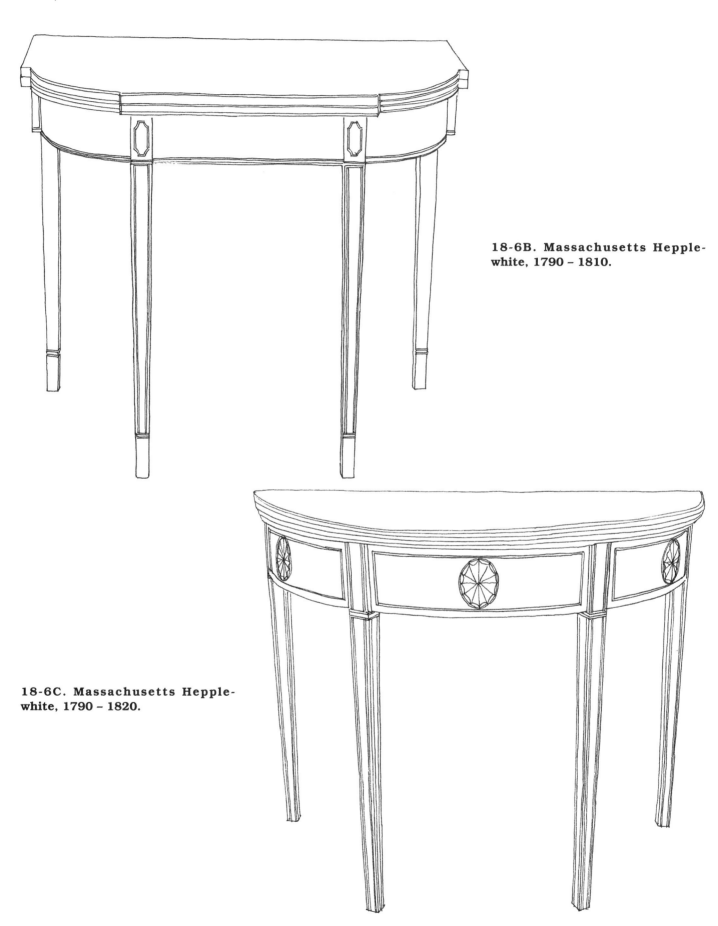

**18-6B. Massachusetts Hepple-
white, 1790 – 1810.**

**18-6C. Massachusetts Hepple-
white, 1790 – 1820.**

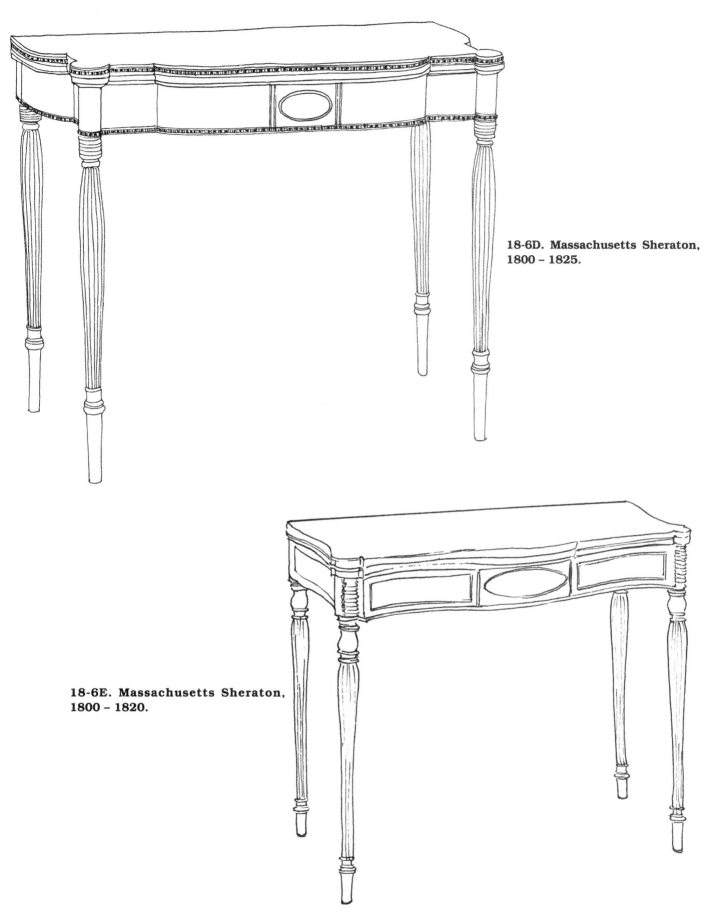

18-6D. Massachusetts Sheraton, 1800 – 1825.

18-6E. Massachusetts Sheraton, 1800 – 1820.

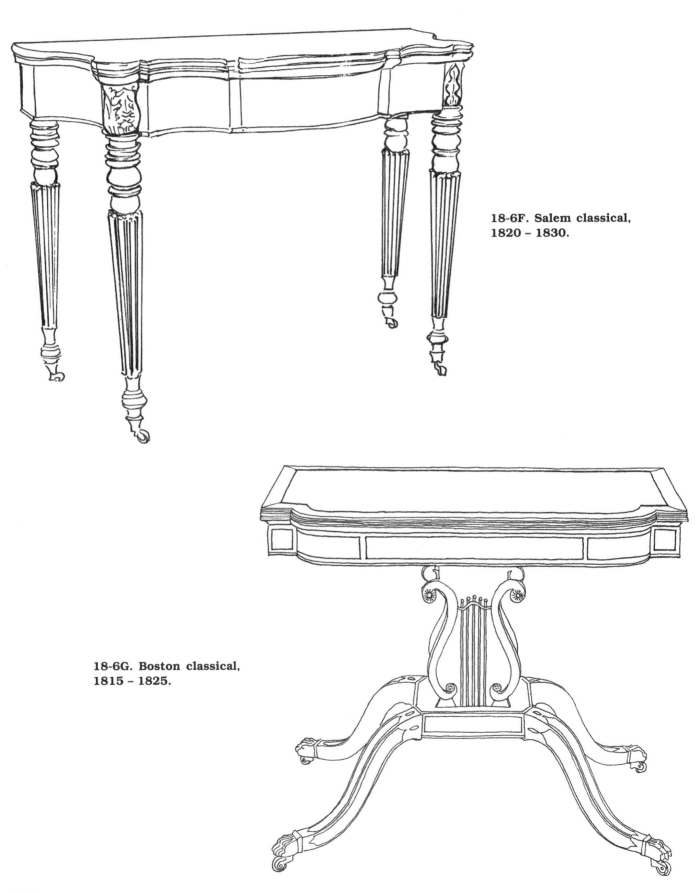

**18-6F. Salem classical,
1820 – 1830.**

**18-6G. Boston classical,
1815 – 1825.**

18-7 Rhode Island neoclassical card tables. In this section we will discuss two neoclassical Rhode Island card tables, but actually there are three, for we have already seen a square Rhode Island card table, which although described as Chippendale in the auction catalog, had tapering neoclassical legs and should more properly have been identified as Federal or Hepplewhite rather than Chippendale (18-2B). Although Providence and Newport are less than a hundred miles from Boston, we will see that Rhode Island card tables are more Middle Atlantic than New England in design and construction.

The two most common shapes of Providence card tables are two of the three most common in Massachusetts: those with circular and ovolo tops. This seems to have been in part due to the influence of Newport, where the circular or demilune tables were much favored, and also to the many Massachusetts cabinetmakers who moved down after the Revolution to seek opportunity in this growing city. Although similar in shape to Massachusetts card tables, Rhode Island tables are very different in design and construction. An ovolo corner card table like that shown in figure 18-6B, if made in Providence, will probably have knuckle rather than finger hinges, no filler blocks between the inner and outer rails, a flyleg that fits under the back rail, and one or two little beveled tenons to help support the leaf — all in all, a better-made table.

While circular and ovolo card tables are found everywhere, there is one table that is suggestive of Providence workmanship, and although it appears to have been only moderately popular, it is seldom seen elsewhere. This table has a D-shape with a slightly bowed front, as illustrated in figure 18-7A — what was called "square with rounded corners." Unlike ovolo tables, the ends were simply rounded and not inset, although to soften the curve, the front was given a slight elliptical curve. These unusual tables were also produced to some extent in Newburyport and Salem, but here there should be no confusion as to origin, for as has been noted, Massachusetts workmanship was very different. The form was also produced to some extent in New York City, but in the Sheraton style and with a fifth swing leg. Here it might be noted that Rhode Island cabinetmakers often decorated the edges of the tops and leaves of card tables with rows of stringing or banding. Alternatively, you will sometimes observe the rows of gouged notches that are so often seen on square Rhode Island tables (18-2A).

In Newport, the new neoclassical style was treated very conservatively. The most common card tables are circular with square, tapered Hepplewhite legs. The turned and reeded Sheraton leg is never seen in Newport card tables, and only seldom in those from Providence. Although the Newport card table in figure 18-7B looks much like the Massachusetts table we saw in the previous section, it is a very different table. It is well made, with the bookend inlay so often seen in Rhode Island and Connecticut. Look at the back you will see neatly made knuckle hinges, and that both the rear legs pivot out to provide support to the folding leaf. When there are not two swing legs, there will be four fixed legs and a fifth — and sometimes a sixth — flyleg.

Lastly, it might be noted that in addition to white pine, poplar, birch, and maple, you are quite likely to see some chestnut in a Rhode Island table, often in the fly rail, or fly rails.

18-7A. Providence Hepplewhite, c. 1805.

18-7B. Newport Hepplewhite, 1790 – 1810.

18-8 Connecticut neoclassical card tables. Connecticut card tables are relatively uncommon in spite of the popularity of card tables after the Revolution and the amount of surviving Connecticut furniture. This may be in part because most card tables, even in Connecticut, were made of mahogany, and there is a significant amount of Connecticut workmanship that is not identified as such simply because it is not made of cherry. This problem is compounded by the many Massachusetts and New York influences seen in Connecticut furniture.

As you would expect of pieces made in a rural environment, most identified Connecticut card tables are either square or circular, with the Massachusetts ovolo shape coming in a distant third. In Rhode Island and New York fashion, they tend to have knuckle hinges and will usually employ one or two beveled tenons each to help support the leaves. Most have the tapered Hepplewhite legs that were the norm in rural New England, then the four fixed and one flyleg that are so often seen in New York.

Perhaps half are square in shape with tapered Hepplewhite legs like those on the cherry card table illustrated in Figure 18-8A. Aside from the remarkable lower legs, which would seem to have been a Boston Seymour inspiration, this table is typical of a number of Connecticut tables in having a rectangular bed with a gadrooned skirt. Many of these tables, in New York fash-

ion, have single small drawers tucked in behind the flylegs. Applied gadrooning is often seen on Connecticut casework, the idea perhaps having been borrowed from New York.

The circular cherry table in figure 18-8B exhibits the naive enthusiasm so often seen in Connecticut furniture. Although simply made of local woods, it is generously decorated with an inlaid sunburst at the rear of the leaf, paterae at the top of the legs, then rather strange icicles extending down the legs. In lieu of the usual swinging flyleg, the fifth leg slides out to support the folding leaf, a feature employed in other Connecticut tables. This was probably done to avoid the complication of a swinging leg. That sliding legs are seen in rural Connecticut card tables does not mean that this unusual feature is unique to this area, for this simple and logical workaround is seen in rural tables from other regions.

Also, while cherry is indeed suggestive of Connecticut workmanship, this prince of cabinet woods was used elsewhere in card tables. As noted earlier, there is a lovely cherry card table with the label of John Dunlap II in the Garvan Collection at Yale University. What is more suggestive of Connecticut workmanship is the somewhat naive embellishment and idiosyncratic design.

18-8A. Connecticut Hepplewhite, 1790 – 1800.

18-8B. Connecticut Hepplewhite, c. 1800.

18-9 New York neoclassical card tables. Now we arrive at the other major source of neoclassical card tables. The city of New York grew rapidly in population and wealth following the Revolution, first as the temporary home of the new Federal government, then as a center of commerce. Perhaps nowhere is this better expressed than in the quality and diversity of New York card tables. However, before covering specific types, we will, as before, pause to discuss the features common to these tables.

The affluence of a city is usually expressed in its furniture, and this is very evident in New York card tables. As a group, they are well made of the best woods, with generous use of choice mahogany veneers. For strength and stability, they normally have four fixed legs and a separate flyleg, employ horizontally and vertically laminated rails with many laminations, often has a medial brace, and almost always have either one, two, or three beveled tenons to support the folding leaf. Facades are typically single units whose design then repeated on the sides, as seen in the table in figure 18-9A. Veneer is normally laid on a base of white pine, laminations are made-up of white pine or poplar, and cherry is employed for the swing rails.

By far the most common New York Hepplewhite card table is the "square with ovolo corners" form that was also very popular in Boston. However, it is not difficult to tell the two apart. The card table illustrated in figure 18-9A is a perfect expression of New York taste: a single large oval in the facade that is repeated on the side panels, four fixed legs and one flyleg, and elegantly thin legs. The flyleg will pivot on either finger or knuckle hinges. The curved corners will be made up of multiple thin vertical laminations — very different from the parallel saw cuts seen in Massachusetts. Although card tables with a fifth leg are not rare in Massachusetts, you will never see the double taper shown in figure 18-6A.

New York circular or demilune tables are also very likely to have five legs, and not infrequently, six legs, as shown in figure 18-9B. Circular tables often have inlaid fans of light wood at the backs of the tops, and conforming fan-shaped mahogany veneer panels extending out from the fans to the edges of the leaves, which make for spectacular tops. The legs on this large table are decorated with oval floral panels and inverted cup inlay, but you will often see oval paterae and bellflowers, the bellflowers often separated, in New York fashion, by light wood oval stringing. Most card tables are of a standard 36" width, but this table is 39" wide, and to stiffen the top there are two diagonal braces extending from the front legs to a block at the center of the back rail. Unfortunately, oversize card tables are not region specific. From time to time, they were produced in all the major urban centers.

New York was so fashion conscious that the new Hepplewhite style was soon superseded by Sheraton, and shortly thereafter by Empire and Classical, and to survey these changes I will show you half a dozen fashionable Sheraton and Classical tables. With the advent of the Sheraton style, both New York and Philadelphia cabinetmakers turned to dark, monochromatic mahogany veneers, while Massachusetts cabinetmakers continued to employ light mahoganies in conjunction with panels of light figured maple and birch, not employing darker veneers until introduction of the classical, and even here often retaining some light wood inlays. Although we will see a number of different designs, the most striking difference between New England and Middle Atlantic card tables is the color. A dark and monochromatic Sheraton card table will probably be from New York or Philadelphia.

Earlier it was noted that canted corners were very popular in New York, and we will start with a Sheraton card table of this form (18-9C). In addition to the canted corners, this table has a number of New York features. First though, it might be mentioned that *not all* New York card tables have five legs, and as was noted in the chapter on dining tables, additional legs should be interpreted as no more than an indication of New York workmanship. However, that this table has only four legs does not mean that one is a flyleg, for by this time swiveling tops were already being introduced in New York.

Aside from the canted corners, what is suggestive of New York in this table is the inverted vase-form feet and the brass casters. Although castors are almost always found on the heavier Classical card tables, they are seldom seen on Sheraton tables except those from New York City, where they are so common as to have evidently been the normal treatment. Lastly, it should be noted that some of these tables have carved paw feet, not always a happy choice, for they tend to overpower the rather slender Sheraton legs.

When surveying breakfast tables, it was noted that New York Pembroke tables often have double- or triple-elliptic shaped leaves. As you might expect, the same shape is frequently seen in New York card tables. The double-elliptic table in figure 18-9D is a perfect expression of New York taste: four fixed and one flyleg, monochromatic veneer, and elegantly thin reeded legs with inverted vase form feet and brass swiveling castors. Double elliptic card tables were also produced to some extent in Philadelphia, but they are a very different product, being heavier in appearance, with four legs rather than five, and having the Philadelphia shape of foot. Also, they are seldom fitted with castors.

Pedestal form card tables present a problem, for the placement of the legs prevents them from being placed flush against walls when not in use. The New York solution was to fit such a table with a mechanical action such that the back legs pivot to parallel when the table is not in use. To accomplish this, the two rear legs were connected by iron rods and hinged iron braces to two hinged flys, so that the legs swing out when the corresponding flys are pulled out. Because the mechanism is hidden in the column and under the top, this kind of table is often called a "trick leg" table. Most New York versions of these very expensive tables have double or triple elliptical tops like the top on the handsome table shown in figure 18-9E. This table also illustrates the acanthus leaf carving so often seen on the legs of New York classical tables.

Although popularly identified with New York, and with Duncan Phyfe, trick-leg tables were also made in Philadelphia, and in greater numbers than is apparently realized, for they are sometimes not correctly identified in auction catalogs. A Philadelphia trick-leg table has a number of features that differ from New York practice: there will normally be a shallow apron under the top which may be decorated with a pair of square dies and acorn drop finials; when the legs are leaf carved, the carving will terminate square across rather than tapering off as seen in figure 18-9E; and lastly, the top and leaves will probably be of the elliptic front and serpentine corner shape seen on many Philadelphia card tables (18-10C). Trick-leg tables are more singular than one might think, for they were only made in America, and then only in New York or Philadelphia. Unlike so much of the furniture we have discussed, there are no bothersome little exceptions.

Trick-leg tables were much more expensive than other card tables, and although made in some quantity in New York and Philadelphia, were produced for no more than about ten years. More common are card tables with four legs, the cost of the additional leg more than offset by avoiding a trick-leg mechanism. The table in figure 18-9F is typical of many fine tables produced in New York in the first decades of the nineteenth century. Most have the canted corners so favored in the city. When a little more money was available, there was leaf carving rather than reeding on the tops of the legs. All the legs are fixed and the top swivels to open. Sadly, within a few short years these handsome tables became heavier and more ornate, and lose the classical elegance of this table.

In chapter 16 we saw a grand New York dining table, on which, in lieu of a pedestal, the top was supported by a cluster of small columns or colonettes that rose from a square base, that in turn was supported by four downswept legs. The form was very fashionable in New York City, from where you will often see colonette tables. There are even a few candlestands in which the pedestal is composed of a cluster of three colonettes. The swivel-top card table in figure 18-9G is typical of New York card tables, having canted corners, acanthus-carved columns, and downswept acanthus-carved legs. Some examples have double elliptic or D-shape tops; later versions may have carved animal-form legs and feet. The form lent itself to all sorts of embellishments, and within a few years cabinetmakers were making card tables that, in lieu of colonettes, had twin lyres, large carved eagles, and carved-acanthus scrolls. On some, the top is supported by gilt and ebonized carved winged caryatids or pairs of gilt and ebonized winged griffins. Although frequently published, these remarkable tables were very expensive, even by New York standards, and are quite rare.

Lastly, it should be noted again that colonette-form tables, while most fashionable in New York City, were produced to some extent in Boston and Philadelphia. Although these may resemble New York tables, they differ in detail, in the shape of the top, in the turning of the colonettes, and in the design of the carving.

Finally, I will venture a bit deeper into the classical and illustrate a late Federal card table that was fashionable in New York in the 1820s (18-9H). Unlike trick-leg card tables, which are often attributed to the shop of Duncan Phyfe (in spite of there being no labeled examples), a number of these tables carry the label of Mr. Phyfe's Cabinet Warehouse at 170 Fulton Street. Similar card tables, usually with a pair of columns at each end, were made in Boston.

18-9A. New York Hepplewhite, 1790 – 1805.

18-9B. New York Hepplewhite, 1790 – 1805.

18-9C. New York Sheraton, 1800 – 1810.

18-9D. New York Sheraton, 1800 – 1810.

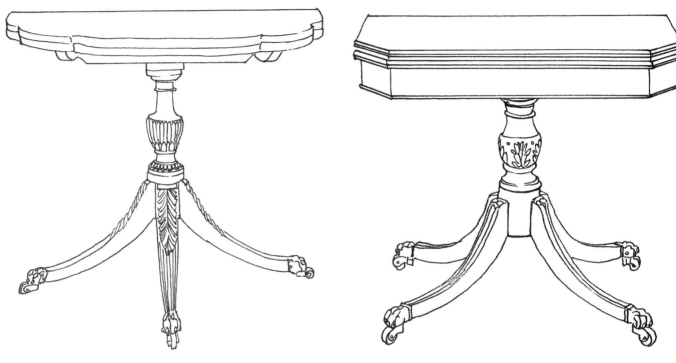

18-9E. New York classical, 1805 – 1815.

18-9F. New York classical, c. 1810.

18-9G. New York classical, 1805 – 1815.

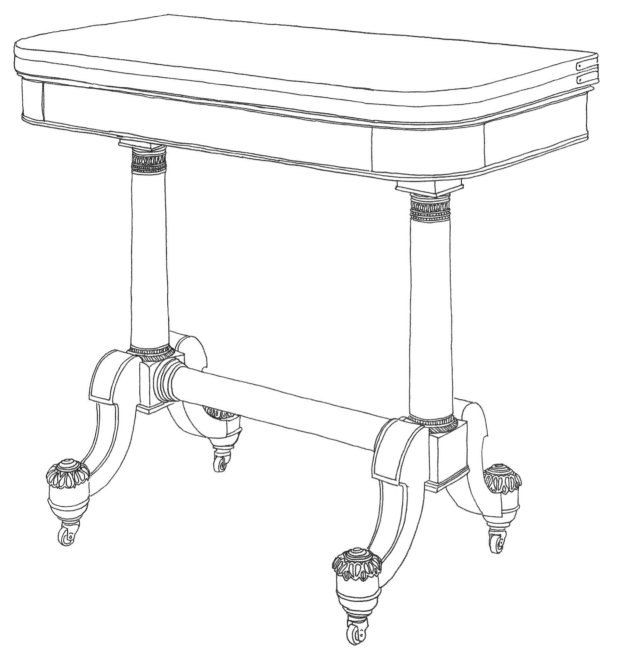

18-9H. New York classical, c. 1820.

18-10 Pennsylvania neoclassical card tables. For all the size of the city, which at the end of the century was still the largest urban center in America, Philadelphia had notably little diversity in gaming tables. In part this may have been due to a continuing affection for the rococo and a somewhat tardy acceptance of the new neoclassical styles. In any event, the result seems to have been no lack of card tables, but not as many different types.

Earlier, in section 18-4, we saw that square card tables with Marlborough legs were favored in Colonial Philadelphia. As you might expect, square card tables carry over into the Federal period, although in the process they acquire some neoclassical features. The table in figure 18-10A is typical of many produced in and around Philadelphia in the last decades of the eighteenth century. Although much the same form as the earlier Chippendale card table (18-4C), it is lighter and slimmer in proportion, has lost the pierced rococo brackets and acquired tapered neoclassical legs and spade feet. When not given spade feet, the legs will often be molded. Card tables of this type were made throughout the Delaware Valley, frequently of local woods: walnut, cherry, and occasionally maple. In the next section you will see a similar table that was made in the South.

Chapter 14 illustrated two Philadelphia sideboards with rounded ends and recessed serpentine centers, the kidney shape that was so fashionable in federal Philadelphia. This same shape, identified in price books as "kidney end, serpentine middle," is also the best-known form of Philadelphia card tables, even though it is but one of three fashionable types, and in any event, is also employed in Baltimore card tables. The table in figure 18-10B is typical of a great many of these tables, with four legs and a single unit facade bordered with light wood stringing. Often there will be a square tablet, either an inlay of light wood, or a slightly raised reserve, centered in the facade. Some tables are of a more complex form: the rounded corners are inset, the same ovolo shape seen in so many New York and

Massachusetts tables. Most of these card tables are Hepplewhite in style with square tapering legs. It is interesting that the word kidney was used to describe the shape in price books published in the early nineteenth century. It is not a modern invention.

With the introduction of the Sheraton style there comes a change in the shape of Philadelphia card tables. These somewhat later tables are "square with elliptic front, serpentine corners", as seen in figure 18-10C. Simpler versions of these popular tables will have rounded rather than serpentine ends. In chapter 16 we see the same shape in the leaves of Pennsylvania breakfast tables. Most of these Sheraton card tables are monochromatic, lacking even the stringing shown in the table in the previous illustration. The edges of the top and leaf are reeded, a feature also seen in many New York and Baltimore tables. The ball and button feet on this table is a common Pennsylvania pattern.

Although perhaps one in three Philadelphia card tables are circular in shape, I will not show you an example, for in truth, there is not much to show. Most are quite similar to the Massachusetts table illustrated in figure 18-6C, although you are unlikely to see paterae in the center of each panel. However, there are features that can tell us if such a table is likely to be from Philadelphia. In additional to a general conservatism, the table will be solidly built, the outer rail fastened directly to the inner rail, the flyleg pivoting on knuckle hinges. The fly rail will usually be made of either oak or yellow pine, rather than the cherry employed in New York, and the maple, birch, and chestnut seen in New England. Here also it might be noted that while mahogany was the norm for urban Federal card tables, some Philadelphia tables are made of walnut.

There is an old saying that a lyre-base table having a solid or closed lyre is from New England, while an open lyre is from the Middle Atlantic, New York or Philadelphia. Unlike some sayings, this is true, for the solid lyre shown in the table in figure 18-6G is indeed typical of Boston work, and the open lyre shown in the Philadelphia table in figure 18-10D is seen in Philadelphia and New York. However, it is not quite this simple, for both Philadelphia and Boston produced card tables of a hybrid form in which the lyre is somewhat three dimensional by being open in the center, but is not as completely open as illustrated in this figure. Here again, the shape of the top may help us to identify the city: Boston lyre-form tables will usually be square with an elliptic front, as shown in figure 18-6D; New York tables are likely to have either a double elliptic top to have canted corners; and Philadelphia tables are likely to be either square with an elliptic front as shown in figure 18-10G, or to have canted corners, or to have some form of the elliptic front and serpentine ends that were so fashionable in Philadelphia. When there is acanthus leaf carving on the legs, remember that in New York the carving will taper off, and in Philadelphia the carving will terminate square across.

18-10A. Pennsylvania Hepplewhite, 1790 – 1810.

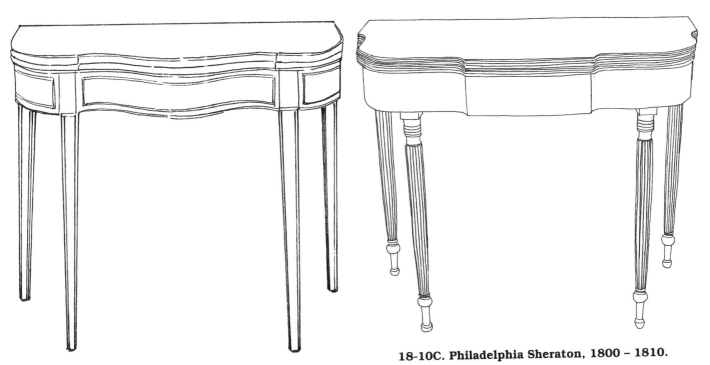

18-10C. Philadelphia Sheraton, 1800 – 1810.

18-10B. Philadelphia Hepplewhite, 1790 – 1810.

18-10D. Philadelphia classical, 1810 – 1820.

18-11 Southern neoclassical card tables. While Queen Anne and Chippendale card tables of Southern origin are very rare, there are quite a number of neoclassical examples, and in this last section we will consider four. Three of these are from Baltimore, which appears to have produced far more neoclassical card tables than any other Southern city. Except for Baltimore, where cabinetmakers were apt to employ popular New York and Philadelphia patterns, most Southern card tables will be either square or circular in shape.

Here we will first consider a common type of neoclassical Southern card table, a rather light, square table with a full-width drawer and Hepplewhite legs. The table shown in figure 18-11A is made of walnut, and the drawer is faced to resemble two short drawers. Similar card tables made of mahogany will most probably be from tidewater Maryland or Virginia. John Shaw was producing tables very much like this in Annapolis both before and after the Revolution. The principal problem in identifying these card tables is that they are very similar to card tables being produced in southeastern Pennsylvania, and indeed, you will sometimes see this type of table identified as either "Pennsylvania or Maryland." Here you might consider the secondary woods. An oak fly rail is not much help, for oak was used for fly rails in Philadelphia, Baltimore, and Annapolis. However, the use of a hard pine for the drawers and drawer slides would suggest a table produced in the South. Here also you might watch for atypical or idiosyncratic design or construction, such as the little bit of vertical facing that makes the drawer on this table appear to be two.

Among the Southern cities of the Federal period, Baltimore is something of a special case, for not only is the great majority of Southern urban furniture from Baltimore, but also, Baltimore cabinet work is distinctive. A Baltimore card table is very different from a New York or Philadelphia card table. Just as urban New England furniture is likely to be from eastern Massachusetts, so also urban Southern furniture is likely to be from Baltimore.

Baltimore card tables are similar to New York tables in that there is often a generous use of decorative inlay; light wood stringing around the edges of the tops and leaves; large shells centered in the tops of the leaves; and square or oval inlaid tablets at the tops of the legs, and a string of bellflowers below. However, here the resemblance ends. The swing legs on a Baltimore table will pivot on knuckle hinges and will overlap the bed of the table. Fly rails will usually be oak rather than cherry. Normally, both the back legs will swing, even on ovolo corner and kidney shaped tables. Lastly, there will generally be a medial brace running from front to back under the apron, not only on deep circular tables, where they might be expected, but also on ovolo and kidney shaped tables. Although Baltimore card tables often emulate popular New York and Philadelphia patterns, they are very different in design and construction.

About two of every three Baltimore card tables are circular, and we might consider one of these first. The demilune Hepplewhite table in figure 18-11B is modest by Baltimore standards, even though the facade and legs are bordered by light wood stringing and there are conch inlays at the top of the legs. Both the rear legs are likely to swing out to support the folding leaf, and there will probably be a front to back medial brace under the apron. Spade feet, fashionable in both England and New York, are often seen on Baltimore and Annapolis card tables. Here it might be noted that if there is a string of bellflowers on the legs, the middle petal will most likely be significantly longer than the two side pedals. Often the petals will be separated by a light wood dot.

When not circular, Baltimore card tables will usually be square, and here we will look at a late Federal example. If the table in figure 18-11C seems familiar, it is because you have seen very much the same design in a Baltimore Sheraton dining table from this same period (16-9B): the top and leaf edged with the same triple round molding; the same untapered legs with large, somewhat sharp-edged reeding; and the same ring turned feet. Also, this card table is unlike much Southern workmanship in having turned and reeded legs.

Baltimore pedestal-form card tables are also distinctive. Here again we have the same square top that was favored in Baltimore, then a pedestal with a wide, reed-carved bowl-shaped urn, and below this deeply reeded downswept legs (18-11D). Most of these tables have triple round molding edging the tops and leaves. In identifying late Federal Baltimore tables, watch for this edge molding and the large, rather exuberant reeding on the legs.

**18-11A. Southern Hepplewhite,
c. 1800.**

**18-11B. Baltimore Hepplewhite,
1795 – 1805.**

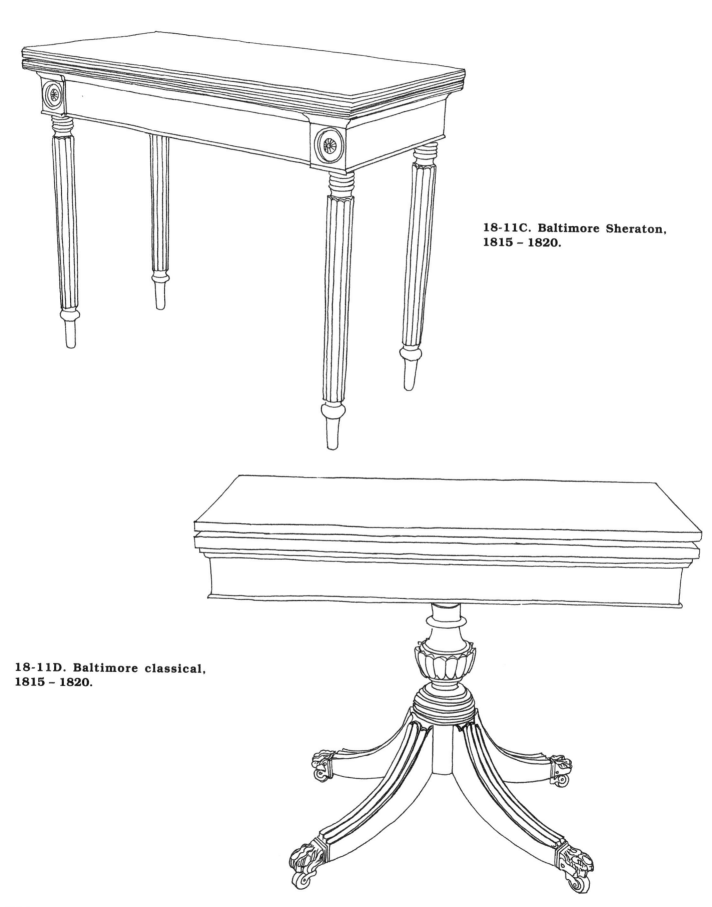

18-11C. Baltimore Sheraton, 1815 – 1820.

18-11D. Baltimore classical, 1815 – 1820.

This chapter covers a variety of small tables: candlestands, light stands, and worktables. Because there is little unanimity in the terms now used to describe these tables, and perhaps not all that much unanimity then, I will employ terms that are historically correct and yet still in use. *Candlestand* may sound modern, but it is actually an old word that fell into disuse when candles finally gave way to oil lamps. These small three-leg tables, when fitted with tilting tops and latches, were also called "snap tables," or sometimes just "snaps." Today they are identified both as stands and candlestands in books on period furniture, and as candle stands, stands, tables, and tip tables in auction catalogs. However, most often they are just called candlestands.

The ubiquitous little four-leg Federal side tables are also something of a muddle, being variously identified as stands, light stands, lamp stands, side tables, and worktables. Here we will call them light stands, which is both an old name and reflects what was once their primary function.

In deference to history, and to use, sewing tables are called worktables, if for no other reason than that sewing has traditionally been seen as "woman's work," which, of course, ignores the labors of many thousands of hatters, tailors, and sailmakers.

Candlestands have been in use for at least two hundred years, and are seen in William and Mary, Queen Anne, Chippendale, and neoclassical styles. For all their small size and simple form — a top, a column, and three legs — they exhibit remarkable variety. In addition to almost every imaginable shape of column, there are cabriole, arched, downswept, and turned legs, and oval, circular, square, and octagonal tops with dished tops and tray edges and with rounded, ovolo, and serpentine corners. One could fill a house with candlestands and yet have no two alike.

In identifying region we have two other types of tables to assist us. Candlestands are but scaled down pillar-form tea tables, and worktables are apt to be similar in detail to neoclassical card tables. In this chapter we will see Philadelphia candlestands almost identical to Philadelphia tea tables, and Massachusetts worktables that share design elements with Massachusetts card tables. They were all made by the same craftsmen for the same customers. When examining a Sheraton table, remember also that in urban areas the legs were often produced by full-time turners who tended to produce standard patterns for the market. The more common of these turnings, as evidenced in the shape of the feet, are illustrated in figure 16-1.

A serviceable candlestand could be produced by anyone with a few tools and access to a lathe, and there are an extraordinary number of rural examples. While we will see many candlestands in the coming sections, for the most part they are either urban products or based on urban designs. However, you may very well encounter a candlestand unlike any of those illustrated in this chapter, and indeed, unlike anything you will ever see again. Perhaps the best that can be done in this case is to allow the primary and secondary woods to indicate if the subject is likely to be from New England, the Middle Atlantic, or, possibly, the South.

The following chapter is divided into three sections: first candlestands, then light stands, and last, worktables. There are too few examples of each to warrant separate sections on period

and style, and therefore I have just jumbled together Colonial and Federal workmanship. This is not as cavalier as it may seem, for a great many candlestands, most all light stands, and all worktables, are relatively recent, being Federal and neoclassical rather than Colonial and rococo. Whatever the style, the great majority were produced after the Revolution, between about 1790 and 1830.

Candlestands

19-1 New Hampshire candlestands. In this section we will consider three candlestands, the first two very typical of New Hampshire workmanship, the third a popular design that could have been produced either in Portsmouth or along the North Shore of Massachusetts.

The legs of a candlestand are normally joined to the column with blind dovetail joints. The top of each leg is cut to a dovetail shape which then slides up from the bottom into a corresponding slot in the bottom of the column. While this provides a neat joint, if the column is of relatively small diameter, there is not a great deal of wood left between the bottom of the slots. Given downward pressure, the base of the column is likely to break out. There are four solutions to this problem. The first, and most common, is to reinforce the joint with either three iron straps or a Y-shaped iron brace which anchors the underside of the legs to the base of the column. The second, often seen in Connecticut, is simply to increase the diameter of the base of the column so that there is adequate wood between the bottom of the slots. Another approach is to fasten the column and legs to a separate platform base. The fourth solution, most often seen in rural New Hampshire, is to avoid the problem by employing a mortise and tenon rather than a dovetail joint. To facilitate this the base of the column is often six-sided as shown in figure 19-1A. Note that the tenons have been pinned at the top and bottom.

Although neatly made, this candlestand is a very rural product. Similar Dunlap School stands are often far more delicate and graceful, with slim spider legs and thin square or, more often, symmetrical octagonal tops. They are truly elegant, all the more so for being rural workmanship. Note that to provide adequate stock at the bottom of the mortise, the column must be extended below the bottom of the legs, and then is usually terminated with a decorative turning. Although commonly seen in rural New Hampshire candlestands and in New Hampshire tea tables (17-3), mortised and tenoned legs should not be considered certain evidence of New Hampshire work, for they are a logical construction in any rural area where the necessary tools, or the iron strapping, were not available. We will see this joint again in a Southern candlestand.

While the candlestand in figure 19-1A is somewhat unusual, it is nothing compared to the candlestand illustrated in figure 19-1B. Normally I have not shown the very rare, but these candlestands are too remarkable to ignore. Most of the few stands of this type are attributed to the Dunlap family, this fine inlaid birch table to John Dunlap II. What makes these candlestands so unusual is not so much the distinctive square column as the use of four rather than three legs on an early candle-stand. While four legs are common on modern candlestands, they are very rare on period work.

Rural New Hampshire candlestands are typically made of birch, maple and birch, and sometimes cherry. There is a tendency to label every birch stand New Hampshire, but this is a mistake, for birch, which takes well to stain, was employed throughout northern New England as a substitute for the more expensive mahogany. A birch candlestand of conventional design is just as likely to be from Massachusetts.

The most common type of urban New Hampshire candle-stand was not only fashionable in Portsmouth, but was also popular north of Boston, in Salem and Newburyport. This type of table is characterized by an elongated octagonal top edged by a contrasting veneer. Often there will be an inlaid oval in the center, as shown in figure 19-1C. Most of these tables have

arched or spider legs and the small spade feet shown here. For all their popularity, it is difficult to say exactly where one of these stands was made, and you will often see them identified as "North Shore, Massachusetts" or "Portsmouth, New Hampshire." Here we might consider color. A basic mahogany table without veneer or inlay would more likely be Salem; a figured maple top bordered with a dark mahogany would suggest Portsmouth. When surveying chests of drawers, we saw the drawer fronts of Portsmouth chests of drawers treated in much the same manner. On some of these stands the tops tilt sideways, that is, a stand's top will tilt across the narrow axis. This may have been done to minimize warping of a rather large veneered top by having the cleats set crosswise to the grain. This unusual feature seems to be associated with New Hampshire candlestands, perhaps because here it was somewhat more important when the best of cabinet woods were not available.

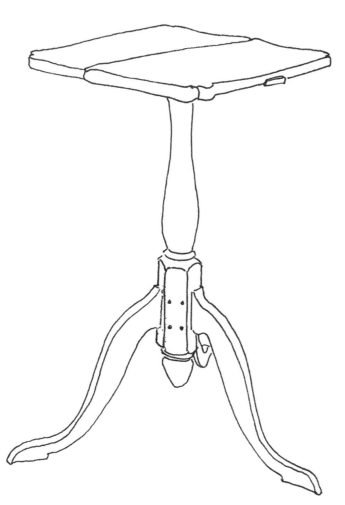

19-1A. New Hampshire, 26" h, 1790 – 1810.

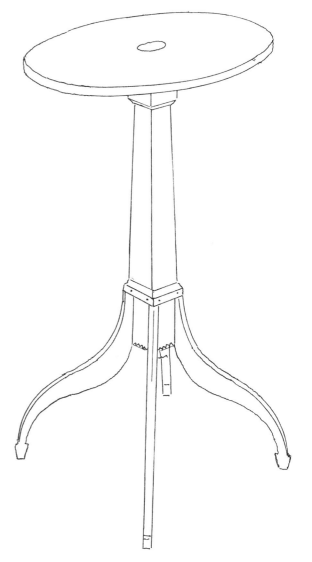

19-1B. New Hampshire neoclassical, 29" h, 1790 – 1800

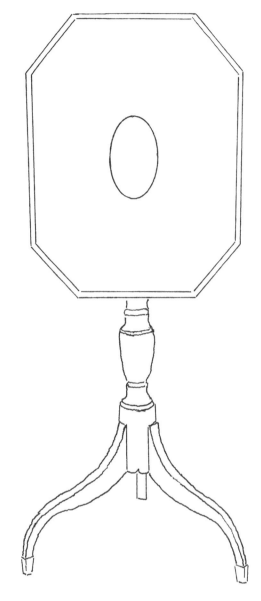

19-1C. New Hampshire neoclassical, c. 1800.

19-2 Massachusetts candlestands. Massachusetts cabinet-makers produced a great many candlestands, and in this section we will see three common types. Actually, there are at least four, for as was noted in the previous section, candlestands with elongated octagonal tops were also fashionable in northeastern Massachusetts, and indeed, these large stands are as likely to be from coastal Massachusetts as from New Hampshire. As with much Portsmouth furniture, the design was probably borrowed from coastal Massachusetts.

However, before starting, we should first discuss a Pilgrim Century stand, for while these are an early form, they are not all that rare, and you occasionally see them at auctions. Although produced in all regions, most of the surviving examples are from New England, most likely eastern Massachusetts which had the largest population in the eighteenth century. The red-painted stand shown in figure 19-2A is an unusually sophisticated example. The well-developed baluster and ring column on

this small table suggests it was produced late in the eighteenth century. For many of these simple candlestands, the appellation *Pilgrim Century* is probably a misnomer.

This stand has the most common type of X-form base, but you will also see T-shaped bases and X-form bases in which the legs have a slight arch. In common with early gateleg tables, Pilgrim Century examples tend to atypical turnings, often a succession of rings rather than the single baluster shown here. In New England they are usually made of local woods, maple or pine, or a combination of local woods, typically maple and pine, but also maple and walnut. Pennsylvania examples are usually all walnut, sometimes with the circular dished tops that become so common later in the century. If you come across an X-base candlestand made of a hard pine, it might be Southern.

Candlestands with serpentine tops and cabriole legs are Chippendale in style, and the Massachusetts stand shown in figure 19-2B is often identified as such, even though the great

397

majority of these handsome candlestands are most likely Federal rather than Colonial. As such, they may reflect the Boston affection for the rococo that continued right up into the opening years of the nineteenth century. Most of these popular stands have the ogee molded top and snake foot legs shown here. There will usually be a thin pad under the foot. Many are given taller, thinner, more vase-shaped urns; and have somewhat larger tops. These are probably later expressions of this popular design. Similar stands, made of cherry, were produced in Connecticut and in western Massachusetts in the Connecticut River Valley. A few Massachusetts examples are fitted with the later neoclassical spider legs.

Massachusetts candlestands with oval tops are so common that we might consider the two principal types: those with the earlier cabriole leg (19-2C), and those with the newer neoclassical arched, or spider, leg (19-2D). The clustered rings on the tall urn of the stand in figure 19-2C are often seen on neoclassical furniture made in Massachusetts and New Hampshire. Turn back to chapter 18 and you will see a similar grouping of rings at the top of the legs on a Sheraton card table (18-6E). Note that although this stand still retains cabriole legs, it is very

much neoclassical in appearance. Somewhat later in style are the spider legs in shown figure 19-2D. When not given some form of urn, a Massachusetts candlestand will usually have the thin, elongated baluster shaped pillar shown here. Often the midpoint of the baluster will be decorated with a small set of rings. In typical New England fashion, this candlestand has double tapered feet, although in this case there is but a very slight taper. More often, spider leg tables will be given small neoclassical spade feet. In budget work the spade is apt to be two dimensional, that is, it will have no thickness, being just shaped out of the sawn leg.

Lastly, it should be noted that while Massachusetts candlestands most often have either oval or serpentine tops, there are a considerable number of other forms, sometimes round, but more often square; frequently with notched, ovolo, or serpentine corners. These can usually be associated with Massachusetts by the shape of the pillar, either an urn at the base of a tapering column, or an elongated baluster, possibly with a cluster of rings at the widest point. The plates or blocks, and the cleats, on New England stands will usually be either birch or soft maple.

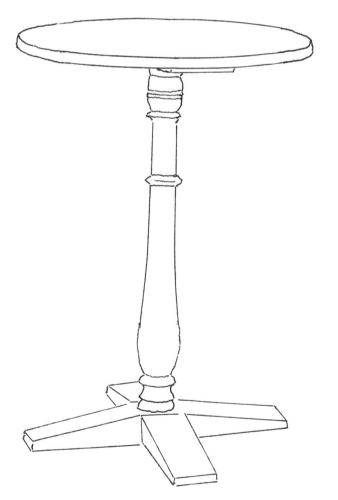

19-2A. New England Pilgrim Century, 24" h, 1750 – 1800.

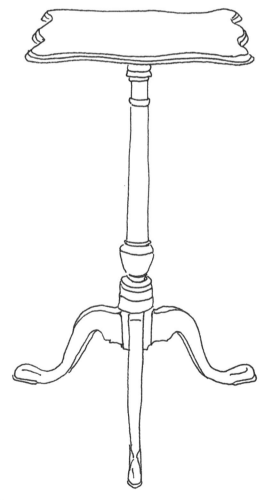

19-2B. Massachusetts Chippendale, 28" h, 1770 – 1800.

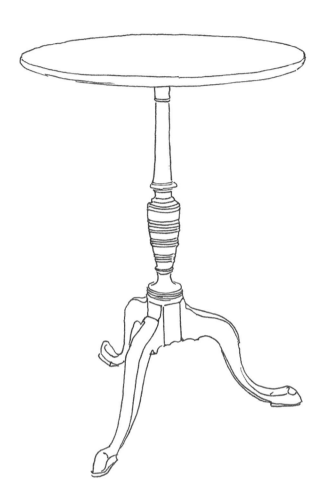

19-2C. Massachusetts neoclassical, 26" h, 1790 – 1810.

19-2D. Massachusetts neoclassical, 29" h, 1790 – 1810.

19-3 Rhode Island candlestands. Candlestands produced in Newport and Providence often resemble New York and Boston stands. Therefore, we might first consider local design and construction practices, for this is a good way to identify Rhode Island workmanship. As a rule a Newport or Providence stand will be well made of good-quality cabinet woods, normally a select mahogany, but sometimes cherry. A stand constructed of an indifferent mahogany is more likely to be from somewhere else, and if a New England product, then probably Massachusetts. The cleats and block may be maple, which suggests only New England, but if chestnut or mahogany, then probably Rhode Island. In chapter 17 it was noted that Newport cabinetmakers did not notch or scallop the bottoms of the columns on pillar-form tea tables, and this feature is also seen in Newport candlestands. Except for New York, south of Boston there was a preference for circular candlestands with tops that were shaped on a lathe to give them a little raised edge, or coaming. A New England candlestand made of mahogany with a circular dished top is likely to be from Rhode Island.

If the following candlestands seem familiar, it is for good reason, for you have seen much the same forms before. In the chapter on tea tables we saw a Newport tea table with a dished top and a "gun-barrel" column, and in figure 19-3A we see it again, this time scaled down to the size of a candlestand. Not only are the tops and columns very similar, but also, the legs have the same rather soft curves more usually seen on English tables. Note also that the bottom of the column is not notched as it would normally be were this stand made in Massachusetts.

The candlestand in figure 19-3B has the same baluster and ring turned column we saw earlier in a Newport tea table, although here the top has not been dished. Later we will see a New York stand with a plain top and similar baluster and ring turned pillar. To tell the difference, remember that Rhode Island tables are likely to employ chestnut in the cleats and blocks, the bases of the columns will not be notched, and the legs will often exhibit the gentle curves shown in this illustration.

Here it might be noted that Rhode Island stands often employ urn and column patterns similar to Boston and New York work. Also, not all Rhode Island stands have these distinctive cabriole legs. Many have more conventional cabriole legs like those illustrated in the Massachusetts stands. Nor are gentle curves unique to Rhode Island, for the legs on both early and rural candlestands are apt to lack the sharp turns at the ankles and the high knees usually seen in later candlestands.

When discussing New Hampshire stands, it was noted that candlestands were sometimes given a platform base. This technique, fairly common in England, is seldom seen in American furniture except in Rhode Island. The handsome platform-base stand in figure 19-3C is typical of Rhode Island workmanship in the dished top, baluster column, and gentle cabriole legs. Interestingly, it is made of walnut rather than the more usual mahogany, perhaps because it is an early example.

Note that all three of these stands are more Queen Anne than Chippendale in style, which should not come as a surprise when we consider the affection for the Queen Anne in Newport and Rhode Island.

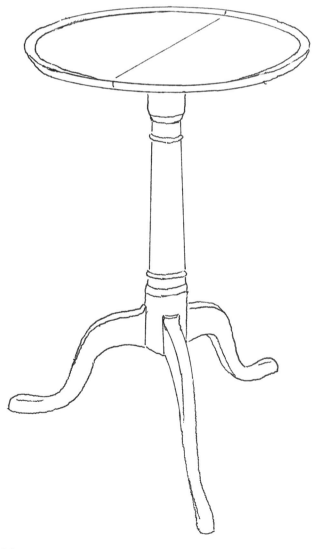

19-3A. Newport Queen Anne, 27" h, 1760 – 1800.

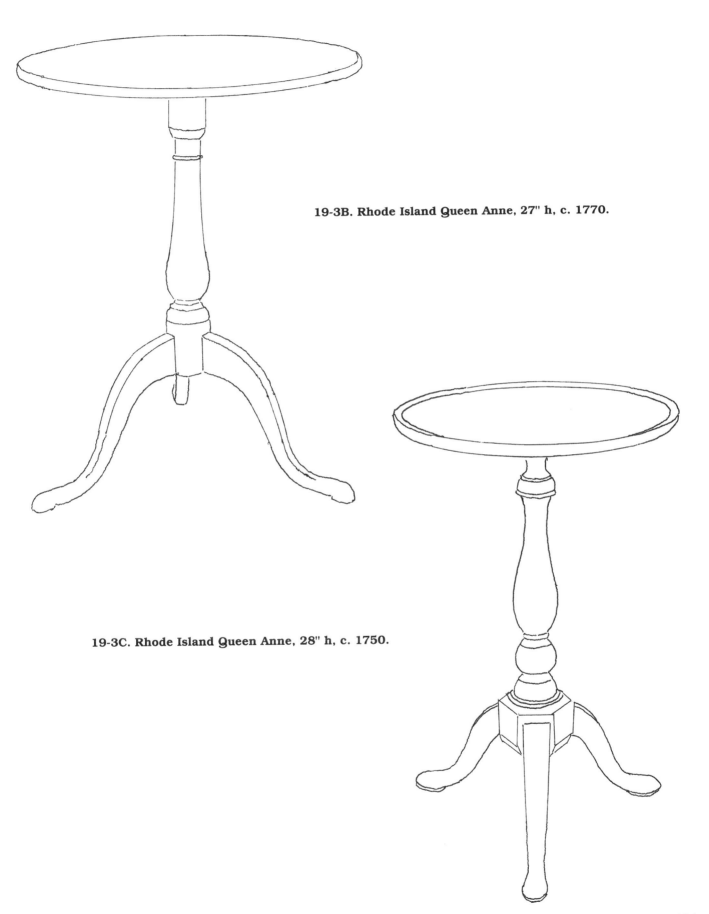

19-3B. Rhode Island Queen Anne, 27" h, c. 1770.

19-3C. Rhode Island Queen Anne, 28" h, c. 1750.

19-4 Connecticut candlestands. Connecticut candlestands exhibit a marvelous diversity, and the five shown in this section illustrate just the more common and more noteworthy types. This section could easily illustrate another half dozen examples. However, this is not a serious deficiency, for whatever the particular shape, there are a number of features that can help us to identify Connecticut workmanship. For the most part, a Connecticut, or Connecticut River Valley, candlestand will be made of cherry. While there are few made of mahogany, or maple, or a combination of woods, perhaps 19 in 20 will be cherry. But then, this ratio may not be all that accurate, for stands made of other woods, perhaps maple or mahogany, are not as likely to be associated with Connecticut workmanship. There may be more or less Connecticut candlestands than is generally realized.

The columns of Connecticut candlestands often display an exuberant, naive eccentricity. There are innumerable turnings, some local, others inspired by Boston, New York, and Philadelphia fashions. Most often Connecticut candlestands will have cabriole rather than spider legs, and these will be quite angular, often almost horizontal at the top. Spider legs are not as common, and those that you see are apt to be rather short and stocky. To avoid strapping the legs, the bottom of the column will often have been thickened. Everywhere there was an affection for tops that would keep small items in place, and you will often see circular dished tops, square tray tops, and even oval tops with applied galleries. While tops that both turn and tilt were rare in northern New England, they began to be seen in Rhode Island and Connecticut. You will see Connecticut candlestands with very tall, spindly, rural-looking birdcages. Stands made in Connecticut tend to be somewhat shorter than the norm, usually 25" – 27" high. They seldom are the 29" and 30" height seen in so many period stands.

The most common type of Connecticut candlestand will have a square top and angular cabriole legs like that shown in figure 19-4A. Often the top is decorated with inlay, in this example with light wood stringing, little fans at the corners, and a neoclassical ellipse in the center. This is a relatively modest example. Some have banding around the edges and large inlaid stars or paterae in the middles. Alternatively, there may be thin molding around the edges to keep things from rolling off. The pillars on some tables have baluster turnings rather than the urn and column shown here.

As you might expect, serpentine-top candlestands were very fashionable throughout the Connecticut River Valley. Here we see two different patterns: the serpentine shape that was so popular in Massachusetts, and a porringer top with ovolo corners like that shown in figure 19-4B. Note that the rather thick top is relieved by the curving under of the edges, a feature also seen in Connecticut tea tables. This stand also illustrates the promi-

nent shallow urn and heavy base seen on so many Connecticut stands. Turn back to the chapter on tea tables and you will see much the same shape in a Connecticut tea table.

If you are reading by the light of a candle, and it is time for a new candle, what is handier than to having a replacement in a little drawer under the top of the candlestand? The idea seems to have had a singular appeal in Connecticut, for most candle-drawer stands are from Connecticut, and naturally, all but a few are made of cherry. They have all sorts of tops: serpentine, square, and circular, the latter often dished on a lathe. In lieu of the single deep transverse support seen in figure 19-4C, some have box structures under the tops that house larger drawers. These may have been intended to be worktables. The stand shown in this figure is a particularly easy study, for not only is it made of cherry and has a tray top, but also, the column has the same form of Hartford compressed ball shown in the tea table in figure 17-6A. Dealers will tell you that these charming little candle drawers are rare, but in truth, they are often seen on Connecticut stands.

Before leaving Connecticut, and New England, something further should be said about the legs on New England candlestands. To keep this survey within reasonable limits, I have shown only stands with conventional cabriole or spider legs, those seen on the great majority of New England stands. However, several other shapes occur with some regularity in New England: a cabriole leg with a ridged or capped top, a very tall and thin downswept leg, and a downswept leg with a double curve. Except for the tall downswept leg, which seems to have been especially favored in New Hampshire, these and other rural inventions do not seem to be particularly area specific. However, ridged or capped cabriole legs like those shown in the stand in figure 19-4D are usually seen on cherry stands associated with Connecticut. Although some of these cherry candlestands are attributed to Nathan Lombard, who worked just to the south of Worcester, in Sutton, Massachusetts, most are probably from somewhere in Connecticut or the Connecticut River Valley.

Finally, we might look at an example from a small group of distinctive kettle stands produced in New London County at the turn of the eighteenth century (19-4E). The top was turned to a dished top with a curved apron, and then the apron was scalloped all around as shown here. Although sometimes identified as candlestands, most of these stands have very small tops, and this, in combination with the use of heat and stain-resistant black paint, would suggest they may have been intended as kettle stands. This is a very nice example, with the fluted urn frequently seen in better-quality Connecticut candlestands. Sometimes in lieu of carving, the urn will have been given a little neoclassical inlay.

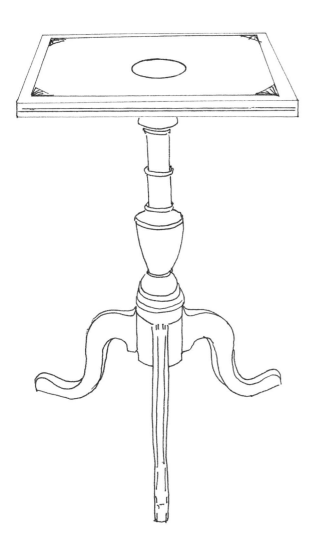

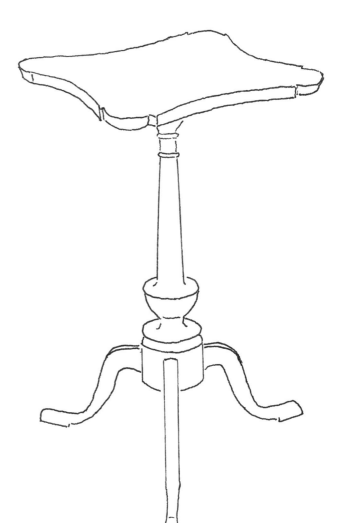

19-4A. Connecticut Queen Anne, 24" h, 1780 – 1810.

19-4B. Connecticut Queen Anne, 26" h, c. 1780.

19-4C. Hartford Queen Anne, 26" h, 1780 – 1800.

19-4D. Connecticut River Valley neoclassical, 1800 – 1810.

19-4E. New London County kettle stand, 29" h, c. 1800.

19-5 New York candlestands. In the previous chapter it was noted that New York was so fashion conscious that new styles were rapidly superseded by even newer styles. This is also true of candlestands, where Queen Anne seems to have been followed almost immediately by classical, with hardly a pause in between. While I will show you a spider-leg candlestand, there are few of these in comparison to the vast number of classical stands.

The most common form of New York cabriole-leg candlestand is a scaled-down version of the New York tea table seen in figure 17-7A. Although some of these stands are probably Federal rather than Colonial, the Queen Anne stand in figure 19-5A is much like New York tea tables: made of mahogany with a plain, rounded top, a baluster or cup turned column, uncarved legs — and a distinctly English look. The principal difference is that tea tables are also apt to have birdcage mechanisms and ball and claw feet. Most of these stands are quite large in scale, about 28" high and 22" across the top. A number carry the label of the hardworking Thomas Burling. Similar mahogany baluster-form stands were made in Rhode Island, but here they will often have dished tops, and may have chestnut blocks. A few have the cup and shaft column shown in the New York tea table in figure 17-7B.

Although it was not easy to locate a representative example, I cannot in good faith go directly from Queen Anne to classical without showing you an early neoclassical candlestand. While the New York spider-leg stand in figure 19-5B appears very similar to the New Hampshire stand in figure 19-1C, it will be different in the details. The primary wood will be a rich, dark mahogany, the cleats and block are likely to be cherry or, perhaps, mahogany rather than birch or soft maple, and the edge of the top is likely be reeded, as shown in the following illustration. On many of these tables, in lieu of the spade feet seen here, the legs will be made somewhat thicker and decorated with reeding. The octagonal top is perhaps a reflection of the New York affection for canted corners. The shape is unlikely to have been borrowed from New England.

Far more common are classical candlestands, and here we will look at two, the first a very typical New York stand with a double elliptical top, a reed-carved urn-shaped column, and downswept reeded legs (19-5C). The top has the reeded edges often seen in New York stands, and indeed, in much New York Federal furniture. This is a high-end stand. Simpler versions will lack the reeding, carving, and brass caster feet.

The second candlestand is a somewhat later table with drum-and-vase turned pillar and acanthus-carved legs of a type that is often attributed to the shop of Duncan Phyfe (19-5D). The top will be mahogany veneered on a base of white pine. Many of these stands have octagonal tops. Both of these stands are fairly large in scale and have the very solid look so often seen in late Federal New York furniture. With the exception of New York City, there appear to be few classical candlestands. While finely made New York examples are common, there are almost no similar Boston and Philadelphia examples. It may be that the form was only fashionable in New York, or only New York candlestands are of such quality that a substantial number have survived.

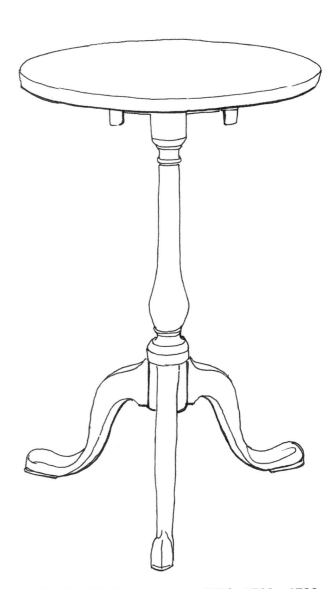

19-5A. New York Queen Anne, 29" h, 1760 – 1790.

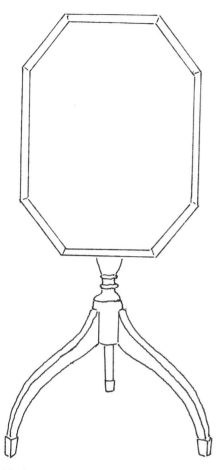

19-5B. New York neoclassical, 30" h (top down), 1800 – 1810.

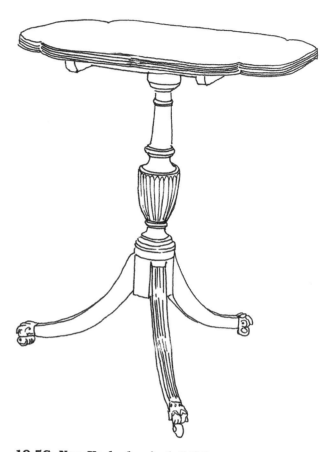

19-5C. New York classical, 29" h, 1810 – 1820.

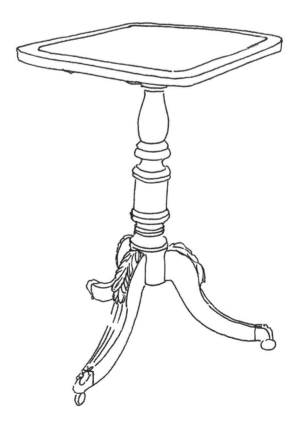

19-5D. New York classical, 30" h, c. 1815.

19-6 Pennsylvania candlestands. As you would expect, Pennsylvania candlestands are more apt to be rococo than neoclassical, and also, a great many employ a reduced version of the immensely popular compressed-ball column. Actually, many are not all that much reduced, for they tend to be quite large, 27" to 29" high, 22" across the top. The Philadelphia stand in figure 19-6A is typical, having solid cabriole legs, a compressed ball at the base of the column, and a birdcage mechanism under the top. Often the ball of such a stand will be only slightly compressed. In Pennsylvania fashion, the widest point of the turning will usually be scored or given a small ridge. The candlestand shown here is a somewhat budget model, for the walnut top is not dished. Other stands may omit birdcages and have either tilting or fixed tops. When a top is both large and walnut, it is often made up of two boards. Although not shown here, most stands have molded collars within the birdcages between the wedge and the lower plate as seen in figure 19-6D. The little pillars that form the birdcage of such a stand are typically a baluster shape. There is much variety in these very fashionable stands. In addition to the birdcage and dished top, some fine examples have ball and claw feet, scalloped tops, or both. Most stands are walnut or mahogany; a few are tiger maple.

Although less common than stands with compressed ball columns, many Pennsylvania candlestands have baluster-form columns, usually with a small ring above the baluster and a larger ring below as illustrated in figure 19-6B. Sometimes there will be an embryonic compressed ball under the baluster. This inexpensive walnut stand is also not dished, and here it might be noted that while dished tops were much favored in the Delaware Valley, dishing, like turning and tilting, added considerably to the cost of a stand, and there are many Pennsylvania tables with neither. While these stands are large enough to carry ball and claw feet, most have the prominent, rounded snake feet shown in these two illustrations.

A great many of these candlestands were made outside of Philadelphia, principally in Chester and Lancaster counties, and before discussing Federal stands, we might first look at a rural interpretation, in this case a candlestand from Chester County (19-6C). That this is Chester County workmanship is suggested by the unusual birdcage, which has a turned and molded lower plate, a feature also seen in Chester County tea tables. Candlestands made in Lancaster County are more conventional, but typically have a heavy, Germanic look, often with rather squatty legs. Products of both counties are likely to have the somewhat melon-shaped column seen in figure 19-6C. Here you will also see the double ring and baluster pattern illustrated in the Lancaster County tea table in figure 17-8C. Similar candlestands, usually with atypical turnings, were produced over a wide area, in southern New Jersey, Delaware, and Maryland.

Soon after the Revolution, neoclassicism reached America, and even in conservative Philadelphia there was accommodation to the new style. From this time we see Pennsylvania candlestands with urn-shaped columns like that shown in figure 19-6D. While these stands sometimes carry earlier dates, I would think that in this instance the urn is a neoclassical influ-

ence, and most all of these stands are Federal rather than Colonial. Often the urn is much taller and thinner in proportion to that shown here. So popular was the turn and tilt mechanism in the Delaware Valley that you will sometimes see stands with birdcages — and then with square or octagonal Federal tops.

Although spider legs seems to have been somewhat less popular in the Middle Atlantic than in New England, we might finish by taking a quick look at a spider-leg candlestand that was probably made in the Delaware Valley. While the stand in figure 19-6E was identified simply as Middle Atlantic in the auction catalog, the use of walnut and the tall, thin urn are seen in many Federal period Pennsylvania stands.

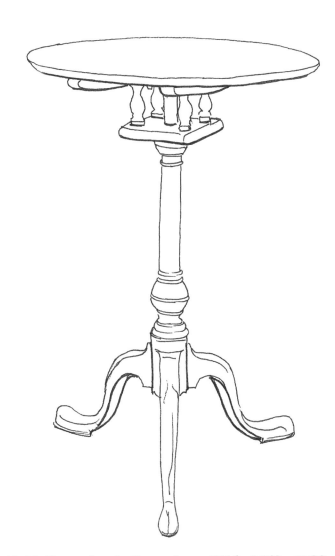

19-6A. Pennsylvania Queen Anne, 28" h, 1750 – 1790.

407

19-6B. Pennsylvania Queen Anne, 28" h, 1770 – 1790.

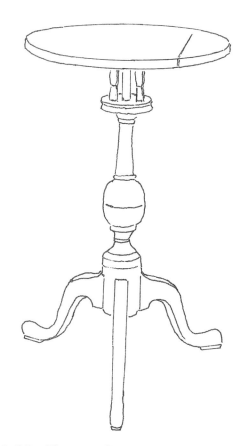

19-6C. Chester County Queen Anne, 30" h, 1760 – 1770.

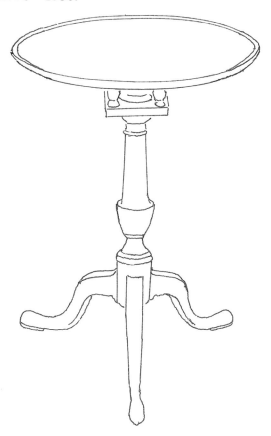

19-6D. Pennsylvania Queen Anne, 28" h, c. 1790.

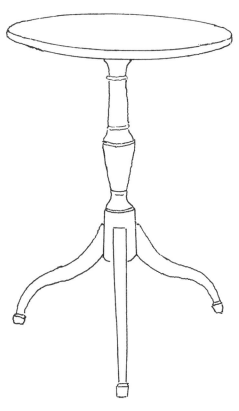

19-6E. Delaware Valley neoclassical, c. 1810.

19-7 Southern candlestand. Very few Southern candle-stands predate the Revolution, and even Federal examples are not all that common, but we should not leave these small tables without discussing the South. In common with so much other furniture from this vast region, there are few centers of production, and I cannot show you a standard urban form as we saw in Boston, New York, and Philadelphia. However, there are common features that suggest Southern workmanship, and it may not be all that difficult to identify a candlestand as Southern, even though the location of manufacture may be obscure unless there is some associated provenance.

The candlestand in figure 19-7 is typical of rural Southern workmanship. Most of these stands are very simple, usually lacking even a tilting mechanism. The legs are mortised and tenoned into the bases of the columns, which avoids having to strap the base of the column. Often there will be rather heavy baluster-form columns like the one shown here. It would be hard to imagine a simpler table. However, stands not too different from this were made everywhere. What suggests the South in this stand is that it is made of walnut, a wood seldom employed elsewhere in such budget work. Here also you might check the plate under the top. If Southern, it may be an unusual wood: perhaps walnut, oak, or yellow pine. Candlestands in the South were also made of cherry and poplar; and if near the coast, sometimes mahogany.

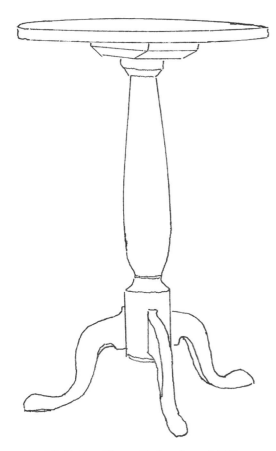

19-7. Southern Federal, c. 1800.

Light Stands

19-8 Light stands. With the introduction of oil lamps at the end of the eighteenth century, the inherent instability in a small three-leg table became a liability. It was one thing to splatter a little hot wax on the floor, quite another to smash a glass lamp full of flammable oil. The solution seems to have been a more stable platform — a square stand with four legs. Since these usually had mortised and tenoned beds or aprons, it was easy to provide small full-width drawers. Such one-drawer stands, uncommon prior to the Revolution, were soon made everywhere, so much so that there is not an auction, and there is hardly an antique shop, that does not have at least a few for sale. That is the good news. The bad news is that not only are most light stands rural products, but also, they are not all that old, and in common with many late arrivals, there is much less regional diversity. While it is usually not too difficult to identify region, it is often impossible to tell where the average grade of lightstand was made. Because of this, we will focus on stands that display features seen in other furniture made in the same area, first touching on some general characteristics that suggest region.

As the great majority of light stands are of rural manufacture, we will start with a simple Hepplewhite stand that could have been produced in any region. That the nicely proportioned little table in figure 19-8A was most probably made in northern New England is suggested by the primary and secondary woods, which are birch and eastern white pine. Further south you are likely to see maple, cherry, or mahogany, and walnut if south of the Mason-Dixon Line. Tulip poplar began to be used as a secondary wood in Rhode Island and coastal Connecticut, and was common throughout the Middle Atlantic and much of the South. A chestnut drawer bottom would suggest Rhode Island or vicinity; an Atlantic white cedar drawer bottom somewhere in the Delaware Valley.

We might next consider one of a group of colorful grain-painted stands produced in Maine in the second and third decades of the nineteenth century. The stand in figure 19-8B is a typical example, although the pen and ink illustration does not do justice to the wonderfully exuberant grain painting so characteristic of these small tables. Many of these light stands have turned legs, and here you may see remarkable turnings, the likes of which you will seldom see elsewhere. The legs on the light stand in figure 19-8B, which have a baluster shape with rather strange cones at the top and bottom, are but a modest example of late Federal Maine workmanship. The distinctive inverted cones at the top and bottom, are also seen in northern New England card tables.

When surveying candlestands, it was noted that stands with serpentine tops were popular in Massachusetts. The fashion carried over into light stands, and today we see many serpentine "turtle-top" stands. The elegant little lightstand in figure 19-8C is typical of these tables, most of which were probably made in Massachusetts. In common with many rural stands, this table is made of several different woods, in this case cherry and mahogany. The drawer will probably be made of white pine.

This carryover is also seen in Connecticut, where light stands are apt to have the tray tops so often seen in candlestands — a four-leg light leg version of the candle-drawer stand shown in figure 19-4C. Although but a small table, the lovely little cherry stand in figure 19-8D is the very model of the best and most charming in Connecticut cabinetry; the top has fan inlay at the corners, a star in the center, and a row of banding around the edges; there are rectangular inlaid dies at the tops of the legs, and light-wood inlaid cuffs at the bottoms. To save a little money, the drawer hardware is a small cast brass pull of the type usually found on the small drawers of desks.

While we have yet to see a light stand produced in an urban center, they do exist, and here we will look at a stand that was probably made in New York City. The inlaid Hepplewhite light-stand in figure 19-8E has the dark mahogany veneers and delicate legs so favored in New York. In New York fashion, the top is not solid, but rather, is made up of thin mahogany veneer on a base of white pine; a construction often seen in New York card tables. Although not evident in this illustration, this table is significantly larger than normal for a light stand. The top is 22" x 20", about 2" larger, in both dimensions, than any of the previous stands.

In chapter 18 we saw a rectangular Pennsylvania card table with Marlborough legs, late rococo bail pulls, and a molding at the base of the apron that extends across the tops of the legs. In figure 19-8F we see very much the same form in a Chippendale stand. This light stand is made of mahogany rather than walnut, suggesting that it was produced in Philadelphia and that the form is more than simply a rural survival. Although this is the only Chippendale-style stand illustrated in this section, light stands and kettle stands with Marlborough legs were also produced in Rhode Island.

The rather ordinary light stand shown in figure 19-8G illustrates why it can be so difficult to place these small tables. That it is the product of a rural cabinetmaker is evident in the general simplicity and rather solid proportions. The primary wood is walnut, the secondary tulip poplar, which would suggest either the Delaware Valley or somewhere in the South. Only the provenance, long ownership in a family from North Carolina, indicates it is most probably of Southern manufacture. Should you pull out a drawer, you may find it is made of very thick stock. Here again it might be noted that rural Southern tables tend to be Federal rather than Colonial, and have tapered Hepplewhite rather than turned Sheraton legs.

The large stand in figure 19-8H presents no such problem, for it is entirely constructed of yellow pine. In addition, the lack of the normal drawer, the imaginative apron, and the very unusual chamfered legs suggest a rural cabinetmaker working much on his own. The stand was probably made about the middle of the nineteenth century.

19-8A. New England Hepplewhite, 28" h, 1790 – 1810.

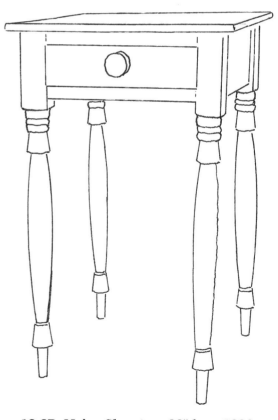

19-8B. Maine Sheraton, 29" h, c. 1820.

19-8C. Massachusetts Hepplewhite, 29" h, 1790 – 1820.

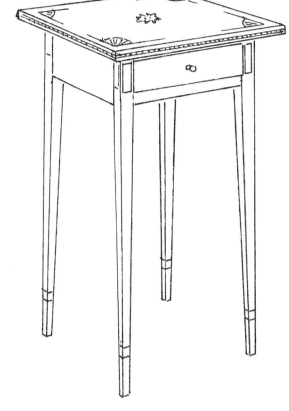

19-8D. Connecticut Hepplewhite, 29" h, c. 1810.

19-8E. New York Hepplewhite, 29" h, c. 1790.

19-8F. Philadelphia Chippendale, 28" h, c. 1790.

19-8G. North Carolina Hepplewhite, 29" h, 1800 – 1820.

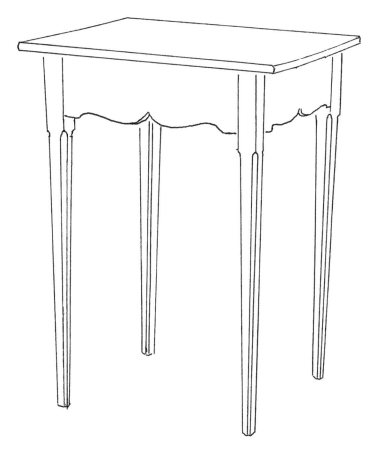

19-8H. Southern Hepplewhite, 33" h, c. 1850.

WORKTABLES

Although small tables for sewing and writing appear in Europe in the last decades of the eighteenth century, very few were produced in America until about 1800, and unlike candle and light stands, they all are both Federal and neoclassical. Identifying an American worktable as one or the other is correct but not necessary, for all are both. However, their late arrival is more than offset by their remarkable popularity in Federal America, for they were produced in large numbers in all regions, first in Hepplewhite, then in Sheraton, and finally in Empire and classical styles.

You may hear that New England worktables are square or square with canted corners, New York tables have lift tops and rounded astragal ends, and Pennsylvania tables are oval or kidney shaped, but this is only a generalization, and in the following sections we will see exceptions to this rule. Also, it is not always easy to tell the difference between a worktable and a light stand. Here we might define stands having two or more drawers as worktables, for why else pay for additional drawers? The reverse is not always true, though, for many delicate little one drawer stands, with or without a sewing bag, are very obviously worktables.

19-9 New England worktables. Worktables were enormously popular throughout New England, and if you encounter a square worktable with white pine drawers, you can pretty safely appear knowledgeable and casually remark that it is from New England. There is also much variety, and in this section we will see no less than six fashionable Hepplewhite and Sheraton designs.

Among the more singular New England products are a group of worktables having a medial shelf with the applied scalloped edge shown in figure 19-9A. While a few may have been produced elsewhere, most were made either along the North Shore of Massachusetts or in adjacent coastal New Hampshire, particularly in and around Portsmouth. Those produced in New Hampshire are likely to be made of birch or maple with flame birch or bird's-eye maple veneer on the drawer fronts. There is much variation in the placement of the drawers. The most common form has two drawers above the shelf as shown here, but you will also see one drawer under the top and the second under the shelf, or just one drawer under the top, or just one drawer under the shelf. The latter may have been intended as night tables rather than worktables, the shelves for chamber pots. These handsome worktables were produced in Hepplewhite and Sheraton styles with either square tapered or the turned legs shown here. Note that the legs are embellished with the stacked rings so often seen in Massachusetts and New Hampshire Federal furniture. Today these practical tables are reproduced as bedside tables — the tops large enough for both lamps and alarm clocks, the shelves used for books and magazines.

Next we might consider a fine-quality worktable that was probably made in Boston about the turn of the century (19-9B).

In New England fashion, the sewing bag is attached to a sliding frame. You can see the small brass pull on the right side of the case. Similar New York worktables are more likely to have the bag suspended on sham drawers. Most New England worktables are far less grand than this urban example, and omit the sewing bag and the brass castors. Many also have turned rather than square tapering legs, for by the first decade of the nineteenth century Hepplewhite was giving way to Sheraton.

As you would expect, with the advent of the Sheraton style, New England worktables not only acquire turned legs, but also the outset or cookie corners so often seen in New England case work. The North Shore worktable in figure 19-9C is typical of a great many produced throughout New England. In lieu of the simple stacked ring turnings shown here, the legs on some Salem tables have delicate carving beside the drawers. These are often attributed to the shop of Samuel McIntire, the carving to the hand of Mr. McIntire himself. Good quality examples may have serpentine cases. These will usually be from either Boston or Salem.

We can tell that this worktable was produced in or near Salem by the shape of the feet. Here it might be noted that the feet on Sheraton worktables do not exhibit the regional consistency seen in dining and card tables, and the regional shapes shown in figure 16-1 may be little help in identifying origin. This is perhaps because worktables are more varied than dining or card tables, the upper section of the legs having to be planned to provide corners for a one- two- or three-drawer case; and here cabinetmakers may have found it more economical to do their own turning.

Work tables with octagonal tops and canted corners were fashionable in Massachusetts, particularly in Boston and Salem, and in figure 19-9D we see a very fine example that is attributed to the shop of John and Thomas Seymour. The best of these tables are quite striking; the flat surfaces and drawer fronts are veneered in light maple or birch and bordered in darker mahogany. There are three forms of legs: a tapered Hepplewhite legs, the more common Sheraton legs shown here, and cookie corner–type legs that extend up across the faces of the canted corners. The feet of this worktable — pronounced rings above tapering posts — have a turning often seen in urban New England worktables. Generally, turned legs will be reeded. On later tables, in all regions, they are apt to be spiral turned.

With time worktables acquired pairs of small drop leaves to provide a little extra working surface. The table in figure 19-9E is a better-than-average example of a great many of these late Federal tables, which were made in all regions and tend to be pretty much alike. The shape of the legs on this table suggest that it is from the Middle Atlantic rather than New England, probably Philadelphia as it does not have the distinctive New York baluster feet. Here again we might remember the common use of secondary woods. Drawers made of white pine would suggest somewhere in New England, tulip poplar somewhere in the Middle Atlantic, or maybe Southern.

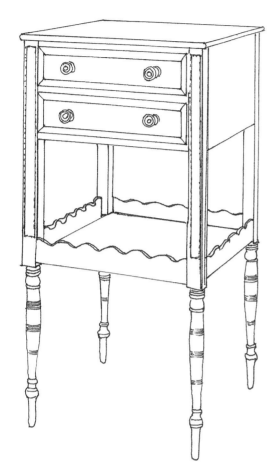

19-9A. New England Sheraton, 32" h, 1800 – 1810.

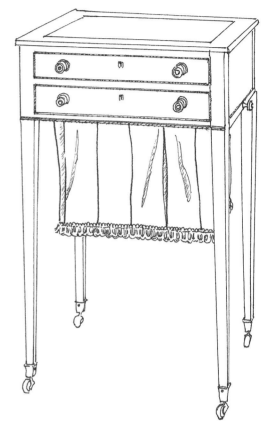

19-9B. Boston Hepplewhite, 30" h, 1790 – 1810.

19-9C. Massachusetts Sheraton, 29" h, 1800 – 1810.

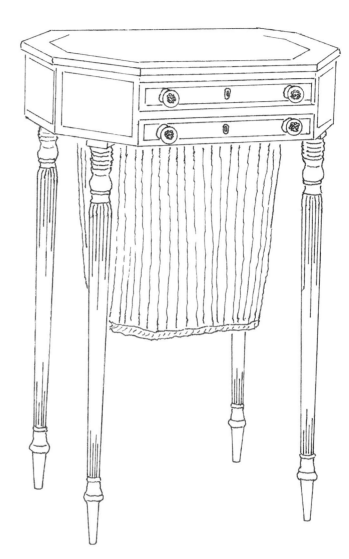

19-9D. Boston Sheraton, 29" h, 1800 – 1810.

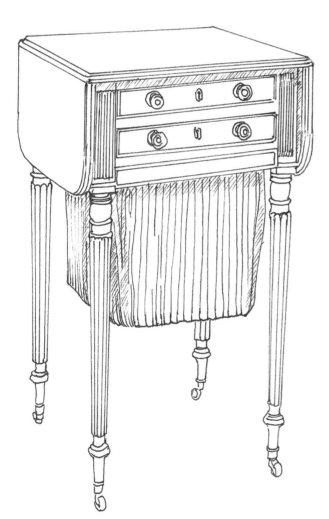

19-9E. Middle Atlantic Sheraton, 29" h, 1810 – 1820.

19-10 Middle Atlantic worktables. If you see a worktable with semicircular ends, you are looking at a product of the Middle Atlantic or the near South: New York, Philadelphia, or Baltimore. Work tables with round ends, whether astragal, kidney shaped, or oval, were never, or perhaps were only very rarely, produced in New England.

The astragal-end worktable in figure 19-10A is typical of many Middle Atlantic worktables. That this is a New York table is suggested by the unusual flared feet, a feature also seen in some Baltimore worktables. Other New York tables of this type have reeded Sheraton legs, the lack of flare doing little to improve their unfortunate top-heavy look. Worktables are identified as "astragal end" when the semicircular ends are stepped in a little, as shown in this illustration.

In common with much other New York Federal furniture, the majority of New York worktables are Empire or classical rather than Hepplewhite or Sheraton, and here we will look at two fashionable types. Both may seem familiar, and this for good reason, for they employ elements of other New York classical furniture. The first has a square case resting on turned legs with a low shelf set between the legs (19-10B). If this worktable gives you a feeling of déjà vu, it is for good reason, for you have seen the same basic form in a classical New York dressing table, a classical New York secretary, and a classical New York serving table. Note that this table has the same inverted baluster or vase form feet seen in much New York furniture. Later versions of these popular worktables have spiral turned legs, and some omit the lower shelf. However, all tend to be somewhat large in scale and decorated with rich, dark mahogany veneer. Most are fitted with the brass swiveling castors so often seen in New York furniture.

Perhaps the most successful New York worktable is based on the same urn-shaped column and downswept legs employed for innumerable New York breakfast and card tables. In figure 19-10C we see this platform serving equally well for one of an extended group of worktables. The tambour doors are often seen on New York classical worktables. Behind these there will usually be a couple of small sliding shelves. Other versions of these worktables have rectangular cases with either canted or concave inset rounded corners. Like many worktables, they served for both sewing and writing. Lift the hinged top and you will usually see a fold-up writing surface that can be adjusted to a comfortable angle.

When surveying New York dining and card tables we saw a design in which the top was supported by four small columns, or colonettes. As you might expect, the same platform was employed for worktables. To the base of the card table illustrated in figure 18-9G, add the astragal-end case shown in the previous figure and you will see how they appear. The cases on these large worktables may also have canted corners rather than the astragal ends shown in figure 19-10C.

Philadelphia worktables are quite different from New York City tables, although also unmistakably products of the Middle Atlantic. Aside from rural workmanship, Pennsylvania worktables tend to be Sheraton rather than Hepplewhite, and this again may reflect the delay in coming to terms with the new neoclassical styles.

While represented in a number of fine collections, the kidney shape so often seen in Philadelphia sideboards and card tables is not often seen in worktables. More common are deep astragal-end tables like that shown in figure 19-10D. Although this rather simple worktable may not actually have been made in Philadelphia, it was most probably made somewhere in the area, as is suggested by the shape of the feet. Notice the pulls on either end of the case. In common with many of these worktables, the ends are compartments that pivot out from the case.

The most notable feature of many Philadelphia worktables is their depth. The astragal-end table in the previous illustration is unusually deep for a worktable, and so also is the square Philadelphia table in figure 19-10E. Here the depth seems due to the use of a deep drawer rather than a cloth bag for the sewing scraps. The ball feet on both these worktables are of a pattern often seen in Pennsylvania furniture. Note that while this worktable is both square and has cookie corners, its solid look is very different from a product of New England.

Earlier we saw classical card tables with lyre bases, and in figure 19-10F we see the same motif in a late Federal Philadelphia worktable. That this table is a product of the Middle Atlantic is suggested by the open lyre. A closed or solid lyre would more likely be from somewhere in New England. This table is also most likely to be from the Philadelphia area, for lyre-base worktables do not seem to have been as popular in New York City. Here it might also be noted that by this time the ring turnings so often associated with Massachusetts and New Hampshire Federal furniture may be found anywhere.

With the advent of the classical there is a veritable explosion of designs, and supporting the case section you will see all sorts of lyres, carved columns, colonettes, foliate pedestals, and Doric columns. Because a single thick pedestal is so common, we might end this section with a classical worktable that might have been produced in any urban area (19-10G), although the additional carving on the case of this fine worktable suggests that it may have been made in New York. When examining these many late Federal worktables, remember what was said about secondary woods: drawers made of white pine suggest New England, tulip poplar the Middle Atlantic or, perhaps, the South.

19-10A. New York Hepplewhite, 29" h, c. 1800.

19-10B. New York classical, 32" h, 1810 – 1830.

19-10C. New York classical, 30" h, 1805 – 1815.

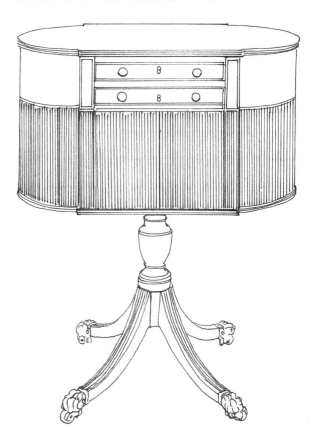

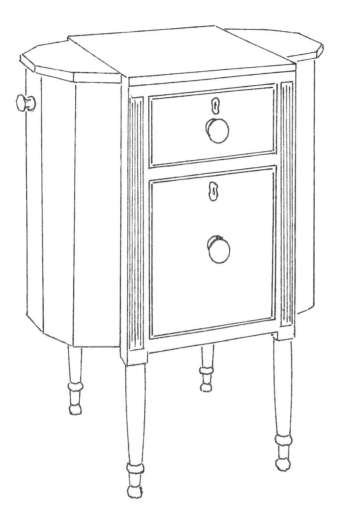

19-10D. Pennsylvania Sheraton, 27" h, c. 1810.

19-10E. Philadelphia Sheraton, 29" h, 1810 – 1820.

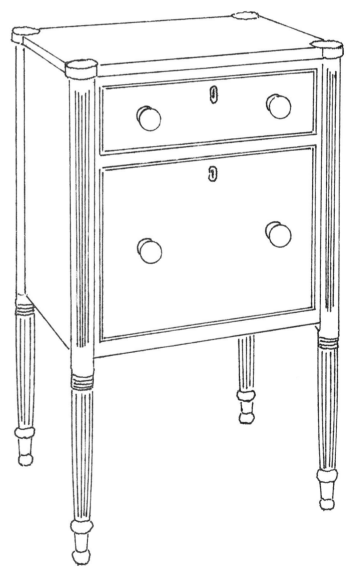

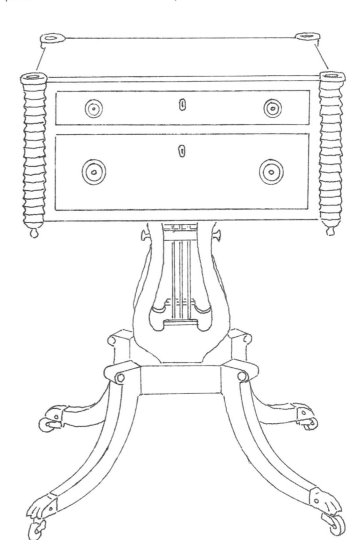

19-10F. Philadelphia classical, 29" h, c. 1815.

19-10G. New York classical, 29" h, c. 1830.

19-11 Southern worktables. While worktables were probably made to some extent throughout the South, most surviving high-style tables are from Maryland, particularly Baltimore. We will see two examples from this city. First, though, it might be noted that Baltimore features we saw earlier in dining and card tables are also seen in worktables, notably the rather strange oversize, unta-pered fluting seen on the legs of Baltimore dining and card tables, and the standard Baltimore table pedestal with a wide, reed-carved bowl-shaped urn and deeply reeded downswept legs.

Astragal-end worktables fitted with large sewing bags in lieu of solid, half-round compartments were produced in both Pennsylvania and Maryland. The kidney-shaped Philadelphia tables were also fashioned this way. Here we will look at a very fine-quality mahogany and satinwood astragal-end table that was probably made in Maryland, very possibly Baltimore (19-11A). Not all Baltimore astragal-end worktables have sewing bags. Others have solid half-round compartments; and if not Sheraton legs, then square tapered legs and the same unusual flared feet that we saw earlier in a New York worktable.

Oval worktables were sometimes made elsewhere, but were particularly favored in Baltimore, where today they are often called "bandbox" tables. The elegantly simple worktable in figure 19-11B is a very fine example with plum pudding mahogany veneer and inlaid satinwood panels.

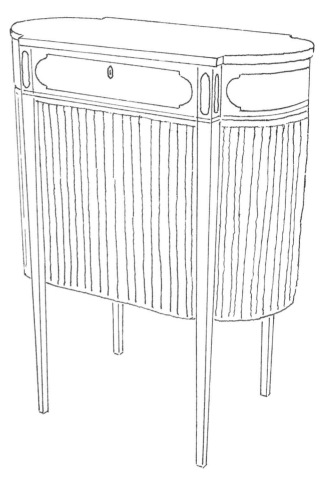

19-11A. Maryland Hepplewhite, 30" h, c. 1790.

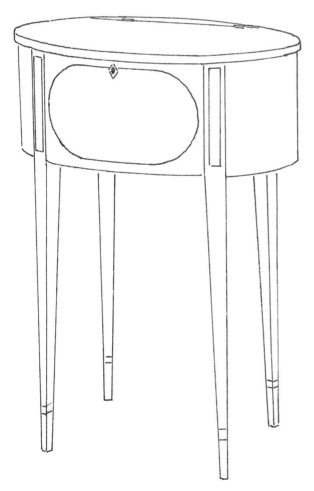

19-11B. Baltimore Hepplewhite, 30" h, c. 1790.

Chapter 20 – Tavern and Farm Tables

The last four chapters have discussed tables for dining, entertainment, and sewing, many high-style furniture pieces made by urban cabinetmakers of imported mahogany. Now in his last chapter on tables we will consider a group of simpler tables made of local woods, some undoubtedly by craftsmen in small towns and villages for whom cabinetmaking was but a part-time avocation. Most are of two basic types: small stretcher-base tables now called tavern tables, and larger rural tables that are usually identified as either tavern or farm tables, even though a great many were simply kitchen tables. This chapter will also cover the scarce Windsor table and two variations of the tavern table, the tuckaway and the butterfly table. Hutch and chair tables, while very much rural farm tables, are largely confined to New England and are therefore covered in the last chapter on miscellaneous regional furniture.

The title of this chapter may be something of a misnomer. Today small stretcher-base tables are almost invariably called either tap or tavern tables, but they were not identified this way in probate records. In any event, both the great many surviving examples, and the small number made of walnut or mahogany, suggest that they were employed everywhere as occasional tables. Also, they are often fitted with a drawer, which would have added about half again to the cost, and would seem to serve little purpose in a tavern.

Larger tables of the sort you would expect to see in the kitchen or dining area of a farmhouse are also a problem, for there seems no good way to describe them. In auction catalogs they are usually called tavern or farm tables, although they might equally well have served in the kitchen of an urban home. Here we will identify them as farm tables, although they might also have been employed in taverns as communal dining tables. Most New England examples are so simple that they were probably used in kitchens or keeping rooms, both in the preparation of food, and then as dining tables if the dwelling was too modest to have a dining room. Pennsylvania tables are often better made, and of better woods, and some were undoubtedly employed as dining tables in the large and prosperous farm houses you can still see in Chester and Lancaster counties.

Like the turned chairs that were placed around them, tavern and farm tables tend to be unsophisticated rural forms and frequently are both difficult to place and to date. Most can be located no closer than a general area. Also, like much rural workmanship, many are a lot newer than dealers would like to admit. The top of a kitchen table that is scrubbed every day soon acquires considerable wear.

20-1 New England tavern tables. In this section we will discuss four typical New England tavern tables, two of which are quite common and two of which you are unlikely to encounter, but nevertheless, are very characteristic of New England workmanship. Lastly, we will take a quick look at a Windsor table, for most of the relatively few surviving examples seem to be from New England.

The most common type of New England tavern table has the oval top and double-baluster splayed legs shown in figure 20-1A. These handsome tables were produced all over New England, usually of local woods: maple, maple and pine, or birch and pine. In common with many turned chairs, they probably are not all as rural as they look, for some have quite sophisticated turnings, and also, there are a small number made of walnut and mahogany. Often the legs are not splayed, but are straight up and down as shown in the next illustration. Many have lost all or most of their turned feet and are a couple of inches lower than their original 25" – 27" height.

The other common type of New England tavern table has a square top, and here we might look at an early table made in Massachusetts, probably in coastal Essex County (20-1B). Many of these tables are fitted with a drawer, again suggesting that they were intended for the home rather than the tavern. A few have square Marlborough legs. Some are made of cherry rather than the usual maple. These are likely to be from Connecticut. This table illustrates the atypical turnings often seen in early tables, a feature also seen in gate-leg tables. New England tables usually have some form of the symmetrical double-baluster and ring turning shown in figure 20-1A, but here the balusters are somewhat compressed and divided by pronounced rings, and there are additional short balusters at the tops and bottoms. Atypical turning patterns are not always indications of early work. They may simply be the products of novice turners. In general, early turnings are apt to be large and bold. With time they tend to become simpler and more standardized.

Perhaps the best-known New England tavern tables are also among the earliest, and the scarcest, for you will seldom see a table like that illustrated in figure 20-1C outside of a museum or a major auction. Today they are called butterfly tables, a term that seems to have been invented by early collectors in the last decades of the nineteenth century. In form, the small drop-leaf table might be seen as a cross between a gate-leg and a Pembroke table; a gate-leg in that the leaf supports pivot on the stretchers, a Pembroke in that there are no swing legs. Most appear to have been produced in either Connecticut or Massachusetts in the first half of the eighteenth century. They are usually a mixture of local woods: maple, cherry, birch, and white pine. While the legs of this table are the standard New England double-baluster turning pattern, you will sometimes see either a single baluster or an early, ornate version of the standard double baluster. The table illustrated here would seem to be a later product, not only because of the conventional turnings, but also because the leaves butt against the top with rule joints rather than the early tongue-and-groove joint. You need to be very careful in identifying one of these tables, for they were once so popular with collectors that quite a number were created from other furniture. Remember that if the feet are not worn down, they should be 26" – 27" inches high. Also, there are many reproductions, some of which are now almost a century old. These are often made of tiger maple.

The other early and rare table is the tuckaway, a design that also seems to be unique to New England. In form, it is a small, very narrow gate-leg table having two fixed legs and supported by a trestle base like that shown in figure 20-1D. Most are made

421

of maple, or maple and pine, although the very fine Massachusetts table shown here is a combination of maple and walnut. Simpler examples of these charming little tables have fewer turnings: the gates of a table may pivot on a square stretcher rather than the turned stretcher shown here, and sometimes the gates themselves are square rather than turned.

Every so often you will come across a small table that is constructed like a Windsor chair, that is, instead of having a bed that links together the legs and the top, the legs extend right up to the underside of the top, as shown in figure 20-1E. These simple utilitarian tables were made everywhere, and probably were once quite common. They appear to have been especially popular in New England, for today most of the relatively few surviving examples are from this region. The legs are usually maple and the tops pine, sometimes with breadboard ends. Unlike Windsor chairs, the shape of the leg turnings are not much help in determining region, for most of these tables have some form of the elongated baluster shown here. A few have three rather than four legs. These seem to be from the Philadelphia area.

Interestingly, Windsor tables are made in different ways. The tops may be pinned to the tops of the legs, or the legs may be tenoned through the tops, or the legs may be tenoned to cleats that are fastened to the tops as seen in this illustration. This suggests that these tables could have been produced either by turners, Windsor chair makers, or cabinetmakers. They are so simple, and originally were so inexpensive, that they may indeed have been tavern tables.

20-1A. New England William & Mary tavern table, 25" h 1740 – 1760.

20-1B. Massachusetts William & Mary tavern table, 27" h, c. 1750.

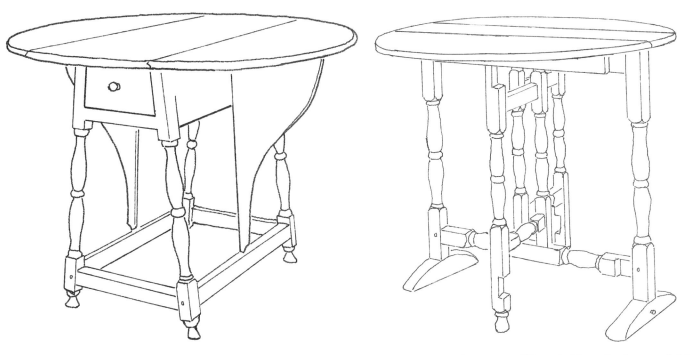

20-1C. New England William & Mary butterfly table, 27" h, 1725 – 1750.

20-1D. Massachusetts William & Mary tuckaway table, 27" h, c. 1750.

20-1E. New England Windsor tavern table, 25" h, 1780 – 1810.

20-2 *Middle Atlantic tavern tables.* The most notable characteristic of Middle Atlantic tavern tables is not that they are usually made of walnut, which they are, but how relatively few there appear to be when compared to the many hundreds of surviving New England tavern tables. If it is indeed true that numbers now are roughly proportionate to numbers then, they would not seem to have been very common. Either that, or the ordinary grade of tavern table was of such little merit that only the better have survived.

Here we will consider three examples, all probably from southeastern Pennsylvania, the first an early table of the sort that could have been produced anywhere in Colonial America from Long Island to Virginia (20-2A). This solid stretcher-base tavern table has the single baluster and ring turning seen in many Pennsylvania gate-leg and tea tables, and which we will see again in a Delaware Valley farm table.

Rural Pennsylvania furniture tends toward the massive, and tavern tables are not the exception. The walnut tavern table in figure 20-2B is quite unlike anything produced in New England. Although but 28" high, it is almost 3' long. Note that the stretchers are as thick as the legs, quite heavy enough to serve as foot rests. Also note that this table has the same horizontal molding below the drawer that is often seen in Delaware Valley card and side tables.

The third example is both lighter in proportion and far more sophisticated in design (20-2C). It might very well have been made in Philadelphia, and should probably be identified as a side table rather than a tavern table. The thin columnar turnings have a distinctly urban look, and the stretchers have been finished off with a small bead molding. Similar turnings are seen in Southern furniture, particularly Virginia, although here they are more likely to be given a slight taper reminiscent of an attenuated gun barrel turning.

Pennsylvania tavern tables are usually made of walnut and often are fitted with brass drawer pulls, which would indicate that most were probably intended for use in the home. The drawers are likely to be made of poplar, perhaps with white cedar bottoms. Most of these tables appear to date no later than the first half of the eighteenth century, suggesting that they did not enjoy the long run seen by similar stretcher-base tables in New England.

20-2A. Pennsylvania William & Mary tavern table, 29" h, 1730 – 1750.

20-2B. Delaware Valley William & Mary tavern table, 28" h x 35" l, 1740 – 1760.

20-2C. Pennsylvania William & Mary side table, 28" h, 1730 – 1750.

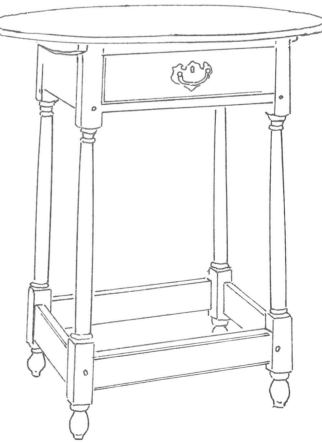

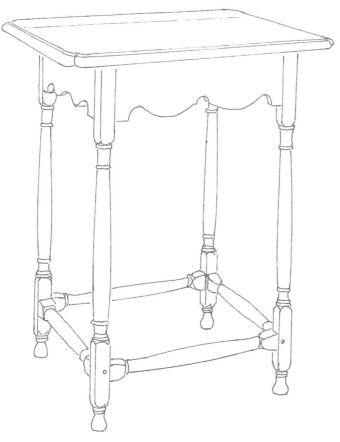

20-3A. Virginia William & Mary side table, 27" h, c. 1750.

20-3 Southern tavern tables. Although you are unlikely to encounter a Southern tavern table, they exhibit such diversity that we might look at two examples, both probably made in Virginia. The first is a delicate little walnut side table that one would think would have been intended for the home rather than the tavern (20-3A). That this small table was most probably made in the South is indicated by the use of walnut, the turned stretchers, and the general simplicity of execution. The South is also suggested by what the table is not. The use of walnut in a somewhat rural product would point to southeastern Pennsylvania or somewhere in the South, but there is little in the somewhat unusual design to suggest the Delaware Valley. This leaves the South, and perhaps tidewater Virginia, for this is a very sophisticated little table. Like much Southern workmanship, it may have been one of only a small group of similar tables, and may now be the only survivor.

The second table, also made of walnut and also probably from Virginia, is typical of many Virginia and Maryland tables in that it exhibits Pennsylvania features, in this case the cleat-fastened top, the baluster and ring turning of the legs, and the small flattened button feet. Similar Southern tables may have gun barrel rather than baluster turnings. The late rococo bail handle shown here is often seen on Southern furniture. South of the Mason-Dixon Line, the drawers on rural furniture are likely to employ yellow pine rather than the poplar and white cedar used in the Delaware Valley. Here it might be mentioned that some Southern drawers are made of such heavy stock that the drawer bottoms are simply fastened with cut nails driven in from the sides.

20-3B. Virginia William & Mary tavern table, 28" h, c. 1770.

20-4 New England farm tables. New England kitchen or farm tables are both plentiful and exhibit much variation in design. Unlike tavern tables, many do not have stretcher bases, and in this and the following sections we will also see tables with turned cabriole and square tapered legs.

Although a fairly diverse group, the great majority of New England farm tables are made of just two local, inexpensive woods: the legs and stretchers will be soft maple, the top eastern white pine. A few are all pine, or all maple, and a rare few have cherry legs. Further south along the Connecticut coast we begin to see the tulip poplar that was employed throughout the Middle Atlantic. A farm table constructed of maple and white pine will most probably be from somewhere in New England, or if a late model, then perhaps to the west in northern New York State.

The table shown in figure 20-4A is typical of a great many New England stretcher-base farm tables, having square stretchers, double-baluster turned maple legs and a white pine top that is stiffened with a pair of cleats across the ends, what are known as breadboard ends and often called breadboard tops. The rather uninspired double-baluster turnings suggest that this may be a relatively late example. Early tables usually have bolder turnings: single large balusters, or additional rings above and below the double balusters, or additional small balusters at the tops and bottoms as seen earlier. This table is somewhat unusual in that it still retains its turned feet. In a great many of these tables the feet are either restored or so worn down that the stretchers are no more than an inch or two above the floor.

This basic sort of kitchen or keeping room table was produced all over New England throughout the eighteenth century; overlapping into New York where it was sometimes executed in cherry and walnut. The stretchers and pinned mortise-and-tenon

joints make for a very strong table, and a number survive from the Pilgrim Century, although often without their original tops or feet. A few New England stretcher-base tables have square, untapered Marlborough legs. These probably date from the late eighteenth century. Nor do all have the square box stretchers shown in figure 20-4A. A few early tables have turned stretchers of the type more commonly seen in the Middle Atlantic and Southern colonies. In this case , such a table will usually have a pair of block and turned stretchers across the ends, then a block and turned medial stretcher. A smaller, but similar, table from Lancaster County is illustrated in figure 20-5B.

The second common form of New England farm table also has turned legs, but has no stretchers. The turnings on these tables are usually very basic, normally either simple straight tapers or elongated balusters. Button feet are very common, now often worn down to a mere nubbin. The table in figure 20-4B is a somewhat better-than-average example with a thumbnail molded drawer and neatly turned offset feet. In common with most such tables, the top is made of white pine boards kept flat with breadboard ends. In the next section we will see a Pennsylvania farm table that is similar in form but very different in detail and proportion.

Farm tables had a long run in New England, and to finish this section we might look at a Hepplewhite table that was most probably made in the early decades of the nineteenth century (20-4C). A few of these tables have straight Marlborough legs rather than the tapered Hepplewhite legs shown here. These are probably a little earlier, perhaps the last decades of the century when the Marlborough leg was very much in fashion. There is an old saw that the greater the overhang of the top the earlier the table, and this is indeed true, but remember that it is no more than a generalization. Some New England Sheraton and Hepplewhite tables have very bold overhangs.

20-4A. New England William & Mary farm table, 29" h, 1750 – 1800.

20-4B. New England Queen Anne farm table, 27" h x 40" w, c. 1780.

20-4C. New England Hepplewhite farm table, 30" h, 1790 – 1820.

20-5 Middle Atlantic farm tables. In surveying Middle Atlantic farm tables, we will focus on Pennsylvania, not only because there are many fine examples from this area, but also because fewer appear to have been made in, or perhaps fewer have survived from, New York and New Jersey.

Pennsylvania farm tables are singularly easy to identify, for they have no less than four noteworthy regional characteristics: they tend to be of better-than-average quality, they very often are made of walnut, they normally have an asymmetric drawer arrangement, and they almost always have some form of removable cleated top. In common with Pennsylvania tavern tables, they are likely to be entirely made of hardwood, principally walnut, and to be fitted with brass rather than wood pulls. If not made of a hardwood, they will usually be made of tulip poplar, or a mixture of woods in conjunction with pine: walnut and pine, poplar and pine, or oak and pine.

Look at a the top of a Pennsylvania farm table and you will usually see that the boards are dovetailed to a pair of crosswise cleats which are then fastened to the bed of the table. The dovetailed cleats kept the boards level and allowed them to be fastened to the table bed without the maker having to drive any fastenings through the top. On better work, the dovetail slot is stopped so that it does not show from the front. Often the top is removable, being kept in place by little "belaying pins" that fit into matching holes in the cleats and bed of the table. While this is thought to have been done to allow the top to be taken outside to be scrubbed and left to dry in the sun, I would wonder also that it was not a help in moving these large and very heavy hardwood tables. Cleated tops are seen on all sorts of Delaware Valley tables, both large and small. They are a handy indication of Pennsylvania workmanship.

Most Delaware Valley stretcher-base farm tables are similar to the table shown in figure 20-5A, a large walnut table with a cleated top, two drawers of different sizes, brass bail pulls, baluster turned legs, and square stretchers. Typically one drawer will be about double the width of the other. While the table

in the next illustration has but a single drawer, there will usually be two drawers, and on large tables, three. You will even see pairs of unequal drawers on quite small tables for which you would think that one drawer would have sufficed. Perhaps the smaller was intended for candles?

Sometimes the stretchers on these tables will be given footboards, a Continental feature that was probably introduced by settlers from Germany. Alternatively, some have flat stretchers similar to those seen on William and Mary highboys, although here they are heavy enough to serve as footboards.

Not all Pennsylvania stretcher-base farm tables have box stretchers. A considerable number employ a medial arrangement, that is, the end stretchers are joined at the middle by a center or medial stretcher. Usually these stretchers are square, and aside from the medial arrangement, these tables look much like the table in figure 20-5A. However, sometimes the stretchers are turned as we see in the Lancaster County table in figure 20-5B. Turned stretchers are also seen in some Southern tables. Aside from the stretchers, this is a fairly typical Delaware Valley table, made of walnut with a cleated top and baluster turned legs. The style is not evident, for it lacks the robust turnings and box stretchers of William and Mary and the cabriole leg of the Queen Anne.

When Pennsylvania farm tables are not given stretchers, the legs are still turned, sometimes just a simple taper, but more often neatly offset turned with a pad foot like that shown in the walnut and pine table in figure 20-5C. Some of these tables have a small horizontal molding at the base of apron like that seen in the tavern table in figure 20-2B. A rare few have shaped cabriole legs and trifid feet. Similar tables were made in the South, principally in Virginia and North Carolina. Here the drawers may be fabricated of yellow pine rather than tulip poplar. Although this table may very well have been produced after the Revolution, in form and construction it is much like other Pennsylvania farm tables. The only acquiesce to modernity are the Queen Anne legs. As such, it again demonstrates the innate conservatism that so often characterizes rural workmanship.

20-5A. Pennsylvania William & Mary farm table, 30" h x 54" w, 1760 – 1800.

20-5B. Lancaster County farm table, 30" h x 38" w, c. 1760.

20-5C. Pennsylvania Queen Anne farm table, 27" h x 48" w, 1760 – 1800.

20-6 Southern farm table. Aside from local interpretations of the standard Pennsylvania farm table, the South seems to have produced relatively few of the large rural tables of the sort that might have been employed in a kitchen or a rural dining room. However, many smaller tables survive, and here we might consider a typical example. The solid little table in figure 20-6 has a Georgia provenance, although it could have been produced anywhere in the South. In common with a great many rural Southern tables, it is made of yellow pine and has simple tapered legs. Many of these tables are not fitted with drawers, and for some reason, when there is a drawer, it frequently will not extend the full width of the apron as was usually done elsewhere.

20-6. Southern Hepplewhite farm table, 30" h x 32" w, c. 1800.

Chapter 21 – Daybeds and Bedsteads

This short chapter will survey the domestic furniture made for napping and sleeping — daybeds and bedsteads. As so frequently is the case, the words used to describe this furniture have changed over the years. Daybeds were originally called couches, and until the end of the eighteenth century there seems to have been a distinction between bed and bedstead, between the expensive mattress and hangings and the much less expensive frame. Here we will mix periods and words, identifying couches by the newer term and beds by the older term, the latter because almost invariably all that remains is the bedstead, into which we now insert that wonderful nineteenth century invention — the box spring and padded mattress.

Daybeds and bedsteads are an anomaly among domestic furniture in that there is so little overlap between the two: daybeds went pretty much out of use and out of production well before the outbreak of the Revolution, and the great majority of surviving bedsteads actually postdate the Revolution. While a prosperous colonial family might have had a daybed in the parlor and a number of bedsteads in the sleeping rooms, very few of the latter survive today. Most were no more than simple frames made of local woods. They went into the kindling pile when the mattress and hangings were no longer of use. Not many daybeds remain either, for they do not seem to have been widely popular and are very much a single purpose furniture. Nothing is more inimical to survival than to go out of fashion, and then to have no other use.

Daybeds

21-1 Daybeds. Daybeds are not difficult to place, for they emulate the designs of chairs, and better yet, they do so at a time when chairs are regionally very distinct. They are little more than an elongated chair with six or eight legs and an adjustable back, and in the following illustrations you will see all sorts of similarities between daybeds and Queen Anne and Chippendale chairs.

There are two basic types of daybeds: those assembled from turnings like the chairs discussed in chapter 6, and those made of sawn and shaped components like the chairs covered in chapter 5. While the former are rare in New England, we might start with an example that probably dates from the first half of the eighteenth century (21-1A). Turn back to chapter 6 and in figure 6-3C you will see a banister-back side chair with a similar arched crest rail. These early New England daybeds are usually made of maple which was then either painted black or given a walnut finish. Although this banister-back daybed is identified only as being from New England, it would appear to be an urban product, for the turnings are sophisticated and the stiles have been offset turned so as to give the back a slight rake.

Perhaps due to the earlier settlement, daybeds are more common in New England than in the Middle Atlantic. Most of the surviving examples are in the later Queen Anne style with cabriole legs and pad feet like that shown in figure 21-1B. Aside from the extended rails and additional legs, this walnut daybed is very similar to a great many Massachusetts Queen Anne chairs. The arrised cabriole legs, block and turned stretchers, and the pronounced disks under the pad feet are seen everywhere on chairs in eastern Massachusetts.

By the second half of the eighteenth century, the limited popularity of the daybed was coming to an end, and in New England, Chippendale-style daybeds like that shown in figure 21-1C are less common than Queen Anne. Like many later New England Chippendale side chairs, the stretchers have been omitted. As would be expected of early New England furniture, most of these cabriole-leg daybeds are made of either walnut or maple. A rare few are made of mahogany. Most are also from eastern Massachusetts, with a few from Rhode Island. Note that the splats on both of these daybeds are fairly common New England patterns.

While daybeds were most probably produced to some extent throughout the Middle Atlantic, very few survive that are not from the Philadelphia area, and even these are scarce. Here again though, we might look at an example of each basic form, the first a Pennsylvania daybed having the same cylinder-and-ball turning pattern seen in so much Delaware Valley seating furniture (21-1D). Note that this maple daybed has the same leg and stretcher pattern employed in the immensely popular Delaware Valley ladder-back chairs (6-7A), and also, that the arched crest rail resembles that seen in early Pennsylvania banister-back chairs (6-3G). Unlike New England daybeds, all, or most all, Pennsylvania William and Mary daybeds of this period have rounded seat rails and rush seats.

In contrast to New England, Pennsylvania daybeds in the Queen Anne style are quite rare, and while we will look at one, it may the only example you will ever see. Aside from the additional pairs of legs, the daybed in figure 21-1E is not all that different from a great many Philadelphia chairs of this time in the shape of the splat, the trifid feet, and the lack of stretchers. The deep rails are very probably tenoned through the stiles. As you would expect, this very solid daybed is made of walnut.

With these five examples we come to the end of daybeds, for while they were produced in all regions, I know of only one surviving Southern example. This is a turned daybed, thought to be have been made in Charleston, South Carolina, in the collection of the Museum of Early Southern Decorative Arts in Winston-Salem, North Carolina.

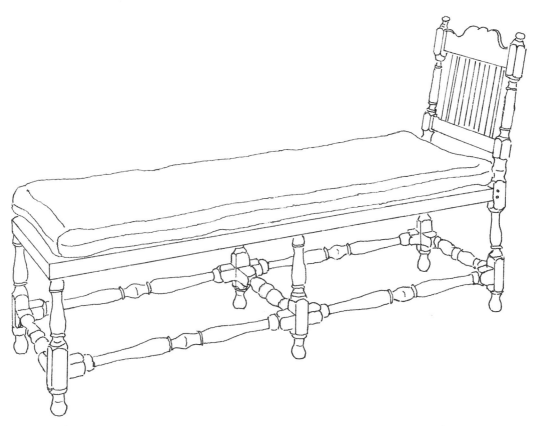

21-1A. New England William & Mary daybed, 60" l, 1730 – 1750.

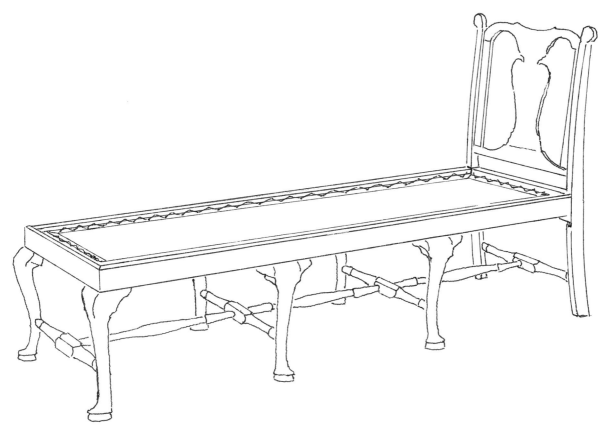

21-1B. Massachusetts Queen Anne daybed, 68" l, 1750 – 1760.

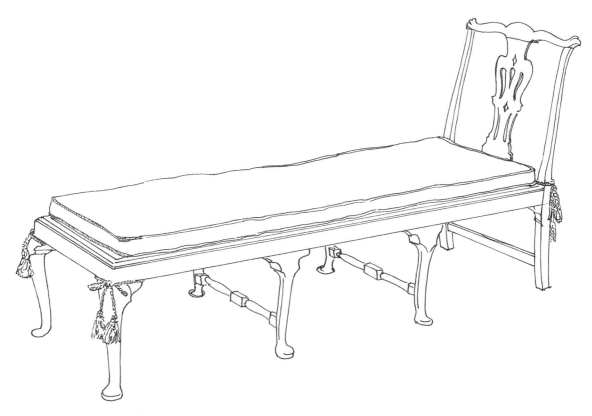

21-1C. New England Chippendale daybed, 74" l, c. 1770.

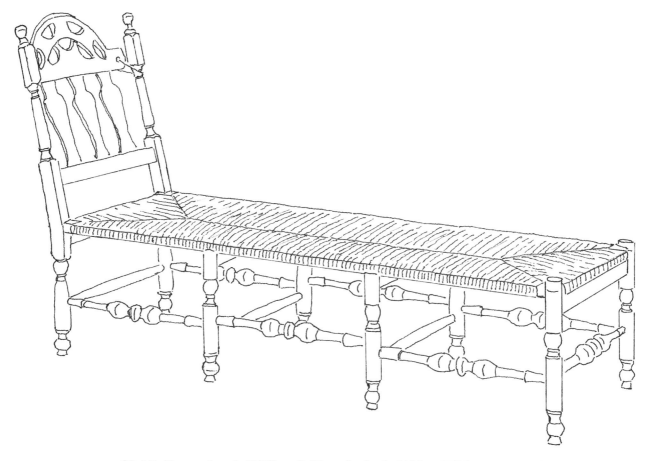

21-1D. Pennsylvania William & Mary daybed, 41" h x 75" l, 1730 – 1750.

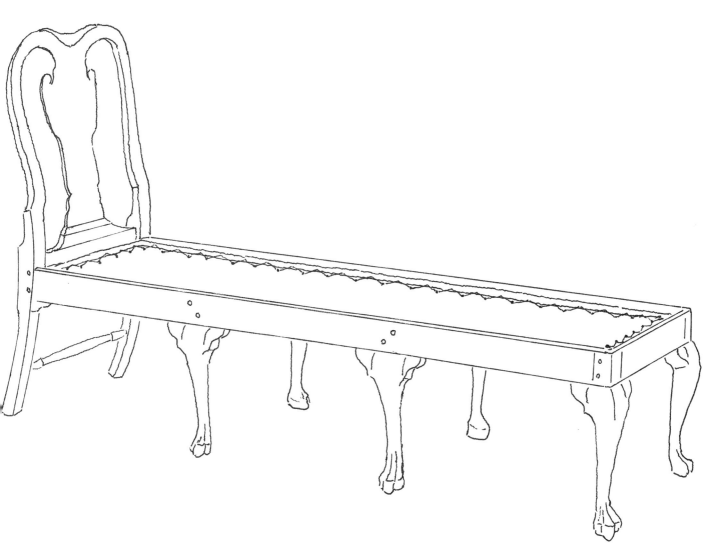

21-1E. Philadelphia Queen Anne daybed, 1740 – 1760.

Bedsteads

Bedsteads are more of a challenge, for unlike daybeds, they are not just an atypical expression of a common form. They are their own class of furniture. Also, bedsteads tend toward variation, to be one off products. While I will show you some representative types, they are not nearly as standardized as seating furniture and case work, and here you may have to consider secondary woods and regional motifs to determine where a bedstead was made. Fortunately, the foot posts of high post beds often incorporate regional features, particularly if the bed was produced in or near an urban center. Better yet, old bedsteads are amply supplied with what might be seen as secondary woods, for the structure that does not show under the hangings, the side and head rails, the head posts, and the headboard, will frequently be made of less expensive local woods. Only the foot rail and foot posts will be imported mahogany. In northern New England these components will usually be birch, maple and white pine, from Connecticut south maple and tulip poplar, and in the South, tulip poplar and yellow pine.

Although in the following sections I use style terms such as Chippendale and Hepplewhite, many old bedsteads, particularly rural low post beds and the popular pencil post bed, resist any particular designation. These are simply identified by form.

21-2 New England bedsteads. New England bedsteads would seem to exhibit greater diversity than those from any other region, and in this section we will see four very different designs. They are all easy studies in that all four display features associated with New England workmanship. In addition, we will take a brief look at a common type of folding bedstead, if for no other reason than that most of the relatively few surviving examples seem to be from New England.

High- and low-post bedsteads having cabriole legs are quite rare, even though they were produced to some extent in all the major urban centers: Boston, New York, Philadelphia, and Charleston. That the bedstead in figure 21-2A was produced in eastern Massachusetts, and most probably in Boston, is suggested by the creased or arrised knees on the cabriole legs and the ball and claw feet in which the toes slope to the rear of the ball. Turn back to chapter 5 and you will see the same retracted claw foot in figure 5-1A. A rare few of these New England beds have pad rather than ball and claw feet. The head posts, side and head rails of this mahogany bedstead are most probably either birch or maple, the headboard white pine. However, here we need to be careful, for often these components have been replaced at a later time, and then perhaps with other woods.

Earlier, when surveying card and breakfast tables, it was noted that the English feature of blocking the ends of Marlborough legs was common in Pennsylvania. Thus, you might think that the mahogany bedstead in figure 21-2B would be from the Philadelphia area. But it is not, because both Marlborough legs and blocked feet are often seen on New England bedsteads, and beds like that shown here were produced in Massachusetts and Rhode Island, and possibly New Hampshire. This is a better-than-average bed, for the headboard is neatly finished, and the

head posts have been turned to match the carved and reeded foot posts. Like the previous example, the roping or canvas sacking is held in place by a row of small turned knobs. Blocked Marlborough legs were particularly fashionable in Rhode Island, and here you will often see them in conjunction with stop-fluting on either the legs or the posts. You might also think that these bedsteads predate the Revolution, and while many Rhode Island examples are indeed Colonial, this example with its slender proportions and urn and baluster posts is very much neoclassical. Only the legs are rococo. As such, it is perhaps in keeping with the lingering New England affection for the rococo that is seen in so much case furniture.

The bedstead in figure 21-2C is very obviously a product of the northeast, for the double taper on the foot posts is seen everywhere in New England. When not given a double taper, New England Hepplewhite bedsteads will often have pronounced spade feet. The elongated neoclassical urn shape just above the rails is often seen on these beds. Although the foot posts on this bed are reeded and given a little string inlay, this bedstead is a somewhat budget product, for there has been no attempt to shape the head posts to match the foot posts.

Sheraton bedsteads are far more common than Hepplewhite, and here there is no difficulty in illustrating a representative example. The field bed in figure 21-2D is typical of many Massachusetts bedsteads, particularly in the inverted baluster and ring turning of the legs. Sometimes these will be given a flattened button feet. The other common pattern is a taper with a step at the foot, what looks like, and is often called, a turned spade foot. The prevalence of these two patterns suggest, that at least in urban centers, that cabinetmakers obtained the foot and head posts from full-time turners.

The shape of the foot posts above the rail of this bedstead, with the inverted tulip-shaped carved section in the middle, is seen in many Massachusetts beds, particularly those made in Salem. The same pattern is seen in late Federal Salem card tables. Later versions of these popular beds will have spiral turning rather than fluting above and below the center section. Some better-quality bedsteads have inlaid rectangular figured birch panels where the foot posts are left square to join the rails, a feature also seen in many New England sofas.

Somewhere I need to illustrate a fold-up or press bed, and since they are most often seen in New England auctions, we will discuss them here, even though they might have been produced anywhere for a home where space was at a premium. In the past they were called slaw beds; slaw being a corruption of the sixteenth century word "slough," which meant "clothed." When folded up, these beds were stowed behind curtains hung from the overhead frame, and were, in effect, clothed. The bed in figure 21-2E is typical of New England press beds, made of maple and given only the most simple inverted baluster shaped legs; although in this case the roping or canvas sacking is supported by the small turned knobs usually seen in better quality beds. Simpler examples just have holes bored in the rails for roping. In form they are basically just low beds with the head posts extended to support the overhead frames. Some omit the frame, and perhaps were just folded up against the wall.

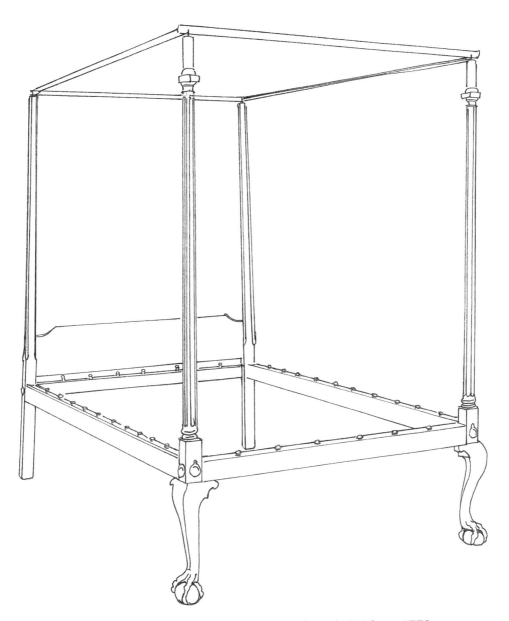

21-2A. Massachusetts Chippendale bedstead, 69" h, c. 1770.

21-2B. New England Federal bedstead, 89" h, 1790 – 1810.

21-2C. New England Hepplewhite bedstead, 80" h, 1790 – 1815.

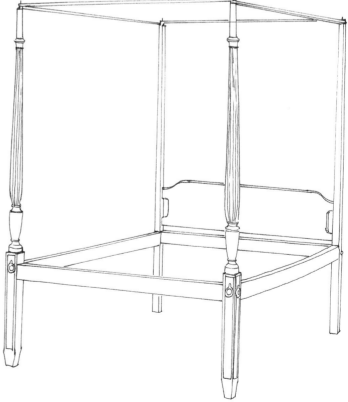
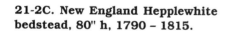

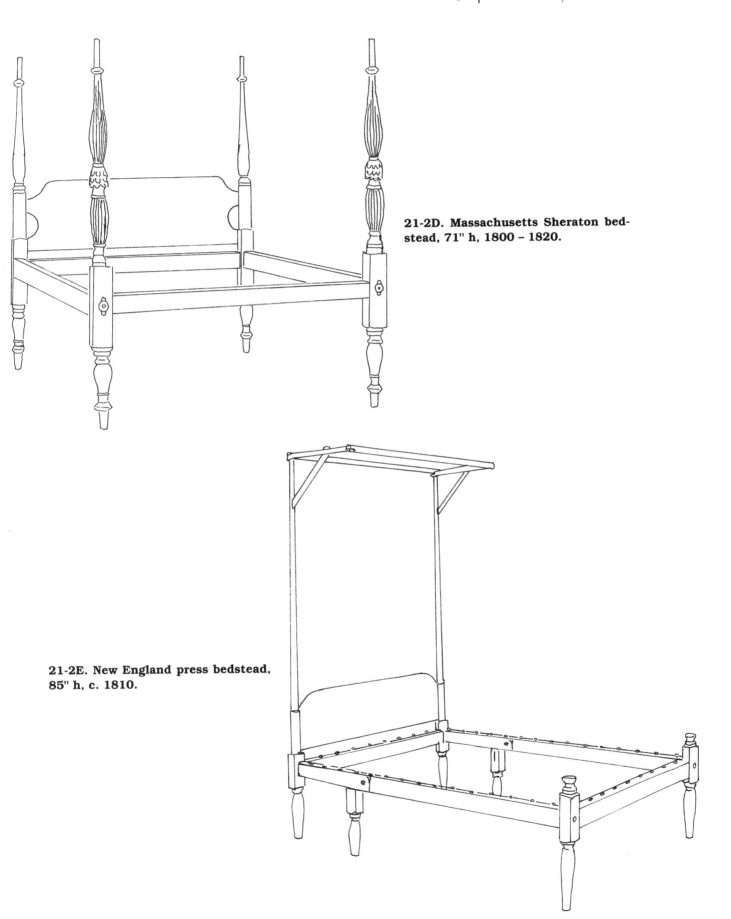

21-2D. Massachusetts Sheraton bedstead, 71" h, 1800 – 1820.

21-2E. New England press bedstead, 85" h, c. 1810.

21-3 Middle Atlantic bedsteads. In this section we will discuss four very different bedsteads, the first a typical product of New York City, the second a typical product of Philadelphia, then two common rural forms that might be covered here because they were produced in all regions, and the Middle Atlantic is roughly midway between New England and the South.

High-style New York bedsteads are usually fairly easy to identify, for they employ decorative features seen in other New York furniture of the period. The foot posts of the bedstead in figure 21-3A have much the same fluted urn and waterleaf carving seen in many New York classical tables. The baluster legs with the cup-shaped foot are often seen on New York bedsteads. Their general simplicity, in contrast with the carving and fluting above the rails, suggest that the legs may have once been covered with a skirt. In common with other New York furniture of this time, these bedsteads tend to be of good quality, in this case having turned head posts and a finished headboard. While this bed might be considered Sheraton in style, the decoration of the foot posts is very much New York classical.

Philadelphia bedsteads have a feature, that while not unique, can help in identification. Frequently the head and foot posts just above the rails are deeply chamfered as shown in the Philadelphia bedstead in figure 21-3B. Like many other furniture "rules," this is not a sure thing, for chamfering is often seen on head and foot posts. The New England bedstead illustrated in figure 21-2B is treated in a similar manner, although here the chamfered section is much longer, and also, this bedstead is lighter and more New England in feeling.

This mahogany bedstead is very different from New York workmanship in that the elongated urns above the chamfered sections have drapery, cord and tassel carving rather than fluting that would most likely have been employed in New York. Also note the square notches in the side rails. The mattress is supported by crosswise slats rather than the usual roped sacking. This made for a somewhat cooler bed during the hot summer months. It is also seen in many Southern bedsteads.

You may read that both the foot and head posts of Philadelphia high-post beds will be finished, but this is no more than a generalization, for all the posts on some New York beds are carved and reeded, and everywhere on quality workmanship the head posts are apt to be turned to emulate the carved and reeded foot posts. This has been done in the New England bedstead shown in figure 21-2B. Finished head posts are more likely an indication of a climate where all the winter hangings are put away during the hot summer months.

Now we come to perhaps the most definitive American bedstead, the aptly named pencil-post bed. Although most of the surviving examples are from New England, we will cover them here to emphasize that they were made in all regions. They are American beds, not New England beds. Of the two bedsteads illustrated in Hurst and Prown's *Southern Furniture 1680 – 1830*, one is a pencil-post. The reason for their abundance is evident if one considers the difficulty in turning a 7' or 8' 4" square billet. Turning a bed post requires an unusually powerful lathe with a long bed. Until well into the nineteenth century, this was probably the providence of professionals in urban centers, which may be why we see local turning patterns. In comparison, the head and foot posts on a pencil-post bed could be worked out with no more than a saw, a plane, and a spokeshave.

While the simplest of high-post bedsteads, there are some differences among pencil posts, principally in the shaping of the legs. The New England bedstead in figure 21-3C has square Malborough legs, but more often you will see either Hepplewhite legs, or tapered, chamfered legs that echo the eight-sided chamfered posts. For some reason, Middle Atlantic and Southern beds are more apt to be given footboards, perhaps to provide a rest for turned-back sheets and blankets on warm nights, but I must admit that this observation is based on a very small sample. Aside from chance provenance, the best indication of region lies in the woods employed for the posts, rails, and headboards. As noted earlier, in northern New England we would expect to see birch, maple, and eastern white pine, then from Connecticut south, maple and poplar, and in the South, perhaps poplar and yellow pine. However, as neither the posts nor the headboards require large stock, you may see timber from smaller trees, perhaps red gum, river birch, cedar, or mulberry. Get lucky and you may find one made of cypress. While the thin chamfered posts give these beds an early look, most all are probably Federal rather than Colonial.

Lastly, while on the subject of rural bedsteads, we should discuss an early low-post bed. While fewer survive, at one time these must have been much more common than high-post beds. The shaping of the posts and legs suggest the low-post bedstead in figure 21-3D was produced in New England, although similar beds were made in all regions. Here again, Middle Atlantic beds seem to be more apt to be fitted with footboards, although by the second decade of the nineteenth century low-post beds everywhere were likely to have both headboards and footboards. These beds are frequently not as early as their simplicity would suggest. When looking at a paint-decorated bedstead, remember that while black and red finishes may be eighteenth century, milk-base paints and grain painting are nineteenth century.

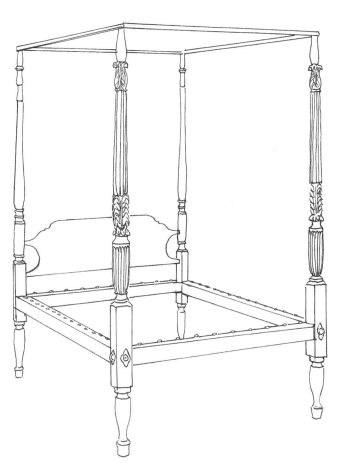

21-3A. New York classical bedstead, 91" h, c. 1810.

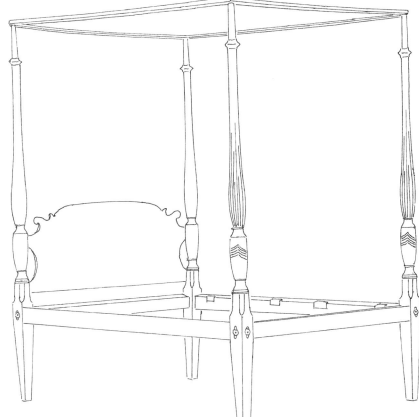

21-3B. Philadelphia Hepplewhite high-post bedstead, 91" h, c. 1810.

21-3C. New England pencil-post bedstead, 77" h, 1780 – 1810.

21-4 Southern bedsteads. This will be the only section for which there is not a single illustration. The reason is that among the thousands of illustrations assembled in the research that led to this book, I do not have a single suitable illustration of an early Southern high-post bedstead. Although the major collections of Southern furniture have some fine examples, they must be quite rare.

However, I can suggest what to look for. As might be expected in a region with long, hot summers, Southern high post beds tend to be elevated well off the floor, to be extra wide, and to be unusually tall. Many — if not reduced in height — have eight-foot posts. The mattress will often be supported by slats rather than the usual roped sacking. Better-quality beds may be fitted with castors, probably so that the bed could be pulled away from the wall on hot nights.

Given the rural nature of much of the South and the desirability of mosquito nettings, pencil-post beds must have been quite common. While the posts might be made of local hardwoods, a hard Southern pine would have served equally well. To keep the netting away from the occupants of the bed, there might be a headboard and footboard.

Charleston bedsteads, like so much Charleston furniture, are in a class by themselves. First off, mahogany was so common in coastal South Carolina that with the exception of headboards, bedsteads are apt to be made entirely of mahogany. A bed with mahogany rails will generally be from Charleston. For some reason, perhaps the heat, the headboards are usually removable, being held in place with pairs of parallel slats. Like mahogany rails, these are not unique to the area, but both together are a pretty good indication of Charleston workmanship. Lastly, the foot posts are distinctive. Most Charleston bedsteads are neoclassical rather than rococo, and have Hepplewhite legs that terminate in spade feet. Above the legs, the squared section where the posts join the rails is usually given a little neoclassical inlay. Above the rails the posts are turned, usually first with an elongated urn decorated with carved overlapping leafage, then above this often the famous rice carving at the base of a reeded post. Should you have never seen rice outside of an Uncle Ben's box, this looks like a small sheaf of wheat in which the grains in the tassels are clearly delineated, and the left and right side tassels bow over to face straight down.

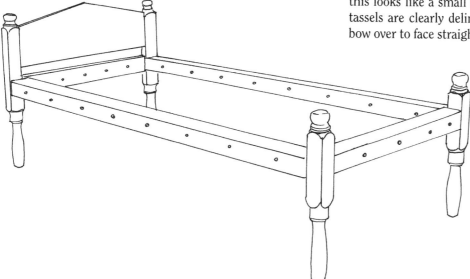

21-3D. New England low-post bedstead, 29" h x 79" l, c. 1780.

In every survey there are inevitably a few things that should be covered that do not fit any particular category, and yet, if just put somewhere would be difficult to locate, not unlike a book returned to the wrong shelf in a library, is lost for years. An additional difficulty is that some of these, although themselves well-known regional forms, are largely the products of one area, with no more than a minimal overlap into adjacent regions. While they should be discussed, they perversely refuse to follow the logical north to south format of the other furniture in this book.

First I might note what is not covered. This chapter does not discuss the small household furniture that usually lacks any significant regional character: pipe boxes, cradles, and fire screens. Also omitted are a number of primarily English forms: tea caddies, knife boxes, knife urns, writing boxes, and canterburies, which, while produced to some extent in America, do not exhibit any particular regional characteristics. American examples are usually identified on the basis of American secondary woods, but here we need to be careful, for much timber, both hardwoods and softwoods, was exported to England. White pine provided just as good a base for veneer in England as it did in America.

In the sections that follow, the furniture is discussed in alphabetical order, commencing with boxes and ending with tables. Although this is the last chapter and, indeed, something of a catchall, it nevertheless covers some of the most interesting regional furniture.

22-1 Spice boxes. Of all small regional furniture, perhaps the most famous is the Pennsylvania spice box or spice chest. There are two things to keep in mind about these charming little storage chests: although "spice box" and "spice case" are early terms, many were probably not used for spices; also, not all spice boxes were produced in southeastern Pennsylvania. It is possible that they originally were intended to hold spices, and some indeed appear to have been used in this manner. However, most have a door and a lock, suggesting that they were more often used to hold small valuables: silver spoons, coins, jewelry, eyeglasses, documents, and the like. The door permitted all the little inside drawers to be secured with a single lock; and keeping family valuables in a single place made for easy removal in event of a fire. It is easy to forget that in a time before thousand gallon pumpers, a house fire, once well established, would have been very difficult to put out.

To show that not all spice boxes are from Pennsylvania, we might start with a small chest probably made in eastern Massachusetts about the turn of the seventeenth century (22-1A). That this is an early box is suggested by the applied geometric moldings on the door, a feature more commonly seen in early Jacobean paneled chests of drawers. Spice chests were not nearly as successful a form in New England as in Pennsylvania, for not only are they quite rare, but most exhibit the base molding and ball feet of the William and Mary style. They do not seem to have been produced after the early years of the eighteenth century.

The great majority of spice boxes are from southeastern Pennsylvania, principally Philadelphia or Chester County. Most are made of walnut. Many have a charming little arched Queen Anne "tombstone" door like that illustrated in figure 22-1B. They were a popular and long lived form, being successively produced in William and Mary, Queen Anne, Chippendale, and Hepplewhite styles from about the 1740s right up into the early years of the nineteenth century. In addition to the straight bracket feet and arched door shown here, you will see ball, ogee bracket, and French feet, and square paneled and flush doors. A few chests have two doors. Behind the door there will normally be a symmetrical grouping of 7 to 12 small drawers around a somewhat larger center drawer. Simpler versions, made of pine rather than walnut, often lack the covering door. These may indeed have been used for keeping spices and herbs.

Similar spice boxes were produced to some extent in Virginia, and most probably also in North Carolina, the form having come south with settlers from Pennsylvania. These are usually less sophisticated than Pennsylvania chests, and are sometimes made of yellow pine.

Before leaving spice boxes, we might take a quick look at the high end of the market, those made in the form of a high chest of drawers. The spice chest in figure 22-1C is typical of these remarkable cabinets, although it is made of cherry rather than the more usual walnut. In form, most are similar to Pennsylvania high chests with either slipper, ball and claw, Spanish, or trifid feet, then usually the distinctive four-square, two-over-two drawer arrangement so often seen in rural Pennsylvania high chests and dressing tables. A rare few are William and Mary in style with trumpet turned legs, flat stretchers, and ball feet. Like high chests, they are constructed in two parts, the upper case resting within a mid-molding fastened to the top of the lower case. They vary in size between three and four feet in height, and one might wonder if they were not intended as children's furniture were not the cabinet doors fitted with a lock.

22-1A. New England William & Mary spice box, 18" h, c. 1700.

22-1B. Pennsylvania Queen Anne spice box, 22" h, 1740 – 1780.

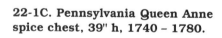

22-1C. Pennsylvania Queen Anne spice chest, 39" h, 1740 – 1780.

22-2 Bottle case. Bottle cases are small lift-top chests for holding bottles of alcoholic beverages. In probate records they are variously identified as bottle, gin, or brandy cases, or cases of bottles. While popularly thought to be a Southern form, they were in fact produced to some extent in all regions. In the South they are normally raised on frames. Sometimes you will see a sliding shelf, or sliding shelves on either side of the frame, but more often a case will have a single full-width drawer like that shown in figure 22-2. While this is very grand mahogany veneered and inlaid example, even simpler rural versions are neatly made and are apt to be given some inlay in the new neoclassical manner. Although seen in some major collections, bottle cases with square Marlborough legs are quite rare. While Chippendale in style, most of these are probably also Federal rather than Colonial.

Lift the top and inside you will see a dozen or so square compartments. These reputedly were sized to fit the standard square Dutch gin bottle, which when emptied would be refilled with something equally lethal. The case is usually fitted with a pair of brass carrying handles so that it could easily be taken out for refilling the bottles.

Bottle cases like that shown here were produced in northeastern North Carolina and tidewater Virginia. Inland they become simpler, usually made of walnut or cherry, and with flat rather than cased tops. A few produced in coastal Maryland are very different, being wider and constructed as single units without the usual carrying handles.

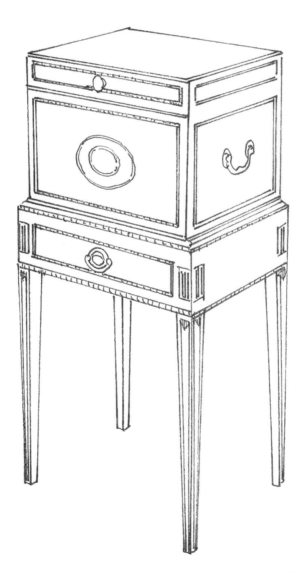

22-2. Virginia Hepplewhite bottle case, 37" h, c. 1800.

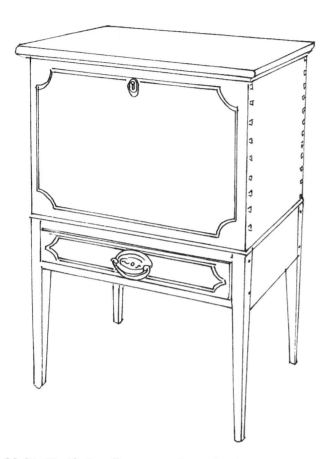

22-3A. North Carolina sugar chest, 31" h, 1800 – 1810.

22-3 Sugar chests. Sugar chests are always, or almost always, of Southern manufacture. Most are also products of the backcountry, principally Tennessee and Kentucky, but also Virginia and North Carolina. In the rural South before the Civil War, sugar was such a luxury that it was often kept, together with tea and coffee, in a locked chest.

Unlike bottle cases, sugar chests postdate the Revolution and always seem to be neoclassical in style. While most are both rural and Sheraton, a small number are more urban, having tapered Hepplewhite legs, neoclassical brasses, and inlay, similar to the Southern bottle case illustrated in the previous section. The handsome sugar chest in figure 22-3A could easily be mistaken for a bottle case but that it lacks carrying handles and the inside is not divided into square compartments for bottles.

More typically, sugar chests are Sheraton in style and have turned legs like that shown in the walnut chest in figure 22-3B. Some resemble bottle cases in having a separate frame, but instead of bottle compartments there will be two or three large bins for light and dark sugar, coffee, and perhaps tea. Some have a dovetailed liners that can be removed for scrubbing out. A few are made with compartments for bottles so as to serve as both bottle cases and sugar chests. Others have overhanging tops and resemble small tables, these to provide handy surfaces to break chunks of sugar off the cones or loaves. Some are in the form of small desks.

Like bottle cases, these sugar chests must have been much prized, for they are neatly made, very often of cherry rather than walnut. The majority are Sheraton in style, and some are probably very late Sheraton at that, for such was the affection for them that they continued to be made right up through the middle of the nineteenth century, probably long after sugar ceased to be so rare and expensive in the backcountry. Like the two-drawer chest shown here, they often employ the paneled construction that everywhere returns to case furniture in the second quarter of the nineteenth century.

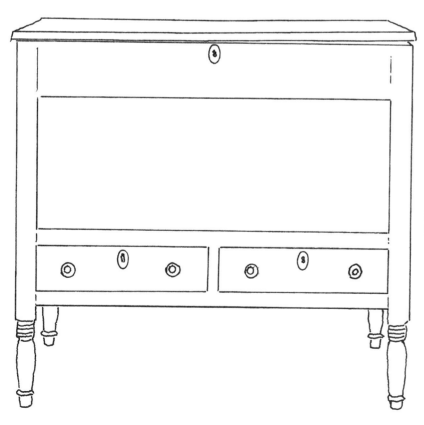

22-3B. Southern Sheraton sugar chest, 34" h, c. 1820.

22-4 Hanging cupboards. In the past, houses were filled with inquisitive small children and hungry small rodents, and from this time we have all sorts of wall-mounted storage containers: pipe boxes, candle boxes, sugar boxes, and a great many small cupboards. Most of the latter are very simple, little more than a rectangular box with a door, with no decoration other than perhaps a molded cornice. They tell us no more of region than is suggested by the species of wood employed in their construction. Here we might look at three better-than-average examples whose form and primary wood is suggestive of region, the first a white pine cupboard that was probably made in Connecticut (22-4A). That this cupboard might well be a product of Connecticut is suggested not only by the inventive arched cornice, but also by the applied carved pinwheel so often seen in Connecticut case work.

Quite the most notable hanging cupboards were made in southeastern Pennsylvania, and here we will consider two typical forms, the first a simple cupboard (22-4B) that was probably made about the end of the eighteenth century. Although a somewhat budget product, being made of poplar rather than walnut, and having the simplest of moldings, it is typical of a great many Pennsylvania cupboards in having a drawer under the cupboard and being given both cornice and base moldings. Some Pennsylvania cupboards are quite elegant, having swan's-neck pediments, flanking quarter columns, and complex moldings. Earlier versions are apt to be made of walnut or cherry and have a paneled arched door like the spice box illustrated in figure 22-1B.

Perhaps the most distinctive Pennsylvania cupboards are a group of rural Chester County and Lancaster County cupboards having an open bases with scrolled sides that flank narrow shelves (22-4C). The form would appear to have been introduced from the Continent, for they have a distinctly Germanic look. Frequently the doors swing on rat's-tail hinges, and sometimes the cupboards will have the applied mid-molding shown in this illustration. Often there will be a small drawer just below the door. The narrow shelf would seem too shallow for pewter or china. Maybe it held clay pipes, the small drawer for the tobacco, iron strikers and flints. These early cupboards are usually made of walnut. Later cupboards, like that in the previous illustration, are generally made of pine or poplar.

22-4A. New England hanging cupboard, 27" h, 1800 – 1820.

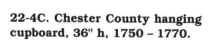

22-4B. Pennsylvania hanging cupboard, 25" h, c. 1800.

22-4C. Chester County hanging cupboard, 36" h, 1750 – 1770.

22-5 Tabletop desks. Lap desks are very common, but most date from the nineteenth century and are English, made in London by firms that specialized in these small portable desks. In this section we will instead examine a box and two tabletop desks that are both American and early enough to still speak to us of region.

The first is the New England tabletop box shown in Figure 22-5A. These early lift-top boxes are frequently called Bible boxes in the fond belief that they once held large family Bibles, and indeed they may have, but they would also have provided a container for valuables at a time when house fires were all too common. The slanting top could have provided a comfortable reading surface for a large Bible, or may have been used as a desk, the case holding quill pens, ink, and paper. If used as a desk, a box might have been placed on a stool to bring the top to a comfortable height. Like much other early domestic furniture, we can only guess how such a box was actually used.

American tabletop boxes of this period are quite rare; most of those you see will be either English or Continental. Generally, American boxes will be carved only on the front rather than on the front and sides, and will be made of a combination of woods, generally with oak sides and a softwood top and bottom. Most of these Pilgrim Century boxes are products of New England, principally Massachusetts and Connecticut. Massachusetts boxes normally have white pine tops and bottoms, Connecticut boxes either yellow pine or tulip poplar or a mix of both. Sometimes the carving can be associated with a particular New England joiner.

Somewhat later, New England tabletop boxes acquire the base molding and ball feet of the William and Mary style as shown in the pine and oak box in figure 22-5B. That this handsome little box may have been intended for writing is suggest by the interior, which is divided into two compartments, although the slant top would seem too small to provide a useful writing surface. That it may simply have been a storage box, as is suggested by the presence of a lock. Like other New England boxes of this period, it is of very basic construction, made of local woods and fastened together with simple lap joints and nails. A similar Pennsylvania box would probably be made of walnut and joined with dovetails.

In common with spice boxes, Pennsylvania tabletop desks are more plentiful and generally far better made than those few that survive from New England. That there are more may be because of their greater popularity or simply because they were better made and more likely to survive. In either event, they are charming small furniture, neatly made of walnut with dovetailed cases. While some are William and Mary in style, others are Queen Anne or Chippendale like the handsome little desk shown in figure 22-5C. Unlike the previous examples, this is a proper desk with a slant lid that opens onto little square lopers. Both the case and the bracket feet are dovetailed, and in Delaware Valley fashion, the dovetails are employed as an element of the decoration.

22-5A. New England tabletop box, 10" h, 1680 – 1710.

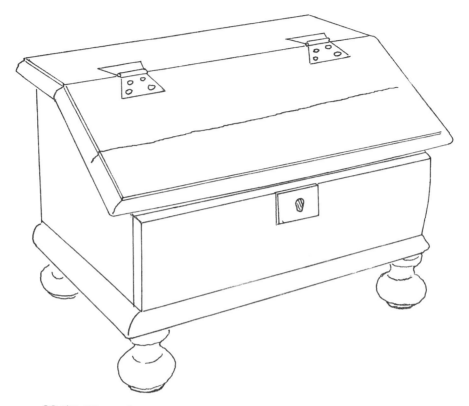

22-5B. Massachusetts writing box, 12" h x 18" w, 1700 – 1740.

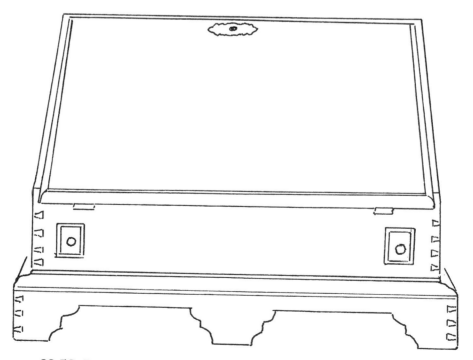

22-5C. Pennsylvania tabletop desk, 16" h x 24" w, 1740 – 1760.

22-6 Children's furniture. Furniture made for children is not rare. The great majority comprises diminutive turned chairs, Windsor chairs, lift-top chests, and chests of drawers. For some reason, perhaps because a small tavern table would serve the purpose, there are very few tables. Far less common, but most enchanting, are little desks like that shown in figure 22-6. Most of these were produced in New England. For the most part, children's furniture is what you would expect would be made for children: both simple and sturdy, and without the veneer, inlay, and carving found in other period work. High-style examples are very rare.

The general simplicity of children's furniture does not always make for easy identification. While the overall design and choice of woods can suggest region, there is seldom enough detail to distinguish a specific area. You will be able to identify New England or Middle Atlantic, and very rarely, Southern, but seldom Massachusetts or New York. The charming little desk in figure 22-6 is a case in point. The use of maple and white pine suggest northern New England, but the interior is too simplified to suggest where.

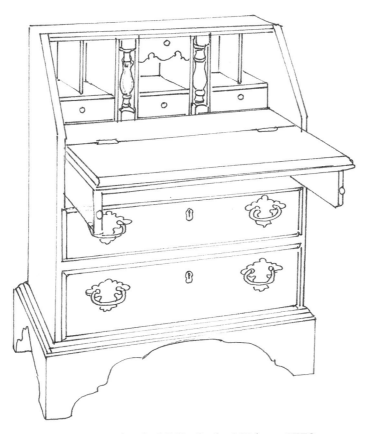

22-6. New England child's desk, 22" h, c. 1770.

22-7 Miniature furniture. While the subject of innumerable myths, most all miniature furniture was simply produced for the enjoyment of children. Most are just children's toys. Unlike children's furniture, they cover the complete range of domestic accouterments, from chests of drawers to fire screens, tea services, and brass andirons. There is almost nothing that cannot be found replicated in miniature. For the most part, they faithfully emulate the fashions of their period, albeit in a somewhat simplified manner. Most common are chests of drawers, followed by beds and chairs — just the furniture a young lady would need with her dolls.

Here we might consider two examples, the first a diminutive mahogany reverse-serpentine chest of drawers that was almost certainly made somewhere in New England (22-7A), and the second a somewhat larger Pennsylvania walnut lift-top chest (22-7B). Both of these are easy studies, and perhaps slightly unfair, for the average grade of miniature turned chair or chest of drawers is usually not this easy to place. Where there is not a popular regional model, you may have to look for elements of style and try to identify the primary and secondary woods. You might also take a careful look for inscriptions, for by nature, miniatures are very personal objects, and while almost never labeled, they sometimes carry ink or pencil notations from the maker to the recipient.

22-7A. New England miniature reverse-serpentine chest of drawers, 7" h, c. 1800.

22-7B. Pennsylvania miniature chest, 12" h x 24" l, 1780 – 1800.

22-8 Washstands. In the eighteenth century, prior to the Revolution, small basin stands were used for washing up. The basin was held by a circular ring and supported by three turned columns that ended in small cabriole legs. In America, they do not seem to have been common even among the well-to-do, for American-made examples are quite rare. Most all that you see in shops and at auctions are English.

By the early years of the nineteenth century, though, increasing wealth brings more comforts into the home, and from this time we see a great many washstands. The most common has a large circular opening in the top for the basin, a median shelf with a small drawer, and a lower shelf that held a pitcher of water, although in some the lower shelf appears too delicate to have done much more than stiffen the legs. Often there will small additional shelves to hold soap, or small holes for turned soap cups. Usually there is a splashboard to keep water off the wall. There are two basic forms of these washstands: square stands designed to stand flush against bedroom walls and, more commonly, triangular stands that fit into corners. We might look at two regional examples of each.

The most common type of corner stand has three slender legs, the front two flaring out at the bottom to provide additional stability. They might be seen as Hepplewhite in style, although the legs normally lack taper. The washstand in figure 22-8A with the scalloped apron under the top and the distinctively shaped lower shelf is one of a large group of similar stands produced in eastern Massachusetts.

Variations on this design were produced in all regions from Portsmouth, New Hampshire, down to Charleston, South Carolina. Outside of New England, the delicate lower shelf is often omitted. Southern washstands are apt to omit the flaring legs and have either Marlborough or tapered legs, sometimes with a fourth leg in the middle to provide additional stability. Most are fitted with a small drawer in the center of the middle shelf. South of New England, this drawer will usually be framed of tulip poplar rather than white pine.

New York Hepplewhite-style washstands are much like other New York Hepplewhite furniture: well made, with generous use of fine veneer and inlay. More common are the somewhat later Sheraton stands, and here we might look at a fine example (22-8B). This large, solid washstand with reeded legs and dark veneers is typical of New York City workmanship in the first decades of the nineteenth century. It is noticeably larger and more solid looking than the previous New England washstand. Because the corner legs do not flare out at the bottom, a

middle leg has been fitted to provide additional stability. The median shelf is so low that it probably was used to hold the pitcher, while the lower shelf is mostly a stretcher to stiffen the unsupported middle leg.

Aside from a great many later rural examples, square washstands are less common than corner stands, perhaps because it was easier to find wall space in the corner of a bedroom. They also seem to have been most popular in New England, and here we might look at two examples, the first a handsome little stand that was probably made in eastern Massachusetts (22-8C). Why Massachusetts? Well, if you look at the apron under the top, you will see that it is the same shape as we saw in figure 22-8A, a shape very common in eastern Massachusetts. Also, the feet are of a standard Boston turning (16-1B). The little drawer will most probably be made of white pine.

The other New England example is the distinctive classical washstand shown in figure 22-8D. These English-type stands were fashionable in the Boston area, particularly in Salem and the North Shore. The design seems to have spread throughout northern New England, for there are painted and stenciled versions attributed to New Hampshire and Vermont. While an urban product, this is a relatively simple example. Grander versions are of the same general shape, but are open in the middle, the rear of the top supported by turned extensions of the back legs, the front by a pair of carved and reeded scrolls, and then an incurved lower drawer to leave room for the user's legs.

This section ends without illustrating either a Philadelphia or a Southern washstand. It is because among the thousands of illustrations assembled in research for this book, I have not a single representative example of either. For some reason, washstands, or perhaps more correctly, surviving washstands, seem to be far less common south of New York City. However, I can suggest what to look for. As Philadelphia was slow to accept the neoclassical following the Revolution, we would expect to see a conservative washstand, perhaps a rococo form that is nevertheless neoclassical in feeling like the square stand with thin Marlborough legs illustrated in Plate 413 of *Hornor's Blue Book of Philadelphia Furniture*. The few Southern washstands I've seen are atypical in detail and exhibit a similar conservatism. They omit the lower shelf and have straight Marlborough or Hepplewhite legs. Washstands were produced in Charleston, South Carolina; and if you encounter a nicely made, but rather atypical urban stand, you might check to see if there is some bald cypress among the secondary woods.

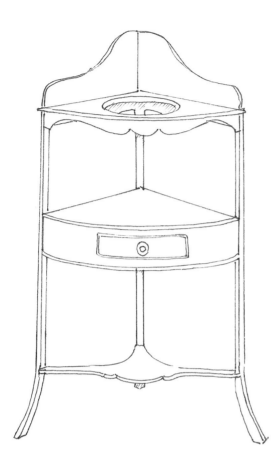

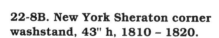

22-8A. Massachusetts Hepplewhite corner washstand, 39" h, c. 1800.

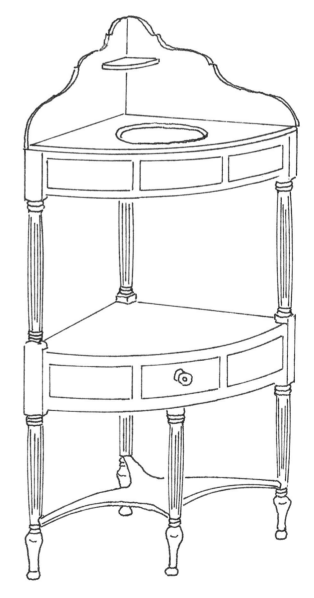

22-8B. New York Sheraton corner washstand, 43" h, 1810 – 1820.

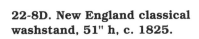

22-8C. Massachusetts Sheraton washstand, 42" h, 1800 – 1820.

22-8D. New England classical washstand, 51" h, c. 1825.

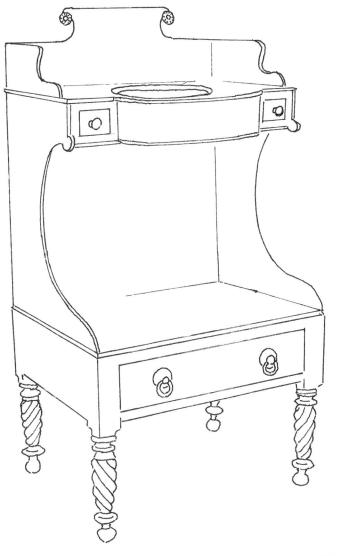

22-9 Hutch tables. Finally in this chapter, and finally for the whole subject of regional furniture, we should look at hutch tables, the best-known Colonial dual purpose furniture. With the top upright, they resemble a simple sort of Jacobean wainscot chair with a wide back to keep off drafts; with the top down they form a small dining table. The name itself is something of a misnomer, for we will see a New England example that lacks the hutch or storage box, and might properly be called a chair table. Hutch and chair tables had a long run, appearing near the close of the seventeenth century, then continuing in production right up into the first decades of the nineteenth. Like much rural furniture, they are not easy to date, and the dates shown with the illustrations are admittedly very rough estimates. Many are not nearly as early as their simple construction would suggest.

The most basic type of New England hutch table is built on a simple box structure like that illustrated in figure 22-9A. Usually the boards that make the sides are just lapped and nailed. Under the seat will be a shortage box or hutch, hutch being an old word for chest. Normally the vertical sides will be tenoned into a trestle base as seen here. Often the box section is raised above the feet and the sides below the box are curved, which provides a lighter and better looking table. New England hutch tables are made of a variety of local woods: all pine, all maple, or a mixture of woods: pine and maple, pine and birch, or pine and oak. They are most often from New England and northern New York, perhaps because when employed as a chair, the large top protected the sitter from cold drafts.

The other common form of New England hutch table is based on a joined chair as seen in figure 22-9B. Most of these handsome tables lack any storage under the seat other than a drawer, and are actually chair tables rather than hutch tables. Some are considerably smaller than this example and have square rather than round or oval tops. While the legs are usually turned, you will also see simpler square or chamfered legs. A few have turned stretchers. Later versions may lack stretchers and at times have a distinctly late Sheraton look, which is probably what they are. The turnings on this table suggest that it was made some time prior to the middle of in the eighteenth century. Note that the top of both this and the previous table are made up of just two very wide pine boards. Later tables are more likely to have three-board tops. In a general way, New England chair tables are better made than hutch tables. Some are entirely maple, and if the top is white pine, then the legs will be maple, birch, or sometimes cherry.

Outside of New England, hutch tables are far less common, and chair tables even more so. Most come from rural New York state, which interestingly, is about the same latitude as New England — and is just as cold in winter. The most distinctive New York examples are the early tables that were probably produced in the Hudson River Valley before the northern and western sections of the state were opened to settlement after the Revolution. The table in figure 22-9C is a fine example of this type, made entirely of maple with a dovetailed case, heart-shaped sides, and a large trestle base with shoe feet. Many of these tables have the through-tenoned and pinned-cross stretcher shown here. They would seem to have been made in Dutch settlements, for they have a distinctly European look. Other New York hutch tables are similar to the New England table shown in figure 22-9A. These may have been produced somewhat later in the northern part of the state that lies just to the west of the New England colonies.

South of New York, there are relatively few surviving hutch tables, but before ending this section I will show you a Pennsylvania table with a square top (22-9D). In common with other Pennsylvania hutch tables, the seat is more the width of a small bench than a chair. Although made of pine rather than walnut, the large drawer and the cleated top, held in place with nicely shaped removable "belaying pins," is suggestive of a great many Pennsylvania farm tables.

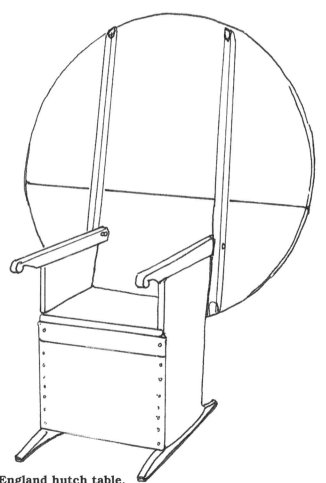

22-9A. New England hutch table, 27" h (top down), 1760 – 1790.

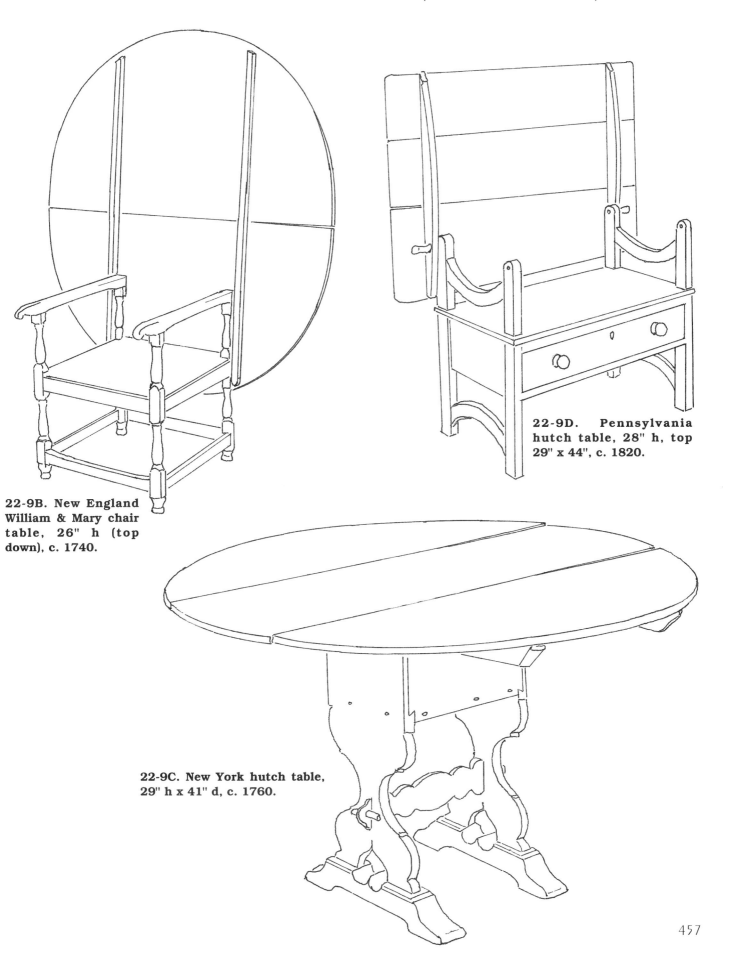

22-9B. New England William & Mary chair table, 26" h (top down), c. 1740.

22-9D. Pennsylvania hutch table, 28" h, top 29" x 44", c. 1820.

22-9C. New York hutch table, 29" h x 41" d, c. 1760.

Every book on old furniture includes a bibliography at the end, and lest you think me lazy, or ignorant, or both, I include one also. The bibliography that follows is tailored to the subject, focusing on the museum collections, exhibition publications, historical society publications, and magazine articles most useful in determining region and location. For convenience, they are presented two ways: first an alphabetical listing; then a listing by major region: New England, the Middle Atlantic, and the South.

Many of the listed publications are long out of print, and are found only in libraries and secondhand-book shops. If not in your local library, you may wish to look further afield. This usually is not difficult, for in this day and age library holdings are linked by computers into regional networks, and from a terminal you can search all over your state for a publication, and, if successful, have it forwarded to your local library.

It is also easy to locate and purchase an out-of-print book, for there are Internet firms that list selections from the stocks of many hundreds of used-book stores. Unless the book is rare, you will be presented with a number of choices and can decide on the quality you can afford — provided, of course, that you can afford any, for some museum publications have become quite expensive.

When looking for information, I would suggest that you favor the more recent publications. American furniture has been the subject of much study during the last half century, and in general, the newer the book, the more the detailed and informative the descriptions. You will find that many of the well-known early books are strong on prose and light on detail. However, they sometimes illustrate rare and uncommon forms.

Books and Museum and Historical Society Publications

Bacot, H. Parrott. *Southern Furniture and Silver: The Federal Period, 1788 – 1830*. Baton Rouge: Louisiana State University Press, 1968.

Baltimore Museum of Art. *The Work of Baltimore and Annapolis Cabinetmakers from 1760 to 1810*. Baltimore: The Baltimore Museum of Art, 1947.

Barquist, David L. *American Tables and Looking Glasses in the Mabel Brady Garvan and Other Collections at Yale University*. Yale University Press, 1992.

Bivens, John Jr. *The Furniture of Coastal North Carolina, 1700 – 1820*. Winston Salem, N.C.: Museum of Early Southern Decorative Arts, 1988.

——. *Wilmington Furniture, 1720 - 1860*. St. John's Museum of Art and Historic Wilmington Foundation, 1989.

Bivens, John Jr., and Forsyth Alexander. *The Regional Arts of the Early South — A Sampling From the Collection of the Museum of Early Southern Decorative Arts*. Museum of Early Southern Decorative Arts, Winston Salem, North Carolina, 1991.

Brainard, Newton C., Houghton Bulkeley and Phyllis Kihn. *Connecticut Cabinetmakers*. Connecticut Historical Society Bulletin, October 1967 and January 1968.

Burton, E. Milby. *Charleston Furniture, 1700 – 1825*. Charleston: Charleston Museum, 1955.

Butler, Joseph T., and Ray Skibinski. *Field Guide to American Antique Furniture*. New York: Facts On File Publications (Roundtable Press), 1985.

Carpenter, Ralph E. Jr. *The Arts and Crafts of Newport, Rhode Island, 1640-1820*. Newport: Preservation Society of Newport County, 1954.

Clunie, Margaret Burke, Anne Farnham, and Robert Trent. *Furniture at the Essex Institute*. Salem, Mass.: Essex Institute, 1980.

Comstock, Helen. *American Furniture: Seventeenth, Eighteenth, and Nineteenth Century Styles*. The Viking Press, 1962. Bonanza Books (reprint), New York, NY.

Conger, C. E., Alexandra W. Rollins, Mary K. Itsell, and Will Brown. *Treasures of State: Fine and Decorative Arts in the Diplomatic Reception Rooms of the Department of State*. Harry N. Abrams, Inc., New York, 1991.

Connecticut Historical Society. *Connecticut Chairs in the Collection of the Connecticut Historical Society*. Hartford: Connecticut Historical Society, 1956.

Craig, James. *Arts and Crafts in North Carolina 1699 – 1840*. Winston-Salem, North Carolina, 1965.

Currier Gallery of Art. *Decorative Arts of New Hampshire, 1723 – 1825*. Manchester, NH: Currier Gallery of Art, 1964.

——. *The Dunlaps and Their Furniture*. Manchester, NH: Currier Gallery of Art, 1970.

Downs, Joseph. *American Furniture: Queen Anne and Chippendale Periods in the Henry Francis du Pont Winterthur Museum*. New York: Viking, 1967.

Elder, William Voss, III. *Baltimore Painted Furniture, 1800 – 1840*. Baltimore, MD: The Baltimore Museum of Art, 1972.

——. *Maryland Queen Anne and Chippendale Furniture of the Eighteenth Century*. Baltimore, MD: The Baltimore Museum of Art, 1968.

Elder, William Voss, III, and Jayne E. Stokes. *American Furniture 1680 – 1880 from the Collection of the Baltimore Museum of Art*. Baltimore, MD: The Baltimore Museum of Art, 1987.

Elder, William Voss, III, and Lu Bartlett. *John Shaw: Cabinetmaker of Annapolis*. Baltimore, MD: The Baltimore Museum of Art, 1983.

Evans, Nancy Goyne. "American Windsor Chairs." Hudson Hills Press, New York, in association with The Henry Francis du Pont Winterthur Museum, 1996.

——. "Unsophisticated Furniture Made and Used in Philadelphia and Environs, ca. 1750 – 1800." In Winterthur Conference Report 1969: Country Cabinetwork and Simple Case Furniture, edited by John D. Morse, 151 – 203. Charlottsville, VA.: University Press of Virginia, 1970.

Fabian, Monroe H. *The Pennsylvania-German Decorated Chest*. Clinton, NJ: Main Street Press, 1978.

Failey, Dean F. *Long Island Is My Nation*. Setauket, NY: Society for the Preservation of Long Island Antiqueties, 1976.

Fairbanks, Jonathan L., and Elizabeth Bidwell Bates. *American Furniture 1620 to the Present*. New York: Richard Marek, 1981.

Fales, Dean A., Jr. *American Painted Furniture, 1660 – 1880*. New York: Dutton, 1979.

——. *The Furniture of Historic Deerfield*. New York: Dutton, 1976.

——. *Essex County Furniture: Documented Treasures from Local Collections, 1660 – 1860*. Salem, MA: Essex Institute, 1965.

Flanigan, J. Michael. *American Furniture from the Kaufman Collection*. National Gallery of Art, 1986.

Forman, Benno M. *American Seating Furniture, 1630 – 1730: An Interpretive Catalog*. W. W. Norton, 1988.

Garvin, Donna-Belle, James L. Garvin and John F. Page. *Plain & Elegant, Rich and Common. Documented New Hampshire Furniture, 1750 – 1850*. Concord, NH: Historical Society, 1978.

Greene, Jeffrey P. *American Furniture of the 18th Century*. The Taunton Press, Inc., Newtown, CT, 1996.

Greenlaw, Barry. *New England Furniture at Williamsburg*. Williamsburg, VA: Colonial Williamsburg Foundation, 1974.

Griffen, William, Florence Griffen, et al. Neat Pieces. *The Plain-Style Furniture of 19th Century Georgia*. Atlanta, GA: Atlanta Historical Society, 1983.

Gusler, Wallace B. *Furniture of Williamsburg and Eastern Virginia, 1710 – 1790*. Richmond, VA: Virginia Museum, 1979.

Hageman, Jane Sikes, and Edward M Hageman. *Ohio Furniture Makers, Volume 1, 1790 to 1845, Volume 2, 1790 – 1860*. (privately published).

——. *Ohio Furniture Makers, Volume 2, 1790 – 1860*. (privately published).

Hagler, Katharine Bryant. *American Queen Anne Furniture, 1720 – 1755*. Dearborn: The Edison Institute, 1976.

Harsh, Nathan, and Derita C. Williams. *The Art and Mystery of Tennessee Furniture and its Makers Through 1850*. Tennessee Historical Society, 1988.

Heckscher, Morrison H. *American Furniture in the Metropolitan Museum of Art - Late Colonial period: The Queen Anne and Chippendale Styles —- Vol II*. Random House, 1985.

Hewitt, Benjamin A., Patrica E. Kane, and Gerald W. R. Ward. *The Work of Many Hands: Card Tables in Federal America, 1790 – 1820*. Yale University Art Gallery: 1982.

Hornor, William M. *Blue Book of Philadelphia Furniture: William Penn to George Washington*. 1935. Reprinted by Highland House Publishers, Inc., 1977.

Horton, Frank L. *The Museum of Early Southern Decorative Arts: A Collection of Southern Furniture, Paintings, Ceramics, Textiles, and Metalware*. Old Salem, Inc., Winston-Salem, NC: 1979.

Horton, Frank L., and Carolyn J. Weekly. *The Swisegood School of Cabinetmaking, Museum of Early Southern Decorative Arts*. Winston-Salem, NC: Hall Printing Company, 1980.

Hummel, Charles F. *A Winterthur Guide to American Chippendale Furniture: Middle Atlantic and Southern Colonies*. New York: Crown Publishers, 1976.

Hurst, Ronald L., and Jonathan Prown. *Southern Furniture 1680 – 1830: The Colonial Williamsburg Collection*. The Colonial Williamsburg Foundation Harry N. Abrams, Inc. 1997.

Jobe, Brock. *Portsmouth Furniture: Masterworks from the New Hampshire Seacoast*. Society for the Preservation of New England Antiquities, University Press of New England, 1993.

Jobe, Brock, and Myrna Kaye. *New England Furniture — The Colonial Era*. Boston, MA: Houghton Mifflin Company, 1984.

Kane, Patrica E. *300 Years of American Seating Furniture*. Boston, MA: New York Graphic Society, 1976.

Ketchem, William, Jr. *American Cabinetmakers; Marked American Furniture, 1640 – 1940*. Crown Publishers, 1995.

Kettell, Russell Hawes. *The Pine Furniture of Early New England*. Doubleday, Doran and Company, Inc. New York, 1929 (later reprint available).

Kindig, Joseph K., III. *The Philadelphia Chair, 1685 – 1785*. The Historical Society of York, 1978.

Kirk, John T. *American Chairs: Queen Anne and Chippendale*. New York: Knopf, 1972.

——. *American Furniture and the British Tradition to 1830*. New York: Knopf, 1982.

——. *Connecticut Furniture: Seventeenth and Eighteenth Centuries*. Hartford, CT: Wadsworth Atheneum, 1967.

Kugelman, Thomas B., Alice K. Kugelman and Robert J. Lionetti. *Connecticut Valley Furniture by Eliphalet Chapin and his Contempories, 1750 – 1800*. Hartford, CT: Connecticut Historical Society, 2005.

Lindsey, Jack L. *Worldly Goods — The Arts of Early Pennsylvania 1680 – 1758*. Philadelphia Museum of Art, 1999.

Litchfield Historical Society. *Litchfield County Furniture, 1730 – 1850*. Litchfield, CT: Litchfield Historical Society, 1969.

Madigan, Mary Jean, and Susan Colgan. *Early American Furniture From Settlement to City: Aspects of form, style and regional design from 1620 to 1830*. An Art and Antiques Book. Billboard Publications, 1983.

Miller, V. Isabelle. *Furniture by New York Cabinetmakers, 1650 – 1860*. New York: Museum of the City of New York, 1956.

Montgomery, Charles F. *American Furniture: The Federal Period in the Henry Francis du Pont Winterthur Museum*. New York: Viking, 1966.

Moses, Michael. *Master Craftsmen of Newport: The Townsends and Goddards*. Tenafly, NJ: MMI American Press, 1984.

Mussey, Robert D. Jr. *The Furniture Masterworks of John & Thomas Seymour*. Peabody Essex Museum, 2003. (University Press of New England)

Myers, Minor, Jr., and Edgar deN. Mayhew. *New London County Furniture: 1640 – 1840*. New London, CT: Lyman Allyn Museum, 1974.

Newbern, Thomas R. J., and James R. Melchor. *Classical Norfolk Furniture, 1810 – 1840*.

New Hampshire Historical Society. *Plain & Elegant, Rich & Common: Documented New Hampshire Furniture, 1750 – 1850*. Concord, NH: New Hampshire Historical Society, 1979.

Ormsbee, Thomas H. *Field Guide to Early American Furniture*. Little, Brown and Company, 1951.

Randall, Richard H., Jr. *American Furniture in the Museum of Fine Arts, Boston*. Boston: Museum of Fine Arts, 1965.

Rauschenberg, Bradford L., and John Bivens, Jr. *The Furniture of Charleston, 1680 – 1820*. (3 Volumes) Museum of early Southern Decorative Arts, Old Salem Inc., 2003.

Richards, Nancy E. "Furniture of the Lower Connecticut River Valley, The Hartford Area, 1785 – 1801." In *Winterthur Portfolio 4*, edited by Richard K. Doud, 1 – 25. Charlottesville, VA: University Press of Virginia, 1968.

Richards, Nancy E., and Nancy Goyne Evans. *New England Furniture at Winterthur; Queen Anne and Chippendale Periods*. (A Winterthur Book) University Press of New England, 1997.

Sack, Albert. *American Antiques from Israel Sack Collection (Volumes 1 – 10)*. Highland House Publishers, Inc.

Santore, Charles. *The Windsor Style in America*. Running Press, 1981.

——. *The Windsor Style in America. Volume II*. Running Press, 1987.

Schaffner, Cynthia V. A., and Susan Klein. *American Painted Furniture, 1790 – 1880*. New York: Clarkson Potter, 1997.

Scherer, John L. *New York Furniture at the New York State Museum*. Highland House Publishers, 1984.

Schiffer, Margaret B. *Furniture and Its Makers of Chester County, Pennsylvania*. Philadelphia: University of Pennsylvania Press, 1966.

Schwartz, Marvin D. *American Furniture of the Colonial Period*. New York: Metropolitan Museum of Art, 1976.

Shea, John C. *The Pennsylvania Dutch and Their Furniture*. New York: Van Nostrand Reinhold Co., 1980.

Snyder, John J. Jr. *Philadelphia Furniture and Its Makers*. Antiques Magazine Library.

Theus, Mrs. Charlton M. *Savannah Furniture 1735 – 1825*. 1967.

Tracy, Berry B., and William H. Gerdts. *Classical America, 1815 – 1845*. Newark, NJ: The Newark Museum Association, 1963.

Trent, Robert F. *Hearts & Crowns: Folk Chairs of the Connecticut Coast, 1720-1840*. New Haven: New Haven Colony Historical Society.

Trent, Robert F., and Nancy Lee Nelson. *New London County Joined Chairs The Connecticut Historical Society Bulletin*. Volume 50, Number 4. Fall, 1985.

Venable, Charles L. *American Furniture in the Bybee Collection*. Austin, Texas: University of Texas Press, 1989.

Voss, Thomas M. *Antique American Country furniture — A Field Guide*. J. P. Lippincott Co., 1978.

Ward, Gerald W. R. *American Case Furniture in the Mabel Brady Garvan and Other Collections at Yale University*. Yale University Press, 1988.

Warren, David B. *Bayou Bend, American Furniture, Paintings and Silver from the Bayou Bend Collection*. Houston: Museum of Fine Arts, 1975.

Weidman, Gregory R. *Furniture in Maryland, 1740 – 1940: The Collection of the Maryland Historical Society*. Baltimore: Maryland Historical Society, 1984.

Weidman, Gregory R., Jennifer F. Goldsborough, et. al. *Classical Maryland 1815 – 1845 — Fine and Decorative Arts from the Golden Age*. Maryland Historical Society, the Museum and Library of Maryland History, 1993.

Winters, Robert E. Jr. (Editor) *North Carolina Furniture 1700 – 1900*. Raleigh: North Carolina Museum of History Associates, 1977.

Zogry, Kenneth Joel. *The Best the Country Affords: Vermont Furniture, 1765 – 1850*. Bennington, VT: Bennington Museum, 1995.

Magazine Articles

Andrus, Vincent D. "American Furniture from the Blair Collection." *Antiques* 61 (February 1952): 292 – 294.

Bartlett, Lu. "John Shaw, Cabinetmaker of Annapolis." *Antiques* 111 (February 1977): 362 – 377.

Bivins, John, Jr. "Furniture of Lower Cape Fear, North Carolina." *Antiques* 137 (May 1990): 1202 – 1213.

Blackburn, Roderic H. "Branded and Stamped New York Furniture." *Antiques* 119 (May 1981): 1130 – 1145.

Brown, Michael K. "Scalloped-Top Furniture of the Connecticut River Valley." *Antiques* 117 (May 1980): 1092 – 1099.

Burroughs, Paul H. "Furniture Widely Made in New Hampshire." *American Collector* 6 (June 1937): 6 – 7, 14 – 15.

Burton, E. Milby. "The Furniture of Charleston." *Antiques* 61 (January 1952): 44 – 57.

Cain, Helen, and Charles F. Hummel. "The Carnation Chests: New Discoveries in Pennsylvania-German Art." *Antiques* 122 (September 1982): 552 – 557.

Carpenter, Charles H., Jr. and Mary Grace Carpenter. "Nantucket Furniture." *Antiques* 133 (May 1988): 1160 – 1173.

Carpenter, Ralph E., Jr. "Discoveries in Newport Furniture and Silver." *Antiques* 68 (July 1955): 44 – 49.

Childs, Elizabeth Taylor. "Living With Antiques - The Southern Furniture Collection of Mr. and Mrs. Willam C. Adams Jr." *Antiques* 113 (May 1978): 1070 – 1077.

Chillingworth, Peter W. "Inlaid Furniture of Southwestern Pennsylvania, 1790 – 1840." *Antiques* 123 (May 1983): 1040 – 1043.

Churchill, Edwin A., and Thomas B. Johnson. "The Painted Furniture of Maine." *Antiques* 157 (May 2000): 778 – 787.

Comstock, Helen. "Furniture of Virginia, North Carolina, Georgia, and Kentucky." *Antiques* 61 (January 1952): 58 – 100.

——. "Southern Furniture Since 1952." *Antiques* 91 (January 1967): 102 – 119.

Connell, E. Jane, and Charles R. Muller. "Ohio Furniture 1788 – 1888." *Antiques* 125 (February 1984): 462 – 468.

Cooper, Wendy A. "American Chairback Settees: Some Sources and Related Examples." *American Art Journal* 9 (November 1977): 34 – 45.

De Julio, Mary Antoine. "New-York-German Painted Chests." *Antiques* 127 (May 1985): 1156 – 1165.

Dibble, Ann W. "Major John Dunlap: The Craftsman and His Community." *Old Time New England* 68 (Winter-Spring 1978): 50 – 58.

Downes, Joseph. "American Japanned Furniture." *Old-Time New England* 28 (October 1937): 61 – 67.

Ducoff-Barone, Deborah. "Philadelphia Furniture Makers." *Antiques* 139 (May 1991): 982 – 995.

Elder, William Voss III. "Maryland Furniture, 1760 – 1840." *Antiques* 111 (February 1977): 354 – 361.

Ellesin, Dorothy E. "Collector's Notes: Signed Savannah Furniture." *Antiques* 110 (September 1976): 560 – 561.

Evans, Nancy Goyne. "Design Sources for Windsor Furniture." *Antiques* 133 (May 1988): 1128 – 1143.

Fabian, Monroe H. "The Pennsylvania-German decorated Chest." *Antiques* 113 (May 1978): 1044 – 1051.

Failey, Dean F. "Seventeenth- and Eighteenth-century Long Island Furniture." *Antiques* 112 (October 1977): 732 – 741.

Fairbanks, Jonathon L. "American Antiques in the Collection of Mr. and Mrs. Charles L. Bybee." Parts 1 – 2. *Antiques* 92 (December 1967): 823 – 839, (January 1968): 76 – 82.

Farnam, Anne. "Furniture at the Essex Institute, Salem, Massachusetts." *Antiques* 111 (May 1977): 958 – 973.

Federhen, Deborah Anne. "The Serpentine-front chests of Drawers of Jonathan Gostelowe and Thomas Jones." *Antiques* 133 (May 1988): 1174 – 1183.

Forman, Benno M. "The Crown and York Chairs of Coastal Connecticut and the Work of the Durands of Milford." *Antiques* 105 (May 1974): 1147 – 54.

Garrett, Wendell D. "The Goddard and Townsend Joiners of Newport." *Antiques* 111 (May 1982): 1153 – 1155.

——. "Providence Cabinetmakers, Chairmakers, Upholsterers and Allied Craftsmen, 1756 – 1838." *Antiques* 90 (October 1966): 514 – 519.

George Dudley Seymour's Furniture Collection in The Connecticut Historical Society. Hartford, Connecticut: The Connecticut Historical Society, 1958.

Ginsburg, Benjamin. "The Barbour Collection of Connecticut Furniture in the Connecticut Historical Society." *Antiques* 105 (May 1974): 1092 – 1111.

Golovin, Anne Castrodale. "Cabinetmakers and chairmakers of Washington, D.C., 1791 – 1840." *Antiques* 107 (May 1975): 898 – 922.

Green, Henry D. "Furniture of the Georgia Piedmont Before 1830." *Antiques* 110 (September 1976): 550 – 559.

Griffith, Lee Ellen. "The Pennsylvania Spice Box." *Antiques* 129 (May 1986): 1062 – 1067.

Gronning, Erik K. "New Haven's Six-Board Chests." *Antiques* 163 (May, 2003): 116 – 121.

Gronning, Eric K., and Dennis Carr. "Rhode Island Gateleg Tables." *Antiques* 165 (May 2004): 122 – 127.

Gunnion, Vernon S. "The Pennsylvania-German Schrank." *Antiques* 123 (May 1983): 1022 – 1026.

Gusler, Wallace B. "Queen Anne Style Desks from the Virginia Piedmont." *Antiques* 104 (October 1973): 665 – 673.

Gusler, Wallace B., and Sumpter Priddy III. "Furniture of Williamsburg and Eastern Virginia." *Antiques* 114 (August 1978): 282 – 293.

Hall, Elton W. "New Bedford Furniture." *Antiques* 113 (May 1978): 1105 – 1127.

Hardiman, Thomas, Jr. "Veneered Furniture of Cumstan and Buckminster, Saco, Maine." *Antiques* 159 (May 2001): 754 – 761.

Hardiman, Thomas, Jr., Thomas B. Johnson, and Laura Fecych Sprague. "Maine Cabinetmakers of the Federal Period and the Influence of Coastal Massachusetts Design." *Antiques* 165 (May 2004): 128 – 143.

Heckscher, Morrison H. "Form and Frame: New Thoughts on the American Easy Chair." *Antiques* 100 (December 1971): 886 – 893.

——. "John Townsend's Block-and-Shell Furniture" and "The Goddard and Townsend Joiners of Newport." *Antiques* 121 (May 1982): 1144 – 1155.

Heckscher, Morrison H., and Frances Gruber Safford. "Boston Japanned Furniture in the Metropolitan Museum of Art." *Antiques* 129 (May 1986): 1046 – 1061.

Hewett, Benjamin A. "Regional Characteristics of Inlay on American Federal Period Card Tables." *Antiques* 121 (May 1982): 1164 – 1171.

Hicks, Robert, and Benjamin Hubbard Caldwell, Jr. "A Short History of the Tennessee Sugar Chest." *Antiques* 164 (September 2001): 128 – 133.

Hosley, William N., Jr., and Philip Zea. "Decorated Board Chests of the Connecticut River Valley." *Antiques* 119 (May 1981): 1146 – 1151.

Hummell, Charles F. "Queen Anne and Chippendale Furniture in the Henry Francis duPont Winterthur Museum." Parts 1 – 2. *Antiques* 97 (June 1970): 896 – 903, (December 1970): 900 – 909.

Hurst, Ronald L., and Sumpter T. Priddy III. "The Neoclassical Furniture of Norfolk, Virginia, 1770 – 1820." *Antiques* 137 (May 1990): 1140 – 1153.

Johnston, Philip. "Eighteenth and Nineteenth Century Furniture in the Wadsworth Atheneum." *Antiques* 115 (May 1979): 1016 – 1027.

Jones, Karen M. "American Furniture in the Milwaukee Art Center." *Antiques* 111 (May 1977): 974 – 985.

Joy, Edward T. "English Furniture Exports to America, 1697 – 1830." *Antiques* 85 (January 1964): 92 – 98.

Kane, Patrica E. "Furniture owned by the Massachusetts Historical Society." *Antiques* 109 (May 1976): 960 – 969.

Kaye, Myrna. "Marked Portsmouth Furniture." *Antiques* 113 (May 1978): 1098 – 1104.

Kenny, Peter M. "Honore Lannuier's Furniture and Patrons: Recent Discoveries." *Antiques* 153 (May 1998): 712 – 721.

Kirk, John T. "The Distinctive Character of Connecticut Furniture." *Antiques* 92 (October 1967): 524 – 529.

——. "Sources of Some American Regional Furniture." *Antiques* 88 (December 1965): 790 – 798.

Kugelman, Thomas P., and Alice K. Kugelman. "The Hartford Case Furniture Survey." *Maine Antique Digest* (March 1993): 36A-38A.

——. "Case Furniture of the Chapin School, 1775 – 1800." *Antiques* 167 (February 2005): 58 – 65.

Kugelman, Alice K., Thomas P. Kugelman, and Robert Lionetti. "The Hartford Case Furniture Survey, Part II — The Chapin School of East Windsor, Connecticut." *Maine Antique Digest* (January 1994): 12D-14D.

——. "The Hartford Case Furniture Survey, Part III — The Connecticut Valley Oxbow Chest." *Maine Antique Digest* (October 1995): 1C-3C.

Landman, Hedy B. "The Pendleton House at the Museum of Art, Rhode Island School of Design." *Antiques* 112 (May 1975): 923 – 938.

Lionetti, Joseph, and Robert F. Trent. "New Information about Chapin Chairs." *Antiques* 129 (May 1986): 1082 – 1095.

Lovell, Margaretta Markle. "Boston Blockfront Furniture" in *Boston Furniture of the Eighteenth Century*. Pages 77 – 135 Boston: Colonial Society of Massachusetts, 1974.

Lyle, Charles T., and Philip D. Zimmerman. "Furniture of the Monmouth County Historical Association." *Antiques* 117 (January 1980): 186 – 205.

McDonald, Janet Strain. "Furniture Making in Arbemarle County, Virginia, 1750 – 1850." *Antiques* 153 (May 1998): 746 – 751.

McPherson, Anne S. "Southern Bottle Cases." *Antiques* 166 (August 2004): 76 – 83.

Monahon, Eleanore Bradford. "The Rawson Family of Cabinetmakers in Providence, Rhode Island." *Antiques* 118 (July 1980): 134 – 147.

Mooney, James E. "Furniture at the Historical Society of Pennsylvania." *Antiques* 113 (May 1978): 1034 – 1043.

Moore, J. Roderick. "Painted Chests from Wythe County, Virginia." *Antiques* 122 (September 1982): 516 – 521.

Moses, Lisa and Michael. "Authenticating John Townsend's and John Goddard's Queen Anne and Chippendale Tables." *Antiques* 121 (May 1982): 1130 – 1143.

——. "Authenticating John Townsend's Later Tables." *Antiques* 119 (May 1981): 1152 – 1163.

Ott, Joseph K. "Exports of Furniture, Chaises, and Other Wooden Forms from Providence and Newport, 1783 – 1795." *Antiques* 102 (January 1975): 135 – 141.

——. "Some Rhode Island Furniture." *Antiques* 107 (May 1975): 940 – 951.

——. "Lesser-known Rhode Island Cabinetmakers: the Carliles, Holmes Weaver, Judson Blake, and Thomas Davenport." *Antiques* 121 (May 1982): 1156 – 1163.

Page, John F. "Documented New Hampshire Furniture." *Antiques* 115 (May 1979): 1004 – 1015.

Pierce, Donald C. "New York Furniture at the Brooklyn Museum." *Antiques* 115 (May 1979): 994 – 1003.

Pizer, Laurence R., Eleanor A. Driver and Alexandra B. Earle. "Furniture and Other Decorative Arts in Pilgrim Hall Museum in Plymouth, Massachusetts." *Antiques* 127 (May 1985): 1112 – 1120.

Podmaniczky, Michael. "The Incredible Elastic Chairs of Samuel Gragg." *Antiques* 163 (May 2003): 138 – 145.

Randall, Richard H., Jr. "Boston Chairs." *Old-Time New England* 54 (Summer 1963): 12 – 20.

Rauschenberg, Bradford L., and John Bivens, Jr. "Robert Walker, Charleston Cabinetmaker." *Antiques* 163 (February 2003): 62 – 69.

Rhoads, Elizabeth, and Brock Jobe. "Recent Discoveries in Boston Japanned Furniture." *Antiques* 105 (May 1974): 1082 – 1091.

Sack, Harold. "The Development of the American High Chest of Drawers." *Antiques* 133 (May 1988): 1112 – 1127.

Sack, Harold, and Deanne Levison. "American Roundabout Chairs." *Antiques* 139 (May 1991): 934 – 947.

Scherer, John L. "Labeled New York Furniture at the New York State Museum, Albany." *Antiques* 119 (May 1981): 1113 – 1129.

Scott, G. W., Jr. "Lancaster and Other Pennsylvania Furniture." *Antiques* 115 (May 1979): 984 – 993.

Scotti, N. David. "Notes on Rhode Island Cabinetmakers." *Antiques* 87 (May 1965): 572.

Seibert, Peter S. "Decorated Chairs of the Lower Susquehanna River Valley." *Antiques* 159 (May 2001): 780 – 787.

Shettleworth, Earle G. "The Radford Brothers: Portland Cabinetmakers of the Federal Period." *Antiques* 106 (August 1974): 285 – 289.

Smith, Michael O. "North Carolina Furniture, 1700 – 1900." *Antiques* 115 (June 1979): 1266 – 1277.

Smith, Robert C. "The Furniture of Anthony G. Quervelle, Part III: The Worktables." *Antiques* 104 (August 1973): 260 – 268.

Snyder, John J. "New Discoveries in Documented Lancaster County Chippendale Furniture." *Antiques* 124 (May 1985): 1150 – 1155.

Somerville, Romaine S. "Furniture at the Maryland Historical Society." *Antiques* 109 (May 1976): 970 – 989.

Stover, Donald E. "Early Texas Furniture." *Antiques* 150 (May 1974): 1112 – 1118.

Swan, Mabel Munson. "Furnituremakers of Charleston." *Antiques* 46 (October 1944): 203 – 206.

———. "John Goddard's Sons." *Antiques* 57 (June 1950): 448 – 449.

———. "Major Benjamin Frothingham, Cabinetmaker." *Antiques* 52 (November 1962): 392 – 395.

———. "Newburyport Furnituremakers." *Antiques* 47 (April 1945): 222 – 225.

Sweeney, Kevin M. "Furniture and Furniture Making in Mid-Eighteenth Century Wethersfield, Connecticut." *Antiques* 125 (May 1984): 1156 – 1163.

Talbott, Page. "Boston Empire Furniture: Part I." *Antiques* 107 (May 1975): 878 – 887.

———. "Boston Empire Furniture: Part II." *Antiques* 109 (May 1976): 1004 – 1013.

———. "Seating Furniture in Boston, 1810 – 1835." *Antiques* 139 (May 1991): 956 – 969.

Trent, Robert F. "Sources for the Heart-and-Crown Chairs." *Antiques* 113 (February 1978): 410 – 417.

Trice, Harley N. II. "Decorated Furniture of Soap Hollow, Somerset County, Pennsylvania." *Antiques* 123 (May 1983): 1036 – 1039.

Vincent, Gilbert T. "The Bombe Furniture of Boston." In Boston Furniture of the Eighteenth Century, 137 – 96. Boston: Colonial Society of Massachusetts, 1974.

Waters, Deborah Dependahl. "Delaware Furniture, 1740 – 1890." *Antiques* 127 (May 1985): 1144 – 1155.

Widmer, Kemble II, and Judy Anderson. "Furniture from Marblehead, Massachusetts." *Antiques* 163 (May 2003): 96 – 105.

Wood, David F. "A Group of Concord, Massachusetts, Furniture." *Antiques* 151 (May 1997): 742 – 747.

Zea, Philip. "A Revolution in Taste: Furniture Design in the American Backcountry." *Antiques* 159 (January 2001): 186 – 195.

Zimmerman, Philip D. "The American Sofa Table." *Antiques* 155 (May 1999): 744 – 753.

———. "Dating Dunlap-style Side Chairs." *Antiques* 157 (May 2000): 796 – 803.

———. "Eighteenth Century Chairs at Stenton." *Antiques* 163 (May, 2003): 122 – 129.

———. "Delaware River Valley Chests of Drawers 1725 – 1800." *Antiques* 159 (May 2001) 788 – 794.

———. "Philadelphia Queen Anne Chairs in Wright's Ferry Mansion." *Antiques* 149 (May 1996): 736 – 745.

———. "Queen Anne and Chippendale Chairs in Delaware." *Antiques* 160 (September 2001) 330 – 339.

———. "Eighteenth-century Philadelphia Case Furniture at Stenton." *Antiques* 161 (May 2002) 94 – 101.

———. "Early American Furniture in the New Castle Historical Society in Delaware." *Antiques* 167 (May 2005) 130 – 141.

Zogry, Kenneth Joel. "Urban Precedents for Vermont Furniture." *Antiques* 147 (May 1995): 762 – 768.

Books and Museum and Historical Society Publications: Multiple Regions

Barquist, David L. *American Tables and Looking Glasses in the Mabel Brady Garvan and Other Collections at Yale University*. Yale University Press, 1992.

Butler, Joseph T., and Ray Skibinski. *Field Guide to American Antique Furniture*. New York: Facts On File Publications (Roundtable Press), 1985.

Comstock, Helen. *American Furniture: Seventeenth, Eighteenth, and Nineteenth Century Styles*. The Viking Press 1962. Bonanza Books (reprint), New York.

Conger, C. E., Alexandra W. Rollins, Mary K. Itsell, and Will Brown. *Treasures of State: Fine and Decorative Arts in the Diplomatic Reception Rooms of the Department of State*. Harry N. Abrams, Inc., New York, 1991.

Downs, Joseph. *American Furniture: Queen Anne and Chippendale Periods in the Henry Francis du Pont Winterthur Museum*. New York: Viking, 1967.

Elder, William Voss, III, and Jayne E. Stokes. *American Furniture 1680 – 1880 from the Collection of the Baltimore Museum of Art*. Baltimore: The Baltimore Museum of Art, 1987.

Evans, Nancy Goyne. "American Windsor Chairs." Hudson Hills Press, New York — in association with The Henry Francis du Pont Winterthur Museum, 1996.

Fairbanks, Jonathan L., and Elizabeth Bidwell Bates. *American Furniture 1620 to the Present*. New York: Richard Marek, 1981.

Fales, Dean A., Jr. *American Painted Furniture, 1660 – 1880*. New York: Dutton, 1979.

Flanigan, J. Michael. *American Furniture from the Kaufman Collection*. National Gallery of Art, 1986.

Forman, Benno M. *American Seating Furniture, 1630 – 1730: An Interpretive Catalog*. W. W. Norton, 1988.

Greene, Jeffrey P. *American Furniture of the 18th Century*. The Taunton Press, Inc., Newtown, CT 1996.

Hagler, Katharine Bryant. *American Queen Anne Furniture, 1720 – 1755*. Dearborn: The Edison Institute, 1976.

Heckscher, Morrison H. *American Furniture in the Metropolitan Museum of Art - Late Colonial period: The Queen Anne and Chippendale Styles - Vol II*. Random House. 1985.

Hewitt, Benjamin A., Patrica E. Kane, and Gerald W. R. Ward. *The Work of Many Hands: Card Tables in Federal America, 1790 – 1820*. Yale University Art Gallery, 1982.

Kane, Patrica E. *300 Years of American Seating Furniture*. Boston: New York Graphic Society, 1976.

Ketcham, William, Jr. *American Cabinetmakers; Marked American Furniture, 1640 – 1940*. Crown Publishers, 1995.

Kirk, John T. *American Chairs: Queen Anne and Chippendale*. New York: Knopf, 1972.

———. *American Furniture and the British Tradition to 1830*. New York: Knopf, 1982.

Madigan, Mary Jean, and Susan Colgan. *Early American Furniture From Settlement to City: Aspects of form, style and regional design from 1620 to 1830*. An Art and Antiques Book. Billboard Publications, 1983.

Montgomery, Charles F. *American Furniture: The Federal period in the Henry Francis du Pont Winterthur Museum*. New York: Viking, 1966.

Ormsbee, Thomas H. *Field Guide to Early American Furniture*. Little, Brown and Company, 1951.

Randall, Richard H., Jr. *American Furniture in the Museum of Fine Arts, Boston*. Boston: Museum of Fine Arts, 1965.

Sack, Albert. *American Antiques from Israel Sack Collection (Volumes 1 – 10)*. Highland House Publishers, Inc.

Santore, Charles. *The Windsor Style in America*. Running Press, 1981.

———. *The Windsor Style in America. Volume II*. Running Press, 1987.

Schaffner, Cynthia V. A., and Susan Klein. *American Painted Furniture, 1790 – 1880*. Clarkson Potter, New York, 1997.

Schwartz, Marvin D. *American Furniture of the Colonial Period*. New York: Metropolitan Museum of Art, 1976.

Tracy, Berry B., and William H. Gerdts. *Classical America, 1815 – 1845*. Newark, NJ: The Newark Museum Association, 1963.

Venable, Charles L. *American Furniture in the Bybee Collection*. Austin, Texas: University of Texas Press, 1989.

Voss, Thomas M. *Antique American Country furniture – A Field Guide*. J. P. Lippincott Co., 1978.

Ward, Gerald W. R. *American Case Furniture in the Mabel Brady Garvan and Other Collections at Yale University*. Yale University Press, 1988.

Warren, David B. *Bayou Bend, American Furniture, Paintings and Silver from the Bayou Bend Collection*. Houston: Museum of Fine Arts, 1975.

Zogry, Kenneth Joel. *The Best the Country Affords: Vermont Furniture, 1765-1850*. Bennington, VT: Bennington Museum, 1995.

Books and Museum and Historical Society Publications: New England Region

Brainard, Newton C., and Houghton Bulkeley and Phyllis Kihn. *Connecticut Cabinetmakers*. Connecticut Historical Society Bulletin, October, 1967 & January, 1968.

Carpenter, Ralph E. Jr. *The Arts and Crafts of Newport, Rhode Island, 1640-1820*. Newport: Preservation Society of Newport County, 1954.

Clunie, Margaret Burke, Anne Farnham, and Robert Trent. *Furniture at the Essex Institute*. Salem, Mass.: Essex Institute, 1980.

Connecticut Historical Society. *Connecticut Chairs in the Collection of the Connecticut Historical Society*. Hartford: Connecticut Historical Society, 1956.

Currier Gallery of Art. *Decorative Arts of New Hampshire, 1723 – 1825*. Manchester, N.H.: Currier Gallery of Art, 1964.

——. *The Dunlaps and Their Furniture*. Manchester, N.H. Currier Gallery of Art, 1970.

Fales, Dean A., Jr. *The Furniture of Historic Deerfield*. New York: Dutton, 1976.

——. *Essex County Furniture: Documented Treasures from Local Collections, 1660 – 1860*. Salem, Mass.: Essex Institute, 1965.

Garvin, Donna-Belle, and James L. Garvin and John F. Page. *Plain & Elegant, Rich and Common*. Documented New Hampshire Furniture, 1750 – 1850. Concord, New Hampshire Historical Society, 1978.

Greenlaw, Barry. *New England Furniture at Williamsburg*. Williamsburg, VA: Colonial Williamsburg Foundation, 1974.

Gronning, Erik K. "New Haven's Six-Board Chests." *Antiques* 163 (May 2003): 116 – 121.

Jobe, Brock, and Myrna Kaye. *New England Furniture - The Colonial Era*. Boston, MA: Houghton Mifflin Company, 1984.

Jobe, Brock. *Portsmouth Furniture: Masterworks from the New Hampshire Seacoast*. Society for the Preservation of New England Antiquities, University Press of New England, 1993.

Kettell, Russell Hawes. *The Pine Furniture of Early New England*. Doubleday, Doran and Company, Inc. New York, 1929 (later reprint available).

Kirk, John T. *Connecticut Furniture: Seventeenth and Eighteenth Centuries*. Hartford: Wadsworth Atheneum, 1967.

Kugelman, Thomas B., Alice K. Kugelman and Robert J. Lionetti. *Connecticut Valley Furniture by Eliphalet Chapin and his Contempories, 1750 – 1800*. Hartford, CT: Connecticut Historical Society, 2005.

Litchfield Historical Society. *Litchfield County Furniture, 1730 – 1850*. Litchfield, CT: Litchfield Historical Society, 1969.

Moses, Michael. *Master Craftsmen of Newport: The Townsends and Goddards*. Tenafly, NJ: MMI Americana Press, 1984.

Mussey, Robert D. Jr. *The Furniture Masterworks of John & Thomas Seymour*. Peabody Essex Museum, 2003. (Distributed by University Press of New England)

Myers, Minor, Jr., and Edgar deN. Mayhew. *New London County Furniture: 1640 – 1840*. New London, CT: Lyman Allyn Museum, 1974.

New Hampshire Historical Society. *Plain & Elegant, Rich & Common: Documented New Hampshire Furniture, 1750 – 1850*. Concord, NH: New Hampshire Historical Society, 1979.

Richards, Nancy E. "Furniture of the Lower Connecticut River Valley, The Hartford Area, 1785 – 1801." In *Winterthur Portfolio* 4, edited by Richard K. Doud, 1 – 25. Charlottsville, VA: University Press of Virginia, 1968.

Richards, Nancy E., and Nancy Goyne Evans. *New England Furniture at Winterthur; Queen Anne and Chippendale Periods* (A Winterthur Book) University Press of New England, 1997.

Trent, Robert F. *Hearts & Crowns: Folk Chairs of the Connecticut Coast, 1720-1840*. New Haven, CT: New Haven Colony Historical Society.

Trent, Robert F., and Nancy Lee Nelson. *New London County Joined Chairs*. The Connecticut Historical Society Bulletin. Volume 50, Number 4. Fall, 1985.

Books and Museum and Historical Society Publications: Middle Atlantic Region

Evans, Nancy Goyne. "Unsophisticated Furniture Made and Used in Philadelphia and Environs, ca. 1750 – 1800." In Winterthur Conference Report 1969: Country Cabinetwork and Simple Case Furniture, edited by John D. Morse, 151 – 203. Charlottsville, VA: University Press of Virginia, 1970.

Fabian, Monroe H. *The Pennsylvania-German Decorated Chest*. Clinton, NJ: Main Street Press, 1978.

Failey, Dean F. *Long Island Is My Nation*. Setauket, N.Y.: Society for the Preservation of Long Island Antiquities, 1976.

Hageman, Jane Sikes, and Edward M Hageman. *Ohio Furniture Makers - Volume 1, 1790 to 1845, Volume 2, 1790 – 1860*. (privately published).

——. *Ohio Furniture Makers - Volume 2, 1790 – 1860*. (privately published).

Hornor, William M. *Blue Book of Philadelphia Furniture: William Penn to George Washington*. 1935. Reprinted by Highland House Publishers, Inc. 1977.

Hummel, Charles F. *A Winterthur Guide to American Chippendale Furniture: Middle Atlantic and Southern Colonies*. New York: Crown Publishers, 1976.

Kindig, Joseph K., III. *The Philadelphia Chair, 1685 – 1785*. The Historical Society of York, 1978.

Lindsey, Jack L. *Worldly Goods - The Arts of Early Pennsylvania 1680 - 1758*. Philadelphia Museum of Art, 1999.

Miller, V. Isabelle. *Furniture by New York Cabinetmakers, 1650 – 1860*. New York: Museum of the City of New York, 1956.

Scherer, John L. *New York Furniture at the New York State Museum*. Alexandria, VA: Highland House Publishers, 1984.

Schiffer, Margaret B. *Furniture and Its Makers of Chester County, Pennsylvania*. Philadelphia: University of Pennsylvania Press, 1966.

Shea, John C. *The Pennsylvania Dutch and Their Furniture*. New York: Van Nostrand Reinhold Co. 1980.

Snyder, John J., Jr. *Philadelphia Furniture and Its Makers*. Antiques Magazine Library.

Books and Museum and Historical Society Publications: Southern Region

Bacot, H. Parrott. *Southern Furniture and Silver: The Federal Period, 1788 – 1830*. Baton Rouge, LA: Louisiana State University Press, 1968.

Baltimore Museum of Art. *The Work of Baltimore and Annapolis Cabinetmakers from 1760 to 1810*. Baltimore: The Baltimore Museum of Art, 1947.

Bivens, John Jr., and Forsyth Alexander. *The Regional Arts of the Early South - A Sampling From the Collection of the Museum of Early Southern Decorative Arts*. Museum of Early Southern decorative Arts, Winston Salem, NC, 1991.

Bivens, John, Jr. *The Furniture of Coastal North Carolina, 1700 – 1820*. Winston-Salem, NC: Museum of Early Southern Decorative Arts, 1988.

——. *Wilmington Furniture, 1720 - 1860*. St. John's Museum of Art and Historic Wilmington Foundation, 1989.

Burton, E. Milby. *Charleston Furniture, 1700 – 1825*. Charleston: Charleston Museum, 1955.

Craig, James. *Arts and Crafts in North Carolina 1699 – 1840*. Winston-Salem, NC, 1965.

Griffen, William, Florence Griffen, et al. Neat Pieces. *The Plain-Style Furniture of 19th Century Georgia*. Atlanta Historical Society, 1983.

Elder, William Voss, III. *Baltimore Painted Furniture, 1800 – 1840*. Baltimore: The Baltimore Museum of Art, 1972.

——. *Maryland Queen Anne and Chippendale Furniture of the Eighteenth Century*. Baltimore: The Baltimore Museum of Art, 1968.

Elder, William Voss, III, and Lu Bartlett. *John Shaw: Cabinetmaker of Annapolis*. The Baltimore Museum of Art, Baltimore, Maryland, 1983.

Gusler, Wallace B. *Furniture of Williamsburg and Eastern Virginia, 1710 – 1790*. Richmond, VA: Virginia Museum, 1979.

Harsh, Nathan, and Derita C. Williams. *The Art and Mystery of Tennessee Furniture and its Makers Through 1850*. Tennessee Historical Society, 1988.

Horton, Frank L. *The Museum of Early Southern Decorative Arts: A Collection of Southern Furniture, Paintings, Ceramics, Textiles, and Metalware*. Winston-Salem, NC: Old Salem, Inc., 1979.

Horton, Frank L., and Carolyn J. Weekly. *The Swisegood School of Cabinetmaking*, Museum of Early Southern Decorative Arts. Winston Salem, NC, Hall Printing Company, 1980.

Hummel, Charles F. *A Winterthur Guide to American Chippendale Furniture: Middle Atlantic and Southern Colonies*. New York: Crown Publishers, 1976.

Hurst, Ronald L., and Jonathan Prown. *Southern Furniture 1680 – 1830: The Colonial Williamsburg Collection The Colonial Williamsburg Foundation - Harry N*. Abrams, Inc. 1997.

Newbern, Thomas R. J., and James R. Melchor. *Classical Norfolk Furniture, 1810 – 1840*.

Rauschenberg, Bradford L., and John Bivens, Jr. *The Furniture of Charleston, 1680 – 1820*. (3 Volumes) Museum of early Southern Decorative Arts, Old Salem Inc., 2003.

Theus, Mrs. Charlton M. *Savannah Furniture 1735 – 1825*. 1967.

Weidman, Gregory R. *Furniture in Maryland, 1740 – 1940: The Collection of the Maryland Historical Society*. Baltimore: Maryland Historical Society, 1984.

Weidman, Gregory R., and Jennifer F. Goldsborough, et. al. *Classical Maryland 1815 – 1845 - Fine and Decorative Arts from the Golden Age*. Maryland Historical Society, the Museum and Library of Maryland History, 1993.

Winters, Robert E. Jr. (Editor) *North Carolina Furniture 1700 – 1900*. Raleigh, NC: North Carolina Museum of History Associates, 1977.

Magazine Articles: Multiple Regions

Andrus, Vincent D. "American Furniture from the Blair Collection" *Antiques* 61 (February 1952): 292 – 294.

Cooper, Wendy A. "American Chairback Settees: Some Sources and Related Examples." *American Art Journal* 9 (November 1977): 34 – 45.

Downes, Joseph. "American Japanned Furniture" *Old-Time New England* 28 (October 1937): 61 – 67.

Evans, Nancy Goyne. "Design Sources for Windsor Furniture." *Antiques* 133 (May 1988): 1128 – 1143.

Fairbanks, Jonathon L. "American Antiques in the Collection of Mr. and Mrs. Charles L. Bybee." Parts 1 – 2. *Antiques* 92 (December 1967): 823 – 839, (January 1968): 76 – 82.

Heckscher, Morrison H. "Form and Frame: New Thoughts on the American Easy Chair." *Antiques* 100 (December 1971): 886 – 893.

Hewett, Benjamin A. "Regional Characteristics of Inlay on American Federal Period Card Tables." *Antiques* 121 (May 1982): 1164 – 1171.

Hummell, Charles F. "Queen Anne and Chippendale Furniture in the Henry Francis duPont Winterthur Museum." Parts 1 – 2. *Antiques* 97 (June 1970): 896 – 903, 98 (December 1970): 900 – 909.

Johnston, Philip. "Eighteenth and Nineteenth Century Furniture in the Wadsworth Atheneum." *Antiques* 115 (May 1979): 1016 – 1027.

Jones, Karen M. "American Furniture in the Milwaukee Art Center." *Antiques* 111 (May 1977): 974 – 985.

Joy, Edward T. "English Furniture Exports to America, 1697 – 1830." *Antiques* 85 (January 1964): 92 – 98.

Kirk, John T. "Sources of Some American Regional Furniture." *Antiques* 88 (December 1965): 790 – 798.

Sack, Harold. "The Development of the American High Chest of Drawers." *Antiques* 133 (May 1988): 1112 – 1127.

Sack, Harold, and Deanne Levison. "American Roundabout Chairs." *Antiques* 139 (May 1991): 934 – 947.

Zimmerman, Philip D. "The American Sofa Table." *Antiques* 155 (May 1999): 744 – 753.

Magazine Articles: New England Region

Brown, Michael K. "Scalloped-Top Furniture of the Connecticut River Valley." *Antiques* 117 (May 1980): 1092 – 1099.

Burroughs, Paul H. "Furniture Widely Made in New Hampshire." *American Collector* 6 (June 1937): 6 – 7, 14 – 15.

Carpenter, Charles H., Jr. and Mary Grace Carpenter. "Nantucket Furniture." *Antiques* 133 (May 1988): 1160 – 1173.

Carpenter, Ralph E. Jr. "Discoveries in Newport Furniture and Silver." *Antiques* 68 (July 1955): 44 – 49.

Churchill, Edwin A., and Thomas B. Johnson. "The Painted Furniture of Maine." *Antiques* 157 (May 2000): 778 – 787.

Dibble, Ann W. "Major John Dunlap: The Craftsman and His Community." *Old Time New England* 68 (Winter-Spring 1978): 50 – 58.

Farnam, Anne. "Furniture at the Essex Institute, Salem, Massachusetts." *Antiques* 111 (May 1977): 958 – 973.

Forman, Benno M. "The Crown and York Chairs of Coastal Connecticut and the Work of the Durands of Milford." *Antiques* 105 (May 1974): 1147 – 1154.

Garrett, Wendell D. "The Goddard and Townsend Joiners of Newport." *Antiques* 111 (May 1982): 1153 – 55.

——. "Providence Cabinetmakers, Chairmakers, Upholsterers and Allied Craftsmen, 1756 – 1838." *Antiques* 90 (October 1966): 514 – 519.

George Dudley Seymour's Furniture Collection in The Connecticut Historical Society. Hartford, Connecticut: The Connecticut Historical Society, 1958.

Ginsburg, Benjamin. "The Barbour Collection of Connecticut Furniture in the Connecticut Historical Society." *Antiques* 105 (May 1974): 1092 – 1111.

Gronning, Eric K., and Dennis Carr. "Rhode Island Gateleg Tables." *Antiques* 165 (May 2004): 122 – 127.

Hall, Elton W. "New Bedford Furniture." *Antiques* 113 (May 1978): 1105 – 1127.

Hardiman, Thomas, Jr. "Veneered Furniture of Cumstan and Buckminster, Saco, Maine." *Antiques* 159 (May 2001): 754 – 761.

Hardiman, Thomas, Jr., Thomas B. Johnson, and Laura Fecych Sprague. "Maine Cabinetmakers of the Federal Period and the Influence of Coastal Massachusetts Design." *Antiques* 165 (May 2004): 128 – 143.

Heckscher, Morrison H. "John Townsend's Block-and-Shell Furniture." and "The Goddard and Townsend Joiners of Newport." *Antiques* 121 (May 1982): 1144 – 1155.

Heckscher, Morrison H., and Frances Gruber Safford. "Boston Japanned Furniture in the Metropolitan Museum of Art." *Antiques* 129 (May 1986): 1046 – 1061.

Hosley, William N., Jr., and Philip Zea. "Decorated Board Chests of the Connecticut River Valley." *Antiques* 119 (May 1981): 1146 – 1151.

Kane, Patrica E. "Furniture owned by the Massachusetts Historical Society." *Antiques* 109 (May 1976): 960 – 969.

Kaye, Myrna. "Marked Portsmouth Furniture." *Antiques* 113 (May 1978): 1098 – 1104.

Kirk, John T. "The Distinctive Character of Connecticut Furniture." *Antiques* 92 (October 1967): 524 – 529.

Kugelman, Thomas P., and Alice K. Kugelman. "The Hartford Case Furniture Survey." *Maine Antique Digest* (March 1993): 36A-38A.

——. "Case Furniture of the Chapin School, 1775 – 1800." *Antiques* 167 (February 2005): 58 – 65.

Kugelman, Alice K., Thomas P. Kugelman, and Robert Lionetti. "The Hartford Case Furniture Survey, Part II - The Chapin School of East Windsor, Connecticut." *Maine Antique Digest* (January 1994): 12D-14D.

——. "The Hartford Case Furniture Survey, Part III - The Connecticut Valley Oxbow Chest." *Maine Antique Digest* (October 1995): 1C-3C.

Landman, Hedy B. "The Pendleton House at the Museum of Art, Rhode Island School of Design." *Antiques* 112 (May 1975): 923 – 938.

Lionetti, Joseph, and Robert F. Trent. "New Information about Chapin Chairs." *Antiques* 129 (May 1986): 1082 – 1095.

Lovell, Margaretta Markle. "Boston Blockfront Furniture" in Boston Furniture of the Eighteenth Century. Pages 77 – 135 Boston, MA: Colonial Society of Massachusetts, 1974.

Monahon, Eleanore Bradford. "The Rawson Family of Cabinetmakers in Providence, Rhode Island." *Antiques* 118 (July 1980): 134 – 147.

Moses, Lisa and Michael. "Authenticating John Townsend's and John Goddard's Queen Anne and Chippendale Tables." *Antiques* 121 (May 1982): 1130 – 1143.

——. "Authenticating John Townsend's Later Tables." *Antiques* 119 (May 1981): 1152 – 1163.

Ott, Joseph K. "Exports of Furniture, Chaises, and Other Wooden Forms from Providence and Newport, 1783 – 1795." *Antiques* 102 (January 1975): 135 – 141.

——. "Some Rhode Island Furniture." *Antiques* 107 (May 1975): 940 – 951.

——. "Lesser-known Rhode Island Cabinetmakers: the Carliles, Holmes Weaver, Judson Blake, and Thomas Davenport." *Antiques* 121 (May 1982): 1156 – 1163.

Page, John F. "Documented New Hampshire Furniture." *Antiques* 115 (May 1979): 1004 – 1015.

Pizer, Laurence R., Eleanor A. Driver and Alexandra B. Earle. "Furniture and Other Decorative Arts in Pilgrim Hall Museum in Plymouth, Massachusetts." *Antiques* 127 (May 1985): 1112 – 1120.

Podmaniczky, Michael. "The incredible elastic chairs of Samuel Gragg." *Antiques* 163 (May 2003): 138 – 145.

Randall, Richard H., Jr. "Boston Chairs" *Old-Time New England* 54 (Summer 1963): 12 – 20.

Rhoads, Elizabeth, and Brock Jobe. "Recent Discoveries in Boston Japanned Furniture." *Antiques* 105 (May 1974): 1082 – 1091.

Scotti, N. David. "Notes on Rhode Island Cabinetmakers." *Antiques* 87 (May 1965): 572.

Shettleworth, Earle G. "The Radford Brothers: Portland Cabinetmakers of the Federal Period." *Antiques* 106 (August 1974): 285 – 289.

Swan, Mabel Munson. "John Goddard's Sons." *Antiques* 57 (June 1950): 448 – 449.

——. "Major Benjamin Frothingham, Cabinetmaker." *Antiques* 52 (November 1962): 392 – 395.

——. "Newburyport Furnituremakers." *Antiques* 47 (April 1945): 222 – 225.

Sweeney, Kevin M. "Furniture and Furniture Making in Mid-Eighteenth Century Wethersfield, Connecticut." *Antiques* 125 (May 1984): 1156 – 1163.

Talbott, Page. "Boston Empire Furniture: Part I." *Antiques* 107 (May 1975): 878 – 887.

——. "Boston Empire Furniture: Part II." *Antiques* 109 (May 1976): 1004 – 1013.

——. "Seating Furniture in Boston, 1810 – 1835." *Antiques* 139 (May 1991): 956 – 969.

Trent, Robert F. "Sources for the Heart-and-Crown Chairs." *Antiques* 113 (February 1978): 410 – 417.

Vincent, Gilbert T. "The Bombe Furniture of Boston." In Boston Furniture of the Eighteenth Century, 137 – 96. Boston, MA: Colonial Society of Massachusetts, 1974.

Widmer, Kemble II, and Judy Anderson. "Furniture from Marblehead, Massachusetts." *Antiques* 163 (May 2003): 96 – 105.

Wood, David F. "A Group of Concord, Massachusetts, Furniture." *Antiques* 151 (May 1997): 742 – 747.

Zea, Philip. "A revolution in taste: Furniture design in the American backcountry." *Antiques* 159 (January 2001): 186 – 195.

Zimmerman, Philip D. "Dating Dunlap-style Side Chairs." *Antiques* 157 (May 2000): 796 – 803.

Zogry, Kenneth Joel. "Urban Precedents for Vermont Furniture." *Antiques* 147 (May 1995): 762 – 768.

Magazine Articles: Middle Atlantic Region

Blackburn, Roderic H. "Branded and Stamped New York Furniture." *Antiques* 119 (May 1981): 1130 – 1145.

Cain, Helen, and Charles F. Hummel. "The Carnation Chests: New Discoveries in Pennsylvania-German Art." *Antiques* 122 (September 1982): 552 – 557.

Chillingworth, Peter W. "Inlaid Furniture of Southwestern Pennsylvania, 1790-1840." *Antiques* 123 (May 1983): 1040 – 1043.

Connell, E. Jane, and Charles R. Muller. "Ohio Furniture 1788 – 1888." *Antiques* 125 (February 1984): 462 – 468.

De Julio, Mary Antoine. "New York-German Painted Chests." *Antiques* 127 (May 1985): 1156 – 1165.

Ducoff-Barone, Deborah. "Philadelphia Furniture Makers." *Antiques* 139 (May 1991): 982 – 995.

Fabian, Monroe H. "The Pennsylvania-German decorated Chest." *Antiques* 113 (May 1978): 1044 – 1051.

Failey, Dean F. "Seventeenth- and Eighteenth-century Long Island Furniture." *Antiques* 112 (October 1977): 732 – 741.

Federhen, Deborah Anne. "The Serpentine-front chests of Drawers of Jonathan Gostelowe and Thomas Jones." *Antiques* 133 (May 1988): 1174 – 1183.

Griffith, Lee Ellen. "The Pennsylvania Spice Box." *Antiques* 129 (May 1986): 1062 – 1067.

Gunnion, Vernon S. "The Pennsylvania-German Schrank." *Antiques* 123 (May 1983): 1022 – 1026.

Kenny, Peter M. "Honore Lannuier's Furniture and Patrons: Recent Discoveries." *Antiques* 153 (May 1998): 712 – 721.

Lyle, Charles T., and Philip D. Zimmerman. "Furniture of the Monmouth County Historical Association." *Antiques* 117 (January 1980): 186 – 205.

Mooney, James E. "Furniture at the Historical Society of Pennsylvania." *Antiques* 113 (May 1978): 1034 – 1043.

Pierce, Donald C. "New York Furniture at the Brooklyn Museum." *Antiques* 115 (May 1979): 994 – 1003.

Scherer, John L. "Labeled New York Furniture at the New York State Museum, Albany." *Antiques* 119 (May 1981): 1113 – 1129.

Scott, G. W., Jr. "Lancaster and Other Pennsylvania Furniture." *Antiques* 115 (May 1979): 984 – 993.

Seibert, Peter S. "Decorated chairs of the lower Susquehanna River Valley." *Antiques* 159 (May 2001): 780 – 787.

Smith, Robert C. "The Furniture of Anthony G. Quervelle, Part III: The Worktables." *Antiques* 104 (August 1973): 260 – 268.

Snyder, John J. "New Discoveries in Documented Lancaster County Chippendale Furniture." *Antiques* 124 (May 1985): 1150 – 1155.

Trice, Harley N. II. "Decorated Furniture of Soap Hollow, Somerset County, Pennsylvania." *Antiques* 123 (May 1983): 1036 – 1039.

Waters, Deborah Dependahl. "Delaware Furniture, 1740 – 1890." *Antiques* 127 (May 1985): 1144 – 1155.

Zimmerman, Philip D. "Delaware River Valley chests of drawers 1725 – 1800." *Antiques* 159 (May 2001) 788 – 795.

——. "Philadelphia Queen Anne Chairs in Wright's Ferry Mansion." *Antiques* 149 (May 1996): 736 – 745.

——. "Eighteenth Century Chairs at Stenton." *Antiques* 163 (May 2003): 122 – 129.

——. "Eighteenth-century Philadelphia case furniture at Stenton". *Antiques* 161 (May 2002) 94 – 101.

——. "Queen Anne and Chippendale chairs in Delaware". *Antiques* 160 (September 2001) 330 – 339.

——. "Early American furniture in the New Castle Historical Society in Delaware". *Antiques* 167 (May 2005) 130 – 141.

Magazine Articles: Southern Region

Bartlett, Lu. "John Shaw, Cabinetmaker of Annapolis." *Antiques* 111 (February 1977): 362 – 377.

Bivins, John, Jr. "Furniture of Lower Cape Fear, North Carolina." *Antiques* 137 (May 1990): 1202 – 1213.

Burton, E. Milby. "The Furniture of Charleston." *Antiques* 61 (January 1952): 44 – 57.

Childs, Elizabeth Taylor. "Living With Antiques - The Southern Furniture Collection of Mr. and Mrs. Willam C. Adams Jr." *Antiques* 113 (May 1978): 1070 – 1077.

Comstock, Helen. "Furniture of Virginia, North Carolina, Georgia, and Kentucky." *Antiques* 61 (January 1952): 58 – 100.

——. "Southern Furniture Since 1952." *Antiques* 91 (January 1967): 102 – 119.

Elder, William Voss III. "Maryland Furniture, 1760 – 1840." *Antiques* 111 (February 1977): 354 – 361.

Ellesin, Dorothy E. "Collector's Notes: Signed Savannah Furniture." *Antiques* 110 (September 1976): 560 – 561.

Golovin, Anne Castrodale. "Cabinetmakers and chairmakers of Washington, D.C., 1791 – 1840." *Antiques* 107 (May 1975): 898 – 922.

Green, Henry D. "Furniture of the Georgia Piedmont Before 1830." *Antiques* 110 (September 1976): 550 – 559.

Gusler, Wallace B. "Queen Anne Style Desks from the Virginia Piedmont" *Antiques* 104 (October 1973): 665 – 673.

Gusler, Wallace B., Sumpter Priddy III. "Furniture of Willaimsburg and Eastern Virginia." *Antiques* 114 (August 1978): 282 – 293.

Hicks, Robert, and Benjamin Hubbard Caldwell Jr. "A Short History of the Tennessee Sugar Chest." *Antiques* 164 (September 2001): 128 – 133.

Hurst, Ronald L., and Sumpter T. Priddy III. "The Neoclassical Furniture of Norfolk, Virginia, 1770 – 1820." *Antiques* 137 (May 1990): 1140 – 1153.

McDonald, Janet Strain. "Furniture Making in Arbemarle County, Virginia, 1750- 1850." *Antiques* 153 (May 1998): 746 – 751.

McPherson, Anne S. "Southern Bottle Cases." *Antiques* 166 (August 2004): 76 – 83.

Moore, J. Roderick. "Painted Chests from Wythe County, Virginia." *Antiques* 122 (September 1982): 516 – 521.

Rauschenberg, Bradford L., and John Bivens, Jr. "Robert Walker, Charleston Cabinetmaker." *Antiques* 163 (February, 2003): 62 – 69.

Smith, Michael O. "North Carolina Furniture, 1700 – 1900." *Antiques* 115 (June 1979): 1266 – 1277.

Somerville, Romaine S. "Furniture at the Maryland Historical Society." *Antiques* 109 (May 1976): 970 – 989.

Stover, Donald E. "Early Texas Furniture." *Antiques* 150 (May 1974): 1112 – 1118.